Thirteenth Edition

Business Communication

Thirteenth Edition

Business Communication

KITTY O. LOCKER
The Ohio State University

JEANINE ELISE AUNE
Iowa State University

JO MACKIEWICZ
Iowa State University

DONNA S. KIENZLER
Iowa State University

McGraw Hill

BUSINESS COMMUNICATION, THIRTEENTH EDITION

2 3 4 5 6 7 8 9 LKV 27 26 25 24 23 22

ISBN 978-1-264-06751-0 (bound edition)
MHID 1-264-06751-8 (bound edition)
ISBN 978-1-266-07742-5 (loose-leaf edition)
MHID 1-266-07742-1 (loose-leaf edition)

Portfolio Director: *Anke Weekes*
Senior Product Developer: *Anne Leung*
Marketing Manager: *Trina Maurer*
Project Manager, Core Content: *Amy Gehl*
Project Manager, Assessment Content: *Vanessa McClune*
Senior Buyer: *Susan K. Culbertson*
Design: *Matt Diamond*
Content Licensing Specialist: *Gina Oberbroeckling*
Cover Image: *DrAfter123/Getty Images*
Compositor: *MPS Limited*

Library of Congress Cataloging-in-Publication Data

Names: Locker, Kitty O., author. | Mackiewicz, Jo, author. | Aune, Jeanine
  Elise, author. | Kienzler, Donna S., author.
  Title: Business communication / Kitty O. Locker, The Ohio State University,
  Jo Mackiewicz, Iowa State University, Jeanine Elise Aune, Iowa State
  University, Donna S. Kienzler, Iowa State University.
  Other titles: Business and administrative communication
  Description: Thirteenth edition. | New York, NY : McGraw Hill, [2023] |
  Includes index.
  Identifiers: LCCN 2021054457 (print) | LCCN 2021054458 (ebook) |
  ISBN 9781264067510 (hardcover) | ISBN 9781266077425 (spiral bound) |
  ISBN 9781266080623 (ebook)
  Subjects: LCSH: Business communication. | Communication in management.
  Classification: LCC HF5718 .L63 2023 (print) | LCC HF5718 (ebook) |
  DDC 651.7—dc23/eng/20211110
  LC record available at https://lccn.loc.gov/2021054457
  LC ebook record available at https://lccn.loc.gov/2021054458

Dedication

In memory of Kitty Locker. We are honored to continue her legacy.
For the instructors in the Advanced Communication program at Iowa State University.

The Authors

Jo Mackiewicz is a Professor of Rhetoric and Professional Communication at Iowa State University. Her research has been published in a range of journals, including *Journal of Business and Technical Communication, Technical Communication Quarterly, IEEE Transactions on Professional Communication,* and the *WAC Journal.* With Isabelle Thompson, she wrote *Talk about Writing: The Tutoring Strategies of Experienced Writing Center Tutors.* She also wrote *The Aboutness of Writing Center Talk: A Corpus-Driven and Discourse Analysis* and *Writing Center Talk over Time: A Mixed-Method Study.* The latter won the International Writing Center Association's 2019 Outstanding Book award.

Jeanine Elise Aune is a Teaching Professor at Iowa State University, where she serves as the Advanced Communication Director. Her work has appeared in the *Journal of Natural Resource & Life Sciences Education,* the *WAC Journal,* and the *Journal of Microbiology & Biology Education.* She has received several awards for her work with Iowa State's learning communities, including the LAS Learning Community Leadership Award, and in 2017 she received the Outstanding Achievement in Teaching Award from her college.

Donna S. Kienzler is a Professor Emeritus of English at Iowa State University, where she taught in the Rhetoric and Professional Communication program. As the Director of Advanced Communication, she oversaw more than 120 sections of business and technical communication annually. She was also an Assistant Director of the university's Center for Excellence in Learning and Teaching, where she taught classes, seminars, and workshops on pedagogy; directed graduate student programming; and directed the Preparing Future Faculty program, a career-training program for graduate students and postdoctoral fellows. Her research focused on pedagogy and ethics.

Brief Contents

Business Communication

While staying true to its tradition of delivering a high standard of business communication pedagogy and resources, the 13th edition further modernizes the chapter content and organization to make it more relevant to students today. As in each prior edition, the foundation of the 13th edition is a rhetorical approach to business communication. Each chapter underscores the importance of analyzing each communicative situation in terms of audience, purpose, and context. This rhetorical approach gives students the ability to choose the most applicable genre and to generate an effective business message no matter the situation. Finally, the 13th edition includes many updated exercises and several new exercises, as well as new instructor resources.

What's New?

We have worked hard to update *Business Communication* from its 12th edition to its 13th. We have added new content that instructors have asked for, such as examples of business plans and sales proposals and elaborated discussion of social media use for business. We've updated content, particularly in relation to communication during the COVID-19 pandemic. We have painstakingly cut repetitious content, streamlining each section within each chapter so that it makes its point clearly and efficiently. We have also reorganized, regrouping like with like, so that students can more readily find the content they need. We've also used singular *they, them,* and *their* as generic third-person pronouns when the pronoun referent is indefinite (for example, *everyone*) and when a person's gender is unknown, in accordance with APA style. And we've simplified the page layout, eliminating unnecessary design elements, such as horizontal lines before and after bulleted lists. In short, we have overhauled the textbook to create a modernized and elegant 13th edition.

The following list delineates some of the specific changes that we made.

CHAPTER 1

- Replaced the chapter-opening case with a new case about Wells Fargo.
- Reorganized and updated content about basic criteria for effective messages and about questions for analyzing a rhetorical situation. Both sections now stress ethical choices.

CHAPTER 2

- Replaced the chapter-opening case with a new case about Stitch-Fix.
- Updated benefits and descriptions of potential communication channels, including newer social media.
- Updated material on and examples about *you*-attitude, positive emphasis, and tone.
- Added a section on creating inclusivity.
- Updated platform-specific best practices for creating goodwill.

CHAPTER 3

- Added chapter-opening case study about disinformation having a direct negative effect on a business.
- Updated material about research from previous edition's chapter about writing reports, including conducting primary research, analyzing search results, and using secondary research.
- Developed content about evaluating sources and reading sources critically.
- Updated and elaborated content on citation and documentation.

CHAPTER 4

- Introduced the concepts of oppressive language and inclusive language.

CHAPTER 5

- Revised and updated content throughout the chapter.

CHAPTER 6

- Updated chapter-opening case to focus on the increased and increasing expectation that people work collaboratively.
- Added content about innovation coming from working collaboratively in diverse teams.
- Elaborated content on the configuration and purpose of teams.
- Streamlined chapter by removing separate sections on technology and incorporated content about working virtually throughout the chapter.

CHAPTER 7

- Revised and updated content throughout the chapter.

CHAPTER 8

- Clearly differentiated between charts and graphs.
- Added discussion about text tables, flow charts, organizational charts, and scatter-plot graphs.
- Added new examples of text tables, flow charts, organizational charts, scatter-plot graphs, and infographics.
- Trimmed extraneous discussion and examples of maps.

CHAPTER 9

- Updated the chapter-opening case.
- Shifted content about platform-specific communication to Chapter 2.

CHAPTER 10

- Reorganized sections.
- Shifted content about platform-specific communication to Chapter 2.

CHAPTER 11

- Updated the chapter-opening case.
- Updated visuals.
- Shifted content about platform-specific communication to Chapter 2.

CHAPTER 12

- Added a new chapter-opening case about a rejected proposal.
- Added a section on typical proposal content and organization.
- Added annotated examples of sales, grant, and business proposals.

CHAPTER 13

- Added a section on white papers.

CHAPTER 14

- Updated the chapter-opening case.
- Revised examples of presentation slides.
- Added a section about online presentations (e.g., via WebEx).

CHAPTER 15

- Updated online resources for job listings, job-search advice, company information.

CHAPTER 16

- Added a section on online interviews.
- Updated the section on interview attire.

Features

Application-Based Activities in Connect

Application-Based Activities in Connect are highly interactive, assignable exercises that provide students a safe space to apply the concepts they have learned to real-world, course-specific problems. Each Application-Based Activity involves the application of multiple concepts, allowing students to synthesize information and use critical thinking skills to solve realistic scenarios.

Writing Assignment in Connect

Available within Connect, the Writing Assignment tool delivers a learning experience to help students improve their written communication skills and conceptual understanding. As an instructor you can assign, monitor, grade, and provide feedback on writing more efficiently and effectively.

Test Builder in Connect

Available within Connect, Test Builder is a cloud-based tool that enables instructors to format tests that can be printed, administered within a Learning Management System, or exported as a Word document of the test bank. Test Builder offers a modern, streamlined interface for easy content configuration that matches course needs, without requiring a download.

Test Builder allows you to:

- Access all test bank content from a particular title.
- Easily pinpoint the most relevant content through robust filtering options.
- Manipulate the order of questions or scramble questions and/or answers.
- Pin questions to a specific location within a test.
- Determine your preferred treatment of algorithmic questions.
- Choose the layout and spacing.
- Add instructions and configure default settings.

Test Builder provides a secure interface for better protection of content and allows for just-in-time updates to flow directly into assessments.

Proctorio

Remote Proctoring & Browser-Locking Capabilities

Remote proctoring and browser-locking capabilities, hosted by Proctorio within Connect, provide control of the assessment environment by enabling security options and verifying the identity of the student.

Seamlessly integrated within Connect, these services allow instructors to control students' assessment experience by restricting browser activity, recording students' activity, and verifying students are doing their own work.

Instant and detailed reporting gives instructors an at-a-glance view of potential academic integrity concerns, thereby avoiding personal bias and supporting evidence-based claims.

OLC-Aligned Courses

Implementing High-Quality Online Instruction and Assessment through Preconfigured Courseware

In consultation with the Online Learning Consortium (OLC) and our certified Faculty Consultants, McGraw Hill has created pre-configured courseware using OLC's quality scorecard to align with best practices in online course delivery. This turnkey courseware contains a combination of formative assessments, summative assessments, homework, and application activities, and can easily be customized to meet an individual's needs and course outcomes. For more information, visit https://www.mheducation.com/highered/olc.

 ReadAnywhere

Read or study when it's convenient for you with McGraw Hill's free ReadAnywhere app. Available for iOS or Android smartphones or tablets, ReadAnywhere gives users access to McGraw Hill tools, including the eBook and SmartBook 2.0 and Adaptive Learning Assignments in Connect. Take notes, highlight, and complete assignments offline—all of your work will sync when you open the app with WiFi access. Log in with your McGraw Hill Connect username and password to start learning—anytime, anywhere!

Create

Your Book, Your Way

McGraw Hill's Content Collections Powered by Create® is a self-service website that enables instructors to create custom course materials—print and eBooks—by drawing upon McGraw Hill's comprehensive, cross-disciplinary content. Choose what you want from our high-quality textbooks, articles, and cases. Combine it with your own content quickly and easily, and tap into other rights-secured, third-party content such as readings, cases, and articles. Content can be arranged in a way that makes the most sense for your course, and you can include the course name and information as well. Choose the best format for your course: color print, black-and-white print, or eBook. The eBook can be included in your Connect course and is available on the free ReadAnywhere app for smartphone or tablet access as well. When you are finished customizing, you will receive a free digital copy to review in just minutes! Visit McGraw Hill Create®—https://www.mcgrawhillcreate.com—today and begin building!

Instructors: Student Success Starts with You

Tools to enhance your unique voice

Want to build your own course? No problem. Prefer to use an OLC-aligned, prebuilt course? Easy. Want to make changes throughout the semester? Sure. And you'll save time with Connect's auto-grading too.

65% Less Time Grading

Laptop: McGraw Hill; Woman/dog: George Doyle/Getty Images

Study made personal

Incorporate adaptive study resources like SmartBook® 2.0 into your course and help your students be better prepared in less time. Learn more about the powerful personalized learning experience available in SmartBook 2.0 at **www.mheducation.com/highered/connect/smartbook**

Affordable solutions, added value

Make technology work for you with LMS integration for single sign-on access, mobile access to the digital textbook, and reports to quickly show you how each of your students is doing. And with our Inclusive Access program you can provide all these tools at a discount to your students. Ask your McGraw Hill representative for more information.

Padlock: Jobalou/Getty Images

Solutions for your challenges

A product isn't a solution. Real solutions are affordable, reliable, and come with training and ongoing support when you need it and how you want it. Visit **www.supportateverystep.com** for videos and resources both you and your students can use throughout the semester.

Checkmark: Jobalou/Getty Images

Students: Get Learning that Fits You

Effective tools for efficient studying

Connect is designed to help you be more productive with simple, flexible, intuitive tools that maximize your study time and meet your individual learning needs. Get learning that works for you with Connect.

Study anytime, anywhere

Download the free ReadAnywhere app and access your online eBook, SmartBook 2.0, or Adaptive Learning Assignments when it's convenient, even if you're offline. And since the app automatically syncs with your Connect account, all of your work is available every time you open it. Find out more at **www.mheducation.com/readanywhere**

> *"I really liked this app—it made it easy to study when you don't have your text-book in front of you."*
>
> - Jordan Cunningham,
> Eastern Washington University

Calendar: owattaphotos/Getty Images

Everything you need in one place

Your Connect course has everything you need—whether reading on your digital eBook or completing assignments for class, Connect makes it easy to get your work done.

Learning for everyone

McGraw Hill works directly with Accessibility Services Departments and faculty to meet the learning needs of all students. Please contact your Accessibility Services Office and ask them to email accessibility@mheducation.com, or visit **www.mheducation.com/about/accessibility** for more information.

Top: Jenner Images/Getty Images, Left: Hero Images/Getty Images, Right: Hero Images/Getty Images

Acknowledgments

This 13th edition, like each before, builds upon the ideas and advice of many instructors, students, and researchers. We would like to thank the following people who reviewed the 12th edition and suggested changes, many of which we incorporated into the 13th edition:

Brock Adams, *Weber State University*

Kathryn Archard, *University of Massachusetts-Boston*

Gretchen M. Arthur, *Lansing Community College*

Samuel Ascoli, *Iowa State University*

William Carland Caldwell Beckham, *Horry-Georgetown Technical College*

Lisa Branham, *Greenville Technical College*

Chloe Clark, *Iowa State University*

Christina Force, *Bloomsburg University of Pennsylvania*

Stephen David Grover, *Park University*

Albert Haley, *Abilene Christian University*

David Jalajas, *Long Island University*

Eduardo Landeros, *San Diego Mesa College*

Molly Mayer, *University of Cincinnati*

Natalie Meyer, *Iowa State University*

Smita Jain Oxford, *University of Mary Washington*

Joseph Evan Ray, *University of Nevada-Reno*

Jacqueline Staley, *Yakima Valley College*

We also would like to thank the following instructors who contributed to the development of the previous editions:

Matt Alberhasky, *Des Moines Area Community College and Iowa State University*

Mark Alexander, *Indiana Wesleyan University*

Bill Allen, *University of LaVerne*

Vanessa Arnold, *University of Mississippi*

Eve Ash, *Oklahoma State University-Tulsa*

Lynn Ashford, *Alabama State University*

Tracy Austin, *Sam Houston State University*

Monique Babin, *Clackamas Community College*

Jean Baird, *Brigham Young University-Idaho*

Lenette Baker, *Valencia Community College*

Dennis Barbour, *Purdue University-Calumet*

Laura Barelman, *Wayne State College*

Fiona Barnes, *University of Florida*

Jan Barton-Zimerman, *University of Nebraska-Kearney*

Jaye Bausser, *Indiana University-Purdue University at Fort Wayne*

Sallye Benoit, *Nicholls State University*

Michael Benton, *Bluegrass Community and Technology College*

Raymond W. Beswick, *formerly of Synerude, Ltd.*

Carole Bhakar, *The University of Manitoba*

Cathie Bishop, *Parkland College*

Randi Meryl Blank, *Indiana University*

Sarah Bleakney, *Georgia Institute of Technology*

Yvonne Block, *College of Lake County*

Bennis Blue, *Virginia State University*

John Boehm, *Iowa State University*

Maureen S. Bogdanowicz, *Kapi'olani Community College*

Kendra S. Boggess, *Concord College*

Melanie Bookout, *Greenville Technical College*

Christy Ann Borack, *California State University-Fullerton; Orange Coast College-Costa Mesa*

Mary Young Bowers, *Northern Arizona University*

Charles P. Bretan, *Northwood University*

Paula Brown, *Northern Illinois University*

Vincent Brown, *Battelle Memorial Institute*

William Brunkan, *Augustana College*

John Bryan, *University of Cincinnati*

Phyllis Bunn, *Delta State University*

Trudy Burge, *University of Nebraska-Lincoln*

Dennis V. Burke, *Coker College*

Janice Burke, *South Suburban College of Cook County*

Brian Burmmeister, *Iowa State University*

Aaron Butler, *Warner Pacific College*

Nicole Buzzetto-More, *University of Maryland-Eastern Shore*

Robert Callahan, *The University of Texas-San Antonio*

Andrew Cantrell, *University of Illinois*

Danny Cantrell, *West Virginia State College*

Peter Cardon, *University of South Carolina*

John Carr, *The Ohio State University*

Marilyn Chalupa, *Ball State University*

Kelly Chaney, *Southern Illinois University-Carbondale*

Jay Christiansen, *California State University-Northridge*

Lynda Clark, *Maple Woods Community College*

David T. Clements, *Community College of Baltimore County*

Robert Cohn, *Long Island University*

Brendan G. Coleman, *Mankato State University*

Andrea Compton, *St. Charles Community College*

John Cooper, *University of Kentucky*

Mark Courtright, *Elon University*

Donna Cox, *Monroe Community College*

Rosemarie Cramer, *Community College of Baltimore County*

Christine Leigh Cranford, *East Carolina University*

Tena Crews, *University of South Carolina*

Smiljka Cubelic, *Indiana University-South Bend*

Victoria Cumings, *Warner Pacific College*

Carla Dando, *Idaho State University*

Sarah Davis, *Iowa State University*

Aparajita De, *University of Maryland-College Park*

Susan H. Delagrange, *The Ohio State University*

Mark DelMaramo, *Thiel College*

Moira E. W. Dempsey, *Oregon State University*

Gladys DeVane, *Indiana University*

Linda Di Desidero, *University of Maryland-University College*

Veronica Dufresne, *Finger Lakes Community College*

Jose A. Duran, *Riverside Community College*

Dorothy J. Dykman, *Point Loma Nazarene College*

Marilyn Easter, *San Jose State University*

Anna Easton, *Indiana University*

Yvette Essounga-Njan, *Fayetteville State University*

Donna Everett, *Morehead State University*

Joyce Ezrow, *Ann Arundel Community College*

Susan Fiechtner, *Texas A&M University*

Susan Finnerty, *John Carroll University*

Bartlett Finney, *Park University-Parkville*

Gina Firenzi, *Santa Clara University*

Mary Ann Firmin, *Oregon State University*

Melissa Fish, *American River College*

W. Clark Ford, *Middle Tennessee State University*

Louisa Fordyce, *Westmoreland County Community College*

Paula J. Foster, *Foster Communication*

Mildred Franceschi, *Valencia Community College-West Camp*

Linda Fraser, *California State University-Fullerton*

Silvia Fuduric, *Wayne State University*

Lynda Fuller, *Wilmington University*

Robert D. Gieselman, *University of Illinois*

Stacey Durbin Gish, *Western Kentucky University*

Cheryl Glenn, *Pennsylvania State University*

Wade Graves, *Grayson County College*

Mary Greene, *Prince George's Community College*

Daryl Grider, *West Virginia State College*

Peter Hadorn, *Virginia Commonwealth University*

Ed Hagar, *Belhaven College*

Elaine Hage, *Forsythe Technical Community College*

Barbara Hagler, *Southern Illinois University*

Robert Haight, *Kalamazoo Valley Community College*

Mark Hama, *Angelo State University*

Les Hanson, *Red River Community College-Canada*

Kathy Harris, *Northwestern State University*

Mark Harstein, *University of Illinois*

Maxine Hart, *Baylor University*

Vincent Hartigan, *New Mexico State University*

David Hawes, *Owens Community College*

Charles Hebert, *The University of South Carolina*

Tanya Henderson, *Howard University*

Paulette Henry, *Howard University*

Deborah Herz, *Salve Regina University*

Kathy Hill, *Sam Houston State University*

Robert Hill, *University of LaVerne*

Kenneth Hoffman, *Emporia State University*

Elizabeth Hoger, *Western Michigan University*

Carole A. Holden, *County College of Morris*

Carlton Holte, *California State University-Sacramento*

Cynthia Houlden, *University of Nebraska-Kearney*

Glenda Hudson, *California State University-Bakersfield*

Elizabeth Huettman, *Cornell University*

Melissa Ianetta, *University of Southern Indiana*

Susan Isaacs, *Community College of Philadelphia*

Daphne A. Jameson, *Cornell University*

Lorri Jaques, *South Florida State College*

Elizabeth Jenkins, *Pennsylvania State University*

Carolyn Jewell, *Fayetteville State University*

Lee Jones, *Shorter College*

Paula R. Kaiser, *University of North Carolina-Greensboro*

Jeremy Kemp, *San Jose State University*

Robert W. Key, *University of Phoenix*

Joy Kidwell, *Oregon State University*

Susan E. Kiner, *Cornell University*

Lisa Klein, *The Ohio State University*

Gary Kohut, *University of North Carolina-Charlotte*

Sarah McClure Kolk, *Hope College*

Patti Koluda, *Yakima Valley Community College*

Keith Kroll, *Kalamazoo Valley Community College*

Claire Kruesel, *Iowa State University*

Milton Kukon, *Southern Vermont College*

Linda M. LaDuc, *University of Massachusetts-Amherst*

Suzanne Lambert, *Broward Community College*

Jamie Strauss Larsen, *North Carolina State University*

Newton Lassiter, *Florida Atlantic University*

Barry Lawler, *Oregon State University*

Sally Lawrence, *East Carolina University*

Cheryl Ann Laws, *City University*

Gordon Lee, *University of Tennessee*

Paul Lewellan, *Augustana College*

Kathy Lewis-Adler, *University of North Alabama*

Luchen Li, *Iowa State University*

Barbara Limbach, *Chadron State College*

Jodi Lindseth, *Amarillo College*

Dana Loewy, *California State University-Fullerton*

Bobbi Looney, *Black Hills State University*

Joyce Lopez, *Missouri State University*

Andrea A. Lunsford, *Stanford University*

Catherine MacDermott, *Saint Edwards University*

Elizabeth Macdonald, *Thunderbird Graduate School of International Management*

John T. Maguire, *University of Illinois*

Michael D. Mahler, *Montana State University*

Margaret Mahoney, *Iowa State University*

Pamela L. Martin, *The Ohio State University*

Iris Washburn Mauney, *High Point College*

Robin McCarter, *North Greenville University*

Patricia McClure, *West Virginia State College*

Lynn McCool, *Drake University*

Kelly McCormick-Sullivan, *Saint John Fisher College*

Nancie McCoy-Burns, *University of Idaho*

Robert McEachern, *Southern Connecticut State University*

Brian R. McGee, *Texas Tech University*

Virginia Melvin, *Southwest Tennessee Community College*

Yvonne Merrill, *University of Arizona*

Elizabeth Metzger, *University of South Florida*

Carol Meyer, *American Public University*

Julia R. Meyers, *North Carolina State University*

Jack Miao, *Southern Methodist University*

Julianne Michalenko, *Robert Morris University*

Paul Miller, *Davidson College*

Danielle Mitchell, *Pennsylvania State University-Fayette*

Karl Mitchell, *Queens College-CUNY*

Mialisa Moline, *University of Wisconsin-River Falls*

Jayne Moneysmith, *Kent State University-Stark*

Josef Moorehead, *California State University-Sacramento*

Gregory Morin, *University of Nebraska-Omaha*

Evelyn Morris, *Mesa Community College*

Rodger Glenn Morrison, *Troy University*

Frederick K. Moss, *University of Wisconsin-Waukesha*

Andrea Muldoon, *University of Wisconsin-Stout*

Anne Nail, *Amarillo College*

Frank P. Nemecek Jr., *Wayne State University*

Cheryl Noll, *Eastern Illinois University*

Nancy Nygaard, *University of Wisconsin-Milwaukee*

Tanya Patrick, *Clackamas Community College*

Greg Pauley, *Moberly Area Community College*

Jean E. Perry, *University of Southern California*

Linda N. Peters, *University of West Florida*

Florence M. Petrofes, *University of Texas-El Paso*

Melinda Phillabaum, *IUPUI*

Evelyn M. Pierce, *Carnegie Mellon University*

Allison Piper-Geber, *Miller, Hall & Triggs*

Cathy Pleska, *West Virginia State College*

Susan Plutsky, *California State University-Northridge*

Virginia Polanski, *Stonehill College*

Janet Kay Porter, *Leeward Community College*

Susan Prenzlow, *Minnesota State University-Mankato*

Brenda Price, *Bucks County Community College*

Brenner Pugh, *Virginia Commonwealth University*

David Ramsey, *Southeastern Louisiana University*

Greg Rapp, *Portland Community College*

Kathryn C. Rentz, *University of Cincinnati*

Janetta Ritter, *Garland County Community College*

Naomi Ritter, *Indiana University*

Jeanette Ritzenthaler, *New Hampshire College*

Betty Jane Robbins, *University of Oklahoma*

Cassie Rockwell, *Santa Monica College*

Ralph Roberts, *University of West Florida*

Carol Roever, *Missouri Western State College*

Kara Romance, *Indiana University of Pennsylvania*

Deborah Roper, *California State University-Dominguez Hills*

Joseph A. Rosendale, *Indiana University of Pennsylvania*

Tim Rowe, *SUNY Fredonia*

Mary Jane Ryals, *Florida State University*

Mary Saga, *University of Alaska-Fairbanks*

Bobbie Schnepf, *South Central Louisiana Technical College-River Parishes*

Betty Schroeder, *Northern Illinois University*

Nancy Schullery, *Western Michigan University*

Kelly Searsmith, *University of Illinois*

Sherry Sherrill, *Forsythe Technical Community College*

Stacey Short, *Northern Illinois University*

Frank Smith, *Harper College*

Pamela Smith, *Florida Atlantic University*

Helen W. Spain, *Wake Technical Community College*

Valarie Spiser-Albert, *University of Texas-San Antonio*

Janet Starnes, *University of Texas-Austin*

Natalie Stillman-Webb, *University of Utah-Salt Lake City*

Ron Stone, *DeVry University*

T. Reneé Stovall, *Amarillo College*

Bruce Todd Strom, *University of Indianapolis*

Judith A. Swartley, *Lehigh University*

Christine Tachick, *University of Wisconsin-Milwaukee*

Mel Tarnowski, *Macomb Community College*

Bette Tetreault, *Dalhousie University*

Barbara Z. Thaden, *St. Augustine's College*

Lori Townsend, *Niagara County Community College-Sanborn*

Linda Travis, *Ferris State University*

Lisa Tyler, *Sinclair Community College*

Donna Vasa, *University of Nebraska-Lincoln*

David A. Victor, *Eastern Michigan University*

Robert Von der Osten, *Ferris State University*

Catherine Waitinas, *University of Illinois-Champaign-Urbana*

Vicky Waldroupe, *Tusculum College*

Randall Waller, *Baylor University*

George Walters, *Emporia State University*

Jie Wang, *University of Illinois-Chicago*

Craig Warren, *Pennsylvania State-Erie Behrend College*

Linda Weavil, *Elon College*

Judy West, *University of Tennessee-Chattanooga*

Gail S. Widner, *University of South Carolina*

Rebecca Wiggenhorn, *Clark State Community College*

Paula Williams, *Arkansas Northeastern College*

Marsha Daigle Williamson, *Spring Arbor University*

Bennie Wilson, *University of Texas-San Antonio*

Rosemary Wilson, *Washtenaw Community College*

Janet Winter, *Central Missouri State University*

Annette Wyandotte, *Indiana University Southeast*

Bonnie Thames Yarbrough, *University of North Carolina-Greensboro*

Sherilyn K. Zeigler, *Hawaii Pacific University*

Chris Ziemnowicz, *University of North Carolina at Pembroke*

We are honored to carry on the tradition that Kitty Locker began and that Donna Kienzler fostered.

Jo Mackiewicz

Janine Aune

Association for Business Communication

An international, interdisciplinary organization committed to advancing business communication research, education, and practice.

Benefits of The Association for Business Communication

- Annual international and regional conferences
- Award & grant opportunities for you and your students
- Access to decades of online archives
- Over 25 committees and special interest groups (SIGs)
- Two journals: *Business and Professional Communication Quarterly & International Journal of Business Communication*

Visit www.businesscommunication.org
Learn about ABC; join our community with its affordable membership levels, including special graduate student rates.

Contents

moovstock/123RF

Part One

The Building Blocks of Effective Messages

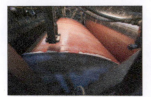

Nati Harnik/AP Images

Part Two

The Communication Process

6　Working and Writing in Teams　154

2018 Guardian News and Media Limited or its affiliated companies/Alamy Stock Photo

Part Three

Design of Communication

7　Designing Documents　186

limbitech/123RF

Part Four

Basic Business Messages

LittleRedDragon/Shutterstock

Part Five

Common Genres

Casey Rodgers/AP Images

Part Six

The Job Hunt

Appendices

Thirteenth Edition

Business Communication

1

Succeeding in Business Communication

Chapter Outline

DrAfter123/Getty Images

Costly Communications: Wells Fargo's Second Mistake

moovstock/123RF

Poorly done business communications can have severe consequences, as Wells Fargo learned in the wake of its 2016 fraud scandal. The second-largest bank in the U.S., Wells Fargo had pressured employees at local branches to meet quotas that led the employees to order debit cards and create fake checking and savings accounts in customers' names—all without the customers' consent. Clients noticed the new accounts as fees appeared on their bank statements. For its illegal actions, Wells Fargo was fined $185 million by regulatory bodies such as the Consumer Financial Protection Bureau.

Testifying before Congress after the story broke in 2016, then-CEO and President John Stumpf seemed to blame 5,300 low-level employees—employees who were then fired. In addition, he failed to concede the corporate policies—the unattainable quotas—that had pushed employees toward unethical and illegal behavior. In initial public statements, Wells Fargo expressed only "regret" for what it had done. It took weeks for the company to apologize.

In 2020, Wells Fargo agreed to a $3 billion settlement of criminal and civil charges. Its reputation remains marred.[1] Poor business practices started the bank's problems; poor business communication compounded them.

Business communication takes many forms: face-to-face, phone, or online conversations, presentations, emails, text messages, reports, blogs, tweets, social media posts, and websites. All of these methods typically use **verbal communication**, or communication that uses words. **Nonverbal communication** does not use words. Photographs, graphs, and company logos are nonverbal. Nonverbal interpersonal communication includes how and where people sit at meetings, how people use gestures, how they organize office spaces, and how long they keep a visitor waiting.

Learning Objectives

After studying this chapter, you should be able to

LO 1-1 Describe the benefits of good communication.

LO 1-2 Explain why you need to be able to communicate well.

LO 1-3 Describe the costs of poor communication.

LO 1-4 Describe what communication on the job can look like.

LO 1-5 Explain the basic criteria for effective messages.

LO 1-6 Analyze a business communication situation.

The Benefits of Good Communication Skills

LO 1-1

Good communication—whether verbal or nonverbal—is worth every minute it takes and every penny it costs. Companies that communicate effectively with their employees enjoy, for example, lower turnover rates.[2]

Good communication skills also will benefit you, even in your first job. You may have wonderful ideas for your workplace, but unless you can communicate them to the relevant people, they will get you nowhere. You must understand how to persuade, to explain complex material, and to adapt information to particular audiences. No software program will replace these skills. Even in your first job, you'll communicate. As a result, communication ability consistently ranks first among the qualities that employers look for in college graduates.[3]

The National Commission on Writing surveyed 120 major corporations, employing nearly 8 million workers. Almost 70% of respondents said that at least two-thirds of their employees have specific writing responsibilities included in their position descriptions. These writing responsibilities include

- Email (100% of employees).

- Presentations with visuals, such as PowerPoint slides (100%).

- Memos and correspondence (70%).

- Formal reports (62%).

- Technical reports (59%).

Respondents also noted that communication functions were least likely to be outsourced.[4] In fact, good communicators earn more. Research has shown that among people with two- or four-year degrees, workers in the top 20% of writing ability earn, on average, more than three times as much as workers whose writing falls into the bottom 20%.[5]

The Need for Good Communication Skills

LO 1-2

Despite the frequency of on-the-job writing and the importance of overall communication skills, college graduates often don't demonstrate the necessary writing skills as they enter the workforce. A survey of employers conducted on behalf of the Association of American Colleges and Universities found that writing was one of the weakest skills of college graduates.[6] In another large survey, respondents noted that a lack of "effective business communication skills appears to be a major stumbling block among new [job] entrants—even at the college level."[7]

Some students think that an administrative assistant will do their writing, that they can use form letters if they do have to write, that only technical skills matter, or that they'll call or text rather than write. Each of these claims is fundamentally flawed.

Claim 1: An administrative assistant will do all my writing.

Reality: Because of automation and restructuring, job responsibilities in offices have changed. Administrative assistants perform complex tasks such as training, research, and database management for several managers. Managers are likely to take care of their own writing, data entry, and phone calls.

Claim 2: I'll use form letters or templates when I need to write.

Reality: A form letter is designed to cover only routine situations, many of which are computerized or outsourced. Also, the higher you rise, the more frequently you'll face situations that aren't routine, that demand creative solutions.

Claim 3: I'm being hired as an accountant, not a writer.

Reality: Almost every entry-level professional or managerial job requires you to write email messages, speak to small groups, write documents, and present your work for annual reviews. People who do these things well are likely to be promoted beyond the entry level. Employees in jobs as diverse as firefighters, security professionals, and construction project managers all are being told to polish their writing and speaking skills.[8]

Claim 4: I'll just pick up the phone.

Reality: Important phone calls require follow-up letters or emails. People in organizations put things in writing to make themselves visible, to create a record, to convey complex data, to save money, and to convey their own messages more effectively. "If it isn't in writing, it didn't happen" is a maxim at many companies. Writing is an essential way to record agreements, to make yourself visible, and to let your accomplishments be known.

The Costs of Poor Communication

LO 1-3

Poor communication can cost billions of dollars. For example, according to the presidential commission, inadequate communication among British Petroleum (BP), Halliburton, and Transocean, as well as within their own companies, was a contributing factor in BP's massive oil spill, which caused extensive damage, as well as fatalities, in the Gulf of Mexico.[9] BP agreed to a $4 billion fine for its role in the Gulf of Mexico oil spill. That sum is in addition to the $36.5 billion BP already had spent, or committed to spend, in additional fines, cleanup costs, and settlements to individuals and businesses.

Costs of poor communication are not just financial. People died in the explosion of BP's oil well. Not all communication costs are so dramatic, however. When communication isn't as good as it could be, you and your organization pay a price in wasted time, wasted effort, lost goodwill, and legal problems.

Wasted Time

Bad writing takes longer to read as we struggle to understand what we're reading. How quickly we can comprehend written material is determined by the difficulty of the subject matter and by the document's organization and writing style.

British Petroleum spilled oil into the Gulf of Mexico for 87 days. The explosion that caused the spill killed 11 people and injured 17 others.

NOAA

Second, bad writing needs to be rewritten. Poorly written documents frequently cycle to others for help, thus wasting time of people other than the original writer.

Third, ineffective communication may obscure ideas so that discussions and decisions are needlessly drawn out.

Fourth, unclear or incomplete messages may require the receiver to gather more information. Some receivers may not bother to do so, leading to wrong decisions or a refusal to act.

Wasted Efforts

Ineffective messages don't get results. A receiver who has to guess what the sender means may guess wrong. A reader who finds a letter or email unconvincing or insulting simply won't do what the message asks.

Like many business projects, the *Mars Climate Orbiter* involved a wide range of people in a range of locations. The programmers who wrote the software that controlled the spacecraft's engines worked in Great Britain and used metric measurements in their calculations, while the engineers who made the satellite's engines worked in the United States and used English measurements. Both teams assumed they were using the same measurement standards, neither team made any attempt to check, and no one else caught the error. With that failure, NASA lost a $125 million satellite and years of effort, while gaining a major public embarrassment.[10]

Lost Goodwill

Whatever the literal content of the words, every communication serves either to build or to undermine the image the audience has of the communicator.

One example of wasted effort arising from communication problems occurred when the *Mars Climate Orbiter* spacecraft lost contact with NASA mission control just after it arrived at Mars. A subsequent investigation revealed the main problem was a minor software-programming error caused by communication errors.

NASA

Part of building a good image is taking the time to write correctly. Even organizations that have adopted casual dress still expect writing to appear professional and to be free from typos and grammatical errors.

Legal Problems

Poor communication choices can lead to legal problems for individuals and organizations. The news is full of examples. Papa John's pizza was hit with a lawsuit of a quarter billion dollars for text advertisements that customers claimed were spam.[11] Capital One Financial, the large credit card company, agreed to pay $210 million to settle allegations that its call center pressured customers into buying credit-protection products such as credit monitoring.[12]

Individual communications also can have legal consequences. For example, text messages revealed an affair between Detroit Mayor Kwame Kilpatrick and one of his aides; both the messages and the affair contradicted testimony the mayor had given under oath. Consequences included loss of office, jail time, and a $1 million fine.

In particular, communications such as emails and text messages create legal obligations for organizations. When a lawsuit is filed against an organization, the lawyers for the plaintiffs have the right to subpoena documents written by the organization's employees. These documents then may be used as evidence, for instance, that an employer fired an employee without adequate notice or that a company knew about a safety defect but did nothing to correct it.

Careful writers and speakers think about the larger social context in which their words may appear. What might those words mean to other people in the field? What might they mean to a judge and jury? What might they mean to an unintended audience in the general public?

Communicating on the Job

LO 1-4

Communication—verbal and nonverbal, spoken and written—goes to both internal and external audiences. **Internal audiences** are other people in the same organization: subordinates, superiors, and peers. **External audiences** are people outside the organization: customers, suppliers, distributors, unions, stockholders, potential employees, trade associations, special interest groups, government agencies, the press, and the general public.

People in organizations produce a large variety of documents. Figures 1.1 and 1.2 list a few of the specific documents produced at Ryerson, a company that fabricates and sells steel, aluminum, other metals, and plastics to a wide variety of industrial clients and has sales offices across the United States, Canada, and China.

All of the documents in Figures 1.1 and 1.2 have one or more of the three basic purposes of organizational writing: (1) to inform, (2) to request or persuade, and (3) to build goodwill. In fact, most messages have multiple purposes. When you answer a question, for instance, you're informing, but you also want to build goodwill by suggesting that you're competent and perceptive and that your answer is correct and complete.

Figure 1.1	Internal Documents Produced in One Organization	
Document	**Description of document**	**Purpose(s) of document**
Transmittal	Memo accompanying document, telling why it's being forwarded to the receiver	Inform; persuade reader to read document; build image and goodwill
Monthly or quarterly report	Report summarizing profitability, productivity, and problems during period; used to plan activity for next month or quarter	Inform; build image and goodwill (report is accurate, complete; writer understands company)
Policy and procedure bulletin	Statement of company policies and instructions (e.g., how to enter orders, how to run fire drills)	Inform; build image and goodwill (procedures are reasonable)
Request to deviate from policy and procedure bulletin	Persuasive message arguing that another approach is better for a specific situation than the standard approach	Persuade; build image and goodwill (request is reasonable; writer seeks good of company)
Performance appraisal	Evaluation of an employee's performance	Inform; persuade employee to improve
Memo of congratulations	Congratulations to employees who have won awards, been promoted	Build goodwill

Figure 1.2	External Documents Produced in One Organization	
Document	**Description of document**	**Purpose(s) of document**
Quotation	Letter giving price for a specific product or service	Inform; build goodwill (price is reasonable)
Claims adjustment	Letter granting or denying customer request to be given credit for defective goods or service	Inform; build goodwill
Job description	Description of qualifications and duties of job; used for performance appraisals, salaries, and hiring	Inform; persuade good candidates to apply; build goodwill (job duties match level, pay)
10-K report	Report filed with the Securities and Exchange Commission detailing financial information	Inform
Annual report	Report to stockholders summarizing financial information for year	Inform; persuade stockholders to retain stock and others to buy; build goodwill (company is a good corporate citizen)
Thank-you letter	Letter to suppliers, customers, or other people who have helped individuals or the company	Build goodwill

Basic Criteria for Effective Messages

LO 1-5

Good business communication meets seven basic criteria.

- **It's clear.** An effective message clearly imparts its intended meaning. The audience doesn't have to work to figure out what the author means. Often, you'll need to revise entire paragraphs to phrase your ideas more clearly and to incorporate more accurate or more precise words.

- **It's complete.** All of the audience questions are answered. The audience has enough information to evaluate the message and act on it.

- **It's correct.** The message is free from errors in spelling, capitalization, word choice, and grammar.

- **It follows conventions. Conventions** are widely accepted practices that help people recognize, produce, and interpret different kinds of communications. The key to using conventions effectively is to remember that they always need to fit the rhetorical situation—they always need to be adjusted for the particular audience, context, and purpose.

- **It saves the audience's time.** The style, organization, and visual or aural impact of the message help the audience read or hear, understand, and act on the information as quickly as possible. For example, effective messages use forecasting statements for organization, "Employee stock ownership programs (ESOPs) provide four benefits." Such statements tell readers what information will follow.

- **It builds goodwill.** The message presents a positive image of the communicator and their organization. It treats the message recipient as a person, not a number. It cements a good relationship between the communicator and the audience.

- **It's ethical.** Ethical communication enacts certain values; for example, it is responsible, careful, truthful, and relevant.

Whether a message meets these seven criteria depends on the interactions among the communicator, the audience, and the rhetorical situation. No single set of words will work in all possible situations.

Questions for Analyzing a Business Communication Situation

LO 1-6

When you're faced with the need to communicate, you need to analyze the **rhetorical situation.** You can ask the questions posed in this section in order to analyze any communication situation that you encounter.

1. What Is Your Purpose in Communicating?

What must this message do to meet the organization's needs? What must it do to meet your own needs? What do you want your audience to do? To think or feel? List all your purposes, major and minor.

Even in a simple message, you may have several related purposes: to announce a new policy; to make the audience aware of the policy's provisions and requirements; and to have them feel that the policy is a good one, that the organization cares about its employees, and that you are a competent communicator and manager.

When you convey information to which the audience's basic reaction will be neutral, the message is an **informative message**. If you convey information to which the audience's reaction will be positive, the message is a **positive or good-news message**. Unlike a **persuasive message**, neither informative nor positive messages ask the audience to do something. However, you will want the audience to take a positive attitude toward the information they are receiving, so in a sense, even an informative message has a persuasive element. Chapter 11 discusses persuasive messages—messages that aim to change beliefs or behavior. Chapter 10 discusses negative messages—messages that convey news the audience will not welcome. Chapter 9 covers positive and informative messages.

Keep in mind that many messages can be positive, informative, negative, or persuasive, depending on your purpose. A transmittal, for example, can be positive when you want to let your audience know about glowing sales figures; it can be persuasive when you want the audience to act on the information. A performance appraisal is positive when you evaluate someone who's doing superbly, negative when your purpose is to compile a record to justify firing someone, and persuasive when you want to motivate a satisfactory worker to continue to improve.

2. Who Is Your Audience?

What audience characteristics are relevant for this particular message? If you are writing or speaking to more than one person, how do the people in your audience differ? Some characteristics of your audience will be irrelevant; focus on ones that matter *for this message*. Whenever you address several people or a group, try to identify the economic, cultural, or situational differences that may affect how various subgroups may respond to what you have to say.

Identifying Audiences   The first step in analyzing your audience is to decide who your audience is. Organizational messages have multiple audiences:

1. A **gatekeeper** has the power to stop your message instead of sending it on to other audiences. The gatekeeper therefore controls whether your message even gets to the primary audience. Sometimes the supervisor who assigns the message is the gatekeeper; sometimes the gatekeeper is higher in the organization. In some cases, gatekeepers may exist outside the organization.

2. The **primary audience** decides whether to accept your recommendations or act on the basis of your message. You must reach the primary audience to fulfill your purposes in any message.

3. The **secondary audience** may be asked to comment on your message or to implement your ideas after they've been approved. Secondary audiences also include lawyers who may use your message—perhaps years later—as evidence of your organization's culture and practices.

4. An **auxiliary audience** may encounter your message but will not have to interact with it. This audience includes the "read-only" people.

5. A **watchdog audience**, though it does not have the power to stop the message and will not act directly on it, has political, social, or economic power. The watchdog pays close attention to the transaction between you and the primary audience and may base future actions on its evaluation of your message.

Figure 1.3	Strategies for Documents with Multiple Audiences

Content and number of details

- Provide an overview or executive summary for readers who want just the main points.
- In the body of the document, provide enough detail for the primary audience (i.e., decision makers) and for anyone else who could veto your proposal.
- If the primary audience doesn't need details that other audiences will want, provide those details in appendices.

Organization

- Use headings and a table of contents so readers can turn to the portions that interest them.
- Organize your message based on the primary audience's attitude toward it.

Level of formality

- Avoid personal pronouns. The pronoun "you" ceases to have a specific meaning when several different audiences use a document.
- If both internal and external audiences will use a document, use a slightly more formal style than you would in an internal document.
- Use a more formal style when you write to international audiences.

Technical level

- In the body of the document, assume the degree of knowledge of the primary audience.
- Put background and explanatory information under separate headings. Then readers can use the headings and the table of contents to read or skip these sections, as their knowledge dictates.
- If the primary audience has more knowledge than other audiences, provide a glossary of terms. Early in the document, let readers know that the glossary exists.

Here's an example: Fernanda works in the information technology department of a large financial institution. She must write an email explaining a major software change. Her boss is the *gatekeeper*; the software users in various departments are the *primary audience*. The *secondary audience* includes the tech people who will be helping the primary audience install and adjust to the new software. The *auxiliary audience* includes department program assistants who forward the email to appropriate people in each department. A *watchdog audience* is the board of directors.

When it is not possible to meet everyone's needs, meet the needs of gatekeepers and decision makers first. Figure 1.3 offers strategies for creating documents for multiple audiences.

Although you will probably use different styles, and sometimes include different content, when communicating with multiple audiences, you need to keep your core message consistent. For example, engineers might need more technical information than managers, but the core messages that the two audiences receive should not be conflicting in any way.

Analyzing Members of Groups   In many organizational situations, you'll analyze your audience not as individuals, but as members of a group. When creating your message, first determine the relationship between the audience and your organization, what separates them from the public: "taxpayers who must be notified that they owe more income tax," "customers who use our accounting services," or "employees with small children." Focus on what group members have in common. After determining the relationship between the audience and your organization, focus on what these audience members have in common.[13] Although generalizations won't be true for all members of the group, generalization is necessary when you must appeal to a large group of people with one message. In some cases, no research is necessary: It's easy to guess the attitudes of people who must be told they owe more taxes. In other cases, databases may yield useful information. In still other cases, you may want to do original research.

Figure 1.4	Some Generational Differences in the Workplace			
	Baby boomers	**Generation X**	**Millennials**	**Generation Z**
Birth dates	1946–1964	1965–1980	1980–1995	1996–2010
Attitude toward career	Loyal to employer	Loyal to profession	Digital entrepreneurs	Flexible, able to shift
Characteristics	Experimental, liberal, free-spirited	Ethical, independent, adaptable	Optimistic, adventurous, open-minded	Internet savvy, innovative, impatient
Preferred channels	Face-to-face, email	Texting, email	Texting, social media	Online face-to-face

Sources: "The Generation Guide—Millennials, Gen X, Y, Z and Baby Boomers," *FourHooks*, April 26, 2015, http://fourhooks.com/marketing/the-generation-guide-millennials-gen-x-y-z-and-baby-boomers-art5910718593/; and Jen Wieczner, "Are Generational Differences Impacting Your Business? Are You Communicating Effectively?" My RIA Lawyer, n.d., https://www.myrialawyer.com/generational-differences/?utm_medium=social&utm_source=linkedin.company&utm_campaign=postfity&utm_content=postfityee71c.

Demographic Characteristics   Databases enable you to map demographic and psychographic profiles of customers or employees. **Demographic characteristics** are measurable features that can be counted objectively, such as income, education level, geographic region, and age.

For most companies, income is a major demographic characteristic. In 2011, Walmart quietly returned to advertising its "everyday low prices" after experimenting with low-priced sale products balanced by slightly higher prices elsewhere. The new pricing had not appealed to Walmart's financially strapped customers. The chain also returned guns and fishing equipment to the shelves of many of its stores in an attempt to attract more men as customers.[14]

Location is yet another major demographic characteristic. You can probably think of many differences among regional audiences or between urban and rural audiences in the U.S. See Chapter 5 for more information on communicating across cultures.

Age certainly matters. One aspect of age that gets much press is the differences between generations in the office. Many older people believe younger workers have a sense of entitlement, that they expect great opportunities and perks without working for them. On the other hand, many younger workers see their older colleagues as rigid. Figure 1.4 shows some of the frequently mentioned differences among baby boomers, Gen Xers, millennials, and Gen Zers. While awareness of generational differences may help in some communication situations, such lists are also a good place to warn against stereotypes.

Psychographic Characteristics   **Psychographic characteristics** include personalities, values, interests, opinions, attitudes, beliefs, goals, and lifestyles. Knowing what your audience finds important allows you to choose information that the audience will find persuasive.

Marketing companies obtain psychographic data from consumers' web surfing records, including use of social media, and personal offline data from sources such as the Census Bureau, consumer research firms such as Nielsen, credit card and shopping histories, and real estate and motor vehicle records. The combined data allow marketers to reach narrowly defined audiences.

3. How Will the Audience Initially React to the Message?

Will the Audience See This Message as Important?   Audiences will read and act on messages they see as important, and they may ignore messages that seem unimportant to them. When the audience may see your message as unimportant, you need to (1) use a subject line or first paragraph that shows your reader this message is important and relevant, (2) make the action as easy as possible, (3) keep the message as short as possible, and (4) suggest a realistic deadline for action.

Is the Audience Opposed to Your Message?   People who have already made up their minds are highly resistant to change. When the audience will oppose what you have to say, you need to start your message with any areas of common ground that you share with your audience and show that your solution is the best solution currently available, even though it isn't perfect. You might also limit your statement or request. If parts of your message could be delivered later, postpone them.

How Will the Fact That the Message Is From You Affect the Audience's Reaction?   The audience's experience with you and your organization shapes the response to this new message. Someone who thinks well of you and your organization will be prepared to receive your message favorably; someone who thinks poorly of you and the organization will be quick to find fault with what you say and the way you say it. When your audience has negative feelings about your organization, your position, or you personally, you need to use positive emphasis (see Chapter 2) to counteract the natural tendency to sound defensive.

4. What Information Must Your Message Include?

Make a list of all the points that you must include; check your draft to make sure you include them all. To include information without emphasizing it, put it in the middle of a paragraph or document and present it as briefly as possible.

How Much Does the Audience Already Know about This Subject?
It's easy to overestimate the knowledge an audience has. People outside your own immediate unit may not really know what it is you do. Even people who once worked in your unit may have forgotten specific details now that their daily work is in management. People outside your organization won't know how *your* organization does things.

Does the Audience's Knowledge Need to Be Updated or Corrected?
Our personal experience guides our expectations and actions, but sometimes it needs to be corrected. If you're trying to change someone's understanding of something, you need to acknowledge the audience's initial understanding early in the message; use examples, statistics, or other evidence to show the need for the change; allow the audience to save face by suggesting that changed circumstances call for new attitudes or action.

How Much Detail Does the Audience Want?   A message that does not give the audience the desired amount or kind of detail may fail. Sometimes you can ask your audience how much detail they want. When you write to people you do not know well, you can provide all the detail needed to understand and act on your message. You should group chunks of information under headings so that readers can go directly to the parts of the message they find most interesting and relevant.

   Always provide enough detail to be vivid and concrete, especially when you are proposing an idea that the audience may not have thought of before or that will take some time to pay off.

Are There Hot Buttons or "Red Flag" Words That May Create an Immediate Negative Response?   You don't have time to convince the audience that a term is broader or more neutral than their understanding. When you need agreement or approval, you should avoid terms that carry emotional charges for many people, such as *criminal* and *fundamentalist*.

5. What Benefits Will Your Audience Find Convincing?

Use your analysis of your audience to create effective **audience benefits**, advantages that the audience gets by using your services, buying your products, following your policies, or adopting your ideas. In informative messages, benefits give reasons to comply with the information you announce and suggest that the information is good. In persuasive messages, benefits give reasons to act and help overcome audience resistance. Negative messages do not use benefits.

Good benefits meet five criteria. Each of these criteria suggests a technique for writing good benefits.

Adapt Benefits to the Audience

When you write to different audiences, you may need to stress different benefits. Suppose that you want to persuade people to come to the restaurant you manage. It's true that everybody needs to eat, but telling people they can satisfy their hunger needs won't persuade them to come to your restaurant rather than going somewhere else or eating at home. Depending on what features your restaurant offered, you could appeal to one or more of the following subgroups:

Subgroup	Features to meet the subgroup's needs
People who work outside the home	A quick lunch; a relaxing place to take clients or colleagues
Parents with small children	High chairs, children's menus, and toys to keep the kids entertained while they wait for their order
People who eat out a lot	Variety both in food and in decor
People on tight budgets	Economical food; a place where they don't need to tip (cafeteria or fast food)
People on special diets	Low-sodium and low-carb dishes; vegetarian food; kosher or halal food
People to whom eating out is part of an evening's entertainment	Music or a floor show; elegant surroundings; reservations so they can get to a show or event after dinner; late hours so they can come to dinner after a show or game

Stress Intrinsic as Well as Extrinsic Motivators

Intrinsic motivators come automatically from using a product or doing something. **Extrinsic motivators** are "added on." Someone in power decides to give them; they do not necessarily come from using the product or doing the action. Figure 1.5 gives examples of extrinsic and intrinsic motivators for three activities.

Intrinsic motivators or benefits are better than extrinsic motivators; there just aren't enough extrinsic motivators for everything you want people to do. You can't give a prize to every customer every time they place an order or to every subordinate who does what they are supposed to do. In addition, research shows that extrinsic motivators actually may make people *less* satisfied with the products they buy or the procedures they follow.

Figure 1.5	Extrinsic and Intrinsic Motivators	
Activity	**Extrinsic motivator**	**Intrinsic motivator**
Making a sale	Getting a commission	Pleasure in convincing someone; pride in using your talents to think of a strategy and execute it
Turning in a suggestion to a company suggestion system	Getting a monetary reward when the suggestion is implemented	Solving a problem at work; making the work environment a little more pleasant
Writing a report that solves an organizational problem	Getting praise, a good performance appraisal, and maybe a raise	Pleasure in having an effect on an organization; pride in using your skills to solve problems; solving the problem itself

Prove Benefits with Clear Logic and Explain Them in Adequate Detail
An audience benefit is a claim or assertion that the audience will benefit if they do something. Convincing the audience, therefore, involves two steps: making sure the benefit really will occur and explaining it to the audience.

If the logic behind a claimed benefit is faulty or inaccurate, there's no way to make that particular benefit convincing. Revise the benefit to make it logical.

Faulty logic: Moving your account information into Excel will save you time.

Analysis: If you have not used Excel before, in the short run it will probably take you longer to work with your account information using Excel. You may have been pretty good with your old system!

Revised benefit: Moving your account information into Excel will allow you to prepare your monthly budget pages with a few clicks of a button.

Overcome Potential Obstacles
Everyone has a set of ideas and habits and a mental self-image. If we're asked to do something that seems to violate any of those, we first have to be persuaded to change our attitudes or habits or self-image—a change we're reluctant to make. In these cases, show that what you ask is consistent with some aspect of what the audience believes.

When your request is time-consuming, complicated, or physically or psychologically difficult, you need to show how the audience (not just you or your organization) will benefit when the action is completed. You should also make the action as easy as possible. For complex procedures, create a list of actions so that the audience can check off each step when it's done.

Phrase Benefits in *You*-Attitude
If benefits aren't worded with *you*-attitude (see Chapter 2), they'll sound selfish and won't be as effective as they could be. It doesn't matter how you phrase benefits while you're brainstorming and developing them, but in your final draft, check to be sure that you've used *you*-attitude.

Lacks *you*-attitude: We have the lowest prices in town.

You-attitude: At Havlichek Cars, you get the best deal in town.

Using *you*-attitude also means showing how your organization's policy or product meets the audience's needs. Link features to audience needs and provide details that make the benefit vivid.

Weak: You get quick service.

Better: If you only have an hour for lunch, try our Business Buffet. Within minutes, you can choose from a variety of main dishes, vegetables, and a make-your-own-sandwich-and-salad bar. You'll have a lunch that's as light or filling as you want, with time to enjoy it—and still be back to the office on time.

6. How Can You Ensure That You Communicate Ethically?

Business communication occurs at multiple levels: between coworkers, between organizations, and between organizations and the communities in which they operate. Throughout these levels, ethical business communication begins with telling the truth.

The National Communication Association developed a "Credo for Ethical Communication." In the credo, the NCA focuses on concrete actions as opposed to abstract philosophies. Besides calling for truthfulness, it advocates diversity of perspective, reason, and respect in communication practices.

Figure 1.6 elaborates on ethical components of communication. As it suggests, language, graphics, and document design—basic parts of any business document—can be

Figure 1.6	Ethical Issues in Business Communications
Manner of conveying the message	**Qualities of the message**
■ Is the language clear to the audience? Does it respect the audience? ■ Do the words balance the organization's right to present its best case with its responsibility to present its message honestly? ■ Do graphics help the audience understand? Or are graphics used to distract or confuse? ■ Does the design of the document make reading easy? Does document design attempt to make readers skip key points?	■ Is the message honest and sensitive to all stakeholders? ■ Have interested parties been able to provide input? ■ Does the audience get all the information it needs to make a good decision, or is information withheld? ■ Is information communicated so the audience can grasp it or are data "dumped" without any context? ■ Are the arguments logical? Are they supported with adequate evidence? ■ Are the emotional appeals used fairly? Do they supplement logic rather than substitute for it? ■ Does the organizational pattern lead the audience without undue manipulation? ■ Does the message use good sources? Are the sources used honestly? Are they documented?

ethical or manipulative. Persuading and gaining compliance—activities at the heart of business and organizational life—can be done with respect or contempt for customers, co-workers, and subordinates.

In these days of instant communication, you, like the organization in which you work, always must act in an ethical manner.

Summary by Learning Objectives

LO 1-1   **Describe the benefits of good communication.**

Communication helps organizations and the people in them achieve their goals. People put things in writing to create a record, to convey complex data, to make things convenient for the reader, to save money, and to convey their own messages more effectively.

LO 1-2   **Explain why you need to be able to communicate well.**

- The three basic purposes of business communication are to inform, to request or persuade, and to build goodwill. Most messages have more than one purpose.
- The ability to write and speak well becomes increasingly important as you rise in an organization.

LO 1-3   **Describe the costs of poor communication.**

Poor writing wastes time, wastes effort, and jeopardizes goodwill.

LO 1-4   **Describe what communication on the job can look like.**

- Communication goes to both internal and external audiences.
- People in organizations produce a large variety of documents.

LO 1-5   **Explain the basic criteria for effective messages.**

Good business writing meets seven basic criteria: it's clear, complete, and correct; it follows conventions; it saves the reader's time; it builds goodwill; and it's ethical.

LO 1-6   **Analyze a business communication situation.**

1. What is your purpose in communicating?
2. Who is your audience?
3. How will the audience initially react to the message?
4. What information must your message include?
5. What benefits will your audience find convincing?
6. How can you ensure that you communicate ethically?

Exercises and Cases

1.1   Reviewing the Chapter

Why do you and your business need to be able to communicate well? (LO 1-1)

What are some flawed assumptions about workplace communication? What is the reality for each myth? (LO 1-2)

What are the costs of poor communication? (LO 1-3)

What is the difference between internal and external audiences? (LO 1-4)

What are the basic criteria for effective messages? (LO 1-5)

What are the questions for analyzing a business communication situation? (LO 1-6)

Who are the five different audiences your message may need to address? (LO 1-6)

What are five characteristics of good audience benefits? (LO 1-6)

1.2   Assessing Your Punctuation and Grammar Skills

To help you see where you need to improve in grammar and punctuation, take the Diagnostic Test, B.1, Appendix B.

1.3   Messages for Discussion I—Asking for a Class

The following are emails from various students to Dr. Destiny Sands, who is a professor in the English Department. These students are wondering if Dr. Sands would let them register for her already-full class (English 320: Business Communication).

Each email shows a different way a student could make a request of Dr. Sands. How well does each message meet the needs of the reader and the writer? Is the message clear, complete, and correct?

1.
> Hi Destiny,
>
> My name is Jake and I was wondering if you had any extra seats in your English 320 class. See, I'm a senior and I really need to take your class so I can graduate. I don't know what else to do. I didn't take it last year cuz I really didn't want to.
>
> I'm desperate. Help me out.
>
> Jake

2.
> Hello Sands,
>
> I'm sorry to bother you, but I really, really need to get into your English 320 class. My advisor totally screwed up my schedule and I didn't know I needed to take this class. It's so weird because I shouldn't have to take this class anyway, but whatever. So, if you could just add me into your class, that would be great.
>
> Thanks,
>
> Ally

3.
> Dr. Sands,
>
> Good morning. I hate to email you right before the semester begins, but I have a request. When I tried to register for your Eng 320 course, the website stated the course was full. I was wondering if I could possibly be put on a list to add the course just in case someone drops it? I am very interested in this course and would love to take it this semester if at all possible.
>
> Thank you so much for your time,
>
> Christine

4.

> Dear Dr. Sands,
>
> Do u have anymore seats open in your class? I think its 302 or 320 or something like that. Anyways, it would be cool if you would let me into the class. Sorry for emailing right at the last minute, but I didn't know what else to do.
>
> You are the best,
>
> Andrew

1.4   Messages for Discussion II—Responding to Rumors

The Acme Corporation has been planning to acquire Best Products, and Acme employees are worried about how the acquisition will affect them. Ed Zeplin, Acme's human resource manager, has been visiting the Acme chat sites and sees a dramatic rise in the number of messages spreading rumors about layoffs. Most of the rumors are false.

The following messages are possible responses that Ed can post to the chat sites. How well does each message meet the needs of the reader, the writer, and the organization? Is the message clear, complete, and correct? Does it save the reader's time? Does it build goodwill?

1.

> It Will Be Great!
>
> Author: L. Ed Zeplin, HR
>
> Date: Tuesday, May 23
>
> I am happy to tell you that the HR news is good. Two months ago, the CEO told me about the merger, and I have been preparing a human resource plan ever since.
>
> I want you to know about this because morale has been bad, and it shouldn't be. You really should wait for the official announcements, and you'll see that the staffing needs will remain strong. My department has been under a lot of pressure, but if you'll be patient, we'll explain everything—the staffing, the compensation.
>
> Our plan should be ready by Monday, and then if you have any questions, just contact your HR rep.

2.

> HR Staffing
>
> Author: HR Boss
>
> Date: Tuesday, May 23
>
> The rumors are false. Just ask anyone in HR. There will be no layoffs.

3.

> Don't Believe the Rumors
>
> Author: lezeplin@acme.com
>
> Date: Tuesday, May 23
>
> Acme has 475 employees, and Best Products has 132 employees. Our human resource plan for next year calls for 625 employees. If you do the math, you can see that there will be no layoffs. Rather, we will be hiring 18 employees. Of course, as we consolidate operations with Best, there will be some redeployments. However, our plan indicates that we will be able to retain our current staff. All employees are valued at Acme, as our current benefits package testifies.

Our HR plan is based on the best analytic techniques and a business forecast by a top consulting firm. If you're an employee, you should review our business plan, at the Our Goals page on Acme's intranet. Everyone should read Acme's mission statement on our home page, www.acme.com.

4.

Layoff Rumors Do Acme a Disservice

Author: Zeplin in HR

Date: Tuesday, 23 May

If you come here to get your company information, you aren't getting the straight story. The people posting to this discussion board are spreading false rumors, not the truth. If you want to know the truth about Acme, ask the people who have access to the information.

As HR manager, I can assure you we won't be laying off employees after the merger with Best Products. I'm the one who approves the staffing plan, so I should know. If people would ask me, instead of reading the negative, whining lies at this site, they would know the facts, too.

If people really cared about job security, they would be working and exceeding their goals, rather than wasting their time in rumor-mongering on message boards. Hard work: that's the key to success!

5.

The True Story about Layoffs

Author: lezeplin@acme.com

Date: Tuesday, 23 May

Whenever there is a merger or acquisition, rumors fly. It's human nature to turn to rumors when a situation seems uncertain. The case of Acme acquiring Best Products is no exception, so I'm not surprised to see rumors about layoffs posted on this message board.

Have no fear! I am working closely with our CEO and with the CEO and human resource manager at Best Products, and we all agree that our current staff is a valuable asset to Acme, to Best, and to our combined companies in the future. We have no plans to lay off any of our valued people. I will continue monitoring this message board and will post messages as I am able to disclose more details about our staffing plans. In the meantime, employees should watch for official information in the company newsletter and on our intranet.

We care about our people! If employees ever have questions about our plans and policies, they should contact me directly.

L. Ed Zeplin, HR Manager

1.5   Understanding the Role of Communication in Your Organization

Interview your work supervisor to learn about the kinds and purposes of communication in your organization. Your questions could include the following:

- What kinds of communication (e.g., emails, presentations) are most important in this organization?

- What communications do you create? Are they designed to inform, to persuade, to build goodwill—or to do a combination?

- What communications do you receive? Are they designed to inform, to persuade, to build goodwill—or to do a combination?

- Who are your most important audiences within the organization?
- Who are your most important external audiences?
- What are the challenges of communicating in this organization?
- What kinds of documents and presentations does the organization prefer?

As your instructor directs,
a. Share your results with a small group of students.
b. Present your results in an email to your instructor.
c. Join with a group of students to make a group presentation to the class.
d. Post your results online to the class.

1.6 Making Ethical Choices

Indicate whether you consider each of the following actions ethical, unethical, or a gray area. Which of the actions would you do? Which would you feel uncomfortable doing? Which would you refuse to do?

Discuss your answers with a small group of classmates. In what ways did knowing you would share with a group change your answers?

1. Inflating your evaluation of a subordinate because you know that only people ranked *excellent* will get pay raises.
2. Updating your Facebook page and visiting the pages of friends during business hours.
3. Writing a feasibility report about a new product and deemphasizing test results that show it could cause cancer.
4. Designing an ad campaign for a cigarette brand.
5. Telling a job candidate that the company "usually" grants cost-of-living raises every six months, even though you know that the company is losing money and plans to cancel cost-of-living raises for the next year.
6. Laughing at the racist or sexist jokes a client makes, even though you find them offensive.

1.7 Identifying Audiences

In each of the following situations, label the audiences as gatekeeper, primary, secondary, auxiliary, or watchdog audiences (all audiences may not be in each scenario) and explain your reasoning:

1. Kent, Carol, and Jose are planning to start a website design business. However, before they can get started, they need money. They have developed a business plan and are getting ready to seek funds from financial institutions for starting their small business.
2. Quinn's boss asked them to write a direct-mail letter to potential customers about the advantages of becoming a preferred member of their agency's travel club. The letter will go to all customers of the agency who are more than 65 years old.
3. Paul works for the mayor's office in a big city. As part of a citywide cost-cutting measure, a blue-ribbon panel has recommended requiring employees who work more than 40 hours in a week to take compensatory time off rather than being paid overtime. The only exceptions

will be the police and fire departments. The mayor asks Paul to prepare a proposal for the city council, which will vote on whether to implement the change. Before they vote, council members will hear from (1) citizens, who will have an opportunity to read the proposal and communicate their opinions to the city council; (2) mayors' offices in other cities, who may be asked about their experiences; (3) union representatives, who may be concerned about the reduction in income that will occur if the proposal is implemented; (4) department heads, whose ability to schedule work might be limited if the proposal passes; and (5) the blue-ribbon panel and good-government lobbying groups. Council members come up for reelection in six months.

4. Sharon, Steven's boss at Bigster Corporation, has asked him to write an email for everyone in her division, informing them of HR's new mandatory training sessions on new government regulations affecting Bigster's services.

1.8 Analyzing Multiple Audiences

Like most major corporations, the U.S. Census Bureau has multiple, conflicting audiences, among them the president, Congress, press, state governments, citizens (both as providers and users of data), statisticians, and researchers.

- For the bureau, who might serve as gatekeeper, primary, secondary, auxiliary, and watchdog audiences?
- What kinds of conflicting goals might these audiences have?
- What would be appropriate benefits for each type of audience?
- What kinds of categories might the bureau create for its largest audience (citizens)?

1.9   Identifying and Developing Audience Benefits

Listed here are several things an organization might like its employees to do:

1. Write fewer emails.
2. Volunteer at a local food pantry.
3. Volunteer to recruit interns at a job fair.
4. Attend team-building activities every other Friday afternoon.
5. Attend HR seminars on health policy changes.

As your instructor directs,

a. Identify the motives or needs that might be met by each of the activities.

b. Develop each need or motive as an audience benefit in a full paragraph. Use additional paragraphs for the other needs met by the activity. Remember to use *you*-attitude.

1.10   Identifying Objections and Audience Benefits

Think of an organization you know something about and answer the following questions for it:

1. Your organization is thinking about developing a knowledge management system that requires workers to input their knowledge and experience in their job functions into the organizational database. What benefits could the knowledge management system offer your organization? What drawbacks are there? Who would be the easiest to convince? Who would be the hardest?

2. New telephone software would efficiently replace your organization's long-standing human phone operator, who has been a perennial welcoming voice to incoming callers. What objections might people in your organization have to replacing the operator? What benefits might your organization receive? Who would be easiest to convince? Who would be the hardest?

3. Your organization is thinking of outsourcing one of its primary products to a manufacturer in another country where the product can be made more cost-efficiently. What fears or objections might people have? What benefits might your organization receive? Who would be easiest to convince? Who would be hardest?

As your instructor directs,

a. Share your answers orally with a small group of students.

b. Present your answers in an oral presentation to the class.

c. Write a paragraph developing the best audience benefit you identified. Remember to use *you*-attitude.

1.11   Analyzing Benefits for Multiple Audiences

The U.S. Census Bureau lists these benefits from cooperating with the census:

1. "Census information affects the numbers of seats your state occupies in the U.S. House of Representatives. And people from many walks of life use census data to advocate for causes, rescue disaster victims, prevent diseases, research markets, locate pools of skilled workers and more.

    "When you do the math, it's easy to see what an accurate count of residents can do for your community. Better infrastructure. More services. A brighter tomorrow for everyone. In fact, the information the census collects helps to determine how more than $400 billion of federal funding each year is spent on infrastructure and services like:

    -   Hospitals
    -   Job-training centers
    -   Schools
    -   Senior centers
    -   Bridges, tunnels and other public works projects
    -   Emergency services"[15]

How well do these benefits meet the characteristics of good audience benefits discussed in this chapter?

Banking on Multiple Audiences

Bruce Murphy, an executive at KeyBank, tackled a new problem: how to extend banking services to a new audience—people who use banks intermittently or not at all. It is a large group, estimated at 73 million people. Together, they spend an estimated $11 billion in fees at places such as check-cashing outlets, money-wire companies, and paycheck lenders (companies offering cash advances on future paychecks).

However, they are a tough audience. Many of them have a deep distrust of banks or believe banks will not serve them. Murphy also faced another tough audience: bank managers who feared attracting forgeries and other bad checks and thus losing money. One manager actually said, "Are you crazy? These are the very people we're trying to keep out of the bank!"

To attract the new customers, KeyBank cashes payroll and government checks for a 1.5% fee, well below the 2.44% average for check-cashing outlets. The bank also started offering free financial education classes. In fact, the bank even has a program to help people with a history of bounced checks to clear their records by paying restitution and taking the financial education class.

The program is growing, among both check-cashing clients and branches offering the services, to the satisfaction of both audiences.[16]

- What are some other businesses that could expand services to underserved populations?
- What services would they offer?
- What problems would they encounter?
- What audience appeals could they use to attract clients or customers?

Notes

1. Emily Flitter, "The Price of Wells Fargo's Fake Account Scandal Grows by $3 Billion," February 25, 2020, The New York Times, https://www.nytimes.com/2020/02/21/business/wells-fargo -settlement.html#; William Comcowich, "6 PR Crisis Management Lessons from the Wells Fargo Scandal," Glean Info, February 25, 2020, https://glean.info/7-pr-crisis-management-lessons-from-the -wells-fargo-scandal; and Andreas Slotosch, "5 Business Communication Failure Examples and How to Avoid Them," Beekeeper, October 8, 2020, https://www.beekeeper.io/blog /3-internal-communication-failures-that-turned-into-pr-disasters.

2. Eric Krell, "The Unintended Word," *HRMagazine* 51, no. 8 (2006): 52.

3. National Association of Colleges and Employers, "Top 10 Skills for Job Candidates," April 3, 2013, http://www.naceweb.org /Publications/Spotlight_Online/2013/0403/Top_10_Skills_for _Job_Candidates.aspx.

4. The National Commission on Writing for America's Families, Schools, and Colleges, "Writing: A Ticket to Work . . . or a Ticket Out: A Survey of Business Leaders," *College Board* (2004): 7–8.

5. Anne Fisher, "The High Cost of Living and Not Writing Well," *Fortune*, December 7, 1998, 244.

6. Peter D. Hart Research Associate Inc., *How Should Colleges Assess and Improve Student Learning? Employers' Views on the Account- ability Challenge: A Survey of Employers Conducted on Behalf of the Association of American Colleges and Universities* (Washington, DC: The Association of American Colleges and Universities, 2008), 3.

7. The Conference Board et al., *Are They Really Ready to Work? Employers' Perspectives on the Basic Knowledge and Applied Skills of New Entrants to the 21st Century U.S. Workforce,* accessed April 10, 2013, http://www.conference-board.org/pdf_free/BED -06-workforce.pdf.

8. Tom DeMint, "So You Want to Be Promoted," *Fire Engineer- ing* 159, no. 7 (2006); Karen M. Kroll, "Mapping Your Career," *PM Network* 19, no. 11 (2005): 28; and Jeff Snyder, "Recruiter: What It Takes," *Security* 43, no. 11 (2006): 70.

9. Selina Williams, "For BP, the Cleanup Isn't Entirely Over," *Wall Street Journal*, February 4, 2013, B2.

10. NASA MCO Mission Failure Mishap Investigation Board, *Mars Climate Orbiter Mishap Investigation Board Phase I Report*, November 10, 1999, ftp://ftp.hq.nasa.gov/pub/ pao/reports/1999 /MCO_report.pdf.

11. Olivia Smith, "Papa John's Faces $250 Million Spam Lawsuit," *CNNMoney*, November 13, 2012, http://money.cnn .com/2012/11/13/technology/mobile/papa-johns/index.html?iid =obinsite.

12. Matthias Rieker, Andrew R. Johnson, and Alan Zibel, "Capital One Dealt Fine for Pitch to Customers," *Wall Street Journal*, July 19, 2012, C1.

13. Mary Anne Moffitt, *Campaign Strategies and Message Design: A Practitioner's Guide from Start to Finish* (Connecticut: Praeger Publishers, 1999), 12–13.

14. Miguel Bustillo, "Wal-Mart Adds Guns Alongside Butter," *Wall Street Journal*, April 28, 2011, B1; and Karen Talley and Shelly Banjo, "With More on Shelves, Wal-Mart Profit Rises," *Wall Street Journal*, May 18, 2012, B3.

15. Quoted from "Why It's Important," U.S. Census Bureau: United States Census 2010, accessed March 6, 2013, http://www.census .gov/2010census/about/why-important.php.

16. Ann Carrns, "Banks Court a New Client: The Low-Income Earner: KeyCorp Experiments with Check Cashing," *Wall Street Journal*, March 16, 2007, A1, A14.

2 Using Goodwill for Effective Communication

Chapter Outline

DrAfter123/Getty Images

Stitch Fix: Showing Customers that They Care

Reliability, convenience, and customer service are paramount features of goodwill—or the relationship that companies develop with their audience. That relationship is essential when 79% of 18- to 65-year-old consumers in the U.S. say that, before they buy anything, they want to see that companies care about their customers. Few businesses can compete with the level of caring that StitchFix offers its customers.

StitchFix is an online personal-styling service that uses data analytics and AI combined with the expertise of human stylists and customer feedback to send millions of clothing items to customers each year. StitchFix uses a wide variety of data—including customers' ratings of clothing items in the StitchFix app—and runs them through algorithms to narrow available clothing items into smaller pools of potential clothing choices. Customers choose how often to receive a "fix," a selection of five items, and the delivery date of the fix. They are also encouraged to provide a note of request for the upcoming fix. While data analytics may start the fix, a human touch completes it. Each fix comes with a personal note from a human stylist that speaks directly to the customer's request, as well as suggestions for how to wear and combine the items. Customers review each fix item on several criteria to help create a better fix the next time.

StitchFix's success is due to customers' willingness to trust the company to make personal clothing choices and the company's ability to make customers feel

Jeanine E Aune

heard throughout the process, including when things do not go right. That communication comes through many channels, some of them surprising. When one of the authors of this book was preparing to undergo a mastectomy, she requested tops that would be easy to wear during recovery. Not only did the company send five tops as requested, it also sent flowers and a note.

Sources: Blake Morgan, "5 Lessons in Personalization from StitchFix," *Forbes*, December 19, 2019, https://www.forbes.com/sites/blakemorgan/2019/12/10/5-lessons-in-personalization-from-stitch-fix/?sh=1367be26b4e8; Ernan Roman, "How Stitch Fix Shows They Truly Care about Their Customers," *CustomerThink*, February 9, 2018, https://customerthink.com/how-stitch-fix-shows-they-truly-care-about-their-customers; Bernard Marr, "Stitch Fix: The Amazing Use of Case of Using Artificial Intelligence in Fashion Retail," *Forbes*, May 25, 2018, https://www.forbes.com/sites/bernardmarr/2018/05/25/stitch-fix-the-amazing-use-case-of-using-artificial-intelligence-in-fashion-retail/?sh=7101905b3292; and "Wunderman Study Reveals 79% of Consumers Only Buy from Brands that Prove They Care about Earning Their Business," *Cision PR Newswire*, January 5, 2017, https://www.prnewswire.com/news-releases/wunderman-study-reveals-79-of-consumers-only-buy-from-brands-that-prove-they-care-about-earning-their-business-300386618.html.

Learning Objectives

Choosing the Appropriate Channel to Reach Your Audience

LO 2-1

Goodwill makes people feel positively toward you and the organization that you work for, helps build the relationships that increase customer loyalty, and eases the challenges of business and administration. Companies have long been aware that treating customers well pays off in more sales and higher profits. Today we work in a service economy: the majority of jobs are in service, where goodwill is even more important.[1]

The importance of building goodwill with audiences outside your organization is perhaps obvious, but goodwill is also important in your internal communications. More and more organizations are realizing that treating employees well is both financially wise and ethically sound. Happy employees result in less staff turnover, which reduces hiring and training costs, and greater willingness to help the organization succeed. Research indicates prioritizing employee satisfaction can lead to a 6.6% increase in productivity per hour.[2] In 2015, Dan Price, CEO of Gravity Payments, a credit card processing company, made headlines for raising the minimum wage at his business to $70,000, while taking a salary cut to fund the increase. This increase in worker salary directly led to an increase in retention and worker happiness rates, as well as a boost in sales, nearly double profits in 2016,[3] and a reported 80% increase in customers by 2018.[4] More recently, the COVID-19 pandemic hit the company hard, but Price met with all of his employees to explain the dire situation, and almost every employee agreed to a voluntary, temporary pay cut in order to avoid layoffs.[5]

Choosing the appropriate communication channel and using *you*-attitude, positive emphasis, appropriate tone, and bias-free language are all ways that you can build goodwill in your business communications. All of these practices will help you achieve your purposes and make your messages friendlier, more persuasive, more professional, and more compassionate. They suggest that you care not just about money, but also about the needs and interests of your customers, employees, and fellow citizens.

A communication **channel** is the means by which you convey your message. Today's communication offers myriad choices when it comes to media; whether letter, email, podcast, tweet, Instagram, TikTok, or some other option, each method of communicating carries distinct advantages and disadvantages. You should select an appropriate channel in order to optimize your communication.

Evolving channels can have enormous impacts on businesses, and depending on the rhetorical situation, including your audience and purpose, one channel may be better than another. For example, Normans Bridal Shoppe in Springfield, Missouri, reaches its teenage market for prom dresses by showcasing available dresses in upbeat TikTok videos.[6] Ad money has been moving out of print and TV channels and into social media advertising, which had a budget of over $40 billion in 2020.[7]

Businesses use Facebook, Twitter, YouTube, and Flickr to highlight new products and services. Many companies have interactive websites and forums where customers can get product information and chat about products; Amazon is a prime example. Manufacturers give perks to bloggers to talk about their products. Nonprofits advertise events, connect with volunteers, and schedule volunteer service on their Instagram accounts and Facebook pages. And all that social network communication now can be mined by software that performs **semantic analyses**, providing feedback to advertisers about both products and audiences.

Choosing the right channel can be tricky sometimes. As Hurricane Katrina approached the Gulf Coast, the National Hurricane Center found its electronic communications about the looming wallop were not enough; officials at the Center determined that they should phone Gulf Coast mayors and governors to hasten their disaster preparations.[8] Even in the office, you will have to decide if your message will be more effective as an email, text message, phone call, visit, or even sticky note posted on a colleague's computer.

In general, a written message makes it easier to

- Present extensive or complex data.
- Present many specific details.
- Minimize undesirable emotions.
- Track details and agreements.

Oral and visual messages make it easier to
- Use emotion to help persuade the audience.
- Focus the audience's attention on specific points.
- Resolve conflicts and build consensus.
- Modify plans.
- Get immediate action or response.

Benefits of Appropriate Communication Channels

Using a well-chosen channel to share messages will help you meet audience expectations, reach your target audience, shorten response time, and make a broader impact.

Meet Audience Expectations   Audiences expect certain messages to be conveyed certain ways—in other words, messages should adhere to delivery-method conventions. Conventions change as technology changes, but audiences expect businesses to keep up. Years ago, it was standard to receive medical test results in a doctor's-office consultation; today, you can log in to your hospital's website and download data from yesterday's blood draw. If a hospital fails to develop the website that stores and delivers test results electronically, it will lose credibility and, possibly, patients because it does not meet current expectations for how to deliver information.

Reach a More Targeted Audience   Using appropriate technology improves business because it affords a more targeted reach to potential customers. Using the appropriate channel also helps in nonbusiness endeavors. For example, an animal shelter uses Facebook to post videos of pets available for adoption.[9] By showcasing the pets' charming qualities to a wide range of viewers—in a format that allows easy sharing with others—the animal shelter can reach potential adopters more quickly and effectively.

Shorten Response Time   The appropriate channel allows communicators to respond more quickly. Letters used to take weeks to arrive; now emails are sent and received nearly instantaneously. In a hospital, patients order meals and receive their made-to-order tray 22 minutes later.[10] Coworkers may text each other or send an instant message and expect a response within minutes. Although the increased expectations of shortened response times for many technological channels may burden today's employees, the sheer variety of available channels allows for improved service and, in some cases (as in the chapter-opening StitchFix case), stronger customer–company relationships.

Make a Broader Impact   As seen in the StitchFix case, companies and individuals can use a communication channel to do more than improve their bottom line. Companies can retweet support of social-justice causes, email their employees about a company drop-off site for donations to a local charity, or post a video to their Facebook page sharing a list of workplace healthy behaviors, such as taking a brisk walk between tasks. A variety of communication channels allows for an array of opportunities for engagement with a broad range of audiences; it enables a positive impact beyond the realm of business.

Common Communication Channels for Sharing Messages

The best approach for your business depends on its size, purposes, circumstances, needs, and budget.

Face-to-Face Conversations   In the office, much communication is most effectively done face-to-face, and some businesses are encouraging their employees to write fewer emails and visit each other's desks more often. They believe such visits contribute to a friendlier, more collaborative work environment. Research with tracking sensors shows they are right; the most productive workers have the most face-to-face contacts.[11] Face-to-face visits are a good choice when

- You know a colleague welcomes your visits.

- You are building a business relationship with a person.

- A real-time connection saves messages (e.g., setting a meeting agenda).

- Your business requires dialogue or negotiation.

- You need something immediately (such as a signature).

- Discretion is vital, and you do not want to leave a paper trail.

- The situation is complex enough that you want as many visual and aural cues as possible.

Use these tips for effective face-to-face contact:

- Ensure the timing is convenient for the recipient and ask permission to pop in (e.g., "Excuse me, but do you have a moment to talk?")

- If you are discussing something complex, have appropriate documents in hand.

- Don't take over the other person's space. Don't place your papers on top of their desk or table without permission. Don't lean over them or their desk.

- Look for "time to go" signs. Some people have a limited tolerance for small talk, especially when they are hard at work on a task.

Phone Calls   Phone calls serve an important role in business communication, whether within a business or between business and customer.[12] The phone call medium demands immediacy, which can help clarify misunderstandings, address urgent needs, or make decisions in the moment. Phone calls also allow for a layer of nonverbal communication that texting does not, such as nuances of the voice like inflection, pace, and volume. Even voicemail captures vocal communication that would be absent from a written message such as a text or email.

Letters   A letter is a short document that uses a block, modified, or simplified letter format that goes to readers outside your organization. (See Appendix A for examples.) There are many common purposes for letters: job applications, recommendations, job offer letters, resignations, commendations, policy changes, notifications, and more. Letters are useful communication tools when you want your audience to have information that they can refer to keep permanently without access to technology. In addition, a well-written letter offers a personal touch, which creates goodwill with your audience.

Websites   Most customers expect to find information online about a company, such as business hours, services offered, and contact information. To control the information its customers find online, and to control the company's narrative, a company needs a website—if not a standalone website with a private domain name, such as http://www.joaniescupcakes.com, then at least a social media-hosted site, such as a business Facebook page. Without an online presence, a company risks appearing out of touch, incompetent, or not audience-focused, and it loses control of its image to online reviews.

Email   Using email to send messages saves companies time and money because it eliminates printing and postage costs. It also conveys messages more quickly than printed messages. Most companies rely on intracompany email as the primary form of communication among employees, and many companies connect with customers via email lists. In communicating with customers, businesses use email to send order confirmations and tracking updates, special discounts, goodwill-building messages such as holiday greetings, or new product announcements.

Email is commonly used for these purposes:

- To accomplish routine, noncontroversial business activities (e.g., setting up meetings and appointments, reminders, notices, quick updates, information sharing).

- To save time: People can look through 60 to 100 emails an hour.

- To save money: One email can go to many people, including globally distributed teams.

- To allow readers to deal with messages at their convenience, when timing is not crucial.

- To communicate accurately.

- To provide readers with details for reference (e.g., meeting information).

- To create a "paper trail," that is, a record of an interaction.

Emails do not work well for some purposes. For example, negative critiques and bad news generally have better outcomes when delivered in person. Avoid passing on any email communication that could be misinterpreted, such as that featuring sarcasm or irony. If your name is attached, you are responsible for how the audience perceives your message—even if your intent was sound.

Memos   A memo is a document using memo format to send messages to readers in your organization (see Appendix A for examples). These days, memos typically cover the same information as email. Indeed, they are typically sent via email as an attachment. However, memo format makes the message a bit more formal.

Text Messages   Text messages allow for quick communication that falls between the immediacy of a phone call and that of an email. Researchers have found that people do not like to use texting for larger tasks, more complex questions or instructions, or messages connected in any way with conflict.[13] For simple communication, texting is an appropriate and efficient choice. For example, patients can request appointment reminders from their doctor's office via text or the doctor's office can request that a client confirm an appointment via text. This practice reduces forgotten appointments, improving overall efficiency, and builds goodwill between doctor and patient. In fact, 70% of patients see value in receiving texts from their health care providers.[14]

Texting is not used just between businesses and clients; it can assist internal communication as well. For example, Canada and parts of Europe have adopted a new system allowing copilots and air-traffic controllers to communicate by texting.[15] The new system helps reduce communication errors that traditionally occur when using radios, mistakes such as misheard instructions and numbers. It saves valuable time when pilots or controllers no longer have to repeat information to make sure they are being understood. Both pilots and controllers alike appreciate this use of texting.

Social Media   Many organizations have adopted multiple social media tools. In addition to reaching thousands of clients in a single message, social media offers a relatively inexpensive way to connect. Employees can post profiles, updates, tweets, blog entries, or useful links, all for free. They also can do all of these activities from the smartphones, laptops, or tablets that many organizations provide their employees.

Of course, like all communication channels, social media sites have some drawbacks. If employees spend much of their day immersed in social media, how much of their regular work routine is not being completed? A survey of 1,400 large U.S. companies reported that more than half have some restrictions on social media use.[16] For businesses, a challenge of social media is figuring out how to harness the positives to increase productivity, particularly when dealing with customers. Some companies monitor what employees do on social media. However, it can be hard to differentiate between social media use for professional and personal purposes, especially when some employees have just a single account.

New social media modes are invented and introduced daily, but some of the most common ways for businesses to connect using social media are Facebook, Twitter, Instagram, and LinkedIn.

Facebook   Facebook is a social networking tool where users create a profile and then can chat and share interests with other users. In 2020, the site had 1.69 billion users worldwide.[17]

Beyond buying advertising space, organizations use Facebook as a communication channel with customers by providing updates about business activities, introducing new products or services, providing tips on old ones, providing information about upcoming events, encouraging participation in philanthropic causes, or offering discounts or incentives. Organizations also can create focus groups where they can receive or share feedback from clients about products and services.

Organizations get data from likes, links clicked, and customer comments. As an added bonus to businesses, Facebook connections can increase awareness about their brand by boosting their presence in search engines. Best of all, Facebook easily integrates with other social media platforms such as Instagram and Twitter, which offers organizations a broad media connection to consumers.

Employees within the same organization can build stronger relationships by friending each other. In some organizations, teams even have established Facebook groups to promote camaraderie and create a place to discuss project documents and other concerns.

Instagram   Instagram is a visuals-based social media platform that allows users to share images with brief descriptions and respond to others' posts with hearts and comments. Like Twitter, Instagram utilizes the **hashtag** system that allows users to categorize their posts under a variety of labels, helping decide how the post will be sorted, and users can filter to view only posts that were tagged with a certain hashtag. For instance, including #dogsofinstagram on your post would mean that anyone searching for the #dogsofinstagram hashtag would see your post (in chronological order or sorted by popularity)—possibly gaining you more followers who want to see dog posts.

Instagram does not allow users to put links in their posts or utilize typical visual organization such as paragraph breaks, so users have developed workarounds. To direct followers to a certain link, a user may state "link in bio!" (see Figure 2.1) and then post the link as part of their user biography—the only place in Instagram that allows a link. To create visual organization in long posts, users will use emojis to create a sense of visual rhythm (see Figure 2.2).

Twitter   Twitter is a microblog that allows users to let their followers know what they're doing by posting tweets—that is, short messages of 280 characters or fewer. Twitter also uses the hashtag system.

| **Figure 2.1** | Apartment Therapy's Post Demonstrates "Link in Bio" Instagram Convention |

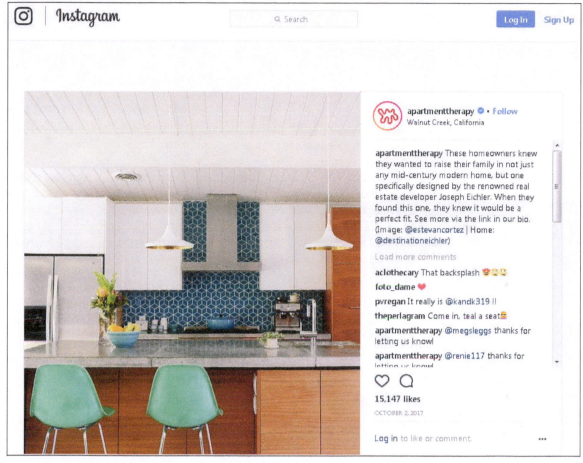

Source: Instagram

Twitter offers another way for organizations to create a following, share information, brand themselves, and even eavesdrop on what people say about their competitors. Organizations can follow what other people tweet about them and use the service to provide an additional form of customer service. For example, when a patron in a Fort Worth branch of Chipotle tweeted about the restaurant lacking corn tortillas, the corporate office called the manager before the customer even left.[18]

Similar to many restaurants and other organizations, Chipotle has service representatives dedicated to social media relations. With more than 500 million tweets sent per day worldwide (as of January 2020),[19] it can be overwhelming for organizations to manage their image and plan appropriate 280-character responses.

TikTok　TikTok is a video-sharing platform where users make their own short videos, typically a few seconds to a minute. In them, users often lipsync and dance to songs. While many users make TikTok videos to entertain family, friends, and followers, some businesses are using TikTok to market their products. As mentioned earlier, Normans Bridal Shoppe in Springfield, Missouri, markets its prom dresses using TikTok videos,[20] and businesses from the NBA to Chipotle to the *Washington Post* keep in touch via TikTok.[21]

LinkedIn　LinkedIn allows professionals to connect with colleagues and other industry members. More than 660 million people use the site.[22] Unlike Facebook or Twitter, which can easily blur the line between professional and personal, LinkedIn profiles tend to remain strictly work oriented.

Figure 2.2   Instagram Utilizes Hashtag System to Categorize Posts

Source: Tami Ulrich Social Media

You can use the site to network and earn recommendations from past and current clients. Another section allows your connections to endorse skills and expertise you may have. These referrals, in turn, could create more business opportunities. You also can join industry associations or alumni groups to expand your network of connections. LinkedIn Answers provides a forum for industry professionals to ask questions and share their expertise, which also may lead to new clients. For job searches,

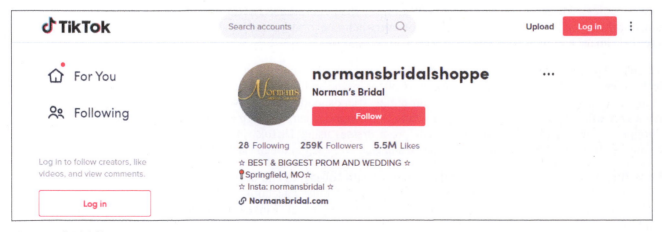

Normans Bridal Shoppe

LinkedIn allows users to search for new job opportunities, post a résumé, or recruit new employees.

Applications (Apps) Smartphones allow users to send and receive email, access websites, conduct word processing, track a shipped order, check inventory, complete a time sheet, stream video and audio, and make phone calls. Some smartphones even have add-on applications, or apps, that allow customers to place orders for goods or services.

Every day more apps become available for these smartphones, and they can enhance productivity and provide special services to customers. For example, Starbucks and Panera Bread have contactless ordering and payment options with their apps. Offering incentives such as loyalty discounts encourages users to dedicate precious space on their phones to a particular company's app.

Web Conferencing With health risks brought on by the COVID-19 pandemic, many businesses began more frequent use of an alternative to traditional face-to-face meetings—namely, web conferencing, a medium with full audio and visual capabilities. Common web conferencing platforms include WebEx, Zoom, Skype, Google Hangouts, Microsoft Teams, GoToMeeting, and Jabber. Such platforms allow employees to connect and collaborate remotely using web cameras and microphones that are standard on laptops, tablets, and smartphones.

Some businesses are using web conferencing to increase engagement with their clients. Consultants for the direct-sales skincare company Rodan+Fields host virtual "parties" on Facebook, using the platform's live video capabilities to share information and

Technology plays a large role in the changing face of business communication, increasingly so since the beginning of the COVID-19 pandemic.

Vadym Pastukh/123RF

personal testimonies about products; while customers post comments, the consultant responds in real time to their queries. The medium allows businesses to create a sense of immediacy and personal connection and, thus, goodwill.

You-Attitude

LO 2-2

You-**attitude** is a communication style that looks at things from the audience's point of view, emphasizing what the audience wants or needs to know, respecting the audience's intelligence, and protecting the audience's ego. We see *you*-attitude often in terms of customer service. In fact, companies are increasingly focusing on improving customer relationships over efficiency to enhance customer experience and happiness by anticipating customers' needs, thus improving customer retention and satisfaction. Satisfied, happy customers are more likely to recommend the organization to their friends and families, and word-of-mouth recommendations from trusted sources are more effective than any advertising or marketing campaign.[23]

For example, Microsoft fought lax enforcement of intellectual property laws in China for years. The software company finally started making progress when it looked at the problem from the Chinese point of view. Government officials were ignoring the problem because many of their people made a living from illegal copies and because Microsoft prices put the products beyond the reach of most citizens. With this new perspective, Microsoft began creating jobs in China and lowering the prices of its products in return for better law enforcement.[24]

Create *You*-Attitude at the Sentence Level

Expressing what you want to say with *you*-attitude is a crucial step in communicating your concern to your audience.

To apply *you*-attitude on a sentence level, use the following techniques:

1. Talk about the audience, not about yourself.
2. Refer specifically to the customer's request or order.
3. Don't talk about feelings, except to congratulate or offer sympathy.
4. In positive situations, use *you* more often than *I*. Use *we* when it includes the audience.
5. In negative situations, avoid the word *you*. Protect the audience's ego. Use passive voice and impersonal expressions to avoid assigning blame.

Revisions for *you*-attitude do not change the basic meaning of the sentence. However, revising for *you*-attitude often makes sentences longer because the revision is more specific and has more information. Long sentences need not be wordy. **Wordiness** means having more words than the meaning requires. You can add information and still keep your writing concise.

1. Talk about the audience, not about yourself.   Your audience wants to know how they benefit or are affected. When you provide this information, you make your message more complete and more interesting.

> Lacks *you*-attitude: We have negotiated an agreement with Apex Rent-a-Car that gives you a discount on rental cars.
>
> *You*-attitude: As a Sunstrand employee, you can now get a 20% discount when you rent a car from Apex.

2. Refer specifically to the customer's request or order.   A specific referral, rather than a generic *your order* or *your policy*, helps show that your customer is important to you. If your customer is an individual or a small business, it's friendly to specify the content of the order. If you're dealing with a company with which you do a great deal of business, give the invoice or purchase order number.

Lacks *you*-attitude: Your order . . .

You-attitude

(to individual):   The desk chair you ordered . . .

You-attitude

(to a large store):   Your invoice #783329 . . .

3. Don't talk about feelings, except to congratulate or offer sympathy.

In most business situations, your feelings are irrelevant and should be omitted.

Lacks *you*-attitude: We are happy to extend you a credit line of $15,000.

You-attitude: You can now charge up to $15,000 on your American Express card.

It *is* appropriate to talk about your own emotions in a message of congratulations or condolence.

You-attitude: Congratulations on your promotion to district manager! I was really pleased to read about it.

Don't talk about your audience's feelings, either. It's distancing to have others tell us how we feel—especially if they are wrong.

Lacks *you*-attitude: You'll be happy to hear that Open Grip Walkway Channels meet OSHA requirements.

You-attitude: Open Grip Walkway Channels meet OSHA requirements.

Maybe the audience expects that anything you sell would meet government regulations. (OSHA—the Occupational Safety and Health Administration—is a federal agency.) The audience may even be disappointed if they expected higher standards. Simply explain the situation or describe a product's features; don't predict the audience's response.

When you have good news, simply give the good news.

Lacks *you*-attitude: You'll be happy to hear that your scholarship has been renewed.

You-attitude: Congratulations! Your scholarship has been renewed.

4. In positive situations, use *you* more often than *I*. Use *we* when it includes the audience.   Talk about the audience, not you or your company.

Lacks *you*-attitude: We provide health insurance to all employees.

You-attitude: You receive health insurance as a full-time Procter & Gamble employee.

Most readers are tolerant of the word *I* in email messages, which seem like conversation. But edit paper documents to use *I* rarely if at all. *I* suggests that you're concerned about personal issues, not about the organization's problems, needs, and opportunities. *We* works well when it includes the reader. Avoid *we* if it excludes the reader (as it would in a letter to a customer or supplier or as it might in an email about what *we* in management want *you* to do).

5. In negative situations, avoid the word *you*. Protect your audience's ego. Use passive voice and impersonal expressions to avoid assigning blame.   When you report bad news or limitations, use a noun for a group of which your audience is a part instead of *you* so people don't feel that they're singled out for bad news.

Lacks *you*-attitude: You must get approval from the director before you publish any articles or memoirs based on your work in the agency.

You-attitude: Agency personnel must get approval from the director to publish any articles or memoirs based on their work at the agency.

Use passive voice and impersonal expressions to avoid blaming people. Passive-voice verbs describe the action performed on something, without necessarily saying who did it. A verb is in **passive voice** if the subject is acted upon. Passive voice is usually made up of a form of the verb *to be* plus a past participle:

were obtained	(in the past)
is endorsed	(in the present)
will be fulfilled	(in the future)

In most cases, active voice is better, but when your audience is at fault, passive voice may be useful to avoid alienation by assigning blame.

Impersonal expressions omit people and talk only about things. Normally, communication is most lively when it's about people—and most interesting to audiences when it's about them. When you have to report a mistake or bad news, however, you can protect your audience's ego by using an impersonal expression, one in which things, not people, do the acting.

Lacks *you*-attitude:	You made no allowance for inflation in your estimate.
You-attitude (passive):	No allowance for inflation has been made in this estimate.
You-attitude (impersonal):	This estimate makes no allowance for inflation.

A purist might say that impersonal expressions are illogical: An estimate, for example, is inanimate and can't "make" anything. In the pragmatic world of business writing, however, impersonal expressions help you convey criticism tactfully.

Create *You*-Attitude beyond the Sentence Level

Good messages apply *you*-attitude beyond the sentence level by using content and organization as well as style to build goodwill.

To create goodwill with content:

- Be complete. When you have lots of information to give, consider putting some details in an appendix. The audience can read them later.

- Anticipate and answer questions that your audience is likely to have.

- Show why information your audience didn't ask for is important.

- Show your audience how the subject of your message affects them.

To organize information to build goodwill:

- Put first the information that most interests your audience.

- Arrange information to meet your audience's needs, not yours.

- Use parallel-structure headings and lists so readers can find and understand key points quickly.

Creating **parallel structure** in headings and lists facilitates readers' comprehension of your message. Headings and list items in parallel structure share the same grammatical structure, such as the verbal-first phrases (*-ing* verbs) in a report titled, "Ways to Increase Volunteer Commitment and Motivation":

- Increasing Training Opportunities

- Improving Supervision

- Providing Emotional Support

- Establishing and Maintaining a Two-Way Information Flow

These headings are in parallel structure when written as noun phrases as well:

- Increased Training Opportunities

- Improved Supervision

- More Emotional Support

- A Two-Way Information Flow

Consider the email in Figure 2.3. As the red marginal notes indicate, many individual sentences in this message lack *you*-attitude. Fixing individual sentences could improve the email. However, it really needs to be totally rewritten.

Figure 2.4 shows a possible revision of this email. The revision is clearer, easier to read, and friendlier. Note that the list items are all in simple present tense: *give, have,* and *give.*

Figure 2.3   An Email Lacking *You*-Attitude

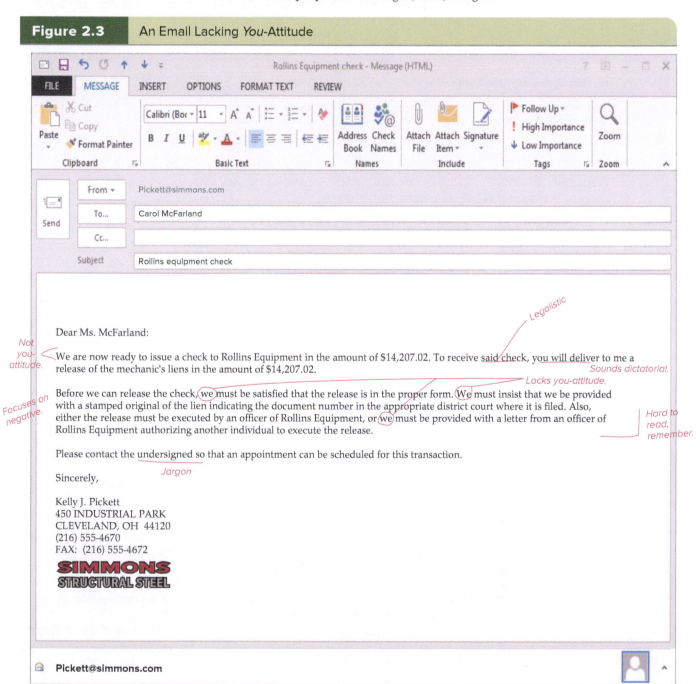

Figure 2.4 An Email Revised to Improve *You*-Attitude

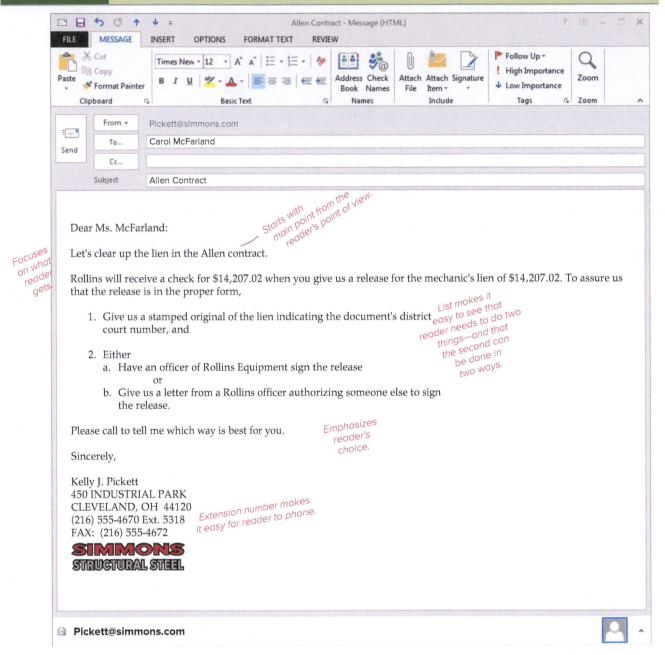

Dear Ms. McFarland:

Starts with main point from the reader's point of view.

Let's clear up the lien in the Allen contract.

Focuses on what reader gets.

Rollins will receive a check for $14,207.02 when you give us a release for the mechanic's lien of $14,207.02. To assure us that the release is in the proper form,

List makes it easy to see that reader needs to do two things—and that the second can be done in two ways.

1. Give us a stamped original of the lien indicating the document's district court number, and

2. Either
   a. Have an officer of Rollins Equipment sign the release
      or
   b. Give us a letter from a Rollins officer authorizing someone else to sign the release.

Please call to tell me which way is best for you.

Emphasizes reader's choice.

Sincerely,

Kelly J. Pickett
450 INDUSTRIAL PARK
CLEVELAND, OH 44120
(216) 555-4670 Ext. 5318
FAX: (216) 555-4672

Extension number makes it easy for reader to phone.

SIMMONS STRUCTURAL STEEL

Pickett@simmons.com

Be Aware of Cultural Differences

When you communicate with international audiences, familiarize yourself with the differences in social norms. Simple actions such as greetings easily can be taken for granted but should be researched to ensure that you do not alienate an audience with your message. Different countries, and even different regions of the same country, have different greetings. They may shake hands, bow, hug, kiss, or a combination of these actions as a method of professional greetings.[25]

In addition to different greetings, measurement systems are likely to be different. The U.S., along with Liberia and Myanmar, clings to the Imperial measurement system, which has been abandoned by the rest of the world in favor of the metric system.[26] When you write for international audiences, use the metric system.

Even pronouns and direction words need attention. *We* may not feel inclusive to readers with different assumptions and backgrounds. *Here* won't mean the same thing to a reader in Bonn, Germany, as it does to one in Boulder, Colorado.

Build Trust

Financial crises, internet scams, and shoddy goods and services all have contributed to a lack of trust of the commercial world. Trust is a vital element in goodwill and is necessary on the personal level and the corporate level. Robert Hurley, author of *The Decision to Trust: How Leaders Can Create High Trust Companies*, says, "Trust comes from delivering every day on what you promise—as a manager, an employee, and a company. It involves constant teamwork, communication and collaboration."[27]

A large part of trust comes from ethical behaviors, including being truthful, using reason, seeking a diversity of perspectives, and showing respect in communication practices, but by themselves, such behaviors are not enough. As Hurley notes, trust is also delivering on our commitments. This delivery is important for you when you start a new job and then move up the organizational rungs. Do you do what you are expected to do? What you say you will do? Or do you say yes to more than you can possibly deliver? Honoring commitments is also important for the organization: Does it deliver the expected quality and quantity of goods and services in a timely fashion?

Trust also comes from the goodwill communication skills described in this chapter, and especially from skill with *you*-attitude. Are you good at discerning the interests of others and fulfilling or promoting those interests fairly and ethically?

Clear, open, and timely communication helps build and maintain trust.

Positive Emphasis

LO 2-3

With some bad news—announcements of layoffs, store closings, product defects and recalls, salary cuts—straightforward negatives build credibility. (See Chapter 10 for how to present bad news.) Sometimes negatives are needed to make people take a problem seriously. In some messages, such as disciplinary notices and negative performance appraisals, one of your purposes is to make the problem clear. Even here, avoid insults or attacks on your audience's integrity.

In most situations, however, it's better to be positive. Researchers have found that businesspeople responded more positively to positive language than to negative language, and were more likely to say they would act on a positively worded request.[28] In groundbreaking research for Met Life, Martin Seligman found that optimistic salespeople sold 37% more insurance than pessimistic colleagues. As a result, Met Life began hiring optimists even when they failed to meet the company's other criteria. These "unqualified" optimists outsold pessimists 21% in their first year and 57% in the next.[29]

Positive emphasis is a way of looking at things. You can create positive emphasis with the words, information, organization, and layout you choose. "Part-time" may be a negative phrase for someone seeking full-time employment, but it may be a positive phrase for college students seeking limited work hours while they pursue their education. It may become even more positive if connected with flexible hours.

How to Create Positive Emphasis

Create positive emphasis by using the following techniques:

1. Avoid negative words and words with negative connotations.
2. Beware of hidden negatives.
3. Focus on what the audience can do rather than on limitations.

Figure 2.5	Negative Words to Avoid		
afraid	impossible	**Some *dis*- words:**	**Many *un*- words:**
anxious	lacking	disapprove	unclear
avoid	loss	dishonest	unfair
bad	neglect	dissatisfied	unfortunate
careless	never		unfortunately
damage	no		unpleasant
delay	not	**Many *in*- words:**	unreasonable
delinquent	objection	inadequate	unreliable
deny	problem	incomplete	unsure
difficulty	reject	inconvenient	
eliminate	sorry	insincere	
error	terrible	injury	
except	trivial		
fail	trouble		
fault	wait	**Some *mis*- words:**	
fear	weakness	misfortune	
hesitate	worry	missing	
ignorant	wrong	mistake	
ignore			

4. Justify negative information by giving a reason or linking it to an audience benefit.

5. Put the negative information in the middle and present it compactly.

Choose the technique that produces the clearest, most accurate communication.

1. Avoid negative words and words with negative connotations.

Figure 2.5 lists some common negative words. If you find similar words in a draft, try to substitute a more positive word. When you must use a negative, use the least negative term that will convey your meaning:

Negative:	We have failed to finish taking inventory.
Better:	We haven't finished taking inventory.
Still better:	We will be finished taking inventory Friday.
Negative:	If you can't understand this explanation, feel free to call me.
Better:	If you have further questions, just call me.
Still better:	Omit the sentence.

Omit double negatives.

Negative:	Never fail to back up your documents.
Better:	Always back up your documents.

When you must use a negative term, use the least negative word that is accurate.

Negative:	Your balance of $835 is delinquent.
Better:	Your balance of $835 is past due.

Getting rid of negatives has the added benefit of making what you write easier to understand. Sentences with three or more negatives are hard to interpret correctly.[30]

2. Beware of hidden negatives.   Some words are not negative in themselves

but become negative in context. *But* and *however* indicate a shift, so, after a positive statement, they are negative. *I hope* and *I trust that* suggest that you aren't sure. *Patience* may sound like a virtue, but it is a necessary virtue only when things are slow. Even positives about a service or product may backfire if they suggest that in the past the service or product was bad.

Negative:	I hope this is the information you wanted. [Implication: I'm not sure.]
Better:	Enclosed is a brochure about road repairs scheduled for 2022.
Still better:	The brochure contains a list of all roads and bridges scheduled for repair during 2022, specific dates when work will start, and alternate routes.
Negative:	Please be patient as we switch to the automated system. [Implication: You can expect problems.]
Better:	If you have questions during our transition to the automated system, please call Melissa Morgan.
Still better:	You'll be able to get information instantly about any house on the market when the automated system is in place. If you have questions during the transition, please call Melissa Morgan.
Negative:	Now Crispy Crunch tastes better. [Implication: it used to taste terrible.]
Better:	Now Crispy Crunch tastes even better.

Removing negatives does not mean being arrogant or pushy.

Negative:	I hope that you are satisfied enough to place future orders.
Arrogant:	I look forward to receiving all of your future business.
Better:	Whenever you need computer chips, a call to Mercury is all it takes for fast service.

When you eliminate negative words, be sure to maintain accuracy. Words that are exact opposites will usually not be accurate. Instead, use specifics to be both positive and accurate.

Negative:	The exercycle is not guaranteed for life.
Not true:	The exercycle is guaranteed for life.
True:	The exercycle is guaranteed for 10 years.

Legal phrases also have negative connotations for most readers and should be avoided whenever possible.

3. Focus on what the audience can do rather than on limitations.

When there are limits, or some options are closed, focus on the alternatives that remain.

Negative:	We will not allow you to charge more than $5,000 on your Visa account.
Better:	You can charge $5,000 on your new Visa card.
or:	Your new Visa card gives you $5,000 in credit that you can use at thousands of stores nationwide.

As you focus on what will happen, check for *you*-attitude. In the previous example, "We will allow you to charge $5,000" would be positive, but it lacks *you*-attitude.

When you have a benefit and a requirement the audience must meet to get the benefit, the sentence is usually more positive if you put the benefit first.

Negative:	You will not qualify for the student membership rate of $55 a year unless you are a full-time student.
Better:	You get all the benefits of membership for only $55 a year if you're a full-time student.

4. Justify negative information by giving a reason or linking it to an audience benefit.
A reason can help your audience see that the information is necessary; a benefit can suggest that the negative aspect is outweighed by positive

factors. Be careful, however, to make the logic behind your reason clear and to leave no loopholes.

> Negative: We cannot sell individual pastel sets.
>
> Loophole: To keep down packaging costs and to help you save on shipping and handling costs, we sell pastel sets in packages of 12.

Suppose the customer says, "I'll pay the extra shipping and handling. Send me six." If you truly sell only in packages of 12, you need to say so:

> Better: To keep down packaging costs and to help customers save on shipping and handling costs, we sell pastel sets only in packages of 12.

If you link the negative element to a benefit, be sure it is a benefit your audience will acknowledge. Avoid telling people that you're doing things "for their own good." They may have a different notion of what their own good is. You may think you're doing customers a favor by limiting their credit so they don't get in over their heads and go bankrupt. They may think they'd be better off with more credit so they could expand in hopes of making more sales and more profits.

5. Put the negative information in the middle and present it compactly.

Put negatives at the beginning or end only if you want to emphasize the negative. To de-emphasize a written negative, put it in the middle of a paragraph rather than in the first or last sentence and in the middle of the message rather than in the first or last paragraph.

When a letter or memo runs several pages, remember that the bottom of the first page is also a position of emphasis, even if it is in the middle of a paragraph, because of the extra white space of the bottom margin. (The first page gets more attention because it is on top and the reader's eye may catch lines of the message even when they aren't consciously reading it; the tops and bottoms of subsequent pages don't get this extra attention.) If possible, avoid placing negative information at the bottom of the first page.

Giving a topic lots of space emphasizes it. Therefore, you can de-emphasize negative information by giving it as little space as possible. Give negative information only once in your message. Don't list negatives with bulleted or numbered lists. These lists take space and emphasize material.

How to Check Positive Emphasis

All five of the strategies just listed help create positive emphasis. However, you always should check to see that the positive emphasis is appropriate, sincere, and realistic.

As you read at the beginning of this section, positive emphasis is not always *appropriate*. Some bad news is so serious that presenting it with a positive tone is insensitive, if not unethical. Layoffs, salary cuts, and product defects are all topics in this category.

Some positive emphasis is so overdone that it no longer seems sincere. The used-car sales rep selling a rusting auto is one stereotype of insincerity. A more common example for most businesspeople is the employee who gushes praise through gritted teeth over your promotion. Most of us have experienced something similar, and we know how easy it is to see through the insincerity.

Positive emphasis also can be so overdone that it clouds the reality of the situation. If your company has two finalists for a sales award, and only one award, the loser does not have second place, which implies a second award. On the other hand, if all sales reps win the same award, top performers will feel unappreciated. Too much praise also can make mediocre employees think they are doing great. Keep your communications realistic.

Restraint can help make positive emphasis more effective. Conductor Otto Klemperer was known for not praising his orchestra. One day, pleased with a particularly good rehearsal, he spoke a brusque "good." His stunned musicians broke into spontaneous applause. Klemperer rapped his baton on his music stand to silence them and said, "Not *that* good."[31]

Tone is the implied attitude of the communicator toward the audience. If the words of a document seem condescending or rude, tone is a problem. Norms for politeness are cultural and generational; they also vary from office to office.

Tone is tricky because it interacts with context and power. Language that is acceptable within one group may be unacceptable if used by someone outside the group. Words that might seem friendly from a superior to a subordinate may seem audacious if used by the subordinate to the superior. Similarly, words that may be neutral among peers may be seen as negative if sent by a superior to a subordinate.

The form letter printed in Figure 2.6 failed because it was stuffy and selfish. The comments in red show specific problems with the letter:

- **The language is stiff and legalistic.** Note the sexist "Gentlemen:" and obsolete "Please be advised" and "herein."

- **The tone is selfish.** The letter is written from the writer's point of view; there are no benefits for the reader. (The writer says there are, but without a shred of evidence, the claim isn't convincing.)

- **The main point is buried.** The main point is in the middle of the long first paragraph. The middle is the least emphatic part of a paragraph.

- **The request is vague.** How many references does the supplier want? Are only vendor references OK, or would other credit references, such as banks, work too? Is the name of the reference enough, or is it necessary also to specify the line of credit, the average balance, the current balance, the years credit has been established, or other information? What "additional financial information" does the supplier want? Annual reports? Bank balance? Tax returns? The request sounds like an invasion of privacy, not a reasonable business practice.

- **Words are misused.** The use of *herein* for *therein* suggests either an ignorant writer or one who doesn't care enough about the subject and the reader to use the right word.

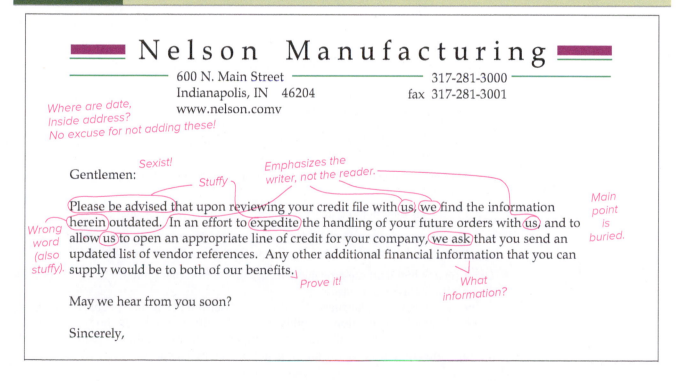

The desirable tone for business writing is businesslike but not stiff, friendly but not phony, confident but not arrogant, polite but not groveling. The guidelines below will help you achieve the tone you want.

Use Courtesy Titles for People You Don't Know Well

Most U.S. organizations use first names for everyone, whatever their age or rank. But many people don't like being called by their first names by people they don't know or by someone much younger. When you talk or write to people outside your organization, use first names only if you've established a personal relationship. If you don't know someone well, use a courtesy title (discussed later in this chapter).

Be Aware of the Power Implications of Word Choice

"Thank you for your cooperation" is generous coming from a superior to a subordinate; it's not appropriate in a message to your superior. Different ways of asking for action carry different levels of politeness.[32]

Order: (lowest politeness)	Turn in your time card by Monday.
Polite order: (midlevel politeness)	Please turn in your time card by Monday.
Indirect request: (higher politeness)	Time cards should be turned in by Monday.
Question: (highest politeness)	Would you be able to turn in your time card by Monday?

Higher levels of politeness may be unclear. In some cases, a question may seem like a request for information to which it's acceptable to answer, "No, I can't." In other cases, it will be an order, simply phrased in polite terms.

You need more politeness if you're asking for something that will inconvenience the audience and help you more than the person who does the action. Generally, you need less politeness when you're asking for something small, routine, or to the audience's benefit. Some discourse communities, however, prefer that even small requests be made politely.

Creating Inclusivity

LO 2-5

The makeup of the U.S. population is changing. According to the U.S. Census Bureau:

- Women outnumber men.

- More women than men are attaining associate's, bachelor's, and master's degrees.

- For people 16 and older, more women than men work in management, professional, and related occupations.[33]

- The Hispanic population is the fastest growing in the country; it numbered 60.48 million in 2019.[34]

- Projections show non-Hispanic whites becoming a minority soon after 2040.[35]

- The number of people 65 and older also is growing; that population now numbers more than 49 million, and by 2026, 22 million of them will still be in the workforce.[36]

These figures highlight the growing diversity of the workplace and the need to communicate with inclusive language.

Inclusive language is language that does not discriminate against people on the basis of gender, physical condition or ability, race, ethnicity, age, religion, body size, or any other category. It includes all audience members, helps to sustain goodwill, is fair and friendly, and complies with the law. It is not **oppressive language**.

Check to be sure that your language is inclusive. Doing so is ethical; it also can avoid major problems and lawsuits.

Making Language Nongendered

Nongendered language treats gender neutrally. Check to be sure your messages are free from bias in four areas: job titles, courtesy titles and names, pronouns, and other words and phrases.

Job Titles Use neutral titles that do not imply a job is held only by people of a certain gender. Many job titles are already neutral: *accountant, banker, doctor, engineer, inspector, manager, nurse, pilot, secretary, technician*, to name a few. Other titles reflect gender stereotypes and need to be changed.

Instead of	Use
Businessman	A specific title: executive, accountant, department head, owner of a small business, businessperson
Chairman	Chair, chairperson, moderator
Fireman	Firefighter
Foreman	Supervisor
Mailman	Mail carrier
Salesman	Salesperson, sales representative
Waitress	Server
Woman lawyer	Lawyer
Workman	Worker, employee. Or use a specific title: crane operator, bricklayer, etc.

Courtesy Titles and Names Emails to people you know normally do not use courtesy titles. However, letters and emails to people with whom you have a more formal relationship require courtesy titles in the salutation *unless* you're on a first-name basis with your reader. (See Appendix A for examples of email and letter formats.)

When you know your reader's name and gender, use courtesy titles that do not indicate marital status: *Mr.* for men and *Ms.* for women. *Ms.* is particularly useful when you do not know what a woman's marital status is. However, even when you happen to know that a woman is married or single, you still use *Ms.* unless you know that she prefers another title. There are, however, two exceptions:

1. If the woman has a professional title, use that title.

    Dr. Kristen Sorenson is our new company physician.

    The Rev. Elizabeth Townsley gave the invocation.

2. If the woman prefers to be addressed as *Mrs.* or *Miss*, use the title she prefers rather than *Ms.* (*You*-attitude takes precedence over nongendered language: address the reader as the reader prefers to be addressed, taking note if the reader has listed personal pronouns.) To find out if a woman prefers a traditional title:

    ■ Check the signature block in previous correspondence. If a woman types her name as *Miss Elaine Anderson* or *Mrs. Kay Royster*, use the title she designates.

    ■ Notice the title a woman uses in introducing herself on the phone. If she says, "This is Robin Stine," use Ms. when you write to her. If she says, "I'm Mrs. Stine," use the title she specifies.

    ■ When you're writing job letters or crucial correspondence, call the company and ask the receptionist which title your reader prefers.

In addition to using parallel courtesy titles, use parallel forms for names.

Not Parallel	Parallel
Members of the committee will be Mr. Jones, Mr. Yacone, and Lisa.	Members of the committee will be Mr. Jones, Mr. Yacone, and Ms. Melton. or Members of the committee will be Irving, Ted, and Lisa.

When you know your reader's name but not the gender, either

- Call the company and ask.

- Use the reader's full name in the salutation:
  Dear Chris Crowell:
  Dear J. C. Meath:

When you know neither the reader's name nor gender, you have three options:

- Omit the salutation and use a subject line in its place. (See Figure A.2, Simplified Format, in Appendix A.) SUBJECT: Recommendation for Ben Wandell

- Use the reader's position or job title:
  Dear Loan Officer:
  Dear Registrar:

- Use a general group to which your reader belongs:
  Dear Investor:
  Dear Admissions Committee:

Pronouns   When you refer to a specific person, use the correct personal pronouns for your audience. That pronoun may be a plural pronoun (*they*, *them*, *their*).

In his speech, Pat Jones said . . .

In her speech, Alex Jones said . . .

In their speech, Chris Jones said . . .

When you are referring not to a specific person but to anyone who may be in a given job or position, traditional gender pronouns are sexist.

Incorrect: a.   Each supervisor must certify that the time sheet for his department is correct.

Incorrect: b.   When the nurse fills out the accident report form, she should send one copy to the Central Division Office.

Business communication uses three ways to eliminate gendered generic pronouns: use plural pronouns, use second-person *you*, or revise the sentence to omit the pronoun. Whenever you have a choice of two or more ways to make a phrase or sentence nongendered, choose the alternative that is the smoothest and least conspicuous.

The following examples use these methods to revise sentences *a* and *b* above.

1. Use plural nouns and pronouns, even when you must focus on the action of an individual.

   Correct plural: a.   Supervisors must certify that the time sheets for their departments are correct.

   Correct singular: b.   When the nurse fills out the accident report, they should send one copy to the Central Division Office.

   Correct singular: c.   The supervisor must certify that the time sheet for their department is correct.

2. Use *you*.

    Correct: a.   You must certify that the time sheet for your department is correct.

    Correct: b.   When you fill out an accident report form, send one copy to the Central Division Office.

You is particularly good for instructions and statements of the responsibilities of someone in a given position.

3. Substitute an article (*a, an,* or *the*) for the pronoun, or revise the sentence so that the pronoun is unnecessary.

    Correct: a.   The supervisor must certify that the time sheet for the department is correct.

    Correct: b.   The nurse will

           1.   Fill out the accident report form.

           2.   Send one copy of the form to the Central Division Office.

Other Words and Phrases If you find any terms similar to those in the first column in Figure 2.7 in your messages or your company's documents, replace them with terms similar to those in the second column.

Not every word containing *man* carries bias. For example, *manager* is nongendered. Avoid terms that assume that everyone is married.

    Biased: You and your husband or wife are cordially invited to the reception.

    Better: You and your guest are cordially invited to the reception.

Making Language Nonracist and Nonageist

Language is **nonracist** and **nonageist** when it treats all races and ages fairly, avoiding negative stereotypes of any group. Use the following guidelines to check for bias in documents you write or edit.

Figure 2.7	Getting Rid of Gendered Terms and Phrases	
Instead of	**Use**	**Because**
The girl at the front desk	The woman's name or job title: "Ms. Browning," "Rosa," "the receptionist"	Refer to women as *women*, not *girls*. When you talk about a specific woman, use her name, just as you use a man's name to talk about a specific man.
The ladies on our staff	The women on our staff	Use parallel terms for all individuals regardless of gender. Therefore, use *ladies* only if you refer to the men on your staff as *gentlemen*. Few businesses do because social distinctions are rarely at issue and to avoid excluding those who do not identify along binary gender lines.
Manpower Manhours Manning	Personnel Hours or worker hours Staffing	The power in business comes from all people who do the labor.

Give someone's race or age only if it is relevant to your story.   When you do mention age, race, or other categories, give them for everyone in your story.

Refer to a group by the term it prefers. As preferences change, change your usage.   If you must refer to a group, refer to the group using the term it prefers.

Fifty years ago, *Negro* was a more dignified term than *colored* for African Americans. As times changed, both *Negro* and *colored* are offensive, while *Black American* and *African American* replaced the terms.

Oriental has now been replaced by *Asian*, as in *Asian American*.

The term *Latinx* is the most acceptable gender-neutral group term to refer to Mexican Americans, Cuban Americans, Puerto Ricans, Dominicans, Brazilianos, and other people with Central and Latin American backgrounds. *Latino* is masculine, while *Latina* is feminine.[37] Better still is to refer to the precise group. The differences among various Latinx groups are at least as great as the differences among Italian Americans, Irish Americans, Armenian Americans, and others descended from various European groups.

Baby Boomers, older people, and *mature customers* are more generally accepted terms than *senior citizens* or *golden agers*.

Avoid terms that suggest competent people are unusual.   The statement "He is an asset to his race" suggests excellence in the race is rare. "He is a spry 70-year-old" suggests the writer thinks anyone that old has mobility issues.

Referring to People with Disabilities and Diseases

A disability is a physical, mental, sensory, or emotional impairment that interferes with the major tasks of daily living. According to the U.S. Census Bureau, 26% of Americans currently have a disability.[38] The number of people with disabilities will rise as the population ages.

To keep trained workers, more and more companies are making accommodations such as telecommuting, flexible hours, work shift changes, and assignment changes.

When referring to people with conditions and disabilities, use **people-first language**. People-first language names the person first. Use it instead of the traditional noun phrases that imply the condition defines the person, for example, "people being treated for cancer" rather than "cancer patients." Figure 2.8 lists more examples.

Avoid negative terms, unless the audience prefers them. *You*-attitude takes precedence over positive emphasis: Use the term a group prefers. People who lost their hearing as infants, children, or young adults often prefer to be called *deaf*, or *Deaf* in recognition of Deafness as a culture. But people who lose their hearing as older adults often prefer to be called *hard of hearing*, even when their hearing loss is just as great as that of someone who identifies as part of the Deaf culture.

Figure 2.8	Using People-First Language	
Instead of	**Use**	**Because**
Confined to a wheelchair	Uses a wheelchair	Wheelchairs enable people to escape confinement.
AIDS victim	Person with AIDS	Someone can have a disease without being victimized by it.
Abnormal	Atypical	People with disabilities are atypical but not necessarily abnormal.

Finding the best term requires keeping up with changing preferences. If your target audience is smaller than the whole group, use the term preferred by that audience, even if the group as a whole prefers another term.

Some negative terms, however, are never appropriate. Negative terms such as *afflicted, suffering from*, and *struck down* also suggest an outdated view of any illness as a sign of divine punishment.

Choosing Inclusive Visuals

When you produce a document with photographs or illustrations, check the visuals for possible inclusivity. Do they show people of different genders, races, abilities, ages, and so on? It's okay to have pictures that show individual people, but the general impression of your document should suggest that diversity is welcome and normal.

In addition, check how visuals portray relationships. For example, if in a document's photographs only men appear in business suits, the visuals convey bias.

Platform-Specific Best Practices for Creating Goodwill

LO 2-6

With new communication technology comes new conventions. In addition to the medium-specific best practices discussed in this section, you should carefully consider your message's rhetorical situation and keep in mind the potential permanence of any electronic communication.

Whatever communication technology your company embraces, you must take care to integrate it into your business in a scaffolded way that allows less tech-savvy customers to learn it at their own pace. For example, if a bank starts offering electronic scans of deposited checks on its online banking platform, it should allow users access to physical scans of checks for a reasonable adaptation period.

Consider your audience and purpose when using informal language or abbreviations. Although even the *Oxford English Dictionary* lists LOL, BFF, IMHO, and OMG, some people will not recognize other abbreviations. In many organizations, text messages to all but close friends are expected to look professional.

Not this: that time should work. bring the donuts and coffee!!! i'm hungry! CU L8r

But this: 3 works for me, too. I'll bring copies of the Wolford schedule. See you there.

Remember that electronic messages can be saved, forwarded, and printed. They too leave a paper trail and many businesses monitor them. Do not use them to send sensitive information, such as passwords, and always keep them professional.

When making phone calls, writing emails, or managing social media accounts such as Facebook, Twitter, or Instagram, you should consider the following best practices.

Phone Calls

Phone calls provide fewer contextual cues than face-to-face conversations, but more cues than written messages. Phone calls are a good choice when

- Tone of voice is important.
- A real-time connection saves multiple phone calls or emails (e.g., setting a meeting time).
- You need something immediately.

Use these tips for effective phone calls (also see Figure 2.9 for things to avoid):

- Ensure the timing is convenient for the recipient; try to limit phone calls to business hours.
- Promptly return calls to your voicemail.

Figure 2.9	Voicemail Pet Peeves

- Callback numbers that are mumbled or given too quickly.
- Messages longer than 30 seconds.
- Messages that require serious note taking (when an email would have been better).
- Too much or too little information.
- Demands to return the call without saying why.
- Messages expecting an immediate response.
- Angry messages.

- Speak clearly, especially when giving your name and phone number. Speaking clearly is even more important when you're leaving your name and phone number on voicemail. Do not assume the recipient has a phone that records your number.

- Use an information hook: I am calling about. . . .

- Keep the call short and cordial. If you need to leave a message, keep it brief; use one or two sentences. Most people resent long voicemail messages.

- Repeat your phone number at the end of the call. Too often, people don't write the number down at the beginning of the call.

- Focus on the call; do not do other work. Most people can tell if you are reading email or webpages while talking to them, and they get the message that their concern is not important to you.

Remember that unplanned phone calls are an interruption in a busy worker's day. If that person works in an open office, as many do, the call also will interrupt other employees to some extent. For this reason, and also because of the increase in texting, voicemail messages are declining. Voicemail retrieval is declining even more rapidly, so even if you leave a message, you cannot be sure it will be heard.[39]

Email

To successfully craft effective email messages, you should adhere to best practices and save your audience time.

Best Practices   Use To/CC/BCC lines to your advantage:

- **To:** Send your email only to people who will want or need it. If you are sending to multiple people, decide in which order to place the names. Is organizational rank important? Should you alphabetize the list? Don't hit "reply all" unless all will appreciate your doing so.

- **CC:** CC stands for "carbon copy," from the days of typewriters when carbon paper was used to make multiple copies. CC people who are not directly involved in the business of the email but are interested in it. Marketing may not be helping you produce your new software, but the department may want to stay abreast of the changes to start generating marketing ideas. A committee might CC an assistant who does not attend committee meetings but does maintain the committee's paper records. Sometimes, the CC line is used politically. For example, an administrative assistant doing routine business may CC the boss to give added weight to the email.

- **BCC:** BCC stands for "blind carbon copy," a copy that the listed receivers do not know is being sent. Blind copies can create ill will when they become known, so be careful in their use.

Use appropriate subject lines for your message. Subject lines for informative and positive messages (Chapter 9), negative messages (Chapter 10), and persuasive messages (Chapter 11) are discussed later in the textbook.

Use appropriate **salutations**: *Dear* is saved mostly for formal emails; *Hey* is generally considered too informal for business use. Many writers are now starting their emails with *Hi* or *Hello* (e.g., "Hi Abhinav,"). And when emailing people with whom they are in constant contact, many writers use no salutation at all.

Remember that emails are public documents and may be widely forwarded. Use standard capitalization and spelling; save lowercase and instant message abbreviations for friends, if you use them at all. Features that express emotion, such as underlining, all caps, exclamation points, and emoticons, should be used with great caution. Even a quick confirmation to your boss should look professional.

Keep in mind the possibility that your email may not be read. Emails outside your company may be deflected by a misspelled address, an in-box filter, or an internet malfunction. With the high volume of items in most in-boxes, it is easy for an email to move off the screen and out of the receiver's awareness. If you do not receive a response within a reasonable time, follow up.

Remember that many people do not consider a one- to two-hour turnaround time reasonable for email. If the item is that urgent, you should choose another means of communication, such as a phone call.

WARNING: Never put anything in an email that would embarrass you or harm your career if your employer saw it.

Finally, you should take care to avoid common email mistakes (see Figure 2.10).

Figure 2.10	Email Pet Peeves

- Missing or vague subject lines.
- Copying everyone ("Reply all"), rather than just the people that might find the information useful.
- Too much information or too little information.
- Too many instant messaging abbreviations.
- Lack of capitalization and punctuation.
- Long messages without headings or bullets.
- Delayed response emails that don't include the original message. Sometimes readers have no idea what the emails are about.
- Writers who send a general request to multiple people, creating confusion about who is responsible for handling the request.
- People who expect an immediate answer (within one to three hours) and do not select a more rapid means of communication, such as a phone call.
- People who never respond to queries.
- People who don't read their email carefully enough to absorb a simple message.
- People who send too many unimportant emails.
- Superfluous images and attachments.
- Overuse of high-priority markers or subject line words such as URGENT or READ NOW.
- Flaming (angry messages, frequently with extreme language).

Save Your Audience Time   Email overload has become a serious problem; workers now spend about one-third of their working days responding to emails.[40] To save your audience time—whether a coworker or a client—send an email only when necessary; write specific subject lines; be clear about whether you expect an action from the recipient, and if so, what it is and when you expect it; and avoid sending an email impulsively so you can accurately assess whether it's necessary and whether multiple messages could be combined into one.

Use these tips to value your readers' time by designing your email to help them:

- Put the most important information in the first sentence.

- If your email is more than one screen long, use an overview, headings, and enumeration to help draw readers to successive screens.

- Limit your email to one topic. Delete off-topic material.

- If you send messages with an attachment, put the most vital information in the email, too. Don't make readers open an attachment merely to find out the time or location of a meeting.

- Check your message for accuracy and completeness. In emails about meetings, remember to include the time, place (whether a physical location or a web-conference link), and date.

To help you with all these best practices toward saving your audience time, Gmail offers an undo-send option that allows you to undo sending up to 30 seconds after pushing the "send" button.[41]

> **WARNING:** You do not want to be the person whose emails or voicemail messages are opened last because they take so long to get to the point or, even worse, the person whose messages are rarely opened at all because you send so many that aren't important or necessary.

Social Media

Facebook   Because of its interactivity, Facebook requires a lot of attention. Customers posting to a corporate site expect prompt responses. They also can post misinformation and vulgarities, so it is important that organizations have policies to help guide their social media writers.

If you are creating a business Facebook page, be sure to include key information such as business hours, link to an external company website, and contact information such as email address and phone number. Select cover and profile photos that are easily rendered on multiple platforms: laptops, tablets, and smartphones. And use the page to interact with customers in a way that builds goodwill and generates meaningful interest in your company.

If users post complaints to your page, you should respond promptly, courteously, and publicly. When the company holds itself accountable to customer complaints and fixes any problems, it encourages potential customers to become actual customers.

If you are responsible for responding to customers from a company's Facebook profile, respond promptly and courteously, even if you do not yet have the answer; Facebook logs response time and posts it publicly. If you need time to research an answer, you still should respond as soon as you see a message to let the sender know you have acknowledged their query and are processing it. This will improve the response-time metrics of your Facebook page.

Employees with personal Facebook pages need to remember the public nature of the site. In fact, poor judgment has cost some workers their jobs as a result of posting controversial updates about their employers or uploading inappropriate photos.[42] For example, an Atlanta police officer was terminated after posting sensitive job information; Virgin Atlantic fired 13 crew members after they posted mean comments about passengers and spiteful opinions about the airline's safety standards.[43]

You should carefully consider the privacy settings of your personal Facebook posts; you can set all posts to a conservative setting such as "Friends only" and expand the availability of individual posts as needed. Be aware that your current profile photo will always be publicly visible.

Twitter   Although Twitter messages as business communications are still relatively new compared to letters and emails, they have developed some commonly accepted guidelines:

- Clarity is important. Although tweets are limited to 280 characters, they still need to use enough words so they are not cryptic.

- Don't waste people's time with tweets. If the audience response could be, "Who cares?" don't send it. This guideline particularly applies to most tweets describing what you are doing at the moment.

- Be sparing with hashtags and abbreviations.

- Slang is generally inappropriate for workplace tweets.

Companies can use Twitter to reinforce the desired narrative about their company. You should share informative or positive content about what your company is doing, ideally using stories, humor, or interesting information. Include links when relevant so interested followers can learn more. And use hashtags when appropriate to categorize your content as desired.

As an employee, you should consider your audience and context before tweeting, just as you should with all other forms of business communication. Avoid sending tweets like the following:

> @bossman_GGSA I'm totes going to be late for work today. whacky traffic and coffee shop line is ridic UGH! #suckydaysofar #fail #IhateMondays

This person has probably selected the wrong medium to communicate with the boss, and the slang, uncommon abbreviation, and multiple hashtags are not appropriate for workplace communication. Instead, be upbeat and positive with workplace tweets:

> Had a great presentation today with bossman. Lots of great feedback and excited to move onto the next phase!

Remember that if your Twitter account is connected to your workplace followers, your tweets not only represent your views, but also should reflect positively on your organization. As is true with all social media, you must be careful what you say. Tweets can be searched on Google and can be recalled in defamation lawsuits.

Instagram   Instagram offers users a visually driven way to influence how followers view a company. Use an Instagram account to illustrate your company's desired narrative, to connect with followers, and to gain new followers via hashtag cross-referencing.

Figure 2.11   YogaFit Reaffirms Positive and Inclusive Narrative in Instagram Posts

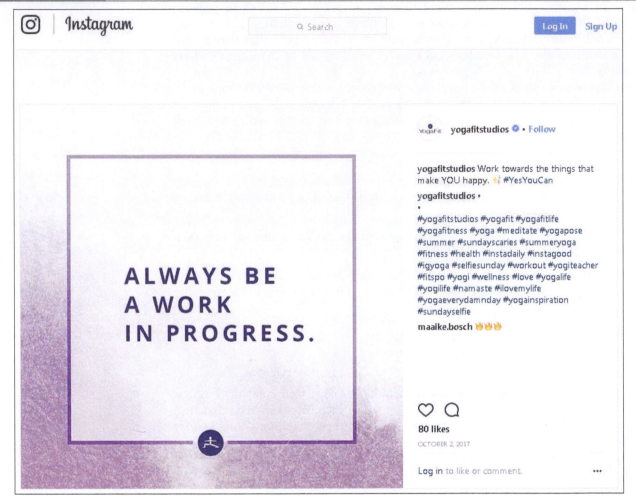

Source: Instagram/yogafitstudios

Determine how your company wants to be seen, then use images and illustrated text to establish and continually reaffirm that narrative. For example, YogaFit, an international yoga certification program, posts positive messages across a purple-watercolor background, framed in a purple box with the YogaFit logo placed unobtrusively at the bottom (see Figure 2.11 for one example; other messages include "Never Give Up" and "Keep Shining, Keep Smiling"). By regularly posting images that are similar in both message and visuals, the company plays an active role in illustrating the narrative of its company, continually reestablishing its image as positive and inclusive.

YogaFit also uses Instagram to interact with and connect with followers. In another post (Figure 2.12), it asked followers, "What is your favorite YogaFit class and why?" Notice how the design follows a similar aesthetic, with a purple frame and the company's logo at the bottom. You should use Instagram to ask your followers questions and thus to make their voices feel heard; it is even better if you follow up on those

Figure 2.12   YogaFit Interacts with Followers in Instagram Posts

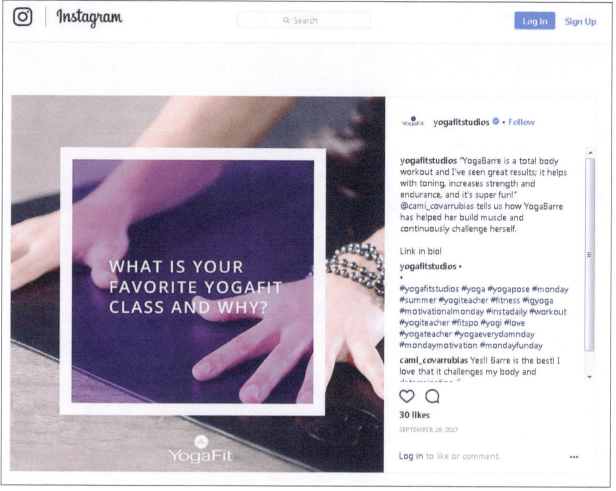

Source: Instagram/yogafitstudios

comments in a later post by acknowledging comment trends. YogaFit posted a photo of smiling participants at a barre class, which had been identified (in a response to the post depicted in Figure 2.12) as a favorite class.

Finally, you can use hashtags in your Instagram posts to cross-reference in order to gain additional followers.

Many businesses create hashtags specific to worker groups or projects. In communicating with the public, hashtags can help organize a certain promotion, such as a contest (#NameOurNewCereal), build goodwill by adding levity to a post (#IsItFridayYet?), and help connect with more followers (i.e., potential customers). For example, in Figure 2.13, YogaFit posted a smoothie recipe with several hashtags, including #yogafitness, #summer, #healthyeating, and #smoothie. Users who searched for #smoothie might find this recipe, enjoy it, and start following YogaFit because of this one strategically hashtagged post.

| Figure 2.13 | YogaFit Connects with New Followers via Hashtags in Instagram Posts |

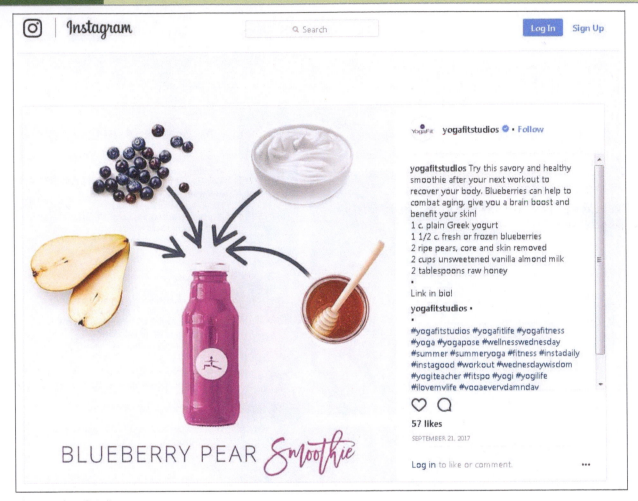

Source: Instagram/yogafitstudios

Summary by Learning Objectives

LO 2-1   **Select an appropriate channel for your message.**

A communication channel is the means by which you convey your message. You should select an appropriate channel in order to optimize your communication. Using a well-chosen channel to share messages will help you meet audience expectations, reach your target audience, shorten response time, and make a broader impact.

The best channel for your business message depends on its size, purposes, circumstances, needs, and budget. Choices include face-to-face conversations, phone calls, websites, email, memos, text messages, social media, applications (i.e., apps), and web conferences.

LO 2-2   **Create *you*-attitude.**

You-attitude is a style of communication that looks at things from the audience's point of view, emphasizing what the audience wants to know, respecting the audience's intelligence, and protecting the audience's ego. To create *you*-attitude:

1. Talk about the audience, not about yourself.
2. Refer to the audience's request or order specifically.
3. Don't talk about feelings except to congratulate or offer sympathy.
4. In positive situations, use *you* more often than *I*. Use *we* when it includes the audience.
5. In negative situations, avoid the word *you*. Protect the audience's ego. Use passive verbs and impersonal expressions to avoid assigning blame.

Apply *you*-attitude beyond the sentence level by using organization and content as well as style to build goodwill.

LO 2-3   **Create positive emphasis.**

Positive emphasis means focusing on the positive rather than the negative aspects of a situation. To create positive tone:

1. Avoid negative words and words with negative connotations.
2. Beware of hidden negatives.
3. Focus on what the audience can do rather than on limitations.
4. Justify negative information by giving a reason or linking it to an audience benefit.
5. Put the negative information in the middle and present it compactly.

Check to see that your positive emphasis is appropriate, sincere, and clear.

LO 2-4   **Improve tone in business communication.**

The desirable tone for business communication is businesslike but not stiff, friendly but not phony, confident but not arrogant, polite but not groveling.

LO 2-5   **Create inclusive business communication.**

Inclusive language is fair and friendly, it complies with the law, it includes all members of your audience, and it helps sustain goodwill.

- Check to be sure your language is nonoppressive.
- Communication should be nongendered; pay special attention to job titles, courtesy titles and names, pronouns, and other words and phrases.

- *Ms.* is the default courtesy title for women. Use *Ms.* unless the woman has a professional title or unless you know she prefers a traditional title.
- Three ways to make pronouns nongendered are to use plural pronouns, to use *you*, and to revise the sentence to omit the pronoun.
- When you talk about people with disabilities or diseases, use the term they prefer.
- When you produce documents with photos and illustrations, include in the image a sampling of the whole population, not just part of it.

LO 2-6   **Employ platform-specific best practices for creating goodwill.**

When making phone calls, writing emails, or managing social media accounts on Facebook, Twitter, or Instagram, you should consider best practices specific to the medium.

- Phone calls: Speak clearly; repeat key information; keep your message concise; do not multitask.
- Emails: Use specific subject lines; keep your message concise; clearly state expectations.
- Facebook: Interact with clients; respond promptly; use your personal page responsibly.
- Twitter: Make your message clear and concise; reinforce your company's desired narrative.
- Instagram: Illustrate your company's narrative; interact with followers; cross-reference with hashtags.

Exercises and Cases

2.1   Reviewing the Chapter

1. Why might you choose a phone call, an email, a memo, a text message, or a particular social media for a given business message? (LO 2-1)
2. What are five ways to create *you*-attitude? (LO 2-2)
3. What are five ways to create positive emphasis? (LO 2-3)
4. How can you improve the tone of business messages? (LO 2-4)
5. What are different categories to keep in mind when you are trying to increase inclusivity in business messages? (LO 2-5)
6. What are some platform-specific best practices for building goodwill? (LO 2-6)

2.2   Choosing a Channel to Reach a Specific Audience

Suppose your organization wants to target a product, service, or program for each of the following audiences. What would be the best channel(s) to reach that group in your city? To what extent would that channel reach all group members?

1. Parents of children with autism.
2. Ballroom dancers.
3. Nontraditional college students.
4. Parents whose children play basketball.
5. People who are blind.
6. Mothers who are vegan.
7. People who are interested in improvisation.
8. Dog owners.

2.3   Evaluating a New Channel

To combat software piracy, Microsoft tried an unusual communication channel. A new software update turned screens black on computers using pirated software; the update also posted a message to switch to legitimate software copies. The update did not prevent people from using their machines, and they could manually change their wallpaper back to its previous design. But the black screen returned every 60 minutes. Microsoft said there was little protest except in China, where the software piracy problem is greatest.[44]

In small groups, discuss this practice.

1. What do you think of this channel?
2. Is it ethical?

3. Do you think it helped or hurt Microsoft profits in China?
4. How do you think receivers of the black screen reacted?

As your instructor directs,

a. Post your findings electronically to share with the class.
b. Present your findings in an email to your instructor.
c. Present your findings in an oral presentation to the class.

2.4   Evaluating the Ethics of Positive Emphasis

The first term in each pair is negative; the second is a positive term that is sometimes substituted for it. Which of the positive terms seem ethical? Which seem unethical? Briefly explain your choices.

cost	investment
second mortgage	home equity loan
tax	user fee
nervousness	adrenaline
problem	challenge
price increase	price change
for-profit hospital	tax-paying hospital
used car	pre-owned car
credit card fees	usage charges

2.5   Eliminating Negative Words and Words with Negative Connotations

Revise each of the following sentences to replace negative words with positive ones. Be sure to keep the meaning of the original sentence.

1. You will lose the account if you make a mistake and the customer is dissatisfied.
2. Avoid errors on customer reports by carefully proofreading.

3. Your account, #82654, is delinquent. If you neglect to pay this balance, your account will be sent to collections.
4. When you write a report, do not make claims that you cannot support with evidence.
5. Don't drop in without an appointment. Your counselor or caseworker may be unavailable.
6. I am anxious to discuss my qualifications in an interview.

2.6   Focusing on the Positive

Revise each of the following sentences to focus on the options that remain, not those that are closed off.

1. Applications that are postmarked after January 15 will not be accepted.
2. All new employees will not be able to receive benefits for 90 days.

3. I will not be available by phone on Saturdays and Sundays.
4. Overtime cannot be processed without the supervisor's signature.
5. Travel reimbursement forms will only be processed at the end of the month.

2.7   Identifying Hidden Negatives

Identify the hidden negatives in the following sentences and revise to eliminate them. In some cases, you may need to add information to revise the sentence effectively.

1. The seminar will help you become a better manager.
2. Thank you for the confidence you have shown in us by ordering one of our products. It will be shipped to you soon.
3. This publication is designed to explain how your company can start a recycling program.

4. I hope you find the information in this brochure beneficial to you and a valuable reference as you plan your move.
5. In thinking about your role in our group, I remember two occasions where you contributed something.
6. [In job letter] This job in customer service is so good for me; I am so ready to take on responsibility.

2.8 Improving *You*-Attitude and Positive Emphasis

Revise these sentences to improve *you*-attitude and positive emphasis. Eliminate any awkward phrasing. In some cases, you may need to add information to revise the sentence effectively.

1. You'll be happy to learn that the cost of tuition will not rise next year.
2. Although I was only an intern and didn't actually make presentations to major clients, I was required to prepare PowerPoint slides for the meetings and to answer some of the clients' questions.
3. At DiYanni Homes we have more than 30 plans that we will personalize just for you.
4. Please notify HR of your bank change as soon as possible to prevent a disruption of your direct deposit.
5. I'm sorry you were worried. You did not miss the deadline for signing up for a flexible medical spending account.
6. You will be happy to hear that our cell phone plan does not charge you for incoming calls.
7. The employee discount may only be used for purchases for your own use or for gifts; you may not buy items for resale. To prevent any abuse of the discount privilege, you may be asked to justify your purchase.
8. I apologize for my delay in answering your inquiry. The problem was that I had to check with our suppliers to see whether we could provide the item in the quantity you say you want. We can.
9. If you mailed a check with your order, as you claim, we failed to receive it.
10. This job sounds perfect for me.

2.9 Creating Inclusive Language

Explain the source of bias in each of the following and revise for inclusivity.

1. Mr. Brady, Mr. Barnes, and the new intern, Jodi, will represent our company at the job fair.
2. Although he is blind, Mr. Morin is an excellent group leader.
3. Please join us for the company potluck! Ladies, please bring a main dish. Men, please bring chips and dip (store bought is fine).
4. Lee Torsad
   Pacific Perspectives
   6300 West Coronado Blvd.
   Los Angles, CA
   Dear Sir:
5. I would prefer if you hired a female secretary; women are typically friendlier than men.
6. Please do not use the side elevator because it is reserved for people who can't walk.
7. Because older customers tend to be really picky, we will need to give a lot of details in our ads.

2.10 Analyzing Goodwill Ethics

In the U.S., credit card companies make offers to people fresh out of bankruptcy. They do this because they know that those targeted people cannot file for Chapter 7 bankruptcy again for eight years. If someone fails to pay back what they owe the credit card company, the company can sue to collect the debt.

In small groups, discuss whether you think this practice is ethical. Why or why not? What reasons exist for not offering new credit to people who have just gone through bankruptcy? Why might such people need new credit cards?

2.11 Advising a Hasty Subordinate

Three days ago, one of your subordinates forwarded to everyone in the office a bit of email humor he'd received from a friend. Titled "You know you're Southern when . . . ," the message poked fun at Southern speech, attitudes, and lifestyles. Today you get this message from your subordinate:

> Subject: Should I Apologize?
>
> I'm getting flamed left and right because of the Southern message. I thought it was funny, but some people just can't take a joke. So far I've tried not to respond to the flames, figuring that would just make things worse. But now I'm wondering if I should apologize. What do you think?

Answer the message.

2.12   Responding to a Complaint

You're the director of corporate communications and the employee newsletter is produced by your office. Today you receive this email message from Tonya Freira:

> Subject: Complaint
>
> The section on the back of the employee newsletter referred to Mindy Kelso and me as "the girls at the front desk." We are not "girls," and we don't see why our gender was even pointed out in the first place. We are customer service representatives and would like to be referred to that way.

Write a response to Tonya Freira. Also, draft a message to your staff, reminding them to edit newsletter stories as well as external documents to replace oppressive language.

2.13   Dealing with Negative Clients

An executive at one of your largest client companies is known for his negative attitude. He is feared for his sharp tongue and scathing attacks, and he bullies everyone. Everyone you know, including yourself, is afraid of him. Unfortunately, he is also the one who decides whether you get your annual contract. Your contract is up for renewal and you have some new services you think his company would like.

In small groups, discuss at least four ways to handle Mr. Bully. Write up your two best to share with the whole class. Also write up the reasons you think these two approaches will work. Share your two approaches with the whole class, as a short oral presentation or online.

As a class, select the two best approaches from those offered by the small groups. Discuss your criteria for selection and rejection.

2.14   Writing Business Thank-You Notes

Some businesses make a practice of sending goodwill messages to some of their customers.

Pick a business you patronize that might logically send some thank-you notes. Write a suitable note and design a tasteful visual for it. In a separate document, write an email to your instructor explaining your design and content decisions.

Questions you might want to consider:

- Who is your audience? Will you write to everyone? Will you target big spenders? Trendsetters? People who might become long-term customers? How will you identify your categories?
- What tone did you select? What words and phrases help produce that tone? What words and phrases did you avoid? What diction choices did you make to convey sincerity?
- What content did you choose? Why? What content choices did you discard?
- What design features did you choose? Why? What design features did you discard?

Notes

1. Frances Frei and Anne Morriss, *Uncommon Service: How to Win by Putting Customers at the Core of Your Business* (Boston: Harvard Business Review Press, 2012), 1.
2. Petri Böckerman and Pekka Ilmakunnas, "The Job Satisfaction-Productivity Nexus: A Study Using Matched Survey and Register Data," *Cornell University Industrial & Labor Relations Review* 65, no. 2 (2012): 259.
3. Rheana Muray, "Gravity Payments' $70K Minimum Salary: CEO Dan Price Shares Results over a Year Later," *Today,* August 11, 2016, https://www.today.com/money/gravity-payments-70k-minimum-salary-ceo-dan-price-shares-results-t101678.
4. Jim Ludema and Amber Johnson, "Gravity Payment's Dan Price on How He Measures Success after His $70k Experiment," *Forbes,* August 28, 2018, https://www.forbes.com/sites/amberjohnson-jimludema/2018/08/28/gravity-payments-dan-price-on-how-he-measures-success-after-his-70k-experiment/?sh=7faf6df3174b.
5. John Sowell, "He Employs 50 Boise Workers. They Took Pay Cuts to Avoid Layoffs. The Choice Paid Off," *Idaho Statesman,* August 21, 2020, https://www.idahostatesman.com/news/business/article244968805.html.
6. Normans Bridal Shoppe, "New Arrivals under 60 Seconds," November 21, 2020, https://www.tiktok.com/@normansbridalshoppe/video/6897639010378845446.
7. A. Guttman, "Social Network Advertising Spending in the United States from 2016 to 2022," Statistica, December 11, 2020, https://www.statista.com/statistics/736971/social-media-ad-spend-usa/#.
8. Nate Silver, *The Signal and the Noise: Why So Many Predictions Fail–But Some Don't* (New York: Penguin, 2012), 139–40.
9. Ames Animal Shelter, https://www.facebook.com/AmesAnimalShelter.
10. Steve Sullivan, "Everybody Eats!" *Health Connect,* Mary Greeley Medical Center, Fall 2017, 7.

11. Rachael Emma Silverman, "Tracking Sensors Invade the Workplace," *Wall Street Journal*, March 7, 2013, B1.

12. Corilyn Shropshire, "Americans Prefer Texting to Talking, Report Says," *Chicago Tribune*, March 26, 2015.

13. Pilar Pazos, Jennifer M. Chung, and Marina Micari, "Instant Messaging as a Task-Support Tool in Information Technology Organizations," *Journal of Business Communication* 50, no. 12 (2013): 68–86.

14. Jim Tierney, "Healthcare Providers Need to Adapt to Real-Time Customer Engagement," *Loyalty 360*, July 24, 2015.

15. Scott McCartney, "In-Flight Texting Makes Pilot :-)," *Wall Street Journal*, May 16, 2013, D1.

16. "Social Networking Rules Vary among Businesses," *Des Moines Register*, October 19, 2009, 6E.

17. J. Clement, "Number of Facebook Users Worldwide from 2015 to 2020," Statistica, November 15, 2019, https://www.statista.com/statistics/490424/number-of-worldwide-facebook-users/#.

18. Serena Dai, "Tweeting Diners Get Quick Response," *Des Moines Register*, September 25, 2010, 3E.

19. "60 Incredible and Interesting Twitter Stats and Statistics," Brandwatch, January 2, 2020, https://www.brandwatch.com/blog/twitter-stats-and-statistics.

20. Normans Bridal Shoppe, "New Arrivals under 60 Seconds," November 21, 2020, https://www.tiktok.com/@normans bridalshoppe/video/6897639010378845446.

21. Pamela Bump, "How 7 Brands Are Using TikTok," *HubSpot*, June 4, 2020, https://blog.hubspot.com/marketing/brands-on-tiktok.

22. Ying Lin, "10 LinkedIn Statistics Every Marketer Should Know in 2021 [Infographic]", *Oberlo*, January 20, 2020, https://www.oberlo.com/blog/linkedin-statistics#.

23. "Word-of-Mouth Recommendations Remain the Most Credible," *Nielsen*, October 7, 2015, http://www.nielsen.com/id/en/press-room/2015/word-of-mouth-recommendations-remain-the-most-credible.html.

24. Pino G. Audia, "Train Your People to Take Others' Perspectives," *Harvard Business Review* 90, no. 10 (November 2012): 28.

25. Tim Gibson, "A Guide to Business Greetings around the World," *The Telegraph*, September 7, 2015, http://www.telegraph.co.uk/sponsored/business/business-etiquette/11834830/business-greetings.html.

26. "Appendix G: Weights and Measures," *The World Factbook*, 2017, https://www.cia.gov/library/publications/the-world-factbook/appendix/appendix-g.html.

27. Robert Hurley, "Trust Me," *Wall Street Journal*, October 24, 2011, R4.

28. Annette N. Shelby and N. Lamar Reinsch, "Positive Emphasis and You-Attitude: An Empirical Study," *Journal of Business Communication* 32, no. 4 (1995): 303–27.

29. Martin E. P. Seligman, *Learned Optimism: How to Change Your Mind and Your Life*, 2nd ed. (New York: Pocket Books, 1998), 96–107.

30. Mark A. Sherman, "Adjectival Negation and Comprehension of Multiply Negated Sentences," *Journal of Verbal Learning and Verbal Behavior* 15 (1976): 143–57.

31. Jeffrey Zaslow, "In Praise of Less Praise," *Wall Street Journal*, May 3, 2007, D1.

32. Margaret Baker Graham and Carol David, "Power and Politeness: Administrative Writing in an 'Organized Anarchy,'" *Journal of Business and Technical Communication* 10, no. 1 (1996): 5–27.

33. "Women's History Month: March 2013," U.S. Census Bureau Newsroom, February 7, 2013, http://www.census.gov/newsroom/releases/archives/facts_for_features_special_editions/cb13-ff04.html.

34. U.S. Census Bureau, "The Hispanic Population in the United States: 2019," https://www.census.gov/data/tables/2019/demo/hispanic-origin/2019-cps.html.

35. "Rise of Latino Population Blurs US Racial Lines," *Associated Press*, May 17, 2013, http://www.npr.org/templates/story/story.php?storyId=174546756.

36. Administration for Community Living, April 2018, "2017 Profile of Older Americans," https://acl.gov/sites/default/files/Aging%20and%20Disability%20in%20America/2017Older AmericansProfile.pdf; and David Wagner, "More Seniors Are Working—Some by Choice, Others by Necessity," *Marketplace*, May 19, 2019, https://www.marketplace.org/2019/05/01/more-seniors-are-working-some-choice-others-without-one.

37. Amy Molina, "Latina, Latino, Latinx. What Is This New Term, Latinx?" *NASPA*, August 31, 2016, https://www.naspa.org/constituent-groups/posts/latina-latino-latinx.-what-is-this-new-term-latinx.

38. Centers for Disease Control and Prevention, "Disability Impacts All of Us," September 16, 2020, https://www.cdc.gov/ncbddd/disabilityandhealth/infographic-disability-impacts-all.html#.

39. John Brandon, "Voicemail Is Now Officially Dead. Here's What Killed It. We never really liked it anyway," *Inc.*, January 12, 2018, https://www.inc.com/john-brandon/voicemail-is-now-officially-dead-heres-what-killed-it.html; and Dan Kedmey, "4 Reasons You Should Never Leave Another Voicemail Again," *Time*, December 23, 2014, https://time.com/3645710/no-more-voicemail.

40. Danie-Elle Dubé, "This Is How Much Time You Spend on Work Emails Every Day, According to a Canadian Survey," *Global News*, April 21, 2017.

41. Chandra Steele, Lance Whitney, and Jason Cohen, "How to Manage 'Undo Send' in Gmail," *PC Magazine*, February 19, 2019, https://www.pcmag.com/how-to/how-to-manage-undo-send-in-gmail.

42. Dylan Love, "17 People Who Were Fired for Using Facebook," *Business Insider*, July 4, 2014, https://www.businessinsider.com/17-people-who-were-fired-for-using-facebook-2014-7.

43. Christopher Steiner and Helen Coster, "11 Career Ending Facebook Faux Pas," *Forbes*, April 13, 2010, http://www.forbes.com/2010/04/13/how-facebook-ruined-my-career-entrepreneurs-human-resources-facebook_slide.html.

44. Loretta Chao and Juliet Ye, "Microsoft Tactic Raises Hackles in China: In Antipiracy Move, Software Update Turns Screens Black and Urges Users to Buy Legal Windows Copies," *Wall Street Journal*, October 23, 2008, B4.

3 Researching and Evaluating Source Material

Chapter Outline

Research Strategies

Primary Research

- Surveys
- Research Interviews
- Focus Groups
- Using Online Networks
- Observations of Customers and Users
- Using Technology for Research

Analyzing Your Research Results

- Analyze Numbers
- Analyze Patterns
- Check Your Logic

Secondary Research

- Effectively Searching for Secondary Sources
- Sifting through Search Results
- Using Preliminary Results to Find More Sources

Recognizing Types of False or Misleading Information

- Categories of Information Pollution
- Types of Problematic Content

Strategies for Evaluating Sources

- How to Spot Fabricated News, Spam, and Phishing
- Stop the Spread of Fabricated or Misleading Information
- Use the CRAAP Test to Evaluate Sources

Source Citation and Documentation

- Quotations
- Paraphrases
- Summaries
- Documentation Requires Precision
- Ethical versus Unethical Practice

Summary by Learning Objectives

DrAfter123/Getty Images

Disinformation Hurts Business

"Why are you still open?" "Why are you selling human meat?"

Shrina Begum and her employees answered hundreds of phone calls with callers screaming at them over a 24-hour period. After one of her employees was able to calm one of the callers down, the employee learned that the caller had been sent an article on social media claiming that the restaurant was selling human meat, that nine bodies were found in the freezer, and that the owner had been arrested. Included in the article was a picture of Begum's restaurant.

Begum was eventually able to track the article down. It was created on website that invites people to prank others with fake news stories, but the article published through that website looked like any mainstream news article when shared on social media. Once it appeared on one social media platform, it could be quickly shared and cross-referenced on other platforms. A quick search of the pranking website revealed that six Indian restaurants were targeted with the accusation of selling human meat; five used almost the exact same narrative as the article targeting Begum's restaurant.

If people would have clicked on the article's link, they would have seen the

DEBUNKED

Trolls Are Targeting Indian Restaurants With A Create-Your-Own Fake News Site

At least 30 websites invite people to make up a fake news story and share it on Facebook. Over the past 12 months the articles have generated more than 13 million engagements on the social network.

Craig Silverman
BuzzFeed News Media Editor

Sara Spary
BuzzFeed Staff

Posted on May 29, 2017, at 2:58 p.m. ET

ASIAN RESTAURANT SHUT DOWN FOR USING HUMAN MEAT

FAKE

BuzzFeed, Inc

message "You've Been Pranked! Now Create A Story & Trick Your Friends!" to the right of the fake article, but apparently not everyone did, and suddenly Begum's restaurant, established by her father in 1957, was in danger of closing.

Discerning accurate information from false information is a critical component of the research process. This chapter covers methods for analyzing the accuracy and credibility of online sources, as well as gathering your own data via surveys, interviews, and other methods.

Sources: Eleanor Rose, "New Cross Indian Restaurant Hit by Fake News Story Claiming It 'Served Human Meat,'" *Evening Standard,* May 17, 2017, https://www.standard.co.uk/news/london/new-cross-restaurant-hit-by-fake-news-story-claiming-it-served-human-meat-a3541956.html; "Restaurant Hit by 'Human Meat' Fake News Claims," *BBC News,* May 18, 2017, https://www.bbc.com/news/newsbeat-39966215; and Craig Silverman and Sara Spary, "Trolls Are Targeting Indian Restaurants with a Create-Your-Own Fake News Site," *BuzzFeed News,* May 29, 2017, https://www.buzzfeednews.com/article/craigsilverman/create-your-own-fake-news-sites-are-booming-on-facebook-and.

Learning Objectives

After studying this chapter, you should be able to

LO 3-1 Explain strategies of primary research.

LO 3-2 Collect and analyze research results from primary research.

LO 3-3 Effectively search for secondary research.

LO 3-4 Recognize types of false or misleading information.

LO 3-5 Critically evaluate potential source material.

LO 3-6 Use and document source material ethically.

Research Strategies

Quality research is important for a variety of reasons. With it, we build our understanding of how the world—including how business—works. Through research, businesses learn how to operate more efficiently and effectively. Research also helps businesses improve products and services. For example, engineers have designed furniture that reduces employees' injuries; agronomists have generated crops that resist pests and drought; programmers have created apps that enable bank customers to deposit checks with their smartphones; and web designers have built agile websites that adapt to users based on their differing needs, such as impaired vision or mobility.

Research can also inform business decisions and actions. A manager might gather data on how customers move through the store before planning a redesign or restocking of shelves, study how customers enter and leave the parking lot to redesign the lot for increased parking spaces and fewer accidents, analyze how customers land on their website before changing marketing strategies, or investigate the feasibility of changing suppliers.

Depending on the question that needs answering, research may be as simple as retrieving a printout of sales for the last month; it may involve locating material published in a trade journal; or it might involve developing and disseminating a survey or interviewing people. The research strategy, or a combination of strategies, that you choose must be determined carefully and with the rhetorical situation in mind. Your research strategy must

- Provide you with the data you need.

- Advance your purpose for communicating.

- Generate enough evidence for your audience to accept and, if needed, act.

There are several different research strategies at your disposal. **Primary research** gathers new information. Surveys, interviews, focus groups, and observations are common primary-research methods for gathering new information for business reports. **Secondary research** retrieves information that someone else gathered. Library research and online searches are the most common kinds of secondary research.

Primary Research

LO 3-1

Sometimes you can use data that someone else has collected and possibly interpreted as well, but you may find that the data that you need do not yet exist. In such cases, you—possibly working with a team—have to gather the data. This section covers some common primary-research methods: surveys, interviews, focus groups, use of online networks, and observations of customers and users.

Surveys

A **survey** questions a group of people. The easiest way to ask many questions is to create a **questionnaire**, a written list of questions that people fill out. An **interview** is a structured conversation with someone who will be able to give you useful information. Organizations use surveys and interviews to research both internal issues, such as employee satisfaction, and external issues, such as customer satisfaction.

When you consider using a survey's data for your own work, examine the survey's construction, dissemination, data, and interpretation closely.

Figure 3.1 lists questions to ask about surveys.

1. Who did the survey and who paid for it? Unfortunately, it is far too easy to introduce bias into surveys. Thus, a good place to start when examining survey results is to determine the survey producers. Who are they? How were they financed? For example, how comfortable should you be with the results of a survey about a medical device when the survey was financed by the maker of the device? Was a survey about car satisfaction financed by the maker of the car?

2. How many people were surveyed and how were they chosen? To keep research costs reasonable, usually only a **sample** of the total **population** is polled. A sample is a subset of the population; the population is the group you want to make statements about. The way that sample was chosen and the attempts made to get responses from nonrespondents will determine whether you can infer that what is true of the sample is also true of the population as a whole.

A **convenience sample** is a group of participants who are easy to get: students who walk through the student union, people at a shopping mall, workers in your own unit. Convenience samples are useful for a rough pretest of a questionnaire and may be acceptable for some class research projects. However, you cannot generalize from a convenience sample to a larger group. If, for instance, you survey people entering your local library about their opinion of the proposed library bond (which has to be voter approved), you are taking a convenience sample and one that will not tell you what non-library users think.

A purposive or **judgment sample** is a group of people whose views seem useful. Someone interested in surveying the kinds of writing done on campus might ask each department for the name of a faculty member who cared about writing and then send surveys to those people.

In a **random sample**, each person in the population theoretically has an equal chance of being chosen. When people say they did something *randomly* they often mean *without conscious bias*. However, unconscious bias exists. Someone passing out surveys in front of the library may be more likely to approach people who seem friendly and less likely to ask people who seem intimidating; are in a hurry; are much older or younger; or are of a different race or gender. True random samples rely on random digit tables, published in texts and online.

If you take a truly random sample, you can generalize your findings to the whole population from which your sample comes. Consider, for example, a random phone

Figure 3.1	Questions to Ask about Surveys
	1. Who did the survey and who paid for it?
	2. How many people were surveyed, and how were they chosen?
	3. How was the survey conducted?
	4. What was the response rate?
	5. What questions were asked?

survey that shows 65% of respondents approve of a presidential policy. Measures of variability always should be attached to survey-derived estimates like this one. Typically, a **confidence interval** provides this measure of variability. Using the confidence interval, we might conclude it is likely that between 58% and 72% of the population approve of the presidential policy when the margin of error is 6% to 7%. The confidence interval is based on the size of the sample and the expected variation within the population. Statistical texts tell you how to calculate measures of variability.

Do not, however, confuse **sample size** with randomness. A classic example is the 1936 *Literary Digest* poll that predicted Republican Alf Landon would beat Democrat incumbent President Franklin Roosevelt. *Literary Digest* sent out 10 million ballots to its magazine subscribers as well as people who owned cars and telephones, most of whom in 1936 were richer than the average voter—and more Republican.[1]

3. How was the survey conducted?
Face-to-face surveys are convenient when you are surveying a fairly small number of people in a specific location. In a face-to-face survey, however, the interviewer's gender, race, and nonverbal cues can bias results. Most people prefer not to say things they think their audience will dislike. For example, women may be more likely to agree that sexual harassment is a problem if the interviewer is also a woman.

Phone surveys are popular because they can be closely supervised. Interviewers can read the questions from a computer screen and key in answers as the respondent gives them. The results can then be available just a few minutes after the last call is completed.

Phone surveys also have limitations. First, they reach only people who have phones and thus underrepresent some groups such as people who cannot afford a phone. Voice-mail, caller ID, and cell phones also make phone surveys more difficult. Most people do not answer or return calls from unknown sources, nor are their cell phone numbers readily available in most cases.

Mail surveys can reach anyone who has an address. Some people may be more willing to fill out an anonymous questionnaire than to give sensitive information to a stranger over the phone. However, mail surveys are not effective for respondents who don't read and write well. Further, it may be more difficult to get a response from someone who doesn't care about the survey or who sees the mailing as junk mail.

Online surveys deliver questions over the internet. The researcher can contact respondents with an email containing a link to a webpage with the survey or can ask people by mail or in person to log on and visit the website with the survey.

Another alternative is to post a survey on a website and invite the site's visitors to complete the survey. This approach does not generate a random sample, so the results probably do not reflect the opinions of the entire population. In addition, volunteers for online surveys are more educated, more likely to be white, and more likely to be at the ends of the age spectrum than the general population.[2] Nevertheless, with online surveys costing about one-tenth of phone surveys, they are increasing their acceptance among experts and growing in popularity.

4. What was the response rate?
A major concern with any kind of survey is the **response rate**, the percentage of people who respond. People who refuse to answer may differ from those who respond, and you need information from both groups to be able to generalize to the whole population. Low response rates pose a major problem, especially for phone surveys. Answering machines and caller ID are commonly used to screen incoming calls, resulting in decreased response rates.

5. What questions were asked?
Surveys and interviews can be useful only if the questions are well designed. Good questions have these characteristics:

- They ask only one thing.

- They are phrased neutrally.

- They are asked in an order that does not influence answers.

- They avoid making assumptions about the respondent.

- They mean the same thing to different people.

At a telecommunications firm, a survey asked employees to rate their manager's performance at "hiring staff and setting compensation." Although both tasks are part of the discipline of human resource management, they are different activities. A manager might do a better job of hiring than of setting pay levels, or vice versa. The survey gave respondents—and the company using the survey—no way to distinguish performance on each task.[3]

Phrase questions in a way that won't bias the response, either positively or negatively. Respondents tend to agree more than disagree with statements. If a survey about managers asks employees whether their manager is fair, ethical, intelligent, knowledgeable, and so on, they are likely to assign all of these qualities to the manager—and to agree more and more as the survey goes along. To correct for this, some questions should be worded to generate the opposite response. For example, a statement about ethics can be balanced by a statement about corruption, and a statement about fairness can be balanced by a statement about bias or stereotypes.[4]

The order in which questions are asked matters. Asking about the economy—and its impact on families—before asking about the president will lower opinions of the president during bad economic times; the opposite is true for good economic times.[5]

Avoid questions that make assumptions about your subjects. The question "Does your spouse have a job outside the home?" assumes that your respondent is married.

Words like *often* and *important* mean different things to different people. To catch questions that can be misunderstood, avoid terms that are likely to mean different things to different people and pretest your questions with several people who are like those who will fill out the survey. Even a small pretest with 10 people can help you refine your questions.

Survey questions can be categorized in several ways. **Closed questions** have a limited number of possible responses. **Open questions** do not lock the subject into any sort of response. Figure 3.2 gives examples of closed and open questions. The second question in Figure 3.2 is an example of a **Likert scale**.

Closed questions are faster for subjects to answer and easier for researchers to score. However, because all answers must fit into prechosen categories, they cannot probe the complexities of a subject. You can improve the quality of closed questions by conducting a pretest with open questions to find categories that matter to respondents. Analyzing the responses from open questions is usually less straightforward than analyzing responses from closed questions.

Use closed multiple-choice questions for potentially embarrassing topics. Seeing their own situation listed as one response can help respondents feel that it is acceptable. However, very sensitive issues are perhaps better asked in an interview, where the interviewer can build trust and reveal information about themself to encourage the interviewee to answer.

Use an "Other, Please Specify" category when you want the convenience of a closed question but cannot foresee all the possible responses. These responses can be used to improve choices if the survey is to be repeated.

What is the single most important reason that you ride the bus?

_____ I don't have a car.

_____ I don't want to fight rush-hour traffic.

_____ Riding the bus is cheaper than driving my car.

_____ Riding the bus conserves fuel and reduces pollution.

_____ Other (please specify): _____

Figure 3.2	Closed and Open Questions

Closed questions

1. Are you satisfied with the city bus service? (yes/no)

2. How good is the city bus service?

   Excellent   5   4   3   2   1   Terrible

3. Indicate whether you agree (A) or disagree (D) with each of the following statements about city bus service.

   A   D The schedule is convenient for me.

   A   D The routes are convenient for me.

   A   D The drivers are courteous.

   A   D The buses are clean.

4. Rate each of the following improvements in the order of their importance to you (1 = most important and 6 = least important).

   _____ Buy new buses.

   _____ Increase non-rush-hour service on weekdays.

   _____ Increase service on weekdays.

   _____ Provide earlier and later service on weekdays.

   _____ Buy more buses with wheelchair access.

   _____ Provide unlimited free transfers.

Open questions

1. How do you feel about the city bus service?

2. Tell me about the city bus service.

3. Why do you ride the bus? (or, Why don't you ride the bus?)

4. What do you like and dislike about the city bus service?

5. How could the city bus service be improved?

When you use multiple-choice questions, make the answer categories mutually exclusive and exhaustive. This means you make sure that any one answer fits in only one category and that a category is included for all possible answers. In the following example of overlapping categories, a person who worked for a company with exactly 25 employees could check either *a* or *b*. The resulting data would be hard to interpret.

Overlapping categories: Indicate the number of full-time employees in your company on May 16:

   _____ a. 0–25

   _____ b. 25–100

   _____ c. 100–500

   _____ d. over 500

Discrete categories: Indicate the number of full-time employees on your payroll on May 16:

   _____ a. 0–25

   _____ b. 26–100

   _____ c. 101–500

   _____ d. more than 500

Branching questions direct different respondents to different parts of the question-naire based on their answers to earlier questions.

10. Have you talked to an academic adviser this year?   yes   no

     (If "no," skip to question 14.)

Generally, put questions that will be easy to answer early in the questionnaire. Put questions that are harder to answer or that people may be less willing to answer (e.g., age and income) near the end of the questionnaire. Even if people choose not to answer such questions, you'll still have the rest of the survey filled out.

If subjects will fill out the questionnaire themselves, pay careful attention to the physical design of the document. Use indentations and white space effectively; make it easy to mark and score the answers. Label answer scales frequently so respondents remember which end is positive and which is negative. Include a brief statement of purpose if you (or someone else) will not be available to explain the questionnaire or answer questions. Pretest the questionnaire to make sure the directions are clear. One researcher mailed a two-page questionnaire without pretesting it. One-third of the respondents didn't realize there were questions to answer on the back of the first page.

See Figure 3.3 for an example of a questionnaire for a student report.

Research Interviews

Interviews can be structured or unstructured. In a **structured interview**, the interviewer uses a detailed list of questions to guide the interview. Indeed, a structured interview may use a questionnaire just as a survey does.

In an **unstructured interview**, the interviewer has three or four main questions. Other questions build on what the interviewee says. To prepare for an unstructured interview, learn as much as possible about the interviewee and the topic. Go into the interview with three or four main topics you want to cover.

Interviewers sometimes use closed questions to start the interview and set the interviewee at ease. The strength of an interview, however, is getting at a person's attitudes, feelings, and experiences. **Situational questions** let you probe what someone does in a specific circumstance. **Hypothetical questions** that ask people to imagine what they would do generally yield less reliable answers than questions about **critical incidents** or key past events.

Situational question:	How do you tell an employee that their performance is unsatisfactory?
Hypothetical question:	What would you say if you had to tell an employee that their performance was unsatisfactory?
Critical incident question:	You've probably been in a situation where someone who was working with you wasn't carrying their share of the work. What did you do the last time that happened?

A **mirror question** paraphrases the content of the last answer: "So you confronted him directly?" "You think that this product costs too much?" Mirror questions are used both to check that the interviewer understands what the interviewee has said and to prompt the interviewee to continue talking.

Probes follow up an original question to get at specific aspects of a topic:

Question:	What do you think about the fees for campus parking?
Probes:	Would you be willing to pay more for a reserved space? How much more? Should the fines for vehicles parked illegally be increased? Do you think fees should be based on income?

Figure 3.3 Questionnaire for a Student Report Using Survey Research

An interesting title can help.

In your introductory paragraph,
① *tell how to return the survey*
② *tell how the information will be used*

Survey: Why Do Students Attend Athletic Events?

The purpose of this survey is to determine why students attend sports events, and what might increase attendance. All information is to be used solely for a student research paper. Please return completed surveys to Elizabeth or Vicki at the Union help desk. Thank you for your assistance!

Start with easy-to-answer questions.

1. What is your class year? (Please circle) 1 2 3 4 Grad Other

2. Gender (Please circle one) M F Nonbinary Other

The words below each number anchor responses, while still allowing you to average the data.

Seeing a response in a survey can make respondents more willing to admit to feelings they may be embarrassed to volunteer.

3. How do you feel about women's sports? (Please circle)

1	2	3	4	5
I enjoy watching women's sports		I'll watch, but it doesn't really matter		Women's sports are boring/ I'd rather watch men's sports

4. Do you like to attend MSU men's basketball games? (Please circle)
Y N

5. How often do you attend MSU women's basketball games? (Please circle)

1	2	3	4	5
All/most games	Few games a season	Once a season	Less than once a year	Never

6. If you do not attend all of the women's basketball games, why not? (Please check all that apply. If you attend all the games, skip to #7.)

__I've never thought to go.
__I don't like basketball.
__I don't like sporting events.
__The team isn't good enough.
__My friends are not interested in going.
__I want to go; I just haven't had the opportunity.
__The tickets cost too much ($10).
__Other (please specify) _____

Think about factors that affect the problem you're studying and write survey questions to get information about them.

7. To what extent would each of the following make you more likely to attend an MSU women's basketball game? (please rank all)

1	2	3
Much more likely to attend	Possibly more likely	No effect

__Increased awareness on campus (flyers, chalking on the Oval, more articles in the *Gazette*)
__Marketing to students (give-aways, days for residence halls or fraternities/sororities)
__Student loyalty program (awarding points towards free tickets, clothing, food for attending games)
__Education (pocket guide explaining the rules of the game provided at the gate)
__Other (please specify) _____

Thank you!
Please return this survey to Elizabeth or Vicki at the Union help desk.

Repeat where to turn in or mail completed surveys.

Probes are not used in any definite order. Instead, they are used to keep the interviewee talking, to get at aspects of a subject that the interviewee has not yet mentioned, and to dig more deeply into points that the interviewee brings up.

If you read questions to subjects in a structured interview, use fewer options than you might in a written questionnaire.

> I'm going to read a list of factors that someone might look for in choosing a restaurant. After I read each factor, please tell me whether that factor is Very Important to you, Somewhat Important to you, or Not Important to you.

If the interviewee hesitates, reread the scale.

Schedule interviews in advance; tell the interviewee about how long you expect the interview to take. A survey of technical writers (who get much of their information from interviews) found that the best days to interview subject matter experts are Tuesdays, Wednesdays, and Thursday mornings.[6] People are frequently swamped on Mondays, and on Fridays they are looking forward to the weekend or trying to finish their week's work.

Always record the interview. Test your equipment ahead of time to make sure it works. If you think your interviewee may be reluctant to be recorded, offer to give a copy of the recording to the interviewee.

Focus Groups

A **focus group,** yet another form of qualitative research, is a small group of people convened to provide a more detailed look into some area of interest—a product, service, process, concept, and so on. Because the group setting allows members to build on each other's comments, carefully chosen focus groups can provide detailed feedback; they can illuminate underlying attitudes and emotions relevant to particular behaviors.

Focus groups also have some problems. The first is the increasing use of professional respondents drawn from databases, a practice usually driven by cost and time limitations. The *Association for Qualitative Research Newsletter* labeled these respondents as a leading industry problem.[7] To get findings that are consistent among focus groups, the groups must accurately represent the target population. A second problem with focus groups is that such groups sometimes aim to please rather than offering their own evaluations.

Using Online Networks

An updated version of the focus group is the online network. These networks, first cultivated as research tools by technology and video game companies, are being employed by various producers of consumer products and services, including small companies. The networks are often cheaper and more effective than traditional focus groups because they have broader participation and allow for deeper and ongoing probing. Companies can use them for polls, real-time chats with actual consumers, and product trials.[8]

A still larger online community comes from Twitter and other social media. These communities are the least controllable of feedback groups but are becoming more important. Many companies are hiring employees or technology services to monitor comments on social networks and respond quickly. They also use data from Twitter, Facebook, and other sites to track trends and preferences.

Observations of Customers and Users

Answers to surveys and interviews may differ from actual behavior—sometimes greatly. To get more accurate consumer information, many marketers observe users. Before designing new ketchup packets, Heinz watched fast-food customers in their vehicles wrestle with traditional packets. The new packets allow users to dip or squeeze.[9] Intuit, a leader in observation studies, sends employees to visit customers and watch how they use Intuit products such as QuickBooks. Watching small businesses struggle with Quick-Books Pro told the company of the need for a new product, QuickBooks Simple Start.[10]

Observation also can be used for gathering in-house information such as how efficiently production systems operate and how well employees serve customers. Some businesses use "mystery shoppers." For instance, McDonald's has used mystery shoppers to check cleanliness, customer service, and food quality. The company posts store-by-store results online, giving store operators an incentive and the information they need to improve quality on measures where they are slipping or lagging behind the region's performance.[11] So many organizations use mystery shoppers that there is a Mystery Shopping Providers Association.

Observation often is combined with other techniques to get the most information. **Think-aloud protocols** ask users to voice their thoughts as they use a document or product: "First I'll try. . . ." These protocols are recorded and later analyzed to understand how users approach a document or product. **Interruption interviews** interrupt users to ask them what's happening. For example, a company testing a draft of computer instructions might interrupt a user to ask, "What are you trying to do now? Tell me why you did that." **Discourse-based interviews** ask questions based on documents that the interviewee has written: "You said that the process is too complicated. Tell me what you mean by that."

Using Technology for Research

Within the past few years, social media such as Twitter and TikTok have also been playing a larger role in organizations' marketing research and marketing campaigns. Market research is analyzing Twitter comments to investigate customers' brand associations and product preferences, to understand forces behind spikes and dips in demand, and to plan product-development and marketing strategies. Marketing is being encouraged to take advantage of TikTok's 500 million users worldwide (it was also the #2 downloaded app in 2019)[12] to introduce products, or even their company, to potential customers.[13]

One major limitation of data mining in social media is that users are not a representative sample—let alone a random sample—of the population. They tend to be younger, more educated, more urban, more affluent, and less likely to have children than nonusers. TikTok, for example, is primarily used by those 16–24 years old.[14] Another significant limitation is that thanks to language complexity, it is not always obvious—even to human researchers, let alone data-mining programs—what opinion is being expressed in an online comment.[15]

One notable outcome of all this data collection is that the job of data scientist—composed of a combination of mathematician, statistician, computer scientist, and business guru—is predicted to be one of the hottest jobs of the decade.[16]

Analyzing Your Research Results

LO 3-2

After you've conducted your primary research, you'll need to analyze the data you've gathered, which means analyzing your numbers, looking for patterns in your data, and checking your logic.

Analyze Numbers

Many reports analyze numbers—either numbers from databases and sources or numbers from a survey you have conducted. The numerical information, properly analyzed, can make a clear case in support of your ideas.

When you have multiple numbers for salaries or other items, an early analysis step is to figure the average (or mean), the median, and the range. The **average** or **mean** is calculated by adding up all the figures and dividing by the number of samples. The **mode** is the number that occurs most often. The **median** is the number that is exactly in the middle in a ranked list of observations. When you have an even number, the median will be the average of the two numbers in the center of the list. The **range** is the difference between the high and low figures for that variable.

Averages are particularly susceptible to a single extreme figure. Three different surveys reported the average cost of a wedding at nearly $30,000. Many articles picked up that figure because weddings are big business. However, the median cost in those three surveys was "only" about $15,000. Even that amount is probably on the high side because the samples were convenience samples for a big wedding website, a bride magazine, and a maker of wedding invitations, and thus probably did not include smaller, less elaborate weddings.[17]

Often it's useful to simplify numerical data by rounding off or combining similar elements. Graphing also can help you see patterns in your data. (See Chapter 8 for a full discussion of tables and graphs as a way of analyzing and presenting numerical data.) Look at the raw data as well as at percentages. For example, a 50% increase in shoplifting incidents sounds alarming. An increase from two to three shoplifting incidents sounds less so but could be the same data, just stated differently.

Analyze Patterns

Patterns can help you draw meaning from your data. In your secondary-research sources, on which points do experts agree? Which disagreements can be explained by early theories or numbers that have now changed? Which disagreements are the result of different interpretations of the same data? Which are the result of having different values and criteria?

In your primary-research data, what patterns do you see?

- Have things changed over time?

- Does geography account for differences?

- Do demographics such as gender, age, or income account for differences?

- What similarities do you see?

- What differences do you see?

- What confirms your hunches?

- What surprises you?

Many descriptions of trends, in sales, business technology, corporate social responsibility, and marketing are descriptions of patterns derived from data.

Check Your Logic

A common logic error is confusing causation with correlation. **Causation** means that one thing causes or produces another. **Correlation** means that two things are positively or negatively related to some extent. One might cause the other, but both might be caused by a third. For instance, consider a study that shows pulling all-nighters hurts grades: Students who pull all-nighters get lower grades than those who do not pull all-nighters. But maybe it is not the all-nighter causing the poor grades; maybe students who need all-nighters are weaker students to begin with.

Correlation and causation are easy to confuse, but the difference is important. The Census Bureau publishes figures showing that greater education levels are associated with greater incomes. A widely held assumption is that more education causes greater earnings. But might people from richer backgrounds seek more education? Or might some third factor, such as grit, lead to both greater education and higher income?[18]

When faced with a business-related problem, search for at least three possible causes for the problem you've observed and at least three possible solutions for the problem. The more possibilities you brainstorm, the more likely you are to find good options. In your report, discuss in detail only the possibilities that will occur to readers and that you think are the real reasons and the best solutions.

When you have identified causes of the problem or the best solutions, check these ideas against reality. Can you find support in primary or secondary research? Can you answer claims of people who interpret the data in other ways?

Make the nature of your evidence clear to your reader. Do you have observations that you yourself have made? Or do you have inferences based on observations or data collected by others? Old data may not be good guides to future action.

If you can't prove the claim you originally hoped to make, modify your conclusions to fit your data. Even when your market test is a failure or your experiment disproves your hypothesis, you still can write a useful report:

- Identify changes that might yield a different result. For example, selling the product at a lower price might enable the company to sell enough units.

- Divide the discussion to show the parts of the test that succeeded.

- Discuss circumstances that may have affected the results.

- Remember that negative results aren't always disappointing to the audience. For example, the people who commissioned a feasibility report may be relieved to have an impartial outsider confirm their suspicions that a project isn't feasible.

A common myth associated with numbers is that numbers are more objective than words: "Numbers don't lie." But as the previous discussion shows, numbers can be subject to widely varying interpretations.

Secondary Research

Conducting secondary research involves searching for sources of information, evaluating them to determine whether they meet your research needs, and finding more sources with the relevant sources that you've already found. In other words, the research process, like the writing process, is recursive. You can keep track of your secondary research by using reference management software, such as Mendeley or Zotero. While you're searching for and evaluating sources, you should take notes on the relevant sources that you find. Some reference management software—Zotero is one—can incorporate your notes.

LO 3-3

Effectively Searching for Secondary Sources

Secondary research retrieves information that someone else gathered. Library research and online searches are the most common kinds of secondary research. Many college and university libraries provide workshops and resources on research techniques, as well as access to databases and research librarians who have areas of specializations—including business.

Categories of sources that may be useful include:

- Google Scholar to find scholarly articles, books, and other resources, such as dissertations and conference proceedings. Google Scholar indexes resources such as academic publishers, professional organizations, and online repositories. You may have to access some of the materials that you find through your library's databases, but even so, Google Scholar is a good place to begin your secondary research.

- Databases to find articles and company information. Gale Business Insights Essentials provides information about companies around the world; EBSCO Business Source Elite provides access to over 1,600 business-related journals; BCC Research provides market-research reports for science- and technology-related businesses.

- Specialized encyclopedias for introductions to a topic, such as *Encyclopedia of Business in Today's World*[19] and *Oxford Research Encyclopedia of Business and Management.*[20]

- Newspapers for information about recent events. *The Wall Street Journal, Financial Times, Crain's Chicago Business,* and *The Economist* are all good sources of business information.

- Magazines covering business, such as *Forbes, Bloomberg Businessweek, Entrepreneur,* and *Fortune.*

- Trade journals for information specific to a type of business. For example, trade journals covering the construction sector include *Engineering News Record, Contract Design, Construction Executive,* and *Builder.* You can find trade journals for most any sector of business. ABI/Inform Global and Business Source Elite are two databases that allow you to limit your search to trade journals.

- U.S. Census Bureau reports. Census reports cover a variety of business and demographic information. These reports are available at www.census.gov.

In your searches, you'll need to determine which words and phrases will lead to relevant sources. A **key word** search will locate resources based on the importance of the word or phrase in a document. You can search only in titles, abstracts, the full text, among other options. If you're not sure what terms to use, check the ABI/Inform Thesaurus, which you are likely to find in your library's list of databases. Under the Advanced Search option, you'll see a link for the thesaurus. The thesaurus will help you find alternatives for the key words you thought of on your own and thus help you find more sources. For example, entering "dividends" leads to five narrower terms that might be of interest: constructive dividends, dividend reinvestment plans, ex-dividend, patronage dividends, and policyholder dividends. Without the thesaurus, it might be difficult to generate all of these terms for further database searching.

When you conduct secondary research through Google or another search engine, note that these engines personalize your search results with algorithms. Google's algorithms limit your current searches based on your past searches and reading choices. This personalization means that someone with environmental concerns—say, a member of the Sierra Club—who Googles "global climate change" will be led to widely different sources than someone with big oil connections. You can use a tool like Chrome's "Incognito" mode or Safari's "Private" mode to avoid results influenced by your search history.

Sifting through Search Results

Not everything you find as you search for information will be relevant and useful. In fact, most sources won't be. Your task is to sift through the results you get when you use your key words to search Google Scholar, your library's databases, and the internet in general.

When you find a scholarly source, such as a journal article, that might be useful, read its abstract first. An abstract is a brief description or summary of the article that follows. In many cases, you can tell from an abstract whether an article will be useful for your needs. Once you obtain the article, read the article's introduction and then ask yourself whether you still think the source is helpful for your purposes. If it seems to be, you should read the conclusion to the article next to ensure that the article is indeed useful. If a source passes these tests, you can read the middle—where the details lie. There's no sense in using your time trying to understand the details of an author's argument or study if the author's work won't fit your needs.

Using Preliminary Results to Find More Sources

Once you've found some useful sources, you can use them to find even more sources. First, you can look at the works cited or references list from a useful article to see the sources that the author used. Those sources of information might be useful to you as well.

Second—and perhaps more important—you can use library databases and Google Scholar to find more recent sources that cited your useful article. If you enter the title of your original article in Google Scholar, for example, you'll see a link called "Cited by" with a number after it. That number represents the number of times that resource has been cited by other authors. In the example in Figure 3.4, the article "Small Business Uniqueness and the Theory of Financial Management" has been cited 950 times by other authors. You could search through these 950 sources, limiting that next search by date, for example, 2020 to the present, to winnow those 950 sources. Or you might conduct another search within those 950 sources, using another key word search. Figure 3.5 shows the results narrowed to five sources when the additional key words "social capital theory Putnam" were used to search within the 950 sources that cited the original article.

Figure 3.4	Article Cited 950 Times by Other Sources in Google Scholar

Below an article's opening lines of text in Google Scholar, you can see the number of times that article has been cited. For example, the article "Small Business Uniqueness and the Theory of Financial Management" has been cited 950 times by other authors.

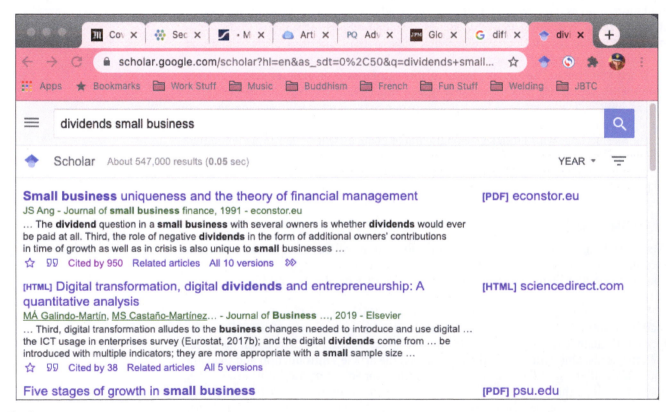

Google

Figure 3.5 | Narrowed Search Results

The results narrowed to five sources when the additional key words "social capital theory Putnam" were used to search within the 950 sources that cited the original article, "Small Business Uniqueness and the Theory of Financial Management."

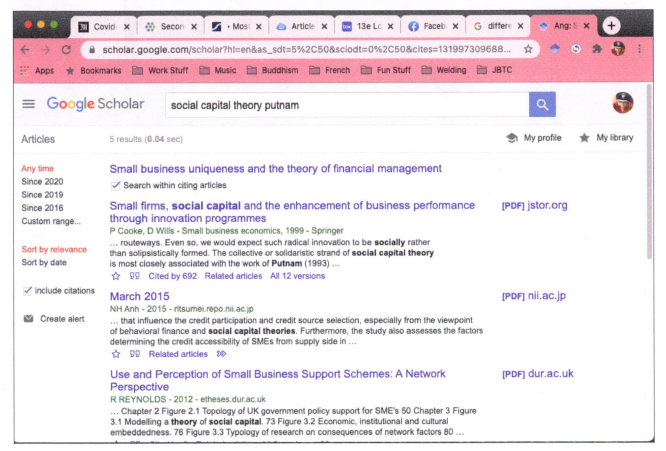

Google

The same idea applies in many library databases, including databases for business-related research, such as EBSCO Business Source Elite. The idea here is to use the most useful sources that you've found to find other, more recent sources that might also be useful.

Recognizing Types of False or Misleading Information

LO 3-4

As you conduct online searches for information or identify potential sources on social media, scrutinize what you find for false or misleading information. False and misleading information is not new, it has exponentially increased in the wake of the internet in general and social media in particular. "Information pollution," as Wardle and Derakhshan call it, comes in many forms: false headlines, altered photos, altered videos, push polls, decontextualized facts and data, and more.[21] It can compete and, in some cases, overshadow accurate news.

Information pollution can be shared, cross-referenced, retweeted, and so on, by thousands, hundreds of thousands, even millions, in a matter of minutes or hours (see Figure 3.6). The information pollution passes as legitimate, and people then use it to make decisions

Figure 3.6   Social Media Allows the Rapid Sharing of Information

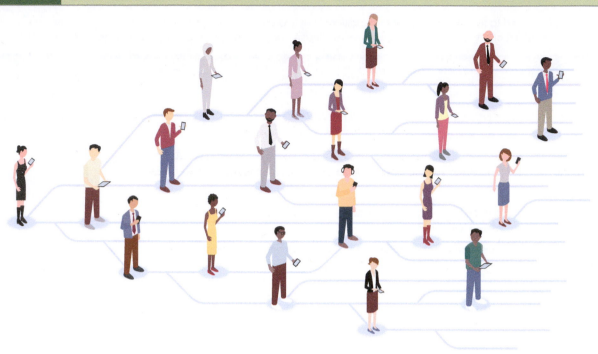

and to change or verify their current beliefs. They then share it with others, continuing the cycle. In a recent study published in *Science,* it was found that "It took the truth about six times as long as falsehood to reach 1,500 people."[22]

While people adeptly navigate content on social media, they typically are not sufficiently critical of its content. A study by the Stanford History Education Group found that[23]

- More than 80% of middle schoolers believed sponsored content on a website was real news.

- Only 9% of an AP history class were able to discern that a website was actually a front for a lobbying organization. College students performed worse; only 7% failed to look beyond the website.

- Nearly 40% of high schoolers accepted the content of an *Imgur* (photo-sharing site) post without questioning whether the source was credible, whether the image was taken where the post said it was taken, or whether the image was altered in some way.

- Less than a third of college students could fully explain that a tweet's content could be swayed by the political agenda of the tweeting organization.

Technological advances are making the development and dissemination of false photos and videos easier.[24] For example, fake videos can now be made using a generative adversarial network, an algorithmic model for generating synthetic data that can pass for genuine data.[25] The caliber of the counterfeits, their capacity to deceive, and the ease with which they disseminate should make us highly critical of any content we consume.

Categories of Information Pollution

While false or misleading information is sometimes referred to as "fake news," Wardle and Derakhshan argue that the term is an inadequate descriptor of a much larger problem: the wide dissemination (whether intended or unintended) of misleading or false information.[26] As noted earlier, they call this problem "information pollution," and they specify three types based on the information content (false or real), the motivation of those creating or sharing the information (to harm or not to harm), and the creator's/ sharer's awareness of disseminating the content (knowingly or unknowingly):

- **Misinformation.** Sharing false information without any intent of harm. It is the equivalent of sharing a funny meme or a shocking news article without checking its content.

- **Disinformation.** When you knowingly share false information in order to cause harm. Examples include instances of false news reports about politicians or medicine.

- **Mal-information.** When real information is shared with the purpose of causing harm. It happens most often when private information is shared publicly, like leaked information, a photo or video meant for an intimate partner, or even hate speech.

These three categories help us analyze the combination of the content and the intent behind the information with the purchase of being ethical consumers and users of information.

Types of Problematic Content

Identifying misleading and false content can be difficult. Wardle's typology helps in identifying the kinds of content you should avoid as you conduct research for your business communication:[27]

1. **Satire or parody** ("no intention to cause harm but has potential to fool").
2. **False connection** ("when headlines, visuals, or captions don't support the content").
3. **Misleading content** ("misleading use of information to frame an issue or an individual").
4. **False context** ("when genuine content is shared with false contextual information").
5. **Impostor content** ("when genuine sources are impersonated" with false, made-up sources).
6. **Manipulated content** ("when genuine information or imagery is manipulated to deceive," as with a "doctored" photo).
7. **Fabricated content** ("new content is 100% false, designed to deceive and do harm").

While it's tempting to think that problematic content is someone else's problem and nothing to worry about, the truth is that we all encounter problematic information every day. And eventually, if not already, you will be communicating as an employee or representative of an organization. As an ethical communicator, you must be aware of the accuracy of the information that you rely on, use, and share in all your communications.

Strategies for Evaluating Sources

LO 3-5

In a survey of U.S. adults by the Pew Research Center at the beginning of 2019, 10% of respondents reported having knowingly shared fabricated news and 49% reported having shared news that they later learned was fabricated.[28] The first step in disrupting the cycle of information pollution is to commit to being ethical and not participating in the accepting or sharing of false or misleading information; the second step is to recognize information pollution when we see it.

How to Spot Fabricated News, Spam, and Phishing

Recognizing Fabricated News There are eight simple steps that we can take to spot false or misleading news:[29]

1. **Consider the source.** One of the simplest ways to review content is to take a close look at the URL to make sure that it matches the name of the source. FactCheck. org, for example, has reviewed content from abcnews.com.co, but that is not the

URL for ABC News. In addition, look for the site's mission and credentials, usually on an About Us page, as satirical or parodies might be slightly or fully disguised so as not to appear as satire or parody.

2. **Read beyond the headline.** Headlines do not always fully match the content of the article, not even in mainstream news. So if you come across a headline that's salacious or shocking, read all the way through the article. Don't just stop at the title; it could just be clickbait.

3. **Check the author.** Do not rely on the credentials given on the article's page. Open a new tab or window and search for information about the author. If the authors claim to have won accolades or awards, cross-check them. Award winners are often listed by giving organization and written about in the news.

4. **Verify the support.** Just as you shouldn't accept the author's credentials at face value, don't trust the support. Verify supporting facts and reasons by conducting separate searches.

5. **Check the date.** Make sure that the content is current. Verify that the described events happened when the article says they did. If the article summarizes another information source, go back to the original text to ensure the article you are checking is true to the original article.

6. **Find out if it's a joke.** If it sounds too good or too "off" to be true, take time to verify the source, content, author, support, and date. You could very well be reading a satire or parody not meant to be understood literally (as many students reading Jonathan Swift's "A Modest Proposal" have discovered).

7. **Check your biases.** It's easier to accept ideas that fit your current beliefs, so you must be extra vigilant when the content you read is easy for you to accept.

8. **Ask the experts.** Several organizations check facts, news, and stories, including FactCheck.org, PolitiFact.com, and Snopes.com, so take advantage of their expertise.

The International Federation of Library Associations (IFLA) has created an infographic that illustrates these eight steps for spotting false or misleading news (Figure 3.7).[30]

Recognizing Spam   The term *spam* refers to **unsolicited** bulk email, also called junk mail, or text messages (or other types of messages), most often made from addresses and cell phone numbers purchased from similar businesses or organizations. The low cost and ease of sending emails and texts in bulk make it tempting for companies to spam.

In fact, text spam is believed to be 95% of all emails worldwide are spam.[31] However frustrating clearing spam from your inbox is, typically, its intent is not to do harm. Often, spam senders want to sell goods and services or convey persuasive or proselytizing messages.

The organization you work for likely has a spam filter on its email program. If spam messages make it through the filter, mark the message as spam and forward it to your organization's technology department. Do not click on any attached files or links, including the unsubscribe option, which spam senders use to verify that your email account is active. If you have not yet installed a spam filter on your personal email account, you should contact your provider about options. The same advice—to mark the message as spam and to avoid clicking on attached files and links—applies for personal email accounts too.

You can take several steps to avoid spam text messages. Put your phone number on the Federal Trade Commission's *National Do Not Call Registry*.[32] Contact your carrier to see if it offers a number-blocking service that can proactively block potential spam calls, and check your phone's settings, as you are likely able to block messages from individual numbers directly. Do not respond to spam messages or click on any links that might be in the message, and review your phone bill carefully to make sure you haven't been charged for spam text messages.

Figure 3.7 How to Spot Fake News

HOW TO SPOT FAKE NEWS

CONSIDER THE SOURCE
Click away from the story to investigate the site, its mission and its contact info.

READ BEYOND
Headlines can be outrageous in an effort to get clicks. What's the whole story?

CHECK THE AUTHOR
Do a quick search on the author. Are they credible? Are they real?

SUPPORTING SOURCES?
Click on those links. Determine if the info given actually supports the story.

CHECK THE DATE
Reposting old news stories doesn't mean they're relevant to current events.

IS IT A JOKE?
If it is too outlandish, it might be satire. Research the site and author to be sure.

CHECK YOUR BIASES
Consider if your own beliefs could affect your judgement.

ASK THE EXPERTS
Ask a librarian, or consult a fact-checking site.

IFLA
International Federation of Library Associations and Institutions
With thanks to www.FactCheck.org

International Federation of Library Associations

Remember to be exceptionally judicious when sharing your personal information, such as email addresses and phone numbers. You might not be able to completely avoid spam, but at least you can make the work of spam senders more difficult.

Finally, if your organization considers using unsolicited bulk email (UBE), consider the reaction that you have to spam emails and text messages. Rather than gaining clients or new business, your organization may actually lose goodwill.

Recognizing Phishing

The term *phishing* arose in the 1990s to describe computer hackers' theft of email-account passwords. The word plays on *fishing,* as in fishing in a sea of internet users.[33] While phishing started with stealing passwords, it now encompasses more crimes.

Senders of phishing emails and texts purposefully try to deceive recipients so that they will provide personal information, such as their social security number, credit card numbers, or bank account numbers. Phishing messages might also try to convince the recipient to send money. Since the 1990s, phishing scams have become more common and sophisticated. The Internet Crime Complaint Center of the FBI recorded $3.5 million in losses to both businesses and individuals due to phishing in 2019.[34]

Phishing emails and texts appear as though they come from an organization that you trust, such as your employer, your bank, your credit card company, a social media site, or a business where you regularly shop. However, most phishing messages—at least for now—make mistakes of various sorts:

- They may use the same or similar-looking logo to a company you regularly do business with, but the color or look is "off" somehow.

- They might use a colleague's name and username in an email, but the name might be misspelled or the domain is not the official company email address.

- They impersonate a colleague but the message doesn't sound like your colleague at all. For example, a colleague who normally sends text messages in complete sentences would likely not say "U got a sec need 2 talk" or send an email without punctuation or capitalization.

- They include dubious links. Hover over links without clicking—does the link match the title? That is, will the link send you to the location it claims? Will it download something? If the link doesn't match or looks strange, do not click on it.

- They offer something that sounds too good to be true.

Phishing messages trying to get your personal information will tempt you with something you might want (e.g., coupons or a refund), provide you with information you think you need (e.g., a fabricated invoice), or scare you (e.g., a problem with your account, a late payment, or suspicious activity).

If the message is suspicious, do not respond to it or click on anything in it. Many organizations, especially banks and other financial institutions (such as credit card companies), have special email address that you can forward suspicious messages to for verification. Such institutions like to be aware of potential cheats to help their clients avoid costly financial scams. You should delete the message and block the sender.

Phishing can also be done over the phone. One of the most recent and common phishing calls claims to be from the Social Security Administration. The caller tells the call recipient that there has been suspicious activity on their social security number and that their account will be suspended—a serious concern for people living mostly or solely on their social security income. The caller tells the recipient that before the call can continue, they must confirm their social security number. In other words, the caller tries to get the call recipient to state their social security number.[35] As the risk of repeating this advice too much, do not give out your personal information without verifying the identity of the sender.

Stop the Spread of Fabricated or Misleading Information

You have a responsibility to be ethical about the information you produce and share. As an employee, your responsibility to your employer might seem obvious. However, even outside work hours, you are perceived as a representative of your organization. Your personal communication, therefore, has implications for your job. Perception counts. For example,

- A CEO of a large health system told employees in an email that he didn't need to wear a mask after recovering from COVID-19 and lost his position.[36]

- An oncology nurse bragged on TikTok that, during the COVID-19 pandemic, she doesn't wear a mask unless she's at work. The nurse was put on administrative leave.[37]

- A daycare worker lost her job after complaining on Facebook about how much she hates being around the kids at her job.[38]

As these examples suggest, you should be as careful on your personal social media accounts as you are on your work accounts. Aim to practice good information hygiene:

1. **Pause.** Don't let your emotions take over. Stop to think and evaluate what you have just seen, read, or heard.
2. **Glance through the comments.** Review how people are reacting to the content and consider whether you want your name and profile connected to it. If so, check to see if anyone as already fact-checked the content.
3. **Do a quick search.** Open a new browser tab and conduct your own search. Follow the steps in the previous section, "Recognizing Fabricated News."
4. **Ask for the source.** Ask the person who has posted the information for the original source or for additional supporting material.

If you discover the content is false or misrepresented, consider letting others know in a reply or send a private message to the poster. The cycle of information disorder, which affects us all, can only be stopped if we actively help to stop the cycle.

Use the CRAAP Test to Evaluate Sources

Source evaluation goes beyond asking whether a source contains misinformation, disinformation, or mal-information. You need to go further to ensure that the information that you use in your communications is quality information.

If you have taken an information literacy course or learned about source evaluation in writing classes, you might already be familiar with the CRAAP test. The test asks you to evaluate a source using five criteria:

1. **Currency.** The timeliness of the information.
2. **Relevance.** The importance of the information for your needs.
3. **Authority.** The source of the information.
4. **Accuracy.** The correctness of the content.
5. **Purpose.** The reason the information exists.

For each criterion, there is a list of questions to ask about each source, for the purpose you are communicating, and for the audience you are communicating (see Figure 3.8).

Figure 3.8 Evaluate a Source's Currency, Relevance, Authority, Accuracy, and Purpose before Using it in Any Documents

Evaluating Information – Applying the CRAAP Test
Meriam Library 📖 California State University, Chico

When you search for information, you're going to find lots of it . . . but is it good information? You will have to determine that for yourself, and the **CRAAP Test** can help. The **CRAAP Test** is a list of questions to help you evaluate the information you find. Different criteria will be more or less important depending on your situation or need.

Key: ■ indicates criteria is for Web

Evaluation Criteria

Currency: *The timeliness of the information.*
- When was the information published or posted?
- Has the information been revised or updated?
- Does your topic require current information, or will older sources work as well?
- Are the links functional?

Relevance: *The importance of the information for your needs.*
- Does the information relate to your topic or answer your question?
- Who is the intended audience?
- Is the information at an appropriate level (i.e. not too elementary or advanced for your needs)?
- Have you looked at a variety of sources before determining this is one you will use?
- Would you be comfortable citing this source in your research paper?

Authority: *The source of the information.*
- Who is the author/publisher/source/sponsor?
- What are the author's credentials or organizational affiliations?
- Is the author qualified to write on the topic?
- Is there contact information, such as a publisher or email address?
- Does the URL reveal anything about the author or source?
  examples: **.com .edu .gov .org .net**

Accuracy: *The reliability, truthfulness and correctness of the content.*
- Where does the information come from?
- Is the information supported by evidence?
- Has the information been reviewed or refereed?
- Can you verify any of the information in another source or from personal knowledge?
- Does the language or tone seem unbiased and free of emotion?
- Are there spelling, grammar or typographical errors?

Purpose: *The reason the information exists.*
- What is the purpose of the information? Is it to inform, teach, sell, entertain or persuade?
- Do the authors/sponsors make their intentions or purpose clear?
- Is the information fact, opinion or propaganda?
- Does the point of view appear objective and impartial?
- Are there political, ideological, cultural, religious, institutional or personal biases?

Sarah Blakeslee, Meriam Library, California State University, Chico

Source Citation and Documentation

An essential element of ethical communication is the ethical use of source material, which includes how you give credit to the author of your source material. The benefits of using source material ethically include

- Building credibility.

- Demonstrating honesty.

- Showing the audience the breadth and depth of completed research.

- Showing the amount of knowledge communicator has about the subject.

- Showing respect for the original authors.

- Reflecting the critical thought and planning on the type and number of source material in order to ensure the best possible product for clients.

Ethical communication cites and documents sources and, at best, does so smoothly and unobtrusively. **Citing** a source means attributing an idea or fact to its source in the body text of your document. You will need to include either a parenthetical citation or a number referring to a **footnote** or **endnote.** Which one you use will depend on the style guide you are using. A popular style guide for business is APA style, where the APA stands for American Psychological Association. In an APA-style citation, you would use the name of the author (usually a person sometimes an organization), the year of publication, and the page number, like this in-text citation for a quotation:

> Documentation is ethical writing because it "gives formal credit to a person, organization, or publication for an idea or information that is not original or is not common knowledge of the field" (Finkelstein, 2008, p. 256).

In addition to citing your source in the body text, you'll need to **document** your source as well with a reference-list entry. The reference-list entry is included in the reference list, which is also called a works cited list or a bibliography. Whatever you call it, this list of references comes at the end of your document. This list provides the information readers would need to find the original source, such as the author's name, the title of the work, and the year of publication. The form that your reference-list entries will take will depend on the style guide that you're following. A reference-list entry for Finkelstein's book would look like this in APA style:

> Finkelstein, L. (2008). *Pocket book of technical writing for engineers and scientists* (3rd ed.). McGraw-Hill Education.

The citation and the reference-list documentation together allow your reader to find the original source and go directly to page 256 to find the original quotation.

Quotations

If you quote a source, that is, use exact words from a source, you must use quotation marks around those words. However, the quotation marks alone are not enough. As noted and exemplified above with APA style, you will also need to provide a citation in your document's body text and a reference-list entry.

Long quotations (four typed lines or more) are used sparingly in business communication. Many readers skip quotes, so it is often most effective to summarize the main point of the quotation in a single sentence before the quotation itself. End the introductory sentence with a colon, not a period, because it introduces the quote. For example, you might introduce a long quotation in this way:

> Finkelstein explains that determining what is common knowledge is a judgment call, but it is best to cite when in doubt:
>
>> Whether something is common knowledge of the field is often a judgment call. Normally, we think of something as being common knowledge when the average skilled person in field should already be familiar with it. However, the best approach is to document any source when you are in doubt. (Finkelstein, 2008, p. 256)

Indent long quotations on the left to set them off from your text. Indented quotations do not need quotation marks; along with citation, the indentation shows the reader that the passage is a quotation.

Whether you use a short quotation or a long one, you should limit your use of quotations to authors' opinions, as opposed to facts and data. Another use of quotations is to draw attention to way the original author expressed an idea. Keep in mind that in some disciplines, there is a perception that if you have to quote it, you do not actually understand it. In sum, minimize your use of quotations.

Paraphrases

When you put the source's idea or findings into your own words, you are **paraphrasing** that source. You're also paraphrasing when you condense ideas from a source or synthesize information from multiple sources. In such uses of other people's work, you don't need to use quotation marks, but you definitely still need to cite each source in the body text of your document and provide a reference-list entry for each source at the end of your document. For example, you might paraphrase Finkelstein, the author of the quotation used as an example above, like this:

> Finkelstein said that it's often difficult to tell what information is common knowledge; it helps to consider whether a person in the relevant discipline would know the information. Even so, he said, when in doubt, cite the source (2008, p. 256).

In this case, because Finkelstein's name appears in the body text as a lead-in to the paraphrase (*Finkelstein said*), it's not necessary to put his name in the in-text citation at the end of the paraphrase. The same rule applies to quotations; if you use the author's name in a lead-in to a quotation, you don't need to include it in the citation.

And, as with the quotation examples above, the author's name, Finkelstein, will lead the reader to the correct reference-list entry at the end of the text.

The benefits of paraphrasing source material are that you can highlight an idea (but not misrepresent or take it out of context) that you need for your own message. You can also synthesize information from multiple sources, using those sources to support your own claims. All the while, you can maintain a consistent tone throughout your document because you are using your own words.

Summaries

A summary reports the main idea and supporting arguments or findings from a source. The length of a summary depends on your purpose in summarizing, the needs of the audience, and the length of the original text. A summary can be a few sentences or several paragraphs. Summaries differ depending on the type of source being summarized; however, in general, an effective summary follows the organization of the original source and includes the following:

- A topic sentence that includes the author's name, the title, and the main point (i.e., thesis).

- A brief overview of the source's content.

- An explanation of the author's support for their argument or their discussion of their findings.

Note too what a summary does *not* include:

1. What you, the reader, took away from the source. That is, a summary should not contain your opinion, evaluation, or interpretation.
2. Quotations. Use your own words.

Imagine that you need to provide a one-paragraph summary for this entire chapter; in APA style, it would look something like this:

> In chapter 3 of *Business Communication*, Locker, Mackiewicz, Aune, and Kienzler (2021) explain that effective communicators can employ a variety of primary and secondary research strategies when collecting the data and information they need. In their second-ary research, they should make sure to critically evaluate all potential source material, staying on the alert for false or misleading information. They should evaluate potential source material for its currency, relevance, accuracy, authority, and purpose. They must also use sources ethically. Effective communicators always cite and document all source material that they use in their communications.

This summary begins with the main point of the chapter. Then it describes the content of the chapter. It *doesn't* contain any evaluation or interpretation of the chapter.

Documentation Requires Precision

So far in this section, we've used APA style in our examples. How you will format your in-text citations and your reference-list documentation will depend on the style that you use. Some common citation styles guides besides the *APA Style Guide* include these:

- The *MLA Handbook* from the Modern Language Association.

- *Scientific Style and Format* from the Council of Scientific Editors (CSE); this guide contains three documentation systems: citation-sequence, citation-name, and name-year.

- The *Chicago Manual of Style*, which contains two documentation systems: author-date and notes and bibliography.

In addition, your organization might follow a style based on one of these styles but modified for its own purposes. Such a style is called a **house style;** for example, the notes in this text are (mostly) set according to McGraw Hill's house style. You'll need to know which style your organization uses.

Regardless of which style you follow, you will need to follow it precisely, including matters such as these:

- The information to include

- The order of the information

- Spacing

- Punctuation

- Capitalization

- Formatting

Take this textbook that you're reading, for example. Here is how its bibliographic entry (an entry for a book with multiple editions) would look in several different documentation styles:

Modern Languages Association (MLA)

Locker, Kitty O., Jo Mackiewicz, Jeanine Elise Aune and Donna Kienzler. *Business Communication,* 13th ed., McGraw-Hill Education, 2021.

American Psychological Association (APA)

Locker, K. O., Mackiewicz, J., Aune, J. E. & Kienzler, D. (2021). *Business communication* (13th ed.). McGraw-Hill Education.

Chicago Style (Author-Date System)

Locker, Kitty O., Jo Mackiewicz, Jeanine Elise Aune, and Donna Kienzler. 2021. *Business Communication.* New York: McGraw-Hill Education.

Council of Scientific Editors (Citation-Sequence System)

1 Locker, KO, Mackiewicz, J, Aune, JE, D Kienzler. Business communication. 13th ed. New York: McGraw-Hill Education; 2021.

From this small sample, you can see that some styles use authors' complete names and other styles prioritize efficiency, using authors' initials. Following your style precisely builds your credibility, whereas inaccurate and sloppy documentation detracts from your credibility.

Ethical versus Unethical Practice

As noted above, ethical communication requires the ethical use of source material. Using source material ethically means maintaining the meaning that the author intended. That is, you should avoid taking material out of context in such a way that its meaning no longer accords with its meaning in context. Such a lapse can occur accidentally if you don't fully understand the entire text. It can also happen if you **cherry-pick** details or facts from the source. Whether or not the intent to mislead is present, using source material out of context to convey a different meaning is unethical.

Another unethical practice is the failure to cite and document sources, referred to as academic dishonesty in a university setting or, more commonly, as **plagiarism.** Plagiarism is the passing off of the words or ideas of others as one's own. It might be using someone else's responses in an exam, posting an exam questions and answers to an online study site, submitting an entire paper written by someone else (a friend's paper or a new paper you paid someone to write for you), using portions of someone else's paper, or using material from sources without giving attribution. Plagiarism can lead to nasty consequences, from failure of a class to losing your job.

While plagiarism is unethical, it is not illegal. Copyright infringement is. Copyright is a type of intellectual property that protects the expression of ideas and it comes with federal and international protection. Copyright does not protect the ideas themselves, but it does protect the creator's rights to control how their work is reproduced, is used to create similar works (i.e., derivatives), how it is displayed publicly, and by whom their work can be used.[39] Copyright infringement can result in serious legal consequences.

Summary by Learning Objectives

LO 3-1   **Explain strategies of primary research.**

- A survey questions a large group of people, called respondents. A questionnaire is a written list of questions that people fill out. An interview is a structured conversation with someone who will be able to give you useful information.

- Because surveys can be used to show almost anything, people need to be careful when analyzing the results of surveys or designing their own. These are questions commonly asked about surveys:

  - Who did the survey and who paid for it?

  - How many people were surveyed and how were they chosen?

  - How was the survey conducted?

  - What was the response rate?

  - What questions were asked?

- Good questions ask just one thing, are phrased neutrally, avoid making assumptions about the respondent, and mean the same thing to different people.

- A convenience sample is a group of people who are easy to get. A judgment sample is a group of people whose views seem useful. In a random sample, each person in the population theoretically has an equal chance of being chosen. A sample is random only if a formal, approved random sampling method is used. Otherwise, unconscious bias can exist.

- Qualitative research also may use interviews, focus groups, online networks, and technology.

LO 3-2   Collect and analyze research results from primary research.

After you've conducted your primary research, you'll need to analyze the data you've gathered, which means analyzing your numbers, looking for patterns in your data, and checking your logic.

LO 3-3   Effectively search for secondary research.

- Use indexes and directories to find information about a specific company or topic.

- Sift through your results and choose the relevant sources for your project.

- Use the "cited by" function in databases to find additional source material.

LO 3-4   Recognize types of false or misleading information.

Information pollution comes in many forms: false headlines, altered photos, altered videos, push polls, decontextualized facts and data, and more.

LO 3-5   Critically evaluate potential source material.

It is important to critically evaluate any and all potential source material before using in your communications and recognize fabricated news, spam, and phishing. A common strategy is the "What the CRAAP" method.

LO 3-6   Use and document sources ethically.

An essential element of effective communication is the ethical use of source material, which includes how source material is used and documented. There are important benefits to ethically and responsibly using source material, including building your credibility as an author and showing the breadth and depth of your knowledge.

- Citation means attributing an idea or fact to its source in the body of your text, no matter how you incorporate it.
  - Quoting is when you use the exact wording of the original source.
  - Paraphrasing with when you put the source's ideas into your own words.
  - Summarizing is when you explain the main idea and supporting content of the entire source or a section of it.

- Documentation means providing the bibliographic information readers would need to go back to the original source.

- Documentation requires precision.

- Plagiarism is the passing off of the words or ideas of others as one's own and it comes with serious consequences.

- Copyright is a type of intellectual property that protects the expression of ideas and it comes with federal and international protection. Copyright infringement comes with serious legal consequences.

Exercises and Cases

3.1   Reviewing the Chapter

1. What are strategies of primary and secondary research? (LO 3-1)

2. What questions should you use to analyze a survey? (LO 3-1)

3. What are some criteria for good survey questions? (LO 3-1)

4. What is a random sample? (LO 3-1)

5. What are some disadvantages of focus groups and online networks? (LO 3-1)

6. What are three steps involved in analyzing data? (LO 3-2)

7. What kinds of patterns should you look for in your data and text? (LO 3-2)

8. What are the strategies for effective secondary research searches? (LO 3-3)

9. What are the categories of information pollution and how are they determined? (LO 3-4)

10. What are the types of problematic content available on the internet? (LO 3-4)

11. What are the strategies for identifying fabricated news? (LO 3-5)

12. What are the strategies for identifying spam? (LO 3-5)
13. What are the strategies for identifying phishing scams? (LO 3-5)
14. What are the steps for stopping the spread of fabricated or misleading information? (LO 3-5)
15. What are the criteria for evaluating sources using the CRAAP test? What does each criterion look for? (LO 3-5)

16. What is the difference between citation and documentation? (LO 3-6)
17. What is the difference among quotation, paraphrase, and summary? (LO 3-6)
18. What is needed to cite a source correctly in a text? (LO 3-6)
19. How do you know which documentation style to use? (LO 3-6)

3.2   Choosing Research Strategies

For each of the following reports, indicate the kinds of research that might be useful. If a survey is called for, indicate the most efficient kind of sample to use.

1. How can Twitter and Facebook users on campus be more connected to school events?
2. Is it feasible to send all XYZ organization's communication through email?
3. How can XYZ store increase sales?
4. What is it like to live and work in [name of country]?
5. Should our organization have a dress code?
6. Is it feasible to start a monthly newsletter for students in your major?
7. How can we best market to people who have retired?
8. Can compensation programs increase productivity?
9. What skills are in demand in our area? Of these, which could the local community college offer courses in?

3.3   Comparing Search Results

Do a Google search on these terms:

- COVID-19 vaccine
- Global warming
- Immigration
- Gun control
- Fake news
- BLM movement

Print off the first 10 sources Google gives you for each. In small groups, compare your listings. How do they differ? Pick one of the three topics and present the differences you found to your classmates.

3.4   Evaluating Websites

Choose five websites that are possible resources for an upcoming assignment. Evaluate them on the currency, authority, accuracy, and purpose of their information. Consider the following questions and compare and contrast your findings.

- What person or organization sponsors the site? What credentials do the authors have?
- Does the site give evidence to support its claims? Does it give both sides of controversial issues?
- Is the tone professional?

- How complete is the information? What research is it based on?
- How current is the information?

Based on your findings, which sites are best for your upcoming assignment and why?

As your instructor directs,

a. Write an email to your instructor summarizing your results.
b. Share your results with a small group of students.
c. Present your results to the class in an oral presentation.

3.5   Choosing Samples for Surveys and Interviews

For the following topics, indicate the types of sample(s) you would use in collecting survey data and in conducting interviews.

1. How can your school improve the usability of its website?
2. How can your school use social media to increase communication with students?
3. How can your school save money to limit tuition increases?
4. How can your favorite school organization attract more student members?
5. How can your school improve communication with international students?
6. How should your school deal with hate speech?
7. How can instructors at your school improve their electronic presentations for students?

3.6   Evaluating Survey Questions

Evaluate each of the following questions. Are they acceptable as they stand? If not, how can they be improved?

a. Survey of clerical workers:

Do you work for the government? ☐
or the private sector? ☐

b. Questionnaire on grocery purchases:

1. Do you *usually* shop at the same grocery store?

a. Yes

b. No

2. Do you use credit cards to purchase items at your grocery store?

a. Yes

b. No

3. How much is your average grocery bill?

a. Under $25

b. $25–50

c. $50–100

d. $100–150

e. Over $150

c. Survey on technology:

1. Would you generally welcome any technological advancement that allowed information to be sent and received more quickly and in greater quantities than ever before?

2. Do you think that all people should have free access to all information, or do you think that information should somehow be regulated and monitored?

d. Survey on job skills:

How important are the following skills for getting and keeping a professional-level job in U.S. business and industry today?

	Low				High
Ability to communicate	1	2	3	4	5
Leadership ability	1	2	3	4	5
Public presentation skills	1	2	3	4	5
Selling ability	1	2	3	4	5
Teamwork capability	1	2	3	4	5
Writing ability	1	2	3	4	5

3.7   Designing Questions for an Interview or Survey

Submit either a one- to three-page questionnaire or questions for a 20- to 30-minute interview *and* the information listed below for the method you choose.

Questionnaire

1. Purpose(s), goal(s).

2. Respondents (who, why, how many).

3. How and where to be distributed.

4. Any changes in type size, paper color, etc., from submitted copy.

5. Rationale for order of questions, kinds of questions, wording of questions.

6. References, if building on questionnaires by other authors.

Interview

1. Purpose(s), goal(s).

2. Interviewees (who, and why).

3. Proposed site, length of interview.

4. Rationale for order of questions, kinds of questions, wording of questions, choice of branching or follow-up questions.

5. References, if building on questions devised by others.

As your instructor directs,

a. Create questions for a survey on one of the following topics:

■ Survey students on your campus about their knowledge of and interest in the programs and activities sponsored by a student organization.

■ Survey workers at a company about what they like and dislike about their jobs.

■ Survey people in your community about their willingness to pay more to buy products using recycled materials and to buy products that are packaged with a minimum of waste.

■ Survey two groups on a topic that interests you.

b. Create questions for an interview on one of the following topics:

■ Interview an international student about the forms of greetings and farewells, topics of small talk, forms of politeness, festivals and holidays, meals at home, size of families, and roles of family members in their country.

■ Interview a TV producer about what styles and colors work best for people appearing on TV.

■ Interview a worker about an ethical dilemma they faced on the job, what the worker did and why, and how the company responded.

■ Interview the owner of a small business about problems the business has; what strategies the owner has already used to increase sales and profits and how successful these strategies were; and the owner's attitudes toward possible changes in product line, décor, marketing, hiring, advertising, and money management.

■ Interview someone who has information you need for a report you're writing.

3.8   Reviewing Motivations of a Website

Using the tools provided to you in this chapter, conduct a comprehensive review one of the websites listed below. Is it a reliable resource without underlying motivations?

- MinimumWage.com
- Citizens.org
- AmericansforProsperity.org

a. Write an email to your instructor explaining the results of your evaluation.

b. Share your results orally with a small group of students.

c. Present your results to the class.

3.9   Researching Damage Caused by Fabricated or Misleading News

Research and find at least three reports of fabricated or misleading news causing damage to a company or organization. Consider how the news was created and disseminated. What could have been done, when, and by whom to reduce or mitigate the damage?

a. Write an email to your instructor explaining the results of your evaluation.

b. Share your results orally with a small group of students.

c. Present your results to the class.

3.10   Researching University Policies

Locate and carefully read your university's academic dishonesty or plagiarism policies. What constitutes academic dishonesty and plagiarism? What are the procedures if an instructor suspects a student of such actions? What are the consequences?

Synthesize your findings and share.

a. Write an email to your instructor explaining the results of your evaluation.

b. Share your results orally with a small group of students.

c. Present your results to the class.

Notes

1. Cynthia Crossen, "Fiasco in 1936 Survey Brought 'Science' to Election Polling," *Wall Street Journal,* October 2, 2006, B1.

2. Andrew O'Connell, "Reading the Public Mind," *Harvard Business Review* 88, no. 10 (October 2010): 28.

3. Palmer Morrel-Samuels, "Getting the Truth into Workplace Surveys," *Harvard Business Review* 80, no. 2 (February 2002): 111–18.

4. Ibid.

5. Sheldon R. Gawiser and G. Evans Witt, "20 Questions Journalists Should Ask about Poll Results," *Public Agenda Archives*, accessed June 25, 2013, http://www.publicagendaarchives.org/pages/20-questions-journalists-should-ask-about-poll-results.

6. Earl E. McDowell, Bridget Mrolza, and Emmy Reppe, "An Investigation of the Interviewing Practices of Technical Writers in Their World of Work," in *Interviewing Practices for Technical Writers,* ed. Earl E. McDowell (Amityville, NY: Baywood Publishing, 1991), 207.

7. Peter Noel Murray, "Focus Groups Are Valid When Done Right," *Marketing News,* September 1, 2006, 21, 25.

8. Emily Steel, "The New Focus Groups: Online Networks: Proprietary Panels Help Consumer Companies Shape Products, Ads," *Wall Street Journal,* January 14, 2008, B6.

9. Sarah Nassauer, "Old Ketchup Packet Heads for Trash," *Wall Street Journal,* September 9, 2012, B1.

10. Christopher Meyer and Andre Schwager, "Understanding Customer Experience," *Harvard Business Review* 85, no. 2 (February 2007): 116–26.

11. Daniel Kruger, "You Want Data with That?" *Forbes* 173, no. 6 (2004): 58.

12. "50 TikTok Stats that Will Blow You Away," *InfluencerMarketingHub,* https://influencermarketinghub.com/tiktok-stats, Accessed December 29, 2020.

13. Syed Balkhi, "How to Use TikTok to Promote Your Business," *Entrepreneur,* October 23, 2019, https://www.entrepreneur.com/article/340216, accessed December 29, 2020.

14. Ibid.

15. Carl Bialik, "Tweets as Poll Data? Be Careful," *Wall Street Journal,* February 11, 2012, A2.

16. Mark Abadi, "The 50 Best Jobs in America for 2019," *Business Insider,* January 22, 2019, https://www.businessinsider.com/best-jobs-in-america-2019-1.

17. Carl Bialik, "Weddings Are Not the Budget Drains Some Surveys Suggest," *Wall Street Journal,* August 24, 2007, B1.

18. Jakob Nielsen, "Risks of Quantitative Studies," *Alertbox,* March 1, 2004, http://www.useit.com/alertbox/20040301.html; and Dan Seligman, "The Story They All Got Wrong," *Forbes,* November 25, 2002, 124.

19. C. Wankel, *Encyclopedia of Business in Today's World* (Sage, 2009).

20. C. Kulich and M. K. Ryan, *Oxford Research Encyclopedia of Business and Management* (2017).

21. Claire Wardle and Hossein Derakhshan, *Information Disorder: Toward an Interdisciplinary Framework for Research and Policy Making,* Council of Europe report DGI(2017)09, September 17, 2017, https://firstdraftnews.org/wp-content/uploads/2017/11/PREMS-162317-GBR-2018-Report-de%CC%81sinformation-1.pdf?x55001.

22. Soroush Vosoughi, Deb Roy, and Sinan Aral, "The Spread of True and False News Online," *Science* 359, no. 6380 (March 9, 2018), https://science.sciencemag.org/content/359/6380/1146.

23. Stanford History Education Group, "Evaluating Information: The Cornerstone of Civic Online Learning," 2016, https://stacks.stanford.edu/file/druid:fv751yt5934/SHEG%20Evaluating%20Information%20Online.pdf.

24. "Fake News: How Disinformation Is Spread & Technological Advances Are Making It More Dangerous," *Maine Calling*, October 18, 2019, https://internews.org/news/fake-news-how-disinformation-spread-technological-advances-are-making-it-more-dangerous.

25. Oscar Schwartz, "You Thought Fake News Was Bad? Deep Fakes Are Where Truth Goes to Die," *The Guardian*, November 12, 2018, https://www.theguardian.com/technology/2018/nov/12/deep-fakes-fake-news-truth.

26. Claire Wardle and Hossein Derakhshan, *Information Disorder: Toward an Interdisciplinary Framework for Research and Policy Making,* Council of Europe report DGI(2017)09, September 17, 2017, https://firstdraftnews.org/wp-content/uploads/2017/11/PREMS-162317-GBR-2018-Report-de%CC%81sinformation-1.pdf?x55001.

27. Claire Wardle, "Fake News. It's Complicated," *First Draft*, February 16, 2017, https://firstdraftnews.org/latest/fake-news-complicated.

28. Amy Watson, "Share of Adults Who Have Ever Shared Fake News or Information Online in the United States as of March 2019," *Statista*, October 12, 2020, https://www.statista.com/statistics/657111/fake-news-sharing-online.

29. Eugene Kiely and Lori Robertson, "How to Spot Fake News," *Fact Check.org: A Project of The Annenberg Public Policy Center*, November 18, 2016, https://www.factcheck.org/2016/11/how-to-spot-fake-news.

30. International Federation of Library Associations, "How to Spot Fake News" (infographic), https://www.ifla.org/publications/node/11174.

31. Francis West, "How to Identify spam," *WestTek*, July 17, 2018, https://www.westtek.co.uk/blog/story/9-tips-on-how-to-identify-a-spam-email.

32. Federal Trade Commission, *National Do Not Call Registry*, https://www.donotcall.gov.

33. Russell Kay, "Sidebar: The Origins of Phishing," *Computer World*, January 19, 2004, https://www.computerworld.com/article/2575094/sidebar–the-origins-of-phishing.html.

34. FBI, "2019 IC3 Complaints," February 11, 2020, https://www.fbi.gov/news/stories/2019-internet-crime-report-released-021120.

35. American Association of Retired Persons (AARP), "Social Security Scams," https://www.aarp.org/money/scams-fraud/info-2019/social-security.html.

36. Associated Press, "Health System CEO Out after He Refused to Wear Mask, Said He Was Immune from COVID-19," *Chicago Tribune*, November 25, 2020, https://www.chicagotribune.com/business/ct-biz-covid-19-health-ceo-no-mask-20201125-qeoru-vw6rvaktb4ff2pi3lj3vq-story.html.

37. Andrea Salcedo, "An Oregon Nurse Bragged on TikTok about Not Wearing a Mask Outside of Work. She's Now on Administrative Leave," *The Washington Post*, November 30, 2020, https://www.washingtonpost.com/nation/2020/11/30/oregon-nurse-tik-tok-covid.

38. Peter Holley, "Day-Care Employee Fired for Facebook Post Saying She Hates 'Being around a Lot of Kids'," *The Washington Post*, May 4, 2015, https://www.washingtonpost.com/news/morning-mix/wp/2015/05/04/day-care-employee-fired-for-facebook-post-noting-she-hates-being-around-a-lot-of-kids.

39. U.S Copyright Office, "Copyright in General," https://www.copyright.gov/help/faq/faq-general.html, accessed November 4, 2020.

4 Planning, Composing, and Revising

Chapter Outline

DrAfter123/Getty Images

The Power of Words

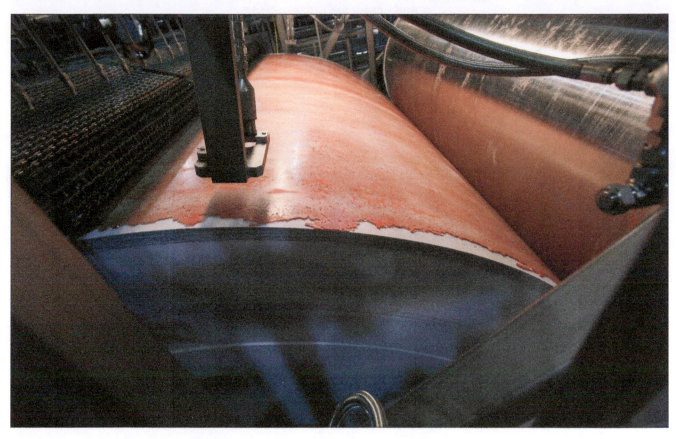

Nati Harnik/AP Images

In September 2012, Beef Products Inc. (BPI) sued ABC News for $1.2 billion over two words: *pink slime*.

For years, BPI produced "lean, finely textured beef," a product made from beef trimmings treated with ammonia and added as filler in some ground beef. Although cleared by the U.S. Department of Agriculture (USDA), its safety came into question from some 2011 news reports.

ABC News reports described BPI's product as *pink slime*, a term coined by a USDA microbiologist in 2002. The term caught on and quickly spread through social media.

The effect of *pink slime* was swift. Restaurant chains, grocery stores, and school cafeterias eliminated products that contained it. In 28 days, BPI's business dropped by 80%, and the company was forced to shut three of its plants and lay off more than 700 employees.

BPI's attorney blamed the losses on ABC News: "To call a food product slime is the most pejorative term that could be imagined. ABC's constant repetition of it . . . had a huge impact on the consuming public." ABC's lawyers disagreed, calling *pink slime* "the sort of 'loose, figurative, or hyperbolic language' that courts recognize demands protection under the First Amendment."

ABC settled the lawsuit in June 2017. While the terms of the settlement were not disclosed, Walt Disney Co., ABC's parent company, indicated in its August 2017 financial statement that it spent $177 million to settle the case. A lawyer for BPI indicated that the settlement was even costlier than that amount as Disney's insurance covered some of the cost.

Two small but powerful words nearly destroyed BPI—which has since changed its name—and cost ABC a lot of money. In preparing documents, professionals always should be careful of the words they use and the impression those words convey to an audience.

Sources: Bill Tomson, "ABC Sued for '*Pink Slime*' Defamation," *Wall Street Journal,* September 14, 2012, B3; Daniel P. Finney, "'*Pink Slime*': Two Small Words Trigger Big Lawsuit," *Des Moines Register,* September 14, 2012, 1A; Timothy Mclaughlin and P. J. Huffstutter, "Meat Packer Blames ABC's '*Pink Slime*' for Nearly Killing Company," *Reuters,* June 5, 2017, https://www.reuters.com/article/us-abc-pinkslime/meat-packer-blames-abcs-pink-slime-for-nearly-killing-company-idUSKBN18W0KJ; and Christine Hauser, "ABC's '*Pink Slime*' Report Tied to $177 Million in Settlement Costs," *New York Times,* August 10, 2017, https://www.nytimes.com/2017/08/10/business/pink-slime-disney-abc.html?mcubz=1.

Learning Objectives

After studying this chapter, you should be able to

LO 4-1 Implement activities involved in the composing process.

LO 4-2 Apply guidelines for effective word choice, sentence construction, and paragraph organization.

LO 4-3 Apply techniques to revise, edit, and proofread your communications.

Skilled performances look easy and effortless. In reality, as every dancer, musician, and athlete know, they're the products of hard work, hours of practice, attention to detail, and intense concentration. Like skilled performances in other arts, writing rests on a base of work.

The Ways Good Writers Write

No single writing process works for all writers all of the time. However, good writers and poor writers seem to use different processes.[1] Good writers are more likely to break big tasks into smaller chunks, revise their first drafts, identify their purpose and audience, and edit only after completing a draft.

Research also shows that good writers differ from poor writers in identifying and analyzing the initial problem more effectively, understanding the task more broadly and deeply, drawing from a wider repertoire of strategies, and seeing patterns more clearly. Good writers also are better at evaluating their own work.

Thinking about the writing process and consciously adopting the processes of good writers will help you become a better writer.

Activities in the Composing Process

LO 4-1

Composing can include many activities: planning, brainstorming, gathering, organizing, writing, evaluating, getting feedback, revising, editing, and proofreading. The activities do not have to come in this order. Not every task demands all activities.

Planning

- Analyzing the problem, defining your purposes, and analyzing the audience.

- Brainstorming information to include in the document.

- Gathering the information you need—from the message you're answering, a person, printed sources, or the web.

- Selecting the points you want to make and the examples, data, and arguments to support them.

- Choosing a pattern of organization, making an outline, creating a list.

Writing

- Putting words on paper or a screen. Writing can be lists, possible headings, fragmentary notes, stream-of-consciousness writing, and partial drafts.

- Creating a rough draft.

- Composing a formal draft.

Revising

- Evaluating your work and measuring it against the requirements of the rhetorical situation. The best evaluation results from *re-seeing* your draft as if someone else had written it. Will your audience understand it? Is it complete? Convincing? Friendly?

- Getting feedback from someone else. Is all the necessary information there? Is there too much information? Is your pattern of organization appropriate? Does a revision solve an earlier problem? Are there obvious mistakes?

- Adding, deleting, substituting, or rearranging. Revision can be changes in single words or in large sections of a document.

Editing

- Checking the draft to see that it is as clear and concise as possible.

- Correcting spelling and mechanical errors, such as punctuation and capitalization.

- Checking to ensure that the formatting is consistent and readable.

- Proofreading the final copy to see that it's free from typographical errors. Unlike revision, which can produce major changes in meaning, editing focuses on the surface of writing.

Note the following points about these activities:

- **The activities do not have to come in this order.**   For example, you might have to gather data *after* writing a draft when you see that you need more specifics to achieve your purpose.

- **You do not have to finish one activity to start another.**   Some writers plan a short section and write it, plan the next short section and write it, and so on through the document. Evaluating what is already written may cause a writer to do more planning or to change the original plan.

- **Most writers do not use all activities for all the documents they write.**   You'll use more of these activities when you write more complex or difficult documents about new subjects or to audiences that are new to you.

For many workplace writers, prewriting is not a warm-up activity to get ready to write the "real" document. It's a critical series of activities designed to gather and organize information, take notes, brainstorm with colleagues, and plan a document before writing a complete draft. And for many people, these activities do not include outlining. Traditional outlining may lull writers into a false sense of confidence about their material and organization, making it difficult for them to revise their content and structure if they deviate from the outline developed early in the process.

Using Your Time Effectively

To get the best results from the time you have, spend about one-third of your time actually "writing." Spend about another one-third of your time analyzing the rhetorical situation (including your audience), gathering information, and organizing what you have to say. Spend the final third evaluating what you've said, revising the draft(s) to meet your purposes and the needs of the audience and the organization, editing a late draft to remove any errors in grammar and mechanics, and proofreading the final copy.

Do realize, however, that different situations may call for different time divisions, especially when documents are produced by teams. Geographic distance can add even more time to the process. Chapter 6 covers the basics of managing face-to-face and online collaborative writing.

Not all writing has to be completed in office settings. Some people work better outside, in coffee shops, or from home.

Nicolas McComber/Getty Images

Brainstorming, Planning, and Organizing Business Documents

Spend substantial time planning and organizing before you begin to write. The better your ideas are when you start, the fewer drafts you'll need to produce a good document. Start by using the analysis questions from Chapter 1 to identify your audience and audience benefits. Gather information you can use for your document. Select the points you want to make—and the examples and data to support them.

Overcoming Writer's Block

Many people encounter writer's block. You can use these strategies to help you overcome it:

1. **Prepare for writing.**   Collect and arrange material. Talk to people in your audience. The more you learn about the rhetorical situation, especially your audience, the easier it will be to write—and the better your writing will be.
2. **Practice writing regularly and in moderation.**   Write daily. Keep sessions to a moderate length; an hour to an hour and a half is ideal for many people.
3. **Talk positively to yourself:**   "I can do this." "If I keep working, ideas will come." "It doesn't have to be perfect; I can make it better later."
4. **Talk to other people about writing.**   Value the feedback you get from them. Talking to other people expands your repertoire of strategies and your writing community.

In addition, you can try these techniques to get the writing process started:

- **Brainstorming.**   Think of all the ideas you can, without judging them. Consciously try to get at least a dozen different ideas before you stop. Good brainstorming depends on generating many ideas.

- **Freewriting.[2]**   Make yourself write, without stopping, for 10 minutes or so, even if you must write "I will think of something soon." At the end of 10 minutes, read what you've written, identify the best point in the draft, then set it aside, and write for another 10 uninterrupted minutes. Read this draft, marking anything that's good and should be kept, and then write again for another 10 minutes. By the third session, you will probably produce several sections that are worth keeping—maybe even a complete draft that's ready to be revised.

- **Clustering.**[3] Write your topic in the middle of the page and circle it. Write down the ideas the topic suggests, circling them, too. (The circles are designed to tap into the nonlinear half of your brain.) When you've filled the page, look for patterns or repeated ideas. Use different colored pens to group related ideas. Then use these ideas to develop your content.

For an oral presentation, a meeting, or a document with lots of visuals, try creating a **storyboard**, with a rectangle representing each page or unit. Draw a box with a visual for each main point. Below the box, write a short caption or label.

Writing Good Business Documents

After you have a collection of ideas, it is time to put them in a draft of your document. In *Bird by Bird: Some Instructions on Writing and Life*, writer Anne Lamott calls this first draft the "down draft": you just get your ideas down—without worrying about writing skills such as supporting detail, organization, or mechanics.[4] Don't even worry about completeness at this point.

Lamott calls the second draft the "up draft": you start fixing up the first draft.[5] It is at this stage that you start turning your writing into professional writing.

Good business writing is closer to conversation and less formal than the style of writing that has traditionally earned high marks in college essays and term papers (see Figure 4.1).

Figure 4.1	Different Levels of Style		
Feature	**Conversational style**	**Good business style**	**Traditional term paper style**
Formality	Highly informal	Conversational; sounds like a real person talking	More formal than conversation would be but retains a human voice
Use of contractions	Many contractions	Okay to use occasional contractions	Few contractions, if any
Pronouns	Uses first- and second-person pronouns	Uses first- and second-person pronouns	First- and second-person pronouns kept to a minimum
Level of friendliness	Friendly	Friendly	No effort to make style friendly
How personal	Personal; refers to specific circumstances of conversation	Personal; may refer to reader by name; refers to specific circumstances of audiences	Impersonal; may generally refer to readers but does not name them or refer to their circumstances
Word choice	Short, simple words; slang	Short, simple words but avoids slang	Many abstract words; scholarly, technical terms
Sentence and paragraph length	Incomplete sentences; no paragraphs	Short sentences and paragraphs	Longer sentences and paragraphs
Visuals	Not applicable or quickly made (e.g., memes)	Carefully designed for visual impact (e.g., page design, graphs, infographics)	No particular attention to visual impact

Most people have several styles of talking, which they vary instinctively depending on the audience. Good writers have several styles, too. An email to your boss about the delays from a supplier will be informal, perhaps even chatty; a letter to the supplier demanding better service will be more formal.

Reports tend to be more formal than letters, memos, and emails because they may be read many years in the future by audiences the writer can barely imagine. Reports tend to avoid contractions, personal pronouns, and second person (because so many people read reports, *you* doesn't have much meaning). See Chapter 13 for more about report style.

Of course, good business style allows for individual variation. Warren Buffett is widely known for the style of his shareholder letters in the Berkshire Hathaway annual reports. His letters are known for humor, colorful language, and originality. Carol Loomis, a senior editor at *Fortune* who has been the editor of Buffett's letters since 1977, notes she makes few changes to the letters.[6] Figure 4.2 shows excerpts from his 2012 letter. Buffett's direct style suggests integrity and openness.

Figure 4.2	Excerpts from Warren Buffett's 2012 Letter to Shareholders

---

BERKSHIRE HATHAWAY INC.

To the Shareholders of Berkshire Hathaway Inc.:

Buffett's letter starts with a short financial summary of the past year.

In 2012, Berkshire achieved a total gain for its shareholders of $24.1 billion. We used $1.3 billion of that to repurchase our stock, which left us with an increase in net worth of $22.8 billion for the year. The per-share book value of both our Class A and Class B stock increased by 14.4%. Over the last 48 years (that is, since present management took over), book value has grown from $19 to $114,214, a rate of 19.7% compounded annually.*

If this is the bad news, think how great the good news will be.

A number of good things happened at Berkshire last year, but let's first get the bad news out of the way.

When the partnership I ran took control of Berkshire in 1965, I could never have dreamed that a year in which we had a gain of $24.1 billion would be subpar, in terms of the comparison we present on the facing page.

. . .

Contextualizes good news to make it even more impressive.

Despite tepid U.S. growth and weakening economies throughout much of the world, our "powerhouse five" had aggregate earnings of $10.1 billion, about $600 million more than in 2011.

. . .

Todd Combs and Ted Weschler, our new investment managers, have proved to be smart, models of integrity, helpful to Berkshire in many ways beyond portfolio management, and a perfect cultural fit. We hit the jackpot with these two. In 2012 each outperformed the S&P 500 by double-digit margins. They left me in the dust as well.

Uses humor (plus tiny type) and humility to underscore his point.

. . .

Supports green initiatives.

MidAmerican's electric utilities serve regulated retail customers in ten states. Only one utility holding company serves more states. In addition, we are the leader in renewables: first, from a standing start nine years ago, we now account for 6% of the country's wind generation capacity. Second, when we complete three projects now under construction, we will own about 14% of U.S. solar-generation capacity.

---

* All per-share figures used in this report apply to Berkshire's A shares. Figures for the B shares are 1/1500th of those shown for A.

Source: Warren Buffett, "Letters 2012," Berkshire Hathaway Inc., accessed March 4, 2013, http://www.berkshirehathaway.com/letters/2012ltr.pdf.

Half-Truths about Business Writing

Many generalizations about business writing are half-truths and must be applied selectively, if at all.

Half-Truth 1: "Write as You Talk."

Most of us use a colloquial, conversational style in speech that is too informal for writing. We use slang, incomplete sentences, and grammatical errors.

Unless our speech is exceptionally fluent, "writing as we talk" can create awkward, repetitive, and badly organized prose. It's okay to write as you talk to produce your first draft, but revise and edit to create a good written style.

Half-Truth 2: "Never Use *I*."

Using *I* too often can make your writing sound self-centered; using it unnecessarily will make your ideas seem tentative. However, when you write about things you've done or said or seen, using *I* is both appropriate and smoother than resorting to awkward passives or phrases like *this writer*.

Half-Truth 3: "Never Use *You*."

Certainly writers should not use *you* in formal reports, as well as other situations where the audience is not known or *you* may sound too informal. But *you* is widely used in situations such as writing to familiar audiences like our office mates, describing audience benefits, and writing sales text.

Half-Truth 4: "Never Begin a Sentence with *And* or *But*."

Beginning a sentence with *and* or *also* makes the idea that follows seem like an afterthought. That's okay when you want the effect of spontaneous speech in a written document, as you may in a sales letter. If you want to sound as though you have thought about what you are saying, put the *also* in the middle of the sentence or use another transition such as *moreover* or *furthermore*.

But tells the reader that you are shifting gears and that the following point not only contrasts with but also is more important than the preceding ideas. Presenting such verbal signposts to your reader is important. Beginning a sentence with *but* is fine if doing so makes your paragraph read smoothly.

Half-Truth 5: "Never End a Sentence with a Preposition."

Prepositions are those useful little words that indicate relationships: *with, in, under, to, at*. In job application letters, business reports, and important presentations, avoid ending sentences with prepositions. Most other messages are less formal; it's okay to end an occasional sentence with a preposition. Noting exceptions to the rule, Sir Winston Churchill famously scolded an editor who had presumptuously corrected a sentence ending with a preposition, "This is the kind of impertinence up with which I will not put."[7] Analyze your audience and the situation and use the language that you think will get the best results.

Half-Truth 6: "Never Have a Sentence with More Than 20 Words, or a Paragraph with More Than 8 Lines."

While it is true that long sentences and paragraphs may sometimes be hard to read, that is not always the case. A long sentence with parallel phrases and clauses may be quite clear. A longer paragraph with a bulleted list may be quite readable. The rhetorical situation should guide length decisions. Instructions for complicated new software may need shorter sentences and paragraphs, but an instruction paragraph on the six criteria for legitimate travel expenses may be longer than eight lines and still quite clear.

Half-Truth 7: "Big Words Impress People."

Learning an academic discipline requires that you master its vocabulary. After you get out of school, however, no one will ask you to write just to prove that you understand something. Instead, you'll be asked to write or speak to people who need the information you have.

Sometimes you may want the sense of formality or technical expertise that big words create. But much of the time, big words just distance you from your audience and increase the risk of miscommunication. If you use big words, make sure your audience will understand them, and make sure that you use them correctly. When people misuse big words, they look foolish.

Half-Truth 8: "Business Writing Does Not Document Sources."

It is true that much business writing does not use sources and that many businesses frequently use their own boilerplate. However, if you borrow the words or ideas of someone outside your business, you must acknowledge your source or you will be plagiarizing. Even inside a business, if the source is not widely known or the material was particularly good or controversial, it is common to acknowledge the source.

Ten Ways to Make Your Writing Easier to Read

LO 4-2

Direct, simple writing is easier to read. One study tested two versions of a memo report. The "high-impact" version was written with the "bottom line" (the purpose of the report) in the first paragraph, simple sentences in normal word order, active verbs, concrete language, short paragraphs, headings and lists, and first- and second-person pronouns. The high-impact version took 22% less time to read. Readers said they understood the report better, and tests showed that they really did.[8] Another study showed that high-impact instructions were more likely to be followed.[9]

In 2010, the Plain Writing Act became law. It requires all federal agencies to use clear prose that the public can readily understand. In addition, more and more organizations are trying to simplify their communications. For example, in the financial world, the U.S. Securities and Exchange Commission's *A Plain English Handbook: How to Create Clear SEC Disclosure Documents* asks for short sentences, everyday words, active voice, bullet lists, and descriptive headings. It cautions against legal and highly technical terms.

Building an easy-to-read style takes energy and effort, but it's well worth the work. Below you'll find 10 guidelines to help you build good style.

As You Choose Words

The best word depends on the rhetorical situation, especially your audience and their expectations.

1. Use words that are accurate, appropriate, and familiar.   Accurate words mean what you want to say. Appropriate words convey the attitudes you want and fit well with the other words in your document. Familiar words are easy to read and understand.

Use Accurate Words   Some meanings are negotiated as we interact with other people. Individuals are likely to have different ideas about value-laden words such as *fair* or *rich*. Some word choices have profound implications. For example, because Super Storm Sandy was not labeled a hurricane by the National Weather Service or the National Hurricane Center (technically, it made landfall as a post-tropical depression), some officials and residents did not take it seriously enough, leading to damaging inaction. But once it hit, officials hastened to keep it labeled as a post-tropical depression so their residents could get more insurance money. (Many insurance policies limit hurricane payments.)[10]

To be accurate, a word's **denotation** must match the meaning the writer wishes to convey. Denotation is a word's literal or dictionary meaning. Most common words in English have more than one denotation. The word *pound*, for example, means, or denotes, a unit of weight, a place where stray animals are kept, a unit of money in the British system, and the verb *to hit*. Coca-Cola spends millions each year to protect its brand names so that *Coke* will denote only that brand and not just any cola drink.

When two people use the same word or phrase to denote different things, **bypassing** occurs. For example, a large mail-order drug company notifies clients by email when their prescription renewals get stopped because the doctor has not verified the prescription. Patients are advised to call their doctor and remind them to verify. However, the company's website posts a sentence telling clients that the prescription is *being processed*. The drug company means the renewal is in the system, waiting for the doctor's verification. The patients believe the doctor has checked in and the renewal is moving forward. The confusion results in extra phone calls to the company's customer service number, delayed prescriptions, and general customer dissatisfaction.

Problems also arise when writers misuse words.

> Three major divisions of Stiners Corporation are poised to strike out in opposite directions.

(Three different directions can't be opposite each other.)

> Stiners has grown dramatically over the past five years, largely by purchasing many smaller, desperate companies.

This latter statement probably did not intend to be so frank. More likely, the writer relied on a computer's spell checker, which accepted *desperate* for *disparate*, meaning "fundamentally different from one another."

Use Appropriate Words   Words are appropriate when their **connotations**—that is, their emotional associations or colorings—convey the attitude you want. A great many words carry connotations of approval or disapproval, disgust or delight. Consider *firm* or *obstinate*, *flexible* or *wishy-washy*. Some businesses offer a *cash discount*; you rarely hear of a *credit surcharge*. Some companies offer an insurance discount if their employees follow specified good-health practices; the employees who do not follow those practices are paying a penalty, although it is not publicized that way.

A supervisor can "tell the truth" about a subordinate's performance and yet write either a positive or a negative performance appraisal, based on the connotations of the words in the appraisal. Consider an employee who pays close attention to details. A positive appraisal might read, "Terry is a meticulous team member who takes care of details that others sometimes ignore." But the same behavior might be described negatively: "Terry is hung up on trivial details."

Advertisers carefully choose words with positive connotations.

Connotations change over time. The word *charity* had acquired such negative connotations by the 19th century that people began to use the term *welfare* instead. Now, *welfare* has acquired negative associations. Most states have *public assistance programs* instead.

How positively can we present something and still be ethical? We have the right to package our ideas attractively, but we have the responsibility to give the public or our superiors all the information they need to make decisions.

Word choices have ethical implications in technical contexts as well. When scientists refer to 100-year floods, they mean a flood so big that it has a 1% chance of happening in any given year. However, a "1% annual chance flood" is awkward and has not become standard usage. On the other hand, many nonscientists believe a 100-year flood will happen only once every hundred years. After a 100-year flood swamped the Midwest in 1993, many people moved back into flood-prone homes; some even dropped their flood insurance. Unfortunately, both actions left them devastated by a second 100-year flood in 2008.[11]

Use Familiar Words   Familiar words are in almost everyone's vocabulary. Use the word that most exactly conveys your meaning, but whenever you can choose between two words that mean the same thing, use the shorter, more common one. Some writers mistakenly believe that using long, learned words makes them seem smart. However, experimental evidence shows the opposite is usually true: Needlessly pretentious word choice is generally taken as a sign of lower intelligence—and causes low credibility.[12] Try to use specific, concrete words. They're easier to understand and remember.[13]

The following list gives a few examples of short, simple alternatives:

Formal and stuffy	Short and simple
ameliorate	improve
commence	begin
enumerate	list
finalize	finish, complete
prioritize	rank
utilize	use
viable option	choice

There are some exceptions to the general rule that "shorter is better."

- Use a long word if it is the only word that expresses your meaning exactly.

- Use a long word or phrase if it is more familiar than a short word: *a word in another language for a geographic place or area* is better than *exonym*.

- Use a long word if its connotations are more appropriate. *Exfoliate* is better than *scrape off dead skin cells*.

- Use a long word if your audience prefers it.

2. Use technical jargon sparingly; eliminate business jargon.   There are two kinds of **jargon**. The first is the specialized terminology of a technical field. Many public figures enjoy mocking this kind of jargon. Even the *Wall Street Journal* does its share, mocking quotes like this one from a computer industry press release announcing a new "market offering":

> [The] offerings are leading-edge service configuration assurance capabilities that will help us to rapidly deploy high-demand IP services, such as level 3 virtual private networks, multi-cast and quality of service over our IP/MPLS network.[14]

A job application letter is one of the few occasions when it's desirable to use technical jargon: Using the technical terminology of the reader's field helps suggest that you're a peer who also is competent in that field—that you're a member of the **discourse community**. In other kinds of messages, use technical jargon only when the term is essential and known to the reader. If a technical term has a plain-English equivalent, use the simpler term.

The second kind of jargon is the **businessese** that some writers still use: *as per your request, enclosed please find, please do not hesitate*. None of the words in this second category of jargon are necessary. Indeed, some writers call these terms *deadwood* because they are no longer living words. If any of the terms in the first column of Figure 4.3 appear in your writing, replace them with more modern language.

As You Write and Revise Sentences

At the sentence level, you can do many things to make your writing easy to read.

3. Use active voice most of the time. "Who does what" sentences with active voice make your writing more forceful.

A verb is in **active voice** if the grammatical subject of the sentence does the action the verb describes. A verb is in **passive voice** if the subject is acted upon. Passive voice is usually made up of a form of the verb *to be* plus a past participle. *Passive* has nothing to do with *past*. Passive voice can be past, present, or future:

were received	(in the past)
is recommended	(in the present)
will be implemented	(in the future)

Figure 4.3	Getting Rid of Business Jargon	
Instead of	**Use**	**Because**
At your earliest convenience	The date you need a response	If you need it by a deadline, say so. It may never be convenient to respond.
As per your request; 65 miles per hour	As you requested; 65 miles an hour	*Per* is a Latin word for *by* or *for* each. Use *per* only when the meaning is correct; avoid mixing English and Latin.
Enclosed please find	Enclosed is; Here is	An enclosure isn't a treasure hunt. If you put something in the envelope, the reader will find it.
Hereto, herewith	Omit	Omit legal jargon.
Please be advised; Please be informed	Omit—simply start your response	You don't need a preface. Go ahead and start.
Please do not hesitate	Omit	Omit negative words.
Pursuant to	According to; or omit	*Pursuant* does not mean *after*. Omit legal jargon in any case.
This will acknowledge receipt of your letter.	Omit—start your response	If you answer a letter, the reader knows you got it.

To spot a passive voice, find the verb. If the verb describes something that the grammatical subject is doing, the verb is in active voice. If the verb describes something that is being done to the grammatical subject, the verb is in passive voice.

Active voice	Passive voice
The customer received 500 widgets.	Five hundred widgets were received by the customer.
I recommend this method.	This method is recommended by me.
The state agencies will implement the program.	The program will be implemented by the state agencies.

To change from passive voice to active voice, you must make the agent—the "doer" of the action—the new subject. If no agent is specified in the sentence, you must supply one to make the sentence active.

Passive voice	Active voice
The request was approved by the plant manager.	The plant manager approved the request.
A decision will be made next month. No agent in sentence.	The committee will decide next month.
A letter will be sent informing the customer of the change. No agent in sentence.	[You] Send the customer a letter informing her about the change.

Passive voice has at least three disadvantages:

- If all the information in the original sentence is retained, passive voice makes the sentence longer and thus more time-consuming to understand.[15]

- If the agent is omitted, it's not clear who is responsible for doing the action.

- Using much passive voice, especially in material that has a lot of big words, can make the writing boring and pompous.

However, passive voice has its place on occasion. Figure 4.4 lists these occasions and provides examples.

4. Use verbs—not nouns—to carry the weight of your sentence.
Put the weight of your sentence in the verb to make your sentences more forceful and

---

Figure 4.4	When to Use Passive Voice	
Using passive voice	**Example**	**Explanation**
To emphasize the object receiving the action, not the agent.	Your order was shipped November 15.	The customer's order, not the shipping clerk, is important.
To provide cohesion within a paragraph. A sentence is easier to read if "old" information comes at the beginning of a sentence. When you have been discussing a topic, use the word *again* as your subject even if that requires passive voice.	The bank made several risky loans in the late 1990s. These loans were written off as "uncollectible" in 2001.	Using *loans* as the subject of the second sentence provides a link between the two sentences, making the paragraph easier to read.
To avoid assigning blame.	The order was damaged during shipment.	Active voice would require the writer to specify *who* damaged the order. The passive voice is more tactful here.

up to 25% easier to read.[16] When the verb is a form of the verb *to be*, revise the sentence to use a more forceful verb.

Weak: The financial advantage of owning this equipment instead of leasing it is 10% after taxes.

Better: Owning this equipment rather than leasing it will save us 10% after taxes.

Nouns ending in *-ment, -ion,* and *-al* often hide verbs.

Weak	Better
make an adjustment	adjust
make a payment	pay
make a decision	decide
reach a conclusion	conclude
take into consideration	consider
make a referral	refer
provide assistance	assist

Use verbs to present the information more forcefully.

Weak: We will perform an investigation of the problem.

Better: We will investigate the problem.

Weak: Selection of a program should be based on the client's needs.

Better: Select the program that best fits the client's needs.

5. Eliminate wordiness.

Writing is **wordy** if the same idea can be expressed in fewer words. Unnecessary words increase writing time, bore your reader, and make your meaning more difficult to follow.

Good writing is concise, but it still may be lengthy. Concise writing may be long because it is packed with ideas. Chapter 2 shows how revisions to create *you*-attitude and positive emphasis and to develop benefits are frequently *longer* than the originals because the revision adds information not given in the original. Below are three strategies for making your writing more concise.

Eliminate Words That Add Nothing   Cut words if the idea is already clear from other words in the sentence. Substitute single words for wordy phrases.

Wordy: Keep this information on file for future reference.

Better: Keep this information for reference.

or: File this information.

Wordy: The reason we want to see changing our hardware manager to Hanson's is because Hanson's is able to collect hardware from a larger number of vendors than our current supplier.

Better: We recommend changing our hardware manager to Hanson's for its larger number of vendors.

Phrases beginning with *of, which,* and *that* often can be shortened.

Wordy: the question of most importance

Better: the most important question

Wordy: the estimate that is enclosed

Better: the enclosed estimate

Wordy: We need to act on the suggestions that our customers offer us.

Better: We need to act on customer suggestions.

Figure 4.5	Words to Cut		
Cut the following words	**Cut redundant words**	**Substitute a single word for a wordy phrase**	
quite	a period of three months	at the present time	now
really	during the course of the negotiations	due to the fact that	because
very	during the year of 2020	in order to	to
	maximum possible	in the event that	if
	past experience	in the near future	soon (or give the date)
	plan in advance	on a regular basis	regularly
	refer back	prior to the start of	before
	the color blue	until such time as	until
	the month of November		
	true facts		

Sentences beginning with *There are* or *It is* often can be more concise.

Wordy: There are three reasons for the success of the project.

Tighter: Three reasons explain the project's success.

Wordy: It is the case that college graduates earn more money.

Tighter: College graduates earn more money.

Check your draft. If you find these phrases, or any of the unnecessary words shown in Figure 4.5, eliminate them.

Combine Sentences to Eliminate Unnecessary Words   In addition to saving words, combining sentences focuses the reader's attention on key points, makes your writing sound more sophisticated, and sharpens the relationship between ideas, thus making your writing more coherent.

Wordy: I conducted this survey by telephone on Sunday, April 21. I questioned two groups of upperclass students—men and women—who, according to the Student Directory, were still living in the dorms. The purpose of this survey was to find out why some upperclass students continue to live in the dorms even though they are no longer required by the University to do so. I also wanted to find out if there were any differences between men and women upperclass students in their reasons for choosing to remain in the dorms.

Tighter: On Sunday, April 21, I phoned upperclass men and women living in the dorms to find out (1) why they continue to live in the dorms even though they are no longer required to do so and (2) whether men and women gave the same reasons.

Put the Meaning of Your Sentence into the Subject and Verb to Cut the Number of Words
Put the core of your meaning into the subject and verb of your main clause.

Wordy: The reason we are recommending the computerization of this process is because it will reduce the time required to obtain data and will give us more accurate data.

Better: Computerizing the process will give us more accurate data more quickly.

Wordy: The purpose of this letter is to indicate that if we are unable to mutually benefit from our seller/buyer relationship, with satisfactory material and satisfactory payment, then we have no alternative other than to sever the relationship. In other words, unless the account is handled in 45 days, we will have to change our terms to a permanent COD basis.

Better: A good buyer/seller relationship depends upon satisfactory material and payment. You can continue to charge your purchases from us only if you clear your present balance in 45 days.

6. Vary sentence length and sentence structure. Readable prose mixes sentence lengths and varies sentence structure. A short sentence (under 10 words) can add punch to your prose. Long sentences (over 30 words) can be danger signs. You can vary sentence patterns in several ways. First, you can mix simple, compound, and complex sentences. (See Appendix B for more information on sentence structure.) **Simple sentences** have one main clause:

We will open a new store this month.

Compound sentences have two main clauses joined with *and, but, or,* or another conjunction. Compound sentences work best when the ideas in the two clauses are closely related.

We have hired staff, and they will complete their training next week.
We wanted to have a local radio station broadcast from the store during its grand opening, but the DJs were already booked.

Complex sentences have one main and at least one subordinate clause; they are good for showing logical relationships.

When the stores open, we will have specials in every department.
Because we already have a strong customer base in the northwest, we expect the new store to be just as successful as the store in the City Center Mall.

You also can vary sentences by changing the order of elements. Normally the subject comes first.

We will survey customers later in the year to see whether demand warrants a third store on campus.

To create variety, occasionally begin the sentence with some other part of the sentence.

Later in the year, we will survey customers to see whether demand warrants a third store on campus.

Use these guidelines for sentence length and structure:

- Always edit sentences for conciseness. Even a short sentence can be wordy.

- When your subject matter is complicated or full of numbers, make a special effort to keep sentences short.

- Use longer sentences to show how ideas are linked to each other; to avoid a series of short, choppy sentences; and to reduce repetition.

- Group the words in long and medium-length sentences into chunks that the reader can process quickly.

- When you use a long sentence, keep the subject and verb close together.

Let's see how to apply the last three guidelines.

Use long sentences to show how ideas are linked to each other; to avoid a series of short, choppy sentences; and to reduce repetition. The following sentence is hard to read not simply because it is long, but because it fails to connect one idea to another. Just cutting it into a series of short, choppy sentences doesn't help. The best revision uses medium-length sentences to show the relationship between ideas.

Too long: It should also be noted in the historical patterns presented in the summary, that though there were delays in January and February which we realized were occurring, we are now back where we were about a year ago, and that we are not off line in our collect receivables as compared to last year at this time, but we do show a considerable over-budget figure because of an ultraconservative goal on the receivable investment.

Choppy: There were delays in January and February. We knew about them at the time. We are now back where we were about a year ago. The summary shows this. Our present collect receivables are in line with last year's. However, they exceed the budget. The reason they exceed the budget is that our goal for receivable investment was very conservative.

Better: As the summary shows, although there were delays in January and February (of which we were aware), we have now regained our position of a year ago. Our present collect receivables are in line with last year's, but they exceed the budget because our goal for receivable investment was very conservative.

Group the words in long and medium-length sentences into chunks. The "better" revision above has seven chunks. At 27 and 24 words, respectively, these sentences aren't short, but they're readable because no chunk is longer than 10 words. Any sentence pattern will get boring if it is repeated sentence after sentence. Use different sentence patterns—different kinds and lengths of chunks—to keep your prose interesting.

Keep the subject and verb close together. Often you can move the subject and verb closer together if you put the modifying material in a list at the end of the sentence. For maximum readability, present the list vertically.

Hard to read: Movements resulting from termination, layoffs and leaves, recalls and reinstates, transfers in, transfers out, promotions in, promotions out, and promotions within are presently documented through the Payroll Authorization Form.

Better: The Payroll Authorization Form documents the following movements:

- Termination
- Layoffs and leaves
- Recalls and reinstates
- Transfers in and out
- Promotions in, out, and within

7. Use parallel structure.

Parallel structure puts words, phrases, or clauses in the same grammatical and logical form. In the following faulty example, by reviewing is a gerund, while *note* is an imperative verb. Make the sentence parallel by using both gerunds or both imperatives.

Faulty: Errors can be checked by reviewing the daily exception report or note the number of errors you uncover when you match the lading copy with the file copy of the invoice.

Parallel: Errors can be checked by reviewing the daily exception report or by noting the number of errors you uncover when you match the lading copy with the file copy of the invoice.

Also parallel: To check errors, note

1. The number of items on the daily exception report.

2. The number of errors discovered when the lading copy and the file copy are matched.

Note that a list in parallel structure must fit grammatically into the lead-in sentence that introduces the list.

Faulty: The following suggestions can help employers avoid bias in job interviews:

1. Base questions on the job description.

2. Questioning techniques.

3. Selection and training of interviewers.

Parallel: The following suggestions can help employers avoid bias in job interviews:

1. Base questions on the job description.

2. Ask the same questions of all applicants.

3. Select and train interviewers carefully.

Also parallel: Employers can avoid bias in job interviews by

1. Basing questions on the job description.

2. Asking the same questions of all applicants.

3. Selecting and training interviewers carefully.

Words also must be logically parallel. In the following faulty example, *juniors*, *seniors*, and *athletes* are not three separate groups. The revision groups words into non-overlapping categories.

Faulty: I interviewed juniors and seniors and athletes.

Parallel: I interviewed juniors and seniors. In each rank, I interviewed athletes and non-athletes.

Parallel structure is a powerful device for making your writing tighter, smoother, and more forceful.

Faulty: Our customers receive these benefits:

- Use tracking information.
- Our products let them scale the software to their needs.
- The customer can always rely on us.

Parallel: Our customers receive these benefits:

- Tracking information
- Scalability
- Reliability

8. Put your readers in your sentences. Use second-person pronouns (*you*) rather than third-person (*he, she, one*) to give your writing more impact. *You* is both singular and plural; it can refer to a single person or to every member of your organization.

Third-person: Funds in a participating employee's account at the end of each six months will automatically be used to buy more stock unless a "Notice of Election Not to Exercise Purchase Rights" form is received from the employee.

Second-person: Once you begin to participate, funds in your account at the end of each six months will automatically be used to buy more stock unless you turn in a "Notice of Election Not to Exercise Purchase Rights" form.

However, remember to use *you* only when it refers to your reader.

Incorrect: My visit with the outside sales rep showed me that your schedule can change quickly.

Correct: My visit with the outside sales rep showed me that schedules can change quickly.

As You Write and Revise Paragraphs

Paragraphs are visual and logical units. Use them to chunk your sentences.

9. Begin most paragraphs with topic sentences.

A good paragraph has **unity**; that is, it discusses only one idea, or topic. The **topic sentence** states the main idea and provides a scaffold to structure your document. Audiences who skim reports can follow your ideas more easily if each paragraph begins with a topic sentence. Your writing will be easier to read if you make the topic sentence explicit and put it at the beginning of the paragraph.[17]

Hard to read (no topic sentence):   Another main use of ice is to keep the fish fresh. Each of the seven kinds of fish served at the restaurant requires one gallon twice a day, for a total of 14 gallons. An additional 6 gallons a day are required for the salad bar.

Better (begins with topic sentence):   Twenty gallons of ice a day are needed to keep food fresh. Of this, the biggest portion (14 gallons) is used to keep the fish fresh. Each of the seven kinds of fish served at the restaurant requires one gallon twice a day. An additional 6 gallons a day are required for the salad bar.

Hard to read (no topic sentence):   In fiscal 2018, the company filed claims for refund of federal income taxes of $3,199,000 and interest of $969,000 paid as a result of an examination of the company's federal income tax returns by the Internal Revenue Service (IRS) for the years 2014 through 2016. It is uncertain what amount, if any, ultimately may be recovered.

Better (paragraph starts with topic sentence):   The company and the IRS disagree about whether the company is responsible for back taxes. In fiscal 2018, the company filed claims for a refund of federal income taxes of $3,199,000 and interest of $969,000 paid as a result of an examination of the company's federal income tax returns by the Internal Revenue Service (IRS) for the years 2014 through 2016. It is uncertain what amount, if any, ultimately may be recovered.

A good topic sentence forecasts the structure and content of the paragraph.

Plan B also has economic advantages.

(Prepares the reader for a discussion of B's economic advantages.)

We had several personnel changes in June.

(Prepares the reader for a list of the month's terminations and hires.)

Employees have complained about one part of our new policy on parental leaves.

(Prepares the reader for a discussion of the problem.)

When the first sentence of a paragraph is not the topic sentence, readers who skim may miss the main point. If the paragraph does not have a topic sentence, you will need to write one. If you can't think of a single sentence that serves as an "umbrella" to cover every sentence, the paragraph probably lacks unity. To solve the problem, either split the paragraph or eliminate the sentences that digress from the main point.

Figure 4.6	Transition Words and Phrases		
To show addition or continuation of the same idea and also first, second, third in addition likewise similarly	**To introduce an example** for example (e.g.,) for instance indeed to illustrate namely specifically	**To show that the contrast is more important than the previous idea** but however nevertheless on the contrary	**To show time** after as before in the future next then until when while
To introduce another important item furthermore moreover	**To contrast** in contrast on the other hand or	**To show cause and effect** as a result because consequently for this reason therefore	**To summarize or end** finally in conclusion

10. Use transitions to link ideas.   Transition words and sentences signal the connections between ideas to the reader. Transitions tell whether the next sentence continues the previous thought or starts a new idea; they can tell whether the idea that comes next is more or less important than the previous thought.

These sentences use transition words and phrases:

Kelly wants us to switch the contract to Ames Cleaning, and I agree with her. (continuing the same idea)

Kelly wants us to switch the contract to Ames Cleaning, but I prefer Ross Commercial. (contrasting opinions)

As a result of our differing views, we will be visiting both firms. (showing cause and effect)

Figure 4.6 lists some of the most common transition words and phrases.

These are transitional sentences:

Now that we have examined the advantages of using Ames Cleaning, let's look at potential disadvantages. (shows movement between two sections of evaluation)

These pros and cons show us three reasons we should switch to Ross Commercial. (shows movement away from evaluation sections; forecasts the three reasons)

Revising, Editing, and Proofreading

LO 4-3

Once you have your document written, you need to polish it.

A popular myth about revising is that Abraham Lincoln wrote the Gettysburg address, perhaps the most famous of all American presidential speeches, on the back of an envelope as he traveled by train to the battlefield's dedication. The reality is that Lincoln wrote at least a partial draft of the speech before leaving for the trip and continued to revise it up to the morning of its delivery. Furthermore, the speech was on a topic he passionately believed in, one he had been pondering for years.[18]

Like Lincoln, good writers work on their drafts; they make their documents better by judicious revising, editing, and proofreading.

What to Look for When You Revise

When you're writing to a new audience or have to solve a particularly difficult problem, plan to revise the draft at least three times. The first time, look for content and clarity: Have I said enough, and have I said it clearly? The second time, check the organization and layout: Have I presented my content so it can be easily absorbed? Finally, check style and tone: Have I used you-attitude? Have I used **inclusive language**? The Thorough-Revision Checklist in Figure 4.7 summarizes the questions you should ask.

Figure 4.7	Thorough-Revision Checklist

Content and clarity

☐   Does your document meet the needs of the organization and of the reader—and make you look good?

☐   Have you given readers all the information they need to understand and act on your message?

☐   Is all the information accurate and clear?

☐   Is the message easy to read?

☐   Is each sentence clear? Is the message free from apparently contradictory statements?

☐   Is the logic clear and convincing? Are generalizations and benefits backed up with adequate supporting detail?

Organization and layout

☐   Is the pattern of organization clear? Is it appropriate for your purposes, audience, and context?

☐   Are transitions between ideas smooth? Do ideas within paragraphs flow smoothly?

☐   Does the design of the document make it easy for readers to find the information they need? Is the document visually inviting?

☐   Are the points emphasized by layout ones that deserve emphasis?

☐   Are the first and last paragraphs effective?

Style and tone

☐   Does the message use *you*-attitude and positive emphasis?

☐   Is the message friendly?

☐   Does the message use inclusive language, and is it free from **oppressive language?**

☐   Does the message build goodwill?

Figure 4.8	Light-Revision Checklist

☐   Have you given readers all the information they need to understand and act on your message?

☐   Is the pattern of organization clear and helpful?

☐   Is the logic clear and convincing? Are generalizations and benefits backed up with adequate supporting detail?

☐   Does the design of the document make it easy for readers to find the information they need?

☐   Are the first and last paragraphs effective?

Often you'll get the best revision by setting aside your draft, getting a blank page or screen, and redrafting. This strategy takes advantage of the thinking you did on your first draft without locking you into the sentences in it.

As you revise, be sure to read the document through from start to finish. Reading the entire document is particularly important if you've composed in several sittings or if you've used text from other documents. Such drafts tend to be choppy, repetitious, or inconsistent. You may need to add transitions, cut repetitive parts, or change words to create a uniform level of formality throughout the document.

If you're really in a time bind, do a light revision, as outlined in the Light-Revision Checklist (see Figure 4.8). The quality of the final document may not be as high as with a thorough revision, but even a light revision is better than skipping revision altogether.

What to Look for When You Edit

Even good writers need to edit because no one can pay attention to surface correctness while thinking of ideas. As a matter of fact, even history-shaping documents like the Declaration of Independence became better with editing.

Sometimes revising and proofreading are more pleasant if done in an informal setting.

Tim Robberts/The Image Bank/Getty Images

Editing should always *follow* revision. There's no point in taking time to fix a grammatical error in a sentence that may be cut when you clarify your meaning or tighten your style. Some writers edit more accurately when they print out a copy of a document and edit the hard copy.

Check your material to make sure you have acknowledged all information and opinions borrowed from outside the organization. Using material from outside the organization without acknowledging the source is **plagiarism**. Check also that you have acknowledged company information that is controversial or not widely known.

Check your communication to make sure your sentences say what you intend.

Not: Take a moment not to sign your policy.

But: Take a moment now to sign your policy.

Not: I wish to apply for the job as assistant manger.

But: I wish to apply for the job as assistant manager.

One of the most famous editing errors in history was the so-called Wicked Bible, which left out a crucial *not*, thus changing one of the Ten Commandments into "Thou shalt commit adultery."

When you edit, you also need to check that the following are accurate:

- Sentence structure.

- Subject–verb and noun–pronoun agreement.

- Punctuation.

- Word usage—words that are often confused.

- Spelling—including spelling of names.

- Numbers.

Appendix B reviews grammar, punctuation, numbers, and words that are often confused.

Most writers make a small number of errors over and over. If you know that you have trouble with subject–verb agreement, for example, specifically look for them in your draft. Also look for any errors that especially bother your boss and correct them.

How to Catch Typos

To catch typos use a **spell-checker**. But you still need to proofread by eye. Spell-checkers work by matching words; they will signal any group of letters not listed in their dictionaries. However, they cannot tell you when you've used the wrong word but spelled it correctly (e.g., *now* versus *not*).

Proofreading is hard because writers tend to see what they know should be there rather than what really is there. It's easier to proof something you haven't written, so you may want to swap papers with a classmate.

To proofread:

- Read once quickly for meaning, to see that nothing has been left out.

- Read a second time, slowly. When you find an error, correct it and then *reread that line*. Readers tend to become less attentive after they find one error and may miss other errors close to the one they've spotted.

- To proofread a document you know well, read the lines backward or the pages out of order. Also, you can try reading the document out loud.

- Always triple-check numbers, headings, the first and last paragraphs, and the reader's name.

Getting and Using Feedback

Getting feedback almost always improves a document. In many organizations, it's required. All external documents must be read and approved before they go out. The process of drafting, getting feedback, revising, and getting more feedback is called **cycling**. One researcher reported that documents in her clients' firms cycled an average of 4.2 times before reaching the intended audience.[19] Another researcher studied a major 10-page document whose 20 drafts made a total of 31 stops on the desks of nine reviewers on four different levels.[20] Being asked to revise a document is a fact of life in business.

You can improve the quality of the feedback you get by telling people which aspects you'd especially like comments about. For example, when you give a reader the outline or planning draft, you probably want to know whether the general approach and content are appropriate, and if you have included all major points. After your second draft, you might want to know whether the reasoning is convincing. When you reach the polishing draft, you'll be ready for feedback on style and grammar. The Questions to Ask Readers Checklist (see Figure 4.9) offers suggestions.

Figure 4.9	Questions to Ask Readers Checklist

Outline or planning draft

☐ Does the plan seem on the right track?

☐ What topics should be added? Should any be cut?

☐ Do you have any other general suggestions?

Revising draft

☐ Does the message satisfy all its purposes?

☐ Is the message adapted to the audience(s)?

☐ Is the organization effective?

☐ What parts aren't clear?

☐ What ideas need further development and support?

☐ Do you have any other suggestions?

Polishing draft

☐ Are there any problems with word choice or sentence structure?

☐ Did you find any inconsistencies?

☐ Did you find any typos?

☐ Is the document's design effective?

Technology helps with both giving and receiving feedback. Word documents can be edited using review features such as Track Changes, a word-processing feature that records alterations made to a document. It is particularly useful when you are collaborating with a colleague to create, edit, or revise documents. Track Changes will highlight any text that has been added to or deleted from your document, and it also allows you to decide whether to accept each change or reject it and return to your original text. In addition to Track Changes, many word processors include a comment feature that allows you to ask questions or make suggestions without altering the text itself. Documents also can be posted in the cloud using Google Docs and then can be edited by multiple people.

It's easy to feel defensive when someone criticizes your work. If the feedback stings, put it aside until you can read it without feeling defensive. Even if you think that the reader hasn't understood what you were trying to say, the fact that the reader complained usually means that you could improve the section. If the reader says, "This isn't true," and you know the statement is true, several kinds of revision might make the truth clear to the reader: rephrasing the statement, giving more information or examples, or documenting the source.

Reading feedback carefully is a good way to understand the culture of your organization. Are you told to give more details or to shorten messages? Does your boss add headings and bullet points? Look for patterns in the comments and apply what you learn in your next document.

Using Boilerplate

Boilerplate is language—sentences, paragraphs, even pages—from a previous document that a writer legitimately includes in a new document. In academic papers, material written by others must be quoted and documented—to neglect to do so would be plagiarism. However, because businesses own the documents their employees write, old text may be included without attribution.

Many legal documents, including apartment leases and sales contracts, are almost completely boilerplate. Writers also may use boilerplate they wrote for earlier documents. For example, a section from a proposal describing the background of the problem also could be used in the final report. A section from a progress report describing what the writer had done could be used with only a few changes in the methods section of the final report.

Writers use boilerplate both to save time and energy and to use language that already has been approved by the organization's legal staff. However, research has shown that using boilerplate creates two problems.[21] First, using unrevised boilerplate can create a document with incompatible styles and tones. Second, boilerplate can allow writers to ignore subtle differences in situations and audiences.

Summary by Learning Objectives

LO 4-1   **Implement activities involved in the composing process.**

Processes that help writers write well include not expecting the first draft to be perfect, writing regularly, modifying the initial task if it's too hard or too easy, having clear goals, knowing many different strategies, using rules as guidelines rather than as absolutes, and waiting to edit until after the draft is complete.

Writing processes can include many activities: planning, gathering, brainstorming, organizing, writing, evaluating, getting feedback, revising, editing, and proofreading. *Revising* means changing the document to make it better satisfy the writer's purposes and the audience. *Editing* means making surface-level changes that make the document grammatically correct. *Proofreading* means checking to be sure the document is free from typographical errors. The activities do not have to come in any set order. It is not necessary to finish one activity to start another. Most writers use all activities only when they write a document whose genre, subject matter, or audience is new to them.

To think of ideas, try brainstorming, freewriting (writing without stopping for 10 minutes or so), and clustering (brainstorming with circled words on a page).

LO 4-2 Apply guidelines for effective word choice, sentence construction, and paragraph organization.

Good style in business and administrative writing is less formal, more friendly, and more personal than the style usually used for term papers.

Use the following techniques to make your writing easier to read.

As you choose words:

1. Use words that are accurate, appropriate, and familiar. Denotation is a word's literal meaning; connotation is the emotional coloring that a word conveys.
2. Use technical jargon sparingly; eliminate business jargon.

As you write and revise sentences:

3. Use active voice most of the time. Active voice is better because it is shorter, clearer, and more interesting.
4. Use verbs—not nouns—to carry the weight of your sentence.

5. Eliminate wordiness. Writing is wordy if the same idea can be expressed in fewer words.
    a. Eliminate words that add nothing.
    b. Combine sentences to eliminate unnecessary words.
    c. Put the meaning of your sentence into the subject and verb to cut the number of words.
6. Vary sentence length and sentence structure.
7. Use parallel structure. Use the same grammatical form for ideas that have the same logical function.
8. Use second-person pronoun "you" to put your readers in your sentences.

As you write and revise paragraphs:

9. Begin most paragraphs with topic sentences so that readers know what to expect in the paragraph.
10. Use transitions to link ideas.

LO 4-3 Apply techniques to revise, edit, and proofread your communications.

- If the writing situation is new or difficult, plan to revise the draft at least three times. The first time, look for content and completeness. The second time, check the organization, layout, and reasoning. Finally, check style and tone.

- Edit for surface-level changes to make your document grammatically correct.

- Finally, proofread to catch typos. Use available technologies to help you.

Exercises and Cases

4.1 Reviewing the Chapter

1. What are some techniques of good writers? Which ones do you use regularly? (LOs 4-1, 4-2, 4-3.)
2. What are ways to get ideas for a specific communication? (LO 4-1)
3. What activities are part of the composing process? Which one should you be doing more often or more carefully in your writing? (LO 4-1)
4. What are some half-truths about style? (LO 4-2)
5. What are some ways you can make your sentences more effective? (LO 4-2)

6. What are some ways you can make your paragraphs more effective? (LO 4-2)
7. How can you adapt good style to organization preferences? (LO 4-2)
8. How do revising, editing, and proofreading differ? Which one do you personally need to do more carefully? (LO 4-3)
9. How can you get better feedback on your writing? (LO 4-3)

4.2 Interviewing Writers about Their Composing Processes

Interview someone about the composing process(es) they use for on-the-job writing. Questions you could ask include the following:

- What kind of planning do you do before you write? Do you make lists? formal or informal outlines?
- When you need more information, where do you get it?

- How do you compose your drafts? Do you dictate? Draft with pen and paper? Compose on screen? How do you find uninterrupted time to compose?
- When you want advice about style, grammar, and spelling, what source(s) do you consult?
- Does your superior ever read your drafts and make suggestions?
- Do you ever work with other writers to produce a single document? Describe the process you use.
- Describe the process of creating a document where you felt the final document reflected your best work. Describe

the process of creating a document you found difficult or frustrating. What sorts of things make writing easier or harder for you?

As your instructor directs,
a. Share your results orally with a small group of students.
b. Present your results in an oral presentation to the class.
c. Present your results in an email to your instructor.
d. Share your results with a small group of students and write a joint email reporting the similarities and differences you found.

4.3   Analyzing Your Own Writing Processes

Save your notes and drafts from several assignments so that you can answer the following questions:

- Which practices of good writers do you follow?
- Which of the activities discussed in this chapter do you use?
- How much time do you spend on each of the activities?
- What kinds of revisions do you make most often?
- Do you use different processes for different documents, or do you have one process that you use most of the time?
- What parts of your process seem most successful? Are there any places in the process that could be improved? How?

- What relation do you see between the process(es) you use and the quality of the final document?

As your instructor directs,
a. Discuss your process with a small group of other students.
b. Write an email to your instructor analyzing in detail your process for composing one of the papers for this class.
c. Write an email to your instructor analyzing your process during the term. What parts of your process(es) have stayed the same throughout the term? What parts have changed?

4.4   Evaluating the Ethical Implication of Connotations

In each of the following pairs, identify the more favorable term. When is its use justifiable?

1. wasted/sacrificed
2. illegal alien/immigrant
3. bring about/cause
4. terminate/fire
5. inaccuracy/lying
6. budget/spending plan
7. feedback/criticism
8. credit/blame
9. discrepancy/difference

4.5   Correcting Errors in Denotation and Connotation

Identify and correct the errors in denotation or connotation in the following sentences:

1. In our group, we weeded out the best idea each person had thought of.
2. She is a prudent speculator.
3. The three proposals are diametrically opposed to each other.
4. While he researched companies, he was literally glued to the web.
5. Our backpacks are hand sewn by one of roughly 16 individuals.
6. Raj flaunted the law against insider trading.

4.6   Eliminating Jargon and Simplifying Language

Revise these sentences to eliminate jargon and to use short, familiar words.

1. When the automobile company announced its strategic downsizing initiative, it offered employees a career alternative enhancement program.

2. Any alterations must be approved during the 30-day period commencing 60 days prior to the expiration date of the agreement.

3. As per your request, the undersigned has obtained estimates of upgrading our computer system. A copy of the estimated cost is attached hereto.

4. Please be advised that this writer is in considerable need of a new computer.

5. Enclosed please find the proposed draft for the employee negative retention plan. In the event that you have alterations which you would like to suggest, forward same to my office at your earliest convenience.

4.7   Changing Verbs from Passive to Active Voice

Identify passive voice in the following sentences and convert it to active voice. In some cases, you may need to add information to do so. You may use different words as long as you retain the basic meaning of the sentence. Remember that imperative verbs are active voice, too.

1. It has been suggested by the corporate office that all faxes are to be printed on recycled paper.

2. The office carpets will be cleaned professionally on Friday evening. It is requested that all staff members put belongings up on their desks.

3. The office microwave is to be cleaned by those who use it.

4. When the vacation schedule is finalized it is recommended that it be routed to all supervisors for final approval.

5. Material must not be left on trucks outside the warehouse. Either the trucks must be parked inside the warehouse or the material must be unloaded at the time of receiving the truck.

4.8   Using Strong Verbs

Revise each of the following sentences to replace hidden verbs with action verbs.

1. An understanding of stocks and bonds is important if one wants to invest wisely.

2. We must undertake a calculation of expected revenues and expenses for the next two years.

3. The production of clear and concise documents is the mark of a successful communicator.

4. We hope to make use of the company's website to promote the new product line.

5. If you wish to be eligible for the Miller scholarship, you must complete an application by January 31.

6. When you make an evaluation of media buys, take into consideration the demographics of the group seeing the ad.

7. We provide assistance to clients in the process of reaching a decision about the purchase of hardware and software.

4.9   Reducing Wordiness

1. Eliminate words that say nothing. You may use different words.

   a. There are many businesses that are active in community and service work.

   b. The purchase of another computer for the claims department will allow us to produce form letters quickly. In addition, return on investment could be calculated for proposed repairs. Another use is that the computer could check databases to make sure that claims are paid only once.

   c. Our decision to enter the South American market has precedence in the past activities of the company.

2. Combine sentences to show how ideas are related and to eliminate unnecessary words.

   a. Some customers are profitable for companies. Other customers actually cost the company money.

   b. If you are unable to come to the session on HMOs, please call the human resources office. You will be able to schedule another time to ask questions you may have about the various options.

   c. Major Japanese firms often have employees who know English well. U.S. companies negotiating with Japanese companies should bring their own interpreters.

   d. New procedure for customer service employees: Please be aware effective immediately, if a customer is requesting a refund of funds applied to their account a front and back copy of the check must be submitted if the transaction is over $500.00. For example, if the customer is requesting $250.00 back, and the total amount of the transaction is $750.00, a front and back copy of the check will be needed to obtain the refund.

4.10   Improving Parallel Structure

Revise each of the following sentences to create parallelism.

1. The orientation session will cover the following information:
   - Company culture will be discussed.
   - How to use the equipment.
   - You will get an overview of key customers' needs.

2. Five criteria for a good webpage are content that serves the various audiences, attention to details, and originality. It is also important to have effective organization and navigation devices. Finally, provide attention to details such as revision date and the webmaster's address.

3. When you leave a voice mail message,
   - Summarize your main point in a sentence or two.
   - The name and phone number should be given slowly and distinctly.
   - The speaker should give enough information so that the recipient can act on the message.
   - Tell when you'll be available to receive the recipient's return call.

4.11   Revising Paragraphs

1. Make each of the following paragraphs more readable by opening each paragraph with a topic sentence. You may be able to find a topic sentence in the paragraph and move it to the beginning. In other cases, you'll need to write a new sentence.

   a. At Disney World, a lunch put on an expense account is "on the mouse." McDonald's employees "have ketchup in their veins." Business slang flourishes at companies with rich corporate cultures. Memos at Procter & Gamble are called "reco's" because the model P&G memo begins with a recommendation.

   b. The first item on the agenda is the hiring for the coming year. George has also asked that we review the agency goals for the next fiscal year. We should cover this early in the meeting since it may affect our hiring preferences. Finally, we need to announce the deadlines for grant proposals, decide which grants to apply for, and set up a committee to draft each proposal.

   c. Separate materials that can be recycled from your regular trash. Pass along old clothing, toys, or appliances to someone else who can use them. When you purchase products, choose those with minimal packaging. If you have a yard, put your yard waste and kitchen scraps (excluding meat and fat) in a compost pile. You can reduce the amount of solid waste your household produces in four ways.

2. Revise each paragraph to make it easier to read. Change, rearrange, or delete words and sentences; add any material necessary.

   a. Once a new employee is hired, each one has to be trained for a week by one of our supervisors at a cost of $1,000 each which includes the supervisor's time. This amount also includes half of the new employee's salary since new hires produce only half the normal production per worker for the week. This summer $24,000 was spent in training 24 new employees. Absenteeism increased in the department on the hottest summer days. For every day each worker is absent we lose $200 in lost production. This past summer there was a total of 56 absentee days taken for a total loss of $11,200 in lost production. Turnover and absenteeism were the causes of an unnecessary expenditure of over $35,000 this summer.

   b. One service is investments. General financial news and alerts about companies in the customer's portfolio are available. Quicken also provides assistance in finding the best mortgage rate and in providing assistance in making the decision whether to refinance a mortgage. Another service from Quicken is advice for the start and management of a small business. Banking services, such as paying bills and applying for loans, have long been available to Quicken subscribers. The taxpayer can be walked through the tax preparation process by Quicken. Someone considering retirement can use Quicken to ascertain whether the amount being set aside for this purpose is sufficient. Quicken's website provides seven services.

4.12   Revising, Editing, and Proofreading an Email

Dana Shomacher, an enthusiastic new hire at Bear Foods, wants Stan Smith, regional head of HR at the grocery chain, to allow her to organize and publicize a food drive for Coastal Food Pantry. Revise, edit, and proof her email.

> Hey Stan,
>
> I have this great idea for great publicity for Bear Foods that won't cost anything and will get us some really great publicity. Its something great we can do for our community. I wont Bear to conduct a food drive for Coastal Food Pantry. Their was an article

in the Tribune about how they were having trouble keeping up with food requests and I thought what a great fit it would be for Bear.

All our employees should donate food and we should also get our customer to donate also. We could set out some shopping carts for the donations. I could write an announcement for the Tribune and get some postures made for our front windows.

I am willing to take care of all details so you won't have to do anything except say yes to this email.

Dana

After you have fixed Dana's email, answer these questions in an email to your instructor.

- What revisions did you make? Why?
- Many grocery stores already contribute to local food pantries. In addition to some staples, they provide items such as bakery goods that are past their sale date but still quite tasty, sacks for bagging groceries at the pantry, and even shopping carts to transport groceries to the cars of pantry clients. If Bear already contributes to Coastal, how should that fact change the content of Dana's email?

- What edits did you make? Why?
- What impression do you think this email made on the head of human resources? Explain. Do you think he granted Dana's request? Why or why not?

Submit both your version of Dana's email and your analysis email.

4.13   Identifying Buzzwords and Jargon

This is an actual press release published in the *Des Moines Register* with an article on buzzwords.

Wal-Mart Stores, Inc., the largest private employer with more than 1.8 million employees and the largest corporate mover of people, selected Capital Relocation Services as the sole source provider for the implementation of its Tier III and Tier IV relocation programs. These two programs account for the vast majority of the company's relocations. Capital was awarded the business following an intensive RFP and due diligence process.

"We're very excited about the synergy that Wal-Mart's selection of Capital brings to both companies," commented Mickey Williams, Capital's CEO. "We are also pleased to welcome to Capital the existing Wal-Mart PMP Relocation team that has been on-site at Wal-Mart's Bentonville headquarters for 14 years. They will continue to serve Wal-Mart and Sam's Club's Associates and will have an active role in the implementation of the new policy."

"What really enabled us to stand out was our focus on the strategic results Wal-Mart was looking for, and connecting that to their relocation program," added Williams. "Additionally, we demonstrated what would need to be done to achieve those results."

Mr. Williams continued, "Several years ago, we realized that traditional relocation solutions weren't enough. The challenge was that relocation management had become a logistics focused straightjacket. The emphasis was on efficiency and not on effectiveness. In a time of unprecedented change, relocation management programs were becoming increasingly inflexible."

"We realized that our continued success required us to stop thinking of ourselves solely as a relocation management company—we had to start thinking and acting as a talent management support company; after all that is the underlying purpose of relocation management in the first place. Wal-Mart's selection of Capital is a big confirmation that our approach is the right one."[22]

Now answer these questions:

1. What is this press release about? What is it saying?
2. Why did Capital Relocation Services get the new contract?
3. Underline the buzzwords and jargon in the press release. What do these words do in the press release?
4. What is the purpose of this press release? Does it meet its purpose? Why or why not?

Write an email to your instructor evaluating the press release as an effective document.

4.14   Revising Documents Using Track Changes

For this exercise, you will electronically exchange a document with one of your classmates. With the Track Changes feature turned on, you will review each other's documents, make comments or ask questions, insert additions, and make deletions to improve the writing, and then revise your work based upon the changes and comments.

As your instructor directs, select the electronic file of a document you have created for this class. Exchange this file with your peer review partner. Open your partner's file and select Track Changes. Review the document and make suggestions that will help your peer improve the writing. For instance, you can

- Look for accurate, appropriate, and ethical wording as well as instances of unnecessary jargon.
- Look for active voice and concise prose.

- Look for structural issues like topic sentences, tightly written paragraphs, varied sentence structure and length, and focus upon the thesis statement. Suggest where sentences can be combined or where sentences need parallel structure.
- Look for *you*-attitude.
- Ask questions (using comments) when the text isn't clear or make suggestions to tighten the writing or improve word choices.

Return the document to its author and open yours to review the changes and comments your partner added to your document. For each change, decide whether to accept or reject the suggestion.

Continue to revise the document. Then submit a copy of your original version and the revised version to your instructor.

4.15   Using the SEC's *A Plain English Handbook*

Go to the Securities and Exchange Commission's *A Plain English Handbook* at http://www.sec.gov/pdf/handbook.pdf. Scroll down to Appendix B and look at the four before and after examples. What kinds of changes have been made? What are examples of each kind? Can you understand the revised version? Did you understand the original version?

4.16   Evaluating a Letter to Stockholders

Figure 4.2 provides excerpts from Warren Buffett's annual letter to his stockholders. The complete letter is found at Warren Buffett, "Letters 2012," Berkshire Hathaway Inc., http://www.berkshirehathaway.com/letters/2012ltr.pdf. Answer these questions about the letter:

1. How many people are praised by name?
2. This chapter offers some examples of his colorful style. What other examples can you find?

3. Buffett is known for explaining general financial issues in these letters. In the 2012 letter, what does he say about newspapers? Dividends? Are these explanations clear? What phrases and sentences support your opinion?

4.17   Analyzing Your Own Writing

Collect five pages of writing you have prepared for college courses. Now review "Ten Ways to Make Your Writing Easier to Read." Mark places in your writing where you have had problems with those guidelines and identify which of the guidelines those places violate. Which guideline seems to give you the most trouble in your five pages? Would you agree with your findings? Or do you think your five pages are atypical of your writing? If you do not agree with your findings, which of the guidelines do you think generally gives you the most trouble?

Now trade pages with a partner. Read your partner's pages and mark places where they had problems with the 10 guidelines.

Retrieve your own pages. Did your partner find some problems you missed?

On the basis of this exercise, as well as your knowledge of your own writing, write an email to your instructor explaining which of the guidelines (choose just two or three) you most need to work on. Give problem sentences from your writing as evidence.

Below the text of the email, correct the problem sentences you used as evidence.

Notes

1. See especially Linda Flower and John R. Hayes, "The Cognition of Discovery: Defining a Rhetorical Problem," *College Composition and Communication* 31, no. 1 (February 1980): 21-32; Mike Rose, *Writer's Block: The Cognitive Dimension,* published for Conference on College Composition and Communication, 1984; and essays in two collections: Charles R. Cooper and Lee Odell, *Research on Composing: Points of Departure* (Urbana, IL: National Council of Teachers of English, 1978); and Mike Rose, ed., *When a Writer Can't Write: Studies in Writer's Block and Other Composing-Process Problems* (New York: Guilford Press, 1985).

2. Peter Elbow, *Writing with Power: Techniques for Mastering the Writing Process* (New York: Oxford University Press, 1981), 15-20.

3. See Gabriela Lesser Rico, *Writing the Natural Way* (Los Angeles: J. P. Tarcher, 1983), 10.

4. Anne Lamott, *Bird by Bird: Some Instructions on Writing and Life* (New York: Anchor, 1994), 25.

5. Ibid., 25.

6. Carol Loomis, ed., *Tap Dancing to Work: Warren Buffett on Practically Everything, 1966-2012: A Fortune Magazine Book* (New York: Portfolio/Penguin, 2012), 34.

7. Richard Lederer and Richard Dowis, *Sleeping Dogs Don't Lay: Practical Advice for the Grammatically Challenged* (New York: St. Martin's Press, 1999), 91-92.

8. James Suchan and Robert Colucci, "An Analysis of Communication Efficiency between High-Impact and Bureaucratic Written Communication," *Management Communication Quarterly* 2, no. 4 (1989): 464-73.

9. Hiluard G. Rogers and F. William Brown, "The Impact of Writing Style on Compliance with Instructions," *Journal of Technical Writing and Communication* 23, no. 1 (1993): 53-71.

10. Roger Pielke Jr., "Dear Expert, Please Cook the Books," *Wall Street Journal,* January 30, 2013, A11; and Doyle Rice, "Why Didn't Sandy Warrant a Warning?" *Des Moines Register,* December 2, 2012, 14A.

11. Betsy Taylor, "Experts: Flood Terms Can Deceive," *Des Moines Register,* July 1, 2008, 9A.

12. Daniel M. Oppenheimer, "Consequences of Erudite Vernacular Utilized Irrespective of Necessity: Problems with Using Long Words Needlessly," *Applied Cognitive Psychology* 20 (2006): 139-56.

13. Richard C. Anderson, "Concretization and Sentence Learning," *Journal of Educational Psychology* 66, no. 2 (1974): 179-83.

14. Ben Worthen, "Oracle's Hot New Offering: Corporate Technobabble," *Wall Street Journal,* February 12, 2008, B4.

15. Pamela Layton and Adrian J. Simpson, "Deep Structure in Sentence Comprehension," *Journal of Verbal Learning and Verbal Behavior* 14 (1975); and Harris B. Savin and Ellen Perchonock, "Grammatical Structure and the Immediate Recall of English Sentences," *Journal of Verbal Learning and Verbal Behavior* 4 (1965): 348-53.

16. Christopher Toth, "Revisiting a Genre: Teaching Infographics in Business and Professional Communication Courses," *Business and Professional Communication Quarterly* 76, no. 4 (2014): 446-57.

17. Thomas N. Huckin, "A Cognitive Approach to Readability," in *New Essays in Technical and Scientific Communication: Research, Theory, Practice,* eds. Paul V. Anderson, R. John Brockmann, and Carolyn R. Miller (Farmingdale, NY: Baywood, 1983), 93-98.

18. Doris Kearns Goodwin, *Team of Rivals: The Political Genius of Abraham Lincoln* (New York: Simon & Schuster, 2005), 583-87.

19. Dianna Booher, "Cutting Paperwork in the Corporate Culture," *New York: Facts on File Publications* (1986): 23.

20. Susan D. Kleimann, "The Complexity of Workplace Review," *Technical Communication* 38, no. 4 (1991): 520-26.

21. Glenn J. Broadhead and Richard C. Freed, *The Variables of Composition: Process and Product in a Business Setting,* Conference on College Composition and Communication Studies in Writing and Rhetoric (Carbondale, IL: Southern Illinois University Press, 1986), 57.

22. Larry Ballard, "Decipher a Honcho's Buzzwords, such as 'Unsiloing.'" *The Des Moines Register,* January 29, 2008.

CHAPTER

5 Communicating across Cultures

Chapter Outline

Cultural Awareness

Intercultural Competence

Global Agility
- Local Culture Adaptations
- Outsourcing and Offshoring
- International Career Experience

Diversity in the U.S. and Canada
- Beyond Stereotypes

Ways to Look at Culture

Values, Beliefs, and Practices

Global English

Nonverbal Communication across Cultures
- Listening
- Body Language
- Eye Contact
- Facial Expressions
- Gestures
- Proxemics
- Touch
- Time

Writing to International Audiences

Learning More about International Business Communication

Summary by Learning Objectives

DrAfter123/Getty Images

"McStakes" Were Made

Picture what a contemporary coffee shop looks like and you will likely imagine a glass storefront with light, bare wood; open beams; and living-room seating—a hip, cozy design made ubiquitous by Starbucks. This design has proved a winning model for Starbucks locations to flourish in local markets all over the world, even in places that did not have an existing coffee culture before Starbucks expanded there, such as China and South Korea. Why, then, was it nearly impossible for Starbucks to expand its locations within the well-established coffee culture of Australia? Why did Australians reject Starbucks stores at the same time they embraced coffeeshops that adopted the Starbucks design model? The answer is that those other shops don't carry the Starbucks corporate logo.

The Starbucks corporate brand has more than 31,000 locations, and over half are outside the United States. While this makes Starbucks a reassuring and comforting choice for many who instantly recognize its logo and associate it with a reliable, consistent coffeeshop experience, its ubiquity has an adverse effect on a population that prides itself on local flair and resourcefulness. It is not the quality of the coffee and not the amber-toned, modern design of the shops turning Aussies away: Sydney citizens want to shop locally, as in "the corner store," and not "the big-box store." Starbucks has a winning formula for opening shops

Justin Sullivan/Getty Images

on tens of thousands of corners, but it failed to adapt to local cultural trends that require a business to be agile and flexible in determining the aspects of its marketing plan to keep and in determining the most opportune times to branch out into diverse markets.

Given the attitude toward corporate brands on Sydney street corners, McDonald's and its McCafé brand would likely be met with the same skepticism and disdain. However, McDonald's learned from Starbucks' mistakes and found a solution.

Applying cultural analysis and global agility, McCafé reinvented and rebranded itself as "The Corner." This involved not just a name and menu change. The local markets demanded specific food and drink offerings, primarily healthier and fresher, but also required an agility with McDonald's long-standing image and brand promotion. The new McCafé locations are visually nothing like a typical "Mickey Ds" with its golden arches, bright colors, and McCoffee. The Corner closely follows the cozy Starbucks design model. The environment is made for leisure instead of fast food, and not one item on the entire menu carries the prefix "Mc." Because McDonald's paid attention to culture, The Corner has taken off where Starbucks failed.

Sources: Ashley Lutz, "Starbucks Was a Complete Failure in Australia," *Business Insider*, May 29, 2014, https://www.businessinsider.com.au/starbucks-closing-stores-in-australia-2014-5; and Daniel Palmer, "Starbucks: What Went Wrong?" *Australian Food News*, July 31, 2008, http://www.ausfoodnews.com.au/2008/07/31/starbucks-what-went-wrong.html.

Learning Objectives

After studying this chapter, you should be able to

LO 5-1 Explain why having cultural awareness and avoiding stereotypes is important.

LO 5-2 Explain why global agility in business is important.

LO 5-3 Explain why diversity is important.

LO 5-4 Explain how our values and beliefs affect our responses to other people.

LO 5-5 Discover how the global use of English affects business communication.

LO 5-6 Discover how to use nonverbal communication across cultures.

LO 5-7 Construct your written communication to meet the needs of global audiences.

Cultural Awareness

LO 5-1

Culture is a shared set of attitudes, beliefs, behaviors, and customs passed on and learned by the members of a community. This set of cultural practices becomes intuitive and habitual for anyone within the community and includes attitudes about the customary ways that people conduct business, trade, and commerce. Culture influences all of us—the ways we act, speak, think, behave, and even perceive the appearance and behaviors of others. The culture in which we grow up shapes our values, priorities, and practices. Understanding that others are shaped by their home culture and that no one culture is better than another is crucial if you want to be successful in this era of global business. Business in the 21st century means working with a diverse group of employees, working within a global supply chain, selling products to customers from diverse cultures in your country, selling to multiple countries outside your country's borders, managing an international plant or office, or working for a multinational company headquartered in another country.

A successful intercultural communicator is

- Aware of the values, beliefs, languages, and practices in their own culture.

- Sensitive to differences among individuals within their own culture.

- Aware of the values, beliefs, languages, and practices in other cultures.

- Aware that their preferred values and behaviors are not necessarily better or right.

- Interested in the cultures of others and willing to ask questions about preferences and behaviors.

- Flexible and open to adapting some of their own preferences and behaviors.

- Aware that English, as the most common language for business communication, is not the first language of the vast majority of people who speak English.

Intercultural Competence

The attributes of a successful intercultural communicator listed in the previous section are also best practices for any business communication. They are founded on the basic principles of good listening and speech skills, and they enhance all interactions. Dr. Janet Bennett of the Intercultural Communications Institute defines **intercultural competence** as "a set of cognitive, affective, and behavioral skills and characteristics that support effective and appropriate interaction in a variety of cultural contexts."[1] The first step to increasing intercultural competence is to realize that other people may do things differently than you do and that the difference is neither bad nor inferior.

Ethnocentrism is assuming one's own culture is the norm while judging different approaches and behaviors as nonstandard. Ethnocentrism is one of the dangers of lacking a multicultural, international perspective. The inability to see the world with greater neutrality and acceptance can lead to cross-cultural conflict. For example, many developing nations that were under colonial rule tend to carry the effects of colonialism into their current world view. The imposed language, institutions, and culture often lead to ethnocentrism and a perception of cultural superiority or exceptionalism.[2] Cultural attitudes develop over many generations, and historical events have current relevance when it comes to intercultural relations.

Being interested in differences among cultures is quite different from generalizing to the point of labeling and prejudging people based on **stereotypes**. Just as it is difficult to label yourself in broad terms without explaining your own nuances, it can be dangerous to do the same to others. For example, how many misconceptions might people make from your general labels—your nationality, your race, your gender, your age, your religion, your socioeconomic status, your major? How many ways do you fit the stereotypes associated with these labels? How wrong could people be about you and people you know if they relied on these labels to form judgments?

> **WARNING:** When pushed too far, the kinds of differences discussed in this chapter can turn into stereotypes, which can be just as damaging as ignorance.

Psychologists have shown that stereotypes have serious consequences and that they come into play even when we don't intend. Studies show that biases people hold toward established stereotypes not only create prejudice toward others, but also adversely affect the people holding the biases. Asking African American students to identify their race before they answered questions taken from the standardized test used for admission to graduate schools cut in half the number of items those students got right. Similarly, asking students to identify their biological sex at the beginning of Advanced Placement (AP) calculus tests lowered the scores of females but not males. If the sex question had been moved to the end of the test, about 5% more females would have received AP credit.[3]

Global Agility

LO 5-2

When people talk about global business communication, they usually focus on differences. In *Global Dexterity*, Andy Molinsky points out that it is unrealistic to expect anyone to memorize the wide variety of cultural differences across situations, contexts, and cultures and even more preposterous to think that we could successfully mimic cultural particularities that are so different from our own.[4] To be culturally aware and globally agile, we must learn about the way our own culture creates our sensitivities and preferences. We also must learn about other cultural preferences in order to increase our communicative flexibility. **Global agility**, then, is not a process of sterilizing our own identity or mimicking that of others; rather, it is a willingness to relax our customary procedures and allow for new ways of interacting in order to achieve our communicative purposes. Gaining a global perspective is what is required in the current business environment where monoculturalism is a thing of the past. Jack Welch, the former CEO of General Motors, addressed his employees on this topic saying, "The future Jack Welch cannot be like me. I spent my entire career in the United States. The next head of General Electric will be somebody who spent time in Bombay, in Hong Kong, in Buenos Aires."[5]

Local Culture Adaptations

The case at the beginning of this chapter, "McStakes Were Made," demonstrates how U.S. retailers are catering to local tastes and customs. Movie studios, for instance, are turning down scripts that would play well in the United States because they would not play well abroad. Such decisions are seen as sound, given that foreign ticket sales now comprise two-thirds of the global film market. Studios are hiring more foreign actors for blockbusters and rewriting scripts for international audiences.[6] The challenge facing business is understanding how cultural differences influence market demand for products or services. The need a business addresses at home may already be met or not exist at all overseas. Agility without cultural awareness means that important details can create major problems down the line. Language and poor translations across languages can create confusion and, worse, misconceptions and loss of brand reputation. Famously, the very popular Chevrolet Nova was marketed in Mexico without a name change, but "no va" means "no go" in Spanish. Chevrolet found itself at the wrong end of many jokes before realizing its costly blindspot to local culture.[7] Figure 5.1 shows some local adaptations McDonald's makes across the globe.

Many large companies have learned about the benefits of cultural agility. When expanding to China, Walmart enraged consumers when its stores sold dead fish and packaged meat, which shoppers saw as old merchandise. Walmart quickly learned to compensate by leaving meat uncovered and installing fish tanks to sell live fish. Johnson's Baby Oil is stocked next to moisturizers containing sheep placenta, a native wrinkle "cure." Stores lure customers on foot or bikes with free shuttle buses and home deliveries for large items. Perhaps the biggest change is Walmart's acceptance of organized labor in China; in July 2006, it accepted its first union ever into its stores.

Other companies adapt their products to local preferences. Yum Brands, one of the most successful companies operating in China, serves fried shrimp and egg tarts at its KFC (formerly Kentucky Fried Chicken) stores, and it serves Thai fried rice and seafood pizza at its Pizza Huts. In the same market, Kraft Foods is offering spicy-chicken Ritz crackers, lobster cheese, and lemon-tea potato chips. In India, Dunkin' Donuts is offering mango doughnuts and smoothies.[8] Burger King sells a burger with squid-ink-flavored catsup in Japan, where McDonald's sells a pie filled with mashed potatoes and bacon.[9]

KFC achieved a marketing coup in Japan by suggesting that traditional American Christmas dinners should center on fried chicken. The campaign was so successful that Christmas takeout meals from KFC now must be reserved well in advance of the holiday. Signs in storefronts tell customers how many reservations are still available. Statues of Colonel Sanders often are dressed in kimonos or costumes for photo opportunities outside KFC stores.[10]

The costs for failing to adapt to local cultures can be high. AlertDriving, a Toronto company that provides driver training, opened its services in more than 20 countries before it became aware of problems. The driving lessons had been poorly translated and the instructions did not fit with local laws and customs. To make matters worse, the company did not learn about some of the problems for years because some clients considered criticism disrespectful. Eventually AlertDriving had to spend a million dollars to retranslate and rework all of its materials for local cultures, a costly lesson in cultural awareness.[11]

Figure 5.1 McDonald's Products around the World

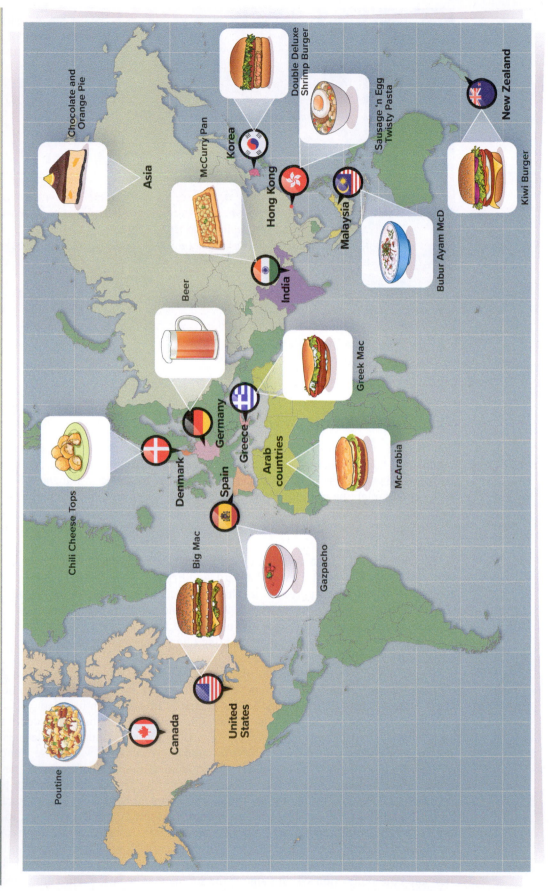

Source: Adapted from Just the Flight (2016). "Brands with Different Names Around the World, https://www.justtheflight.co.uk/blog/28-brands-with-different-names-around-the-world.html.

KFC has adapted to fit the culture of Japan.

Quality Stock Arts/Shutterstock

Outsourcing and Offshoring

Another major aspect of global business is **outsourcing**, sending corporate work to other companies, and **offshoring**, opening whole operational facilities in other countries. In the past, this work was lower level: garment factories might be in Bangladesh; call or help centers might be in India. Now, more companies also are outsourcing higher-level work such as research and accounting.[12] And even outsourcing leaders, such as Tata Consultancy Services of India, are outsourcing; that company has hired thousands of employees in South America.[13]

Outsourcing also has moved from Near East countries to eastern Europe and South America. IBM, Microsoft, Hewlett-Packard, and Ernst & Young all have opened offices in Poland, where they appreciate the highly educated and multilingual young work-force.[14] These arrangements are meant to match demand for specific work skills and resources with available workforce and convenient logistics. However, operational systems that function well in one cultural setting often require awareness and agility to be successful in another.

Toyota has long been a model for success in taking advantage of outsourcing. About 70% of Toyota manufacturing is done outside of Japan, including large operations in the United States.[15] Toyota's success lies primarily in managing its relations with its suppliers by investing tremendous resources in communications and accountability structures. It maintains a tight hold on its quality control standards while nurturing the communications necessary for diverse suppliers to comply with those standards. Boeing tried to capitalize on outsourcing for its innovative design of the brand new 787 model, but the company only superficially followed the Toyota model for face-to-face communications. It relied instead on an electronic data-exchange tool for monitoring its supply chain and for integrating business processes. Boeing expected each user to input the same type of information with the same emphasis on timeliness and accuracy that its home plant used. Unfortunately, this tool was met with varying degrees of mistrust and misunderstanding because it did not provide a way to mediate the diverse information and communication systems among the suppliers. The lack of any communication bridge across widely diverse standards caused the entire supply chain to be severely compromised. Outsourcing was projected to save Boeing $4 billion. Instead, the set-backs caused billions in cost overruns and several years of lost time.

International Career Experience

Most major businesses operate globally, and an increasing share of profits comes from outside the headquarters country. Even small businesses often have global supply chains. When plants, stores, clients, and offices move overseas, people fol-low—from top executives to migrant workers. In fact, managers often find they need international experience if they want top-level jobs. Expatriate experience also has been shown to make them more creative and better problem solvers.[16] This effect, combined with booming overseas growth, means that executive headhunters are looking for people with deep bicultural fluency or experience in several countries, with China, India, and Brazil at the top of the list.[17] Responding to the need for global experience, business schools are stepping up their international offerings with classes, international case studies, overseas campuses, and student/faculty exchanges. For both young and experienced hires, second-language proficiency and multicultural awareness are sought.[18]

Migrant workers benefit the economies of both host and home countries. The money sent home by migrants, more than $554 billion in 2019, is three times the world's total foreign aid. Even during the COVID-19 pandemic, the 270 million people working away from their home countries continued to send money home—in some cases in record amounts.[19]

Thomas Friedman, Pulitzer Prize author and *New York Times* columnist, uses the metaphor of a flat world to describe the increasing globalization. In *The World Is Flat: A Brief History of the Twenty-First Century*, he says:

> What the flattening of the world means is that we are now connecting all the knowledge centers on the planet together into a single global network, which—if politics and terrorism do not get in the way—could usher in an amazing era of prosperity, innovation, and collabora-tion, by companies, communities, and individuals.[20]

Diversity in the U.S. and Canada

LO 5-3

Even if you stay in the U.S. or Canada, you'll work with people whose backgrounds dif-fer from yours. Residents of small towns and rural areas may have different notions of friendliness than do people from big cities. Californians may talk and dress differently than people in the Midwest. The cultural icons that resonate for Baby Boomers may mean little to Millennials. For many workers, local diversity has become as important as international diversity.

The past two decades have seen a growing emphasis on diversity. This diversity comes from many sources:

- Gender
- Race and ethnicity
- Regional and national origin
- Social class
- Religion
- Age
- Sexual orientation
- Physical ability

Many young Americans are already multicultural. According to 2018 U.S. census estimates, only 49.9% of Americans under 15 are non-Hispanic whites.[21] Some of them are immigrants or descendants of immigrants. In 2019, the largest numbers of immigrants to the U.S. have come from Mexico, China, India, and the Philippines.[22]

In 2002, Latinos became the largest minority group in the United States. The U.S. Census Bureau predicts that by 2042, the non-Hispanic white population will be less than 50% of the country's total population.[23] A comparable estimate from the Pew Research Center predicts the change will occur by 2050.[24] Already, California, the District of Columbia, Hawaii, New Mexico, and Texas have a population that is more than 50% minorities; the Census Bureau labels these states as having a "majority-minority" population.[25]

Bilingual Canada has long compared the diversity of its people to a mosaic. But now immigrants from Italy, China, and the Middle East add their voices to the medley of French, English, and Inuit. CHIN Radio in Toronto offers information in more than 30 languages.[26]

According to 2010 U.S. census figures, about 9 million people identified themselves as belonging to two or more races.[27] In 2018, 63.7% of Americans spoke a language other than English at home; in nine states, one in four people did.[28] In cities such as Los Angeles and San Jose, over half the population speaks a language other than English at home (60.5% and 55.0%, respectively).[29]

Faced with these figures, organizations are making special efforts to diversify their workforces. Microsoft, for instance, has 40 employee networks; in addition to various nationality and regional groups such as Arabs, Brazilians, and ex-Yugoslavians, they cover various family roles (e.g., working parents), abilities (e.g., people with visual impairments), age groups (e.g., Baby Boomers), and backgrounds (e.g., U.S. military veterans). The groups help provide a sense of community and also provide resources for recruiting and training.[30]

Diversified companies are smart; new evidence shows that diversity can improve business. Research analyzing the relationship between diversity levels and business performance of 250 U.S. businesses found a correlation between diversity and business success; companies with high levels of racial and ethnic minorities have the highest profits, market shares, and number of customers. On the other hand, organizations with low levels of diversity have the lowest profits, market shares, and number of customers.[31] When the Supreme Court heard arguments on considering race as a factor in admissions at the University of Texas, 57 companies—including Aetna, Dow Chemical, General Electric, Microsoft, Procter & Gamble, and Walmart—filed a brief arguing that a diverse workforce helps profits.[32]

Beyond Stereotypes

Learning about different cultures is important for understanding the different kinds of people we work with. However, leadership coaches Keith Caver and Ancella Livers caution that people are individuals, not just representatives of a cultural group.[33] Based on their work with African American executives and middle managers, Caver and Livers have found that coworkers sometimes treat these individuals first as representatives of African American culture and only second as talented and experienced managers.

As an example, Caver and Livers cite the all-too-common situation of a newly hired Black manager who participates in a management development activity. The new manager is prepared to answer questions about her area of business expertise, but the only questions directed toward her are about diversity and inclusion issues. African American clients of Caver and Livers have complained that they often are called upon to interpret the behavior of famous Black Americans such as Clarence Thomas or Jesse Jackson, and they wonder whether their white colleagues would feel their race qualifies them to interpret the deeds of famous white Americans.

In this example, stereotypes make well-intentioned efforts at communication offensive. Even in less direct interactions involving diverse points of view, our unconscious stereotypes often cause inadvertent biases and prejudices. To avoid such biases, treat people as individuals. Look at the current qualities they present to the current context, understand their role in the business environment, and respect their experiences as unique to them, even though the experiences may include some of their particular cultural perspectives.[34] Embracing inclusion does not mean pretending to be colorblind in a society that is and always has been racialized.[35] Nor does it mean that cultural factors do not have any bearing on how we think and feel. Embracing diversity and inclusion means acknowledging difference in experience without judging the value or the merit of individuals who have different backgrounds. It also means never asking anyone to represent an entire group or expecting that one person's perspective is representative of anything more than that person's individual experience. In other words, avoid gross generalizations.[36]

Ways to Look at Culture

Each of us grows up in a culture that provides patterns of acceptable behavior and belief. We may not be aware of the most basic features of our own culture until we come into contact with people who do things differently. For example, in India, children might be expected to touch the bare feet of elders to show respect, but in the U.S., such touching would be inappropriate.[37] Crossing a leg when sitting may seem natural to most Westerners, but in many cultures raising a foot toward another is extremely rude.

These patterns can be difficult and dangerous to ascribe by nationality, yet there are efforts to categorize them in broader terms. Anthropologist Edward Hall first categorized cultures as high-context or low-context, categories that remain popular in the business milieu although no longer in vogue in anthropology. In **high-context cultures**, most of the information is inferred from the social relationships of the people and the context of a message; little is explicitly conveyed. Chinese, Japanese, Arabic, and Latin American cultures are considered high-context. In **low-context cultures**, context is less important; most information is explicitly spelled out. German, Scandinavian, and Canadian cultures are low-context.

High- and low-context cultures value oral and written communication differently and have different attitudes toward directness and indirectness. As Figure 5.2 shows, low-context cultures like those of the U.S. see the written word as more important than oral statements, so contracts are binding but promises may be broken. Low-context cultures favor direct approaches. For example, many Americans appreciate the time-saving concision of direct, explicit statements. If they receive an email that starts with, "I'd like you to send me the data from the report," they might respond by sending the data. A recipient of that same message in Saudi Arabia or Spain might feel offended. The request does not include

Figure 5.2	Views of Communication in High- and Low-Context Cultures	
	High-context (examples: Japan, Saudi Arabia)	**Low-context (examples: Germany, U.S.)**
Preferred communication strategy	Indirectness, politeness, ambiguity	Directness, confrontation, clarity
Reliance on words to communicate	Low	High
Reliance on nonverbal signs to communicate	High	Low
Importance of relationships	High	Low
Importance of written word	Low	High
Agreements made in writing	Not binding	Binding
Agreements made orally	Binding	Not binding
Attention to detail	Low	High

a greeting asking about the recipient's family nor does it mention how nicely the project or deal is progressing. In addition, the request uses the direct second-person pronoun "you" and lacks hedging language such as "would it be possible . . . ." The gap in cultures' preferences for directness or indirectness generates misunderstandings, but perhaps more important, it can damage relationships and respect.[38]

Another way of looking at cultures is by using Geert Hofstede's cultural dimensions. Based on data collected by IBM, Hofstede's six dimensions are

- Power/inequality
- Individualism/collectivism
- Masculinity/femininity
- Uncertainty avoidance
- Long-term/short-term orientation
- Indulgence/restraint[39]

These dimensions have been applied to 74 countries and regions to produce a generalized snapshot of cultural preferences. To illustrate, Hofstede analyzes the U.S. as extremely high in individualism, but also high in "masculinity," by which Hofstede meant that men dominate a significant portion of the power structure. It ranks low in the power-distance index, indicating more equality at all social levels, and low in the uncertainty avoidance index, meaning it has fewer rules and greater tolerance for a variety of ideas and beliefs than do many countries.[40] Understanding that these preferences are on a continuum and neither extreme is bad nor good can help you to analyze yourself and others for greater understanding when you find yourself with an opposing preference from one of your colleagues, clients, bosses, contractors, or employees.

The preceding framework focuses on national and regional cultures. But diversity in business communication also is influenced by the organizational culture and by personal culture, such as gender, race and ethnicity, social class, and so forth. As Figure 5.3 suggests, all of these intersect to determine what kind of communication is needed in a given situation. This is where diversity is an asset in any workforce as it brings a breadth of perspectives and styles to business communication that could be limited and one-dimensional without it. Sometimes, one kind of culture may be more important than another for finding common ground. For example, in a study of aerospace engineers in Europe, Asia, and the U.S., researchers found that the similarities of the professional discourse community outweighed differences in national cultures.[41]

Figure 5.3   Overlap in the Dimensions of Diversity: National Culture, Organizational Culture, and Personal Culture

Values, Beliefs, and Practices

Values, often unconsciously formed within our cultural experience, affect our response to people and situations. Most Americans, for example, will say they value "fairness." "You're not playing fair" is a sharp criticism calling for changed behavior. However, even the term "fair" carries a meaning or connotation that is culture-bound. Fairness in some contexts could mean that certain groups receive treatment that is divergent from that of other groups but is still in accordance with the established expectations for fairness in that culture. Children, elders, men, women, workers, bosses, and even animals can be treated differently, but that does not mean they are treated "unfairly." This is one example of the way a different cultural practice can be misunderstood as a major difference in "value" when, in fact, it is the context that creates the difference. It also shows how values shape our instincts and choices and can lead us to make value judgments of others if we fail to refrain from evaluating the differences as right or wrong, good or bad.[42]

Belief systems and traditions also affect business communication and business life. Religion often can influence the calendar or even the daily schedule of some businesses. For example, most practicing Muslims, Jews, and Christians observe days of rest and prayer on Friday, Saturday, and Sunday, respectively. During the holy month of Ramadan, Muslims fast from sunup to sundown; scheduling a business luncheon with a Muslim colleague during Ramadan would be inappropriate. Christian observances tend to dominate the vacation and holiday schedules in most Western countries, whereas they are not necessarily significant dates in other parts of the world. Many Asian countries celebrate the lunar new year by reuniting with their families, making it an extremely busy travel time when businesses should expect people to be away. No serious business-person should be ignorant of the main holidays and traditions of people in the country or culture they are communicating with.[43]

Even everyday practices differ from culture to culture. North Americans and Europeans put the family name last; Asians put it first. North American and European printing moves from left to right; Arabic reads from right to left. In the U.S., a meeting on the fourth floor is actually on the fourth floor; in England, it is actually on the fifth floor of the building because the British distinguish between ground and first floors. In China, the building may not have a fourth floor because the word for *four* sounds like the word for *death*, so the number is considered unlucky.[44]

Food practices can lead to interesting business meals, with a variety of ways for serving and eating and a range of unfamiliar delicacies. In some cultures, turning down or refusing offers of food can be taken as a slight offense. You always should do your research about the culture where you will be interacting and be prepared to try something new. In China, as the guest of honor, you might be served the feet of the chicken, which is the most highly prized part, second only to the neck. You might be offered kidney pie in England, snails in France, durian in Indonesia, grasshoppers in Mexico, sheep's head in Saudi Arabia, and haggis in Scotland. Although these may seem unappetizing, remember that eating something you do not prefer will not kill you, and it is best to eat what you are offered as long as it does not violate your beliefs. Remember that consumption of pork would horrify many Muslims, while consumption of beef would disgust many Indians.[45]

Common business practices also differ among cultures (see Figure 5.4 for examples of different business etiquette practices). In Middle Eastern—or predominantly Muslim—countries, business cards are exchanged only with the right hand, never with the "unclean" left hand. Cards should not be kept or put in a pigskin case; in India, avoid leather cases. In China and other places where business cards are exchanged with both hands, the recipient is expected to read both sides carefully and compliment the information and even ask specific questions about the giver's title or company. These also

Figure 5.4 Business Etiquette around the World

Business meetings

	Is small talk common before a meeting dives into official business?			Do participants stick to the meeting's agenda?		Is a direct or indirect communication style used?	
	Yes	Minimal	No	Yes	No	Direct	Indirect
Brazil	Yes				No	Direct	
Canada			No		No		Indirect
USA		Minimal			No		Indirect
Denmark		Minimal		Yes			Indirect
France			No	Yes		Direct	
Germany		Minimal		Yes		Direct	
Ireland		Minimal		Yes		Direct	
Russia			No		No		Indirect
Spain	Yes				No		Indirect
Sweden		Minimal		Yes		Direct	
Switzerland			No	Yes		Direct	
UK		Minimal		Yes		Direct	
Israel	Yes				No	Direct	
UAE	Yes				No		Indirect
Australia		Minimal		Yes		Direct	
Hong Kong	Yes			Yes			Indirect
India	Yes				No		Indirect
Japan	Yes			Yes			Indirect
New Zealand		Minimal		Yes		Direct	
Singapore			No		No		Indirect
South Korea	Yes				No		Indirect
Taiwan	Yes				No		Indirect

Source: Adapted from CT Business Travel, "Business Etiquette around the World," 2015, http://www.ctbusinesstravel.co.uk/news/blog/business-etiquette-around-the-world.

should be put in a card case. In Russia, where hierarchy is important, cards should show your status by including items such as your title and the founding date of your company. In India, where education is specially valued, your card might show your graduate degrees.[46]

In today's electronically connected world, cultural practices can change swiftly. In such fluid contexts, doing research before engaging in communications becomes even more important. If you don't know and can't find out, asking about another's culture is a great way to establish rapport and build relationships, as long as it is done with open-minded and earnest curiosity, respect, and sensitivity.

Global English

LO 5-5

English continues to evolve to reflect the diversity of its users. The changes are not errors but are part of the natural processes involved in the spread of language.[47] English has transformed from a national language to a **lingua franca**—a common language used among speakers of other languages. In *English as a Global Language*, David Crystal explains that English brings a global scope of possible usage, including accent, dialect, and new words. English as a global language has become a standard language for international negotiations.[48]

Some monolingual English speakers meet the prevalence of English with complacency. It is easy to become lazy about making efforts to learn about the languages and cultures of clients, partners, employees, or even employers. Indeed, only 10% of native-born Americans can speak a second language, compared to 56% of European Union citizens. It is even easier to fail to make adjustments in usage that would improve clarity and communications across cultures, such as avoiding idiomatic expressions and culture-specific references.[49]

In 1958, William Lederer and Eugene Burdick published *The Ugly American*, a humorous acknowledgment of how the American tourist is seen abroad: self-centered, overconfident, loud, and expecting the world to speak English. (See Figure 5.5 for an illustration of the world's languages in terms of the number of people who speak them as a native language.)

Sixty years later, the "Ugly American"—or, more broadly, the "Ugly English Speaker"—still exists. Dorie Clark, a marketing strategist, career consultant, and widely published author on successful business messaging, provides advice on avoiding this narrow attitude and expanding one's intercultural competency:

- **Learn some language basics.** Find an online language source or get a handy phrasebook and learn at least place names, greetings and farewells, and *please*, *thank you*, and *excuse me*. Also know the written system so that you can read signs and menus. Make an effort to work on pronunciation—practice it.[50]

- **Learn about the culture and history.** Again, online sources are abundant, but you also should talk to others who are from the region or who have been there. Don't go to India without knowing about main symbols and tenets of Hindu and Muslim religions, or to China without knowing about the building of the Great Wall, or to Mexico without knowing the great accomplishments of the Incas and Aztecs. Also, do not travel to these places thinking their antiquities are who and what they are now. Imagine the frustration of contemporary Egyptians as they explain again and again that the cosmopolitan, modern city of Giza is not just pyramids and Pharaohs in a wide-open desert. Clark also points out that, along with only Liberia and Myanmar, the U.S. does not use the metric system. Learn the basics of the metric system.[51]

- **Learn about basics of oral conversation.** Cultures differ greatly in how they approach oral communication. Is it polite to start a conversation with a stranger? Is it acceptable to praise coworkers? Figure 5.6 delineates some cultural contrasts in oral communication.

Figure 5.5   A World of Languages

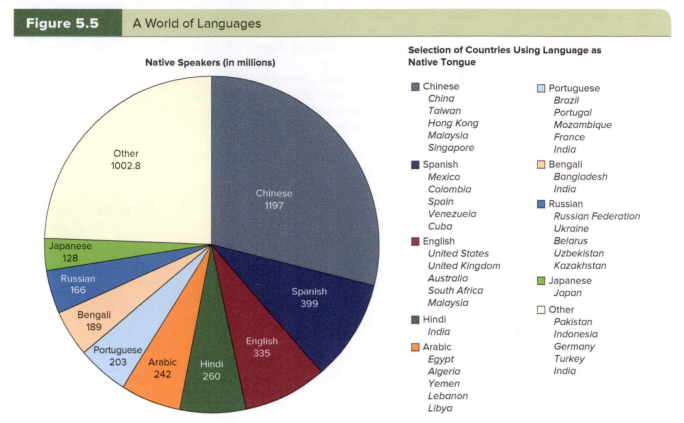

Native Speakers (in millions)

- Chinese 1197
- Spanish 399
- English 335
- Hindi 260
- Arabic 242
- Portuguese 203
- Bengali 189
- Russian 166
- Japanese 128
- Other 1002.8

Selection of Countries Using Language as Native Tongue

- ■ Chinese
  - China
  - Taiwan
  - Hong Kong
  - Malaysia
  - Singapore
- ■ Spanish
  - Mexico
  - Colombia
  - Spain
  - Venezuela
  - Cuba
- ■ English
  - United States
  - United Kingdom
  - Australia
  - South Africa
  - Malaysia
- ■ Hindi
  - India
- ■ Arabic
  - Egypt
  - Algeria
  - Yemen
  - Lebanon
  - Libya
- □ Portuguese
  - Brazil
  - Portugal
  - Mozambique
  - France
  - India
- □ Bengali
  - Bangladesh
  - India
- ■ Russian
  - Russian Federation
  - Ukraine
  - Belarus
  - Uzbekistan
  - Kazakhstan
- ■ Japanese
  - Japan
- □ Other
  - Pakistan
  - Indonesia
  - Germany
  - Turkey
  - India

Source: Adapted from *South China Morning Post,* "A World of Languages—and How Many Speak Them," 2015, http://www.scmp.com/infographics/article/1810040/infographic-world-languages.

Figure 5.6   Cultural Contrasts in Oral Communication

	United States	Europe	Asia
Opening a conversation	Take the initiative	England: take the initiative	Japan: wait for an invitation to speak
Interrupting	Wait until speaker finishes	Italy: interruptions common; more than one person may speak at once	Japan: do not interrupt; silent periods common
Vocal characteristics	Modulated pace and volume	Spaniards may speak louder than the French	Indians speak English much faster than Americans
Disagreements	Often stated calmly and directly	Spain: Often stated strongly and forcefully	Japan: Often communicated with silence
Praise	Key motivational factor	Russia: saved for extraordinary behavior, otherwise seen as false	Indonesia: may be offensive (suggests supervisor surprised by good job)

Source: Adapted from Richard M. Steers, Carlos J. Sanchez-Runde, and Luciara Nardon, *Management across Cultures: Challenges and Strategies* (New York: Cambridge University Press, 2010), 222–23.

Conversely, other populations throughout the world are not just mastering English: they are mastering the ability to provide labor forces, resources, ingenuity, job skills, and locations where the lack of a common language is no longer a barrier, and they can use English to bridge transactions with native and non-native speakers of English alike.

Indeed, English is becoming the common language of multinational corporations even when the communications are within the company's home country and between native users of another shared language. Airbus, Daimler-Chrysler, Nokia, Aventis, Renault, Samsung, SAP, Technicolor, and Microsoft in Beijing are among many who have instituted an English language policy.[52]

One example of why the shift to a shared language is important has to do with employee and operational safety. All mining is dangerous, but platinum mining is particularly so because the mineral is frequently a mile below the surface and in very hard rock. Implementing safety procedures and precautions at Anglo American Platinum's mines in South Africa meant offering English and Afrikaans classes and encouraging all miners, who come from various countries and tribes, to learn one of the two languages.[53] While the need for English to serve as a unifying and simplifying operational tool is real, this transactional form of use does not mean that populations should dispense with their primary languages or that native English populations should dispense with respecting, honoring, and even learning those languages.

Nonverbal Communication across Cultures

LO 5-6

Verbal communication provides information. **Nonverbal communication** adds the "flavor"—attitude, emphasis, and emotion. Both are critical to successful communication across cultures.

Listening

Successful professionals communicate well with different categories of people—coworkers, bosses, clients—among a variety of setting and cultures—institutional, corporate, national, international. To do so, they cultivate skills in listening. To reduce listening errors caused by cultural gaps and misinterpretation,

- During the conversation, paraphrase what the speaker has said, giving them a chance to correct your understanding. Take responsibility for any gaps in understanding.

- At the end of the conversation, check your understanding with the other person. Especially check the actionable items such as who does what next.

- After the conversation, write down key points that affect deadlines or the ways the work will be evaluated. Sometimes these key points need to be confirmed in an email as the transfer from spoken to written language also can shift the interpretation.

- Don't ignore instructions or details that you think are unnecessary. Check to see if there are reasons for them before you use your own intuitions about the necessity. Be careful not to apply your own priorities or preferences to the message.

- Consider the other person's background and experiences but avoid applying stereotypes. What are some of the cultural hallmarks, priorities, and preferences that might shape their needs?

Listening to people is an indication that you're taking them seriously. Acknowledgment responses—nods, *uh-huhs*, smiles, frowns—help carry the message that you're listening. However, remember that listening responses vary in different cultures, including the amount and the direction of head shaking and eye contact. For example, in Balkan countries, both the speed and the direction of head movements can indicate a range of disagreement, and people from India and Pakistan indicate listening with a side-to-side head bobbing that often goes misunderstood by Westerners, who associate head shaking with a negative response.

Body Language

Just as verbal languages differ, body language differs from culture to culture. The Japanese value the ability to sit quietly. They may see the U.S. tendency to fidget and shift as an indication of lack of mental or spiritual balance. Even in North America, interviewers and audiences usually respond negatively to gestures such as fidgeting with a tie, hair, or jewelry; tapping a pencil; or swinging a foot.

People use body language to signal such traits as interest, respect, emotional involvement, confidence, and agreement. Among Arab men, for instance, holding hands is an expression of affection and solidarity. Americans working in the Middle East are cautioned to avoid pointing their finger at people or showing the soles of their feet when seated.[54] Bill Gates made international news when he greeted the president of South Korea by shaking her hand with one hand and keeping his other hand in his pocket (a sign of disrespect in South Korea). Consider that spoken and written languages use symbols that stand for meaning in the same way that gestures are symbols that stand for meaning in a different "language." Thus, the gesture common to you can mean a very different thing to someone from another culture; for example, nodding your head may mean affirmative to you but can signify disagreement for Greeks and Bulgarians.[55] Figure 5.7 shows a few gestures that convey different meanings in different cultural contexts. Your concern should be to use your body as carefully as you use your language for different audiences.

Eye Contact

Most Americans see eye contact as a sign of attention; in fact, to many Americans, lack of eye contact is slightly suspect. But in many cultures, dropped eyes are a sign of appropriate deference to a superior. Japanese show respect by lowering their eyes when speaking to superiors. In some Latin American and African cultures, such as Nigeria, it is disrespectful for lower-status people to engage in prolonged eye contact with their superiors. Similarly, in the U.S., staring is considered rude. For the English, however, polite people pay strict attention to speakers and blink their eyes to show understanding. In China, a widening of the eyes shows anger, but in the U.S. it shows surprise. Among Arab men, eye contact is important; it is considered impolite not to face someone directly.[56] In Muslim countries, women and men are not supposed to have eye contact.

These differences can lead to miscommunication in the multicultural workplace. Superiors may feel that subordinates are being disrespectful when the subordinates are being fully respectful—according to the norms of their culture.

Facial Expressions

The frequency of smiling and the way people interpret smiles may depend on the purpose smiles serve in a particular culture. In the U.S., smiling varies from region to region. In Germany, Sweden, and the "less-smiley" U.S. cultures, smiling is more likely to be reserved for close relationships and genuine joy. Frequent smiles in other situations, therefore, would seem insincere. For other people, including those in Thailand, smiling can be a way to create harmony and make situations pleasant.

Research has shown that when they are interpreting emotions, Americans focus on the mouth, so smiles are important. Japanese often focus on the eyes. This distinction is apparent even in their emoticons. Americans use :) for a happy face and :(for a sad one; Japanese use ^^ for a happy face and ;_; for a sad one.[57]

Gestures

U.S. citizens sometimes assume that they can depend on gestures to communicate if language fails. But the meanings of gestures vary widely in different cultures. Kissing is

Figure 5.7 Gestures and Body Language Variations

BODY LANGUAGE
AROUND THE WORLD

HEAD

In most places,
nodding signals agreement,
with the exception of
Bulgaria and Greece,
where nodding signals "no."

EYES

In the West and in Arab countries,
eye contact is expected, but
in Finland and Japan,
eye contact can make people
uncomfortable.

LIPS

In some cultures,
including Native American and
Latin American cultures,
people use their lips to point.

HANDS

The American gesture for "come over here" signals "goodbye"
in Italy.

The American gesture for goodbye conveys "no" in Latin America
and some parts of Europe.

In Malaysia, individuals point with their thumbs. Pointing with
an index finger is taboo. The "thumbs up" gesture is rude in
Islamic countries, but it is widely used in Brazil. It signals "1" in France.

Source: Adapted from Hult International Business School, "11 Biggest Challenges of International Business in 2017," 2017, http://www.hult.edu/blog
/international-business-challenges.

usually an affection gesture in the U.S. but is a greeting gesture in other countries. In Greece, people may nod their heads to signify *no* and shake their heads to signify *yes*.[58]

Gestures that mean approval in the United States may have very different meanings in other countries. The "thumbs up" sign, which means "good work" or "go ahead" in the U.S. and most of western Europe, is a vulgar insult in Iraq, Iran, and Bangladesh. The circle formed with the thumb and first finger that means *okay* in the U.S. is obscene in Brazil and Germany. In India, the raised middle finger means you need to urinate.[59]

The V-sign is another gesture with multiple meanings. Made with the palm facing out, it was famously used by Churchill during World War II and by the hippies in the 1960s and 1970s. Made with the palm facing in, it is the equivalent of giving someone the finger in countries such as the United Kingdom, Ireland, and Australia. An American president made interesting headlines when he inadvertently used the V-sign on a visit to Australia.[60]

Learning all the appropriate and inappropriate gestures can be confusing, especially when there are regional and local variations, so a good practice is to neutralize many of your customary gestures and use clear words or signs instead.

Here is a list of gesture types to consider modifying:[61]

- Curled finger: Beckoning someone to "come here" by curling your finger should never be done outside the U.S. and Canada. In some places it has very hostile or aggressive meanings.

- Waving: Waving the entire arm should be avoided, although many places are okay with a mild, open, hand wave.

- "Okay" gesture: Placing finger and thumb in an "O" shape to indicate approval is not universal and, in some places, has unintended meanings.

- Thumbs up: Be very careful when using the thumb as a signal; do your homework to find out before you do. A nod and smile works very well to show approval.

With all of these and more, when in doubt, leave it out. Your efforts to increase communication with gestures just might instead cause a misunderstanding.

Proxemics

Proxemics refers to the distance people want between themselves and other people in ordinary, nonintimate interchanges. Some research shows that many Americans, Canadians, North Europeans, and Asians want a larger personal space than do many Latin Americans, French, Italians, and Arabs. Even people who prefer lots of personal space often are forced to accept close contact on a crowded elevator or subway or in a small conference room.

Even within a culture, some people like more personal space than do others. In many cultures, people who are of the same age and gender take less personal space than do mixed-age or mixed-gender groups.

Touch

Some people are more comfortable with touch than others. Each kind of person may misinterpret the other. A person who dislikes touch may seem unfriendly to someone who's used to touching. A toucher may seem overly familiar to someone who dislikes touch.

In U.S. business settings, people generally shake hands when they meet, but little other touching is considered appropriate. In Mexico, greetings may involve greater physical contact. Men may embrace one another, and women may kiss one another. In many European settings, business colleagues may shake hands when they encounter one another throughout the day. In countries along the Mediterranean, hugs and shoulder pats are common as well. In some European countries, greetings include light kisses. The typical pattern is to kiss the person's right cheek and then the left (or, more accurately, to kiss the air near the cheek). In Italy, this pattern stops with two kisses; Belgians may continue for three and the French for four.[62]

Time

Differences in time zones complicate international phone calls and videoconferences. But even more important are different views of time and attitudes toward time. Offices in the U.S. keep track of precise time by the calendar and the clock. Being "on time" is seen as a sign of dependability, and multiple transactions pivot on the appointed time of execution. Other cultures may view time schedules and time frames as desired or projected possibilities but operate with greater flexibility.

Americans who believe that "time is money" often are frustrated in negotiations with people who take a much more leisurely approach. Part of the problem is that people in many other cultures want to establish a personal relationship before they decide whether to do business with each other. They will take several meetings or phone calls simply to establish a baseline for the relationship, which is very important and worth investing the time for them, while the American will feel like they are just "wasting time."

The problem is made worse because various cultures mentally measure time differently. Many North Americans measure time in five-minute blocks. Someone who's five minutes late to an appointment or a job interview feels compelled to apologize. If the executive or interviewer is running half an hour late, the caller expects to be told about the likely delay upon arriving. Some people won't be able to wait that long and will need to reschedule their appointments. But in other cultures, half an hour may be the smallest block of time. To someone who mentally measures time in 30-minute blocks, being 45 minutes late is no worse than being 10 minutes late to someone who measures time in smaller units.

Different cultures have different lead times for scheduling events. In some countries, you need to schedule important meetings at least two weeks in advance. In other countries, people are not booked up so far in advance, and a date two weeks into the future may be forgotten.

Anthropologist Edward Hall distinguishes between **monochronic cultures**, which focus on clock time, and **polychronic cultures**, which focus on relationships. People in monochronic cultures tend to schedule their time and do one task at a time; people in polychronic cultures tend to want their time unstructured and do multiple tasks at the same time. For example, when a U.S. manager feels offended because a Latin American manager also sees other people during "their" appointments, the two kinds of time are in conflict.[63]

Writing to International Audiences

LO 5-7

Cultural preferences are also important in written documents. Germans, for instance, have a reputation for appreciating technical data and scientific detail. They are likely to be intolerant of claims that seem logically unsupportable. An American writing for a German audience should ensure that any claims are literally true.[64] The Muslim calendar, the Hijri, is a lunar one of 354 days. Paperwork for Saudi businesses might carry two sets of dates: Western dates, designated C.E. (Common Era), and Muslim dates, designated H. (Hijri).[65]

Most cultures are more formal in their writing than the U.S. When you write to international audiences, you may need to use titles, not first names. Avoid contractions, slang, and sports metaphors.

Not: Let's knock these sales figures out of the ballpark.

But: Our goal is to increase sales 7%.

Avoid idiomatic expressions, sayings that mean more than the sum of their parts. Such expressions can easily confuse audiences whose native language is not English. Consider the following list of very common office phrases and think about what they mean literally:

- Get ahold of me.

- Shoot me an email (Drop me a line).

- Get to the point.

- It's on my radar.

- Keep me posted.

- Stay on top of things.

- Put it on the back burner.

- Take that to the bank.

While these expressions are what give language color and vitality, they can exclude people from understanding and cause frustration for the listener.

Do write in English unless you're extremely fluent in your reader's language. Be clear, but be adult. Don't write in second-grade English.

> **Not:** We will meet Tuesday. Our meeting room will be Hanscher North. We will start at 9:30 a.m.
>
> **But:** We will meet Tuesday at 9:30 a.m. in Hanscher North.

The patterns of organization that work for U.S. audiences may need to be modified in international correspondence. For instance, most Americans develop an argument linearly; points in a contract such as price, quantity, and delivery date are presented in order, one at a time. However, businesspeople from other cultures may think holistically rather than sequentially, and the business relationship may be far more important than the actual contract, which may not even be considered binding.

As noted earlier, negative messages may need more buffering and requests may need to be indirect. A U.S. manager asking a direct question in an email ("Were the contract numbers checked against Accounting's figures?") could cause hurt feelings among some international recipients, who might take the question as an accusation.

When major difficulties arise affecting a business community, such as accidents or disasters, communications that cross cultures have multiple complexities. Apple CEO Steve Jobs wrote a message that moved audiences in multiple cultures when the 2011 earthquake and tsunami struck Japan. At the time, Apple was preparing to release its latest version of the popular iPad there. It was a critical moment for the company's continued success. Hours after the earthquake, however, Apple suspended the iPad's launch, and all its employees in Japan received this message from CEO Steve Jobs:

> To Our Team in Japan,
>
> We have all been following the unfolding disaster in Japan. Our hearts go out to you and your families, as well as all of your countrymen who have been touched by this tragedy. If you need time or resources to visit or care for your families, please see HR and we will help you. If you are aware of any supplies that are needed, please also tell HR and we will do what we can to arrange delivery.
>
> Again, our hearts go out to you during this unimaginable crisis. Please stay safe.

The message itself was important—a statement of compassion from the CEO.[66] But the way Apple continued to respond made the difference for thousands of employees and even more nonemployees. In cities with no power or internet, Apple's self-contained stores stayed open, providing free wireless access, computer access, phone calls, charging stations, food, and places to sleep for stranded employees. Hundreds crowded into the stores to contact family and friends.[67]

In high-context cultures like Japan's, which place great importance on actions and personal relationships, Apple's response to the disaster was appropriate and culturally sensitive. The message from Jobs and the actions of local employees who helped thousands of people were compassionate gestures from an international company that understands the importance of people-to-people connections and management.

The style, structure, and strategies for written communications that would motivate a U.S. audience may need to be changed for international readers. As Figure 5.8 shows, relationships become more important, as do politeness strategies and the degree of directness versus indirectness of requests and information. Figure 5.8 suggests general patterns, not definitive delineations, but such suggestions help communicators look for ways to be more effective. Writers will benefit from researching a specific culture and audience before composing messages for people in it.

In the aftermath of the 2011 earthquake and tsunami, Japan deserved empathy and cultural awareness from companies doing business there.

Nippon News/Aflo Co. Ltd./Alamy Stock Photo

Response time expectations also may need to be modified. U.S. employees tend to expect fast answers to emails. However, other cultures with hierarchical organization structures may need extra response time to allow for approval by superiors. Pressing for a quick response may alienate the people whose help is needed and may result in false promises.[68]

In international business correspondence, list the day before the month:

Not: April 9, 2021

But: 9 April 2021

Spell out the month to avoid confusion as the document moves between cultural styles. Is the above date 09/04/21 or 04/09/21?

When setting up meeting times, acknowledge and account for differences in time zones. Remember that European countries are six or seven hours ahead of New York.

Figure 5.8	Cultural Contrasts in Written Persuasive Documents		
	United States	**Japan**	**Arab countries**
Opening	Request action or get reader's attention	Offer thanks; apologize	Offer personal greetings
Way to persuade	Immediate gain or loss of opportunity	Waiting	Personal connections; future opportunity
Style	Short sentences	Modesty; minimize own standing	Elaborate expressions; many signatures
Closing	Specific request	Desire to maintain harmony	Future relationship, personal greeting
Values	Efficiency, directness, action	Politeness, indirectness, relationship	Status, continuation

Source: Adapted from Farid Elashmawi and Philip R. Harris, *Multicultural Management 2000: Essential Cultural Insights for Global Business Success* (Houston: Gulf, 1998), 139.

China is 12 hours ahead, and Japan is 13 hours ahead. When referring to a time, indicate the time zone you mean:

Not: 7:00 a.m.

But: 7:00 a.m. (U.S. Central Time)

Businesspeople from Europe and Japan who correspond frequently with Americans are beginning to adopt U.S. directness and patterns of organization. Still, it may be safer to modify your message somewhat; it certainly is more courteous.

Learning More about International Business Communication

Learning to communicate with people from different backgrounds shouldn't be a matter of learning rules. Test the generalizations in this chapter against your experience. Remember that people everywhere have their own personal characteristics. And when in doubt, ask.

You also can learn by seeking out people from other backgrounds and talking with them. Many campuses have centers for international students. Some communities have groups of international businesspeople who meet regularly to discuss their countries. By asking all these people what aspects of the U.S. culture seem strange to them, you'll learn much about what is "right" in their cultures.

Summary by Learning Objectives

LO 5-1   **Explain why having cultural awareness and avoiding stereotypes is important.**

We live and do business in a global society where national boundaries are less important than cross-border interests. No one can afford to build walls between potential partners, clients, and coworkers. Even small businesses now have global supply chains.

LO 5-2   **Explain why global agility in business is important.**

Global agility is not a process of sterilizing our own identity or mimicking that of others. Rather, it is a willingness to relax our customary procedures and allow for new ways of interacting in order to achieve our communicative purposes.

LO 5-3   **Explain why diversity is important.**

Research has found a correlation between diversity and business success; companies with high levels of minority racial and minority ethnic groups have the highest profits, the highest market shares, and the highest number of customers.

LO 5-4   **Explain how our values and beliefs affect our responses to other people.**

Although often unconscious, our values and beliefs affect our cross-cultural communications. Religious beliefs, social values, even everyday practices, all affect communication.

LO 5-5   **Discover how the global use of English affects business communication.**

English as the common language for business communication does not belong to any specific nation. It is the lingua franca of many. Learning a little of the native language of those with whom you will communicate helps to ease the imbalance placed on non-native English speakers.

LO 5-6   **Discover how to use nonverbal communication across cultures.**

Nonverbal communication includes listening, body language, eye contact, facial expressions, gestures, personal space, touch, and perception of time. Our nonverbal communication conveys our attitude, emphasis, and emotion.

LO 5-7   **Construct your written communication to meet the needs of global audiences.**

Awareness of cultural preferences as you draft your written communication is also critical. Most cultures are more formal in their writing than the U.S. Also, the patterns of organization that work for American audiences may need to be modified in international correspondence.

Exercises and Cases

5.1   Reviewing the Chapter

1. Why is having cultural awareness and avoiding stereotypes important? (LO 5-1)
2. What is global agility in business, and why is it important? (LO 5-2)
3. Why is diversity important? (LO 5-3)
4. How do our values and beliefs affect our responses to other people? (LO 5-4)
5. What does the role of global English as a lingua franca mean to you? How will you adjust your use of English to neutralize the predominance of English in business communications? (LO 5-5)
6. What are some nonverbal communication skills necessary for successful cross-cultural communications? (LO 5-6)
7. How might you alter patterns of organization and styles that are typical of American written communications so that they meet the needs of global audiences? (LO 5-7)

5.2   Identifying Sources of Miscommunication

In each of the following situations, identify one or more ways that cultural differences may be leading to miscommunication.

1. Peyton is a U.S. sales representative in South America. They make appointments and are careful to be on time. But the person they're calling on is frequently late. To save time, Peyton tries to get right to business. But their hosts want to talk about sightseeing and their family. Even worse, their appointments are interrupted constantly not only by business phone calls, but also by long conversations with other people and even the customers' children who come into the office. Peyton's first progress report is very negative. They haven't yet made a sale. Perhaps, they decide, South America just isn't the right place to sell their company's products.

2. To help their company establish a presence in Asia, Morgan wants to hire a local interpreter who can advise them on business customs. Kana Tomari has superb qualifications on paper. But when Morgan tries to probe about Kana's experience, Kana just says, "I will do my best. I will try very hard." Kana never gives details about any of the previous positions they've held. Morgan begins to wonder if the résumé is inflated.

3. Finley wants to negotiate a joint venture with an Asian company. They ask Tung-Sen Lee if the local people have enough discretionary income to afford their product. Mr. Lee is silent for a time, and then says, "Your product is good. People in the West must like it." Finley smiles, pleased that Mr. Lee recognizes the quality of their product, and Finley gives Mr. Lee a contract to sign. Weeks later, Finley still hasn't heard anything. If Asians are going to be so nonresponsive, Finley wonders if they really should try to do business with them.

4. Skylar is very proud of her participatory management style. On assignment in India, she is careful not to give orders but to ask for suggestions. But people rarely suggest anything. Even a formal suggestion system doesn't work. And to make matters worse, Skylar doesn't sense the respect and camaraderie of the plant she managed in the U.S. Perhaps, Skylar decides gloomily, people in India just aren't ready for a woman boss.

5.3   Looking at Differences in Time and Directness in Communications

Arden works with United Technologies, a Chicago-based company. They are talking on the phone to Abhinav, the manager of one of United Technologies' vendors for customer service outsourcing.

Arden:	We really need to get all of the customer service representatives trained on our new process in the next two weeks. Can you get this done?
Abhinav:	That timeline is pretty aggressive. Do you think it's possible?
Arden:	I think it will require some creativity and hard work, but I think we can get it done with two or three days to spare.
Abhinav:	Okay.
Arden:	Now that our business is settled, how is everything else?
Abhinav:	All's well, although the heavy monsoons this year are causing a lot of delays getting around the city.

Two weeks later. . .

Abhinav:	We've pooled all of our resources, and I'm happy to say that 60% of the customer service representatives are now trained in the new process. The remaining 40% will complete the training in the next two weeks.
Arden:	Only 60%? I thought we agreed that they all would be trained by now!
Abhinav:	Yes. The monsoon is now over so the rest of the training should go quickly.
Arden:	This training is critical to our results. Please get it done as soon as possible.
Abhinav:	I am certain that it will be done in the next two weeks.

Reflection. . .

- Did Abhinav agree to the initial timeline requested by Arden?
- What might Arden be thinking about Abhinav?

- What might Abhinav be thinking about Arden?
- How will this incident affect their future interactions?

From Shanti Consulting: http://www.shanticonsulting.com/multicultural -communication-case-studies/. Used by permission.

5.4   Interviewing for Cultural Information

Interview a person from an international community about cross-cultural communication. You might want to discuss issues such as these:

- Verbal and nonverbal communication, including body language.
- Tone and organization of professional communications.

- Attitude toward hierarchies and authority.
- Time awareness differences.
- Concepts of personal space.

Compare the person's responses with your own values, and write an email to your instructor reflecting on the similarities and differences.

5.5   Analyzing Ads

Go to Ad Forum's "The Best Ads from China" (https://www .adforum.com/creative-work/best-of/9299/the-best-ads-from -china). In small groups, choose one advertisement to analyze. Compare it to a similar ad created in the U.S.

- What are some differences you see in the advertisements?
- What does the Chinese advertisement say about cultural values in the country it is from?

- What message is the Chinese advertisement sending about a particular product or company?
- Does the Chinese advertisement require an explanation for your classmates' understanding?
- Would the Chinese advertisement be effective if shown in the U.S.?

Discuss your findings in small groups. As a group, prepare a short presentation for your classmates.

5.6   Comparing Company Webpages for Various Countries

Many multinationals have separate webpages for their operations in various countries. For example, Coca-Cola's pages include pages for Belgium, France, and Japan. Analyze three of the country pages of a company of your choice.

- Is a single template used for pages in different countries, or do the basic designs differ?
- Are different images used in different countries? What do the images suggest?
- If you can read the language, analyze the links. What information is emphasized?
- To what extent are the pages similar? To what extent do they reveal national and cultural differences?

As your instructor directs,

a. Write an email analyzing the similarities and differences you find. Attach images of the pages to your email.

b. Make an oral presentation to the class. Paste the webpages into PowerPoint slides.

c. Join with a small group of students to create a group report comparing several companies' webpages in three specific countries. Include images of the pages.

d. Make a group oral presentation to the class.

5.7   Researching Other Countries

Choose two countries on two continents other than North America. Research them on sites such as http://www.cyborlink .com and https://www.business.com/articles/so-international -business-etiquette-from-around-the-world. Note information a new manager in those countries would need to know.

a.   Which country would be the easiest one for a young U.S. manager to gain international experience? Why?
b.   Which country would be the hardest? Why?
c.   To which country would you like to be sent for work? Why?

5.8   Comparing International Information

In small groups, find at least four websites providing information about a specific international community. Also, if possible, meet with a member of that community and discuss your findings. Do you find any clashing sources of evidence? What do the contradictions tell you about your sources? What do they tell you about that international community in general?

Discuss your findings in small groups. As a group, prepare a short presentation for your classmates.

5.9   Planning an International Trip

Assume that you're going to the capital city of another country on business two months from now. (You pick the country.) Use a search engine to find out

- What holidays will be celebrated in that month.
- What the climate will be.
- What current events are in the news there.
- What key features of business etiquette you might consider.
- What kinds of gifts you should bring to your hosts.
- What sightseeing you might include.

As your instructor directs,

a.   Write an email to your instructor reporting the information you found.
b.   Post a message to the class analyzing the pages. Include the URLs.
c.   Make an individual oral presentation to the class.
d.   Join with a small group of students to create a group report on several countries in a region.
e.   Make a group oral presentation to the class.

5.10   Recommending a Candidate for an Overseas Position

Your company sells customized computer systems to businesses around the world. The Executive Committee needs to recommend someone to begin a three-year term as manager of Eastern European marketing.

As your instructor directs,

a.   Write an email to each of the candidates, specifying the questions you would like each to answer in a final interview.
b.   Assume that it is not possible to interview the candidates. Use the information here to write an email to the CEO recommending a candidate.
c.   Write an email to the CEO recommending the best way to prepare the person chosen for their assignment.
d.   Write an email to the CEO recommending a better way to choose candidates for international assignments.
e.   Write an email to your instructor explaining the assumptions you made about the company and the candidates that influenced your recommendation(s). Be mindful of your stereotypes and related assumptions. Remember that individuals must be considered based on their qualifications and experience.

Information about the candidates:

All the candidates have applied for the position and say they are highly interested in it.

1.   **Ziv Gere**, 39, American, white, single. Employed by the company for eight years in the Indianapolis and New York offices. Currently in the New York office as assistant marketing manager, Eastern United States; successful. University of Indiana MBA. Speaks Russian fluently; has translated for business negotiations that led to the setting up of the Moscow office. Good technical knowledge, acceptable managerial skills, excellent communication skills, good interpersonal skills. Excellent health; excellent emotional stability. Swims. One child, age 12. Lived in the then–Soviet Union for one year as an exchange student in college; business and personal travel in Europe.

2.   **Roux Chabot**, 36, French, white, single. Employed by the company for 11 years in the Paris and London offices. Currently in the Paris office as assistant sales manager for the European Community; successful. No MBA, but degrees from MIT in the U.S. and l'Ecole Supérieure de Commerce de Paris. Speaks native French; speaks English and Italian fluently; speaks some German. Good technical knowledge, excellent managerial skills, acceptable communication skills, excellent interpersonal skills. Excellent health, good emotional stability. Plays tennis. No children. French citizen; lived in the U.S. for two years, in London for five years (one year in college, four years in the London office). Extensive business and personal travel in Europe.

3.   **Darby Moss**, 35, American, African American, married. Employed by the company for 10 years in the Atlanta and Toronto offices. Currently assistant manager of Canadian marketing; very successful. Harvard University MBA.

Speaks some French. Good technical knowledge, excellent managerial skills, excellent communication skills, excellent interpersonal skills. Excellent health; excellent emotional stability. Runs marathons. Spouse is an executive at a U.S. company in Detroit; plans to stay in the U.S. with their children, ages 11 and 9. The couple plan to commute every two to six weeks. Has lived in Toronto for five years; business travel in North America; personal travel in Europe and Latin America.

4. **Quinn Hsu**, 42, American, Asian American, married. Employed by the company for 18 years in the Los Angeles office. Currently marketing manager, Western United States; very successful. UCLA MBA. Speaks some Korean. Excellent technical knowledge, excellent managerial skills, good communication skills, excellent interpersonal skills. Good health, excellent emotional stability. Plays golf. Spouse is an engineer who plans to do consulting work in eastern Europe. Children ages 8, 5, and 2. Has not lived outside the United States; personal travel in Europe and Asia.

Your committee has received this email from the CEO.

To:	Executive Committee
From:	Peyton Conzachi
Subject:	Choosing a Manager for the New Eastern European Office

Please write me an email recommending the best candidate for manager of East European marketing. In your email, tell me whom you're choosing and why; also explain why you have rejected the unsuccessful candidates.

This person will be assuming a three-year appointment, with the possibility of reappointment. The company will pay moving and relocation expenses for the manager and their family.

The Eastern European division currently is the smallest of the company's international divisions. However, this area is poised for growth. The new manager will supervise the Moscow office and establish branch offices as needed.

The committee has invited comments from everyone in the company. You've received these emails.

To:	Executive Committee
From:	Leslie Osborne, U.S. Marketing Manager
Subject:	Recommendation for Quinn Hsu

Quinn Hsu would be a great choice to head up the new Moscow office. In the past seven years, Quinn has increased sales in the Western Region by 15%—in spite of recessions, earthquakes, and fires. Quinn has a low-key, participative style that brings out the best in subordinates. Moreover, Quinn is a brilliant computer programmer and probably understands our products better than any other marketing or salesperson in the company.

Quinn is clearly destined for success in headquarters. This assignment will give Quinn the international experience needed to move up to the next level of executive success.

To:	Executive Committee
From:	Logan Exter, Affirmative Action Officer
Subject:	Hiring the New Manager for East European Marketing

Please be sensitive to inclusivity and diversity concerns. The company has a very good record of appointing women and minorities to key positions in the U.S. and Canada; so far our record in our overseas divisions has been less effective.

In part, perhaps, that may stem from a perception that women and minorities will not be accepted in countries less open than our own. But the experience of several multinational firms has been that even exclusionary countries will accept people who have the full backing of their companies. Another concern may be that it will be harder for women to establish a social-support system abroad. However, different individuals have different ways of establishing support. To assume that the best candidate for an international assignment is a man with a stay-at-home wife is discriminatory and may deprive our company of the skills of some of its best people.

We have several qualified women and minority candidates. I urge you to consider their credentials carefully.

To: Executive Committee

From: William E. Dortch, Marketing Manager, European Economic Community

Subject: Recommendation for Ziv Gere

Ziv Gere would be my choice to head the new Moscow office. As you know, I recommended that Europe be divided and that we establish an Eastern European division. Of all the people from the U.S. who have worked on the creation of the new division, Ziv is the best. The negotiations were often complex. Ziv's knowledge of the language and culture was invaluable. Ziv's done a good job in the New York office and is ready for wider responsibilities. Eastern Europe is a challenging place, but Ziv can handle the pressure and help us gain the foothold we need.

To: Peyton Conzachi, President

From: Pierre Garamond, Sales Representative, European Economic Community

Subject: Recommendation for Claude Chabot

Roux Chabot would be the best choice for manager of Eastern European marketing. He is a superb supervisor, motivating us to the highest level of achievement. He understands the complex legal and cultural nuances of selling our products in Europe as only a native can. He also has the budgeting and managerial skills to oversee the entire marketing effort.

You are aware that the company's record of sending U.S. citizens to head international divisions is not particularly good. European Marketing is an exception, but our records in the Middle East and Japan have been poor. The company would gain stability by appointing Europeans to head European offices, Asians to head Asian offices, and so forth. Such people would do a better job of managing and motivating staffs which will be comprised primarily of nationals in the country where the office is located. Ending the practice of reserving the top jobs for U.S. citizens would also send a message to international employees that we are valued and that we have a future with this company.

To: Executive Committee

From: Elaine Crispell, Manager, Canadian Marketing

Subject: Recommendation for Darby Moss

Darby Moss has done well as Assistant Manager for the last two and a half years. Darby is a creative, flexible problem solver whose productivity is the highest in the office. Though Darby could be called a "workaholic," Darby is a warm, caring human being.

As you know, the Canadian division includes French-speaking Montreal and a large Native Canadian population; furthermore, Toronto is an international and intercultural city. Darby has gained intercultural competence on both personal and professional levels.

Darby has the potential to be our first minority CEO 15 years down the road but needs more international experience to be competitive at that level. This would be a good opportunity for Darby, who would do well for the company.

5.11   Researching Inclusion at Your School

Research your university's policies and practices regarding inclusion. Conduct the following research:

- Locate your university's position statement on inclusion (or diversity) for both employment and educational opportunities.
- Find inclusion data for your university's student body.
- Gather pictures of the student body you can find from the internet, brochures, and posters throughout your university.
- Analyze your findings. Do the pictures you find resemble the statistics you find?

As your instructor directs,

a. Write an email to your instructor explaining your findings, opinions, and conclusions.

b. Share your results with a small group of students.

c. Write an email message to the president of the university outlining your opinion on how your university is achieving inclusion and what, if anything, needs to be done to improve its efforts.

d. Make a short oral presentation to the class discussing your findings and conclusions.

Notes

1. Janet Bennett, ed., *Proceedings Developing Intercultural Competence.* Association of International Education Administrators (AIEA), (San Francisco, CA: 2011).

2. Suzy Hansen, "Unlearning the Myth of American Innocence," *The Guardian,* August 8, 2017, https://www.theguardian.com/us-news/2017/aug/08/unlearning-the-myth-of-american-innocence.

3. Sharon Begley, "Studies Take Measure of How Stereotyping Alters Performance," *Wall Street Journal,* February 23, 2007, B1; and Claude Steele and Joshua Aronson, "Stereotype Threat and Intellectual Test Performance of African Americans," *Journal of Personality and Social Psychology* 69, no. 5 (1995): 797–811.

4. Andy Molinsky, *Global Dexterity: How to Adapt Your Behavior Across Cultures without Losing Yourself in the Process* (Cambridge, MA: Harvard Business Review Press, 2013).

5. Ibid.

6. Lauren A. E. Schuker, "Plot Change: Foreign Forces Transform Hollywood Films," *Wall Street Journal,* July 31, 2010, https://www.wsj.com/articles/SB10001424052748704913304575371394036766312.

7. Hult International Business News, "11 Biggest Challenges of International Business in 2017," *HULT News,* December 2016 Section: Careers, http://www.hult.edu/news/international-business-challenges.

8. Laurie Burkitt, "China Loses Its Taste for Yum," *Wall Street Journal,* December 3, 2012, B9; Laurie Burkitt, "Kraft Craves More of China's Snacks Market," *Wall Street Journal,* May 30, 2012, B6; and Margherita Stancati, "Dunkin' Donuts Goes to India," *Wall Street Journal,* May 9, 2012, B3.

9. Dan Myers, "The 5 Craziest McDonald's Pies," *USAToday.com,* January 29, 2013, http://www.usatoday.com/story/travel/destinations/2013/01/29/the-5-craziest-mcdonalds-pies/1873913.

10. Terri Morrison and Wayne A. Conaway, *Kiss, Bow, or Shake Hands: Sales and Marketing: The Essential Cultural Guide—from Presentations and Promotions to Communicating and Closing* (New York: McGraw-Hill, 2012), 140.

11. Emily Maltby, "Expanding Abroad? Avoid Cultural Gaffes," *Wall Street Journal,* January 19, 2010, B5.

12. Vindu Goel, "IBM Now Has More Employees in India Than in the U.S.," *New York Times,* September 28, 2017, https://www.nytimes.com/2017/09/28/technology/ibm-india.html.

13. John Helyar, "Outsourcing: A Passage Out of India," *Bloomberg Businessweek,* March 19, 2012, 36.

14. Ibid.

15. Jonathan Burke, "Outsourcing—To America," *Forbes,* May 29, 2008, https://www.forbes.com/2008/05/25/foreign-labor-auto-oped-cx_jhb_outsourcing08_0529america.html.

16. William W. Maddux, Adam D. Galinshky, and Carmit T. Tadmor, "Be a Better Manager: Live Abroad," *Harvard Business Review* 88, no. 9 (2010): 24.

17. Joann S. Lublin, "Hunt Is on for Fresh Executive Talent: Recruiters List Hot Prospects, Cultural Flexibility in Demand," *Wall Street Journal,* April 11, 2011, B1.

18. Diana Middleton, "Schools Set Global Track, for Students and Programs," *Wall Street Journal,* April 7, 2011, B7.

19. Laura Caron and Erwin R. Tiongson, "Immigrants Are Still Sending Lots of Money Home Despite the Coronavirus Job Losses—for Now," *The Conversation,* October 21, 2020, https://theconversation.com/immigrants-are-still-sending-lots-of-money-home-despite-the-coronavirus-job-losses-for-now-148387.

20. Thomas L. Friedman, *The World Is Flat: A Brief History of the Twenty-First Century,* updated and expanded ed. (New York: Farrar, Straus and Giroux, 2006), 8.

21. William H. Frey, "Less than Half of US Children under 15 Are White, Census Shows," Brookings, June 24, 2019, https://www.brookings.edu/research/less-than-half-of-us-children-under-15-are-white-census-shows.

22. U.S. Department of Homeland Security, "Table 2. Persons Obtaining Lawful Permanent Resident Status by Region and Selected Country of Last Residence: Fiscal Years 2017 to 2019," https://www.dhs.gov/immigration-statistics/yearbook/2019/table2.

23. Conor Dougherty, "Whites to Lose Majority Status in U.S. by 2042," *Wall Street Journal,* August 14, 2008, A3.

24. Jeffery Passel, Gretchen Livingston, and D'Vera Cohn, "Explaining Why Minority Births Now Outnumber White Births," *Pew Research Social & Demographic Trends,* May 17, 2012, http://www.pewsocialtrends.org/2012/05/17/explaining-why-minority-births-now-outnumber-white-births.

25. U.S. Census Bureau, "2010 Census Shows America's Diversity," news release, March 24, 2011, http://www.census.gov/newsroom/releases/archives/2010_census/cb11-cn125.html.

26. CHIN Radio, "CHIN Radio," accessed May 16, 2013, http://chinradio.com/chin-radio.

27. U.S. Census Bureau, "2010 Census Shows America's Diversity."

28. Karen Zeigler and Steven A. Camarota, "67.3 Million in the United States Spoke a Foreign Language at Home in 2018," Center for Immigration Studies, October 29, 2019, https://cis.org/Report/673-Million-United-States-Spoke-Foreign-Language-Home-2018.

29. U.S. Census Bureau, "Statistical Abstract of the United States, Table 54: Language Spoken at Home by State: 2009," accessed May 16, 2013, http://www.census.gov/compendia/statab/2012/tables/12s0054.pdf.

30. Microsoft Corporation, "Employee Resource Groups and Networks at Microsoft," accessed May 14, 2013, http://www.microsoft.com/en-us/diversity/programs/ergen/default.aspx.

31. Cedric Herring, "Does Diversity Pay? Race, Gender, and the Business Case for Diversity," *American Sociological Review* 74 (April 2009): 208–24.

32. Paul M. Barrett, "Selling the Supremes on Diversity," *Bloomberg Businessweek*, October 22, 2012, 38.

33. Keith A. Caver and Ancella B. Livers, "Dear White Boss," *Harvard Business Review* 80, no. 11 (November 2002), 76–81.

34. Ibid.

35. J. D. Vance, "Race Relations Are Getting Worse in America—Why?" *The National Review*, August 29, 2016, http://www.nationalreview.com/article/439431/race-relations-getting-worse-america-why.

36. Derrick A. Watson, "Why There's No Such Thing as Colorblindness," *The Odyssey Online*, April 17, 2017, https://www.theodysseyonline.com/why-there-is-no-such-thing-as-colorblindness.

37. Abhijit Rao, email message to author, August 15, 2013.

38. Ibid.

39. Geert Hofstede, "The 6-D Model of National Culture," accessed September 2, 2021, https://geerthofstede.com/culture-geert-hofstede-gert-jan-hofstede/6d-model-of-national-culture/.

40. Hofstede Centre, "What about the USA?" accessed May 14, 2013, http://www.geert-hofstede.com/hofstede_united_states.shtml.

41. John Webb and Michael Keene, "The Impact of Discourse Communities on International Professional Communication," in *Exploring the Rhetoric of International Professional Communication: An Agenda for Teachers and Researchers*, ed. Carl R. Lovitt and Dixie Goswami (Amityville, NY: Baywood, 1999), 81–109.

42. Christine Chmielewski, "The Importance of Values and Culture in Ethical Decision Making," NACADA Clearinghouse, 2004, http://www.nacada.ksu.edu/Resources/Clearinghouse/View-Articles/Values-and-culture-in-ethical-decision-making.aspx.

43. Morrison and Conaway, *Kiss, Bow, or Shake Hands*, 29, 174–83.

44. Richard M. Steers, Carlos J. Sanchez-Runde, and Luciara Nardon, *Management across Cultures: Challenges and Strategies* (New York: Cambridge University Press, 2010), 205–206.

45. Morrison and Conaway, *Kiss, Bow, or Shake Hands*, 272.

46. Morrison and Conaway, *Kiss, Bow, or Shake Hands*, 94, 178; "Business Cards," *BusinessWeek SmallBiz*, June/July 2008, 28; and Roy A. Cook and Gwen O. Cook, *Guide to Business Etiquette* (New York: Prentice Hall, 2011), 113.

47. Janina Brutt-Griffler, *World English: A Study of Its Development* (Bristol, UK: Multilingual Matters, 2002).

48. David Crystal, *English as a Global Language*, 2nd ed. (Cambridge, UK: Cambridge University Press, 2003).

49. Dorie Clark, "English—The Language of Global Business?" *Forbes Magazine*, October 26, 2012, https://www.forbes.com/sites/dorieclark/2012/10/26/english-the-language-of-global-business/#6fe0c6acb57e.

50. Dorie Clark, "How Not to Be an Ugly American: The Art of Successful Business Travel," *The Huffington Post*, April 21, 2015, https://www.huffpost.com/entry/how-not-to-be-an-ugly-ame_b_783527?.

51. Ibid.

52. Tsedal Neeley, "Global Business Speaks English," May 2012, *Harvard Business Review*, https://hbr.org/2012/05/global-business-speaks-english.

53. Robert Guy Matthews, "A Mile Down, Saving Miners' Lives," *Wall Street Journal*, July 19, 2010, B1.

54. Robert T. Moran, Philip R. Harris, and Sarah V. Moran, *Managing Cultural Differences: Global Leadership Strategies for the 21st Century*, 7th ed. (Boston: Elsevier, 2007), 341–42.

55. Hult International Business News, "11 Biggest Challenges of International Business in 2017," 2017.

56. Moran, Harris, and Moran, *Managing Cultural Differences*, 341–42.

57. Steers, Sanchez-Runde, and Nardon, *Management across Cultures*, 219.

58. Moran, Harris, and Moran, *Managing Cultural Differences*, 579.

59. Mike Kilen, "Watch Your Language: Rude or Polite? Gestures Vary with Cultures," *Des Moines Register*, May 30, 2006, E1–2.

60. "Bush's V-Sign Has Different Meaning for Australians with PM-Bush," *Associated Press*, January 2, 1992, https://apnews.com/article/42939a95e2b694ec6262ff5949d910c9.

61. Forogh Karimipur Davaninezhad, "Cross-Cultural Communication and Translation," *Translation Journal* 13, no. 4 (October 2009), http://translationjournal.net/journal/50culture.htm.

62. Martin J. Gannon, *Understanding Global Cultures: Metaphorical Journeys through 23 Nations*, 2nd ed. (Thousand Oaks, CA: Sage, 2001), 13.

63. Edward Twitchell Hall, *Hidden Differences: Doing Business with the Japanese* (Garden City, NY: Anchor-Doubleday, 1987), 25.

64. Craig Storti, *Old World, New World: Bridging Cultural Differences: Britain, France, Germany, and the U.S.* (Yarmouth, ME: Intercultural Press, 2001); and Morrison and Conaway, *Kiss, Bow, or Shake Hands*, 76.

65. Morrison and Conaway, *Kiss, Bow, or Shake Hands*, 181, 185.

66. "Steve Jobs Responds to Japan Quake," *International Business Times*, March 17, 2011, http://www.ibtimes.com/steve-jobs-responds-japan-quake-276013#.

67. Josh Ong, "Japan Apple Stores Serve as Rallying Point after Massive Quake," *Apple Insider*, March 14, 2011, http://appleinsider.com/articles/11/03/14/japan_apple_stores_serve_as_rallying_point_after_massive_quake.

68. Nick Easen, "Don't Send the Wrong Message," *Business 2.0*, August 2005, 102.

CHAPTER

6 Working and Writing in Teams

Chapter Outline

DrAfter123/Getty Images

154

Stronger Together

More and more, work gets done when people come together—either virtually or in-person—to accomplish business goals. The ability to work in a team is one of the top skills employers seek in job candidates.[1] Teamwork brings together people's varying strengths and talents to create ideas, solve problems, and make decisions—all combining to build, or rebuild, successful businesses.

Rido/Shutterstock

Satya Nadella became CEO of Microsoft in 2014, after Microsoft had just bought Nokia's phone business for more than $7 billion. Most analysts felt the purchase was a bad move for the company, another misstep as the company slipped from its position as an industry leader. After assuming leadership, Nadella diagnosed the company's main problem not as a lack of skill or talent, but instead as a failure to foster a culture that allowed people to make the kinds of innovative products expected of them.

Nadella began to remedy this problem by building a culture that fostered empathy and understanding from top management to ground-floor employees. This switch entailed changing everyday activities and daily routines in order to develop the social capital that could help solve engineering problems. Nadella even hosted training sessions, taking his teams through exercises designed to help them learn about one another as individuals with lives outside of work.

Promoting empathy and community changed the culture at Microsoft. Through proactive, productive team building and teamwork and through structured channels for brainstorming, input, and feedback, Microsoft made operational changes that have helped place it back on track toward being an industry leader in tech engineering and development. One result of its reciprocal flow of team communications from bottom-up, top-down, and lateral channels was the decision that Microsoft would no longer pursue an "arms-race" competition with other tech companies and, instead, would focus more on its areas of expertise, such as cloud computing and artificial intelligence. Through better understanding among its teams, Microsoft capitalizes on both the hard and so-called soft skills of its people.

The result? Microsoft's stock price tripled in four years. Satya Nadella was named *Fortune*'s Businessperson of the Year 2019 and was chosen as the Best CEO for Diversity 2020.

Sources: Martha C. White, "When Microsoft's CEO Joined the Company 3 Years Ago, He Had an Epiphany That Has Guided His Role Ever Since," *Business Insider*, October 4, 2017, http://www.businessinsider.com/microsoft-ceo-says-success-has-nothing-to-do-with-your-skills-2017-10; Jordan Novet, "How Satya Nadella Tripled Microsoft's Stock Price in Just over Four Years," *CNBC*, July 18, 2018, https://www.cnbc.com/2018/07/17/how-microsoft-has-evolved-under-satya-nadella.html; *Fortune*, "Businessperson of the Year 2019," https://fortune.com/businessperson-of-the-year/2019; and "Best CEOs for Diversity 2020," *Comparably*, July 19, 2020, https://www.comparably.com/news/best-companies-for-diversity-2020.

Learning Objectives

After studying this chapter, you should be able to

LO 6-1 Explain the benefits of having multiple perspectives in teams.

LO 6-2 Explain the configuration and purpose of teams.

LO 6-3 Establish ground rules for teams.

LO 6-4 Describe etiquette for working in teams.

LO 6-5 Describe the roles and characteristics of effective team members and teams.

LO 6-6 Describe group decision-making strategies.

LO 6-7 Resolve team conflicts.

LO 6-8 Make meetings effective.

LO 6-9 Write collaboratively.

Innovation from Multiple Perspectives

LO 6-1

"Homogeneity is the enemy of creativity and innovation."[2]

Heterogenous teams bring multiple perspectives to projects, and that multiplicity of perspectives fosters creativity and innovation. When people are brought together in teams, whatever the team's purpose, they bring different information, assumptions, opinions, and insights, and those differences spark thought and discussion in ways that are not possible without diversity. Research shows that socially diverse groups consistently outperform nondiverse groups: "Decades of research by organizational scientists, psychologists, sociologists, economists and demographers show that socially diverse groups (i.e., those with a diversity of race, ethnicity, gender, and sexual orientation) are more innovative than homogeneous groups."[3]

Wherever people go and whatever they do, they bring their backgrounds and experiences with them. For example, residents of small towns and rural areas often have different notions of friendliness than do people from big cities. Differences in perspectives also arise from the experiences people have had in relation to their gender, class, race and ethnicity, religion, age, sexual orientation, physical ability, and even political affiliations. A woman walking alone in a parking lot at night will likely have a different reaction to a man approaching her than a man would, for example. People also differ in working styles. Some people work extremely logically and are detailed oriented, whereas others think in big pictures and sweeping ideas. Some people prefer to work at the crack of dawn, while others are night owls. In addition to differences in background and working style, people also differ in personality type.

Such differences in perspectives can spark creativity and innovation. As mentioned earlier, research shows that socially and ethnically diverse teams produce more and higher quality ideas.[4] One study showed that simply including more women actually increases the team's ability to perform better.[5] Multiple disciplinary perspectives also help create innovative ideas. For example, a biologist (Frank Fish), an aeronautical engineer (Phillip Watts), and inventor (Stephen Dewar) worked together to develop and market more efficient wind-turbine blades based on whale fins, an innovation not possible but for the innovators' varied expertises and backgrounds.[6] Including and listening to multiple voices can also help companies and organizations avoid serious ethical errors in judgment, such as using a sermon by Martin Luther King Jr. to sell trucks,[7] images of a Black woman turning white to sell a body wash,[8] or an image of a Black child with a t-shirt reading "coolest monkey in the jungle" to sell clothing.[9] Hurtful and insulting ideas like these demonstrate the benefits of incorporating multiple perspectives into a decision-making process.

Collaborating with people from different backgrounds and working styles can be frustrating sometimes. For example, it can be difficult to work with people who hold worldviews and opinions that you have never personally encountered before or that are polar opposite to those you hold. Differences also manifest in what people expect from teams and how they behave on teams. For example, in a business negotiation, some people are more likely to view a signed contract as the negotiation's goal,[10] while others might see the development of a relationship between the parties as the goal. Such differences are likely to affect what people talk about and how they talk. Some cultures use direct approaches; other cultures consider such approaches rude and respond by withholding information. Neither approach is right or correct; rather, the team members must be flexible and adaptable in their responses to the differences they encounter.

While differences can cause frustration, research also has found that over time, as team members focus on their task, mission, or profession, differences become less important than being part of the team.[11] Savvy team members play to each other's strengths and devise strategies for dealing with differences. These efforts can benefit the whole team. A study of multicultural teams found that an ideal strategy for surmounting cultural differences is acknowledging cultural gaps openly and cooperatively working through them.[12]

Configuration and Purpose of Teams

LO 6-2

The configuration and purpose of teams vary greatly, but here are some of the most common types of teams:

- **Area or departmental teams** are teams where team members all come from the same area of the organization and report to the same supervisor. These teams tend to be permanent and work on a continuous project or an ongoing series of projects working toward a larger goal.

- **Interarea** or **cross-functional teams** are made with experts from different areas, jobs, or functions within an organization. Some teams produce products; provide services; recommend solutions to problems; or generate communications, documents, or presentations. Some of these teams are permanent and some are temporary.

- **Problem-solving**, **trouble-shooting**, and **task-force teams** tend to be temporary, put together for a single purpose, and have team members whose expertise can inform the problem or the solution. A **task force**, a term first used by the U.S. military to mean "a special operation under a unified command,"[13] is typically limited to an emergency situation.

- **Project teams**, as the name implies, are formed for the purpose of completing a project. Project teams have team members from a variety of areas within an organization, and they are disbanded once the project is completed.

- **Self-managed** or **self-directed teams** are teams that have the power to implement their ideas within an organization. These teams tend to work in an extremely collaborative manner and are fluid and flexible in their hierarchy.

Teams helped Sarasota Memorial Hospital resolve major problems with customer and employee satisfaction. For example, team members from the emergency room recorded every step in the process, from pulling into the parking lot through decisions about patient care, and then eliminated unnecessary steps. The ER team then worked with the laboratory staff to improve the process of getting test results. At Michelin, the French tire maker, teams bring together people from the U.S. and Europe. The exchange between the two continents helps employees on both sides of the Atlantic understand a broader array of perspectives and needs.[14]

Teams are convened when a job is too big or the time is too short for one person to do the work, when the project or task requires more creativity than one person can generate, or when no one person has all the needed knowledge and skills. High-stakes projects especially call for teamwork, both because the efforts of multiple talented people are needed and because no one person should assume the sole responsibility for a possible failure. Many companies see teamwork as a way to foster creativity, to manage risk, and to produce better results—and they expect incoming employees to have the ability to work effectively in teams.

Modes for Team Interactions

The modes for conducting teamwork are on a continuum between fully face-to-face and fully online, with various hybrid combinations in between. The trend towards more virtual teamwork has been growing for some time; companies are spread out geographically, and team members may be scattered across different offices, states, and even countries. Although geographically distanced, teams that work together online must produce results. Thankfully, a variety of technologies provide ways for distributed teams to meet, create schedules and assignments, and collaborate on projects. Online teamwork grew even more prevalent as companies adapted to working at home during the COVID-19 pandemic, and the ubiquity of online teamwork is likely to last.[15]

Virtual work is only possible with software that integrates multiple functionalities, such as internal communications (e.g., chats, email, and voice and video conferencing); data and file-sharing; document, spreadsheet, and presentation collaborations; calendar and schedule booking; job applications and other human resources tasks; and project progress, accountability, and reporting. Some of the most popular and highest rated software programs for internal communications include programs such as Slack, Microsoft Teams, Discord, Jabber, and Hangout Chat. These services take advantage of familiar social-networking features, making them user friendly, but each comes with its own strengths and weaknesses. Software for project management either fully integrates

Konstantin Savusia/Alamy Stock Photo

features like those listed above or allows users to move from their chosen communications platforms into the project management system. For collaborative writing, options include Google Docs and Dropbox Paper, and for online meetings, many companies use Skype, GoToMeeting, Zoom, and WebEx, but others are available.[16]

You should follow any expectations your organization has for such communication platforms. If you are allowed to choose your team's communication platform, be aware of the comfort levels team members have with each platform, and choose accordingly. Student teams can take immediate advantage of the same technology platforms, especially if their educational institutions provide access.

Ground Rules for Teams

LO 6-3

Before beginning work with any team, whether a new team just being formed or an established team taking on a new project, you should develop ground rules to establish social cohesiveness and procedures for meeting and acting. Ground rules are needed for teams that are created for a specific purpose, like project or problem-solving teams, and for teams whose team members come and go, like permanent area or cross-functional teams. Diving immediately into project work without establishing expectations and guidelines for issues like interpersonal communication, methods, and process can hurt the team's long-term productivity. In fact, teams are often most effective when they explicitly adopt ground rules. Figure 6.1 lists some common ground rules used by workplace teams.

The initial meeting between team members can set the tone for successful teamwork. If possible, the discussion can be a free-flowing discussion that moves toward consensus where everyone agrees and establishes team expectations for goals, interactions, procedures, and more. A contribution card can help teams in the formation stage to establish expectations and goals. Team members fill out the card in four areas:

1. Your development goals.
2. Steps you need to take to move toward your goals.
3. The knowledge and experience you can bring to bear on this project.
4. Ways to leverage the range of your knowledge and experience.

After the initial meeting, team members use the cards to monitor and evaluate their progress. The team as a whole revisits the cards during the project to manage expectations and make progress toward goals.[17] Some organizations have their own formal means to start and monitor team progress, and require that each step of the team's work is formally recorded and shared with its supervisor.

Figure 6.1	Ground Rules for Teams

- Start team meetings on time; end on time.
- Attend regularly.
- Come to the meeting prepared.
- Leave the meeting with a clear understanding of what each member is to do next.
- Focus comments on the issues.
- Avoid personal attacks.
- Listen to and respect members' opinions.
- Have everyone speak on key issues and procedures.
- Address problems as you become aware of them. If you have a problem with another person, tell that person, not everyone else.
- Do your share of the work.
- Communicate immediately if you think you may not be able to fulfill an agreement.
- Produce your work by the agreed-upon time.

During the beginning stages of team work, conflicts frequently arise when the team defines tasks and procedures. Successful teams anticipate and resolve conflicts by clarifying what each member is supposed to do. They also set procedures: When and how often will they meet? Will decisions be made by a leader, as is the case with many advisory groups? By consensus or vote? Will the team evaluate individual performances? Who will take notes, that is, keep **minutes**? Successful teams analyze their tasks thoroughly and resolve conflicts through interpersonal communication before they begin to search for solutions.

The longest phase of a team's work is the phase during which most of the team's work is done. While the team's adherence to its ground rules should help maintain the team's direction and friendliness, most of its communication will deal with information needed to complete the work. Good information is essential to good decisions. Successful teams deliberately seek numerous possible perspectives and carefully consider each before making any determinations. They particularly avoid the temptation of going with the first perspective or idea that arises. Conflict may occur as the team debates these perspectives, and that is part of the process. Team members must take care to remain respectful of each other's perspectives and maintain focus on how the conflict is helping to negotiate ideas toward a better idea, that multiple perspectives lead to creativity and innovation.

Etiquette for Working in Teams

LO 6-4

Some people think—erroneously—that etiquette consists of a bunch of stuffy old-fashioned rules. Good manners, of course, include basics such as saying *please, thank you,* and *you're welcome.* But the guiding principle of etiquette is treating people with respect, and respecting others means being courteous, patient, and kind.

For many people, the biggest etiquette breach during teamwork involves misuse of technology. Whether your meeting is in-person or online, you and your team members should follow these basic rules of politeness:

- Set your cell phones on vibrate.

- Turn off your email notifications.

- Refrain from texting or interacting with social media accounts.

In fact, it's simply impolite to multitask during any interpersonal communications. When you do, you send a clear message to other people that they are not as important as your text messages, social media, or email.

Indeed, research shows that so-called multitasking doesn't work, particularly when long-term learning or communication tasks are involved.[18] When we think we are multitasking, we are really switching back and forth between tasks. And because there is always a startup delay involved in returning to a previous task, no matter how brief the delay, we actually slow our progress. In fact, some research shows it can take up to 50% longer to multitask.[19]

Some special etiquette guidelines apply in online team meetings:[20]

- Everyone in the team should test their technology to ensure that their wi-fi, mic, camera, and screen sharing work.

- Everyone in the team should log in a few minutes early. Doing so means that the meeting can start on time and also means that team members will have a bit of time to chat about things other than the project at hand.

- When team members are not speaking, they should mute their mics. Doing so silences background noises, such as from pets. In addition, team members should find a quiet spot to sit during the meeting.

- The meeting host should ensure that they have turned off all notifications on their computer. Doing so will help improve audio transmission.

- If at all possible (i.e., if bandwidth is available), all team members should turn on their video. Doing so promotes team unity and shows goodwill. Depending on the number of people in the meeting, it may also allow team members to raise their real hand to ask a question rather than using the software's hand-raise tool. That said, the hand-raise tool works well for ensuring that team members don't talk at the same time.

- If working from home, make sure the wall behind you is as uncluttered as possible. If you do not have a separate office space, and many people do not, make sure whatever appears behind you looks cleared and clean (e.g., closet doors are closed, laundry basket is not visible, counter-top is cleared).

During online meetings, it's easy to let your attention wander; fight against that impulse. If you maintain your focus, you'll use your own time—and the time of your team members—efficiently, and thus you'll more readily move your project forward.

Roles and Characteristics of Effective Team Members

LO 6-5

Roles of Team Members

Individual members can play multiple roles within teams, and these roles can change and adapt as needed during the team's work. Roles on teams can be positive or negative, as Figure 6.2 explains.

Figure 6.2	Positive and Negative Team Actions

Positive roles and actions that help the team achieve its task goals include the following:
- **Seeking information and opinions**—asking questions, identifying gaps in the team's knowledge.
- **Giving information and opinions**—answering questions, providing relevant information.
- **Summarizing**—restating major points, summarizing decisions.
- **Synthesizing**—pulling ideas together, connecting different elements of the team's efforts.
- **Evaluating**—comparing team processes and products to standards and goals.
- **Coordinating**—planning work, giving directions, and fitting together contributions of team members.

Positive roles and actions that help the team build loyalty, resolve conflicts, and function smoothly include the following behaviors:
- **Encouraging participation**—demonstrating openness and acceptance, recognizing the contributions of members, calling on quieter team members.
- **Relieving tensions**—joking and suggesting breaks and fun activities.
- **Checking feelings**—asking members how they feel about team activities and sharing one's own feelings with others.
- **Solving interpersonal problems**—opening discussion of interpersonal problems in the team and suggesting ways to solve them.
- **Listening actively**—showing team members that they have been heard and that their ideas are being taken seriously.

Negative roles and actions that hurt the team's product and process include the following:
- **Blocking**—disagreeing with everything that is proposed.
- **Dominating**—trying to run the team by ordering, shutting out others, and insisting on one's own way.
- **Clowning**—making unproductive jokes and diverting the team from the task.
- **Overspeaking**—taking every opportunity to be the first to speak; insisting on personally responding to everyone else's comments.
- **Withdrawing**—being silent in meetings, not contributing, not helping with the work, not attending meetings.

Some actions can be positive or negative depending on how they are used. Active participation by members helps teams move forward, but too much talking from one member blocks contributions from others. Critiquing ideas and providing feedback are necessary if the team is to produce the best solution, but criticizing every idea raised without ever suggesting possible solutions blocks a team. Jokes in moderation can defuse tension and make the team's work more fun. Too many jokes or inappropriate jokes can make the team's work more difficult. Note that inappropriate is determined by the listeners, not by the person telling the joke; adding "just joking" or "just kidding" does not make it any less inappropriate.

Attitudes toward teamwork are just as important as behaviors. Dispelling preconceived notions about teamwork can help improve members' attitudes. Some myths surrounding teamwork include the idea that teams are merely quaint cheering sections where harmony comes from everyone agreeing; in fact, effective teams use conflict to generate greater creativity and problem solving. Also, with modern telecommuting technology and global reach, people assume teamwork can be vastly larger with new members coming and going. However, findings show that smaller, stable teams that have meaningful contact are far more productive, efficient, and successful.[21]

Leadership in Teams

You may have noted that "leader" was not one of the roles listed in Figure 6.2. Every team has one or more leaders, and these people also perform some of the actions listed in the figure. Frequently the leader is formally designated or chosen, but sometimes leaders emerge during the teamwork process. Being a leader does *not* mean doing all the work yourself. Indeed, someone who implies that they have the best ideas and can do the best work is likely hindering the work of the team.

When communicating ideas in a team, anyone with a clear message can be a leader.

Jacob Lund/Shutterstock

Effective teams balance three kinds of leadership, which parallel the three team dimensions:

- Informational leaders generate and evaluate ideas and text.

- Interpersonal leaders monitor the team's process, check people's feelings, and resolve conflicts.

- Procedural leaders set the agenda, make sure that everyone knows what's due for the next meeting, communicate with absent team members, and check to ensure assignments are carried out.

While it's possible for one person to assume all these responsibilities, in many teams the three kinds of leadership are taken on by three (or more) different people. Some teams formally or informally rotate or share these responsibilities so that everyone—and no one—is a leader.

Studies have shown that people who talk a lot, listen effectively, and respond nonverbally to other members of the team are considered to be leaders.[22] As team projects progress, team leadership evolves and shifts in response to the needs of the team. For example, in the early brainstorming stages, the informational leader may take charge of meetings. As the team moves into making assignments, however, the procedural leader may take over.

Effective team leaders must be more than simply the boss. Leaders employ interpersonal communication and persuasion to help create a good team environment and to encourage productivity. The best leaders work with other team members, talk *and* listen to followers, help all team members develop their skills, and communicate a clear strategy to achieve the team's goals.

Different projects require different types of leaders. Defining or appointing a leader for a project has been shown to increase productivity and reduce conflict in teams. If too many people attempt to lead, more conflicts arise and productivity goes down. If no one tries to lead, teams experience less conflict, but also much less productivity.[23] Choosing a good leader has a direct effect on productivity. In fact, one study showed that a good leader increases the output of the team as much as if the team had an extra member.[24]

Understanding effective leadership can help teams minimize conflict, generate more and better ideas, and ultimately have a better experience.

Effective Team Members

Much time and effort is spent talking about effective leadership and the qualities of leaders, but the focus on leaders neglects the importance of effective team members. Teams don't exist without team members. Effective team members share several qualities:

1. **They have a positive attitude toward working in the team.** Effective team members start the project with a positive attitude. Even if they prefer working alone and do not often enjoy working in teams, effective team members can reset their attitude for the betterment of the team. The attitude reset might be to focus on the positive outcome from the team's work (e.g., a better grade on the project or a more effective production process), a chance to learn something new (e.g., the ways that other departments or units handle a procedure), or an opportunity to show a supervisor skills that they have not yet seen.

2. **They are self-aware.** Effective team members have an unbiased awareness of their own strengths and weaknesses. It is not easy to be brutally honest with ourselves about things we are not good at, but it is necessary. Volunteer for tasks that you excel at and recommend that someone else take tasks that you know you could not do well. For example, if you are paralyzed at the thought of starting to write a document but are fantastic at revising and proofreading, strongly advocate that you take the lead on ensuring that all the points are well supported and that the text is organized and clear.

3. **They are committed to putting in their best efforts to complete the team's work.**   Effective team members keep the team's work at the top—or at least toward the top—of their priority list, and they do the best work they can for the team. They do not wait for others to do the work, and they do not tell themselves that they'll get to the task when they've completed other things.

4. **They are willing to help team members in need.**   Effective team members are empathetic and flexible. Life happens: Team members can run into difficulties during the course of a team project. A family member or close friend might become ill or pass away, an emergency at work might require a team member's full attention for a short time; any number of challenges can arise. When problems spring up, team members should be flexible and empathetic. They should offer to help, and then they should do as they promise.

5. **They are reliable.**   Effective team members can be relied on to do the work they have volunteered for or have been assigned to do, by the deadline, and with quality work. Teamwork usually involves a series of activities or tasks that must be done in sequence, so when a team member does not complete their task on time or does a poor job, every subsequent task is delayed. Other team members will have to redo the poorly done work, which will delay their own tasks. And other team members will be forced to do their tasks in less time, which will reduce the quality of their work.

6. **They are autonomous.**   Effective team members complete their work on their own, without prompting or constant reassurance. They avoid procrastination and finish their tasks with minimal follow-up questions or clarifications. Think in terms of others' time. How long does it take your team member to compose an email or text that gently and politely prompts you to complete your task? How inconvenient is it for them to interrupt their own work to contact you? How long does it take them to read, process, think, and compose a response to your question or clarification? Is your question or clarification something that you can research and determine on your own? If not, then by all means contact them, but if you can find the answer on your own, do it.

7. **They communicate well.**   Effective team members communicate well on multiple levels. They listen actively are able to acknowledge and paraphrase the ideas, concerns, and frustrations of others (for more, see "Active Listening to Avoid Conflict" later in this chapter). They express themselves constructively, sharing feedback in a manner that makes team members open to incorporating the ideas. Effective team members also make sure team members stay informed, and they help others feel supported and part of the team.

8. **They actively share their ideas.**   Effective team members find ways to actively share their ideas. Even if they are not comfortable speaking aloud in public or in groups, effective team members are able to share their ideas, criticism, or thoughts about the team's work.

Peer Pressure and Groupthink

Teams that never express conflict may be experiencing groupthink. Groupthink is the tendency for teams to put such a high premium on agreement that they directly or indirectly punish dissent.

Research has shown that teams produce better documents when they disagree over substantive issues of content and document design. The disagreement does not need to be angry: Someone can simply say, "Yes, and here's another way we could do it." Deciding among two (or more) alternatives forces the proposer to explain the rationale for an idea. Even when the team adopts the original idea, considering alternatives rather than quickly accepting the first idea produces better writing.[25]

Many people feel so much reluctance to express open disagreement that they will say they agree even when objective circumstances would suggest the first speaker cannot be right. In a series of classic experiments in the 1950s, Solomon Asch showed the influence of peer pressure. People sitting around a table were shown a large card with a line and asked to match it to the line of the same length on another card. It's a simple test: people match the lines correctly almost 100% of the time. However, in the experiment, all but one of the people in the group had been instructed to give false answers for several of the trials. When the group gave an incorrect answer, the focal person accepted the group's judgment 36.8% of the time. When someone else also gave a different answer—even if it was another wrong answer—the focal person accepted the group's judgment only 9% of the time.[26] The experimenters varied the differences in line lengths, hoping to create a situation in which even the most conforming subjects would trust their own senses. But some people continued to accept the group's judgment, even when one line was seven inches longer than the other.

Teams that "go along with the crowd" and suppress conflict ignore the full range of alternatives, seek only information that supports the positions they already favor, and fail to prepare contingency plans to cope with foreseeable setbacks. A business suffering from groupthink may launch a new product that senior executives support but for which there is no demand. Student teams suffering from groupthink turn in inferior documents.

The best correctives to groupthink are to consciously search for additional alternatives, to test one's assumptions against those of a range of other people, and to protect the right of people on a team to disagree. When power roles are a factor, input may need to be anonymous.

Characteristics of Successful Student Teams

Studies of student teams completing class projects have found that students in successful teams were not necessarily more skilled or more experienced than students in less successful teams. Studies by a professor at MIT found patterns of communication to be "the most important predictor of a team's success."[27] Successful and less successful teams communicate differently.

- Successful teams assign specific tasks, set clear deadlines, and schedule frequent meetings. They also regularly communicate as a team about each member's progress. In less successful teams, members are not sure what they are supposed to be doing or when it is needed. Less successful teams meet less often.

- Successful teams meet and talk through plans and conflicts. They use nonverbal cues as well as listening skills to build trust and communicate ideas. Less successful teams rely more on email, text messages, and social networking.

- Successful teams recognize that they have to build trust with each other through goodwill, active listening, and consistent participation. Teams who trust each other tend to work together to solve problems that impact the whole team. Less successful teams expect members to complete their own parts and fail to bring those parts together into a coherent whole, behaviors that also appear in unsuccessful workplace teams.[28]

- Successful teams recognize the contribution of every team member to the team's success and take time to acknowledge each member during team meetings. When team members know that their efforts are noticed and appreciated by their peers, they're much more willing to contribute to the team. Less successful teams take individual contributions for granted.

- Successful teams listen carefully to each other and respond to emotions as well as words. Less successful teams pay less attention to what is said and how it is said.

- In successful teams, members work more evenly and actively on the project.[29] They find ways to cater to each other's schedules and work preferences. Less successful teams have a smaller percentage of active members and frequently have some members who do very little on the final project.

- Successful teams make important decisions together. In less successful teams, a sub-group or an individual makes decisions.

- Successful teams listen to criticism and try to improve their performance on the basis of it. In less successful teams, criticism is rationalized.

- Successful teams deal directly with conflicts that emerge; unsuccessful teams try to ignore conflicts.

As you no doubt realize, these characteristics of good teams actually apply to most teams, not just student teams. A survey of engineering project teams found that 95% of the team members thought that good communication was the reason for team success and poor communication was the reason for team failures.[30]

Decision-Making Strategies

LO 6-6

Probably the least effective decision-making strategy is to let the person who talks first, last, loudest, or most determine the decision. Most teams instead aim to air different points of view with the objective of identifying the best choice, or at least a choice that seems good enough for the team's purposes. The team discussion considers the pros and cons of each idea. In many teams, someone willingly plays **devil's advocate** to look for possible flaws in an idea. To give ideas a fair hearing, someone also should develop an idea's positive aspects.

After the team has considered alternatives, it needs a method for picking one to implement. Typical selection methods include voting and consensus. **Voting** is quick but may leave people in the minority unhappy with and uncommitted to the majority's plan. Coming to **consensus** takes time but usually results in speedier implementation of ideas. Airing preferences early in the process, through polls before meetings and straw votes during meetings, sometimes can help teams establish consensus more quickly. Even in situations where consensus is not possible, good teams ensure everyone's ideas are considered. Most people will agree to support the team's decision, even if it was not their choice, as long as they feel they have been heard.

Two decision-making strategies that are often useful in teams are the standard problem-solving process and dot planning.

The standard problem-solving process has multiple steps:

1. Identify the task or problem. What is the team trying to do?
2. Understand what the team has to deliver, in what form, by what due date. Identify available resources.
3. Gather information, share it with all team members, and examine it critically.
4. Establish criteria. What would the ideal solution include? Which elements of that solution would be part of a less-than-ideal but still acceptable solution? What legal, financial, moral, or other limitations might keep a solution from being implemented?
5. Brainstorm solutions (see Figure 6.3).
6. Measure the alternatives against the criteria.
7. Choose the best solution.

Dot planning offers a way for large teams to choose priorities quickly. First, the team brainstorms ideas, recording each on pages that are put on the wall. Then each individual gets two strips of three to five adhesive dots in different colors. One color represents high priority, the others lower priority. People then walk up to the pages and stick dots by the points they care most about. Some teams allow only one dot from one person on any one item; others allow someone who is really passionate about an idea to put

Figure 6.3	Brainstorming Techniques

Here are some techniques that will help produce successful team brainstorming sessions:

- Identify a clear, concrete goal before you start. When you have a concrete goal, you can establish some boundaries for ideas—about practicality or cost, for example—and you can keep your brainstorming session focused.
- Ensure everyone involved in the meeting knows the goal ahead of time. This step gives everyone a chance to have ideas ready when they come to the meeting.
- Set limits on meeting duration and size. An hour is enough time for a focused discussion, and it's easier for everyone to participate and be heard in a small team.
- Let the ideas flow freely without judgment. Any idea, however impractical, might inspire the best solution, and spending time weeding out weak ideas can stifle creativity.
- Build on each other's ideas.
- Brainstorm with a diverse team. Good ideas come from teams of people with different perspectives.

all their dots on it. The dots make it easy to see which items the team believes are most and least important.

What happens if your team can't agree, or can't reach consensus? Team-building expert Bob Frisch suggests some strategies for working through a deadlock. In addition to using standard group techniques (setting clear goals, brainstorming solutions, and weighing the pros and cons of each solution), you should

- Use the current sticking point as the start for a new round of brainstorming. If there are two solutions that your team can't choose between, break the deadlock by brainstorming new solutions that combine the old ones. That will get the team making progress again and get new ideas on the table.

- Instead of rushing to a decision, allow time for team members to consider the options. Sometimes people refuse to compromise to avoid making a bad snap decision. Giving your team time to consider the options will take the pressure off. For especially complex decisions, schedule multiple meetings with time in between to do research and to digest the pros and cons of each solution.

- Allow team members to make their decisions confidentially. People might refuse to state an opinion—or change an opinion—if they feel their opinions and reasoning will be judged negatively by the group. A secret ballot or other confidential form of "discussion" can help break a deadlock by giving team members an opportunity to voice their opinions without being judged or embarrassed.[31]

Feedback Strategies

As soon as the team begins to put its decisions into play, it needs to begin generating and heeding feedback. Sometimes this feedback will be external; it will come from supervisors, suppliers, clients, and customers. It also, however, should come from within the team. Teams frequently evaluate individual team members' performances, team performance, task progress, and team procedures.

Feedback should be frequent and regular. Many teams have weekly feedback as well as feedback connected to specific stages of their task. Regular feedback is a good way to keep team members contributing their share of the work in a timely fashion. While feedback needs to be honest and incorporate criticism, such critiques can be phrased as positively as possible ("please get your figures in for the Wednesday update" rather than "do you think you can make the Wednesday deadline this time?"). And don't forget to praise. Research shows that teams with a higher ratio of positive-to-negative interactions do better work.[32]

Conflict Resolution

Conflicts are going to arise in any group of people who care about their task. Yet many of us feel so uncomfortable with conflict that we pretend it doesn't exist. Conflict does not mean the team has failed. In fact, conflicts are often the result of working through different perspectives to create opportunities. Although conflicts can be healthy for a project, they must be resolved to maintain effective teamwork. Unacknowledged or unresolved conflicts rarely go away: they fester, making the next interchange more difficult.

Active Listening to Avoid Conflict

Listening is crucial to building trust and avoiding conflict. However, listening on the job may be more difficult than listening in a classroom. Many classroom lectures and activities are well organized, with signposts and repetition of key points to help hearers follow. But workplace conversations usually wander. A key point about when a report is due may be sandwiched among statements about other due dates for other projects.

In a classroom, you're listening primarily for information. In interchanges with co-workers, you need to listen for feelings, too. Feelings such as being rejected or over-worked need to be dealt with as they arise. But you can't deal with a feeling unless you are aware of it.

Challenges to effective listening also can arise from being distracted by your own emotional response, especially when the topic is controversial. Listeners have to be aware of their emotional responses so they can clarify the speaker's intent and also allow time for cooling off, if necessary. A *you*-attitude is as helpful for listening as it is for writing. Listening is more effective if the listener focuses more on understanding than on formulating a reply. Thinking about your own response rather than listening causes people to miss important information.

When dealing with problems, instead of acknowledging what the other person says, many of us immediately respond in a way that analyzes or attempts to solve or dismiss the problem. People with problems first of all need to know that we hear that they're having a rough time. Figure 6.4 lists some responses that block communication.[33] Ordering and threatening convey that we don't want to hear what the person has to say. Preaching attacks the other person. Minimizing the problem suggests the other person's concern is misplaced. It can even attack that person's competency because it suggests that other people are coping just fine with bigger problems. Even advising

Figure 6.4	Troubleshooting Team Problems
Blocking response	**Possible active response**
Ordering, threatening	**Paraphrasing content**
"I don't care how you do it. Just get that report on my desk by Friday."	"You're saying that you don't have time to finish the report by Friday."
Preaching, criticizing	**Mirroring feelings**
"You should know better than to air the department's problems in a general meeting."	"It sounds like the department's problems really bother you."
Minimizing the problem	**Asking for information or clarification**
"You think *that's* bad. You should see what *I* have to do this week."	"What parts of the problem seem most difficult to solve?"
Advising	**Offering to help solve the problem together**
"Well, why don't you try listing everything you have to do and seeing which items are most important?"	"Is there anything I could do that would help?"

shuts off discussion. Giving a quick answer minimizes the stress or pain the person feels and puts them down for not seeing (what is to us) the obvious answer. Even if it is a good answer from an objective point of view, the other person may not be ready to hear it. And too often, the off-the-top-of-the-head solution doesn't address the real problem.

Active listening takes time and energy. Even people who are skilled active listeners can't do it all the time. Active listening can reduce the conflict that results from miscommunication, but it alone cannot reduce the conflict that comes when two people want apparently inconsistent things or when one person wants to change someone else.

In addition to actively listening to your team members, you can reduce conflicts in a team by

- Making responsibilities and ground rules clear at the beginning.

- Discussing problems as they arise, rather than letting them fester until people explode.

- Realizing that team members are not responsible for each others' happiness.

Despite these efforts, most teams experience some conflict, and that conflict needs to be resolved. When a conflict is emotionally charged, people will need a chance to calm themselves before they can arrive at a well-reasoned solution. Meeting expert John Tropman recommends the "two-meeting rule" for controversial matters. The first meeting is a chance for everyone to air a point of view about the issue. The second meeting is the one at which the team reaches a decision. The time between the two meetings becomes a cooling-off period.[34]

Figure 6.5 suggests several possible solutions to conflicts that student teams experience. Often the symptom arises from a feeling of not being respected or appreciated by the team. Therefore, many problems can be averted if people advocate for their ideas in a positive way. One way to do this is to devote as much effort to positive observations as possible. Another technique is to state analysis rather than mere opinions. Instead of "I wouldn't read an eight-page brochure," the member of a team could say, "Tests we did a couple of years ago found a better response for two-page brochures. Could we move some of that information to our website?" As in this example, an opinion can vary from person to person; stating an opinion does not provide a basis for the team to make a decision. In contrast, analysis provides objective information for the team to consider.

Steps in Conflict Resolution

Dealing successfully with conflict requires attention both to the issues and to people's feelings. The following techniques will help you resolve conflicts constructively.

1. Make sure the people involved really disagree. Sometimes different conversational styles, differing interpretations of data, or faulty inferences create apparent conflicts when no real disagreement exists. For example, someone who asks, "Are those data accurate?" may just be asking for source information, not questioning the conclusions the team drew from the data.

Sometimes someone who's under a lot of pressure may explode. But the speaker may just be venting anger and frustration; they in fact may not be angry at the person who receives the explosion. One way to find out if a person is just venting is to ask, "Is there something you'd like me to do?"

2. Check that everyone's information is correct. Sometimes people are operating on outdated or incomplete information. People also may act on personal biases or opinions rather than data.

Figure 6.5	Troubleshooting Team Problems
Symptom	**Possible solutions**
We can't find a time to meet that works for all of us.	*a.* Find out why people can't meet at certain times. Some reasons suggest their own solutions. For example, if someone has to stay home with small children, perhaps the team could meet virtually. *b.* Assign out-of-class work to "committees" to work on parts of the project. *c.* Use technology (e.g., Skype, Google Docs) to share, discuss, and revise drafts.
One person isn't doing their fair share.	*a.* Find out what is going on. Is the person overcommitted? Do they feel unappreciated? Are they unprepared? Those are different problems you'd solve in different ways. *b.* Early on, do things to build team loyalty. Get to know each other as writers and as people. Sometimes do something fun together. *c.* Encourage the person to contribute. "Hanisha, what do you think?" "Abhi, which part of this would you like to draft?" Then find something to praise in the work. "Thanks for getting us started." *d.* If someone misses a meeting, assign someone else to bring the person up to speed. People who miss meetings for legitimate reasons (e.g., job interviews, illness) but don't find out what happened may become less committed to the team. *e.* Consider whether strict equality is the most important criterion. On a given project, some people may have more knowledge or time than others. Sometimes the best team product results from letting people do different amounts of work. *f.* Even if you divide up the work, make all decisions as a team: what to write about, which evidence to include, what graphs to use, what revisions to make. People excluded from decisions become less committed to the team.
I seem to be the only one on the team who cares about quality.	*a.* Find out why other members "don't care." If they received low grades on early assignments, stress that good ideas and attention to detail can raise grades. Perhaps the team should meet with the instructor to discuss what kinds of work will pay the highest dividends. *b.* Volunteer to do extra work. Sometimes people settle for something that's just okay because they don't have the time or resources to do excellent work. They might be happy for the work to be done—if they don't have to do it. *c.* Be sure that you're respecting what each person can contribute. Team members sometimes withdraw when one person dominates and suggests that they are "better" than other members. *d.* Fit specific tasks to individual abilities. People generally do better work in areas they see as their strengths. A visual learner who doesn't care about the written report may do an excellent job on the accompanying visuals.
People in the team don't seem willing to disagree. We end up going with the first idea suggested.	*a.* Brainstorm so you have multiple possibilities to consider. *b.* After an idea is suggested, have each person on the team suggest a way it could be improved. *c.* Appoint someone to be a devil's advocate. *d.* Have each person on the team write a draft. It's likely the drafts will be different, and you'll have several options to mix and match. *e.* Talk about good ways to offer criticism. Sometimes people don't disagree because they're afraid that other team members won't tolerate disagreement.
One person just criticizes everything.	*a.* Ask the person to follow up the criticism with a suggestion for improvement. *b.* Talk about ways to express criticism tactfully. "I think we need to think about x" is more tactful than "You're wrong." *c.* If the criticism is about ideas and writing (not about people), value it. Ideas and documents need criticism if we are to improve them.

3. Discover the needs each person is trying to meet. Sometimes determining the real needs makes it possible to see a new solution. The **presenting problem** that surfaces as the subject of dissension may or may not be the real problem. For example, a worker who complains about the hours they are putting in may, in fact, be complaining not about the hours themselves, but about not feeling appreciated. A supervisor who complains that the other supervisors don't invite them to meetings may really feel that the other managers don't accept them as a peer. Sometimes people have trouble seeing beyond the presenting problem because they've been taught to suppress their anger, especially toward powerful people. One way to tell whether the presenting problem is the real problem is to ask, "If this were solved, would I be satisfied?" If the answer is *no,* then the problem that presents itself is not the real problem. Solving the presenting problem won't solve the conflict. Keep probing until you get to the real conflict.

4. Search for alternatives. Sometimes people are locked into conflict because they see too few alternatives. People tend to handle complexity by looking for ways to simplify. In a team, someone makes a suggestion, so the team members discuss it as if it is the only alternative. The team generates more alternatives only if the first one is unacceptable. As a result, the team's choice depends on the order in which team members think of ideas. When a decision is significant, the team needs a formal process to identify alternatives before moving on to a decision. Many teams use brainstorming when they search for alternatives.

5. Repair negative feelings. Conflict can emerge without anger and without escalating the disagreement, as the next section shows. But if people's feelings have been hurt, the team needs to deal with those feelings to resolve the conflict constructively. Only when people feel respected and taken seriously can they take the next step of trusting others on the team.

Criticism Responses

Conflict is particularly difficult to resolve when someone else criticizes or attacks us directly. When we are criticized, our natural reaction is to defend ourselves—perhaps by counterattacking. The counterattack prompts the critic to become defensive. The conflict escalates; feelings are hurt; issues become muddied and more difficult to resolve.

Just as resolving conflict depends on identifying the needs each person is trying to meet, so dealing with criticism depends on understanding the real concern of the critic. Constructive ways to respond to criticism and get closer to the real concern include paraphrasing, checking for feelings, checking inferences, and buying time with limited agreement.

Paraphrasing To **paraphrase**, repeat in your own words the verbal content of the critic's message. The purposes of paraphrasing are (1) to be sure that you have heard the critic accurately, (2) to let the critic know what their statement means to you, and (3) to communicate that you are taking the critic and their feelings seriously.

> Criticism: You guys are stonewalling my requests for information.
>
> Paraphrase: It sounds like you feel we don't give you the information you need.

Checking for Feelings When you check the critic's feelings, you identify the emotions that the critic seems to be expressing verbally or nonverbally. The purposes of checking feelings are to try to understand (1) the critic's emotions, (2) the importance of the criticism for the critic, and (3) the unspoken ideas and feelings that may actually be more important than the voiced criticism.

Criticism:	You guys are stonewalling my requests for information.
Feelings check:	You sound pretty angry; am I hearing you correctly?

Always *ask* the other person if you are right in your perception. Even the best reader of nonverbal cues is sometimes wrong.

Checking for Inferences   When you check the inferences you draw from criticism, you identify the implied meaning of the verbal and nonverbal content of the criticism, taking the statement a step further than the words of the critic to try to understand *why* the critic is bothered by the action or attitude under discussion. The purposes of checking inferences are (1) to identify the real (as opposed to the presenting) problem and (2) to communicate the feeling that you care about resolving the conflict.

Criticism:	You guys are stonewalling my requests for information.
Inference:	Are you saying that you need more information from our team?

Inferences can be faulty. In the preceding interchange, the critic might respond, "I don't need more information. I just think you should give it to me without my having to file three forms in triplicate every time I want some data."

Buying Time with Limited Agreement   Buying time is a useful strategy for dealing with criticisms that really sting. When you buy time with limited agreement, you avoid escalating the conflict (as an angry statement might do) but also avoid yielding to the critic's point of view. To buy time, restate the part of the criticism you agree to be true. (This is often a fact, rather than the interpretation or evaluation the critic has made of that fact.) *Then let the critic respond, before you say anything else.* The purposes of buying time are (1) to allow you time to think when a criticism really hits home and threatens you, so you can respond to the criticism rather than simply reacting defensively, and (2) to suggest to the critic that you are trying to hear what they are saying.

Criticism:	You guys are stonewalling my requests for information.
Limited agreement:	It's true that the cost projections you asked for last week still aren't ready.

It is critical that you do not go on to justify or explain. A "Yes, but . . . " statement is not a time-buyer.

You-Attitude in Conflict Resolution

You-attitude means looking at things from the audience's point of view, respecting the audience, and protecting the audience's ego (see Chapter 2 for more on *you*-attitude). Resolving conflicts or persuading others involves three kinds of awareness: situational awareness (showing that you understand the situation), personal awareness (showing that you understand the other person), and solution awareness (showing that you understand or are seeking a path to resolution).[35] The way you communicate your awareness comes through in how you employ *you*-attitude.

The *you* statements that many people use when they're angry attack the audience; they do not illustrate *you*-attitude. Instead, substitute statements about your own feelings. In conflict, *I* statements show good *you*-attitude!

Lacks *you*-attitude:	You never do your share of the work
You-attitude:	I feel that I'm doing more than my share of the work on this project.
Lacks *you*-attitude:	Even you should be able to run the report through a spell-checker.
You-attitude:	I'm not willing to have my name on a report with so many spelling errors. I did lots of the writing, and I don't think I should have to do the proofreading and spell checking, too.

Meetings always have taken a large part of the average person's week. Although technology has eliminated some meetings, the increased number of teams means that meetings are even more frequent. Despite their advantages for communication, meetings are not always good. Many productive workers see them too often as a waste of time, interrupting valuable work, while less productive workers see them as a pleasant break. However, meetings easily can be made more effective.

Meetings can have multiple purposes:

- To share information.

- To brainstorm ideas.

- To evaluate ideas.

- To develop plans.

- To make decisions.

- To create a document.

- To motivate members.

When meetings combine two or more purposes, it's useful to make the purposes explicit. For example, in the meeting of a company's board of directors, some items are presented for information. Discussion is possible, but the group will not be asked to make a decision. Other items are presented for action; the group will be asked to vote. A business meeting might specify that the first half hour will be time for brainstorming, with the second half hour devoted to evaluation.

Formal meetings are run under strict rules, like the rules of parliamentary procedure summarized in *Robert's Rules of Order*. Motions must be made formally before a topic can be debated. Each point is settled by a vote. Minutes record each motion and the vote on it. Formal rules help the meeting run smoothly if the group is very large or if the agenda is very long. **Informal meetings**, which are much more common in the workplace, are run more loosely. Votes may not be taken if most people seem to agree. Minutes may not be kept. Informal meetings are better for team building and problem solving.

Planning the **agenda** is the foundation of a good meeting. A good agenda indicates

- A list of items for consideration.

- Whether each item is presented for information, for discussion, or for a decision.

- Who is sponsoring or introducing each item.

- How much time is allotted for each item.

Although a time schedule on an agenda is frequently not followed exactly, it does inform participants about the relative importance of the agenda items. In general, the information on an agenda should be specific enough that participants can come to the meeting prepared with ideas, background information, and any other resources they need for completing each agenda item.

Many groups start their agendas with routine items on which agreement will be easy. Doing so gets the meeting off to a positive start. However, it also may waste the time when people are most attentive. Another approach is to put routine items at the end. If there's a long list of routine items, sometimes you can dispense with them in an omnibus motion. An **omnibus motion** allows a group to approve many items together rather than voting on each separately. A single omnibus motion might cover multiple changes to operational guidelines, or a whole slate of candidates for various offices, or various budget recommendations. It's important to schedule controversial items early in the meeting, when energy levels are high, and to allow enough time for full discussion.

Giving a controversial item only half an hour at the end of the day or evening makes people suspect that the leaders are trying to manipulate them.

Pay attention to people and process as well as to the task at hand. At informal meetings, a good leader observes nonverbal feedback and invites everyone to participate. If conflict seems to be getting out of hand, a leader may want to focus attention on the group process and ways that it could deal with conflict before getting back to the substantive issues. Highly sensitive topics may require two or more meetings, the first to air the subject and people's feelings and the second to vote. The time between the two gives participants an opportunity to cool off and informally discuss the issues involved.

If the group doesn't formally vote, the leader should summarize the group's consensus after each point. At the end of the meeting, the leader should summarize all decisions and remind the group who is responsible for implementing or following up on each item. If no other notes are taken, someone should record the decisions and assignments. Long minutes will be most helpful if assignments are set off visually from the narrative.

Collaborative Writing

LO 6-9

Whatever your career, it is likely that some of the documents you produce will be written with a team. Collaborative writing is often prompted by one of the following situations:

- The task is too big or the time is too short for one person to do all the writing.

- No one person has all the knowledge required to do the writing.

- The stakes for the task are so high that the organization wants the best efforts of as many people as possible; no one person wants the sole responsibility for the success or failure of the document.

Collaborative writing can be done by two people or by a much larger group. The team can be democratic or run by a leader who makes decisions alone. The team may share or divide responsibility for each stage in the writing process.

Teams commonly divide the work in several ways. One person might do the main writing, with others providing feedback. Another approach is to divide the whole project into smaller tasks and to assign each task to a different team member. This approach shares the workload more evenly but is harder to coordinate, although technology, such as wikis or Google Docs, helps. Sometimes team members write together simultaneously, discussing and responding to each other's ideas. This approach helps consensus but can consume more time.

Planning the Work and the Document

Collaborative writing is most successful when the team articulates its understanding of the document's rhetorical situation—its purpose, audience, and context—and explicitly discusses the best way to achieve rhetorical goals. Businesses schedule formal planning sessions for large projects to set up a timeline specifying intermediate and final due dates, meeting dates, who will attend each meeting, and who will do what. Putting the plan in writing reduces misunderstandings during the project.

When you plan a collaborative writing project:

- Make your analysis of the problem, audience, context, and purpose explicit so you know where you agree and where you disagree. It usually helps to put these in writing.

- Plan the organization, format, and style of the document before anyone begins to write to make it easier to blend sections written by different authors. Decide who is going to do what and when each piece of the project will be due.

- Consider your work styles and other commitments when making a time line. A writer working alone can stay up all night to finish a single-authored document. But members of a team need to work together to accommodate each other's styles and to enable members to meet other commitments.

- Decide how you will give constructive feedback on each person's work.

- Build some leeway into your deadlines. It's harder for a team to finish a document when one person's part is missing than it is for a single writer to finish the last section of a document on which they have done all the work.

All team members need to give input on important planning issues, especially to analysis and organization.

Composing the Drafts

When you draft a collaborative writing project:

- Decide who will write what. Will one person write an entire draft? Will each team member be assigned a portion of the draft? Will the whole team write the draft together? Most writers find that composing alone is faster than composing in a group. However, composing together may reduce revision time later, since the group examines every choice as it is made. Even so, it is still generally faster to have individuals compose drafts.

- Decide how you will share drafts. Which technologies will you use so everyone can work on a draft? What technologies will enable you to work on a draft simultaneously, if necessary?

- Carefully label and date drafts so everyone is working on the most current version. Make sure everyone knows the date of the latest draft.

- If the quality of writing is crucial, have the best writer(s) draft the document after everyone has gathered the necessary information.

Revising the Document

Revising a collaborative document requires attention to content, organization, and style. The following guidelines can make the revision process more effective:

- Evaluate the content and discuss possible revisions as a team. Brainstorm ways to improve each section so the person doing the revisions has some guidance.

- Evaluate the organization and discuss possible revisions as a team. Would a different organization make the message clearer?

- Recognize that different people favor different writing styles. If the style satisfies the conventions of business writing, accept it even if you wouldn't say it that way.

- When the team is satisfied with the content of the document, one person—probably the best writer—should make any changes necessary to make the writing style consistent throughout.

Editing and Proofreading the Document

A team report needs careful editing and proofreading. Here are some guidelines:

- Have at least one person check the whole document for correctness in grammar, mechanics, and spelling and for consistency in the way that format elements (particularly headings), names, and numbers are handled.

- Run the document through a spell-checker.

- Even if you use a computerized spell-checker, at least one human being should proofread the document, too.

Like any member of the writing team, those handling the editing tasks need to consider how they express their ideas. In many situations, the editor plays the role of diplomat, careful to suggest changes in ways that do not seem to call the writer's abilities into question. Describing the reason for a change is typically more helpful than stating an opinion. Writers are more likely to support changes to their prose if they know, for example, a sentence has a dangling modifier or a paragraph needs work on parallel structure.

Making the Team Process Work

The information in this chapter can help your team interact effectively, run meetings efficiently, and deal with conflict constructively. The following suggestions apply specifically to writing teams:

- Give yourselves plenty of time to discuss problems and find solutions. Writing a team report may require hours of discussion time in addition to the time individuals spend doing research and writing drafts.

- Take the time to get to know team members and to build team loyalty. Team members will work harder and the final document will be better if the team is important to members.

- Be a responsible team member. Produce your drafts on time.

- Be aware that people have different ways of expressing themselves in writing.

- Because talking is "looser" than writing, people on a team can think they agree when they don't. Don't assume that because the discussion went smoothly, a draft written by one person will necessarily be acceptable.

- Use collaborative technologies wisely to help the writing process rather than hinder it.

- Allow more time at all stages of the writing process than you would if you were writing the document by yourself.

Summary by Learning Objectives

LO 6-1   Explain the benefits of having multiple perspectives in teams.

The heterogenous perspectives of teams foster creativity and innovation. When people are brought together in teams, whatever the team's purpose, they bring different information, opinions, insights, assumptions, and perspectives, and those differences spark thought and discussion in ways that are not possible without diversity. Research shows that socially diverse groups consistently outperform nondiverse groups.

LO 6-2   Explain the configuration and purpose of teams.

The configuration and purpose of teams is determined by need. Some of the most common types are area or departmental teams; inter-area or cross-functional teams; problem-solving, trouble-shooting, and task force teams; project teams; and self-manage or self-directed teams.

LO 6-3   Establish ground rules for teams.

Before beginning work with any team, whether a new team just being formed or an established team taking on

a new project, you should develop ground rules to establish social cohesiveness and procedures for meeting and acting. Ground rules are needed for teams created for a specific purpose, like project or problem-solving teams, and for teams whose team members come and go, like permanent area or cross-functional teams.

LO 6-4   Describe etiquette for working in teams.

The guiding principle of etiquette is treating people with respect, and respecting others means being courteous, patient, and kind.

LO 6-5   Describe the roles and characteristics of effective team members and teams.

Individual members can play multiple roles within teams, and these roles can change and adapt as needed during the team's work. Roles on teams can be positive or negative. Effective team members share several qualities: positive attitude, self-awareness, commitment, willingness to help, reliability, autonomy, effective communication skills, and active participation. Successful teams set clear deadlines, schedule frequent meetings, deal directly with conflict, have an inclusive decision-making style, and have a higher proportion of members who worked actively on the project. Effective teams balance informational, interpersonal, and procedural team roles.

LO 6-6   Describe group decision-making strategies.

Two decision-making strategies that are often useful in teams are the standard problem-solving process and dot planning.

LO 6-7   Resolve team conflicts.

- To resolve conflicts, first be an active listener. Then, make sure the people involved really disagree. Next, check to see that everyone's information is correct. Discover the needs each person is trying to meet. The presenting problem that surfaces as the subject of dissension may or may not be the real problem. Search for alternatives. Repair negative feelings.

- Constructive ways to respond to criticism include paraphrasing, checking for feelings, checking inferences, and buying time with limited agreement.

- Use statements about your own feelings to own the problem and avoid attacking the audience. In conflict, *I* statements are good *you*-attitude!

LO 6-8   Make meetings effective.

To make meetings more effective:

- State the purpose of the meeting at the beginning.

- Distribute an agenda that indicates whether each item is for information, discussion, or action, and how long each is expected to take.

- Allow enough time to discuss controversial issues.

- Pay attention to people and process as well as to the task at hand.

- If you don't take formal votes, summarize the group's consensus after each point. At the end of the meeting, summarize all decisions and remind the group who is responsible for implementing or following up on each item.

LO 6-9   Write collaboratively.

Collaborative writing means working with other writers to produce a single document. Writers producing a joint document need to pay attention not only to the basic steps in the writing process but also to the processes of team formation and conflict resolution. They also need to allow more time than they would for single-authored documents.

Exercises and Cases

6.1   Reviewing the Chapter

1. What are the benefits to including multiple perspectives in teams? (LO 6-1)
2. What are five configurations and purposes of teams? (LO 6-2)
3. In what kinds of circumstances are teams beneficial? (LO 6-2)
4. What modes are available for teams to complete their work? (LO 6-2)
5. What are six types of content that should be included in ground rules for teams? (LO 6-3)
6. What are three basic rules of politeness that should be followed in all meetings, regardless of mode? (LO 6-4)
7. Name at least six guidelines of etiquette that should be followed when meeting virtually. (LO 6-4)
8. What are five positive actions that can help a team achieve its goals? (LO 6-5)
9. What are five negative actions that prevent a team from achieving its goals? (LO 6-5)
10. What are three types of effective leadership in teams? (LO 6-5)
11. What are eight characteristics of effective team members? (LO 6-5)
12. What are five characteristics of successful teams? (LO 6-5)
13. What is groupthink? How can a team avoid it? (LO 6-5)
14. What are some team decision-making strategies? (LO 6-6)
15. What are some techniques for resolving conflict? (LO 6-7)
16. What are some techniques for responding to criticism? (LO 6-8)
17. What are some techniques for making meetings effective? (LO 6-8)
18. What are some techniques for collaborative writing? (LO 6-9)

6.2   Brainstorming Ways to Resolve Conflicts

Suggest one or more ways that each of the following teams could deal with the conflict(s) it faces.

1. Mike and Takashi both find writing hard. Elise has been getting better grades than either of them, so they offer to do all the research if she'll organize the document and write, revise, edit, and proofread it. Elise thinks that this method would leave her doing a disproportionate share of the work. Moreover, scheduling the work would be difficult because she wouldn't know how good their research was until the last minute.

2. Because of their class and work schedules, Lars and Andrea want to hold team meetings from 8 to 10 p.m., working later if need be. But Juan's wife works the evening shift, and he needs to be home with his children, two of whom have to be in bed before 8. He wants to meet from 8 to 10 a.m., but the others don't want to meet that early.

3. Akiko wants to divide the work equally, with firm due dates. Seon is trying to get into medical school. She says she'd rather do the lion's share of the work so that she knows it's good.

4. Jessie's father is terminally ill and his physician has just suggested that he be transferred to a hospice facility. This team isn't very important in terms of what's going on in their life, and they know they may have to miss some team meetings.

5. Jada is aware that she is the person on her team who always points out the logical flaws in arguments: She's the one who reminds the team members that they haven't done all the parts of the assignment. She doesn't want her team to turn in a flawed product, but she wonders whether the other team members see her as too critical.

6. Jim's team missed several questions on the team quiz. Talking to Tae-Suk after class, Jim learns that Tae-Suk knew all the answers. "Why didn't you say anything?" Jim asks angrily. Tae-Suk responds quietly, "Todd said that he knew the answers. I did not want to argue with him. We have to work together, and I do not want anyone to lose face."

6.3   Comparing Meeting Minutes

Have two or more people record the minutes of each class or team meeting for a week. Compare the accounts of the same meeting.

- To what extent do they agree on what happened?
- Does one contain information missing in other accounts?
- Do any accounts disagree on a specific fact?
- How do you account for the differences you find?

As your instructor directs,

a. Discuss your findings with your team.

b. Share your team findings orally with the class.

c. Describe and analyze your findings in an email to your instructor.

6.4   Preparing a Contribution Card

This chapter discussed using a contribution scorecard to help set and measure expectations for teamwork. With a small group, prepare a sample contribution scorecard using the following steps:

- List your development goals.
- Outline steps you need to take to move toward your goals.
- Detail the knowledge and experience you can bring to bear on your project.
- List ways to leverage the range of your knowledge and experience.

With your group, discuss the following questions:

- How does a contribution scorecard set expectations for your team?
- Do you think it will help your team in your day-to-day tasks? How?
- How could a contribution scorecard help you measure your performance as a team?

6.5   Recommending a Policy on Student Entrepreneurs

Assume that your small team comprises the officers in student government on your campus. You receive this email from the Dean of Students:

As you know, campus policy says that no student may use campus resources to conduct business-related activities. Students can't conduct business out of dorm rooms or use university email addresses for business. They can't post business webpages on the university server.

On the other hand, a survey conducted by the Kauffman Center for Entrepreneurial Leadership showed that 7 out of 10 teens want to become entrepreneurs.

What are the multiple perspectives that should be considered in consideration of changing the current policy? For example, would there be an increased load on bandwidth? How would that affect students' studies? Would there be increased costs? If so, who should pay? Would there be an increase in work for on-campus mail services? If so, who should pay? What happens if the business, products, or ideas are perceived as provocative or insensitive, or if they violate the university's mission? What, if any oversight, should there be? If there should be oversight, which university office should be charged with the responsibility? Is the university funded by taxpayers? If so, what concerns would that bring? Think broadly and from multiple perspectives.

Should campus policy be changed to allow students to use dorm rooms and university email addresses for business? Please recommend what support (if any) should be given to student entrepreneurs.

Your team will be writing a report recommending what (if anything) your campus should do for student entrepreneurs and supporting your recommendation. Your report will be best received and considered if it addresses the same concerns that the university has, so make sure your recommendation takes multiple perspectives into consideration.

Hints:

- Does your campus offer other support for entrepreneurs (courses, a business plan competition, a startup incubator)? What should be added or expanded?

- What are the legal considerations involved in allowing students to start businesses and connect to the university, whether directly or implied?

- Is it realistic to ask alumni for money to fund student startups?

- Are campus dorms, email, phone, and delivery services funded by tax dollars? If your school is a public institution, do state or local laws limit business use?

- Send email messages to team members describing your initial point of view on the issue and discussing the various options.

- Help your team write the report.

- If instructed, compose a response to your instructor telling how satisfied you are with

  - The decision your team reached.
  - The process you used to reach it.
  - The document your team produced.

6.6   Recommending a Fair Way to Assign Work around the Holidays

Assume your team comprises a hospital's Labor Management Committee. This email arrives from the hospital administrator:

Subject: Allocating Holiday Hours

It's that time of year again, and we're starting to get requests for time off from every department. We have shifts where every physician and half the nurses want time off. Don't these people realize that we can't close down over a holiday? And what's worse is that some of the shift leads are giving preferential treatment to their friends. The head of the nurses' union has already started complaining to me.

We need a comprehensive, hospital-wide procedure for assigning holiday vacation time that doesn't make us shut down wards. It needs to be flexible because people like to take a week off around the holiday. But we have to set limits: No more than one-quarter of the staff can take time off at any one time. And those nurses like to swap shifts with each other to arrange their days off into larger blocks, so we need to cover that too.

Write up a policy to keep these people in line. Be sure to throw in the safety concerns and regulatory stuff.

Your team will be performing these tasks:

a. Write a team response recommending a new policy and supporting your recommendations. Include two transmittal emails: one to the hospital administrator and one to the hospital's physician and nursing staff. Take care to address the two audiences' different needs and expectations with good *you*-attitude and positive emphasis.

b. Create a one-page notice describing your new policy. This notice should be suitable for posting at the duty desk for each ward—in full view of both your employees and your customers (the patients). Create an effective visual design that emphasizes and organizes the text.

You personally need to

- Research the multiple perspectives that need to be considered in this scenario.
- Send email messages to team members describing your initial point of view on the issue and discussing the various options.
- Help your team write the documents.
- If instructed, compose a response to your instructor telling how satisfied you are with
  - The decisions your team reached.
  - The process you used to reach them.
  - The documents your team produced.

6.7   Recommending a Dress Policy

Assume your small team comprises your organization's Labor Management Committee. This email arrives from the CEO:

> In the last 10 years, we became increasingly casual. But changed circumstances seem to call for more formality. Is it time to reinstate a dress policy? If so, what should it be?

Your team will be writing a response recommending the appropriate dress for employees and supporting your recommendation.

Hint:

Agree on an office, factory, store, or other workplace to use for this problem.

You personally need to:

- Research the multiple perspectives that need to be considered in this scenario.

- Send email messages to team members describing your initial point of view on the issue and discussing the various options.
- Help your team write the response.
- If instructed, compose a response to your instructor telling how satisfied you are with
  - The decision your team reached.
  - The process you used to reach it.
  - The document your team produced.

6.8   Responding to Customer Complaints

Assume your small team comprises the Social Networking Committee at the headquarters of a chain of restaurants. After the managers of one of the restaurants appear on a reality television show, your team begins to receive negative online reviews on sites such as Yelp and Facebook. The negative reviews focus on the character and behavior of the restaurant managers. The CEO of the company asks your team to write a response to the criticisms to post online. He wants you to focus on the company's values and service.

Your team will be writing a group response to online criticisms. You will need to agree on how best to present your company, how to write about the managers who appeared on the TV show, and how to respond to the negative reviews.

You personally need to

- Send email messages to team members describing your initial point of view on the issue and discussing the various options.
- Help your team write the response.
- Write an email to your instructor telling how satisfied you are with
  - The decision your team reached.
  - The process you used to reach it.
  - The document your team produced.

6.9   Answering an Ethics Question

Assume your team comprises your organization's Ethics Committee. You receive the following anonymous note:

> People are routinely using the company letterhead to write letters to members of Congress, Senators, and even the President stating their positions on various issues. Making their opinions known is of course their right, but doing so on letterhead stationery implies that they are speaking for the company, which they are not.
>
> I think that the use of letterhead for anything other than official company business should be prohibited.

Your team will be determining the best solution to the problem and then communicating it in a message to all employees.

You personally need to

- Send email messages to team members describing your initial point of view on the issue and discussing the various options.

- Help your team write the message.
- If instructed, compose a response to your instructor telling how satisfied you are with
  - The decision your team reached.
  - The process you used to reach it.
  - The document your team produced.

6.10   Interviewing Workers about Collaborating

Interview someone who works in an organization about their on-the-job collaboration activities. Possible questions to ask include the following:

- How often do you work on collaborative projects?
- Do your collaborative projects always include people who are in your immediate office? How often do you collaborate with people online?
- How do you begin collaborative projects? What are the first steps you take when working with others?
- How do you handle disagreements?
- What do you do when someone isn't doing their share of the work on a collaborative project?

- What do you do to see every person meets team deadlines?
- How do you handle unexpected problems? Illness? Injury? Broken equipment?
- What advice can you give about effectively collaborating on projects?

As your instructor directs,

a. Share your information with a small team of students in your class.
b. Present your findings orally to the class.
c. Present your findings in an email to your instructor.
d. Join with other students to present your findings in a team report.

6.11   Networking for Team Formation

In this exercise, you are going to participate in a networking event, an abbreviated "talk and walk."

To prepare for the event:

- Prepare business cards for yourself, using a computer application of your choice.
- Prepare a list of people in your class whom you would like to meet (give visual descriptions if you do not know their names).
- Prepare a list of questions you would like to have answered.
- Collect materials to use for taking notes during the event.

During the event, you will have six three-minute sessions to talk with a fellow student and exchange business cards.

Remember, the other person also has questions they want answered. Your instructor will time the sessions and tell you when to change people.

After the event, analyze what you have learned. Here are some questions to get you started:

- Who was the most interesting? Why?
- Whom did you like the most? Why?
- Whom would you most like to have on a team in this class? Why?
- Did you meet anyone you didn't want to work with? Explain.
- What lessons did you learn about networking?

Write a response to your teacher containing your analysis.

6.12   Writing a Team Action Plan

Before you begin working on a team project, develop a team action plan to establish a framework that will hold your team members accountable for their work.

After reading the project assignment sheet and meeting your team, decide upon answers for the following questions:

- Will you have a team leader? If so, who? Why is that person qualified to be the team leader? What are that person's responsibilities? How will you proceed if the team leader is unable to meet those responsibilities?
- What will be each team member's role? What is each team member's qualification for that role?
- How are you dividing your work? Why did you choose to divide the work the way you did?

- What are the tasks your team needs to accomplish? For each task in the assignment, identify a concrete deliverable (What do you need to hand in?), a concrete measure for success (How will your team decide if you completed that task well?), and a work schedule (When does each task need to be done?).
- How will you resolve disagreements that may arise while working on the project? How will your team make decisions: By majority? By consensus?
- When and where will you hold meetings? Decide whether you can hold meetings if all team members are not present. How will you inform team members of what occurred at meetings if they were not present?

- Define what "absence" means for your team. Are all absences equal? How should a team member who's going to be absent let the team know? How far in advance does your team need to know about an absence? How many absences from one team member will be too many? What are the consequences of too many absences?
- Create a policy dealing with people who don't attend class during your preparation days or during your presentation; people who don't attend meetings outside class; and people who miss deadlines, don't do their work at all or

in a timely manner, or consistently turn in incomplete or poor-quality work. What penalties will you apply? (You might consider loss of points, grade reductions, failure, a team firing, or a team intervention.)

- Will you report problem members to your instructor? If so, at what point? What role do you want your instructor to have in dealing with problem members?

After your team determines and agrees on an action plan, one team member should send your answers in an email to your instructor, who will keep the document on file in case a problem arises.

6.13   Writing Team Meeting Minutes

As you work in a collaborative team setting, designate a different member to take minutes for each meeting.

As your instructor directs, your minutes should include

- Name of the team holding the meeting.
- Members who were present.
- Members who were absent.
- Place, time, and date of meeting.
- Work accomplished, and who did it, during the meeting.

- Actions that need to be completed, the person responsible, and the due date.
- Decisions made during the meeting.
- New issues raised at the meeting but not resolved, which should be recorded for future meetings.
- Signature of acting secretary.

Remember to keep your minutes brief and to the point. When the minutes are complete, email them to your fellow team members and copy them to your instructor.

6.14   Keeping a Journal about a Team

As you work on a team, keep a journal after each team meeting.

- Who did what?
- What roles did you play in the meeting?
- What decisions were made? How were they made?
- What conflicts arose? How were they handled?
- What strategies could you use to make the next meeting go smoothly?
- Record one observation about each team member.

At the end of the project, analyze your journals. In an email to your instructor, discuss

- Patterns you see.
- Roles of each team member, including yourself.
- Decision making in your team.
- Conflict resolution in your team.
- Strengths of your team.
- Areas where your team could improve.
- Strengths of the deliverables.
- Areas where the deliverables could be improved.
- Changes you would make in the team and deliverables if you had the project to do over.

6.15   Analyzing the Dynamics of a Team

Analyze the dynamics of a task team of which you were a member. Answer the following questions:

1. Who was the team's leader(s)? How did the leader(s) emerge? Were there any changes in or challenges to the original leader?
2. Describe the contribution each member made to the team and the roles each person played.
3. Did any members of the team officially or unofficially drop out? Did anyone join after the team had begun working? How did you deal with the loss or addition of a team member, both in terms of getting the work done and in terms of helping people work together?

4. What planning did your team do at the start of the project? Did you stick to the plan or revise it? How did the team decide that revision was necessary?
5. How did your team make decisions? Did you vote? Reach decisions by consensus?
6. What problems or conflicts arose? Did the team deal with them openly? To what extent did they interfere with the team's task?
7. Evaluate your team both in terms of its task and in terms of the satisfaction members felt. How did this team compare with other task teams you've been part of? What made it better or worse?

8. What were the strengths of the team? Weaknesses?

9. How did the team's strengths and weaknesses impact the quality of the work produced?

10. If you had the project to do over again, what would you do differently?

As you answer the questions,

- Be honest. You won't lose points for reporting that your team had problems or did something "wrong."

- Show your knowledge of good team dynamics. That is, if your team did something wrong, show that you know what

should have been done. Similarly, if your team worked well, show that you know *why* it worked well.

- Be specific. Give examples or anecdotes to support your claims.

As your instructor directs,

a. Discuss your answers with the other team members.

b. Present your findings in an individual response to your instructor.

c. Join with the other team members to write a collaborative email to your instructor.

6.16   Dealing with a "Saboteur"

It's often said that "there's no *I* in *team*" because on the best teams, everyone works together for the good of the group. What happens when you encounter a team member who believes that "there's a *me* in *team*" and ignores or undermines the team's success in order to achieve personal goals?

Consider this scenario. You're on a team of four students and you've all been working for the past month to complete a major class project. When you were planning your project, one team member—let's say Lee—argued with your team's decisions but agreed to go along with the majority. Lee contributed the bare minimum to your team's work and sat silently during meetings; when you asked for help overcoming a problem with the project, Lee responded with a shrug, "I told you at the start that I thought this was a bad idea. I guess we're all going to get a failing grade."

Now you're at your last team meeting before the assignment is due. Lee reveals a decision to quit the team and turn in a

separate project. Lee doesn't want a grade that "will suffer from all your 'second-rate' efforts" and tells you that they already complained to your instructor about the rest of you.

As your instructor directs,

a. Write an email to your instructor in which you explain your individual response to this scenario. What would you do? How should your team proceed?

b. Work as a group to establish a working policy that might address this scenario before it happens.

  - What policies would you need to protect the group from individual members who are out for themselves?

  - What policies would you need to protect team members from having the team take advantage of them?

  - What is your instructor's role in your team's policy?

  - How would your team evaluate each member's contributions fairly?

Notes

1. "Top 10 Skills for Job Candidates," *NACE*, April 3, 2013, http://www.naceweb.org/Publications/Spotlight_Online/2013/0403/Top_10_Skills_for_Job_Candidates.aspx; "Top 11 Skills Employers Look for in Candidates," *Indeed Career Guide*, December 1, 2020, https://www.indeed.com/career-advice/resumes-cover-letters/skills-employers-look-for; and Ashley Brooks, "7 Skills Employers Look for Regardless of the Job," September 23, 2019, Rasmussen College, https://www.rasmussen.edu/student-experience/college-life/skills-employers-look-for.

2. Joni Goldstein, Bruce and Bridgitt Evans, "Different Perspectives Come Together to Form Better Ideas," *Harvard Innovation Labs*, November 11, 2015, https://innovationlabs.harvard.edu/about/news/different-perspectives-come-together-to-form-better-ideas, accessed January 7, 2021.

3. Katherine W. Phillips, "How Diversity Makes Us Smarter," *Scientific American*, October 1, 2014, https://www.scientificamerican.com/article/how-diversity-makes-us-smarter, accessed January 7, 2021.

4. Phillips, "How Diversity Makes Us Smarter;" Kristina B. Dahlin, Laurie R. Weingart, and Pamela J. Hinds, "Team Diversity and Information Use," *Academy of Management Journal* 68, no. 6 (2005): 1107–23; Susannah B. F. Paletz et al., "Ethnic Composition and Its Differential Impact on Group Processes in Diverse Teams," *Small Group Research* 35, no. 2 (2004): 128–57; and

Leisa D. Sargent and Christina Sue-Chan, "Does Diversity Affect Efficacy? The Intervening Role of Cohesion and Task Interdependence," *Small Group Research* 32, no. 4 (2001): 426–50.

5. Anita Woolley and Thomas Malone, "What Makes a Team Smarter? More Women," *Harvard Business Review* 89, no. 6 (2011): 32.

6. Tyler Hamilton, "Whale-Inspired Wind Turbines," *MIT Technology Review*, March 6, 2008, https://www.technologyreview.com/2008/03/06/221447/whale-inspired-wind-turbines, accessed January 7, 2021; and Gene Quinn, "Inventors Inspired by Humpback Whales Make a More Efficient Wind Turbine," *IPWatchdog*, April 24, 2018, https://www.ipwatchdog.com/2018/04/24/inventors-inspired-humpback-whales-more-efficient-wind-turbine/id=96234, accessed January 7, 2021.

7. Sarah Pulliam Bailey, "Martin Luther King Jr. Sermon Used in Ram Trucks Super Bowl Commercial Draws Backlash," *Washington Post*, February 5, 2018, https://www.washingtonpost.com/news/acts-of-faith/wp/2018/02/04/super-bowl-dodge-commercial-draws-backlash-for-using-a-sermon-from-the-rev-martin-luther-king-jr, accessed January 7, 2021.

8. Cleve R. Wootson, Jr., "A Dove Ad Showed a Black Woman Turning Herself White. The Backlash Is Growing," *Washington Post*, October 9, 2017, https://www.washingtonpost.com/news/business/wp/2017/10/08/dove-ad-that-shows-a-black-woman-turning-herself-white-sparks-consumer-backlash, accessed January 7, 2017.

9. Liam Stack, "H&M Apologizes for 'Monkey' Image Featuring Black Child," *New York Times*, January 8, 2018, https://www.nytimes.com/2018/01/08/business/hm-monkey.html, accessed January 7, 2021.

10. Francesca Bariela-Chiappini et al., "Five Perspectives on Intercultural Business Communication," *Business Communication Quarterly* 66, no. 3 (2003): 73–96.

11. Jeswald W. Salacuse, *The Global Negotiator: Making, Managing, and Mending Deals around the World in the Twenty-First Century* (New York: Palgrave Macmillan, 2003), 96–97.

12. Jeanne Brett, Kristin Behfar, and Mary C. Kern, "Managing Multicultural Teams," *Harvard Business Review* 84, no. 11 (2006): 84–91.

13. "Task Force," *Oxford English Dictionary* (online).

14. Christine Uber Grosse, "Managing Communication within Virtual Intercultural Teams," *Business Communication Quarterly* (2002): 22; and Linda H. Heuring, "Patients First," *HRMagazine*, July 2003, 67–68.

15. Katherine Guyot and Isabel V. Sawhill, "Telecommuting Will Likely Continue Long after the Pandemic," *Brookings Institute*, April 6, 2020, https://www.brookings.edu/blog/up-front/2020/04/06/telecommuting-will-likely-continue-long-after-the-pandemic.

16. Adam C. Uzialko, "Best Online Project Management Software of 2017," *Business News Daily*, June 15, 2017, http://www.businessnewsdaily.com/9977-best-online-project-management-software.html.

17. Heidi K. Gardner, "Coming through When It Matters Most," *Harvard Business Review*, April 2012, 88.

18. Jared Sandberg, "Yes, Sell All My Stocks. No, the 3:15 from JFK. and Get Me Mr. Sister," *Wall Street Journal*, September 12, 2006, B1.

19. Toddi Gutner, "Beat the Clock: E-mails, Faxes, Phone Calls, Oh My. Here's How to Get It All Done," *Business Week SmallBiz*, February/March 2008, 58.

20. Neha Kulshreshtha, "22 Online Meeting Etiquette Rules That Must Be Followed for the Sake of Everyone," Fireflies Blog, May 8, 2020, https://blogs.fireflies.ai/online-meeting-etiquette.

21. J. Richard Hackman, "Six Common Misperceptions about Teamwork," *Harvard Business Review* (blog), June 7, 2011, http://blogs.hbr.org/cs/2011/06/six_common_misperceptions_abou.html.

22. Kevin S. Groves, "Leader Emotional Expressivity, Visionary Leadership, and Organizational Change," *Leadership Organizational Development Journal* 27, no. 7 (2006): 566–83; and Ajay Mehra et al., "Distributed Leadership in Teams: The Network of Leadership Perceptions and Team Performance," *The Leadership Quarterly* 17, no. 3 (2006): 232–45.

23. "Why Hierarchies Are Good for Productivity (and Too Much Testosterone Is Not)," *Inc.*, September 2012, 26.

24. Edward P. Lazear, Kathryn L. Shaw, and Christopher T. Stanton, "The Value of Bosses," National Bureau of Economic Research Working Paper No. 18317, August 2012.

25. Rebecca E. Burnett, "Conflict in Collaborative Decision-Making," in *Professional Communication: The Social Perspective*, ed. Nancy Roundy Blyler and Charlotte Thralls (Newbury Park, CA: Sage, 1993), 144–62; and Rebecca E. Burnett, "Productive and Unproductive Conflict in Collaboration," in *Making Thinking Visible: Writing, Collaborative Planning, and Classroom Inquiry*, ed. Linda Flower et al. (Urbana, IL: NCTE, 1994), 239–44.

26. Solomon F. Asch, "Opinions and Social Pressure," *Scientific American* 193, no. 5 (1955): 31–35. For a review of literature on groupthink, see Marc D. Street, "Groupthink: An Examination of Theoretical Issues, Implications, and Future Research Suggestions," *Small Group Research* 28, no. 1 (1997): 72–93.

27. Alex "Sandy" Pentland, "The New Science of Building Great Teams," *Harvard Business Review* 90, no. 4 (2012): 60.

28. Kimberly Merriman, "Low-Trust Teams Prefer Individualized Pay," *Harvard Business Review* 86, no. 11 (2008): 32.

29. Sari Lindblom-Ylanne, Heikki Pihlajamaki, and Toomas Kotkas, "What Makes a Student Group Successful? Student–Student and Student–Teacher Interaction in a Problem-Based Learning Environment," *Learning Environments Research* 6, no. 1 (2003): 59–76.

30. Sue Dyer, "The Root Causes of Poor Communication," *Cost Engineering* 48, no. 6 (2006): 8–10.

31. Bob Frisch, "When Teams Can't Decide," *Harvard Business Review* 86, no. 11 (2008): 121–26.

32. Sue Shellenbarger, "Work & Family Mailbox," *Wall Street Journal*, February 9, 2011, D3.

33. Thomas Gordon and Judith Gordon Sands, *P.E.T. in Action* (New York: P. H. Wyden, 1976), 117–18.

34. John E. Tropman, *Making Meetings Work*, 2nd ed. (Thousand Oaks, CA: Sage, 2003), 28.

35. Mark Goulston and John Ullmen, "How to Really Understand Someone Else's Point of View," *HBR Blog Network*, April 22, 2013, http://blogs.hbr.org/cs/2013/04/how_to_really_understand_someo.html.

CHAPTER

7

Designing Documents

Chapter Outline

DrAfter123/Getty Images

And the Award Goes to . . .

Robyn Beck/Stringer/Getty Images

PricewaterhouseCoopers (PwC) had already done its job: it had tallied votes for the 2017 Oscar awards and stuffed the envelopes with the names of the winners. Now the award ceremony was under way. It was time to sit back and enjoy the show.

But PwC Chairman Tim Ryan's work had just begun. When presenter Warren Beatty opened the envelope for Best Picture and announced *La La Land* as winner, backstage PwC staffers froze in shock: the winner was supposed to be *Moonlight*. What had happened? And what should they do? Producers of *La La Land* were on their way to the podium to accept the award.

Announcing winners may seem simple, but the Oscars ceremony is a complex live event. It turns out that each award had two identical sets of envelopes: one at each side of the stage. And someone had handed a duplicate envelope to Warren Beatty—the duplicate of a different award that *La La Land* had already won. Speculating on how such a mix-up occurred, the *New York Times* pointed to the envelope's gold-lettered design, new in 2017, that "could have made the lettering harder to read."

As PwC administered damage control and corrected the mistake—the first in PwC's 83-year history with the Oscars—the Twittersphere lit up with accusations of negligence in a simple task, terming the error #envelopegate. Ryan feared the effects on PwC's reputation and set to work drafting apologies, all because of a misread envelope.

Perhaps it's a stretch to blame the envelope: after all, shouldn't humans double- and triple-check in such a high-stakes situation? But designers know the impact a small detail can make. Marc Friedman, the stationer who painstakingly designed 2011's envelopes, called the Oscar's envelope "the most iconic, symbolic envelope in the world . . . There is no more significant moment than the anticipation that comes with opening the envelope."

Friedman's 2011 envelopes carried winners to the stage without a hitch. But perhaps 2017's envelopes needed a few more rounds of usability testing.

Sources: Sandy Cohen, "Oscar's Winners' Envelope Made Over with New Look," *San Diego Union Tribune*, February 16, 2011, http://www.sandiegouniontribune.com/sdut-oscars-winners-envelope-made-over-with-new-look-2011feb16-story.html; and David Gelles and Sapna Maheshwari, "Oscars Mistake Casts Unwanted Spotlight on PwC," *New York Times*, February 27, 2017, https://www.nytimes.com/2017/02/27/business/media/pwc-oscars-best-picture.html.

After studying this chapter, you should be able to

LO 7-1 Explain why document design is important.

LO 7-2 Explain design conventions.

LO 7-3 Explain the four levels of document design.

LO 7-4 Apply design guidelines for each level.

LO 7-5 Incorporate design into the writing process.

LO 7-6 Design inclusively.

LO 7-7 Test your documents for usability.

LO 7-8 Design brochures.

LO 7-9 Design websites.

The ability to effectively design a variety of documents is expected of today's professional. Good design saves time and money, affirms the creator's desired image, and builds goodwill.

Effective design groups ideas visually, structuring the flow of information in an inviting, user-friendly way. Easy-to-use documents enhance credibility and build an image of the creator—whether an individual or a company—as competent, thoughtful, and audience-oriented.

Today, a wide array of documents demands insightful, pragmatic, and accessible design—from brochures, infographics, or websites to more diverse documents such as NFL players' jerseys, a breast cancer self-exam shower card, or even the envelope that will deliver the Oscar winner for Best Picture. Regardless of the document types you anticipate designing, attention to effective design will benefit you professionally. Many workplaces expect their employees to be able to create designs that go beyond the basic templates found in common software programs and adapt to user needs, current technology, and best practices in inclusive design.

Why Document Design Is Important

LO 7-1

Poor document design is more than an annoyance or a missed chance for pleasing aesthetics; improper design can cause both organizations and society to suffer. In one tragic example, the *Challenger* space shuttle blew up because engineers did not effectively convey their concerns about the shuttle's O-rings, which failed in the excessive cold. Poor communication—including charts that de-emphasized data about O-ring performance—contributed to the decision to launch. Unfortunately, this was not an isolated incident. More recently, poor communication played a role in NASA's failure to ensure safety of the spacecraft *Columbia*, which disintegrated upon re-entry. Mission leaders insisted that engineers had not briefed them on the seriousness of the damage caused by a piece of foam that struck the shuttle upon takeoff. But after studying meeting transcripts, Edward R. Tufte, who specializes in the visual presentation of information, concluded that engineers did offer concerns and supporting statistics. Why didn't the mission leaders listen? Because the visuals the engineers used obscured the seriousness of the potential damage.[1]

Visual communication plays an important role in the public sphere, from local to global. The *Des Moines Register* recently faced reader backlash for a poorly juxtaposed cover spread: While the upper front-page article highlighted global leaders coming together to help fight worldwide hunger, the article below it featured a local bar known for serving a five-pound burger.[2] Design ramifications extend beyond public opinion of a local newspaper and even can influence national politics. For instance, in 2000, the badly designed Florida ballot confused enough voters to cloud the outcome of the U.S. presidential election.[3]

The thoughtfulness, functionality, and tone of document design convey a specific image of the document's creator, and without deliberate attention to design, this image may not be the one intended. Does your personal résumé paint a picture you want to present to the world? Does the visual tone of a company's website affirm its commitment to transparency? Does the medical brochure distributed at a doctor's office reinforce the clinic's intended image as friendly and helpful? When it comes to business communication, document design should affirm your desired image or your company's "brand."

Design Conventions

LO 7-2

Like all communication, visual communication adheres to certain conventions: the "design language" and expectations for how a certain type of document will look. For instance, if you received a business card in the shape of a circle, it would gain your attention because most business cards adhere to the convention of a rectangular shape. In this case, the circle might thwart convention in an effective way that makes the recipient remember the person with the circular business card, but in many cases, design conventions serve a useful purpose and should be followed. For example, most computers' graphical user interfaces organize files, folders, and a trash can around a "desktop" metaphor; switching to a completely different way of organizing a computer's contents would likely reduce usability. Similarly, when surfing a shopping website, users have the expectation of being able to add an item to their cart or basket, another design convention that streamlines a user's website experience. In general, violating conventions is risky: it may signal that the author or designer is unreliable or unknowledgeable of how a particular form of communication is typically designed.

Conventions may vary by audience, geographic area, industry, company, or even department. Some conventions work well with some audiences but not with others, so careful audience analysis is necessary. For instance, illustrations in instructions for office equipment usually show female hands using the equipment. Some women readers will relate more readily to the instructions, making this choice an effective one for those readers; others will be offended at the implication that only women perform such low-level office jobs, so the company may want to revisit the conventions it employs for visual instructions.[4]

Conventions also change as technology evolves. Résumés used to be typed documents; now most companies ask for electronic versions. When typewriters were common, it was conventional to type two spaces after each period, but with word-processing software, only one period is necessary. Today, as more and more users navigate websites through smartphones, websites must design for mobile functionality, which creates a new set of website-design conventions.

The Four Levels of Document Design

LO 7-3

Visual communications expert Charles Kostelnick distinguishes four levels of design: intra, inter, extra, and supra. Analyzing others' documents can generate ideas for your own communication, so when you encounter documents in a professional setting, look for Kostelnick's four levels of design.[5] These terms provide an organized way to think about the design choices behind every document:

- **Intra:** design choices for individual letters and words. Intra-level design choices include the font and its size; whether you use bold, italics, or color changes to emphasize key words; and the way you use capital letters. The serif font used for body text on this page and the sans serif font used for headings are intra-level design choices.

- **Inter:** design choices for blocks of text. Inter-level design choices include the ways you use headings, white space, indents, lists, and even text boxes. The headings and bulleted lists that organize information on these pages are inter-level design choices.

- **Extra:** design choices for graphics that accompany text. Extra-level design choices include the use of photographs, charts, graphs, and other visuals, as well as the ways you emphasize information in those visuals. The figures in this chapter are extra-level design choices.

- **Supra:** design choices for entire documents. Supra-level design choices include paper size, headers and footers, and the index and table of contents, as well as color schemes and layout grids that define the look of all sections of a document. The placement of the page numbers in this book and the colors used for headings are supra-level design choices.

The Centers for Disease Control and Prevention (CDC) infographic in Figure 7.1 illustrates all levels of design. At the intra-level, this poster uses a sans serif typeface throughout the whole document. Other intra-level elements include the boldface, all-caps, red headings and the black sentences that are set in a smaller type size than the heading text. Inter-level elements include the centered title at the top of the poster and the chunked text within boxes and above and below dotted line dividers. It also includes the red arrows used like bullet points to organize material. The graphics such as an apple, a martini glass, and a bicycle, as well as the U.S. shaped outline used to frame statistics about high blood pressure risk, are extra-level design elements. These images help reinforce the textual message that encourages viewers to adopt healthy habits that prevent high blood pressure. Supra-level elements include the color scheme and the size of the infographic, which occupies an entire browser window and is intended to be shared on social media. Another supra-level design element that unifies all CDC promotional materials is its blue logo at the bottom center. Visually, this information is treated like a page footer and can be found somewhere on every published piece of CDC promotional material.

Design Guidelines

LO 7-4

Use the guidelines in Figure 7.2 to create documents that are usable and visually attractive.

1. Strategize Font Choices.

Fonts are unified styles of type. Popular fonts are Times Roman, Calibri, Palatino, Helvetica, or Arial, and each comes in various sizes and usually in bold and italic. In **fixed-pitch fonts**, every letter takes up the same amount of space; an *i* takes the same space as a *w.* Courier and Prestige Elite are fixed-pitch fonts. Most fonts are **proportional** and allow wider letters to take more space than narrower letters. Times Roman, Palatino, Helvetica, and Arial are proportional fonts. Most business documents use no more than two fonts.

Serif fonts have little extensions, called serifs, from the main strokes. (In Figure 7.3, look at the feet on the r's in New Courier and the flick on the top of the d in Lucinda.) New Courier, Elite, Times Roman, Palatino, and Lucinda Calligraphy are serif fonts. Helvetica, Arial, Geneva, and Technical are **sans serif fonts** because they lack serifs (*sans* is French for *without*). Sans serif fonts are good for titles, headings, and tables.

- **Use a binary font scheme to create visual interest.**   Use two fonts—one for headings and one for body text—to create visual variety within a cohesive design.

- **Create emphasis with font treatments.**   Bold is easier to read than italics, so use bold type if you need only one method to emphasize text. In a complex document, use bigger

Figure 7.1	Four Levels of Design in an Infographic for the Centers for Disease Control and Prevention

Centers for Disease Control and Prevention

Figure 7.2	Design Guidelines for Usable and Attractive Documents

1. Strategize font choices.
2. Minimize use of words in all capital letters.
3. Use white space.
4. Strategize margin choices.
5. Place elements for deliberate emphasis.
6. Unify elements with grids.
7. Use headings.
8. Unify documents with consistent, sparing decorative strategies.

Figure 7.3	Examples of Different Fonts

This sentence is set in 12-point Times Roman.

This sentence is set in 12-point Arial.

This sentence is set in 12-point New Courier.

This sentence is set in 12-point Lucinda Calligraphy.

This sentence is set in 12-point Broadway.

This sentence is set in 12-point Technical.

type for main headings and smaller type for subheadings and body text. Avoid excessive italic type and underlining because these features can make text hard to read.

- **Use minimum 12-point font.**   Twelve-point type is usually ideal for letters, memos, emails, and reports. Smaller type is harder to read, especially for older readers. If your message will not fit in the available pages, cut it. Putting some sections in tiny type saves space but creates a negative response—a negative response that may extend to the organization that produced the document.

You should choose fonts carefully because they shape reader response. Research suggests that people respond positively to fonts that fit the genre and purpose of the document.[6] For example, a font like Broadway is appropriate for a headline in a newsletter but not for the body text of an email.

2. Minimize Use of Words in All Capital Letters.

We recognize words partly by their shapes.[7] In all capital letters, all words take on a rectangular shape (see Figure 7.4); in all capital letters, words lose the descenders and ascenders that make reading faster and more accurate.[8] In addition, many people interpret text in all capitals as "shouting," especially when that text appears in online documents. In those cases, all capitals might elicit a negative response from your audience. Use words in all capital letters sparingly, if at all.

3. Use White Space.

White space—the empty space on the page—makes material easier to read by emphasizing the material that it separates from the rest of the text. Audiences scan documents for information, so anything you can do visually to help ease their reading will reflect positively on you as the communicator.

Figure 7.4	All Capitals Hide the Shape of a Word

Full capitals hide the shape of a word and slow reading 19%.

FULL CAPITALS HIDE THE SHAPE OF A WORD AND SLOW READING 19%.

To create white space:

- Use headings.

- Use a mix of paragraph lengths. It's okay for a paragraph or two to be just one sentence. First and last paragraphs, in particular, should be short.

- Use lists.

- Use tabs or indents—not spaces—to align items vertically.

- Use numbered lists when the number or sequence of items is exact.

- Use **bullets** (large dots or squares like those in this list) when the number and sequence don't matter.

When you use a list, construct the list items with parallel grammar and ensure they fit into the structure of the sentence that introduces the list. The list above is framed by the phrase "To create white space" and each item that follows completes that sentence with a simple present-tense verb phrase, for example, "To create white space . . . use headings."

Increasing white space can easily improve the look of your message. Figure 7.5 shows an original document. Notice how this document is visually dense and uninviting. In Figure 7.6,

| Figure 7.5 | A Document with Poor Visual Impact |

All capital letters make the title harder to read.

MONEY DEDUCTED FROM YOUR WAGES TO PAY CREDITORS

When you buy goods on credit, the store will sometimes ask you to sign a Wage Assignment form allowing it to deduct money from your wages if you do not pay your bill. When you buy on credit, you sign a contract agreeing to pay a certain amount each week or month until you have paid all you owe. The Wage Assignment Form is separate. It must contain the name of your present employer, your social security number, the amount of money loaned, the rate of interest, the date when payments are due, and your signature. The words "Wage Assignment" must be printed at the top of the form and also near the line for your signature. Even if you have signed a Wage Assignment agreement, Roysner will not withhold part of your wages unless all of the following conditions are met: 1. You have to be more than forty days late in payment of what you owe; 2. Roysner has to receive a correct statement of the amount you are in default and a copy of the Wage Assignment form; and 3. You and Roysner must receive a notice from the creditor at least twenty days in advance stating that the creditor plans to make a demand on your wages. This twenty-day notice gives you a chance to correct the problems yourself. If these conditions are all met, Roysner must withhold 15% of each paycheck until your bill is paid and give this money to your creditor.

Long paragraph is visually uninviting.

If you think you are not late or that you do not owe the amount stated, you can argue against it by filing a legal document called a "defense." Once you file a defense, Roysner will not withhold any money from you. However, be sure you are right before you file a defense. If you are wrong, you have to pay not only what you owe but also all legal costs for both yourself and the creditor. If you are right, the creditor has to pay all these costs.

Important information is hard to find.

Figure 7.6   A Document Revised to Improve Visual Impact

Money Deducted from Your Wages to Pay Creditors

First letter of each main word capitalized. Title split onto two lines.

When you buy goods on credit, the store will sometimes ask you to sign a Wage Assignment form allowing it to deduct money from your wages if you do not pay your bill.

Have You Signed a Wage Assignment Form?

Headings divide document into chunks.

When you buy on credit, you sign a contract agreeing to pay a certain amount each week or month until you have paid all you owe. The Wage Assignment Form is separate. It must contain

- The name of your present employer,
- Your social security number,
- The amount of money loaned,
- The rate of interest,
- The date when payments are due, and
- Your signature.

List with bullets where order of items doesn't matter.

Single-space list when items are short.

The words "Wage Assignment" must be printed at the top of the form and also near the line for your signature.

When Would Money Be Deducted from Your Wages to Pay a Creditor?

Headings must be parallel. Here all are questions.

Even if you have signed a Wage Assignment agreement, Roysner will not withhold part of your wages unless all of the following conditions are met:

1. You have to be more than 40 days late in payment of what you owe;

2. Roysner has to receive a correct statement of the amount you are in default and a copy of the Wage Assignment form; and

3. You and Roysner must receive a notice from the creditor at least 20 days in advance stating that the creditor plans to make a demand on your wage. This 20-day notice gives you a chance to correct the problem yourself.

White space between items emphasizes them.

Numbered list where number or order of items matters.

Double-space between items in list when most items are two lines or longer.

If these conditions are all met, Roysner must withhold fifteen percent (15%) of each paycheck until your bill is paid and give this money to your creditor.

What Should You Do If You Think the Wage Assignment Is Incorrect?

If you think you are not late or that you do not owe the amount stated, you can argue against it by filing a legal document called a "defense." Once you file a defense, Roysner will not withhold any money from you. However, be sure you are right before you file a defense. If you are wrong, you have to pay not only what you owe but also all legal costs for both yourself and the creditor. If you are right, the creditor has to pay all these costs.

Figure 7.7   The FedEx Logo Sends a Message with White Space

tanuha2001/Shutterstock

the same document is improved. It uses white space that organizes the document visually: lists, headings, and shorter paragraphs.

Keep in mind that these devices take space, but white space is a useful tool.[9] When saving space is essential, it's better to cut text to make room for sufficient white space than to keep all the text packed together. A clear mark of an amateur document designer is one who tries to fill an entire page with visuals and text.

In visual-heavy documents such as company logos, white space can do more than provide a visual buffer for text: it can convey its own message. The FedEx logo in Figure 7.7 cleverly shapes white space between the "E" and "x," creating a forward-pointing arrow. Whether customers consciously notice the subtle arrow or not, it implies that FedEx is swift or progressive—and this message is composed completely of white space.

4. Strategize Margin Choices.

Word-processing programs allow you to use **full justification** so that type lines up evenly on both the right and left margins. The text in Figure 7.5 uses full justification. Full justification can give a text a more formal look, but it can create problems too. For example, because the words get stretched out across the line, "rivers" of vertical white space can appear throughout a paragraph.

Margins justified only on the left, sometimes called **ragged-right margins**, have lines ending in different places. Figure 7.6 shows text set ragged-right. Ragged-right text avoids the problems that can occur with full justification. It has a somewhat less formal look than fully justified text, but it will still look professional if you follow the other design guidelines.

5. Place Elements for Deliberate Emphasis.

Readers of English are accustomed to reading pages from left to right. Effective document designers tap into this habit. They know that we start in the upper left-hand corner of the page, read to the right, move down, and then to the right again. Actually, the eye moves in a Z pattern (see Figure 7.8).[10] Therefore, the four quadrants of the page carry different visual weights. The upper left quadrant, where the eye starts, is the most important; the bottom right quadrant, where the eye ends, is next most important.

6. Unify Elements with Grids.

Many document designers use a **grid system** to design pages. In its simplest form, a grid imposes two or three imaginary columns on the page. In more complex grids, these columns can be further subdivided. Then all the graphic elements—text indentations, headings, visuals, and so on—align within the columns. The resulting symmetry creates a more pleasing page and unifies long documents. Figure 7.9 uses grids to organize a page with visuals and a newsletter page.

Figure 7.8   Place Important Elements in Upper Left and Bottom Right Quadrants

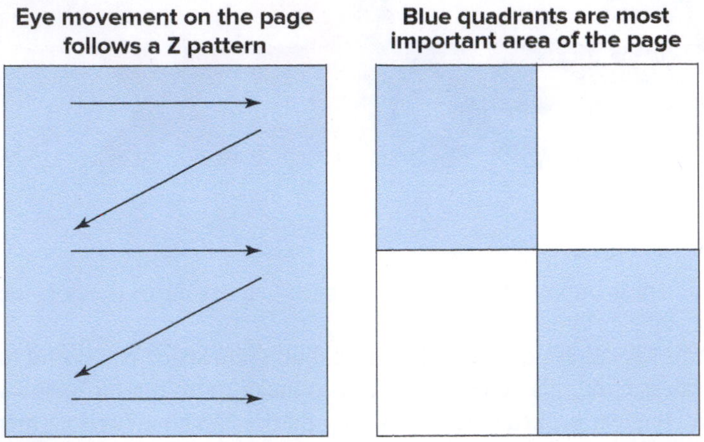

Figure 7.9   Grids Visually Unify Content

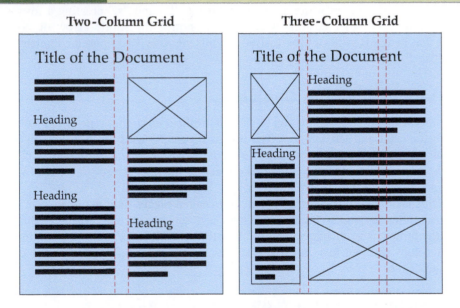

7. Use Headings.

Headings are words, short phrases, or short sentences that group points and divide your document into sections. Headings enable your reader to see at a glance how the document is organized, to turn quickly to sections of special interest, and to compare and contrast points more easily. Headings also break up the page, making it look less formidable and more interesting.

Psychological research shows that short-term memories can hold only five to nine bits of information.[11] Only after those bits are processed and put into long-term memory can we assimilate new information. You'll help your audience process large amounts of information if you group items into three to seven chunks with headings and subheadings rather presenting them with a long list of individual items.

To use headings effectively:

- Write informative and specific headings.

- Write each heading so it covers all the information before the next heading.

- Write headings at the same level with parallel language. For example, all the design tips in this section start with a command-form verb such as "Place" or "Use."

Research continues to show that headings help readers. In a study that examined forensic child-abuse reports from Canadian children's hospitals, researchers examined communication between the physicians who authored the reports and the social workers, lawyers, and police officers who later used them. They discovered that headings and subheadings improved accessibility of crucial information about the severity of the children's injuries.[12]

8. Unify Documents with Consistent, Sparing Decorative Strategies.

Used in moderation, highlighting, color, and other decorative devices add interest to documents. However, don't overdo them. A page or screen that uses every possible decorating device looks busy and is difficult to read.

Because the connotations of colors vary among cultures, do some research before you use color for international or multicultural audiences. In North America, red is appropriate for warnings. Pastel colors such as lavender create a calming impression, while bright colors imply urgency. The brown color of UPS's trucks and uniforms projects an image of reliability; consumers discerning between red- and green-packaged candy bars perceived the green one as healthier, even when content and package text were identical.[13]

To visually unify your document:

- **Match color with purpose.**   Color highlights content and impacts tone.

- **Use a limited, consistent color scheme to create unity.**   Don't overuse color to the point of desensitizing your audience. For example, you might use dark purple for headings and subheadings, captions for visuals in dark blue, and body text in black. You also could use a monochromatic palette, such as dark green headings, medium green frames around visuals, and a light green for the background of text boxes. If you are on a limited printing budget, try a monochrome grayscale palette.

- **Use repetition to create rhythm.**   Repeat design elements such as headings, text boxes, or visuals to create a unified look across pages.

- **Use contrast to create visual interest.**   Consider contrast between text and visuals or between a larger font for headings and a smaller one for text. Note that color contrast is a different concern; see "How to Design Inclusively" later in this chapter.

How to Incorporate Design into the Writing Process

LO 7-5

Seamlessly functional, visually appealing documents require the consideration of design at every step of the writing process. Before you draft or even research your content, consider how the rhetorical situation may influence design strategy.

Analyzing Your Rhetorical Situation

As noted earlier in this book, in all forms of business communication, you should begin by considering your rhetorical situation, including your purpose, medium, and audience.

Purpose   *What design approach or tone does your purpose dictate?* A brochure designed to promote awareness of your company should have a different look than a brochure persuading people to purchase your company's products. For example, a primarily informative brochure may use more graphs or infographics, while a persuasive

Figure 7.10

Figure 7.10   Showerhead Card for Breast Self-Exam

brochure may use images evoking emotional appeals. What is the aim of your communication, and how can your design strategy support that aim?

Medium   *What are the design capabilities and limitations of the medium?* Context-adapted design requires attention to the capabilities, restrictions, and conventions of your communication's particular medium. When working with a new medium, you will need to study preexisting examples, if possible, and use your best judgment in deciding how to design in a way that suits that medium. A billboard medium offers different design possibilities and restrictions than do an email newsletter or a poster on the side of a public bus.

Audience   *What needs, expectations, and concerns does your audience have?* Just as you should adapt written communication to your audience, you also should consider how design can adapt to your audience's needs, expectations, and potential objections. The hanging card for breast self-exams in Figure 7.10, designed to be hung from a showerhead, caters to an audience who do not perform breast self-exams because of forgetfulness or insufficient time. These water-resistant shower cards adapt to those concerns, offering a reminder to perform an exam when in the shower.

Researching Your Topic

As you research your topic, consider whether some content might be better illustrated in a visual rather than textual format. How can you use design to save your audience time or to aid comprehension?

Drafting the Text

As you draft your text, keep in mind how textual content tethers to graphic content. Depending on your medium, you may need to change font size or style or revise for length in order to neatly align textual and graphic content. For example, in the poster from Milwaukee's Safe Sleep campaign, where the headboard looks like a headstone (see Figure 7.11), the text needed to fit within the headboard space and be long enough to remind viewers of text on a headstone.

Selecting Appropriate Visuals

Keep in mind that not all communication needs visuals, but all communication has a visual component—considerations such as white space, font size, and use of bullets or headings. If you decide that visuals suit your rhetorical situation, develop them thoughtfully: Do the visuals tell a story, convey information more effectively than text, or otherwise serve a purpose? Are the visuals free for public use or used with permission, and properly credited? Do visuals representing people account for diversity and inclusion? Do the visuals' style match the tone of your communication?

The Milwaukee-based Safe Sleep Campaign created a series of Public Service Announcements cautioning parents against sleeping with their infants and promoting the use of cribs (see Figures 7.11, 7.12, and 7.13). Notice the difference in tone across the three images, which were created across two years. Which visual do you think was the best choice for the rhetorical situation? Each image is one of several in a set, so for further context, visit the original source.[14]

In 2015, in response to criticism of the "whitewashing" of emojis, Apple released a set of the icons that allows users to select from a scale of skin tones.[15] When portraying a group of people, consider representation of gender, race, ability, age, body shape, ethnicity, and other forms of diversity, and take care to represent people authentically. Audiences want to see themselves represented in visual communication, but there is a fine line between helping your audience imagine themselves as part of the scenario your communication describes and depicting a situation that is not true, which could detract attention away from addressing issues of inequality. If, for example, your company employs only 10% women and wants to recruit more women as employees, it would be inauthentic to feature a photo on your company's HR website with six women and five men working together, implying that such a gender ratio is representative of the company. A photo with two women and three men, depicting a doubling of the current women-employee rate, would be a more appropriate choice to represent the company's hiring goals and help potential women applicants envision themselves working there.

Consider whether you want visuals to downplay or highlight realism. On a sign labeling the compost bin in a company cafeteria, it may be more appropriate to draw a stylized compost pile, or representative food scraps such as an apple core, rather than using a photograph of actual compost. In other situations, a photograph may be preferable for accuracy or realism—if a large amount of farmland is up for auction, for example, an aerial photo with superimposed demarcations of the lot's boundaries would provide more meaningful

Figure 7.11   Safe Sleep Campaign Poster 1: Headboard as Gravestone (January 2010)

Source: http://city.milwaukee.gov

Figure 7.12	Safe Sleep Campaign Poster 2: Baby in Bed with Knife (November 2011)

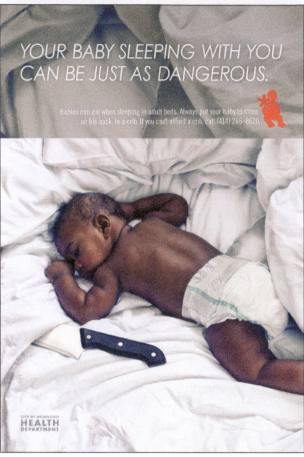

Source: http://city.milwaukee.gov

Figure 7.13	Safe Sleep Campaign Poster 3: Baby in Crib on Words (July 2012)

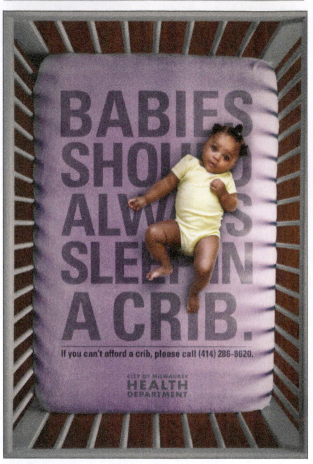

Source: http://city.milwaukee.gov

information to potential buyers than a stylized map of the lot. For additional information about incorporating visuals, including their ethical design and use, see Chapter 8.

Creating the Design

Use design to control and optimize your audience's experience of the document. What does your audience need your document to do and how can good design direct their eyes (or mouse-clicks) to save them time? What are your audience's visual needs? What does your audience expect the document to look like? How will your audience's internal dialogue interact with your design at every word, page, header, navigation bar, or scroll?

Use design guidelines to direct the audience's attention, provide for their visual needs, and meet their expectations. Then employ usability testing, discussed in a later section, to gather feedback on whether your design effectively controls your audience's experience of the document. Then revise and test again until your document achieves optimal usability.

Printing/Publishing

Depending on your medium and budget, some printing can be accomplished on a consumer-grade printer. If your organization demands an even higher professional look or if you have thousands of copies to print, take your brochure to a commercial printer.

Four-color printing on glossy paper often looks best; however, it also will incur greater cost. To get the effect of color with the least expense, try black print on colored paper.

Some media, such as webpages, do not need physical printing, while others, such as a yard sign, require medium-specific printing. Allow time to research the best way to print or publish a new or unusual medium; seek out well-published examples of the same form and inquire about their creation methods.

How to Design Inclusively

Accessibility means designing to account for disabilities or unique perceptive needs such as color blindness or impaired vision; accessible design is required by the Americans with Disabilities Act (ADA), and some examples of accessible accommodations include closed captioning of videos and screen-reader-friendly image tags. **Inclusivity** takes accessibility a step further, using accessibility principles to make your document inviting and usable for all users. Designing for inclusivity shows that the document designer cares about each and every user's needs while treating each user as part of a whole rather than an individual who needs accommodations different from a target user. A welcome side effect? Increasing inclusivity often improves all users' experience of a document. Think of the sloping curbs that accommodate wheelchairs offer increased functionality for many other users, from skateboarders to people who may be prone to tripping to a traveler toting a rolling suitcase.

You might not consider clothing to be a communication "document," but NFL team jerseys are "read" by millions of viewers, and their design undergoes scrutiny just like that of a brochure, memo, or website. In 2015's "Color Rush" game between the Bills and the Jets, viewers with red-green color blindness—approximately 8% of the male population and 0.5% of females—had a hard time distinguishing which player was on which team (see Figure 7.14).

Figure 7.14	NFL's "Color Rush" Jersey Designs Overlooked Viewers with Red-Green Color Blindness

Troy Machir/Sporting News

Responding to criticism, the NFL announced that future "Color Rush" jerseys would account for the needs of viewers with color blindness. To avoid similar accessibility oversights in your documents, you can check them against a color-blindness simulator such as Sim Daltonism[16] or toptal's color blindness webpage filter.[17]

Another way to ensure vision-impaired viewers can access your content is to convert your document to grayscale. This technique checks for appropriate color contrast. Note the two color posters in Figure 7.15: the more saturated image on the left is much more legible even when converted to grayscale, while the less saturated image on the right becomes far less legible.

| Figure 7.15 | Sufficient Contrast Increases Legibility |

Good Contrast

Bad Contrast

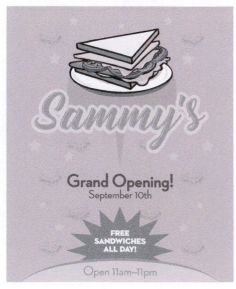

Figure 7.16	Letters of the Proxima Nova Typeface Improve Legibility

The quick brown fox jumps over the lazy dog.

With the team, I moved 111 bushels from farm to bin.

Use of certain fonts also can increase legibility. Asymmetrical fonts in which letters that normally are mirror images, such as "p" and "q," do not mirror each other and fonts such as Proxima Nova (see Figure 7.16) that distinguish between similar characters such as "1" and "I" can increase reading speed and accuracy. However, improving legibility via appropriate contrast or legible fonts benefits everyone, not just viewers with vision impairments, so it demonstrates inclusive design.

How to Test Documents for Usability
LO 7-7

Usability testing, or assessing how well your documents function with real audiences, is an important step in document design. Just because a document has visual appeal does not mean it is functional; in the case of the NFL jerseys, the jerseys looked fine on their own but did not function in the context of paired matches. To assess how well your design serves its purpose, test it with your audience. Then, use feedback to improve your design's usability. If the jersey designers would have shown them to a test group including individuals with red-green color blindness, the unwise pairing of red and green jerseys could have been avoided.

After collecting feedback from both customers and employees, Delta Airlines reimagined the design of its boarding passes. The new look, as shown in Figure 7.17, features a clear hierarchy of information, less clutter, more white space, only one bar code, and a new sans serif typeface. These choices make the new design user-friendly for both Delta employees and passengers.[18]

According to Jakob Nielsen, a usability expert, testing a draft with five users will reveal 85% of the problems with the document.[19] If time and money permit additional testing, revise the document and test the new version with another five users.

To quickly spot design flaws, test the document with the people who are most likely to have trouble with it, such as very old or young users and people who read English as a second language. To design inclusively, test your document with as diverse a group of users as possible; differently abled users and users with perceptual challenges such as color blindness should be able to use your document with ease, which in turn will make your document more functional for all users.

Three kinds of tests yield particularly useful information:

- **Observation.** Watch someone as they use the document to do a task. Where does the user pause, reread, or seem confused? How long does it take? Does the document enable the user to complete the task accurately?

- **User narration/snapshots.** Ask the user to "think aloud" while completing the task or interrupt the user at key points to ask what they are thinking to generate a map of how

Figure 7.17   Before (top) and After (bottom) Redesign of Delta's Boarding Pass

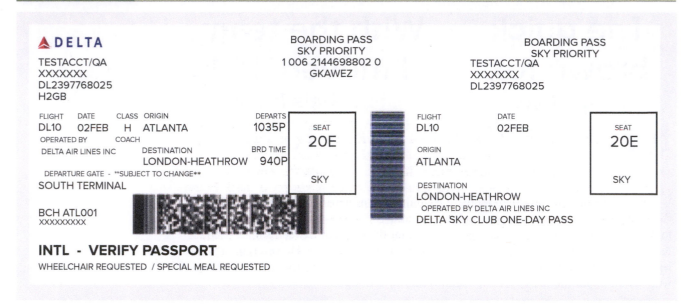

Source: Delta Air Lines, Inc.

the user's mental dialogue interacts with the document. You also can ask the user to describe their thought process after completing the document and the task.

- **User annotation.**   Ask the user to put a plus sign in the margins by any part of the document they agree with or find useful and a minus sign by any part of the document that seems confusing or incorrect. Then use interviews or focus groups to determine the reasons for the plus and minus judgments.

Designing Brochures

LO 7-8

This chapter cannot cover all of the printed documents you are likely to develop as a business communicator; nevertheless, in covering the design of brochures, it provides you with layout ideas that you can transfer to other genres, such as newsletters and posters.

As noted throughout this chapter, engaging design should speak directly to your audience's needs. In designing a brochure, consider why your audience might pick up a brochure and then design to engage with that mental dialogue. For example, the Malaria brochure in Figure 7.18 speaks directly to readers who likely will read the brochure if they are already concerned about contracting malaria; the red, bolded exclamation points draw their attention to key information and the all capital headings in green organize answers to key questions in the readers' minds. The drawings add psychological distance to a potentially scary situation while remaining precise in meaning and, therefore, reassuring. Your content and style may be more formal or informal, but it should affirm the desired image of you or your organization and serve the aim of your communication. The three-fold brochure (also called a tri-fold brochure) of Figure 7.19 depicts the most common brochure layout, but many other arrangements are possible.

Before inserting textual and visual elements into your brochure, optimize layout to consider your audience's viewing tendencies. How will they open the brochure, and which content should they encounter first? How can you guide the audience's eyes using a Z-pattern, grids, or images? Does each panel make sense on its own? Place content to emphasize important points for each spread the reader encounters. In a three-fold brochure, the Z pattern needs to work for the cover alone, for inside pages 1 and 2 (as the reader begins to unfold the brochure), and for inside pages 1, 3, and 4 (when the brochure is fully opened). You even should consider what would happen if the audience doesn't encounter your document as planned: if the brochure is accidentally displayed upside-down, would the information on the back still encourage someone to pick it up?

Figure 7.18 Malaria Brochure Distributed to Zambian Households (also available in local languages)

HOW TO SPOT MALARIA SIGNS

You might have malaria if you have:
- Fever/body heat
- Headache
- Body aches
- Chills
- Vomiting

It you feel sick, it is important to seek treatment right away from your Community Health Worker (CHW). Just one sick person in the household can spread malaria to others in the home through the bite of a mosquito.

Take people with severe malaria *immediately* to the health facility. Severe malaria signs:
- Fever for several days
- Constant vomiting
- Dark urine
- Severe headache and body aches
- Has fits
- Fainting or unconsciousness

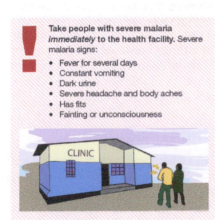

WHAT TO DO IF YOU THINK YOU HAVE MALARIA

Go to your Community Health Worker to get tested and treated for malaria. The CHW will test you for malaria, and if it is positive, give you treatment. The treatment will cure you of malaria.

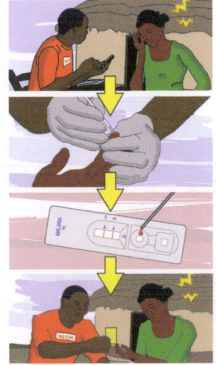

Take all pills given to you. Follow dose instructions carefully. For children under five, crush pills and put into water to dissolve before giving medicine to child.

The CHW will also test and treat others in your household for malaria. It is important that everyone get tested for malaria, even if they feel well, because people can have malaria without signs. After visiting your house, the CHW will visit your neighbors and test and treat them for malaria too. This will help make your community malaria-free.

Bret Smith/PATH

Figure 7.19   Page Setup for a Three-Fold Brochure on 8.5-Inch × 11-Inch Paper

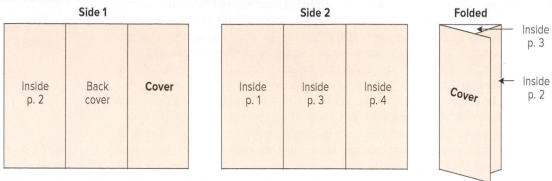

When creating a three-fold brochure, mimic this page setup so your final document prints correctly.

Designing Websites

LO 7-9

This chapter cannot cover all of the online documents you are likely to develop as a business communicator; nevertheless, in covering some of the basics of web design, it provides some guidelines that will transfer to other interactive documents that audiences encounter on screens of various sizes.

To create effective websites, you must attract and maintain the audience's attention, create a helpful home page with useful navigation, follow conventions, and adapt to possible delivery methods. As you design a website, you should also ensure that it is accessible to people with disabilities. Finally, you should test your website to ensure audiences interact with it as intended.

Attracting and Maintaining Attention

Steve Yankovich, vice president for eBay mobile, states, "We've found that people will give us 30 to 60 seconds to connect them with the things they need and love."[20] The amount of time you have to attract and keep an audience's attention on your website is minimal. Researchers tracked how long users took to read or scan webpages; 52% of the visits were shorter than 10 seconds. In fact, 25% were less than four seconds. Only 10% were longer than two minutes. Therefore, you should employ a simple, attractive design strategy that draws your audience in and carefully avoid any design flaws that could cause audiences to leave your website immediately.[21]

Once you've gained your audience's attention, arrange content in a way that will maintain that attention. Jakob Nielsen's research shows that people view websites in an F-shaped pattern. First, they quickly read across the top of the page. Then they move down the page some and read across again, but for a shorter distance. Finally, they scan down the left side. All this happens quickly. The F-shaped pattern means that your most important information must be at the top of the page. In addition, make sure that headings, paragraphs, and items in lists start with words important to your reader.[22]

Creating a Helpful Home Page and Navigation

To keep visitors around long enough to find (or buy) what they want, design your home page and navigation with care. Your home page should load quickly and your navigation should readily orient users to the information they want. Studies show that users grow impatient if they must wait for a page to load, and most will leave the site immediately.[23] In addition, first-time visitors tend not to scroll down beyond the first screen of text; if the audience has to work too hard to figure out how to use your webpage, chances are they will leave the site.

- **Provide a simple, accessible orientation to the website's author or purpose.**   Many websites feature a prominently placed link to an "About" or "FAQ" page; this design choice caters to users who want to assess the site's ethos before reading further or who need the website to quickly answer a question and don't want to have to navigate a complex menu to locate that answer.

- **Provide useful navigation tools.**   A site index, search tool, and navigation bars (vertically on the left of the screen or horizontally on the top and bottom) can help users locate the content they need.

- **Make clear what readers will get if they click on a link.**

Ineffective phrasing:	Employment. Openings and skill levels are determined by each office.
Better phrasing:	Employment. Openings listed by skill level and by location.

- **Make completing a task as easy as possible.**   The donut store, Half a Dozen of One, designed the "Order" button on its website, shown in Figure 7.20, to stand out from other links so users can quickly use the website to perform a desired function—in this case, ordering a late-night snack.

Following Conventions

Nielsen urges his readers to follow conventions of webpages and get back to design basics. He reminds designers that users want quality basics. Here are some of the top web design mistakes he lists:

- Bad search engines.

- Links that don't change color when visited.

- Large text blocks.

- Fixed font size.

- Content that doesn't answer users' questions.

  He also cautions against violating design conventions. Users will expect your website to act like the other sites they visit. If it doesn't, the site will be harder to use and visitors will leave. Nielsen warns that some conventions, such as banner ads, have outlived their usefulness. Banner blindness is so prevalent that anything that looks like a banner will be ignored, as one nonprofit health site discovered. The site had a box at the top of the home page telling users what to do if they thought they were having a heart attack, but research showed that users were ignoring the box because they thought it was an ad.[24]

Figure 7.20   Half a Dozen of One's Donut Website Directs Users to "Order"

©aquariagirl1970/Shutterstock

aquariagirl1970/Shutterstock

As you design webpages, use the following guidelines:

- Use a white or light background for easy scanning.

- Keep visuals small. Specify the width and height so that the text will stay in a fixed location while the graphics load.

- Provide visual variety in your text. Use indentations, bulleted or numbered lists, and headings. Start lists with impact words; remember the F pattern.

- Unify multiple pages with a small logo or label so surfers know who sponsors each page.

- If your webpages include music or sound effects, place an Off button where the user can see it immediately.

As you might guess, you can find many resources about webpage design guidelines; on technical pages regarding HTML, XML, CSS, and Java; and on webpage design programs such as Dreamweaver.

Adapting to Delivery Methods

Today's web users expect to be able to access sites from a variety of devices, such as laptops, smartphones, and tablets. **Mobile-first design** prioritizes functionality and accessibility across many devices. Google encourages app developers to design mobile-friendly apps so that Google can index them for search results, asserting that "users should get the most relevant and timely [search] results, no matter if the information lives on mobile-friendly webpages or apps."[25]

There are two main ways to design a website for mobile viewing: **adaptive design** and **responsive design**. Adaptive design rearranges the full website's content into a mobile window, essentially reshaping the content for a different-sized "frame," whereas responsive design renders content specifically for a mobile screen. A more complex website, such as a health insurance portal, may need adaptive design in order to convey all its content, whereas a website with simpler purpose, such as a pizza-ordering website, may better meet its customers' needs with a responsive website specifically designed for mobile use.

Designing websites for mobile compatibility can affect an organization's bottom line. When United Way redesigned its website with mobile-first, responsive design, traffic increased by over 20% for tablets and 34% for smartphones, with donations growing by 28% compared with the year before.

Designing Inclusive Websites

Inclusive design brings specific consideration to the website medium. Users with hearing impairments need captions for audio material, and users with vision impairments need words, not visuals. Target settled a class action suit with the National Federation of the Blind by agreeing to pay $6 million in damages and to make its site more accessible. More legal proceedings got Apple to agree to make iTunes more accessible. One of the most sought-after features in these legal actions is text attached to links and visuals that can be accessed by screen-reading software.[26]

To make your webpage accessible for people with vision impairments,

- Put a link to a text-only version of the site in the upper left-hand corner.

- Put navigation links, a site map, and search box at the top of the screen, preferably in the upper left-hand corner.

- Arrange navigation links alphabetically so users with loss of vision can use a screen reader to jump to the links they want.

- Provide alternative text (an "alt tag") for all images, applets, and submit buttons.

- Provide a static alternative to flash or animation.

- In linked text, use words that makes sense when read alone. A person listening to a screen reader will not understand "click here." "Click to order a copy" or "Click for details" offers a better clue of what the link leads to.

Testing Websites for Usability

Nielsen recommends usability testing at various stages of the website design process by observing users navigating the site because you may detect behaviors that users might not be aware of themselves, such as viewing websites in an F-pattern.[27] Many apps use "beta testing" on select groups of users—usually volunteers who know the app may not be perfect—to gather usability feedback on how well a new app performs. Using this insight, they can revise the app before rolling out a widely marketed version. This helps preserve a company's reputation by avoiding launching an error-ridden application.[28] You should ask others to beta test your website so you, too, can ensure your electronic communication presents a professional image.

Summary by Learning Objectives

LO 7-1 Explain why document design is important.

- Good document design saves time and money, affirms the creator's desired image, and builds goodwill.
- Effective design groups ideas visually, making the structure of a document more inviting and obvious so the document is easier to use.

LO 7-2 Explain design conventions.

Effective design relies heavily on conventions, which vary by purpose, medium, and audience.

LO 7-3 Explain the four levels of document design.

The four levels of design—intra, inter, extra, and supra—help you organize and analyze design choices.

LO 7-4 Apply design guidelines for each level.

These guidelines help writers create visually attractive and functional documents:

1. Strategize font choices.
2. Minimize use of words in all capital letters.
3. Use white space.
4. Strategize margin choices.
5. Place elements for deliberate emphasis.
6. Unify elements with grids.
7. Use headings.
8. Unify document with consistent, sparing decorative strategies.

LO 7-5 Incorporate design into the writing process.

The best documents are created when you think about design at each stage of the writing process.

- As you plan, think about the needs of your audience.
- As you write, incorporate lists, headings, and visuals.
- Get feedback from people who will be using your document.
- As you revise, check your draft against the guidelines in this chapter.

LO 7-6 Design inclusively.

Inclusive design means accounting for accessibility needs in a way that benefits all users. Some inclusive design considerations include vision impairment, dyslexia, and color blindness.

LO 7-7 Test your documents for usability.

Usability testing is assessing your documents with real audiences. To conduct a usability test, observe people reading the document or using it to complete a task.

LO 7-8 Design brochures.

To create an effective brochure, you must analyze your rhetorical situation, draft the text, select appropriate visuals, create the design, and print.

LO 7-9 Design websites.

To create effective websites, you must attract and maintain the audience's attention, create a helpful home page with useful navigation, follow conventions, adapt to possible delivery methods, design for inclusivity, and test for usability.

Exercises and Cases

7.1   Reviewing the Chapter

1. Why is document design important? (LO 7-1)
2. What are design conventions and what determines the conventions you'll follow? (LO 7-2)
3. What are the four levels of document design? (LO 7-3)
4. What are some critical guidelines for document design? (LO 7-4)

5. How can you incorporate design into your writing process? (LO 7-5)
6. What are considerations for designing inclusively? (LO 7-6)
7. How can you test your document's usability? (LO 7-7)
8. What are some guidelines for designing brochures? (LO 7-8)
9. What are some guidelines for designing websites? (LO 7-9)

7.2   Evaluating Page Designs

Use the guidelines in this chapter to evaluate each of the following page designs. What are their strong points? What could be improved?

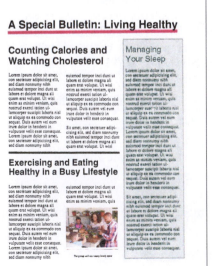

(Roller skates): Waltraud Ingerl/Getty Images; (Family meal): iStock/Getty Images

As your instructor directs,

a. Discuss the design elements you see on these sample pages with a small group of classmates.

b. Write an email to your instructor evaluating the design elements on each of the sample pages. Be sure to address the four levels of design, as well as the guidelines for document design discussed in this chapter.

c. In an oral presentation to the class, explain the process you'd use to redesign one of the sample pages. What design elements would make the page stronger or weaker? What design elements would you change and how? Given the title of the document, what audience characteristics might your design take into account?

7.3   Evaluating the Ethics of Design Choices

Indicate whether you consider each of the following actions ethical, unethical, or a gray area. Which of the actions would you do? Which would you feel uncomfortable doing? Which would you refuse to do?

1. Putting the advantages of a proposal in a bulleted list, while discussing the disadvantages in a paragraph.

2. Using a bigger type size so that a résumé visually fills a whole page.

3. Using tiny print and very little white space on a credit card contract to make it less likely that people will read it.

4. Putting important information on the back of what looks like a one-page document.

5. Putting the services that are not covered by your health plan in full caps to make it less likely that people will read the page.

7.4   Evaluating Page Designs

1. Collect several documents that you receive as a consumer, a student, or an employee: forms, letters, newsletters, emails, announcements, ads, flyers, and reports. Use the document design guidelines in this chapter to evaluate each of them.

2. Compare these documents in a specific category to the documents produced by competing organizations. Which documents are more effective? Why?

As your instructor directs,

a. Discuss the documents with a small group of classmates.

b. Write an email to your instructor evaluating three or more of the documents and comparing them to similar documents produced by competitors. Include originals or photocopies of the documents you discuss in an attachment to your email.

c. Write an email to one of the originating organizations, recommending ways it can improve the document design.

d. In an oral presentation to the class, explain what makes one document strong and another one weak.

7.5   Evaluating Public Service Announcements (PSAs)

Compare the full sets of public service announcements (PSAs) represented by Figures 7.11, 7.12, and 7.13 by visiting http://city.milwaukee.gov/health/Safe-Sleep-Campaign. Which set is most effective? Why? What weaknesses does each set have? Based on the chronological progression of these sets, who do you think the target audience is?

As your instructor directs,

a. Discuss the sets of PSAs with a small group of classmates.

b. Write an email to your instructor evaluating the PSA designs. Include URLs of the PSAs in your email.

c. In an oral presentation to the class, explain what makes the design of one set good and that of another set weak.

d. Post your evaluation in a discussion forum to the class. Include the URLs so classmates can click to the PSAs you discuss.

7.6   Comparing Shopping Websites

In a pair or in small groups, find three online shopping sites that sell similar types of merchandise (e.g., Backcountry.com, Moosejaw.com, REI.com). Consider the following questions:

- Who are the target audiences of the websites?
- What are some of the design features the websites offer customers?

- How easily navigable are the home pages?
- Are the websites organized with an F-shaped pattern?
- How user-friendly are the websites?
- How well do the websites' search engines function?
- How accessible are the websites for people with vision or mobility impairments?

■   Of the three websites, which is the best in terms of usability?

As your instructor directs,
a.   Discuss the websites with your partner or small group.

b.   Share your findings in an informal presentation for the rest of the class.

c.   Write an email to your instructor containing your findings.

7.7   Testing a Document

Ask someone to follow a set of instructions or to fill out a form. (Consider consumer instructions, forms for financial aid, and so forth.) As an alternative, you also might test a document you've created for a course. You also may try ordering food from a website, such as a pizza-delivery chain, as long as you do not process completely through the checkout process.

■   Time the person. How long does it take? Is the person able to complete the task?

■   Observe the person. Where does the person pause, reread, seem confused?

■   Interview the person. What parts of the document were confusing?

As your instructor directs,
a.   Discuss the changes needed with a small group of classmates.

b.   Write an email to your instructor evaluating the document and explaining the changes that are needed. Include the document as an attachment to your email.

c.   Write to the organization that produced the document recommending necessary improvements.

d.   In an oral presentation to the class, evaluate the document and explain what changes are needed.

7.8   Improving a Financial Aid Form

You've just joined the financial aid office at your school. The director gives you the form shown below and asks you to redesign it. The director says:

> We need this form to see whether parents have other students in college besides the one requesting aid. Parents are supposed to list all family members that the parents support—themselves, the person here, any other children in college, and any younger dependent kids.
>
> Half of these forms are filled out incorrectly. Most people just list the student going here; they leave out everyone else.
>
> If something is missing, the computer sends out a letter and a second copy of this form. The whole process starts over. Sometimes we send this form back two or three times before it's right. In the meantime, students' financial aid is delayed—maybe for months. Sometimes things are so late that they can't register for classes, or they have to pay tuition themselves and get reimbursed later.
>
> If so many people are filling out the form wrong, the form itself must be the problem. See what you can do with it. But keep it to a page.

As your instructor directs,
a.   Analyze the current form and identify its problems.

b.   Revise the form. Add necessary information; reorder information; change the chart to make it easier to fill out.

c.   Write an email to the director of financial aid pointing out the changes you made and why you made them.

Hints:

■   Where are people supposed to send the form? What is the phone number of the financial aid office? Should they need to call the office if the form is clear?

■   Does the definition of *half-time* apply to all students or just those taking courses beyond high school?

■   Should capital or lowercase letters be used?

■   Are the lines big enough to write in?

■   What headings or subdivisions within the form would remind people to list all family members whom they support?

■   How can you encourage people to return the form promptly?

Please complete the chart below by listing all family members for whom you (the parents) will provide more than half support during the academic year (July 1 through June 30). Include yourselves (the parents), the student, and your dependent children, even if they are not attending college.

EDUCATIONAL INFORMATION, 202_ – 202_						
FULL NAME OF FAMILY MEMBER	AGE	RELATIONSHIP OF FAMILY MEMBER TO STUDENT	NAME OF SCHOOL OR COLLEGE THIS SCHOOL YEAR	FULL-TIME	HALF-TIME* OR MORE	LESS THAN HALF-TIME
STUDENT APPLICANT						

*Half-time is defined as 6 credit hours or 12 clock hours a term.

When the information requested is received by our office, processing of your financial aid application will resume.

Please sign and mail this form to the above address as soon as possible. Your signature certifies that this information, and the information on the FAF, is true and complete to the best of your knowledge. If you have any questions, please contact a member of the need analysis staff.

_____   _____

Signature of Parent(s)   Date

Notes

1. Edward Tufte, *Beautiful Evidence* (Cheshire, CT: Graphics Press, 2006), 153–55.
2. *Des Moines Register*, Front Page, October 14, 2011.
3. Don Van Natta Jr. and Dana Canedy, "The 2000 Elections: The Palm Beach Ballot: Florida Democrats Say Ballot's Design Hurt Gore," *New York Times*, November 9, 2000, http://www.nytimes.com/2000/11/09/us/2000-elections-palm-beach-ballot-florida-democrats-say-ballot-s-design-hurt-gore.html.
4. Charles Kostelnick and Michael Hassett, *Shaping Information: The Rhetoric of Visual Conventions* (Carbondale, IL: Southern Illinois University Press, 2003), 92, 94.
5. Charles Kostelnick and David Roberts, *Designing Visual Language*, 2nd ed. (Boston: Allyn & Bacon, 2011), 81–83.
6. Jo Mackiewicz, "What Technical Writing Students Should Know about Typeface Personality," *Journal of Technical Writing and Communication* 34, no. 1–2 (2004): 113–31.
7. Jerry E. Bishop, "Word Processing: Research on Stroke Victims Yields Clues to the Brain's Capacity to Create Language," *Wall Street Journal*, October 12, 1993, A6; and Anne Meyer and David H. Rose, "Learning to Read in the Computer Age," in *Reading Research to Practice*, ed. Jeanne S. Chall (Cambridge, MA: Brookline Books, 1998), 4–6.
8. Karen A. Schriver, *Dynamics in Document Design* (New York: Wiley, 1997), 274.
9. Rebecca Hagen and Kim Golombisky, *White Space Is Not Your Enemy: A Beginner's Guide to Communicating Visually through Graphic, Web, and Multimedia Design*, 2nd ed. (New York: Focal Press, 2013), 7.
10. Miles A. Kimball and Ann R. Hawkins, *Document Design: A Guide for Technical Communicators* (Boston: Bedford/St. Martin's, 2008), 49, 125.
11. George A. Miller, "The Magical Number Seven, Plus or Minus Two: Some Limits on Our Capacity for Processing Information," *Psychological Review* 63, no. 2 (1956): 81–97.
12. Marlee M. Spafford, Catherine F. Schryer, Lorelei Lingard, and Marcellina Mian, "Accessibility and Order: Crossing Borders in Child Abuse Forensic Reports," *Technical Communication Quarterly* 19, no. 2 (2010): 118–43.
13. Adapted from Jonathon P. Schuldt, "Does Green Mean Healthy? Nutrition Label Color Affects Perceptions of

Healthfulness," *Health Communication* (2013): 1-8; doi: 10.1080 /10410236.2012.725270.

14. Milwaukee Health Department, "Safe Sleep Campaign," http:// city.milwaukee.gov/health/Safe-Sleep-Campaign.

15. Bill Chappell, "2015 Emoji Update Will Include More Diverse Skin Tones," *The Two Way: Breaking News from NPR*, November 4, 2014, http://www.npr.org/sections/thetwo-way/2014 /11/04/361489535/2015-emoji-update-will-include-more-diverse -skin-tones.

16. Michel Fortin, "Sin Daltonism: The Color Blindness Simulator," https://michelf.ca/projects/sim-daltonism.

17. Toptal, "Colorblind Web Page Filter," https://www.toptal.com /designers/colorfilter.

18. Sarah Nassauer, "Marketing Decoder: Airline Boarding Passes," *Wall Street Journal*, May 3, 2012, D2.

19. Jakob Nielsen, "Why You Only Need to Test with 5 Users," *Nielsen Norman Group: Jakob Nielsen's Alertbox*, March 19, 2000,http://www.nngroup.com/articles/why-you-only-need-to-test -with-5-users.

20. "Lessons, Part 2," *Fast Company*, December 2012/January 2013, 98.

21. Harald Weinreich et al., "Not Quite the Average: An Empirical Study of Web Use," *ACM Transactions on the Web* 2, no. 1 (2008): 18.

22. Jakob Nielsen, "F-Shaped Pattern for Reading Web Content," *Nielsen Norman Group: Jakob Nielsen's Alertbox*, April 17, 2006, http://www.nngroup.com/articles/f-shaped-pattern-reading -web-content.

23. Jakob Nielsen, "Website Response Time," *Nielsen Norman Group: Jakob Nielsen's Alertbox*, June 21, 2010, http://www.nngroup. com/articles/website-response-times.

24. Jakob Nielsen, "Top Ten Mistakes in Web Design," *Nielsen Norman Group: Jakob Nielsen's Alertbox*, January 1, 2011, http://www .nngroup.com/articles/top-10-mistakes-web-design; and Emily Steel, "Neglected Banner Ads Get a Second Life," *Wall Street Journal*, June 20, 2007, B4.

25. Google Webmaster Central Blog, "Finding More Mobile-Friendly Search Results," February 26, 2015, https:// developers.google.com/search/blog/2015/02/finding-more -mobile-friendly-search?hl=en

26. "Corporate News: Target Settles with Blind Group on Web Access," *Wall Street Journal*, August 28, 2008, B4; and Lauren Pollock, "iTunes Eases Access for Blind," *Wall Street Journal*, September 29, 2008, B5.

27. Jakob Nielsen, "Usability 101: Introduction to Usability," *Nielsen Norman Group: Jakob Nielsen's Alertbox*, January 4, 2012, http:// www.nngroup.com/articles/usability-101-introduction-to-usability.

28. Ian Taylor, "The 5 Best Beta-Testing Tools for Your App," *InfoWorld from IDG*, April 24, 2017, https://www.infoworld.com /article/3191442/application-testing/the-5-best-beta-testing-tools -for-your-app.html.

CHAPTER

8 Creating Effective Visuals

Chapter Outline

When to Use Visuals

Types of Visuals

- Images
- Tables
- Charts
- Graphs
- Hybrids

Other Guidelines for Creating Effective Visuals

- Follow Conventions
- Use Color Carefully
- Be Ethical

Integration of Visuals into Your Text

Summary by Learning Objectives

DrAfter123/Getty Images

When Is Correlation Causation?

2018 Guardian News and Media Limited or its affiliated companies/Alamy Stock Photo

An R-value of 1.00 demonstrates perfect correlation. For example, every time it rains, the water level in your rain gauge rises; the R-value is 1.00. So when a scientist published a graph showing a 0.99 correlation between a widely used herbicide and autism rates, many people interpreted the correlation as causation. Alongside this graph (see Figure 8.1) were others charting high correlations between glyphosate application and rates of illnesses such as cancer. And then the International Agency for Research on Cancer declared glyphosate to be "a probable carcinogen."

The public was concerned. And so Monsanto, the company that created glyphosate, the herbicide also known as Roundup, was concerned as well. Roundup-related products (including Roundup-resistant seeds) accounted for about half of Monsanto's profits. If the public—not to mention other scientists—believed that glyphosate causes autism or cancer, it could have drastic consequences for the company—and for farmers and crops worldwide.

Monsanto went to work persuading the public and the scientific community that glyphosate was safe, insisting the chemical did not cause cancer; opponents accused Monsanto of a coverup. A former EPA scientist, on her deathbed due to cancer, declared that the EPA knew the chemical to be carcinogenic. In late 2017, the European Union's Chemical Agency (EChA) re-approved glyphosate after an extended debate over its safety, a seeming win for the chemical, although EChA noted, "this is not the end of the process."

It's true that the lines in the graph align. But the world doesn't yet know whether this alignment is causation or simply correlation: more research is needed. In the meantime, doubt seeded by a graph has upended glyphosate's reputation as a relatively safe herbicide and, possibly, our food supply. The next time you create a visual, such as a data display, craft it with care. Be sure the story it tells is accurate and ethical.

Sources: Nancy Lee Swanson, Bradley C. Wallet, and Andre Frederick Leu, "Genetically Engineered Crops, Glyphosate and the Deterioration of Health in the United States of America," *Journal of Organic Systems* 9, no. 2 (2014), https://www.researchgate.net/profile/Nancy_Swanson/publication/283462716_Genetically_engineered _crops_glyphosate_and_the_deterioration_of_health_in_the_United_States_of_America/links/563fde7d08aec6f17ddb8426/Genetically-engineered-crops-glyphosate -and-the-deterioration-of-health-in-the-United-States-of-America.pdf; International Agency for Research on Cancer, "IARC Monographs Volume 112: Evaluation of Five Organophosphate Insecticides and Herbicides," World Health Organization, March 20, 2015, https://www.iarc.fr/en/media-centre/iarcnews/pdf/MonographVolume112.pdf; "US Court Documents Show Monsanto Manager Led Cancer Cover Up for Glyphosate and PCBs," *Sustainable Pulse*, May 19, 2017, https://sustainablepulse.com/2017/05/19 /us-court-documents-show-monsanto-manager-led-cancer-cover-up-for-glyphosate-and-pcbs; and Arthur Neslen, "Glyphosate Weedkiller, Previously Linked to Cancer, Judged Safe by EU Watchdog," *The Guardian*, March 15, 2017, https://www.theguardian.com/environment/2017/mar/15/no-cancer-risk-to-using-glyphosate-weedkiller-says-eu-watchdog.

Learning Objectives

After studying this chapter, you should be able to

LO 8-1 Determine when to use visuals.

LO 8-2 Use images effectively.

LO 8-3 Use tables effectively.

LO 8-4 Use charts effectively.

LO 8-5 Use graphs effectively.

LO 8-6 Use hybrids (visual clusters, infographics, and dynamic data displays) effectively.

LO 8-7 Explain why it's important to follow conventions, use color effectively, and be ethical when choosing and designing visuals.

LO 8-8 Integrate visuals into text.

Figure 8.1	Graph of High Correlation between Glyphosate Use and Autism Rates Was Interpreted as Causal

Number of children (6–21 yrs) with autism served by IDEA plotted against glyphosate use on corn & soy (R = 0.9893, p <= 3.629e-07)
Sources: USDA:NASS; USDE:IDEA

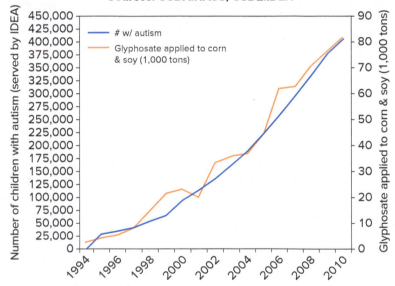

Source: Swanson et al. (2014). Genetically engineered crops, glyphosate and the deterioration of health in the United States of America. *Journal of Organic Systems,* 9(2): 27.

Visuals such as data displays are design elements that help support arguments in your proposals and reports. They also can help communicate your points in brochures, websites, newsletters, social media postings, and other business messages. Besides conveying information, they can add color and emotional appeal. Visuals are often used to enhance oral presentations, which are discussed in Chapter 14.

Data displays such as tables and graphs are particularly useful for presenting numbers dramatically. Suppose you want to give investors information about various stocks' performances. They would not want to read paragraph after paragraph of statements about which stocks went up and which went down. Organizing the daily numbers into tables is much more efficient and useful.

Tables of stock prices have been the norm until recently. Now, the internet offers options such as finviz.com, a dynamic display tool that helps investors see stock performance. Size, color, and other visual elements provide easy cues for spotting the best and worst performers.

When to Use Visuals

LO 8-1

The ease of creating visuals with software such as Excel can make people use them uncritically. Use visuals only to achieve a specific purpose. Never include them in your documents just because you have them; instead, use them to convey information the audience needs or wants. When drafting your document, use visuals

- **To ensure that you've presented your ideas completely.** A table, for example, can show you whether you've included all the items in a comparison.

- **To find relationships.** Charting sales on a map of the U.S. may show that the sales representatives who made quota all have territories on the East or the West Coast. Is the product one that appeals to coastal lifestyles? Is advertising reaching the coasts but not the central states? Even if you don't use the visual in your final document, creating the map may lead you to questions you wouldn't otherwise ask.

In the final presentation or document, use visuals

- **To make points vivid.** Audiences skim documents; a visual catches the eye. The brain processes visuals immediately. Understanding words—written or oral—takes more time.

- **To emphasize material** that your audience might skip if it were buried in a paragraph. Beginnings and endings are places of emphasis. However, something has to go in the middle, especially in a long document. Visuals allow you to emphasize important material, wherever it logically falls.

- **To present material more compactly and with less repetition** than words alone would require. Words can call attention to the main points of the visual, without repeating all of the visual's information.

The number of visuals you will need depends the rhetorical situation, namely, your purposes, the kind of information you want to convey, and your audience. You'll use more visuals when you want to show relationships and to persuade, when the information is complex or contains extensive numerical data, and when the audience values and expects visuals. Some audiences expect presentations and reports to use lots of visuals, particularly data displays such as graphs. Other audiences may see them as frivolous. For these audiences, sharply limit the number of visuals that you use. However, you should still use them when your own purposes and the information call for them.

Types of Visuals

Visuals fall into five main categories:

- Images, such as photographs, drawings, and maps.
- Tables, which can be either textual or numerical.
- Charts, such as flow charts, organizational charts, and Gantt charts.
- Graphs, such as pie graphs, bar graphs, line graphs, and scatterplot graphs.
- Hybrids, such as visual clusters, infographics, and dynamic data displays.

This section explores these categories in more depth.

LO 8-2

Images

Images are pictorial. Business communication relies on three main types: photographs, drawings, and maps.

Photographs convey a sense of authenticity or realism and can show an object in use. The photo of a devastated area can suggest the need for government grants or private donations. The photo of a prototype helps convince investors that a product can be manufactured. If the item is especially big or small, you can include something in the photograph that can serve as a reference point, such as a penny or a person. See Figure 8.2 for an example of a photo that compares a potentially lethal dose of fentanyl to the size of a penny. The photo powerfully demonstrates the opioid's strength.

With **drawings**, the artist can display dimensions, show processes, emphasize detail, represent a theoretical or proposed scenario, or eliminate unwanted detail. Because drawings provide as much or as little detail as needed to make the point, they are more effective than photos for focusing on particular details. Drawings are also better than photos for showing structures underground, undersea, or in the atmosphere. The drawing in Figure 8.3 illustrates important steps in the process of longwall coal mining. The drawings highlight the individual steps in the process.

Use **maps** to emphasize location or to compare items in different locations. Figure 8.4 shows the prevalence of binge drinking among adults by state. In this case, a map is appropriate because the emphasis is on the distribution of binge drinking in various regions. It helps reveal the tendency toward binge drinking in northern states. Several computer software packages now allow users to generate local, state, national, or global maps, adding color or shadings, and labels.

The ethical and effective creation of maps requires consideration of how to manage distortion. Eliminating distortion of a flat map is impossible since a map represents a

Figure 8.2	A Photograph Uses an Object (in this case, a penny) as a Reference Point

Drug Enforcement Administration

Figure 8.3 Drawings Can Show Process

LONGWALL MINING

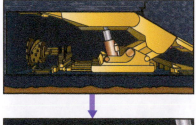
A shearer machine cuts into wide coal seam. Hydraulic supports advance with the machine to keep the roof from collapsing.

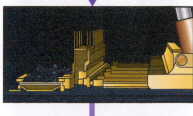
Loosened coal drops onto a conveyor to be removed from the work area.

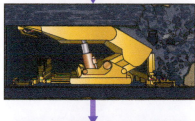
As the equipment moves forward, rock that was supported by coal falls in a controlled manner.

After the maximum amount of coal is recovered safely, the roof is allowed to collapse.

curved area—part of the globe. Distortion certainly has a place, however, when it comes in the form of abstraction that facilitates use. The metro map in Figure 8.5, for example, does not accurately depict distances between subway stops. In this distortion, however, it creates a more usable design.

Tables

LO 8-3

Tables come in two main types: textual and numerical. You've seen several examples of textual tables throughout this book, for example, in Figure 1.1. Use textual tables when you want users to be able to make easy comparisons among different items, such as different product features. They can also help organize discrete textual information, such as the questions, answers, and explanations shown in Figure 8.6. The table in Figure 8.6 is designed to help employees better understand their health care coverage.

Use numerical tables when you want the audience to focus on specific numbers in your data. Numerical tables allow users to focus on particular data points in a way that graphs do not. Figure 8.7 shows a numerical table. The **header row** presents the labels for each column at the top (e.g., Total Average Client Visits). The **stub column** lists the headings for the rows. When constructing tables:

- Use common, understandable units. Round numbers to simplify the data (e.g., 35% rather than 35.27%; 44.5 million rather than 44,503,276).

- Provide column and row totals or averages when they're relevant.

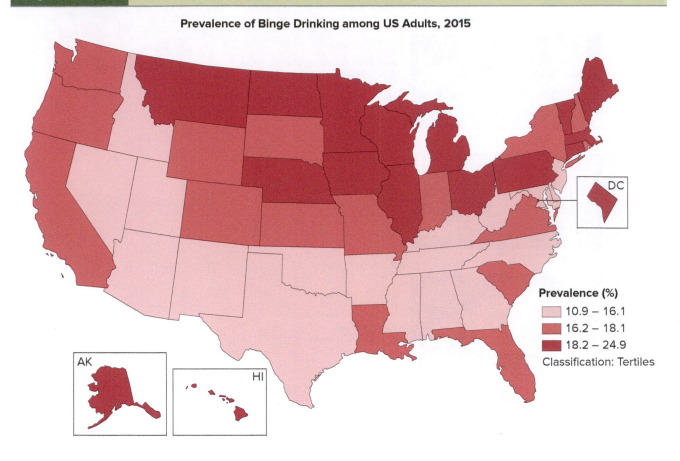

Figure 8.4   Maps Help Compare Information in Different Locations

Prevalence of Binge Drinking among US Adults, 2015

Prevalence (%)
10.9 – 16.1
16.2 – 18.1
18.2 – 24.9
Classification: Tertiles

†**Age-adjusted to the 2000 U.S. Census standard population.**

Source: Centers for Disease Control and Prevention, "Prevalence of Binge Drinking among US Adults, 2015," accessed October 24, 2017, https://www.cdc.gov /alcohol/data-stats.htm.

■ Put the items you want audiences to compare in columns rather than in rows to facilitate mental subtraction and division.

■ When you have many rows, shade alternate rows (or pairs of rows) or double-space after every five rows to help audiences line up items accurately.

LO 8-4

Charts

Charts use spatial relationships to convey information. This section covers three types of charts that commonly appear in business documents.

Flow charts display a process, such as a decision-making or a manufacturing process. Typically, flow charts consistently use shapes, often diamonds and rectangles, to illustrate different types of steps, such as a decision or an action. They may also organize these decisions and actions into "swimlanes," which equate to the person or department responsible for the decision or action. Figure 8.8 shows a flow chart for the fulfillment of a customer order. The diamonds in this flow chart signify decisions, and the rectangles signify actions. The swimlanes show, for example, that the legal department determines whether a nonstandard purchase order can move to fulfillment or whether it gets sent back to the contracts agent.

Figure 8.5   Metro Map of Washington, DC

Martin Shields/Alamy Stock Photo

Figure 8.6   Textual Tables Organize Discrete Textual Information, such as the Questions, Answers, and Explanations

Frequently asked questions	Answer	Explanation
What is my overall deductible?	$0 person per calendar year.	Before this plan pays, you must pay all the costs up to the deductible amount. If you have other family members on the plan, each person must meet their own deductible.
Are any services covered before I meet my deductible?	Yes. Well-child care and independent labs are covered before you meet your deductible.	This plan covers some items and services even if you haven't yet met the deductible amount. But a copayment or coinsurance may apply.
Are there other deductibles for specific services?	No. There are no other deductibles.	You don't have to meet deductibles for specific services.
What is the out-of-pocket limit for this plan?	$1,500/person or $3,000/family per calendar year.	The out-of-pocket limit is the most you could pay in a year for covered services. If you have other family members in this plan, they have to meet their own out-of-pocket limits.
What is not included in the out-of-pocket limit?	Premiums, copayments, and drug-card costs.	Although you pay these expenses, they don't count toward the out-of-pocket limit.

Figure 8.7	Numerical Tables Show Exact Values for FitWorld Gym Average Weekly Client Visits by Age Group in 2020			
Day	**Ages 18–34**	**Ages 35–54**	**Ages 55–older**	**Total average client visits**
Monday	1,212	763	97	2,072
Tuesday	1,132	827	103	2,062
Wednesday	909	811	611	2,331
Thursday	889	794	94	1,777
Friday	168	778	267	1,213
Saturday	389	395	414	1,198
Sunday	135	376	615	1,126
Weekly totals	4,834	4,744	2,201	11,779

Figure 8.8	Flow Charts Illustrate Processes, such as the Process of Fulfilling a Customer Order

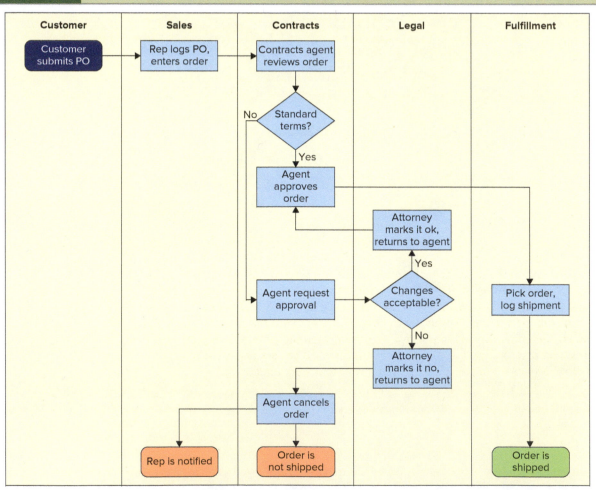

Organizational charts display the structures of and the relationships within a group, particularly hierarchies of individuals or departments in an institution. They use relative position to convey meaning: Positions at the top are the most powerful. Figure 8.9 displays the corporate structure of a company. The CEO directly oversees eight departments and the CFO. In addition, organizational charts can be used to show relationships over time, as in a genealogy tree, where the top positions represent people who lived earlier.

Figure 8.9   Organizational Charts Display the Structures of and the Relationships within a Group, such as this Corporate Structure

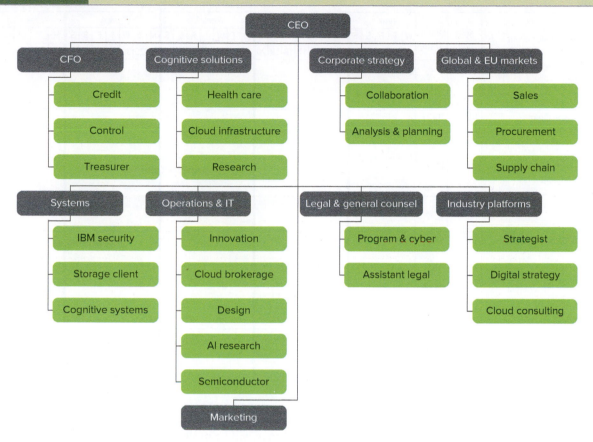

Gantt charts specify tasks in a project and the duration of those tasks. The timetable of the project runs along the top and the tasks are listed on the left. This arrangement allows the viewer to see three variables at once: the sequence of tasks (by scanning the leftmost column from top to bottom), the duration of each task (by scanning from left to right), and the overlap between various tasks, such as polishing the client proposal and rehearsing the presentation in Figure 8.10. Because Gantt charts show schedules, they are most commonly used in proposals to show when the tasks of a project, such as the marketing plan in Figure 8.10, will start and finish. They are also used in progress reports to show work completed, work in progress, and work remaining.

As you develop a Gantt chart:

- Specify the project's critical activities—those tasks that must be completed on time if the project is to be completed by the due date.

- Color code bars to indicate work remaining, work in progress, and work completed.

- Indicate progress reports, major achievements, or other milestones.

- Use parallel structure (e.g., "Hold," "Determine," "Develop") in the list of tasks.

Graphs

LO 8-5

Graphs—also known as data displays—use space to show relationships among numerical, or quantitative, data. Graphs are only as good as their underlying data. Make sure that your data come from a reliable source. If you're questioning the reliability of the

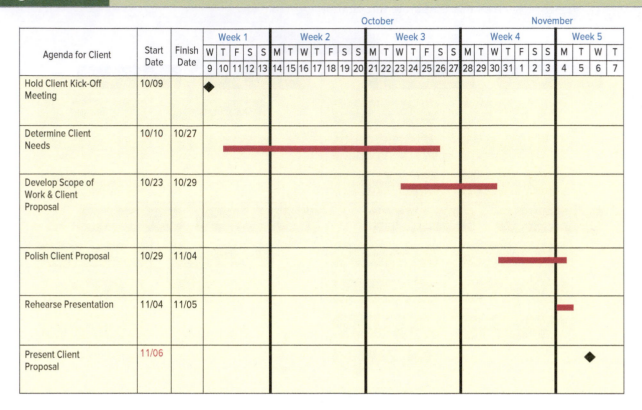

Figure 8.10   Gantt Charts Show the Schedule for Completing a Project

Agenda for Client	Start Date	Finish Date	Week 1					Week 2							Week 3							Week 4							Week 5			
			W	T	F	S	S	M	T	W	T	F	S	S	M	T	W	T	F	S	S	M	T	W	T	F	S	S	M	T	W	T
			9	10	11	12	13	14	15	16	17	18	19	20	21	22	23	24	25	26	27	28	29	30	31	1	2	3	4	5	6	7
Hold Client Kick-Off Meeting	10/09		◆																													
Determine Client Needs	10/10	10/27		▬▬▬▬▬▬▬▬▬▬▬▬▬▬▬▬▬▬																												
Develop Scope of Work & Client Proposal	10/23	10/29																	▬▬▬▬▬												
Polish Client Proposal	10/29	11/04																							▬▬▬▬						
Rehearse Presentation	11/04	11/05																											▬			
Present Client Proposal	11/06																												◆		

data, you're better off not using a graph; the graph will be more powerful than your verbal disclaimer, and the audience will be misled.

Besides being reliable, every graph should tell a story. Stories can be expressed in complete sentences that describe something that happens or changes. The sentence also can serve as the title of the graph.

Not a story: U.S. Sales, 2015–2021

Possible stories: Forty Percent of Our Sales Came from New Customers.

                         Growth Grew Most in the South.

                         Sales Increased from 2015 to 2021.

                         Sales Were Highest in the Areas with More Sales Representatives.

Stories that tell us what we already know are rarely interesting. Instead, good stories may

- Support a hunch.
- Surprise you or challenge so-called common knowledge.
- Show trends or changes the audience didn't know existed.
- Have commercial or social significance.
- Provide information needed for action.
- Be personally relevant to the audience.

To find stories in your data:

1. Focus on a topic (where are the most SUVs bought, who retweets the most, etc.).
2. Simplify the data on that topic and convert the numbers to simple, easy-to-understand units.

Figure 8.11   A Pie Graph Displays the Expenses that Comprise the Total Monthly Expenses of a Startup Company

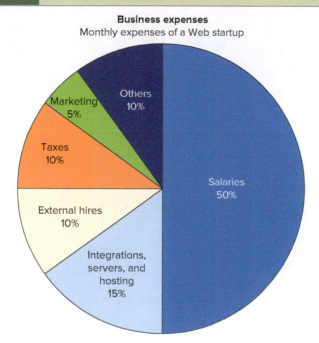

Business expenses
Monthly expenses of a Web startup

3. Look for relationships and changes. For example, compare two or more groups, or look for changes over time.
4. Process the data to find more stories. Find the average and the median. Calculate the percentage change from one year to the next.

When you think you have a story, test it against all the data to be sure it's accurate.

In business communication, four types of graphs commonly appear: pie graphs, bar graphs, line graphs, and scatterplot graphs.

Pie graphs show segments of a whole. In Figure 8.11, the whole equals the total monthly expenses for a startup company. Six segments, including one for "other" expenses, compose 100% of the startup's expenses.

However, when you want to compare one segment to another segment, use a **bar graph** or a **line graph**. In Figure 8.12, notice how it's nearly impossible to tell the difference in graduation rates between the two pie graphs.

Figure 8.12   Comparing Two Pie Graphs with Similar Data Is Difficult

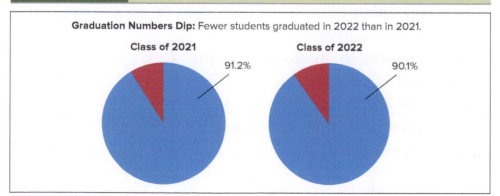

Graduation Numbers Dip: Fewer students graduated in 2022 than in 2021.

Class of 2021 — 91.2%
Class of 2022 — 90.1%

Figure 8.13   Varieties of Bar Graphs

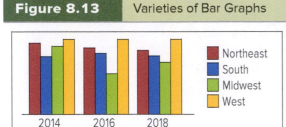 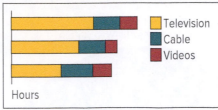 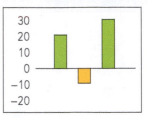

a. **Grouped bar graphs** compare several aspects of each item or several items over time.

b. **Segmented, subdivided,** or **stacked bars** sum the components of an item.

c. **Deviation bar graphs** identify positive and negative values.

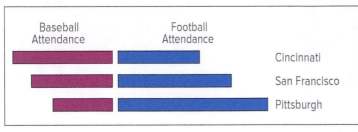 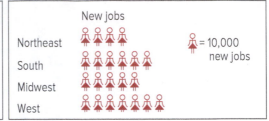

d. **Paired bar graphs** compare two items.

e. **Histograms** or **pictograms** use images to create the bars.

When designing pie graphs, follow these guidelines:

- Limit the number of segments to six or seven. If you use more, the user will have difficulty comparing the segment sizes.

- Use direct labels for the segments, as opposed to a legend.

- Start at "midnight" with the largest segment. Then move to the next largest, and so on.

- If you have an "other" segment, put it to the left of midnight, no matter its size.

Bar graphs are easy to interpret because they ask people to compare distance along a common scale, which most people judge accurately. Bar graphs are useful in a variety of situations: to compare one item to another, to compare items over time, and to show correlations. Several varieties of bar charts exist. See Figure 8.13 for examples.

- **Grouped bar graphs** allow you to compare either several aspects of each item or several items over time. Group the items you want to compare. Figure 8.13a shows that sales were highest in the West each year. If we wanted to show how sales had changed in each region, the bars should be grouped by region, not by year.

- **Segmented, subdivided,** or **stacked bars** sum the components of an item. It's hard to identify the values in specific segments; grouped bar graphs are almost always easier to use.

- **Deviation bar graphs** identify positive and negative values or winners and losers.

- **Paired bar graphs** compare two items.

- **Histograms** or **pictograms** use images to create the bars.

When constructing bar graphs:

- Order the bars in a logical or chronological order.

- Put the bars close enough together to make comparison easy.

- Use horizontal bars when your labels are long; when the labels are short, either horizontal or vertical bars will work.

- Label both horizontal and vertical axes.

Figure 8.14	A Line Graph Shows the Upward Trend of UPS and FedEx Stock during 2020 and the COVID-19 Pandemic

Shares of UPS, FedEx surge as pandemic drives online shopping

- Put all labels inside the bars or outside them. When some labels are inside and some are outside, the labels carry the visual weight of longer bars, distorting the data.

- Make all the bars the same width.

- Use different colors for different bars only when their meanings are different, for example, estimates as opposed to known numbers, negative as opposed to positive numbers.

- Avoid using 3-D perspective; it makes the values harder to read and can make comparison difficult.

Line graphs are also easy to interpret. Use line graphs to compare items over time, to show frequency or distribution, and to show possible correlations. Figure 8.1 in the opening case of this chapter shows this last use of line graphs. Figure 8.14 exemplifies the first purpose, comparing the performance of FedEx and UPS against the S&P 500 Index in 2020.

When constructing line graphs:

- Label both horizontal and vertical axes. When time is a variable, it usually is put on the horizontal axis.

- Avoid using more than three different lines on one graph. Even three lines may be too many if they cross each other.

- Avoid using 3-D perspective. It makes the values harder to read and can make comparison difficult.

Scatterplot graphs show the relationship, or correlation, between two sets of numerical data variables. The x-axis represents one variable, such as the temperature at noon. The y-axis represents the other variable, such as daily iced-coffee sales. A data point represents a combination of the two variables. Figure 8.15 shows a positive correlation—a positive relationship—between iced-coffee sales and the temperature at noon. If, for some strange reason, iced-coffee sales had dropped as the temperature rose, the correlation would be negative.

Figure 8.15   A Scatterplot Shows the Positive Correlation between Temperature and Iced-Coffee Sales

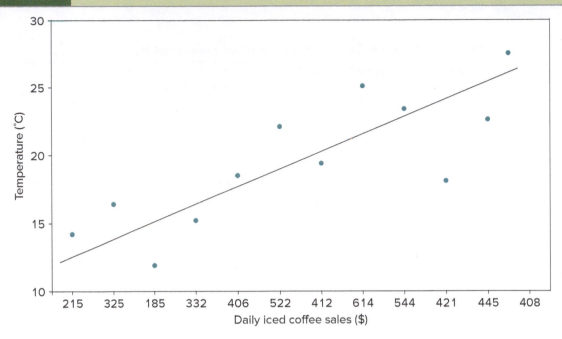

Besides positive and negative correlations between numerical variables, scatterplots also show the strength of a relationship between the variables. You can determine the strength of the relationship through the degree to which the data are scattered throughout the plot. If the data cluster around a line, the relationship between the variables is strong. In the case of daily iced-coffee sales and temperature, the relationship is strong because the data points cluster around a line. This line is called the trend line. If the relationship were weak, the data points would be scattered all over the graph area.

Hybrids

LO 8-6

Newer displays of visuals combine visuals of various types and incorporate interactivity into their design: visual clusters, infographics, and dynamic data displays.

Some stories are simple straight lines, such as "Computer Sales Increased," and require just one visual, such as a line graph. But sometimes, the best story arises from the juxtaposition of two or more stories in a **visual cluster**. Figure 8.16 uses a group of three visuals to tell a more complex story about flu outbreaks.

Almost every data set allows you to tell several stories. Clustering graphs together—and with other types of visuals—can help you tell a complex story.

Informational graphics, or **infographics**, employ visual representations of information to educate an audience about a specific topic. Infographics often depict findings from both **qualitative** and **quantitative** research studies. Presenting data in pictures frames statistics as a story—an easily digestible format.

The infographic in Figure 8.17 tells a story: the benefit of hairstylists and their clients wearing face masks correctly during the COVID-19 pandemic. The infographic conveys the story in three sentences—two that relate a study and its findings, and one that directs people to wear a face covering. It showcases the data in the study by assigning one square for each person who did not contract COVID-19 while getting a haircut.

The infographic in Figure 8.18 tells a story as well: the relationship among personal income, pay raises, and job satisfaction. It combines short blocks of text with visuals to relate its information.

Figure 8.16   A Complex Story about Influenza Outbreaks Using Clustered Visuals

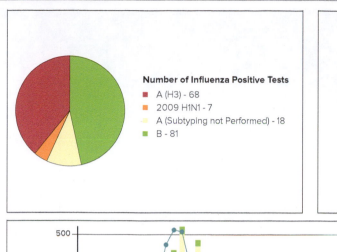

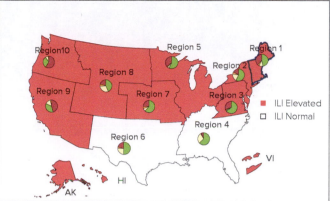

Number of Influenza Positive Tests

- A (H3) - 68
- 2009 H1N1 - 7
- A (Subtyping not Performed) - 18
- B - 81

ILI Elevated
ILI Normal

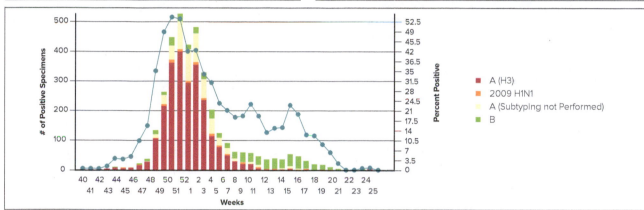

A (H3)
2009 H1N1
A (Subtyping not Performed)
B

Source: Centers for Disease Control and Prevention, "National and Regional Outpatient Illness and Viral Surveillance," *Fluview*, accessed July 3, 2013, http://gis .cdc.gov/grasp/fluview/fluportaldashboard.html.

Figure 8.17   An Infographic Conveys a Powerful Message by Representing Data Visually

Two hair stylists with **COVID-19**
spent at least 15 minutes with 139 clients

EVERYONE WORE FACE COVERINGS   **NO CLIENTS** ARE KNOWN TO BE INFECTED*

WEAR CLOTH FACE COVERINGS CONSISTENTLY AND CORRECTLY TO SLOW THE SPREAD OF COVID-19

*No clients reported symptoms; all 67 customers tested had negative tests

CDC.GOV   bit.ly/MMWR71420   MMWR

CDC

Figure 8.18   An Infographic that Relates a Story about Income and Job Satisfaction

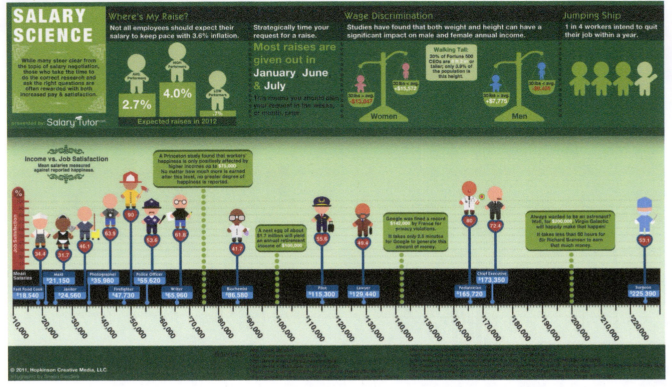

Shaun Sanders/2011 Hopkinson Creative Media

While infographics formerly were found mainly in newspapers and news magazines, professional organizations have quickly adopted them. Many businesses use infographics in their annual reports to communicate with shareholders. Other organizations employ them on websites and social media to connect with customers and promote their business. Infographics thrive in the digital age because they are so easy to share, forward, post, and tweet. Some job hunters even are creating infographic résumés to promote their accomplishments and to get noticed by potential employers.[1]

Technology is expanding the possibilities of data displays. Unlike infographics that are static once published, **dynamic data displays** found on the internet can be updated on the fly. These displays are interactive, allowing users to adapt them to personal needs or interests. During the COVID-19 pandemic, people used dynamic data displays, such as the Johns Hopkins University & Medicine dashboard (https://coronavirus.jhu.edu /us-map), to see the number of cases, hospitalizations, and deaths in different countries. During presidential elections, many news websites such as CNN, *The New York Times,* and *The Wall Street Journal* offer audiences the ability to manipulate what-if scenarios for electoral college votes. Financial investment companies and marketplaces such as Nasdaq produce data displays that help investors evaluate stock performance to make investment decisions, such as this one for the company DavidsTea: https:// www.nasdaq.com/market-activity/stocks/dtea/advanced-charting.

Other Guidelines for Creating Effective Visuals

LO 8-7

The previous section discussed and exemplified five general types of visuals: images, tables, charts, graphs, and hybrids. That discussion included guidelines for using and designing those visuals. This section presents three additional guidelines that apply to all five types of visuals.

Follow Conventions

Follow conventions when creating visuals. When you stray from conventions, you may confuse or alienate your audience.

In many business documents, such as proposals and reports, visuals are divided into tables and figures, and each is numbered separately. That is, a report could contain a Table 1 and a Figure 1. In this system of numbering, a table could be either a textual table or a numerical table. A figure can be anything that isn't a table: a graph, a chart, a photograph, an infographic, and so on.

Figures and tables are numbered and titled, for example, "Figure 1. The Falling Cost of Computer Memory, 2001–2021." In an oral presentation, the title is usually used without the number: "The Falling Cost of Computer Memory, 2001–2021." The title should tell the story so the audience knows what to look for in the visual.

In addition to a number and title, you should provide the source of the visual, even if you designed it yourself using someone else's data. Usually, the source is placed below the visual.

All visuals should have clearly labeled units, such as the units on axes in graphs. You should clearly identify—with labels or with legends—axes, symbols, patterns, and shades of colors.

When preparing visuals, you should also keep in mind cultural differences:

- Make sure any symbols in the visual will have the correct meaning in the culture of your audience. For example, a red cross symbolizes first aid in North America, but in Muslim countries, the symbol with that meaning is typically a green crescent.[2]

- If you use punctuation marks as symbols, be sure they are meaningful to your audience. A question mark in English and certain other languages might signal a help function or answers to questions. But in languages without this symbol, it has no meaning.

- Organize the information according to the reading customs of the audience. For example, English reads from left to right, and Arabic reads from right to left.

- Learn your audience's conventions for writing numbers. In the U.S., a period indicates the decimal point and commas separate groups of three digits. In much of Europe, a comma represents the decimal point and a space goes between each group of three digits. Thus, for American and French readers, 3,333 has different values.

Use Color Carefully

Colors make visuals more dramatic, but they can also create some design challenges. Meanings assigned to colors differ depending on the audience's culture. Red is sometimes used to suggest danger or *stop* in the U.S., but it means *go* and is associated with good fortune in China. Orange suggests courage and love in Japan, while many Middle Eastern countries associate it with mourning and loss. Purple is associated with royalty or honor in the U.S. and with mourning and death in Brazil, but it symbolizes wealth in many Middle Eastern counties.[3] Finally, you would wear black to attend a funeral in the U.S. but white to a funeral in India. These are just a few examples. The point is this: in preparing visuals for international audiences, take special care to research the relevant cultures to inform a strategic use of color.

Be Ethical

As discussed in Chapter 7, visuals wield persuasive power and should be used ethically. To be a trustworthy communicator and to avoid misleading your audience, strive for ethical use of visuals. Doing this includes considering how audiences interact with visuals. For example, graphs communicate quickly; audiences remember the shape more than the labels. If the audience has to study the labels to get an accurate understanding of a graph, the graph is unethical—even if the labels are accurate.

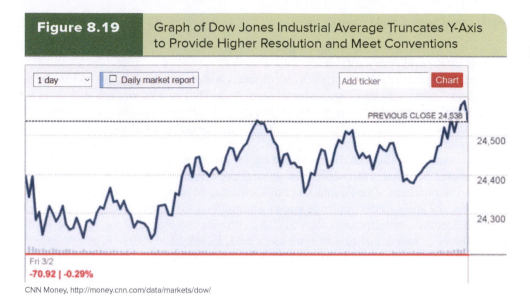

Figure 8.19   Graph of Dow Jones Industrial Average Truncates Y-Axis to Provide Higher Resolution and Meet Conventions

CNN Money, http://money.cnn.com/data/markets/dow/

One convention of ethical graphs is that their y-axis starts at zero. Starting the y-axis at some number other than zero will affect the slope of the lines and can lead to possible misinterpretation. That said, some exceptions exist. **Truncated graphs** are most acceptable when the audience knows the basic data set well. For example, graphs of the stock market almost never start at zero; they are routinely truncated (see Figure 8.19 for an example). Audiences who follow the market closely expect a truncated y-axis; it serves the purpose of depicting market changes at a higher resolution.

When using photographs, use unaltered images or be transparent what edits you've made. For example, you may need to **crop**, or trim, a photo for best results. But a growing problem with photos is that they may be edited or staged, purporting to show something as reality even though it never occurred. If you altered a photograph for good reason, it is better to be up front about the alteration than to be perceived as deceptive.

Integration of Visuals into Your Text

LO 8-8

To make your document's visual and verbal elements work together most effectively, you should integrate its visual elements into its verbal elements.

First, refer in your text to every visual. Normally, you'll use the table or figure number but not the title. Put the visual as soon after your reference to it as space and page design permit.

As Table 2 shows, over 54% of teachers participated in more community service groups—more than members of the other occupations surveyed; 21% of dentists participated in service groups—more than five of the other surveyed occupations.

Over 54% of teachers participated in more community service groups—more than members of the other occupations surveyed; 21% of dentists participated in service groups—more than five of the other surveyed occupations. (See Table 2.)

Summarize the main point of a visual or data display *before* you present it. Then when readers get to it, they'll see it as confirmation of your point.

Weak: Listed below are the results.

Better: As Figure 4 shows, sales doubled in the last decade.

How much discussion a visual needs depends on the audience, the complexity of the visual, and the importance of the point it makes. Use these guidelines:

- If the material is new to the audience, provide a fuller explanation than if similar material is presented to this audience every week or month.

- If the visual is complex, help the reader find key points.

- If the point is important, discuss its implications in some detail.

In contrast, one sentence about a visual may be enough when the audience is already familiar with the topic and the data, when the visual is simple and well designed, and when the information in the visual is a minor part of your proof.

When you discuss visuals, spell out numbers that fall at the beginning of a sentence. If spelling out the number or year is cumbersome, revise the sentence so that it does not begin with a number.

Forty-five percent of the cost goes to pay wages and salaries.

Pay wages and salaries constituted 45% of the cost.

Summary by Learning Objectives

LO 8-1   Determine when to use visuals.

- Visuals help support your arguments.

- In the rough draft, use visuals to see that ideas are presented completely and to see what relationships exist. In the final presentation or document, use visuals to make points vivid, to emphasize material that the reader might skip, and to present material more compactly and with less repetition than words alone would require.

- Use visuals when you want to show relationships and to persuade, when the information is complex or contains extensive numerical data, and when the audience values visuals.

LO 8-2   Use images effectively.

- Photographs convey a sense of authenticity or realism and can show an object in use.

- With drawings, the artist can display dimensions, show processes, emphasize detail, represent a theoretical or proposed scenario, or eliminate unwanted detail.

- Use maps to emphasize location or to compare items in different locations.

LO 8-3   Use tables effectively.

- Use textual tables when you want users to be able to make easy comparisons among different items, such as different product features. They can also help organize discrete textual information, such as questions, answers, and explanations.

- Use numerical tables when you want the audience to focus on specific numbers in your data. Numerical tables allow users to focus on particular data points in a way that graphs do not.

LO 8-4   Use charts effectively.

- Flow charts display a process, such as a decision-making or a manufacturing process. Typically flow charts consistently use shapes, often diamonds and rectangles, to illustrate different types of steps, such as a decision or an action.

- Organizational charts display the structures of and the relationships within a group, particularly hierarchies of individuals or departments in an institution.

- Gantt charts specify tasks in a project and the duration of those tasks.

LO 8-5   Use graphs effectively.

- Pie graphs show segments of a whole.

- Bar graphs compare one item to another, compare items over time, and show correlations.

- Line graphs compare items over time, show frequency or distribution, and show possible correlations.

- Scatterplot graphs show the correlation between two sets of numerical data variables.

LO 8-6   **Use hybrids (visual clusters, infographics, and dynamic data displays) effectively.**

- Visual clusters group visuals to tell a more complex story.
- Infographics depict findings from both qualitative and quantitative research studies.
- Dynamic displays are interactive, allowing users to adapt them to personal needs or interests.

LO 8-7   **Explain why it's important to follow conventions, use color effectively, and be ethical when choosing and designing visuals.**

- Follow conventions when creating visuals. When you stray from conventions, you may confuse or alienate your audience.

- In preparing visuals for international audiences, take special care to research the relevant cultures to inform a strategic use of color.
- To be a trustworthy communicator and to avoid misleading your audience, strive for ethical use of visuals.

LO 8-8   **Integrate visuals into text.**

- Refer in your text to every visual.
- Summarize the main point of a visual before it appears in the text.
- Determine how much discussion a visual needs by considering the audience, the complexity, and the importance of the point it makes.

Exercises and Cases

8.1   Reviewing the Chapter

1. When should you use visuals? (LO 8-1)
2. What are some specific ways to choose effective images? (LO 8-2)
3. Why would you use a numerical table instead of a graph? (LO 8-3)
4. What information does a Gantt chart convey? (LO 8-4)
5. What are some specific ways to choose effective images? (LO 8-5)

6. What are four types of bar graphs, and why would you use one instead of the other? (LO 8-6)
7. What are some concerns that must be addressed to keep your visuals ethical? (LO 8-7)
8. What are some guidelines for integrating visuals into your text? (LO 8-8)

8.2   Evaluating the Ethics of Photo Choices

Indicate whether you consider each of the following actions ethical, unethical, or a gray area. Which of the actions would you do? Which would you feel uncomfortable doing? Which would you refuse to do?

1. Using photos of Hawaiian beaches in advertising for Bermuda tourism, without indicating the location of the beaches.
2. Taking hundreds of photos of students on a mostly white campus, choosing one of a handful of photos that include a Black person, and using that photo on the cover of a recruiting brochure designed to attract minority applicants to the university.
3. Using filters in your photographs so that people look more attractive.
4. Using a fish-eye lens to take real-estate photos that make the rooms look larger than they really are.
5. Including photographs of food arranged by professional "food dressers" in an online restaurant menu. The food looks about 15% brighter and fresher than what is actually delivered. The portion amounts appear larger as well.

8.3   Evaluating Visuals

Evaluate each of the following visuals by answering the following questions.

- Is the visual's message clear?
- Is it the right visual for the story?
- Is the visual designed appropriately? Is color, if any, used appropriately?

- Is the visual free from extraneous lines, shapes, symbols, and so on?
- Does the visual distort data or mislead the reader in any way?

Figure 8.20   Exercise 8.3, Visual 1

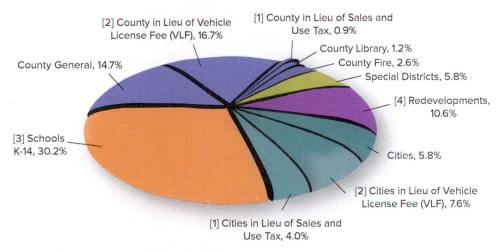

1% Property Tax Revenue Allocation - Fiscal Year 2012–2013
Total Revenue $268,278,928

[1] Represents the exchange of Property Tax for Cities and County Sales and Use Tax as authorized under Assembly Bill 1766, chaptered August 2, 2003.

[2] Represents the exchange of Property Tax for Cities and County Vehicle License Fees as authorized under Senate Bill 1096, chaptered August 5, 2004.

[3] Revenue for Schools has been reduced by the ERAF deficit as authorized under Senate Bill 1096, chaptered August 5, 2004.

[4] Effective February 1, 2012, Redevelopment agencies were dissolved and related revenue will be allocated as provided by Assembly Bill X1 26, chaptered June 29, 2011.

Source: County of Tulare, California. http://www.tularecounty.ca.gov/treasurertaxcollector/index.cfm /property-tax-accounting/faqs/where-do-property-taxes-go.

Figure 8.21   Exercise 8.3, Visual 2

Terrified of bees, snakes and swimming pools?

Thousands of Americans die in accidents every year, but the odds are extremely high that you won't be one of them. A look at what killed Americans in 2003, the most recent year for which data are available, shows that just 4% of fatalities were accidental. So go ahead and take that plane trip or swim in the ocean. Just be careful out there.

Maybe you should worry more about your heart

Even if you exercise regularly and don't smoke or drink, you will probably die of a disease. Two ailments—heart disease and cancer—cause half of all deaths in U.S. Exotic bugs like avian flu and mad cow disease might grab a lot of headlines, but so far they haven't killed a single person in the U.S.

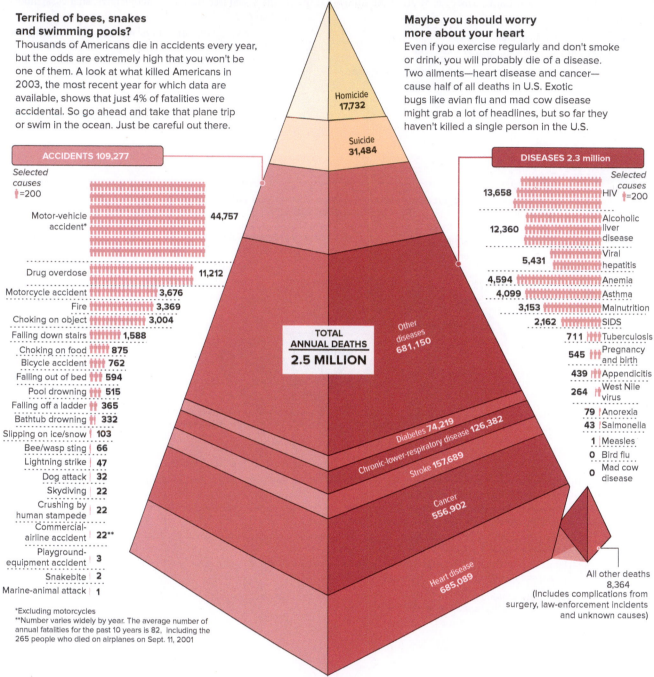

ACCIDENTS 109,277

Selected causes ♂=200

Cause	Deaths
Motor-vehicle accident*	44,757
Drug overdose	11,212
Motorcycle accident	3,676
Fire	3,369
Choking on object	3,004
Falling down stairs	1,588
Choking on food	875
Bicycle accident	762
Falling out of bed	594
Pool drowning	515
Falling off a ladder	365
Bathtub drowning	332
Slipping on ice/snow	103
Bee/wasp sting	66
Lightning strike	47
Dog attack	32
Skydiving	22
Crushing by human stampede	22
Commercial-airline accident	22**
Playground-equipment accident	3
Snakebite	2
Marine-animal attack	1

*Excluding motorcycles
**Number varies widely by year. The average number of annual fatalities for the past 10 years is 82, including the 265 people who died on airplanes on Sept. 11, 2001

DISEASES 2.3 million

Selected causes ♂=200

Deaths	Cause
13,658	HIV
12,360	Alcoholic liver disease
5,431	Viral hepatitis
4,594	Anemia
4,099	Asthma
3,153	Malnutrition
2,162	SIDS
711	Tuberculosis
545	Pregnancy and birth
439	Appendicitis
264	West Nile virus
79	Anorexia
43	Salmonella
1	Measles
0	Bird flu
0	Mad cow disease

Pyramid labels:
Homicide 17,732
Suicide 31,484
Other diseases 681,150
TOTAL ANNUAL DEATHS 2.5 MILLION
Diabetes 74,219
Chronic-lower-respiratory disease 126,382
Stroke 157,689
Cancer 556,902
Heart disease 685,089

All other deaths 8,364 (Includes complications from surgery, law-enforcement incidents and unknown causes)

Source: Centers for Disease Control and Prevention; National Transportation Safety Board.

Figure 8.22 | Exercise 8.3, Visual 3

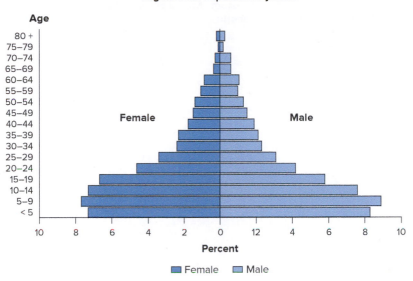

Afghanistan Population Pyramid

Source: MEASURE Demographic and Health Surveys/ICF International, http://www.measuredhs.com.

Figure 8.23 | Exercise 8.3, Visual 4

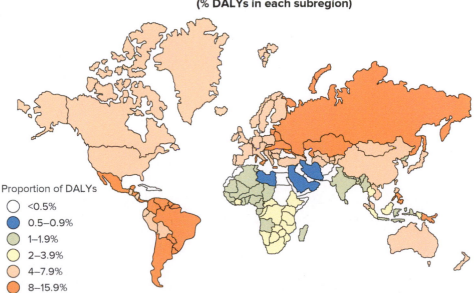

Burden of disease attributable to: ALCOHOL
(% DALYs in each subregion)

Proportion of DALYS

- <0.5%
- 0.5–0.9%
- 1–1.9%
- 2–3.9%
- 4–7.9%
- 8–15.9%

Worldwide alcohol causes 1.8 million deaths (3.2% of total) and 58.3 million (4% of total) of Disability-Adjusted Life Years (DALYs). Unintentional injuries alone account for about one-third of the 1.8 million deaths, while neuro-psychiatric conditions account for close to 40% of the 58.3 million DALYs. The burden is not equally distributed among the countries, as is shown on the map.

Source: World Health Organization, "Alcohol," in *Management of Substance Abuse*, http://www.who.int/substance _abuse/facts/alcohol/en (accessed May 5, 2009).

Figure 8.24   Exercise 8.3, Visual 5

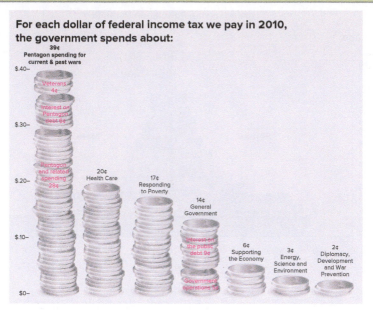

Source: Friends Committee on National Legislation, "Where Do Our Income Tax Dollars Go?," October 2010, http://fcnl.org/assets/issues/budget/Taxes10coin_chart.pdf.

8.4   Evaluating Visuals

With soaring obesity rates in the U.S., the government continues to produce visuals that encourage healthy eating habits. While the food pyramids have been the norm, their messages have been largely ignored by U.S. citizens. The newest version of the visual to encourage healthy eating uses a plate with various portion sizes for fruits, grains, vegetables, protein, and dairy.

Evaluate each of the visuals by answering the following questions.

- Which version of the visual is right for the story?
- Which healthy eating visual is clearest?

- Which is most informative?
- Which visual will most likely encourage healthy eating habits?
- Which visuals contain extraneous text, shapes, lines, and so on?
- Which did you prefer? Why?

Figure 8.25	Exercise 8.4, Visual 1

Former food pyramid

Fats, Oils & Sweets
USE SPARINGLY

KEY
⬒ Fat (naturally occuring and added)
▽ Sugars (added)
Those symbols show fats and added sugars in foods.

Milk, Yogurt & Cheese Group
2–3 SERVINGS

Meat, Poultry, Fish, Dry Beans, Eggs & Nuts Group
2–3 SERVINGS

Vegetable Group
3–5 SERVINGS

Fruit Group
2–4 SERVINGS

Bread, Cereal, Rice & Pasta Group
6–11 SERVINGS

Source: U.S. Department of Agriculture, "Food Pyramid," accessed July 4, 2013, http://www.cnpp.usda.gov/Publications/MyPyramid/OriginalFoodGuidePyramids/FGP/FGPPamphlet.pdf.

Figure 8.26   Exercise 8.4, Visual 2

Anatomy of MyPyramid

One size doesn't fit all

USDA's new MyPyramid symbolizes a personalized approach to healthy eating and physical activity. The symbol has been designed to be simple. It has been developed to remind consumers to make healthy food choices and to be active every day. The different parts of the symbol are described below.

Current Food Pyramid

MyPyramid.gov
STEPS TO A HEALTHIER YOU

Activity

Activity is represented by the steps and the person climbing them, as a reminder of the importance of daily physical activity.

Moderation

Moderation is represented by the narrowing of each food group from bottom to top. The wider base stands for foods with little or no solid fats or added sugars. These should be selected more often. The narrower top area stands for foods containing more added sugars and solid fats. The more active you are, the more of these foods can fit into your diet.

Personalization

Personalization is shown by the person on the steps, the slogan and the URL. Find the kinds and amounts of food to eat each day at Mypyramid.gov.

Proportionality

Proportionality is shown by the different widths of the food group bands. The widths suggest how much food a person should choose from each group. The widths are just a general guide, not exact proportions. Check the Web site for how much is right for you.

Variety

Variety is symbolized by the 6 color bands representing the 5 food groups of the Pyramid and oils. This illustrates that foods from all groups are needed each day for good health.

Gradual Improvement

Gradual improvement is encouraged by the slogan. It suggests that individuals can benefit from taking small steps to improve their diets and lifestyle each day.

U.S. Department of Agriculture
Center for Nutrition Policy
and Promotion
April 2005 CNPP-16
USDA is an equal opportunity provider and employer

| GRAINS | VEGETABLES | FRUITS | OILS | MILK | MEAT& BEANS |

Source: U.S. Department of Agriculture, "Steps to a Healthier You," in MyPyramid.gov, accessed June 10, 2013, http://www.choosemyplate.gov/food-groups/downloads/MyPyramid_Getting_Started.pdf.

| Figure 8.27 | Exercise 8.4, Visual 3 |

Source: U.S Department of Agriculture, www.choosemyplate.gov

8.5   Creating Visuals

As your instructor directs,

a.   Identify other visuals besides tables that you might use to help analyze each of the data sets in Figures 8.28 and 8.29.

b.   Identify and create a visual for one or more of the stories in each set.

c.   Identify additional information that would be needed for other stories related to these data sets.

| Figure 8.28 | Daily Change in Unique Audience (UA) Traffic to NCAA-Related Sports Websites during "March Madness" (U.S., Home and Work). |

Site	Wed: 3/15 UA	Thurs: 3/16 UA	Fri: 3/17 UA
CBS Sportsline.com Network	1,958	3,603	3,135
AOL Sports (web only)	761	999	1,006
FOX Sports on MSN	1,510	1,953	2,237
Yahoo! Sports	2,121	2,601	2,377
SI.com	724*	819*	773*
ESPN	3,074	3,312	2,941
Total Unduplicated UA	**8,005**	**9,659**	**9,573**

*These estimates are calculated on smaller sample sizes and are subject to increased statistical variability as a result.
Source: Enid Burns, "March Madness Invades Office Life," Trends & Statistics: The Web's Richest Resource.

Figure 8.29   Customer Satisfaction with Airlines

	Base-line	95	96	97	98	99	00	01	02	03	04	05	06	07	08	09	10	11	12	13	14	15	16	17	Previous Year % Change	First Year % Change
Delta	77	72	67	69	65	68	66	61	66	67	67	65	64	59	60	64	62	56	65	68	71	71	71	76	7.0	−1.3
American	70	71	71	62	67	64	63	62	63	67	66	64	62	60	62	60	63	63	64	65	66	66	72	76	5.6	8.6
United	71	67	70	68	65	62	62	59	64	63	64	61	63	56	56	56	60	61	62	62	60	60	68	70	2.9	−1.4
Southwest	78	76	76	76	74	72	70	70	74	75	73	74	74	76	79	81	79	81	77	81	78	78	80	80	0.0	2.6
All others	NM	70	74	70	62	67	63	64	72	74	73	74	74	75	75	77	75	76	74	72	70	73	74	74	0.0	5.7
Continental	67	64	66	64	66	64	62	67	68	68	67	70	67	69	62	68	71	64	#						N/A	N/A
US Airways	72	67	66	68	65	61	60	63	64	62	57	62	61	54	59	62	61	65	64	66	#				N/A	N/A

N/A Not available
Company merger
NM Not measured

Source: "Airlines" in *The American Customer Satisfaction Index: Scores by Industry*, accessed October 27, 2017, http://www.theacsi.org/?option=com_content&view=article&id&149&catid=14:acsi-results&Itemid=214&i =Airlines&c=Delta&sort=ChangeAnual.

8.6   Creating Data Displays for a Client

You are volunteering for a local food bank and the director has asked for your assistance. The food bank may be able to receive some state funding if the director can assemble a persuasive proposal about the need for the food bank. The director gives you the following information and asks if you can create visuals for it.

- Food bank is open four days a week.
- One director and four volunteers.
- Food bank feeds 100–150 families per week.
- Of those families, 95% have children under 18.
- Often, food will run out by the end of Thursday.
- If given more support, the food bank could feed many more families in need (the goal would be 250) and could hire more staff members.

As your instructor directs,

a. In a small group, identify and discuss possible visuals for the proposal.

b. Individually, create one (or more) visual(s) using the given data. Write an email to your instructor where you justify your design choices.

c. With a small group, create three visuals that persuade the state agency of the need for funding. Present the visuals to the class in an informal presentation where you justify your design choices.

8.7   Graphing Data from the Web

Find data on the web about a topic that interests you. Sites with data include the following:

Catalyst (women in business)
https://www.catalyst.org/research/?fwp_research_types=quick-take
ClickZ (digital marketing)
http://www.clickz.com/showPage.html?page=stats
FiveThirtyEight (political polls)
http://fivethirtyeight.com
United Nations Environment Program
http://na.unep.net
U.S. Congress Joint Economic Committee
https://www.jec.senate.gov/public/index.cfm/home/

As your instructor directs,

a. Identify at least five stories in the data.

b. Create graphs, visual clusters, or infographics for three of the stories.

c. Write an email to your instructor explaining why you chose these stories and why you chose these visuals to display them.

d. Write an email to a group that might be interested in your findings, presenting your visuals as part of a short report.

e. Print out the data and include them with a copy of your email or report.

8.8   Evaluating Infographics

As a class, select three infographics found online and answer the following questions:

- What are the purposes of the infographics?
- Who do you think are the intended audiences? What makes you say so?
- How informational are the infographics?
- How persuasive are the infographics? If you think they are persuasive, what would make them even more persuasive?
- How do the creators blend visuals and text in the infographics?
- What original contexts would be most appropriate for the infographics?
- What visual design elements attract you to these particular infographics?
- What visual design elements, if any, detract from the main messages of the infographics?

- To what extent do the infographics contain misleading information or data distortion?
- To what extent overall are your three chosen infographics effective or ineffective given the audiences and purpose you have identified?

As your instructor directs,

a. Discuss the infographics and findings with a small group of classmates.

b. Write an email to your instructor evaluating the three infographics. Include URLs of the infographics mentioned in your email.

c. In an oral presentation to the class, explain what makes your three infographics effective or ineffective.

d. Post your evaluation in a discussion forum to the class. Include the URLs of the infographics so classmates can view them.

8.9   Creating a Visual Argument

With a partner, research one of the following topics:

- Introducing new technology into the marketplace.
- Laying off employees during economic downturns.
- Requiring employers to offer insurance plans.
- Integrating social media and branding into an organization.
- Hiring and recruiting underrepresented groups.
- A current/popular business topic.

Then, prepare a four-minute slide show presentation to share with your peers. The presentation should *include only visuals* and *contain no words*. With the visuals, you should take a stand and present an argument about one of the topics. Recall the guidelines outlined in this chapter about effectively using visuals.

Remember that your presentation needs to be captivating to the audience and effectively convey your purpose. Finally, don't forget to cite all source material.

As your instructor directs,

a.   Submit a copy of your slide show presentation to your instructor.

b.   Write a brief email in which you explain in words the argument you were trying to make.

c.   Submit a works cited page that lists each visual you used.

Notes

1.   Mark Smiciklas, *The Power of Infographics* (Indianapolis: Que, 2012), 60–64.
2.   Gerald J. Alred, Charles T. Brusaw, and Walter E. Oliu, *The Business Writer's Handbook,* 10th ed. (New York: St. Martin's Press, 2012), 244–46.
3.   Ibid., 246; and Carrie Cousins, "Color and Cultural Design Association," *Webdesigner Depot*, June 11, 2012, http://www.webdesignerdepot.com/2012/06/color-and-cultural-design-considerations.

Crafting Informative and Positive Messages

Chapter Outline

DrAfter123/Getty Images

Saving Lives 280 Characters at a Time

limbitech/123RF

In September 2020, as Hurricane Sally grew more threatening to the coastlines of Mississippi, Alabama, and Florida, NOAA, the National Oceanic and Atmospheric Agency, posted updates to Twitter—a strategy that differed substantially from the traditional approach the agency took only a decade before. Doug Hilderbrand, who works in NOAA's communications office, notes that while NOAA still updates traditional media outlets, spreading information via social media is a valuable part of the agency's communications because "it is essential that people have multiple ways to get information."

When natural disasters threaten to separate us, Twitter, Facebook, and other social media platforms help us all stay connected—and safer for it.

Informative and positive messages are the most common messages in organizations. When we convey information to which the receiver's basic reaction will be neutral, the message is an **informative message**. If we convey information to which the receiver's reaction will be positive, the message is a **positive or good-news message**. Unlike persuasive messages, neither informative nor positive messages immediately ask the receiver to do anything. However, the sender usually wants to build positive attitudes toward the information they are presenting, so in that sense, even an informative message has a persuasive element. Chapter 10 discusses messages that convey news the receiver will not welcome (negative messages); Chapter 11 discusses messages that aim to change beliefs or behavior (persuasive messages).

Informative and positive messages include acceptances; positive answers to requests; information about meetings, procedures, products, services, or options; goodwill- or community-building messages; announcements of policy changes that are neutral or positive; and changes that are to the receiver's advantage.

Keep in mind that many messages can be informative, negative, or persuasive depending on what you have to say. A transmittal, for example, can be positive when you're sending glowing sales figures or persuasive when you want the reader to act on the information. A performance appraisal is positive when you evaluate someone who's doing superbly, negative when you want to compile a record to justify firing someone, and persuasive when you want to motivate a satisfactory worker to continue to improve. Use your best judgment in evaluating whether you should apply principles of informative, positive, negative, or persuasive messages to your communication.

Source: Douglas MacMillan, "In Irma, Emergency Responders' New Tools: Twitter and Facebook," *The Wall Street Journal*, September 11, 2017.

Learning Objectives

LO 9-1 Explain the purposes of informative and positive messages.

LO 9-2 Describe strategies for building goodwill.

LO 9-3 Implement best practices for organizing informative and positive messages.

LO 9-4 Implement best practices for subject lines in informative and positive messages.

LO 9-5 Implement practices for ending informative and positive messages.

LO 9-6 Implement best practices for organizing transmittals and summaries.

Purposes of Informative and Positive Messages

LO 9-1

Even a simple informative or good-news message usually has several purposes:

Primary purposes

- To give information or good news to the receiver or to reassure the receiver.
- To have the receiver view the information positively.

Secondary purposes

- To build a good image of the sender.
- To build a good image of the sender's organization.
- To cement a good relationship between the sender and the receiver.
- To de-emphasize any negative elements.
- To reduce or eliminate future messages on the same subject.

Informative and positive messages are not necessarily short. Instead, the length of a message depends on the rhetorical situation: your purposes, the audience's needs, and the complexity of the situation.

Building Goodwill

LO 9-2

Although informative and positive messages do not require the audience to act, you still want them to feel considered and important. You should build goodwill in your informative and positive messages by focusing on benefits, framing benefits for a policy change or to build goodwill, connecting with your audience, and avoiding information overload.

Focus on Benefits

Most informative and positive messages should focus on the benefit to your audience. Focusing on the benefit helps establish goodwill: Even though your audience does not need to take action as a result of your message, the message serves the purpose of strengthening a positive connection between audience and sender. To develop benefits for informative and positive messages, employ *you*-attitude; highlight any benefits inherent in the information you want to convey; and try using story, humor, or informative hooks. You also should consider whether focusing on benefits is appropriate for the message.

However, not all informative and positive messages need benefits. You *don't* need benefits when

- You are presenting factual information only.

- The audience's attitude toward the information doesn't matter.

- The benefits may make the audience seem selfish.

- The benefits are so obvious that to restate them insults the audience's intelligence.

You *do* need benefits when

- Presenting policies.

- Shaping your audience's attitudes toward the information or toward your organization.

- Stressing benefits presents the audience's motives positively.

- Presenting benefits that may not be obvious.

Frame Benefits for a Policy Change

Benefits are hardest to develop when you are announcing policies because the policy change was most likely enacted to benefit the organization, not its employees or customers. Yet benefits are most essential in a policy-change message so recipients see the reason for the change and support it. Therefore, when you present benefits, be sure to highlight advantages to the audience. For example, a company may change health care providers to reduce the organization's costs, but the notice of provider change sent to employees should spell out new benefits for employees and their families.

Ineffective notice:	We are changing health care providers to reduce costs to the company by 2% per year. The change shouldn't significantly affect your health care.
Effective notice:	Our new health care provider offers a larger pool of network providers and a convenient internet portal for managing your health-care spending account. Additionally, we were able to negotiate a slightly lower contract cost to the company, so this transition brings benefits across the board.

Frame Benefits to Build Goodwill

When presenting benefits to serve other purposes, such as improving the audience's perception of your company, provide your audience with some benefit. Try using a story, humor, or informative hooks to add value to your communications and, in turn, build goodwill.

Use a Story   Now that employees are used to easy and fast accessibility to information, employers are looking for ways to help information cohere and stick, both among factoids and within employees' minds. One way to achieve this goal that is gaining business attention is through the power of stories.

In the business world, stories are narratives but not fiction, and they are usually brief—a paragraph or two. Nevertheless, these stories enable us to put facts in a context, frequently with emotional underpinnings. The context and the emotion help us to understand and remember information.

- When a popular driver for a city bus company was nearly crushed to death between two parked buses, the company used the story of the driver's accident and agonizing recovery to help drivers remember the safety procedure designed to prevent such accidents in the future.

- Popular business books such as *Fish* and *Who Moved My Cheese?* are told as fables.

- A software company has its experienced technical support personnel help new employees, freshly out of their four-month technical training, by telling stories of a particular problem with a particular customer and how it was solved. The stories help new employees put their technical knowledge into a human context.

- Some companies post personal testimonies—in written, visual before/after, or video form—to their social media sites, featuring the stories of real customers and creating a sense of community.

Use Humor
How do you get people to read information they think is going to be boring?

The Centers for Disease Control and Prevention (CDC) started a zombie apocalypse campaign as a way to direct attention to disaster preparedness (see Figure 9.1).[1] The zombie-themed messages were a unique way to raise interest in the campaign and reached a wider audience with their important safety and natural disaster information. They were particularly effective with younger audiences, who were not familiar with how to prepare for disasters—a primary audience the CDC wanted to reach.

Many emergency departments, like those in the CDC, have a limited budget, so posting humorous blog posts to their websites is one way to bring in readers while still disseminating important safety information. Indeed, 10 minutes after posting the zombie information, the CDC blog site crashed as 30,000 people tried to read it. Once restored, the site had more than 60,000 views per hour. Officials were understandably pleased.

Four decades of research show that skillfully used humor can help in some communication situations. The research also shows that the best executives use humor twice as often as do mediocre managers.[2]

Humor is a risky tool because of its tendency to rile some people. However, if you know your audience well, humor may help ensure that they absorb your message.

If you decide to use humor, these precautions will help keep it useful:

- Do not direct it against other people, even if you are sure they will never see your message. In particular, never aim humor against a specific group of people.

- Avoid political, religious, and sexual humor; it is against discrimination policies in many businesses.

- Use restraint with your humor; a little levity goes a long way.

Used with care, humor in carefully chosen situations can help your communications. An information technology person sent the following email in his nonprofit organization:[3]

> My set of screw driver tips is missing. I may well have loaned them to someone, perhaps weeks ago. If you have them, please return them to me. I use them when someone reports that they have a screw loose.

He got his tips back promptly. Because he had a reputation for clever emails, people regularly read his messages.

Use Informational Hooks
Informational hooks encourage readers to open the email, read the post, or watch the video because they value the content. The informational benefit could be monetary, such as a discount coupon, or content-based, such as a seasonal recipe from a staff member. Even if the content is not novel or used by most audience members, providing information perceived as valuable projects an image of your company as generous, thoughtful, and community-minded.

Gary Nealon, president of the RTA Cabinet Store, builds goodwill with potential customers through a Facebook page titled "We Love Cooking and Baking." He posts recipes, funny memes, and other lighthearted informational-hook content to connect

Figure 9.1	The CDC's Use of Humor to Heighten Interest in a Disaster-Preparedness Campaign

U.S. Department of Health and Human Services Centers for Disease Control and Prevention. http://emergency.cdc.gov
/socialmedia/zombies.asp

with potential customers.[4] He notes that his company tried to use a branded page to generate interest in the company, but this approach was viewed as inauthentic; the hobby-focused page yields much higher engagement and he has been able to successfully shift some of its participants into a mailing list for RTA Cabinet Store. Nealson "compiled a list of the top 10–15 recipes shared throughout the month [on the 'We Love Cooking and Baking' page] and offered a link that took the consumer to the RTA Cabinet Store page to download the recipe book, in exchange for their email address."[5]

Connect with Your Audience

Respond to Complaints   Complaining customers expect organizations to show that they are listening and want to resolve the problem. Although complaints themselves are negative, a satisfactory response is informative or positive. When you grant a customer's request for an adjusted price, discount, replacement, or other benefit to resolve a complaint, do so in the very first sentence of your message.

You can use social media to address complaints in a way that turns the dissatisfied into loyal customers. Jill Castilla, president and CEO of Citizens Bank of Edmond in Oklahoma, started turning around the bank's negative reputation by addressing consumer complaints on social media: "I searched for 'Citizens Bank Sucks' on Twitter and Facebook and found negative references to my institution. I responded to those concerns, even though some were a couple of years old. Over time, we found that people with complaints had become our strongest customer advocates because they know we are listening . . . We've attracted new customers because we're willing to ask the right sorts of questions, listen to the answers, and make the changes."[6]

Express Gratitude   We all like to feel appreciated. Praising or congratulating people can cement good feelings between you and them and enhance your own visibility.

> Congratulations, Sam, on winning the Miller sales award. I bet winning that huge Lawson contract didn't hurt any!

Make your praise sound sincere by offering specifics and avoiding language that might seem condescending or patronizing. For example, think how silly it would sound to praise an employee for completing basic job requirements or to gush that one's mentor has superior knowledge. In contrast, thanks for a kind deed and congratulations or praise on completing a difficult task are rewarding in almost any situation.

Sending a **thank-you note** will make people more willing to help you again in the future. Thank-you notes can be short but must be prompt. They need to be specific to sound sincere.

> Chris, thank you for the extra-short turnaround time. You were a major reason we made the deadline.

Most thank-you notes are emails now, so handwritten ones stand out.

If you make it a habit to watch for opportunities to offer thanks and congratulations, you may be pleasantly surprised at the number of people who extend themselves. During his six-year term, Douglas Conant, chief executive of Campbell, sent more than 16,000 handwritten thank-you notes to employees ranging from top executives to hourly workers.[7] As Kenneth Blanchard and Spencer Johnson, authors of the business best seller *The One Minute Manager*, note, "People who feel good about themselves produce good results."[8]

Thank-you notes can be written on standard business stationery, using standard formats. One student noticed that his professor really liked dogs and told funny dog stories in class, so the student found a dog card for a thank-you note (see Figure 9.2).

Avoid Information Overload

One of the realities of communication today is information overload—having more information than one can process, understand, or act upon. You should build goodwill with others within and outside your organization by avoiding unnecessary or inefficient communication. You can avoid information overload by protecting your audience's time and managing the information you convey.

Figure 9.2   A Handwritten Thank-You Note, Adapted to the Recipient's Interests, Can Make a Positive Impact

Dear Professor Carlton,

Thank you for all your help this semester. My writing skills have improved greatly as have my organizational skills. The extra time you gave me really paid off. I've already had three job interviews due to the job packet I prepared for your course. I will miss your funny dog stories!!! Thanks again for everything!

Pat
Robbins

Both: McGraw Hill

Protect Your Audience's Time   Technology enables other people to bombard us with junk mail, sales calls, advertisements, and spam. Spam clutters computer mailboxes—or leads to filters that stop some needed email. Spam also means that many people do not open email if they do not recognize the sender or the topic.

Even more routine communications are becoming overwhelming. With fast and cheap emails, text messages, instant messages, and tweets, plus the genuine belief in more transparent business procedures, businesses send more announcements of events, procedures, policies, services, and employee news than ever before. Departments send newsletters. Employees send announcements of and best wishes for births, birthdays, weddings, and promotions. Customers send comments about products, service, policies, and advertisements.

Yet another factor in overload is inappropriate emails. This group includes jokes, personal information, and non-job-related emails, as well as emails that are unnecessarily long, trivial, and irrelevant. Too many people forward too many messages to uncaring receivers, and the "Reply All" button has a notorious reputation for being misused.

According to the Radicati Group, a technology market research firm, in 2019, the average corporate email user sent and received 126 emails per day.[9] By one estimate, over 293 billion email messages were sent *daily* in 2019.[10]

With this flood of information, you need to protect your communication reputation and be courteous to others. Follow the best practices for each type of communication you use, and at every step, ask yourself: Is this communication necessary? Is it efficient? Is it clear? Have I considered my audience's needs, and have I done everything I can—within reason—to save them time?

Manage the Information You Convey   Information control is important. You want to give your audience the information they need, but you don't want to overwhelm them with information. Finding the right balance isn't always easy.

For example, pharmaceutical companies struggle with how much information to provide about their drugs. In 2004, the Food and Drug Administration (FDA) publicized an analysis showing that young people on antidepressants had a 4% risk of suicidal thoughts or behavior. The FDA put a black-box warning—the strongest possible warning—on antidepressants. Parents and physicians began backing away from the medications. Two years after the warning, use of antidepressants was down 31% in adolescents and 24.3% in young adults, and a worrying trend emerged. Psychotropic-drug poisoning—used as proxy measure for suicide attempts—increased 21.7% in adolescents and 33.7% in young adults.[11]

Sometimes organizations get in trouble because their information management withholds information that others—shareholders, regulators, and customers—believe should be revealed. For example, Credit Suisse paid $120 million to settle with the Securities and Exchange Commission over allegations that it failed to disclose relevant mortgage practices.[12]

Other concerns about managing information are more prosaic:

- If you send out regularly scheduled messages on the same topic, such as monthly updates of training seminars, develop a system that lets people know immediately what is new. For example, you could put new or changed entries at the top or mark it with a symbol.

- If you are answering multiple questions, use numbers.

- If your email is long (more than one screen), use overviews, headings, and bullets so readers can find the information they need.

- If you are asking people to complete processes involving multiple steps or complicated knowledge, use checklists. Once maligned as too elementary, checklists are being recognized as a major tool to prevent errors.

Organizing Informative and Positive Messages

LO 9-3

This chapter covers patterns of message organization followed in business, nonprofits, and government. Using the appropriate pattern can help you compose more quickly and create a more effective message.

WARNING: The patterns should never be used blindly. You must always consider the rhetorical situation—audience, purpose, and context—warrants the organization.

If you decide to use a pattern:

- Be sure you understand the rationale behind each pattern so that you can modify the pattern when necessary.

- Realize not every message that uses the basic pattern will have all the elements listed.

- Realize sometimes you can present several elements in one paragraph; sometimes you'll need several paragraphs for just one element.

Figure 9.3	How to Organize Informative and Positive Messages

1. **Start with good news or the most important information.** Summarize the main points. If the audience already has raised the issue, make it clear that you're responding.

2. **Give details, clarification, background.** Answer all questions your audience is likely to have; provide all information necessary to achieve your purposes. If you are asking or answering multiple questions, number them. Enumeration increases your chances of giving or receiving all necessary information. Present details in the order of importance to the reader or in some other logical order.

3. **Present any negative elements as positively as possible.** A policy may have limits; information may be incomplete; the audience may have to satisfy requirements to get a discount or benefit. Make these negatives clear, but present them as positively as possible.

4. **Explain any benefits.** Most informative messages need benefits. Show that the policy or procedure helps your audience, not just the company. Give enough detail to make the benefits clear and convincing. In letters, you may want to give benefits of dealing with your company as well as benefits of the product or policy. In a good-news message, it's often possible to combine a short benefit with a goodwill ending.

5. **Use a goodwill ending; make it positive, personal, and forward-looking.** Shifting your emphasis away from the message to the specific audience suggests that serving the audience is your real concern.

Figure 9.3 shows how to organize informative and positive messages.

Figures 9.4 and 9.5 illustrate two ways the basic pattern can be applied.

The letter in Figure 9.4 announces a change in a magazine's ownership. Rather than telling subscribers that their magazine has been acquired, which sounds negative, the first two paragraphs describe the change as a merger that will give subscribers greater benefits from the combined magazine. The third paragraph provides details about how the arrangement will work, along with a way to opt out. A possible negative is that readers who already have subscriptions to both magazines will now receive only one. The company addresses this situation positively by extending the subscription to the jointly published magazine. The goodwill ending has all the desired characteristics: it is positive ("we're confident"), personal ("your continued loyalty"), and forward-looking ("you will enjoy").

The email in Figure 9.5 announces a new employee benefit. The first paragraph summarizes the new benefits. The second and third paragraphs provide major details; further details are saved for the plan's brochure. Negative elements are stated as positively as possible. The last section of the email gives benefits and a goodwill ending.

Subject Lines for Informative and Positive Messages

LO 9-4

A **subject line** is the title of a document. It aids in filing and retrieving the document, tells readers why they need to read the document, and provides a framework in which to set what you're about to say. Subject lines are standard in memos and emails. Letters are not required to have subject lines (see Appendix A).

A good subject line meets three criteria: it is specific, concise, and appropriate to the message type (positive, negative, persuasive).

Making Subject Lines Specific

The subject line needs to be specific enough to differentiate its message from others on the same subject, but broad enough to cover everything in the message.

Too general: Training Sessions

Better: Dates for 2021 Training Sessions

Figure 9.4   A Positive Informational Letter

eBusCompanyToday

P.O. Box 12345
Tampa, FL 33660
813-555-5555

June 17, 2021

Dear Ms. Locker:

Main point presented as good news. — We're excited to share some great news! *eBusCompanyToday* has merged with another business magazine, *High-Tech Business News*. This merged publication will be called *High-Tech Business News* and will continue to be edited and published by the *eBusCompanyToday* staff.

Details focus on benefits to the reader. — The new *High-Tech Business News* is a great tool for navigating today's relentlessly changing marketplace, particularly as it's driven by the internet and other technologies. It reports on the most innovative business practices and the people behind them; delivers surprising, useful insights; and explains how to put them to work. Please be assured that you will continue to receive the same great editorial coverage that you've come to expect from *eBusCompanyToday*.

You will receive the "new" *High-Tech Business News* in about 4 weeks, starting with the combined August/September issue. If you already subscribe to *High-Tech Business News*, your subscription will be extended accordingly. And if you'd rather not receive this — *Option to cancel is offered but not emphasized.* publication, please call 1-800-555-5555 within the next 3 weeks.

Positive, personal, forward-looking ending. — Thank you for your continued loyalty to *eBusCompanyToday*; we're confident that you will enjoy reading *High-Tech Business News* every month.

Sincerely,

Alan Schmidt

Alan Schmidt, Editor and President

High-Tech Business News is published monthly except for two issues combined periodically into one and occasional extra, expanded, or premium issues.

Figure 9.5	A Positive Email, Sent to Chamber of Commerce Employees and Members

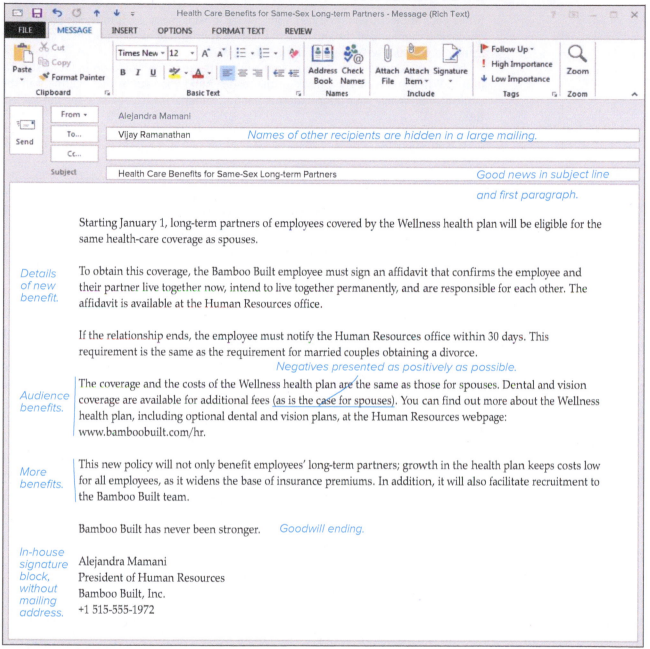

Health Care Benefits for Same-Sex Long-term Partners - Message (Rich Text)

FILE | MESSAGE | INSERT | OPTIONS | FORMAT TEXT | REVIEW

From ▾ Alejandra Mamani

To... Vijay Ramanathan *Names of other recipients are hidden in a large mailing.*

Cc...

Subject Health Care Benefits for Same-Sex Long-term Partners *Good news in subject line and first paragraph.*

Starting January 1, long-term partners of employees covered by the Wellness health plan will be eligible for the same health-care coverage as spouses.

Details of new benefit. To obtain this coverage, the Bamboo Built employee must sign an affidavit that confirms the employee and their partner live together now, intend to live together permanently, and are responsible for each other. The affidavit is available at the Human Resources office.

If the relationship ends, the employee must notify the Human Resources office within 30 days. This requirement is the same as the requirement for married couples obtaining a divorce.

Negatives presented as positively as possible.

Audience benefits. The coverage and the costs of the Wellness health plan are the same as those for spouses. Dental and vision coverage are available for additional fees (as is the case for spouses). You can find out more about the Wellness health plan, including optional dental and vision plans, at the Human Resources webpage: www.bamboobuilt.com/hr.

More benefits. This new policy will not only benefit employees' long-term partners; growth in the health plan keeps costs low for all employees, as it widens the base of insurance premiums. In addition, it will also facilitate recruitment to the Bamboo Built team.

Bamboo Built has never been stronger. *Goodwill ending.*

In-house signature block, without mailing address.
Alejandra Mamani
President of Human Resources
Bamboo Built, Inc.
+1 515-555-1972

Source: Microsoft Inc

Making Subject Lines Concise

Most subject lines are relatively short. While it helps to know whether your audience will read your message on a smartphone or on a computer screen, a "sweet spot" seems to be about 41 characters, or seven words.[13]

Wordy: Communicating with Clients before Preliminary Sales Meeting and Recommendations to Support Client Conversations

Better: Guidance on Communicating with Clients before Sales Meetings

If you can't make the subject both specific and short, be specific.

Making Subject Lines Appropriate for the Pattern of Organization

Since your subject line introduces your reader to your message, it must satisfy the psychological demands of the situation; it must be appropriate to your purposes and to the immediate response you expect from your reader.

In general, do the same thing in your subject line that you would do in the first paragraph. When you have good news for the reader, build goodwill by highlighting it in the subject line. When your information is neutral, summarize it concisely for the subject line.

Not appropriate:	Subject: Your Discount on Rental Cars Is Effective on January 2
	Starting January 2, because you are an employee of Amalgamated Industries, you can receive a 15% discount on cars you rent for either business or personal use from Roadway Rent-a-Car.
Better:	Subject: Rental Car Discount Starts January 2
	Starting January 2, as an employee of Amalgamated Industries, you can get a 15% discount on cars you rent for business or personal use from Roadway Rent-a-Car.

Following Other Pointers for Email Subject Lines

Many people skim through large lists of emails daily, so subject lines in emails are critical. Subject lines must be specific, concise, and catchy. Some email users get so many messages that they don't bother reading messages if they don't recognize the sender or if the subject doesn't catch their interest. Create a subject line that will help your email get read:

- Use important information in the subject line. Many people delete blanks and generic tags such as "hello," "your message," "thank you," and "next meeting" if they don't recognize the sender.

- Put good news in the subject line.

- Name drop to make a connection: Lee Pizer gave me your name.

- Make email sound easy to deal with: Two Short Travel Questions.

- New topics need new subject lines; do not attach a new topic to an email string on a different topic.

- Use specific dates. Do not use indefinite dates such as Today, Tomorrow, Next Week, or even Wednesday as subject lines. They are no longer clear if read at a later time.

- When you reply to a message, check to see that the automatic subject line "Re: [subject line of message to which you are responding]" is still appropriate. If it isn't, you may want to create a new subject line. And if a series of messages arises, you probably need a new subject line. "Re: Re: Re: Re: Question" is not an effective subject line.

The following subject lines would be acceptable for informative and good-news email messages:

Travel Plans for the 8 December Sales Meeting

Your Proposal for the SBA Loan Is Accepted

Reduced Prices during February

Ending Informative and Positive Messages

LO 9-5

Ending a letter or email gracefully can be a problem in short informative and positive messages. In an email in which you have omitted details and proof, you can tell readers where to get more information. In long messages, you can summarize your basic point. In a short message containing all the information readers need, either write a goodwill paragraph that refers directly to the reader or the reader's organization or just stop. In many short emails, just stopping is the best choice.

Goodwill endings should focus on the business relationship you share with your reader rather than on the reader's hobbies, family, or personal life. Use a paragraph that shows you see your reader as an individual. Possibilities include complimenting the reader for a job well done, describing a benefit, or looking forward to something positive that relates to the subject of the message.

> Thank you so much for sending those two extra sales tables. They were just what I needed for Section IV of the report.

When you write to one person, a good last paragraph fits that person so specifically that it would not work if you sent the same basic message to someone else or even to a person with the same title in another organization. When you write to someone who represents an organization, the last paragraph can refer to your company's relationship to the reader's organization. When you write to a group (e.g., to "All Employees"), your ending should apply to the whole group.

> Remember that the deadline for enrolling in this new benefit plan is January 31.

Some writers end every message with a standard invitation:

> If you have questions, please do not hesitate to ask.

That sentence implies both that your message did not answer all questions and that readers will hesitate to contact you. Both implications are negative. But revising the line to say "feel free to call" is rarely a good idea. People in business will call if they need help. Don't make more work for yourself by inviting calls to clarify simple messages. Simply omit this sentence.

> Your Visa bill for a night's lodging has been adjusted to $163. Next month a credit of $37 will appear on your bill to reimburse you for the extra amount you were originally asked to pay.

Don't talk about your own process in making the decision. Don't say anything that sounds grudging. Give the reason for the original mistake only if it reflects well on the company. In most cases, it doesn't, so the reason should be omitted.

Organizing Transmittals and Summaries

LO 9-6

Organizing Transmittals

When you send someone something, you frequently need to attach a transmittal message explaining what you're sending. A transmittal can be as simple as a small yellow sticky note with "FYI" ("for your information") written on it, context written in the body of an email ("Please read the attached proposal, and let me know if there are any errors"), or a separate typed document.

Organize a transmittal message in this order:

1. Tell the reader what you're sending.
2. Summarize the main point(s) of the document.
3. Indicate any special circumstances or information that would help the reader understand the document. Is it a draft? Is it a partial document that will be completed later?
4. Tell the reader what will happen next. Will you do something? Do you want a response? If you do want the reader to act, specify exactly what you want the reader to do and give a deadline.

Frequently, transmittals have important secondary purposes. A transmittal from marketing to a store might have the primary purpose of giving the client a chance to affirm the marketing plan. If there's anything wrong, marketing wants to know *before* spending money developing the plan. But an important secondary purpose is to build goodwill: "I'm working on your plan; I'm earning my fee."

Organizing Summaries

You may be asked to summarize a conversation, a document, or an outside meeting for colleagues or superiors.

In a summary of a conversation for internal use, identify the people who were present, the topic of discussion, decisions made, and who does what next.

To summarize a document, start with the main point. Then go on to summarize supporting evidence or details for that point. Add the subsidiary points if your audience needs them. In some cases, your audience also may want you to evaluate the document. Should others in the company read this report? Should someone in the company write a letter to the editor responding to this newspaper article?

After you visit a client or go to a conference, you may be asked to share your findings and impressions with other people in your organization. Chronological accounts are the easiest to write but the least useful for the reader. Your company doesn't need a second-by-second account of what you did; it needs to know what *it* should do as a result of the meeting.

Summarize a visit with a client or customer in this way:

1. Put the main point from your organization's point of view—the action to be taken, the perceptions to be changed—in the first paragraph.
2. Provide an **umbrella paragraph** to cover and foreshadow the points you will make in the report.
3. Provide necessary detail to support your conclusions and cover each point. Use lists and headings to make the structure of the document clear.

In the following example, the revised first paragraph summarizes the sales representative's conclusions after a call on a prospective client.

Weak original:	On October 10, Rick Patel and I made a joint call on Consolidated Tool Works. The discussion was held in a conference room, with the following people present:
	1. Gail McCloskey (Vice President and General Manager)
	2. Bill Petrakis (Manufacturing Engineer)
	3. Garett Lee (Process Engineering Supervisor)
	4. Courtney Mansor-Green (Project Engineer)
Improved revision:	Consolidated Tool Works is an excellent prospect for purchasing a Matrix-Churchill grinding machine. To get the order, we should
	1. Set up a visit for CTW personnel to see the Matrix-Churchill machine in Kansas City;
	2. Guarantee 60-day delivery if the order is placed by the end of the quarter; and
	3. Extend credit terms to CTW.

Example Problem: Which Email Is Better?

Workplace problems are richer and less well defined than textbook problems and cases. But even textbook problems require analysis before you begin to write. Before you tackle the assignments for this chapter, examine the following problem. Study the two sample solutions to see what makes one unacceptable and the other one good. Note the recommendations for revision that could make the good solution excellent. The checklist at the end of the chapter can help you evaluate a draft.

Problem

At Interstate Fidelity Insurance (IFI), there is often a time lag between receiving a payment—a check—from a customer and recording it. Sometimes, while the payment is in line to be processed, the accounting software sends out additional past-due notices or collection letters. Customers are frightened or angry and ask for an explanation. In most cases, if they just waited a little while, the situation would be straightened out. But policyholders are afraid that they'll be without insurance because the company thinks the bill has not been paid.

IFI doesn't want to spend employee time on determining whether individual checks have been processed. It wants you to write an email that will persuade customers to wait. If something is wrong and the payment never reached IFI, IFI would send a legal notice to that effect saying the policy would be canceled by a certain date (which the notice would specify) at least 30 days after the date on the original premium bill. Continuing customers always get this legal notice as a third chance (after the original bill and the past-due notice).

Prepare a form email that can go out to every policyholder who claims to have paid a premium for automobile insurance and resents getting a past-due notice. The email should reassure readers and build goodwill for IFI.

Analysis of the Problem

1. Who is (are) your audience(s)?

    Automobile insurance customers who say they've paid but have still received a past-due notice. They're afraid they're no longer insured. Because it's a form response, different readers will have different situations. In some cases, payments did arrive late; in some cases, the company made a mistake; in others, the customer never paid (check was lost in mail, unsigned, bounced, etc.).

2. What are your purposes in writing?

    To reassure readers that they're covered for 30 days. To inform them that they can assume everything is okay *unless* they receive a second notice. To avoid further correspondence on this subject. To build goodwill for IFI: (a) we don't want to suggest IFI is error-prone or too cheap to hire enough people to do the necessary work; (b) we don't want readers to switch companies; (c) we do want readers to buy from IFI when they're ready for more insurance.

3. What information must your message include?

    Readers are still insured. We cannot say whether their checks have now been processed (company doesn't want to check individual accounts). Their insurance will be canceled if they do not pay after receiving the second past-due notice (the legal notice).

4. How can you build support for your position? What reasons or benefits will your audience find convincing?

    We provide personal service to policyholders. We offer policies to meet all their needs. Both of these points would need specifics to be interesting and convincing.

    What aspects of the total situation may affect audience response? The economy? The time of year? Morale in the organization? The relationship between the communicator and audience? Any special circumstances?

The insurance business is highly competitive—other companies offer similar rates and policies. The customer could get a similar policy for about the same money from someone else. The economy is making money tight, so customers will want to keep insurance costs low. Yet the fact that prices are steady or rising means that the value of what they own is higher—they need insurance more than ever.

Many insurance companies are refusing to renew policies (car, liability, home). These refusals to renew have gotten lots of publicity, and many people have heard horror stories about companies and individuals whose insurance has been canceled or not renewed after a small number of claims. Readers don't feel very kindly toward insurance companies.

People need car insurance. If they have an accident and aren't covered, they not only have to bear the costs of that accident alone, but also (depending on state law) may need to place as much as $50,000 in a state escrow account to cover future accidents. They have a legitimate worry.

Discussion of Sample Solutions

The solution in Figure 9.6 is unacceptable. The red marginal comments show problem spots. Since this is a form response, we cannot tell customers we have their checks; in some cases, we may not. The email is far too negative. The explanation in the second

Figure 9.6	An Unacceptable Solution to the Sample Problem

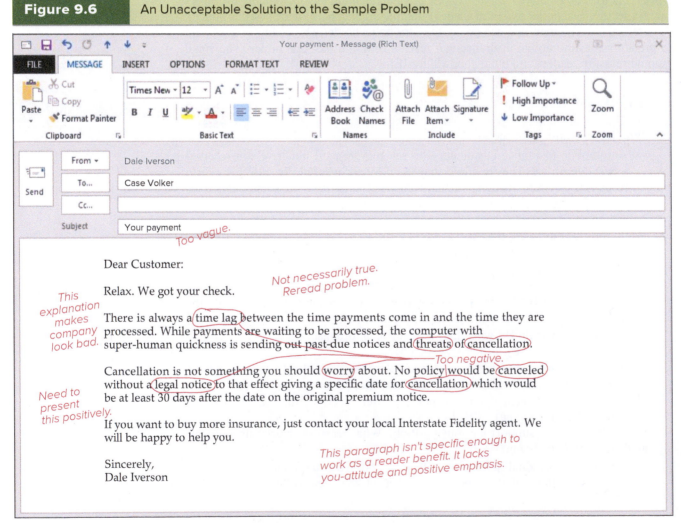

Source: Microsoft Inc

paragraph makes IFI look irresponsible and uncaring. The third paragraph is far too negative. The fourth paragraph is too vague; there are no benefits; the ending sounds selfish. A major weakness with the solution is that it lifts phrases straight out of the problem; the writer does not seem to have thought about the problem or about the words they are using. Measuring the draft against the answers to the questions for analysis suggests that this writer should start over.

The solution in Figure 9.7 is much better. The blue marginal comments show the email's good points. The message opens strongly with the good news that is true for all audiences. The second paragraph explains IFI's policy in more positive terms. The

Figure 9.7	A Good Solution to the Sample Problem

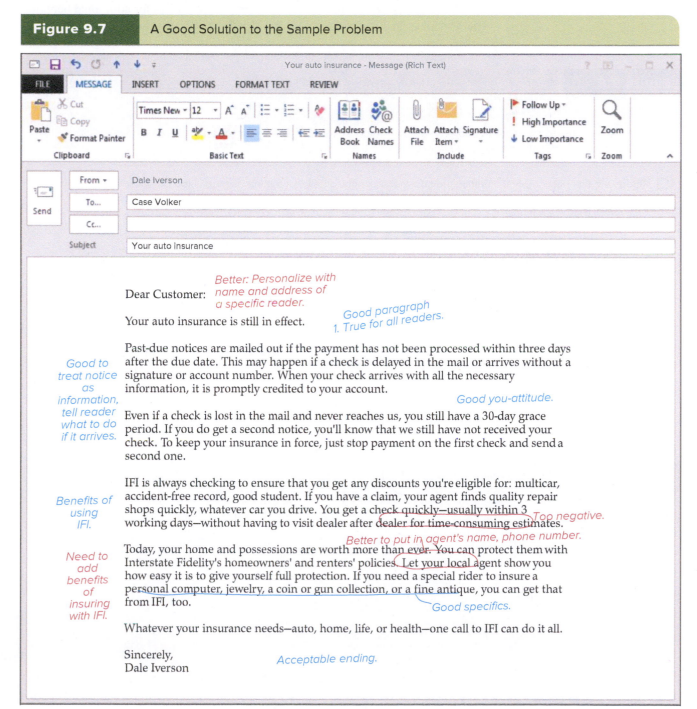

Source: Microsoft Inc

negative information is buried in the third paragraph and is presented positively: the notice is information, not a threat; the 30-day extension is a "grace period." Telling the reader now what to do if a second notice arrives eliminates the need for a second exchange of letters. The fourth paragraph delineates benefits of being insured by IFI. The fifth paragraph promotes other policies the company sells and prepares for the last paragraph.

As the red comments indicate, this good solution could be improved by personalizing the salutation and by including the name and number of the local agent. This good response could be made excellent by revising the fourth paragraph so that it doesn't end on a negative note and by using more benefits. For instance, can agents advise clients about the best policies for them? Does IFI offer quick and friendly service that could be stressed? Are agents well trained? All of these might yield ideas for additional benefits.

The checklists in Figures 9.8 and 9.9 will help you draft informative and positive messages.

Figure 9.8	Informative- and Positive-Messages Checklist

☐ In positive messages, does the subject line give the good news? In either message, is the subject line specific enough to differentiate this message from others on the same subject?

☐ Does the first paragraph summarize the information or good news? If the information is too complex to fit into a single paragraph, does the paragraph list the basic parts of the policy or information in the order in which the message discusses them?

☐ Is all the information given in the message? What information is needed will vary depending on the message, but information about dates, places, times, and anything related to money usually needs to be included. When in doubt, ask!

☐ In messages announcing policies, is there at least one benefit for each segment of the audience? Are all benefits ones that seem likely to occur in this organization?

☐ Is each benefit developed, showing that the benefit will come from the policy and why the benefit matters to this audience? Do the benefits build on the specific circumstances of the audience?

☐ Does the message end with a positive paragraph—preferably one that is specific to the readers, not a general one that could fit any organization or policy?

Figure 9.9	Effective-Messages Checklist

☐ Does the message use *you*-attitude and positive emphasis?

☐ Is the tone friendly?

☐ Is the style easy to read?

☐ Is the visual design of the message inviting?

☐ Is the format correct?

☐ Is the message grammatical? Is it free from typos?

Summary by Learning Objectives

LO 9-1 **Explain the purposes of informative and positive messages.**

Informative and positive messages have a primary purpose of providing information and good news in a positive manner, as well as multiple secondary purposes such as creating a positive image of the sender and the sender's organization.

LO 9-2 **Describe strategies for building goodwill.**

You can build goodwill by providing benefits, framing benefits for policy change or to build goodwill, connecting with your audience, and avoiding information overload.

LO 9-3 **Implement best practices for organizing informative and positive messages.**

Informative and positive messages normally use the following pattern of organization:

1. Start with good news or the most important information; summarize the main points.
2. Give details, clarification, background.
3. Present any negative elements as positively as possible.
4. Explain any benefits.
5. Use a goodwill ending: positive, personal, and forward-looking.

LO 9-4 **Implement best practices for subject lines in informative and positive messages.**

- A subject line is the title of a document. A good subject line meets three criteria: it's specific, it's concise, and it's adapted to the kind of message (positive, negative, persuasive). If you can't make the subject both specific and short, be specific.

- The subject line for an informative or positive message should highlight any good news and summarize the information concisely.

LO 9-5 **Implement best practices for ending informative and positive messages.**

- In short informative and positive messages that contain all the information readers need, either write a goodwill paragraph that refers directly to the reader or the reader's organization or just stop.

- In short informative and positive messages that do not contain all the information readers need, tell readers where to get more information.

- In long messages, summarize your basic point.

LO 9-6 **Implement best practices for organizing transmittals and summaries.**

Organize a transmittal message in this order:

1. Tell the reader what you're sending.
2. Summarize the main point(s) of the document.
3. Indicate any special circumstances or information that would help the reader understand the document.
4. Tell the reader what will happen next.

To summarize a document,

1. Start with the main point.
2. Summarize supporting evidence or details for that point.
3. Add the subsidiary points if your audience needs them.

Exercises and Cases

9.1 Reviewing the Chapter

1. What are some purposes for informative and positive messages? (LO 9-1)
2. What are some strategies for building goodwill in your messages? (LO 9-2)
3. What pattern of organization would you use for an informative or positive message? (LO 9-3)

4. What are some best practices for composing subject lines for informative and positive messages? (LO 9-4)
5. What are some best practices for ending informative and positive messages? (LO 9-5)
6. What are some best practices for organizing transmittals and summaries? (LO 9-6)

9.2 Saying Yes to a Subordinate—Emails for Discussion

Today, you get this request from a subordinate.

> Subject: Request for Leave
>
> You know that I've been feeling burned out. I've decided that I want to take a three-month leave of absence this summer to travel abroad. I've got five weeks of vacation time saved up; I would take the rest as unpaid leave. Just guarantee that my job will be waiting when I come back!

You decide to grant the request. The following subject lines and messages are possible responses.

- How well does each subject line below meet the guidelines in this chapter?

> **Subject Line A:** Re: Request for Leave
>
> **Subject Line B:** Your Request for Leave
>
> **Subject Line C:** Your Request for Leave Granted

- How well does each message below meet the criteria in the checklist for informative and positive messages?

> **Message 1:**
>
> I highly recommend Italy. Spend a full week in Florence, if you can. Be sure to visit the Brancacci Chapel—it's been restored and the frescoes are breathtaking. And I can give you the names of some great restaurants. You may never want to come back!

> **Message 2:**
>
> As you know, we are in a very competitive position right now. Your job is important, and there is no one who can easily replace you. However, because you are a valued employee, I will permit you to take the leave you request, as long as you train a replacement before you leave.

> **Message 3:**
>
> Yes, you may take a three-month leave of absence next summer using your five weeks of accumulated vacation time and taking the rest as unpaid leave. And yes, your job will be waiting for you when you return!
>
> I'm appointing Garrick to take over your duties while you're gone. Talk with him to determine how much training time he'll need, and let me know when the training is scheduled.
>
> Have a great summer! Let us know every now and then how you're doing!

9.3 Critiquing a Letter—Economic Impact Payment Notice

The letter in Figure 9.10 was sent to American households after the U.S. Congress passed a stimulus package in May 2020. Critique it in small groups. Here are some questions to get you started:

1. What are the purposes of this letter?
2. How well does this letter inform the audience of its purpose?
3. Does the letter violate any of the guidelines for constructing informational messages you read about in this chapter? If so, which ones?
4. What kind of impression is given to readers by the document design choices?

As your instructor directs,

a. Write an email to your instructor summarizing your group discussion.

b. As a group, record your answers to the questions, plus other observations you made. Trade summaries with another group. Where did they agree with you? Disagree? What observations did they make that your group did not? Write an email to your instructor summarizing the differences between the two critiques. Submit the email and the two critiques to your instructor.

| **Figure 9.10** | Economic Impact Payment Notice from IRS |

THE WHITE HOUSE
WASHINGTON

NOTICE DATE: May 6, 2020
NOTICE NUMBER: 1444 (EN-SP)

Your Economic Impact Payment Has Arrived

My Fellow American:

Our great country is experiencing an unprecedented public health and economic challenge as a result of the global coronavirus pandemic. Our top priority is your health and safety. As we wage total war on this invisible enemy, we are also working around the clock to protect hardworking Americans like you from the consequences of the economic shutdown. We are fully committed to ensuring that you and your family have the support you need to get through this time.

On March 27, 2020, Congress passed with overwhelming bipartisan support the Coronavirus Aid, Relief, and Economic Security Act (CARES Act), which I proudly signed into law. I want to thank the United States House of Representatives and the United States Senate for working so quickly with my Administration to fast-track this $2.2 trillion in much-needed economic relief to the American people.

This includes <u>fast and direct economic assistance to you</u>.

I am pleased to notify you that as provided by the CARES Act, <u>you are receiving an Economic Impact Payment of $ by direct deposit</u>. We hope this payment provides meaningful support to you during this period.

Every citizen should take tremendous pride in the selflessness, courage and compassion of our people. America's drive, determination, innovation and sheer willpower have conquered every previous challenge---and they will conquer this one too. Just as we have before, America will triumph yet again—and rise to new heights of greatness.

We will do it together, as one nation, stronger than ever before.

President Donald J. Trump

For more information on your Economic Impact Payment, visit IRS.gov/coronavirus or call 800-919-9835.

9.4   Critiquing a Letter—Introducing Kindle

When Amazon brought Kindle to market in 2007, CEO Jeff Bezos sent shareholders a letter telling the story of the creation of the device. Read the letter at http://media.corporate-ir.net/media_files/irol/97/97664/2007letter.pdf. Critique the letter in small groups. Here are some questions to get you started:

1. What are the purposes of this letter?
2. How well are these purposes accomplished?
3. What information does Bezos provide about Kindle? Why do you think he chose this information?
4. How is the information organized?
5. Where do you see *you*-attitude and positive tone? Do they contribute to the letter's effectiveness? Why or why not?

As your instructor directs,

a. Write an email to your instructor summarizing your group discussion.
b. As a group, record your answers to the questions, plus other observations you made. Trade summaries with another group. Where did they agree with you? Disagree? What observations did they make that your group did not? Write an email to your instructor summarizing the differences between the two critiques. Submit the email and the two critiques to your instructor.

9.5   Critiquing a Letter—Company Merger

Visit https://complete-electronics.com/news/companymerger to view the letter sent by the managing director of Electroustic Ltd. before its merger with Complete Electronics Ltd. Critique the letter in small groups. Here are some questions to get you started:

1. What are the purposes of this letter?
2. How well are these purposes accomplished?
3. What information does the letter provide that an ordinary customer would find useful?
4. How is the information organized?
5. Where do you see *you*-attitude and positive tone? Do they contribute to the letter's effectiveness? Why or why not?

As your instructor directs,

a. Write an email to your instructor summarizing your group discussion.
b. As a group, record your answers to the questions, plus other observations you made. Trade summaries with another group. Where did they agree with you? Disagree? What observations did they make that your group did not? Write an email to your instructor summarizing the differences between the two critiques. Submit the email and the two critiques to your instructor.

9.6   Writing Common Informational Emails

Some of the most common emails are meeting announcements, away notices, and maintenance notices. Create these three messages:

1. Write an email announcing a staff meeting to hear a consultant's presentation on business etiquette.
2. Write a computer away notice for your upcoming sales trip.
3. Write an email announcing maintenance work (e.g., updating a server, repaving a parking lot or sidewalk, repairing an entrance).

In small groups, compare messages. Were all messages equally clear? Did some messages accidentally omit necessary information? What kinds of information? Did all messages use *you*-attitude and positive tone? Were benefits included where appropriate? How long did it take each of you to write the three messages?

As your instructor directs,

a. Share your findings with the class.
b. Write an informational email to your instructor summarizing your findings.
c. Write an informational email to your instructor summarizing what you learned about your ability to write short, commonplace emails.

9.7   Managing Overdraft Information

Banks make billions of dollars from overdraft fees. They maintain that the overdraft service allows customers to make vital purchases even when their account is empty.

On the other side, many customers are furious at how the current system allows them to rack up hundreds of dollars in overdraft fees without knowing they are doing so. Many of them claim they did not know they had overdraft service until they saw the fees. They want to be alerted when a purchase will result in an overdraft. They also object to the bank practice of processing a large purchase before several small ones that occurred at almost the same time so that each small purchase gets an overdraft fee that it would not have gotten if the large purchase had been processed last.

In small groups, discuss how much overdraft information should be shared. Here are some questions to get you started:

- For what groups are overdraft services a benefit?
- Which groups do such services hurt most?
- Should people be automatically enrolled in such services, as is now the case for most customers?
- Should banks notify customers that they are about to incur an overdraft fee? How would third-party processors affect such notifications?

Then, decide upon three banks or credit unions and locate the overdraft information on their websites (if possible). How well did the content (or lack of content) adhere to your group's ideas of how much information should be shared?

Write an email to your instructor summarizing your group's discussion.

9.8   Revising a Letter

You work for a local fitness center called Super Fit. The owners of Super Fit would like to expand their business and add a running track and a large pool. They have drafted the following letter to send out to their current members, informing them of the updates and new services.

> Dear Sir or Ma'am,
>
> We are excitedly writing to let you know about some thrilling new changes here at Super Fit! We have decided to expand our current business to fit our clients' needs. So, as of January 2022 we will have a brand new running track and a new lap pool. Both the running track and the pool will be very large, and will be able to accommodate many runners and swimmers. We also will offer a few other new services too.
>
> We are proud to note that your membership fee will not increase at all. We appreciate your business and hope you will consider telling your friends about Super Fit and all that we offer! We also would like to offer you 50% off of one month's fee if you refer a friend to us and they sign a membership contract.
>
> Remember, stay fit with Super Fit!
>
> With love,
>
> Bob and Joanie

1. Bob and Joanie have asked you to look over their letter and make improvements. Write the new letter and an email to Bob and Joanie explaining your changes.

2. Discuss how you would reach out to new customers with this information. Draft a poster or a flyer, designed to grab potential new members' attentions. How will you change the scope of the information for this new audience?

9.9   Critiquing and Revising an Email

In response to complaints about children's pools being left at the city dog park, the parks department sent the following email to those who had registered their dogs at the park:

> Dear Dog Park User,
>
> We have received concerns from users in regards to the use of the small pools near the fountains at the Dog Park. The comments include the lack of cleanliness of the pools, overuse of water, the mess made when the pools are emptied, and more importantly the potential for spreading disease. We understand keeping dogs cool during the hot days, but the dog park is not the place for pools. In an effort to keep dogs and their owners safe while at the Dog Park, pools are not allowed at the Dog Park. If you

(continued)

purchased a pool and left it at the Dog Park, please remove it by Thursday, July 27, or it will be removed and disposed of by staff. Thank you for understanding. If you have any questions or concerns, please contact me at jsmith@city.ia.us.

Thanks,

J. Smith

Park Superintendent

First, critique the email in small groups. Here are some questions to get you started:

1. What are the purposes of this email?
2. How well are these purposes accomplished?
3. What information does the Park Superintendent provide about the policy change? Why do you think the superintendent chose this information?
4. How is the information organized?
5. Where do you see *you*-attitude and positive tone? Do they contribute to the email's effectiveness? Why or why not?

After you have answered these questions, revise the email to be more effective. Consider every level of communication and use the tips from this and other relevant chapters.

As your instructor directs,

Write an email to your instructor summarizing your group's discussion, conveying your revisions, and explaining the reasoning behind your revisions.

9.10   Giving New Information

The Coffee Place, the local coffee shop where you work, has now developed a gluten-free menu at the request of customers.

In a group, list ways The Coffee Place can get this information to customers. What are the benefits of using those particular media?

As a group, design a document that delivers this new information. How can you extend the benefit of developing a gluten-free diet to your customers who don't care about gluten? Share your document with the class.

9.11   Investigating Email

Interview a professional you know about their use of email. You might consider questions such as these:

- How many emails do you receive on an average day? Send?
- How much time do you spend handling emails on an average day?
- What are the most common kinds of emails you receive? Send?

- What are the most difficult kinds of emails for you to write? Why?
- What are your pet peeves about emails?

Write up your findings in an informational email to your instructor.

9.12   Announcing a Tuition Reimbursement Program

Your organization has decided to encourage employees to take courses by reimbursing each eligible employee a maximum of $3,500 in tuition and fees during any one calendar year. Anyone who wants to participate in the program must apply before the first class meeting; the application must be signed by the employee's immediate supervisor. The Office of Human Resources will evaluate applications. That office has application forms; it also has catalogs from nearby schools and colleges.

The only courses employees may choose are those either related to the employee's current position (or to a position in the company that the employee might hold someday) or part of a job-related degree program. Again, the degree must be one that would help the employee's current position or that would qualify them for a promotion or transfer in the organization.

Only tuition and fees are covered, not books or supplies. People whose applications are approved will be reimbursed when they have completed the course with a grade of C or better. An employee cannot be reimbursed until they submit a copy of the approved application, an official grade report, and a statement of the tuition paid. If someone is eligible for other financial aid (scholarship, veterans benefits), the company will pay tuition costs not covered by that aid as long as the employee does not receive more than $3,500 and as long as the total tuition reimbursement does not exceed the actual cost of tuition and fees.

Part-time employees are not eligible; full-time employees must work at the company a year before they can apply to participate in the program. Courses may be at any appropriate level (high school, college, or graduate). However, the Internal Revenue Service currently requires workers to pay tax on any reimbursement for graduate programs. Undergraduate and basic education reimbursements of $3,500 or less a year are not taxed.

As director of human resources, write an email to all employees explaining this new benefit.

Hints:

- Pick an organization you know something about. What do its employees do? What courses or degrees might help them do their jobs better?

- How much education do employees already have? How do they feel about formal schooling?
- The information in the problem is presented in a confusing order. Put related items together.
- The problem stresses the limits of the policy. Without changing the provisions, present them positively.
- How will having a better educated workforce help the organization? Think about the challenges the organization faces, its competitive environment, and so forth.

9.13   Summarizing Information

Summarize one or more of the following:

1. An article from a recent edition of *Bloomberg Businessweek* or *Harvard Business Review*.

2. An article about college, career development, or job searching from LiveCareer, https://www.livecareer.com/resources.

3. Online information about options for recycling or donating used, outdated computers.

4. Options for consolidating student loans and other finances.

5. Online information about protecting your credit card or debit card.

6. An article or webpage assigned by your instructor.

As your instructor directs,

a. Write a summary of no more than 100 words.

b. Write a 250- to 300-word summary.

c. Write a 500-word summary.

d. In a small group compare your summaries. How did the content of the summaries vary? How do you account for any differences?

Notes

1. Sydney Lupkin, "Government Zombie Promos Are Spreading," *abcnews.go.com*, September 7, 2012, http://abcnews.go.com/blogs/health/2012/09/07/government-zombie-promos-are-spreading.
2. Daniel H. Pink, *A Whole New Mind: Why Right-Brainers Will Rule the Future* (New York: Riverhead Books, 2006), 198.
3. Bob Mills, email message to author.
4. Marcia Layton Turner, "How RTA Cabinet Store Finds Hidden Prospects for Its Kitchen Cabinets Using Facebook," *Forbes*, September 28, 2017.
5. Ibid.
6. Joanna Belbey, "Pancakes and Social Media: How One Small Bank Engages Its Community," *Forbes*, September 20, 2017.
7. "Lighting a Fire under Campbell," *BusinessWeek*, December 4, 2006, 96.
8. Kenneth Blanchard and Spencer Johnson, *The One Minute Manager* (New York: William Morrow, 1982), 19.
9. Campaign Monitor, "How Many Emails Does the Average Person Receive Per Day?" n.d., https://www.campaignmonitor.com/resources/knowledge-base/how-many-emails-does-the-average-person-receive-per-day.
10. Nick Gulov, "How Many Emails Are Sent per Day? [And Other 2020 Key Email Statistics]," November 21, 2020, https://review42.com/how-many-emails-are-sent-per-day.
11. Richard A. Friedman, "Antidepressants' Black-Box Warning—10 Years Later," *New England Journal of Medicine*, October 30, 2014, https://www.nejm.org/doi/full/10.1056/nejmp1408480#.
12. Mark Jewell, "New 401(k) Fee Disclosures Are Coming; 4 Key Items to Look for in Documents," *Des Moines Register* July 8, 2012, 1D.
13. Mike Madden, "What Email Subject Line Length Works Best?" Marketo Blog, February 2018, https://blog.marketo.com/2018/02/email-subject-line-length-works-best.html.

Chapter Outline

DrAfter123/Getty Images

The Cost of an Ineffective Apology

How a company responds to negative events can greatly affect its viability as a business.

On April 9, 2017, a United Airlines customer, Dr. David Dao, was forcibly removed from an airplane when he refused to disembark to make room for commuting crew members. During his forceful removal, Dr. Dao suffered a concussion, a broken nose, and lost teeth. United CEO Oscar Munoz issued an insipid apology that Derek Thompson of *The Atlantic* called "the least human sounding statement in crisis-PR history." In his apology, Munoz referred to the violence inflicted on Dr. Dao as an effort to "re-accommodate" a customer. Then, in an email to his employees, Munoz defended United's actions and characterized Dao as "disruptive and belligerent." Munoz's remarks unleashed a firestorm of pushback on social media, including the uploading of videos from other passengers that quickly discredited Munoz's perspective. In the wake of the scandal and Munoz's ineffective apology, the value of the company's stock dropped by $1.4 billion.

After a settlement was reached between Dr. Dao and United, Dao's lawyers praised Munoz for eventually taking full responsibility for the incident "without attempting to blame others." United also amended its policies and procedures, including promises that boarded passengers will not be required to give up their seats and increasing compensation up to $10,000 for customers who voluntarily surrender a seat.

The United Airlines incident illustrates not only the importance of establishing clear policies and procedures for

Nieuwland Photography/Shutterstock

handling negative situations, but also the importance of communicating negative messages effectively to the public. Companies need to be swift when issuing apologies while exercising care to express empathy and avoid blaming victims. Ineffective apologies are costly and diminish a company's goodwill.

In a negative message, the basic information we have to convey is negative; we expect the audience to be disappointed or angry. Some jobs entail conveying more negative messages than others. Customer service representatives, employee relations personnel, and insurance agents all have to say no on a regular basis.

Negative communications such as refusals, rejections, recalls, and apologies are hard to compose. Yet they are so important. Good ones restore corporate reputations as well as customer and employee goodwill. Bad ones can lead to lawsuits. Corporate officers can be promoted or fired on the basis of a negative communication.

Mishandled negative communication can be expensive in terms of both money and reputation. Toyota suffered extensive bad press when it dithered over its response to acceleration problems in its cars; British Petroleum experienced bad publicity when it initially downplayed its oil-well catastrophe in the Gulf of Mexico. Businesses don't have to be large to worry about negative messages; local businesses routinely lose customers when they mishandle complaints.

One Silicon Valley company calculated the costs of negative communications from a salesperson known for poor interpersonal and email skills. The costs included managerial time, human resources time, anger-management training and counseling, among others, and came to $160,000 for just one year.[1] Withholding negative news can be equally expensive. Johnson & Johnson failed to notify the public about problems with its hip implant and was ordered to pay more than $1 billion in damages.[2]

Sources: Lucinda Shen, "United Airlines Stock Drops $1.4 Billion after Passenger-Removal Controversy," *Fortune*, April 11, 2017, http://fortune.com/2017/04/11/united-airlines-stock-drop; Derek Thompson, "The Deeper Scandal of That Brutal United Video," *The Atlantic*, April 10, 2017, https://www.theatlantic.com/business/archive/2017/04/united-video-scandal-law/522552; and Jackie Wattles, "United Airlines Reaches Settlement with Passenger Who Was Dragged Off Plane," *CNN*, April 27, 2017, http://money.cnn.com/2017/04/27/news/companies/united-airlines-dao-settlement/index.html.

Learning Objectives

After studying this chapter, you should be able to

LO 10-1 Explain the different purposes of negative messages.

LO 10-2 Describe the different ways to organize negative messages.

LO 10-3 Construct the different parts of negative messages.

LO 10-4 Improve the tone of negative messages.

LO 10-5 Produce different kinds of negative messages.

LO 10-6 Analyze when and how to apologize.

Purposes of Negative Messages

LO 10-1

Negative messages include rejections and refusals, announcements of policy changes that do not benefit the audience, requests the audience will see as insulting or intrusive, negative performance reviews, disciplinary notices, and product recalls or notices of defects.

A negative message always has several purposes:

Primary purposes

- To give the audience the bad news.
- To have the audience understand and accept the message.
- To maintain as much goodwill as possible.

Secondary purposes

- To maintain, as much as possible, a good image of the communicator and the communicator's organization.
- To reduce or eliminate future communication on the same subject so the message doesn't create more work for the sender.

In many negative situations, the communicator and audience will continue to deal with each other. Even when further interaction is unlikely (e.g., when a company rejects a job applicant or refuses to renew a customer's insurance), the firm wants anything the audience may say about the company to be positive or neutral rather than negative.

Some messages that at first appear to be negative can be structured to create a positive feeling. A decision that may be negative in the short term may be shown to be a positive one in the long term, or the communication of a problem can be directly connected to an effective solution.

Even when it is not possible to make the audience happy with the news that you must convey, you still will want the audience members to feel that

- They have been taken seriously.
- The decision is fair and reasonable.
- If they were in your shoes, they would make the same decision.

Organizing Negative Messages

LO 10-2

The best way to organize a negative message depends on your audience and on the severity of the negative information. This chapter presents several possible patterns and connects them with their most likely contexts.

WARNING: The patterns should never be used blindly. You always must consider whether the rhetorical situation—the audience, purpose, and context—would be better served with a different organization.

Giving Bad News to Clients and Customers

When you must give bad news to clients and customers, you need to be clear, but you also need to maintain goodwill. People are increasingly skeptical and have a hard time trusting organizations. One study found that in order to accept a message as true, more than 70% of people need exposure to it more than three times.[3] Compromises or alternatives can help you achieve clarity and goodwill. See the first column in Figure 10.1 for a way to organize these messages.

Figure 10.2 illustrates another basic pattern for negative messages. This letter omits the reason for the policy change, probably because the change benefits the company, not the customer. Putting the bad news first (though pairing it immediately with an alternative) makes it more likely that the recipient will read the letter. If this letter seemed to be just a routine renewal, or if it opened with the good news that the premium was lower, few recipients would read the letter carefully and many would not read it at all. Then, if they had accidents and found that their coverage was reduced, they'd blame the company for not communicating clearly. Emphasizing the negative here is both good ethics and good business.

Giving Bad News to Superiors

Your superior expects you to solve minor problems by yourself. But sometimes, solving a problem requires more authority or resources than you have. When you give bad news to a superior, also recommend a way to deal with the problem. Turn the negative message into a persuasive one. See the middle column in Figure 10.1.

When you are the superior, be sure that you do not block the transmittal of negative news to you (see Figure 10.3). Don't penalize employees who report negative situations (i.e., whistle-blowers). One study found that 19% of corporate fraud was uncovered by employees.[4]

Figure 10.1	How to Organize Negative Messages

Negative messages to clients and customers	**Negative messages to superiors**	**Negative messages to peers and subordinates**
1. **When you have a reason that the audience will understand and accept, give the reason before the refusal.** A good reason prepares the audience to expect the refusal.	1. **Describe the problem.** Tell what's wrong, clearly and unemotionally.	1. **Describe the problem.** Tell what's wrong, clearly and unemotionally.
2. **Give the negative information or refusal just once, clearly.** Inconspicuous refusals can be missed, making it necessary to say *no* a second time.	2. **Tell how it happened.** Provide the background. What underlying factors led to this specific problem?	2. **Present an alternative or compromise, if one is available.** An alternative not only gives the audience another way to get what they want but also suggests that you care about them and are helping them meet their needs.
3. **Present an alternative or compromise, if one is available.** An alternative not only gives the audience another way to get what they want but also suggests that you care about them and are helping them meet their needs.	3. **Describe the options for fixing it.** If one option is clearly best, you may need to discuss only one. But if your superiors will think of other options, or if different people will judge the options differently, describe all the options, giving their advantages and disadvantages.	3. **If possible, ask for input or action.** People in the audience may be able to suggest solutions. And workers who help make a decision are far more likely to accept the consequences.
4. **End with a positive, forward-looking statement.**	4. **Recommend a solution and ask for action.** Ask for approval so that you can make the necessary changes to fix the problem.	

Figure 10.2   A Negative Letter

Insurance Company

3373 Forbes Avenue
Rosemont, PA 19010
(215) 572-0100

*Negative information
highlighted so reader won't
ignore message.*

**Liability Coverage
Is Being Discontinued—
Here's How to Replace It!**

Negative

Alternative

Dear Policyholder:

Negative

When your auto insurance is renewed, it will no longer include liability coverage
unless you select the new Assurance Plan. Here's why.

*Positive
information
underlined
for emphasis.*

Liability coverage is being discontinued. It, **and the part of the premium which paid for it, will
be dropped** from all policies when they are renewed.

This change could leave a gap in your protection. But you can replace the old Liability Coverage
with Vickers' new Assurance Plan.

*No reason is given. The change
probably
benefits
the
company
rather
than the
reader,
so it is
omitted.*

Alternative

With the new Assurance Plan, you receive benefits for litigation or awards arising from an
accident—regardless of who's at fault. The cost for the Assurance Plan at any level is based on the
ages of drivers, where you live, your driving record, and other factors. If these change before your
policy is renewed, the cost of your Assurance Plan may also change. The actual cost will be listed in
your renewal statement.

To sign up for the Assurance Plan, just check the level of coverage you want on the enclosed form
and return it in the postage-paid envelope within 14 days. You'll be assured of the coverage you
select.

*Forward-looking
ending emphasizes
reader's choice.*

Sincerely,

C. J. Morgan

C. J. Morgan
President

Alternative

P.S. The Assurance Plan protects you against possible legal costs arising from an accident. Sign up
for the plan today and receive full coverage from Vickers.

If employees believe that relaying bad news to you will gain them group support for
solving their problems, you are far more likely to hear of problems at an early stage,
when they are easier to solve. Alan Mulally, president and CEO of Ford from 2006 to
2014, related that when he joined Ford, the first economic forecast was for a $17 billion
loss, yet at his first staff meeting, all the charts were green, indicating financial health.
At the second meeting, one brave executive dared to present a chart with red and everyone present looked to Mulally to see his reaction. His response was to ask everyone
present what they could do to help get that particular vehicle launch back on track. In
the following weeks, charts were all different colors because his staff knew it was safe to
be honest. He and his staff were then able to concentrate on creating ways to turn reds
into greens and move the company forward to financial health.[5]

Figure 10.3	How to Deal with Criticism

1. **Listen carefully,** even if you don't value the person. Focus on the criticism, not your response.
2. **Ask questions.** They will help clarify the criticism, show that you are listening carefully, and probably help you judge the quality of the criticism.
3. **Determine accuracy.** Even a criticism that seems off base may have some elements of truth.
4. **Stay calm and objective.** Save anger and defensiveness for private moments.
5. **Fix the problem.** Sometimes clarifying a misunderstanding is sufficient. Other times you will need to make a change.

Giving Bad News to Peers and Subordinates

When passing along serious bad news to peers and subordinates, many people use the organization suggested in the right-most column in Figure 10.1.

No serious negative (such as being downsized or laid off) should come as a complete surprise, nor should it be delivered by email. Managers may be inclined to use electronic forms of communication to deliver bad news, but they should resist the temptation in most situations. Six factors should be considered when choosing a channel for delivering bad news:

- The severity of the message.

- The degree of surprise involved.

- The context of the problem.

- The type and complexity of the explanation.

- The corporate culture.

- The relationship between the superior and subordinates.

When Chrysler cut 25% of its dealers, it sent the bad news the same day it went public with the list of cut dealerships. Thus, many dealers first heard about their cuts on the news, not from Chrysler's letter, creating even more bad press for the automaker.

People sending bad news must always juggle the efficiency of delivering the message with its impact on receivers. Research shows that managers who deliver bad news in face-to-face settings are more appreciated by employees.[6]

Managers can prepare for possible negatives by giving full information as it becomes available. It is also possible to let the people who will be affected by a decision participate in setting the criteria. Someone who has bought into the criteria for retaining workers is more likely to accept decisions using such criteria. And in some cases, employees may generate ideas that management didn't think of or rejected as "unacceptable."

When the bad news is less serious (see Figure 10.4), try using the pattern in the left-most column of Figure 10.1 unless your knowledge of the audience suggests that another pattern will be more effective.

Figure 10.4	A Negative Email to Subordinates

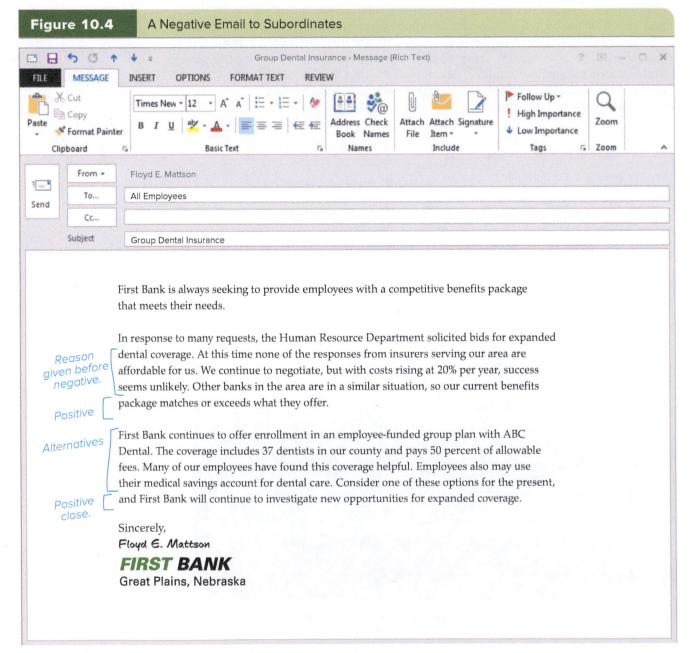

Subject: Group Dental Insurance

First Bank is always seeking to provide employees with a competitive benefits package that meets their needs.

Reason given before negative.
Positive

In response to many requests, the Human Resource Department solicited bids for expanded dental coverage. At this time none of the responses from insurers serving our area are affordable for us. We continue to negotiate, but with costs rising at 20% per year, success seems unlikely. Other banks in the area are in a similar situation, so our current benefits package matches or exceeds what they offer.

Alternatives

First Bank continues to offer enrollment in an employee-funded group plan with ABC Dental. The coverage includes 37 dentists in our county and pays 50 percent of allowable fees. Many of our employees have found this coverage helpful. Employees also may use their medical savings account for dental care. Consider one of these options for the present,

Positive close.

and First Bank will continue to investigate new opportunities for expanded coverage.

Sincerely,

Floyd E. Mattson

FIRST BANK
Great Plains, Nebraska

Source: Microsoft Inc

The Parts of a Negative Message

This section provides more information about wording each part of a negative message.

Subject Lines

Many negative messages put the topic, but not the specific negative, in the subject line.

> Subject: Status of Conversion Table Program

Other negative message subject lines focus on solving the problem.

> Subject: Improving Our Subscription Letter

Use a negative subject line in messages when you think readers may ignore what they believe is a routine message. Also use a negative subject line when the reader needs the information to make a decision or to act.

> Subject: Elevator to Be Out Friday, June 17

Many people do not read all their messages, and a neutral subject line may lead them to ignore the message.

Buffers

Traditionally, textbooks recommended that negative messages open with buffers. A buffer is a neutral or positive statement that allows you to delay the negative. Some research suggests that buffers do not make readers respond more positively,[7] and good buffers are hard to write. However, in special situations, you may want to use a buffer. The first sentence in the First Bank email (Figure 10.4) is a buffer.

To be effective, a buffer must put the reader in a good frame of mind—not give the bad news but not imply a positive answer either—and provide a natural transition to the body of the letter. The kinds of statements most often used as buffers are good news, facts and chronologies of events, references to enclosures, thanks, and statements of principle.

1. Start with any good news or positive elements the letter contains. Here's an example from a letter announcing that the drive-up windows will be closed for two days while new automatic teller machines are installed:

   > Starting Thursday, June 26, you'll have easier access to your money 24 hours a day at First National Bank.

2. State a fact or provide a chronology of events. Here's an example from an announcement of a new dues structure that will raise most members' dues:

   > In December, the Delegate Assembly voted in a new graduated dues schedule.

3. Refer to enclosures in the letter. Here's an example from a letter announcing increase in parking rental rates:

   > A new sticker for your car is enclosed. You may pick up additional ones in the office if needed.

4. Thank the reader for something they have done. Here's an example from a letter refusing a job offer:

   > Thank you for scheduling appointments for me with so many senior people at First National Bank. My visit there March 14 was very informative.

5. State a general principle. Here's an example from a letter announcing that the company will now count traffic tickets, not just accidents, in calculating insurance rates—a change that will raise many people's premiums:

> Good drivers should pay substantially less for their auto insurance. The Good Driver Plan was created to reward good drivers (those with five-year accident-free records) with our lowest available rates. A change in the plan, effective January 1, will help keep those rates low.

Some audiences will feel betrayed by messages whose positive openers delay the central negative point. Therefore, use a buffer only when the audience (individually or culturally) values harmony or when the buffer serves another purpose. For example, when you must thank the reader somewhere in the letter, putting the "thank you" in the first paragraph allows you to start on a positive note.

Buffers are hard to write. Even if you think the reader would prefer to be let down easily, use a buffer only when you can write a good one.

Reasons

Research shows that audiences who described themselves as "totally surprised" by negative news had many more negative feelings and described their feelings as being stronger than did those who expected the negative.[8] A clear and convincing reason prepares the audience for the negative, resulting in people who more easily accept it.

The following reason is inadequate.

Weak reason: The goal of the Knoxville CHARGE-ALL Center is to provide our customers faster, more personalized service. Since you now live outside the Knoxville CHARGE-ALL service area, we can no longer offer you the advantages of a local CHARGE-ALL Center.

If the reader says, "I don't care if my bills are slow and impersonal," will the company let the reader keep the card? No. The real reason for the negative is that the bank's franchise allows it to have cardholders only in a given geographic region.

Real reason: Each local CHARGE-ALL center is permitted to offer accounts to customers in a several-state area. The Knoxville CHARGE-ALL center serves customers east of the Mississippi. You can continue to use your current card until it expires. When that happens, you'll need to open an account with a CHARGE-ALL center that serves Texas.

Don't hide behind "company policy": your audience will assume the policy is designed to benefit you at their expense. If possible, show how your audience benefits from the policy. If they do not benefit, don't mention policy.

Weak reason: I cannot write an insurance policy for you because company policy does not allow me to do so.

Better reason: Gorham insures cars only when they are normally garaged at night. Standard insurance policies cover a wider variety of risks and charge higher fees. Limiting the policies we write gives Gorham customers the lowest possible rates for auto insurance.

Avoid saying that you *cannot* do something. Most negative messages exist because the communicator or company has chosen certain policies or cutoff points. In the preceding example, the company could choose to insure a wider variety of customers if it wanted to do so.

As a middle manager, you will often enforce policies that you did not design and announce decisions that you did not make. Don't pass the buck by saying, "This was a terrible decision." Carelessly criticizing your superiors is never a good idea.

If you have several reasons for saying *no*, use only those that are strong and watertight. If you give five reasons and the audience dismisses two of them, the audience may feel that they've won and should get the request.

Weak reason: You cannot store large bulky items in the dormitory over the summer because moving them into and out of storage would tie up the stairs and the elevators just at the busiest times when people are moving in and out.

If students say they will move large items before or after the two days when most people are moving in or out, you are still not going to grant the request because you do not have the storage room. If you do not have a good reason, omit the reason rather than use a weak one.

Even if you have a strong reason, omit it if it makes the company look bad.

Reason that hurts company: Our company is not hiring at the present time because profits are down. In fact, the downturn has prompted top management to reduce the salaried staff by 5% just this month, with perhaps more reductions to come.

Better: Our company does not have any openings now.

Refusals

Deemphasize the refusal by putting it in the same paragraph as the reason, rather than in a paragraph by itself.

Sometimes you may be able to imply the refusal rather than stating it directly.

Direct refusal: You cannot get insurance for just one month.

Implied refusal: The shortest term for an insurance policy is six months.

Be sure the implication is crystal clear. Any message can be misunderstood, but an optimistic or desperate audience is particularly unlikely to understand a negative message. One of your purposes in a negative message is to close the door on the subject. You do not want to have to send a second message saying that the real answer is *no*.

Alternatives

Giving your audience an alternative or a compromise, if one is available, is a good idea for several reasons:

- It offers the audience another way to get what they want.

- It suggests that you really care about your audience and about helping to meet their needs.

- It enables your audience to reestablish the psychological freedom you limited when you said *no*.

- It allows you to end on a positive note and to present yourself and your organization as positive, friendly, and helpful.

When you give an alternative, give your audience all the information they need to act on it, but don't take the necessary steps. Let your audience decide whether to try the alternative.

Negative messages limit your audience's freedom. People may respond to a limitation of freedom by asserting their freedom in some other arena. This phenomenon, called **psychological reactance**,[9] is at work when a customer who has been denied credit no longer buys even on a cash basis, a subordinate who has been passed over for a promotion gets back at the company by deliberately doing a poor job, or someone who has been laid off sabotages the company's computers.

An alternative allows your audience to react in a way that doesn't hurt you. By letting your audience decide for themselves whether they want the alternative, you allow them to reestablish their sense of psychological freedom. The specific alternative will vary depending on the circumstances. Some stores create goodwill by directing customers to other businesses for out-of-stock items. In Figure 10.2, the company offers the new Assurance Plan.

Endings

If you have a good alternative, refer to it in your ending. In Figure 10.2, the writer explains how to sign up for the Assurance Plan.

The best endings look positively to the future as in this letter refusing to continue a charge account for a customer who has moved:

> Wherever you have your account, you'll continue to get all the service you've learned to expect from CHARGE-ALL, and the convenience of charging items at over a million stores, restaurants, and hotels in the United States and abroad—and in Knoxville, too, whenever you come back to visit!

Avoid endings that seem insincere:

> We are happy to have been of service, and should we be able to assist you in the future, please contact us.

This ending lacks *you*-attitude and would not be good even in a positive message. In a situation where the company has just refused to help, it's likely to sound sarcastic.

Tone in Negative Messages

LO 10-4

Tone—the implied attitude of the author toward the reader and the subject—is particularly important when you want readers to feel that you have taken their requests seriously. Check your draft carefully for positive emphasis and *you*-attitude (see Chapter 2), both at the level of individual words and at the level of ideas. In many situations, empathizing with your audience will help you create a more humane message.

Figure 10.5 lists some words and phrases to avoid in negative messages. Figure 2.5 in Chapter 2 suggests more negative words to avoid.

Even the physical appearance and timing of a message can convey tone. An obvious form rejection letter suggests that the writer has not given much consideration to the reader's application. An immediate negative suggests that the rejection didn't need any thought. A negative delivered just before a major holiday seems especially unfeeling.

Tone is equally important in everyday oral communication of negatives (see Figure 10.6). In these situations, harsh negative tone is frequently labeled incivility or

Figure 10.5	Avoid These Phrases in Negative Messages
Phrase	**Reason**
I am afraid that we cannot	You aren't fearful. Don't hide behind empty phrases.
I am sorry that we are unable	You probably are able to grant the request; you simply choose not to. If you are so sorry about saying no, why don't you change your policy and say *yes*?
I am sure you will agree that	It conveys the assumption that you can read someone's mind.
Unfortunately	*Unfortunately* is negative in itself. It also signals that a refusal is coming.

Figure 10.6	Possible Responses for Some Common Negative Situations
Situation	**Possible response**
Your boss or client asks you to agree on a controversial topic.	I just don't like to get into this topic in the office.
Your coworker is ranting about a controversial topic.	Yes, that is an important topic. (Then leave quickly.)
As a member of a minority group, you are asked how people in your group would respond: As an older worker, how do you think older workers feel about mandatory weight and blood pressure checks?	Turn the question: As a middle-aged worker, how do *you* think middle-aged people will respond? Sometimes careful humor will work: Yes, we older workers do think that. Also, we all got together across the nation and decided that smoothies should be eliminated.
You are using *should have* statements: You should have been checking with clients weekly.	Use *I want* statements and look to future improvement: In the future, I want you to check with your clients weekly.
You are angry about a problem.	Point out how the problem impacts other people or the company (not just yourself). Work together to find ways to prevent the problem from happening in the future.

rudeness. A study of 14,000 people in 17 industries found that 98% of them said they had been treated rudely at work, and half said that rudeness occurred at least once a week. That rudeness was expensive. Among workers receiving it,

48% deliberately decreased work effort.

38% deliberately decreased work quality.

78% reported a loss of commitment to the organization.

25% took out frustration on customers.

12% left their job because of it.[10]

Rudeness to customers is, of course, equally damaging. And the rudeness does not have to be directed at them. Customers witnessing even a single rudeness directed at another employee are unlikely to deal with the company again.[11]

Alternative Strategies for Negative Situations

Whenever you face a negative situation, consider recasting it as a positive or persuasive message. Southwest Airlines, a low-cost airline, is famous for saying no to its customers. It says no to such common perks as reserved seats and meals. But it recasts all those negatives into its two biggest positives, low-cost fares and conveniently scheduled, frequent flights.[12]

Recasting the Situation as a Positive Message

If the negative information will directly lead to a benefit that you know readers want, use the pattern of organization for informative and positive messages:

Situation: Your airline has been mailing out quarterly statements of frequent-flyer miles earned. To save money, you are going to stop mailing statements and ask customers to look up that information at your website.

Negative: Important Notice: This is your last Preferred Passenger paper statement.

Positive emphasis: New, convenient online statements will replace this quarterly mailing. Now you can get up-to-the-minute statements of your miles earned. Choose email updates or round-the-clock access to your statement at our website, www.aaaair.com. It's faster, easier, and more convenient.

In 2015, Chipotle Mexican Grill struggled to overcome negative press surrounding repeated outbreaks of *E. coli*, salmonella, and norovirus that led to the temporary closings of more than 2,000 stores so that the company could conduct food safety training. Chipotle executives worked hard in subsequent years to reestablish the company's image as a fresh and healthy alternative to other fast-food chains. CEO and founder Steve Ells outlined a 2017 advertising campaign intended to restore the company's goodwill by showcasing Chipotle's "taste and great ingredients." Throughout the crisis, executives at Chipotle were quick to identify problems, to accept ownership, and to take steps toward remedying the issue in order to transform a negative situation into a positive one.[13]

Recasting the Situation as a Persuasive Message

Sometimes a negative situation can be recast as a persuasive message. Often, magazines that are raising their rates send a persuasive letter to subscribers urging them to send in renewals early so they can beat the increases.

If your organization has a problem, ask the audience to help solve it. A solution that workers have created will be much easier to implement. If you are criticizing someone, your real purpose may be to persuade the person to act differently. Chapter 11 offers patterns for such problem-solving persuasive messages.

Varieties of Negative Messages

LO 10-5

Some of the most common negative messages are claims and complaints. Three of the most difficult kinds of negative messages to write are rejections and refusals, disciplinary notices and negative performance reviews, and layoffs and firings.

Claims and Complaints

Claims and complaint messages are needed when something has gone wrong: you didn't get the files you needed in time for the report; the supplier didn't send enough parts; the copy machine breaks down daily. Many claims and complaints are handled well with a quick phone call or office visit, but sometimes you will need a paper trail.

When writing a claim or complaint, you generally will use a direct organization. An indirect approach, such as starting with a buffer, may be interpreted as a weak claim.

Follow these guidelines for articulating a complaint:

- Put a clear statement of the problem in the first sentence.

- Give supporting facts—what went wrong, the extent of the damage.

- Give identifiers such as invoice numbers, warranty codes, and order dates.

- If this is a claim, specify what is necessary to set things right, but be realistic.

- Avoid anger and sarcasm; they will only lessen your chances of a favorable settlement. Avoid saying you will never use the company, service, machine again. Such a statement may eliminate your audience's will to rectify the problem.

You may also be in a position to respond to customer complaints. After all, the speed with which complaints travel from one customer to another is increasing; websites such as Amazon, Angie's List, Quora, Wirecutter, and Yelp offer forums for disgruntled customers. To stay on top of the reviews, new electronic tools are emerging that help organizations scan for keywords and monitor reviews related to their brand.

Technology has certainly influenced the way complaints are processed. Delta Air Lines has a team of customer service agents who monitor social media applications such as Twitter for real-time complaints. When travelers complain about the company, the agents try to solve problems before they go viral by offering updated gate information or rebooking details.[14]

However, many reputation-management consultants note that social media are not effective channels to solve customer complaints. It is far better to work out a customer problem on the phone or via chat, as many solutions require personal information, such as the customer's credit card number. After a problem is fixed, companies can respond to further references with a brief, nondefensive statement that they handled the situation (or, even better, fixed the problem) and regret the mistake. In addition, companies also should work on maintaining goodwill before problems arise by posting positive information on their websites and Facebook pages and by answering user questions on the corporate sites.

Rejections and Refusals

When you refuse requests from people outside your organization, try to give an alternative if one is available. For example, you may not be able to replace for free an automotive water pump that no longer is on warranty. But you may be able to offer your customer a rebuilt one that is much less expensive than a new pump.

Politeness and length help. In two studies, job applicants preferred rejection letters that said something specific about their good qualities, that phrased the refusal indirectly, that offered a clear explanation of the procedures for making a hiring decision, that offered an alternative (such as another position the applicant might be qualified for), and that were longer.[15] Furthermore, businesses that follow this pattern of organization for rejection letters will retain applicants who still view the organization favorably, who may recommend the organization to others interested in applying there, and who likely will not file lawsuits.[16]

Double-check the words in a refusal to be sure the reason can't backfire if it is applied to other contexts. The statement that a factory is too dangerous for a group tour could be used as evidence against the company in a worker's compensation claim.

Similarly, writing resignation letters for a variety of reasons—leaving a job, opting out of a fellowship—can be a delicate practice and can have serious future implications. Many audiences will see the letter as a statement that the organization is not good enough. The best letters try to neutralize these feelings. A negative and poorly worded resignation letter can affect your chances for receiving a positive recommendation or reference in the future.

When you refuse requests within your organization, use your knowledge of the organization's culture and of the specific individual to craft your message. Some organizations share more negative information than others. Some individuals prefer a direct no; others may find a direct negative insulting. The sample problem at the end of this chapter is a refusal to someone within the company.

Disciplinary Notices and Negative Performance Reviews

Performance reviews are positive when they are designed to help a basically good employee improve. But when an employee violates company policy or fails to improve after repeated negative reviews, the company may discipline the employee or build a dossier to support firing them.

Present disciplinary notices and negative performance reviews directly, with no buffer. A buffer might encourage the recipient to minimize the message's importance—and might even become evidence in a court case that the employee had not been told to shape up "or else." Cite quantifiable observations of the employee's behavior rather than generalizations or inferences based on it.

Weak: Lee is apathetic about work.

Better: Lee was absent 15 days and late by one hour 6 days in the quarter beginning January 1.

Weak: Vasu is careless with her written documents.

Better: Vasu had multiple spelling errors in her last three client letters; a fourth letter omitted the date of the mandatory federal training seminar.

Not all disciplinary notices are as formal as performance reviews. Blanchard and Johnson, of *One Minute Manager* fame, present what they call the One Minute Reprimand. Much of the effectiveness of these reprimands comes from the fact that supervisors tell their employees from the beginning, before any reprimands are needed, that there will be explicit communication about both positive and negative performances. The reprimand itself is to come immediately after negative behavior and specify exactly what is wrong. It distinguishes between positive feelings for the employee and negative feelings for their performance in the specific situation.[17]

Layoffs and Firings

If a company is in financial trouble, management needs to communicate the problem clearly. Sharing information and enlisting everyone's help in finding solutions may make it possible to save jobs. Sharing information also means that layoff notices, if they become necessary, will be a formality; they should not be new information to employees.

Give the employee an honest reason for the layoff or firing. Based on guidance from your organization's human resource experts, state the reasons in a way that is clear but does not expose the organization to legal liabilities. Research shows that workers given no explanation for being fired are 10 times more likely to sue than workers who receive a complete explanation.[18]

Show empathy for affected employees; think about how you would feel if you were losing your job. Show how the company will help them with severance pay and other aid, such as job search advice. Remember that many studies show that layoffs may temporarily help the bottom line, but they rarely provide long-term savings. They also hurt the productivity of remaining employees.[19]

Firings for unsatisfactory performance always have been a part of business. Now, however, as technology blurs the line between work and home, firings also are happening for personal reasons, even if the behavior is not tied to work and occurs off site. The CEO of HBO was asked to resign after he was accused of assaulting his girlfriend in a parking lot. Kaiser Aluminum's CFO had to resign because of a personal relationship with another employee, as did Boeing's former president and CEO Harry Stonecipher.[20]

Information about layoffs and firings is normally delivered orally but accompanied by a written statement explaining severance pay or unemployment benefits that may be available.

Apologies

LO 10-6

Organizations have to routinely offer apologies, too. The news frequently has stories of corporations providing apologies. United Airlines, for example, apologized for increases in delayed and canceled flights and again for assaulting a customer, as described at the start of this chapter.[21]

Verizon issued an apology in July 2017 after 6 million customer accounts were compromised in a data breach. A third-party vendor's error caused the breach; an employee inadvertently misconfigured an internet-connected database housing user names, addresses, phone numbers, and unique PINs.[22] The data-breach apology letter is quickly becoming a routine negative message that requires careful crafting to assuage customers' fears and reinforce company goodwill.

When and How to Apologize

In business documents, apologize only when you are at fault. If you need to apologize, do it early, briefly, and sincerely. Do so only once, early in the message. Do not dwell on the bad things that have happened. The reader already knows this negative information. Instead, focus on what you have done to correct the situation.

If the news is bad, put the explanation first. If you have good news for the reader, put it before your explanation.

Negative:	I'm sorry that I could not answer your question sooner. I had to wait until the sales figures for the second quarter were in.
Better (neutral or bad news):	We needed the sales figures for the second quarter to answer your question. Now that they're in, I can tell you that . . . .
Better (good news):	The new advertising campaign is a success. The sales figures for the second quarter are finally in, and they show that . . . .

If the error or problem is significant, offer a solution. Even if the customer has some responsibility, offer to fix the problem. The cost of doing so is almost always less than repairing a reputation smeared on social media.

Negative:	I'm sorry that the chairs will not be ready by August 25 as promised.
Better:	Because of a strike against the manufacturer, the desk chairs you ordered will not be ready until November. Do you want to keep that order, or would you like to look at the models available from other suppliers?

Sometimes you will be in a fortunate position where you can pair your apology with an appropriate benefit.

- When Apple sharply cut the price on the iPhone a few months after it came on the market, Steve Jobs offered an apology to earlier buyers and provided them with a $100 Apple store credit.

- Many airlines now have computer programs that generate apology letters for customers on flights with lengthy delays or other major problems; the letters frequently offer additional frequent-flyer miles or discount vouchers for future trips.[23]

Sincere apologies go hand in hand with efforts to rectify the problem. When Toyota apologized to customers for its sticking accelerator problem, the company trained dealers to make the repair and also stopped production of the involved models to concentrate on the repairs.

Some hospitals have found that disclosing medical errors, apologizing, and quickly offering a financial settlement to the victims actually reduces litigation. After a policy of full disclosure and apology was established at the University of Michigan Medical Center to help communicate with wronged patients, the number of lawsuits declined 65%.[24]

When Not to Apologize

Do not apologize when you are not at fault. The phrase "I'm sorry" is generally interpreted in the U.S. to mean the sorry person is accepting blame or responsibility. When you have done everything you can and when a delay or problem is due to circumstances beyond your control, you aren't at fault and don't need to apologize. It may be appropriate, however, to include an explanation so the reader knows you weren't negligent.

No explicit apology is necessary if the error is small and if you are correcting the mistake.

Negative	We're sorry we got the nutrition facts wrong in the recipe.
Better:	You're right. We're glad you made us aware of this. The correct amounts are 2 grams of fat and 4 grams of protein.

Solving a Sample Problem

Solving negative problems requires careful analysis. The checklist in Figure 10.7 at the end of the chapter can help you evaluate your draft.

Problem

You are director of employee benefits for a *Fortune* 500 company. Today, you received the following email:

From: Michelle Jagtiani

Subject: Getting My Retirement Benefits

Date: April 23, 2021

Next Friday will be my last day here. I am leaving to take a position at another firm.

Please process a check for my retirement benefits, including both the deductions from my salary and the company's contributions for the last six and a half years. I would like to receive the check by next Friday if possible.

You have bad news for Michelle. Although the company does contribute an amount to the retirement fund equal to the amount deducted for retirement from the employee's paycheck, employees who leave with fewer than seven years of employment get only their own contributions. Michelle will get back only the money that has been deducted from her own pay, plus 3.5% interest compounded quarterly. Her payments and interest come to just over $17,200; the amount could be higher depending on the amount of her last paycheck, which will include compensation for any unused vacation days and sick leave. Furthermore, because the amounts deducted were not considered taxable income, she will have to pay income tax on the money she will receive.

Figure 10.7	Checklist for Negative Messages

☐ Is the subject line appropriate, for example, focusing on the solving the problem?

☐ Are the organization and content appropriate for the audience?

☐ If a buffer is used, does it avoid suggesting either a positive or a negative response?

☐ Is the reason, if it is given, presented before the refusal? Is the reason watertight, with no loopholes?

☐ Is the negative information clear and complete?

☐ Does the message include details that show it's intended for a specific organization and the specific people in that organization?

☐ Is an alternative given if a good one is available? Does the message provide all the information needed to act on the alternative but leave the choice up to the audience?

☐ Does the last paragraph avoid repeating the negative information?

☐ Is tone acceptable—not defensive, but not cold, preachy, or arrogant either?

You cannot process the check until after her resignation is effective, so you will mail it to her. You have her home address on file; if she's moving, she needs to let you know where to send the check. Processing the check may take two to three weeks.

Write an email to Michelle.

Analysis of the Problem

Use the analysis questions in the first chapter to help you solve the problem.

1. Who is(are) your audience(s)?
   Michelle Jagtiani. Unless she's a personal friend, we probably wouldn't know why she's leaving and where she's going.

   There's a lot we don't know. She may or may not know much about taxes; she may or may not be able to take advantage of tax-reduction strategies. We can't assume the answers because we wouldn't have them in real life.

2. What are your purposes in communicating?
   You have at least three purposes:

   - To tell her that she will get only her own contributions, plus 3.5% interest compounded quarterly; that the check will be mailed to her home address two to three weeks after her last day on the job; and that the money will be taxable as income.

   - To build goodwill so that she feels that she has been treated fairly and consistently. To minimize negative feelings she may have.

   - To close the door on this subject.

3. What information must your message include?
   When the check will come. The facts that her check will be based on her contributions, not the employer's, and that the money will be taxable income. How lump-sum retirement benefits are calculated. The fact that we have her current address on file but need a new address if she's moving.

4. How can you build support for your position? What reasons or benefits will your audience find convincing?
   Giving the amount currently in her account may make her feel that she is getting a significant sum of money. Suggesting someone who can give free tax advice (if the company offers this as a fringe benefit) reminds her of the benefits of working with the company. Wishing her luck with her new job is a nice touch.

5. What aspects of the total situation may be relevant?
   Since this is right after taxes are due, she may be particularly interested in the tax advice. She may have been counting on extra money from a return. On the other hand, most people take another job to get more money, so maybe she is too. We don't know for sure. We don't know about any special circumstances leading to her decision to leave the company.

Discussion of the Sample Solutions

The solution in Figure 10.8 is not acceptable. The subject line gives a bald negative with no reason or alternative. The first sentence has a condescending tone that is particularly offensive in negative messages; it also focuses on what is being taken away rather than what remains. The second paragraph lacks *you*-attitude and is vague. The email ends with a negative. There is nothing anywhere in the email to build goodwill.

The solution in Figure 10.9, in contrast, is effective. The policy serves as a buffer and explanation. The negative is stated clearly but is buried in the paragraph to avoid

Figure 10.8   An Unacceptable Solution to the Sample Problem

Denial of Matching Funds - Message (Rich Text)

FILE   MESSAGE   INSERT   OPTIONS   FORMAT TEXT   REVIEW

Times New ▾ 12 ▾ A˄ A˅ | ☰ ▾ ☰ ▾ | A✎
B I U | ab ▾ A ▾ | ☰ ☰ ☰ | ☰ ☰

Paste — Cut, Copy, Format Painter
Clipboard   Basic Text   Names   Include   Tags   Zoom

From ▾   Lisa Niaz
To...   Michelle Jagtiani
Cc...
Send

Subject   Denial of Matching Funds   *Negative subject line.*

No salutation.   *Negative*   *Paragraph used
                                                                 negative tone
Give   and diction.
reason*   You <u>cannot</u> receive a check the last day of work and you will get <u>only</u> your own
before contributions, <u>not</u> a matching sum from the company, because you have <u>not worked</u> for the
refusal. company for at least seven full years.   *Better to be specific.*

This is lifted   Your payments and interest come to just over $17,200; the amount could be higher
straight from   depending on the amount of your last paycheck, which will include compensation for any
the problem.   unused vacation days and sick leave. Furthermore, since the amounts deducted were not   *More*
The language   considered taxable income, you will have to pay income tax on the money you receive.   *negatives.*
in problems
is often   The check will be sent to your home address. If the address we have on file is <u>incorrect</u>,
negative and   please correct it so that your check is <u>not delayed</u>.   *Negative*
stuffy; information is
disorganized.   *No signature*   *How will reader know what you have on file?*
                      or contact information.   *Better to give current address as you have it.*

Think about the situation and use your own
words to create a satisfactory message.

Microsoft Corporation

overemphasizing it. The second paragraph emphasizes the positive by specifying the amount in the account and the fact that the sum might be even higher.

The third paragraph contains the additional negative information that the amount will be taxable but offers the alternative that it may be possible to reduce taxes. The writer builds goodwill by suggesting a specific person the reader could contact.

The fourth paragraph tells the reader what address is in the company files (Michelle may not know whether the files are up-to-date), asks that she update it if necessary, and ends with the reader's concern: getting her check promptly.

The final paragraph ends on a positive note. This generalized goodwill is appropriate when the writer does not know the reader well.

Figure 10.9 An Effective Solution to the Sample Problem

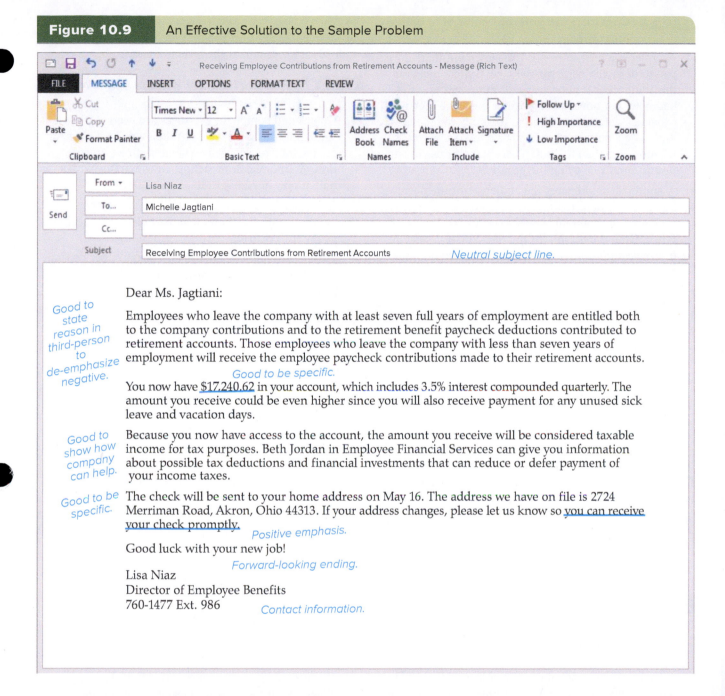

Receiving Employee Contributions from Retirement Accounts - Message (Rich Text)

From ▾ Lisa Niaz

To... Michelle Jagtiani

Cc...

Subject Receiving Employee Contributions from Retirement Accounts *Neutral subject line.*

Dear Ms. Jagtiani:

Good to state reason in third-person to de-emphasize negative.

Employees who leave the company with at least seven full years of employment are entitled both to the company contributions and to the retirement benefit paycheck deductions contributed to retirement accounts. Those employees who leave the company with less than seven years of employment will receive the employee paycheck contributions made to their retirement accounts.

Good to be specific.

You now have $17,240.62 in your account, which includes 3.5% interest compounded quarterly. The amount you receive could be even higher since you will also receive payment for any unused sick leave and vacation days.

Good to show how company can help.

Because you now have access to the account, the amount you receive will be considered taxable income for tax purposes. Beth Jordan in Employee Financial Services can give you information about possible tax deductions and financial investments that can reduce or defer payment of your income taxes.

Good to be specific.

The check will be sent to your home address on May 16. The address we have on file is 2724 Merriman Road, Akron, Ohio 44313. If your address changes, please let us know so you can receive your check promptly. *Positive emphasis.*

Good luck with your new job! *Forward-looking ending.*

Lisa Niaz
Director of Employee Benefits
760-1477 Ext. 986 *Contact information.*

Summary by Learning Objectives

LO 10-1 **Explain the different purposes of negative messages.**

A good negative message conveys the negative information clearly while maintaining as much goodwill as possible. The goal is to make recipients feel that they have been taken seriously, that the decision is fair and reasonable, and that they would have made the same decision. A secondary purpose is to reduce or eliminate future communication on the same subject.

LO 10-2 **Describe the different ways to organize negative messages.**

The best way to organize negative messages depends on the particular audiences and situations involved. Figure 10.1 suggests ways to structure the message.

LO 10-3   **Construct the different parts of negative messages.**

- A buffer is a neutral or positive statement that allows you to delay the negative message. Buffers must put the audience in a good frame of mind, not give the bad news but not imply a positive answer either, and provide a natural transition to the body of the message. Use a buffer only when the audience values harmony or when the buffer serves a purpose in addition to simply delaying the negative.

- A good reason prepares the audience for the negative and must be watertight. Give several reasons only if all are watertight and are of comparable importance. Omit the reason for the refusal if it is weak or if it makes your organization look bad. Do not hide behind company policy.

- Make the refusal crystal clear.

- Giving the audience an alternative or a compromise
  - Offers the audience another way to get what they want.
  - Suggests that you really care about the audience and about helping to meet their needs.
  - Allows you to end on a positive note and to present yourself and your organization as positive, friendly, and helpful.

LO 10-4   **Improve the tone of negative messages.**

Tone—the implied attitude of the author toward the reader and the subject—is particularly important when you have to convey negative news. Check your draft carefully for positive emphasis and *you*-attitude, both at the level of individual words and at the level of ideas.

LO 10-5   **Produce different kinds of negative messages.**

- Claims and complaint messages are needed when something has gone wrong. When writing a claim or complaint, you generally will use a direct organization. An indirect approach, such as starting with a buffer, may be interpreted as a weak claim.

- In a refusal to an external audience, try to give an alternative if one is available. Be polite and specific about any positives.

- Present disciplinary notices and negative performance reviews directly, with no buffer. Be honest and give reasons.

LO 10-6   **Analyze when and how to apologize.**

- In business documents, apologize only when you are at fault.

- If you need to apologize, do it early, briefly, and sincerely. Do so only once, early in the message.

- Do not dwell on the bad things that have happened. The reader already knows this negative information. Instead, focus on what you have done to correct the situation.

- If possible, pair your apology with an appropriate benefit.

Exercises and Cases

10.1   Reviewing the Chapter

1. What are the purposes of negative messages? (LO 10-1)
2. What are the reasons behind the patterns of organization for negative messages in different situations (Figure 10.1)? (LO 10-2)
3. What are the parts of negative messages? How may those parts be changed for different contexts? (LO 10-3)
4. When should you not use a buffer? (LO 10-3)
5. What are some ways you can maintain a caring tone in negative messages? (LO 10-4)
6. What are some different varieties of negative messages? What are some examples from the chapter text? (LO 10-5)
7. When and how should you apologize? (LO 10-6)

10.2   Reviewing Grammar

Negative news is frequently placed in dependent clauses to help deemphasize it. Unfortunately, some dependent clauses and phrases are dangling or misplaced modifiers. Do the exercise from Appendix B on improving modifiers to help you learn to recognize this error.

10.3   Letters for Discussion—Credit Refusal

As director of customer service at C'est Bon, an upscale furniture store, you manage the store's credit. Today you are going to reject an application from Frank Steele. Although his income is fairly high, his last two payments on his college loans were late, and he has three bank credit cards, all charged to the upper limit, on which he's made just the minimum payment for the past three months.

The following letters are possible approaches to giving him the news. How well does each message meet the criteria in the checklist for negative messages?

1.

Dear Mr. Steele:

Your request to have a C'est Bon charge account shows that you are a discriminating shopper. C'est Bon sells the finest merchandise available.

Although your income is acceptable, records indicate that you carry the maximum allowable balances on three bank credit cards. Moreover, two recent payments on your student loans have not been made in a timely fashion. If you were given a C'est Bon charge account, and if you charged a large amount on it, you might have difficulty paying the bill, particularly if you had other unforeseen expenses (car repair, moving, medical emergency) or if your income dropped suddenly. If you were unable to repay, with your other debt you would be in serious difficulty. We would not want you to be in such a situation, nor would you yourself desire it.

Please reapply in six months.

Sincerely,

2.

Dear Frank:

No, you can't have a C'est Bon credit card—at least not right now. Get your financial house in order and try again.

Fortunately for you, there's an alternative. Put what you want on layaway. The furniture you want will be held for you, and paying a bit each week or month will be good self-discipline.

Enjoy your C'est Bon furniture!

Sincerely,

3.

Dear Mr. Steele:

Over the years, we've found that the best credit risks are people who pay their bills promptly. Since two of your student loan payments have been late, we won't extend store credit to you right now. Come back with a record of six months of on-time payments of all bills, and you'll get a different answer.

You might like to put the furniture you want on layaway. A $50 deposit holds any item you want. You have six months to pay, and you save interest charges.

You also might want to take advantage of one of our Saturday Seminars. On the first Saturday of each month at 11 a.m., our associates explain one topic related to furniture and interior decorating. Upcoming topics are

How to Wallpaper a Room	February 5
Drapery Options	March 6
Persian Carpets	April 1

Sincerely,

10.4   Email Situations for Discussion—Sending a Negative News Email

Read the following situations and decide how you would handle them. You know that you will need to inform your boss, but how will you report what happened? Will you apologize? What channel will you use? Discuss as a class.

- Your boss was looking for a new part-time assistant, just for the summer. You knew a friend of yours was looking for a summer job, so you referred them to your boss. Your boss hired your friend on your recommendation, but you've learned from your friend that the job is not quite what they had in mind. Your friend is tired of getting up early to come to the office and doesn't feel like being an assistant anymore. They are thinking about simply not showing up for work next week. How do you let your boss know what is going on?

- You were driving the company car to go pick up some coffee for everyone when you received a text from the office administrative assistant. They added a few more coffee orders to your list, and you texted back: "OK, got it." However, you weren't paying attention and got into a minor fender bender. You know that texting while driving could be a large liability for your company. What should you do? What will you tell your boss?

- You are supervising two interns for the summer, and one has come to you with a complaint about sexual harassment. She noted that the other intern makes her feel uncomfortable by making sexual jokes and comments toward her. You know that you need to report the incidents. What will you say to your boss and the HR representative?

10.5   Emails for Discussion—Ending a Tradition

Your boss has asked you to draft a companywide email that explains a change in policy. Previously, the company would buy a cake for each employee's birthday and there would be a small celebration in the office. However, due to budget cuts, the company will no longer be purchasing cakes for each employee. Your boss is worried that this bad news will hurt office morale and wants you to break the news gently. Analyze the following emails. How well does each relate the news? How well does each message follow the negative messages checklist?

Subject: No more cake

Hello everyone,

We are sending this email to let everyone know that due to budget cuts, we will no longer be purchasing cakes for employee birthday parties. Sorry! If you want to bring in your own cake, that would be fine.

Subject: Budget Cut Information

We regret to inform you that due to some changes to the current budget, we have decided that the company can no longer afford to purchase birthday cakes for each employee's birthday. We do, however, encourage everyone to bring in treats or cake on their own birthday so we can still continue with the office birthday tradition.

Thank you for your understanding!

Management.

Subject: Cake

This email is to inform you that the company will no longer be buying cakes for employee's birthdays. It has simply become too expensive for the company to buy that many cakes every single year.

I would like to remind everyone, before you start sending out angry email replies, that our country has been in an economic downturn and we are still recovering from that. Look at the bigger picture and try to appreciate the fact that you all still have jobs.

Thanks.

10.6 Revising a Negative Message

Rewrite the following negative message so it follows the guidelines for negative messages:

Dear Valued Employee:

I'm afraid the company will not be able to grant you your requested vacation time at this particular time. You recently took your allotted time of maternity leave, and the company has a policy that states employees may not take vacation time so soon after a long leave (even if it was for a baby).

The company also had to pay for your replacement to work here while you were on maternity leave, so we would appreciate it if you would clock some hours in the office.

I can recommend to you that you try submitting your vacation request again in approximately 10–12 weeks. Other than that, there is nothing that I can do for you.

We are so glad to have you as a valued employee here at VegCo.

Have a Veggie-riffic day!

Claire—HR

10.7 Practicing Negative Responses for the Office

Write a brief response for these office situations. Remember, you do not want to alienate your coworkers.

1. Turn down a request to volunteer. (What are some responses that almost guarantee getting recruited?)
2. Turn down a request to contribute to a fund-raiser.
3. Ask a colleague who loves to spread hurtful gossip to please stop sharing it with you.
4. Ask a colleague to wipe their sweat off the piece of equipment they have been using before you in the company gym.
5. Ask colleagues to refrain from using their electronic devices during your meeting.
6. Ask a colleague to take down an unflattering picture of you from their Facebook page.
7. Turn down a lunch request from a colleague who has already asked you several times before.

In small groups, discuss your answers. Pick your best answer for each situation and share it with the class.

10.8 Notifying College Seniors That They May Not Graduate

State University asks students to file an application to graduate one term before they actually plan to graduate. The application lists the courses the student has already had and those they will take in the last term. Your office reviews the lists to see that the student will meet the requirements for total number of hours, hours in the major, and general education requirements. Some students have forgotten a requirement or not taken enough courses and cannot graduate unless they take more courses than those they have listed.

As your instructor directs,

Write form email messages to the following audiences. Leave blanks for the proposed date of graduation and specific information that must be merged into the message:

a. Students who have not taken enough total hours.
b. Students who have not fulfilled all the requirements for their majors.
c. Students who are missing one or more general education courses.
d. Advisers of students who do not meet the requirements for graduation.

10.9 Correcting a Mistake

Today, as you reviewed some cost figures, you realized they didn't fit with the last monthly report you filed. You had pulled the numbers together from several sources and you're not sure what happened. Maybe you miscopied or didn't save the final version after you'd checked all the numbers. But whatever the cause, you've found errors in three categories. You gave your boss the following totals:

Personnel	$2,843,490
Office supplies	$43,500
Company cell phones	$186,240

Email your boss to correct the information.

As your instructor directs,

Write email messages for the following situations:

a. The correct numbers are:

Personnel	$2,845,490
Office supplies	$34,500
Company cell phones	$186,420

b. The correct numbers are:

Personnel	$2,845,490
Office supplies	$73,500
Company cell phones	$368,240

Variations for each situation:

1. Your boss has been out of the office; you know they haven't seen the data yet.

2. Your boss gave a report to the executive committee this morning using your data.

Hints:

- How serious is the mistake in each situation?

- In which situations, if any, should you apologize?

- Should you give the reason for the mistake? Why or why not?

- How do your options vary depending on whether your job title gives you responsibility for numbers and accounting?

10.10   Vetoing an Employee Benefit

Your newspaper ran an article on the front page of the business section featuring a local business that provides employees with unlimited vacation days. Now your Employees Council has come to you requesting the same perk. They say they are all responsible adults who would see that their work is covered and note that it would be an excellent recruitment tool for top-notch people (and you are the owner of an expanding company). You promised to consider their requests carefully, and you have. Now you owe them an answer. Write an email to send to all your employees telling them you will not be offering that perk. When writing, consider these questions:

- Is your audience uniform? Do all your employees think unlimited vacation is a good idea?

- How should you organize your email?

- Where can you use positive tone and *you*-attitude in your email?

- What explanation will you give?

- How will the size of your company affect your explanation? (Twenty employees might need different reasons than 100 employees.)

- Is there an alternative you can propose?

10.11   Composing an Apology Letter

The data-breach apology letter is quickly becoming a routine negative message in the 21st century. In a small group, compose an apology letter to customers whose personal information has been compromised in a data breach. Use strategies from this chapter on crafting negative messages. Before you write, discuss the following:

- Which pattern of organization (see Figure 10.1) should the apology letter use?

- What information does your audience need to know?

- How can you minimize the negative elements?

- How can you rebuild goodwill?

After your group has composed the letter, use the checklist in Figure 10.7 to evaluate your letter.

10.12   Preparing a Class Civility Policy

Create a civility policy for your business communication classroom.

- What oral behaviors do you want to address?

- What nonverbal behaviors should you address?

- What negative consequences could your guidelines have?

Watch the tone of your policy to ensure it follows your own civility guidelines.

1. Write a draft of a policy yourself. Address at least six oral behaviors and four nonverbal behaviors.

2. In a small group, compare policies. Construct a policy as a group, including all the good ideas. Post your group's draft on your class website.

3. Read the policies of the other groups in your class. In your same small group, revise your group policy into a final draft and submit it to your instructor. Include an email explaining your choices for inclusions and their wording. Also explain why you rejected some items.

10.13   Telling Employees to Remove Personal Websites

You are the director of management and information systems in your organization. At your monthly briefing for management, a vice president complained that some employees have posted personal web pages on the company's web server.

"It looks really unprofessional to have stuff about cats and children and musical instruments. How can people do this?"

You took the question literally. "Well, some people have authorization to post material—price changes, job listings, marketing information. Someone who has authorization could put up anything."

Another manager said, "I don't think it's so terrible—after all, there aren't any links from our official pages to these personal pages."

A third person said, "But we're paying for what's posted—so we pay for server space and connect time. Maybe it's not much right now, but the number of people putting up unauthorized pages could grow. We should put a stop to this now."

The vice president agreed. "The website is carefully designed to present an image of our organization. Personal pages are dangerous. Can you imagine the flak we'd get if someone posted links to pornography?"

You said, "I don't think that's very likely. If it did happen, as system administrator, I could remove the page."

The third speaker said, "I think we should remove all the pages. Having any at all suggests that our people have so much extra time that they're playing on the web. That suggests that our prices are too high and may make some people worry about quality. In fact, I think that we need a new policy prohibiting personal pages on the company's web server. And any pages that are already up should be removed."

A majority of the managers agreed and told you to write a message to all employees. Create an email message to tell employees that you will remove the personal pages already posted and that no more will be allowed.

Hints:

- Suggest other ways that people can post personal web pages.
- Give only reasons that are watertight and make the company look good.

10.14   Refusing to Waive a Fee

As the licensing program coordinator for your school, you evaluate proposals from vendors who want to make or sell merchandise with the school's name, logo, or mascot. If you find the product acceptable, the vendor pays a $250 licensing fee and then 6.5% of the wholesale cost of the merchandise manufactured (whether or not it is sold). The licensing fee helps to support the cost of your office; the 6.5% royalty goes into a student scholarship fund. At well-known universities or those with loyal students and alumni, the funds from such a program can add up to hundreds of thousands of dollars a year.

On your desk today is a proposal from a current student, Parker Winston.

I want to silk-screen and sell t-shirts printed with the name of the school, the mascot, and the words "We're Number One!" (A copy of the design I propose is enclosed.) I ask that you waive the $250 licensing fee you normally require and limit the 6.5% royalty only to those t-shirts actually sold, not to all those made.

I am putting myself through school by using student loans and working 30 hours a week. I just don't have $250. In my marketing class, we've done feasibility analyses, and I've determined that the shirts can be sold if the price is low enough. I hope to market these shirts in an independent study project with Professor Doulin, building on my marketing

(continued)

project earlier this term. However, my calculations show that I cannot price the shirts competitively if just one shirt must bear the 6.5% royalty for all the shirts produced in a batch. I will, of course, pay the 6.5% royalty on all shirts sold and not returned. I will produce the shirts in small batches (50–100 at a time). I am willing to donate any manufactured but unsold shirts to the athletic program so that you will know I'm not holding out on you.

By waiving this fee, you will show that this school really wants to help students get practical experience in business, as the catalog states. I will work hard to promote these shirts by getting the school president, the coaches, and campus leaders to endorse them, pointing out that the money goes to the scholarship fund. The shirts themselves will promote school loyalty, both now and later when we're alumni who can contribute to our alma mater.

I look forward to receiving the "go-ahead" to market these shirts.

The design and product are acceptable under your guidelines. However, you've always enforced the fee structure across the board and you see no reason to make an exception now. Whether the person trying to sell merchandise is a student doesn't matter; your policy is designed to see that the school benefits whenever it is used to sell something. Students aren't the only ones whose cash flow is limited; many businesses would find it easier to get into the potentially lucrative business of selling clothing, school supplies, and other items with the school name or logo if they got the same deal Parker is asking for. (The policy also lets the school control the kinds of items on which its name appears.) Just last week, your office confiscated about 400 t-shirts and shorts made by a company that had used the school name on them without permission; the company has paid the school $7,500 in damages.

Write a letter to Parker rejecting their special requests. They can get a license to produce the t-shirts, but only if they pay the $250 licensing fee and the royalty on all shirts made.

10.15   Correcting Misinformation

You're the director of the city's Division of Water. Your mail today contains this letter:

When we bought our pool, the salesman told us that you would give us a discount on the water bill when we fill the pool. Please start the discount immediately. I tried to call you three times and got nothing but busy signals.

Sincerely,

Larry Shadburn-Butler

Larry Shadburn-Butler

The salesperson was wrong. You don't provide discounts for pools (or anything else). At current rates, filling a pool with a garden hose costs from $8.83 (for a 1,800-gallon pool) to $124.67 (for 26,000 gallons) in the city. Filling a pool from any other water source would cost more. Rates are 30% higher in the suburbs and 50% higher in unincorporated rural areas. And you don't have enough people to answer phones. You tried a voice mail system but eliminated it when you found people didn't have time to process all the messages that were left. The city budget doesn't allow you to hire more people.

As your instructor directs,

a.   Write a letter to Mr. Shadburn-Butler.

b.   Write a letter to all the stores that sell swimming pools, urging them to stop giving customers misinformation.

c.   Write a notice for the one-page newsletter that you include with quarterly water bills. Assume that you can have half a page for your information.

10.16   Analyzing Job Rejection Letters

Here are three rejections letters to an applicant who applied for an accounting position.

1.
> We realize that the application process for the accounting position at AlphaBank required a substantial amount of thought, time, and effort on your part. Therefore, we would like to express our sincere appreciation for your willingness to participate in the search process.
>
> The task of selecting a final candidate was difficult and challenging due to the quality of the applicant pool. We regret to inform you that we selected another candidate who we believe will best meet the needs of AlphaBank.
>
> We thank your for your interest in employment at AlphaBank and extend our best wishes as you pursue your professional goals.

2.
> Thank you for your interest in the accounting position at AlphaBank. I'm sorry to inform you that you were not one of the finalists. The position has now been filled.
>
> The search committee and I wish you the best in your future employment searches.

3.
> Thank you for your interest in the accounting position at AlphaBank.
>
> I'm sorry to inform you that the search committee has decided to offer the position to another candidate. This was an extremely difficult decision for us to make. We were all impressed with your résumé and credentials.
>
> Again, thank you for your interest in AlphaBank.

Analyze these three job rejection letters by answering the following questions:

- Do these letters use buffers? If so, how effective are they?
- What reasons do the letters give, if any?
- Does the letter attempt to build goodwill with the audience? If yes, how so?
- Do any of the letters offer an alternative?

- How do you think recipients will react to each of the letters? Which (if any) are more preferable?

As your instructor directs,
a. Discuss your findings in a small group.
b. Present your findings orally to the class.
c. Present your findings in an email to your instructor.

10.17 Creating Equal Work Distribution

You noticed recently that Lane, who works next to you at a call center, takes extended lunches and makes a lot of personal phone calls. As the result of their phone calls and breaks, you and your coworkers complete more work throughout the day. After discussing the situation with a close friend, you decide you are going to tell the boss about this behavior.

As your instructor directs,
a. Write an email to your boss in which you discuss Lane's behavior and ask for a resolution.
b. Partner with a classmate and role-play the situation of telling the boss. One of you is the employee and one of you is the boss.

c. Partner with a classmate and role-play the situation of confronting Lane. One of you is the employee and one of you is Lane.

Hints:
- How can you deliver the negative news without sounding like a tattletale?
- How can you make the situation seem severe enough so that your boss takes action?

10.18 Turning Down a Faithful Client

You are Midas Investment Services' specialist in estate planning. You give talks to various groups during the year about estate planning. You ask nonprofit groups (churches, etc.) just to reimburse your expenses; you charge for-profit groups a fee plus expenses. These fees augment your income nicely, and the talks also are marvelous exposure for you and your company.

Every February for the past five years, Gardner Manufacturing Company has hired you to conduct an eight-hour workshop (two hours every Monday night for four weeks) on retirement and estate planning for its employees who are over 60 or who are thinking of taking early retirement. These workshops are popular and have generated clients for your company. The session last February went smoothly, as you have come to expect.

Today, out of the blue, you got a letter from Ari Goldberger, director of employee benefits at Gardner, asking you to conduct the workshops every Tuesday evening *next* month at your usual fee. They didn't say whether this is an extra series or whether this will replace next February's series.

You can't do it. Your spouse is giving an invited paper at an international conference in Paris next month and the two of you are taking your children, ages 13 and 9, on a three-week trip to Europe. (You've made arrangements with school authorities to have the kids miss three weeks of classes.) You've been looking forward to and planning the trip for eight months.

Unfortunately, Midas Investment Services is a small group, and the only other person who knows anything about estate planning is a terrible speaker. You could suggest a friend at another financial management company, but you don't want Gardner to turn to someone else permanently; you enjoy doing the workshops and find them a good way to get leads.

Write the letter to Ari Goldberger.

10.19   Getting Information from a Co-worker

Your boss has been pressuring you because you are weeks late turning in a termination report. However, you cannot begin your section of the report until your colleague, Matt Churetta, finishes his section. Right now, he is the problem. Here is a series of email exchanges between you and Matt:

> 7/25/2021
>
> Matt,
>
> The boss wants the termination report now. Send over your section as soon as you finish.
>
> Thanks,

Matt's reply:

> 7/30/2021
>
> My apologies about the report.
>
> On another note, I'm waiting to see my oncology surgeon to see what the course of treatment will be for the esophageal cancer. I will keep you posted on the process.
>
> Please let me know if there is anything else coming up.
>
> Thanks,

> 8/3/2021
>
> Matt,
>
> I had no idea that you are dealing with esophageal cancer. Definitely keep me posted on your condition. Best wishes as you work through your treatment.
>
> I need your section of the termination report as soon as you finish it. The boss has been waiting patiently for the finished version.
>
> Thanks,

Matt's reply:

> 8/26/2021
>
> Report is coming along. The last three weeks have been difficult dealing with all the tests, doctors' appointments, etc. I will beat this deal!!!
>
> Take care,

It is now September, and over a month has passed from the termination report's original due date. While you are sympathetic to Matt's situation, the boss is demanding the finished report.

As your instructor directs,

a. Write an email to Matt telling him you have to have his portion of the report as soon as possible. You are concerned for your job security, as well as his, if this report is not finalized soon.

b. Write an email to your boss explaining the situation.

c. Write an email to your instructor that focuses on the ethical choices you had to make while constructing the two messages.

10.20   Sending Negative Messages to Real Audiences

As your instructor directs,

Write a negative letter that responds to one of the following scenarios:

- Write a letter to the owner of a restaurant where you received poor service.

- Write a letter to a company whose product unsatisfactorily met your expectations or needs.

- Identify a current political topic on which you disagree with your congressional representative. Write a letter that outlines your views and calls for change.

- Identify a television advertisement with which you disagree. Write a letter to the company explaining your position and request that the advertisement be altered or taken off the air.

Hints:

- For all of these scenarios, your main goal should be to promote change.

- Express your complaint as positively as possible.

- Remember to consider your audience's needs; how can you build support for your position?

Notes

1. Robert I. Sutton, *The No Asshole Rule: Building a Civilized Workplace and Surviving One That Isn't* (New York: Warner Business Books, 2007), 45–48.
2. "Johnson & Johnson Just Got Hit with a $1B Verdict over Faulty Hip Implants," *Fortune*, December 1, 2016, http://fortune.com/2016/12/02/johnson-johnson-just-got-hit-with-a-1b-verdict-over-faulty-hip-implants.
3. L. Gordon Crovitz, "The Business of Restoring Trust," *Wall Street Journal*, January 31, 2011, A13.
4. Ben Levisohn, "Getting More Workers to Whistle," *BusinessWeek*, January 28, 2008, 18.
5. Alan Mulally, "Get Honest Feedback," *Bloomberg Businessweek*, April 12, 2012, 95.
6. Peter D. Timmerman and Wayne Harrison, "The Discretionary Use of Electronic Media: Four Considerations for Bad News Bearers," *Journal of Business Communication* 42, no. 4 (1005): 379–89.
7. Kitty O. Locker, "Factors in Reader Responses to Negative Letters: Experimental Evidence for Changing What We Teach," *Journal of Business and Technical Communication* 13, no. 1 (January 1999): 21.
8. Ibid., 25–26.
9. Sharon S. Brehm and Jack W. Brehm, *Psychological Reactance: A Theory of Freedom and Control* (New York: Academic Press, 1981), 3.
10. Christine Porath and Christine Pearson, "The Price of Incivility: Lack of Respect Hurts Morale—and the Bottom Line," *Harvard Business Review* 91, no. 1–2 (January–February 2013): 115–21.
11. Ibid., 116, 118.
12. William Ury, *The Power of a Positive No: How to Say No and Still Get to Yes* (New York: Bantam, 2007), 19.
13. John Kell, "Chipotle Has to Finally Shake Off Its E. Coli Slump in 2017," *Fortune*, February 2, 2017, http://fortune.com/2017/02/02/chipotle-sales-decline-2016.
14. Scott McCartney, "The Airlines' Squeaky Wheels Turn to Twitter," *Wall Street Journal*, October 28, 2010, D1, D5.
15. Stephen W. Gilliland et al., "Improving Applicants' Reactions to Rejection Letters: An Application of Fairness Theory," *Personnel Psychology* 54, no. 3 (2001): 669–704; and Robert E. Ployhart, Karen Holcombe Ehrhart, and Seth C. Hayes, "Using Attributions to Understand the Effects of Explanations on Applicant Reactions: Are Reactions Consistent with the Covariation Principle?" *Journal of Applied Social Psychology* 35, no. 2 (2005): 259–96.
16. John P. Hausknecht, David V. Day, and Scott C. Thomas, "Applicant Reactions to Selection Procedures: An Updated Model and Meta-Analysis," *Personnel Psychology* 57, no. 3 (2004): 639–84.
17. Kenneth Blanchard and Spencer Johnson, *The One Minute Manager* (New York: William Morrow, 1982), 59.
18. Dana Mattioli, Joann S. Lublin, and Rachel Emma Silverman, "Bad Call: How Not to Fire a Worker," *Wall Street Journal*, September 9, 2011, B2.
19. Carol Hymowitz, "Though Now Routine, Bosses Still Stumble During Layoff Process," *Wall Street Journal*, June 25, 2007, B1.
20. Carol Hymowitz, "Personal Boundaries Shrink as Companies Punish Bad Behavior," *Wall Street Journal*, June 18, 2007, B1.
21. Jordan Crook, "Tim Cook Apologizes for Apple Maps, Points to Competitive Alternatives," *TechCrunch*, September 28, 2012, https://techcrunch.com/2012/09/28/tim-cook-apologizes-for-apple-maps-points-to-competitive-alternatives; and Lucinda Shen, "United Airlines Stock Drops $1.4 Billion after Passenger-Removal Controversy," *Fortune*, April 11, 2017, http://fortune.com/2017/04/11/united-airlines-stock-drop.
22. Andrew Blake, "Millions of Verizon Customers Affected by Security Breach," *Washingtontimes.com*, July 13, 2017, http://www.washingtontimes.com/news/2017/jul/13/millions-verizon-customers-impacted-security-breac/.
23. Scott McCartney, "What Airlines Do When You Complain," *Wall Street Journal*, March 20, 2007, D1; and Nick Wingfield, "Steve Jobs Offers Rare Apology Credit for iPhone," *Wall Street Journal*, September 7, 2007, B1.
24. Janet Paskin, "Don't Apologize," *Bloomberg Businessweek*, April 22, 2013, 88.

CHAPTER 11

Crafting Persuasive Messages

Chapter Outline

DrAfter123/Getty Images

Successful Fund-Raising Campaigns

From 2018 to 2019, Wikipedia, the world's 13th most popular website and the most visited nonprofit website, raised over $120 million during its annual fund-raising campaign.

During Wikipedia's 2014 fund-raising campaign, critics complained that the organization used exaggerated language that emphasized a financially dire situation to persuade users of the website to give money. For example, critics objected to the use of the phrase "We survive on donations." Also problematic was the advertisement's call to action: "Please help us end the fundraiser and get back to improving Wikipedia," which seemed to imply Wikipedia had temporarily shut down until sufficient funds were donated.

Wikipedia responded to the criticism by softening the language of its 2015 campaign, changing "We survive on donations" to "We're sustained on donations" and revising the call to action: "If Wikipedia is useful to you, please take one minute to keep it online and growing." In 2016, Wikipedia edited the language again to say, "We depend on donations." In November 2020, Pats Pena, Wikipedia's Director of Online Fundraising, urged donations by pointing out, "More people than ever read Wikipedia in 2020, driven in part by the coronavirus pandemic. People depended on Wikipedia for critical, accurate information about COVID-19, viewing pandemic-related articles more than 532 million times."

Wikipedia's communication to potential donors has used effective strategies

We ask you, humbly, to help.

We'll get straight to the point: Today we ask you to defend Wikipedia's independence.

We're a non-profit that depends on donations to stay online and thriving, but 98% of our readers don't give; they simply look the other way. If everyone who reads Wikipedia gave just a little, we could keep Wikipedia thriving for years to come. The price of a cup of coffee is all we ask.

When we made Wikipedia a non-profit, people told us we'd regret it. But if Wikipedia were to become commercial, it would be a great loss to the world.

Wikipedia is a place to learn, not a place for advertising. The heart and soul of Wikipedia is a community of people working to bring you unlimited access to reliable, neutral information.

We know that most people will ignore this message. But if Wikipedia is useful to you, please consider making a donation of $5, $20, $50 or whatever you can to protect and sustain Wikipedia.

Thanks,

Jimmy Wales
Wikipedia Founder

Wikipedia

for crafting persuasive messages—some of the same strategies described in this chapter.

Persuasion is almost universal in good business communications. If you are giving people information, you are persuading them to consider it good information, to remember it, or to use it. If you are giving people negative news, you are trying to persuade them to accept it. If you work for a company, you are a "sales representative" for it. Your job depends on its success.

In our work, some communications seem more obviously persuasive to us than others. Employees try to persuade their supervisors to institute flex hours or casual Fridays; supervisors try to persuade workers to keep more accurate records, thus reducing time spent correcting errors; or employers encourage employees to follow healthier lifestyles, thus reducing health-benefit costs. You may find yourself persuading your colleagues to accept your ideas, your staff to work overtime on a rush project, and your boss to give you a raise.

Whether you're selling safety equipment or ideas, effective persuasion is based on accurate logic, effective emotional appeal, and credibility or trust. Reasons have to be ones the audience finds important; emotional appeal is based on values the audience cares about; credibility depends on your character and reputation.

Sources: Caitlin Dewey, "Wikipedia Has a Ton of Money. So Why Is It Begging You to Donate Yours?" *Washington Post,* December 2, 2015, https://www.washingtonpost.com/news/the-intersect/wp/2015/12/02/wikipedia-has-a-ton-of-money-so-why-is-it-begging-you-to-donate-yours; Alexa Internet, "Top 500 Sites on the Web," accessed January 5, 2020, https://www.alexa.com/topsites; Andrew Littlefield, "The Top 10 Most Visited Nonprofit Websites (And What You Can Learn from Them)," and "Wikipedia: Fundraising statistics," accessed January 5, 2020, https://en.wikipedia.org/wiki/Wikipedia:Fundraising_statistics.

After studying this chapter, you should be able to

LO 11-1	Explain the purposes of persuasive messages.
LO 11-2	Analyze a persuasive situation.
LO 11-3	Identify basic persuasive strategies.
LO 11-4	Produce persuasive direct requests.
LO 11-5	Produce persuasive problem-solving messages.
LO 11-6	Produce performance reviews and letters of recommendation.
LO 11-7	Produce sales and fund-raising messages.

Purposes of Persuasive Messages

LO 11-1

Persuasive messages include requests, proposals and recommendations, sales and fund-raising messages, job application letters, and efforts to change people's behavior, such as collection letters, criticisms or performance reviews where you want people to improve behavior, and public-service ads designed to reduce behaviors such as drunken driving or increase behaviors such as supporting charities. Reports and white papers are persuasive messages if they recommend action.

This chapter gives general guidelines for persuasive messages. Chapter 12 discusses proposals; reports is the subject of Chapter 13. Chapter 15 covers job application letters.

All persuasive messages have several purposes:

Primary purpose

- To have the audience act or change beliefs.

Secondary purposes

- To build a good image of the communicator.

- To build a good image of the communicator's organization.

- To cement a good relationship between the communicator and audience.

- To overcome any objections that might prevent or delay action.

- To reduce or eliminate future communication on the same subject so the message doesn't create more work for the communicator.

Analyzing Persuasive Situations

LO 11-2

Choose a persuasive strategy based on your answers to the five questions in Figure 11.1. Use these questions to analyze persuasive situations.

1. What Do You Want People to Do?

Identify the specific action you want and the person who has the power to do it. If your goal requires several steps, specify what you want your audience to do *now*. For instance, your immediate goal may be to have people come to a meeting or let you make a presentation, even though your long-term goal is a major sale or a change in policy.

Figure 11.1	Questions for Analyzing Persuasive Messages

1. What do you want people to do?

2. What objections, if any, will the audience have?

3. How strong is your case?

4. What kind of persuasion is best for the situation?

5. What kind of persuasion is best for the organization and the culture?

2. What Objections, If Any, Will the Audience Have?

If you're asking for something that requires little time, money, or physical effort and for an action that's part of the person's regular duties, the audience is likely to have few objections. However, that is often not the case, and you'll encounter some resistance. People may be busy and have what they feel are more important things to do. They may have other uses for their time and money. To be persuasive, you need to show your audience that your proposal meets their needs; you need to overcome any objections.

The easiest way to learn about objections your audience may have is to ask. Particularly when you want to persuade people in your own organization or your own town, talk to knowledgeable people. Phrase your questions nondefensively, in a way that doesn't lock people into taking a stand on an issue: "What concerns would you have about a proposal to do X?" "Who makes a decision about Y?" "What do you like best about [the supplier or practice you want to change]?" Ask follow-up questions to be sure you understand: "Would you be likely to stay with your current supplier if you could get a lower price from someone else? Why?"

UNICEF combines photos and text on its website to present persuasive arguments for supporting its efforts to aid people who are hungry, sick, or homeless. This screen persuades audiences to take action by volunteering or sharing a UNICEF story with their friends on social media.

Source: https://www.unicef.org/take-action

People are likely to be most aware of and willing to share objective concerns such as time and money. They will be less willing to tell you their real objection when it is emotional or makes them look bad. People have a **vested interest** in something if they benefit directly from keeping things as they are. People who are in power have a vested interest in retaining the system that gives them their power. Someone who designed a system has a vested interest in protecting that system from criticism. To admit that the system has faults is to admit that the designer made mistakes. In such cases, you'll need to probe to find out what the real reasons are.

Whether your audience is inside or outside your organization, they will find it easier to say *yes* when you ask for something that is consistent with their self-image.

3. How Strong Is Your Case?

The strength of your case is based on three aspects of persuasion: reasoning (also called logos), credibility (also called ethos), and emotional appeal (also called pathos).

Reasoning refers to the argument or logic you offer. Sometimes you may be able to prove conclusively that your solution is best. Sometimes your reasons may not be as strong, the benefits may not be as certain, and obstacles may be difficult or impossible to overcome. For example, suppose you wanted to persuade your organization to offer a tuition reimbursement plan for employees. You'd have a strong argument if you could show that tuition reimbursement would improve the performance of marginal workers or that reimbursement would be an attractive recruiting tool in a tight job market. However, if dozens of fully qualified workers apply for every opening you have, your argument would be weaker. The program might be nice for workers, but you'd have a hard job proving that it would help the company.

Some arguments are weakened by common errors known as logical **fallacies.** Figure 11.2 defines some common logical fallacies.

Credibility is the audience's response to you as the source of the message. Credibility in the workplace has three sources: expertise, image, and relationships.[1] Citing experts can make your argument more credible. In some organizations, workers build credibility by getting assigned to high-profile teams. You build credibility by your track record. The more reliable you've been in the past, the more likely people are to trust you now.

Figure 11.2	Common Logical Fallacies

- **Hasty generalization.** Making general assumptions based on limited evidence. "Most of my friends agree that the new law is a bad idea. Americans do not support this law."

- **False cause.** Assuming that because one event follows another, the first event caused the second. "In the 1990s farmers increased their production of corn for ethanol. Soon after, more Americans began using ethanol fuel in their cars."

- **Weak analogy.** Making comparisons that don't work. "Outlawing guns because they kill people is like outlawing cars because they kill people."

- **Appeal to authority.** Quoting from a famous person who is not really an expert. "Hollywood actor Joe Gardner says this juicer is the best on the market today."

- **Appeal to popularity.** Arguing that because many people believe something, it is true. "Thousands of Americans doubt the reality of climate change, so climate change must not be happening."

- **Appeal to ignorance.** Using lack of evidence to support the conclusion. "There's nothing wrong in the plant; all the monitors are in the safety zone."

- **False dichotomy.** Setting up the situation to look like there are only two choices. "If you are not with us, you are against us."

We are also more likely to trust people we know. That's one reason new CEOs make a point of visiting as many branch offices as they can. Building a relationship with someone—even if the relationship is based on an outside interest, like sports or children—makes it easier for that person to see you as an individual and to trust you.

When you don't yet have the credibility that comes from being expert, high profile, or well known, build credibility by the language and strategy you use:

- **Be factual.** Don't exaggerate. If you can test your idea ahead of time, do so, and report the results. Facts about your test are more convincing than opinions about your idea.

- **Be specific.** If you say, "X is better," show in detail *how* it is better. Show the audience exactly where the savings or other benefits come from so that it's clear the proposal really is as good as you say it is.

- **Be reliable.** If you suspect a project will take longer to complete, cost more money, or be less effective than you originally thought, tell your audience *immediately.* Negotiate a new schedule that you can meet.

Emotional appeal means making the audience *want* to do what you ask. People don't make decisions—even business decisions—based on logic alone. As John Kotter and Holger Rathgeber, authors of the popular business book *Our Iceberg Is Melting*, found, "feelings often trump thinking."[2] Jonah Lehrer, author of *How We Decide*, goes a step further. He offers research that shows people make better decisions—ones that satisfy them better—about large purchases such as cars or homes when they followed their emotions: "The process of thinking requires feeling, for feelings are what let us understand all the information that we can't directly comprehend. Reason without emotion is impotent."[3]

4. What Kind of Persuasion Is Best for the Situation?

Different kinds of people require different kinds of persuasion. What works for your boss may not work for your colleague. But even the same person may require different kinds of persuasion in different situations. Many people who make rational decisions at work do not do so at home, where they may decide to smoke and overeat even though they know smoking and obesity contribute to many deaths.

For years, companies have based their persuasion techniques on the idea that money is most people's primary motivator. And sometimes it is, of course. But research has shown that people also are motivated by other factors, including competition and social norms. Utility companies, for example, have found that people are more likely to conserve energy if they see how their use compares to their neighbors' use.[4] A hotel that posted signs saying that the majority of guests reused their towels increased the reusage rate 26%.[5] These factors, derived from **behavioral economics,** open up new ways to persuade people to act.

Another kind of persuasion that is getting much attention is **choice architecture,** which involves changing the context in which people make decisions to encourage them to make certain choices.

- Companies that automatically enroll new employees in savings and retirement plans are using choice architecture. Instead of having to fill out forms to opt in to saving, employees have to fill out the forms to opt out. Since employees do not like to fill out voluntary forms, more of them remain in the savings programs.

- Asking people the day before the election if they intend to vote increases the probability of their voting by up to 25%.

- A study of 40,000 people that asked them if they intended to buy a car in the next six months increased car purchase rates 35%.

- Officials in Minnesota persuaded more residents to pay their taxes simply by telling them that 90% of their fellow residents obeyed the tax laws. (Neither threats nor information about the good causes funded by taxes had worked.)[6]

In *Drive: The Surprising Truth about What Motivates Us*, Daniel Pink summarizes decades of research that shows many businesses are using the wrong kinds of persuasion on their employees who do knowledge work, work that demands sophisticated understanding, flexible problem solving, and creativity. According to this research, once basic levels of financial fairness are reached, "carrot" motivators, such as financial ones, do not work for employees who are expected to be innovative. In fact, carrot motivators will actually decrease innovation; they turn creative work into drudgery.[7] "Stick" motivators, in the form of ill-chosen goals, are also harmful and can lead to unethical and illegal behavior. Managers hit short-term goals to get performance bonuses, even when they know the short-term goals will cause long-term problems. So what does motivate knowledge workers? Pink says it is three drives: "Our deep-seated desire to direct our own lives, to expend and expand our abilities, and to live a life of purpose."[8]

5. What Kind of Persuasion Is Best for the Organization and the Culture?

Choosing the wrong kind of persuasion can have a deleterious effect on reaching your goals. In the 1980s and 1990s, the U.S. government spent almost a billion dollars on antidrug campaigns, such as the famous "Just Say No" ads, directed at youth. The messages did not have the expected effect. Research showed that young people who had seen the ads were more likely to use drugs than those who had not. Why? The ads proved that lots of young people were using drugs, or all those ads wouldn't exist. The more people seem to be doing something, the more likely it is that other people think they should try it too.[9]

Organizational Culture   In the business world, a strategy that works in one organization may not work somewhere else. One corporate culture may value no-holds-barred aggressiveness. In another organization with different cultural values, an employee who uses a hard-sell strategy for a request would antagonize people. Managers at Google, a culture where job titles do not come with power, have to learn to use ideas and persuasiveness to engage employees. Some businesses are willing to try creative means of persuasion. MGM Resorts produced a talent show starring employees for their corporate training program in diversity and sustainability. The show engaged the talents of 70 employees and ran for 10 performances.[10]

Organizational culture isn't written down; it's learned by imitation and observation. What style do high-level people in your organization use to persuade? When you show a draft to your boss, are you told to tone down your statements or to make them stronger? Role models and advice are two ways organizations communicate their culture to newcomers.

Social Culture   Different kinds of persuasion also work for different social cultures. Texas used a famous antilitter campaign based on the slogan "Don't Mess with Texas." Research showed the typical Texas litterer was 18 to 35 years old, male, a pickup driver, and a lover of sports and country music. He did not respond to authority (Don't litter) or cute owls (Give a hoot; don't pollute). Instead, the campaign aimed to convince this target audience that people like him did not pollute. Ads featured Texan athletes and musicians making the point that Texans don't litter. The campaign was enormously successful: during its first five years, Texas roadside litter decreased 72% and roadside cans 81%.[11] The campaign is still going over 30 years later.

What counts for "evidence" also varies by culture. People control the sample of information they absorb so it supports the conclusions they wish to draw. So someone who wishes to scoff at climate change, for instance, will tend to use sources and see information from a culture that negates the trend. When people do encounter information that counters their beliefs, they tend to ignore it or interpret it differently than other people. People also set the proof standards higher for information that counters their beliefs, both for quality and quantity.[12] In general, people count a scientist as an expert only when that scientist agrees with a position held by most of those who share their cultural values. This remains true even if the scientist got a degree from a major university, is on the faculty at another major university, and is a member of the National Academy of Sciences.[13]

National Cultures   Different native cultures also have different preferences for gaining compliance. In one study, students who were native speakers of American English judged direct statements ("Do this"; "I want you to do this") clearer and more effective than questions ("Could you do this?") or hints ("This is needed"). Students who were native speakers of Korean, in contrast, judged direct statements to be *least* effective. In the Korean culture, the clearer a request is, the ruder and therefore less effective it is.[14]

Choosing a Persuasive Strategy

LO 11-3

If your organization prefers a specific approach, use it. If your organization has no preference, or if you do not know your audience's preference, use the following guidelines to help you choose a strategy. These guidelines work in many cases, but not all.

- Use the **direct request pattern** when
  - The audience will do as you ask without any resistance.
  - You need responses only from people who will find it easy to do as you ask.
  - The audience may not read all of the message.

- Use the **problem-solving pattern** when the audience may resist doing as you ask and you expect logic to be more important than emotion in the decision.

- Use the **sales pattern** when the audience may resist doing as you ask and you expect emotion to be more important than logic in the decision.

WARNING: You always need to consider your audience and situation before choosing your persuasive strategy.

Why Threats and Punishment Are Less Effective Than Persuasion

Sometimes people think they will be able to cause change by threatening or punishing subordinates. Actually, there is a reason for this belief: on a onetime basis, it is frequently true. Most people will not threaten or punish a subordinate unless the behavior is particularly bad. But it is also true of particularly bad behavior that it is out of the ordinary. That is, the next occurrence will be better no matter what the supervisor does. Much research shows that over the long run, persuasion is far more effective than threats or punishment.

Threats are even less effective in trying to persuade people whose salaries you don't pay.

A **threat** is a statement—explicit or implied—that someone will be punished if they do (or don't do) something. Various reasons explain why threats and punishment don't work:

1. **Threats and punishment don't produce permanent change.** Many people obey the speed limit only when a marked police car is in sight.

2. **Threats and punishment won't necessarily produce the action you want.** If you punish **whistleblowers,** you may stop hearing about problems you could be solving—hardly the response you'd want!

3. **Threats and punishment may make people abandon an action—even in situations where it would be appropriate.** Punishing workers for chatting with each other may reduce their overall collaboration.

4. **Threats and punishment produce tension.** People who feel threatened put their energies into ego defense rather than into productive work.

5. **People dislike and avoid anyone who threatens or punishes them.** A supervisor who is disliked will find it harder to enlist cooperation and support on the next issue that arises.

6. **Threats and punishment can provoke counteraggression.** Getting back at a boss can run the gamut from complaints to work slowdowns to sabotage.

Making Persuasive Direct Requests

LO 11-4

When you expect quick agreement, you can generally save your audience's time by presenting the request directly (see Figure 11.3). Also use the direct request pattern for busy people who do not read all the messages they receive and in organizations whose cultures favor putting the request first.

In written direct requests, put the request, the topic of the request, or a question in the subject line.

Subject: Request for Updated Software

My copy of HomeNet does not accept the nicknames for Gmail accounts.

Subject: Status of Account #3548-003

Please get me the following information about account #3548-003.

Subject: Do We Need an Additional Training Session in October?

The two training sessions scheduled for October will each accommodate 20 people. Last month, you said that 57 new staff accountants had been hired. Should we schedule an additional training session in October? Or can the new hires wait until the next regularly scheduled session in February?

Figure 11.4 illustrates a direct request. Note that a direct request does not contain benefits and does not need to overcome objections: it simply asks for what is needed. Direct requests should be clear. Don't make people guess what you want.

Indirect request: Are the updated spreadsheets for our new fall products ready?

Direct request: If the updated spreadsheets for our new fall products are ready, please send them to me.

In more complicated direct requests, anticipate possible responses. Suppose you're asking for information about equipment meeting certain specifications. Explain which

Figure 11.3	How to Organize a Persuasive Direct Request

1. **Consider asking immediately for the information or service you want.** Delay the request if it seems too abrupt or if you have several purposes in the message.

2. **Give your audience all the information they will need to act on your request.** Number your questions or set them off with bullets so readers can check to see that all have been answered.

3. **Ask for the action you want.** Do you want a check? A replacement? A catalog? Answers to your questions? If you need an answer by a certain time, say so. If possible, show why the time limit is necessary.

Figure 11.4   A Direct Request

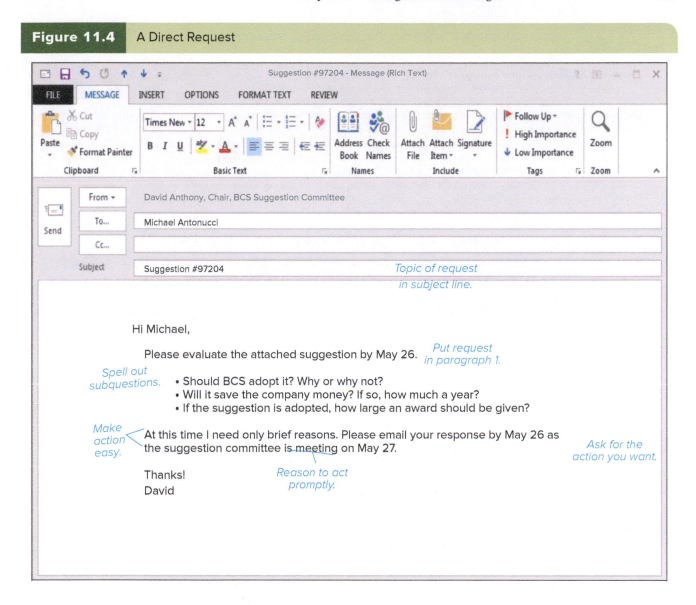

criteria are most important so that the reader can recommend an alternative if no single product meets all your needs. You also may want to tell the reader what your price constraints are and ask whether the item is in stock or must be special-ordered.

Writing Persuasive Problem-Solving Messages

LO 11-5

Generally, you will use an indirect approach and the problem-solving pattern of organization (see Figure 11.5) when you expect resistance from your audience but can show that doing what you want will solve a problem you and your audience share. This pattern allows you to disarm opposition by showing all the reasons in favor of your position before you give your audience a chance to say *no*. As always, you need to analyze your audience and situation before you choose this approach to ensure it is a good one for the occasion.

The message in Figure 11.6 uses the problem-solving pattern of organization. Benefits can be brief in this kind of message since the biggest benefit comes from solving the problem.

Figure 11.5	How to Organize a Persuasive Problem-Solving Message

1. **Catch the audience's interest by mentioning a common ground.** Show that your message will be interesting or beneficial. You may want to catch attention with a negative (which you will go on to show can be solved).

2. **Define the problem you both share (which your request will solve).** Present the problem objectively: Don't assign blame or mention personalities. Be specific about the cost in money, time, lost goodwill, and so on. You have to convince people that *something* has to be done before you can convince them that your solution is the best one.

3. **Explain the solution to the problem.** If you know that the audience will favor another solution, start with that solution and show why it won't work before you present your solution. Present your solution without using the words *I* or *my*. Don't let personalities enter the picture; don't let the audience think they should say *no* just because you've had other requests accepted recently.

4. **Show that any negative elements (cost, time, etc.) are outweighed by the advantages.**

5. **Summarize any additional benefits of the solution.** The main benefit—solving the problem—can be presented briefly since you described the problem in detail. However, if there are any additional benefits, mention them.

6. **Ask for the action you want.** Often your audience will authorize or approve something; other people will implement the action. Give your audience a reason to act promptly, perhaps offering a new benefit. ("By buying now, we can avoid the next quarter's price hikes.")

Subject Lines for Problem-Solving Messages

When you have a reluctant audience, putting the request in the subject line just gets a quick *no* before you've had a chance to give all your arguments. One option is to use a neutral subject line. In the following example, the first is the most neutral. The remaining two increasingly reveal the writer's preference.

> Neutral subject line: A Proposal to Change the Formula for Calculating Retirees' Benefits
>
> Subject line with implied preference: Arguments for Expanding the Marysville Plant
>
> Subject line with explicit preference: Why Cassano's Should Close Its West Side Store

Another option is to use common ground or a benefit—something that shows the audience that this message will help them.

> Subject: Reducing Energy Costs in the Louisville Office
>
> Energy costs in our Louisville office have risen 12% in the last three years, even though the cost of gas has remained constant and the cost of electricity has risen only 5%.

Although your first paragraph may be negative in a problem-solving message, your subject line should be neutral or positive.

Developing a Common Ground

A common ground avoids the me-against-you of some persuasive situations and suggests that both you and your audience have a mutual interest in solving the problems you face. To find a common ground, analyze the audience; understand their biases, objections, and needs; and identify with them to find common goals. This analysis should not be carried out in a cold, manipulative way; it should, rather, be based on a respect for and sensitivity to the audience's position.

Audiences are highly sensitive to manipulation. No matter how much you disagree with your audience members, respect their intelligence. Try to understand why they believe or do something and why they may object to your position. If you can understand your audiences' initial positions, you'll be more effective—and you won't alienate your audience by talking down to them.

Figure 11.6   A Problem-Solving Persuasive Message

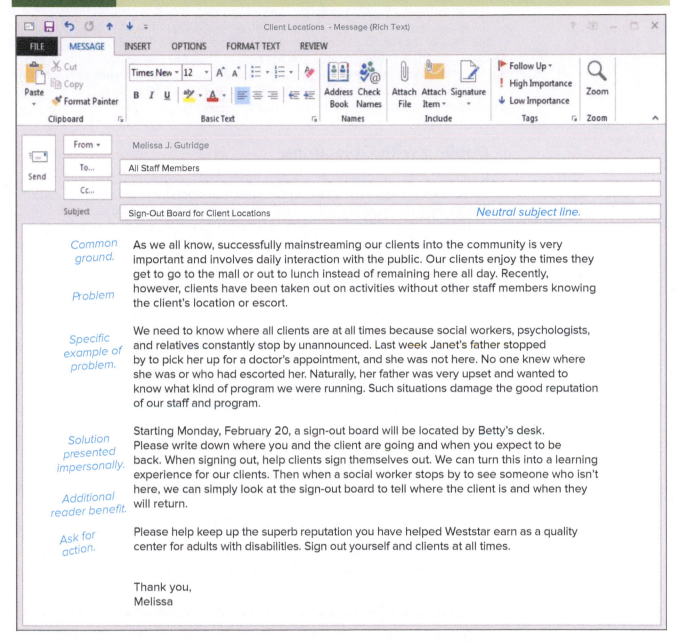

Subject: Sign-Out Board for Client Locations   *Neutral subject line.*

Common ground.

As we all know, successfully mainstreaming our clients into the community is very important and involves daily interaction with the public. Our clients enjoy the times they get to go to the mall or out to lunch instead of remaining here all day. Recently, however, clients have been taken out on activities without other staff members knowing the client's location or escort.

Problem

Specific example of problem.

We need to know where all clients are at all times because social workers, psychologists, and relatives constantly stop by unannounced. Last week Janet's father stopped by to pick her up for a doctor's appointment, and she was not here. No one knew where she was or who had escorted her. Naturally, her father was very upset and wanted to know what kind of program we were running. Such situations damage the good reputation of our staff and program.

Solution presented impersonally.

Starting Monday, February 20, a sign-out board will be located by Betty's desk. Please write down where you and the client are going and when you expect to be back. When signing out, help clients sign themselves out. We can turn this into a learning experience for our clients. Then when a social worker stops by to see someone who isn't here, we can simply look at the sign-out board to tell where the client is and when they will return.

Additional reader benefit.

Ask for action.

Please help keep up the superb reputation you have helped Weststar earn as a quality center for adults with disabilities. Sign out yourself and clients at all times.

Thank you,
Melissa

The best common grounds are specific. Often a negative—a problem the audience will want to solve—makes a good common ground.

Vague common ground:	We all want this plant to be profitable.
Specific common ground:	We forfeited a possible $1,860,000 in profits last month due to a 17% drop in productivity.

Use audience analysis to evaluate possible common grounds. Suppose you want to install a system to play background music in a factory. To persuade management to pay for the system, a possible common ground would be increasing productivity. However, to persuade the union to pay for the system, you'd need a different common ground. Workers would see increasing productivity as a way to get them to do more work for the same pay. A better common ground would be that the music would make the factory environment more pleasant.

Explaining the Solution

If at all possible, present the solution in terms that show how it will benefit the audience. If the situation is complicated, you may need to provide background information and outline the steps of the solution. Don't present the solution as your solution; don't use *I* or *my*. If another solution is being favored, you will need to show why that solution is not as good.

Develop the positives of your solution. Research has shown that when people attempt to make lists of positives and negatives about a decision, whichever side they focus on first has the greatest impact on their choice.[15]

Dealing with Objections

If you know that your audience will hear other points of view, or if your audience's initial position is negative, you have to deal with the objections to persuade the audience. The stronger the objection is, the earlier in your message you should deal with it.

The best way to deal with an objection is to eliminate it. When hail damaged mail-order apples just before harvest, the orchard owner inserted a note in each crate being shipped:

> Note the hail marks which have caused minor skin blemishes in some of these apples. They are proof of their growth at a high mountain altitude where the sudden chills from hailstorms help firm the flesh, develop the natural sugars, and give these apples their incomparable flavor.

No one asked for a refund; in fact, some customers requested the hail-marked apples the next year.[16]

If an objection is false and is based on misinformation, give the response to the objection without naming the objection. (Repeating the objection gives it extra emphasis.) In some communications, you can present responses with a question/answer format.

When objections already have been voiced, you may want to name the objection so that your audience realizes that you are responding to that specific objection. However, to avoid solidifying the opposition, don't attribute the objection to your audience. Instead, use a less personal attribution: "Some people wonder . . ."; "Some citizens are afraid that . . . ."

If real objections remain, try one or more of the following strategies to counter objections:

1. Specify how much time or money is required—it may not be as much as the audience fears.

   Distributing flyers to each house or apartment in your neighborhood will probably take two afternoons.

2. Put the time or money in the context of the benefits they bring.

   The additional $252,500 will (1) allow the Essex Shelter to remain open 24 rather than 16 hours a day, (2) pay for three social workers to help men find work and homes, and (3) keep the Neighborhood Bank open so that men don't have to cash Social Security checks in bars and so they can save for the $800 deposit they need to rent an apartment.

3. Show that money spent now will save money in the long run.

   By buying a $1,000 safety product, we can avoid $5,000 in OSHA fines.

4. Show that doing as you ask will benefit some group or cause the audience supports, even though the action may not help the audience directly. This is the strategy used in fund-raising letters.

   By being a Big Brother or a Big Sister, you'll give a child the adult attention they need to become a well-adjusted, productive adult.

5. Show the audience that the sacrifice is necessary to achieve a larger, more important goal to which they are committed.

   These changes will mean more work for all of us. But we've got to cut our costs 25% to keep the plant open and to keep our jobs.

6. Show that the advantages as a group outnumber or outweigh the disadvantages as a group.

   None of the locations is perfect. But the Backbay location gives us the most advantages and the fewest disadvantages.

Use the following steps when you face major objections:

1. **Find out why your audience members resist what you want them to do.** Sit down one-on-one with people and listen. Don't try to persuade them; just try to understand.

2. **Try to find a win–win solution.** People will be much more readily persuaded if they see benefits for themselves. Sometimes your original proposal may have benefits that the audience had not thought of, and explaining the benefits will help. Sometimes you'll need to modify your original proposal to find a solution that solves the real problem and meets everyone's needs.

3. **Let your audience save face.** Don't ask people to admit that they have been wrong. If possible, admit that the behavior may have been appropriate in the past. Whether you can do that or not, always show how changed circumstances or new data call for new action.

4. **Ask for something small.** When you face great resistance, you won't get everything at once. Ask for a month's trial. Ask for one step that will move toward your larger goal. For example, if your ultimate goal is to eliminate prejudice in your organization, a step toward that goal might be to convince managers to make a special effort for one month to recognize the contributions of women or members of minority groups in group meetings.

5. **Present your arguments from your audience's point of view.** Offer benefits that help the audience, not just you. Take special care to avoid words that attack or belittle your audience. Present yourself as someone helping your audience members achieve their goals, not someone criticizing or giving orders from above.

Organizational changes work best when the audience buys into the solution. And that happens most easily when they find it themselves. Management can encourage employees to identify problems and possible solutions. If that is not possible because of time, sensitive information, or organizational cultural constraints, a good second alternative is to fully explain to employees how the decision for organizational change was made, the reasons behind the change, what alternatives were considered, and why they were rejected. A study of more than 100 employers found that workers who received such explanations were more than twice as likely to support the decision as those workers who did not.[17]

Offering a Reason for the Audience to Act Promptly

The longer people delay, the less likely they are to carry through with the action they had decided to take. In addition, you want a fast response so you can go ahead with your own plans.

Request action by a specific date. Try to give people at least a week or two: they have other things to do besides respond to your requests. Set deadlines in the middle of the month, if possible. If you say, "Please return this by March 1," people will think, "I don't need to do this until March." Ask for the response by February 28 instead. Similarly, a deadline of 5 p.m. Friday will frequently be seen as Monday morning. If such a shift causes you problems, if you were going to work over the weekend, set a Thursday deadline. If you can use a response even after the deadline, say so. Otherwise, people who can't make the deadline may not respond.

Your audience may ignore deadlines that seem arbitrary. Reveal why you need a quick response:

■ **Show that the time limit is real.** Perhaps you need information quickly to use it in a report that has a due date. Perhaps a decision must be made by a certain date to catch the start of the school year, the holiday season, or an election campaign. Perhaps you need to be ready for a visit from out-of-town or international colleagues.

■ **Show that acting now will save time or money.** If business is slow and your industry isn't doing well, then your company needs to act now (to economize, to better serve customers) in order to be competitive. If business is booming and everyone is making a profit, then your company needs to act now to get its fair share of the available profits.

■ **Show the cost of delaying action.** Will labor or material costs be higher in the future? Will delay mean more money spent on repairing something that will still need to be replaced?

Building Emotional Appeal

Emotional appeal helps make people care. Storytelling, audience focus, and psychological description are effective ways of building emotional appeal.

Storytelling   Even when you need to provide statistics or numbers to convince the careful reader that your anecdote is a representative example, telling a story first makes your message more persuasive. In *Made to Stick*, Chip and Dan Heath report on research supporting the value of stories. After completing a survey and receiving cash for their participation, participants received an envelope with a letter requesting they donate to Save the Children. Researchers tested two letters: one was full of grim statistics about starving people in African countries. The other letter told the story of seven-year-old Rokia. Participants receiving the Rokia letter gave more than twice as much money as those receiving the statistics letter. A third group received a letter with both sets of information: the story and the statistics. This group gave a little more than the statistics group but far less than the group that had the story alone. The researchers theorized that the statistics put people in an analytical frame of mind, which canceled the emotional effect of the story.[18]

Audience Focus   As with other appeals, the *emotional appeal* should focus on the audience. To customers who had fallen behind with their payments, one credit card company sent not the expected stern collection notice but a hand-addressed, hand-signed greeting card. The front of the card pictured a stream running through a forest. The text inside noted that sometimes life takes unexpected turns and asked people to call the company to find a collaborative solution. When people called the 800 number, they got credit counseling and help in creating a payment plan. Instead of having to write off bad debts, the company received payments—and created goodwill.[19]

Sometimes emotional appeals go too far and alienate audiences. Germany's Federal Constitutional Court ruled that a PETA ad campaign was an offense against human dignity and not protected by freedom of speech laws. The campaign compared factory farms and animal slaughterhouses to Jewish concentration camps and the Holocaust.[20]

Psychological Descriptions   Sense impressions—what the reader sees, hears, smells, tastes, feels—evoke a strong emotional response. **Psychological description** means creating a scenario rich with sense impressions so readers can picture themselves using your product or service and enjoying its benefits. Restaurant menus are frequently good examples.

You also can use psychological description to describe the problem your product, service, or solution will ease. Psychological description works best early in the message to catch readers' attention.

> Because our smokers take their breaks on the front patio, clients visiting our office frequently pass through a haze of acrid smoke—as well as through a group of employees who are obviously not working.

Tone in Persuasive Messages

The best phrasing for tone depends on your relationship to your audience. When you ask for action from people who report directly to you, polite orders ("Please get me the Ervin file") and questions ("Do we have the third-quarter numbers yet?") will work. When you need action from coworkers, superiors, or people outside the organization, you need to be more polite. See Chapter 2 for a discussion of tone and politeness.

How you ask for action affects whether you build or destroy positive relationships with other employees, customers, and suppliers. Avoiding messages that sound parental or preachy is often a matter of tone. Adding "Please" is a nice touch. Tone also will be better when you give reasons for your request or reasons to act promptly.

Parental:	Everyone is expected to comply with these regulations. I'm sure you can see that they are commonsense rules needed for our business.
Better:	Even on casual days, visitors expect us to be professional. So please leave the gym clothes at home!

Writing to superiors is trickier. You may want to tone down your request by using subjunctive verbs and explicit disclaimers that show you aren't taking a *yes* for granted.

Arrogant:	Based on this evidence, I expect you to give me a new computer.
Better:	If department funds permit, I would like a new computer.

Passive verbs and jargon sound stuffy. Use active imperatives—perhaps with "Please" to create a friendlier tone.

Stuffy:	It is requested that you approve the above-mentioned action.
Better:	Please authorize us to create a new subscription letter.

It can be particularly tricky to control tone in email messages, which tend to sound less friendly than paper documents or conversations. For important requests, compose your message off-line and revise it carefully before you send it. Major requests that require great effort or changes in values, culture, or lifestyles should not be made in email messages.

Performance Reviews and Letters of Recommendation

LO 11-6

Performance reviews and letters of recommendation are two important kinds of persuasive messages.

Performance Reviews

Good supervisors give their employees regular feedback on their performances. The feedback may range from a brief "Good job!" to a hefty bonus.

Companies are recognizing the need to lavish more praise on their workers, especially younger ones. Lands' End and Bank of America hired consultants to teach their supervisors how to compliment workers. Computer-security software maker Symantec has software that allows employees to nominate colleagues for good-work rewards ranging from $25 for everyday good work to $1,000 for outstanding project work.[21] Such companies see the praise as a way to maintain work quality and keep good workers.

Companies also are recognizing the need for more frequent feedback, again especially for younger workers, who are used to instant feedback on Facebook and Twitter. Some companies, including Facebook, have their own social networks where employees seek and give continual feedback—after meetings, presentations, or projects. Other companies are turning to peer reviews, rather than manager reviews, for performance feedback. This system is particularly valuable in offices where employees switch teams frequently and no one leader has insight into all an employee's efforts.[22]

Performance review documents are more formal ways by which supervisors evaluate the performance of their subordinates. In most organizations, employees have access to their reviews; sometimes they must sign the document to show that they've read it. The superior normally meets with the subordinate to discuss the review.

Reviews need to both protect the organization and motivate the employee. Sometimes these two purposes conflict. Most of us will see a candid review as negative; we need praise and reassurance to believe that we're valued and can do better. But the praise that motivates someone to improve can come back to haunt the company if the person does not eventually do acceptable work. An organization is in trouble if it tries to fire someone whose evaluations never mention mistakes.

Problems with Performance Reviews

Problems with Performance Reviews   Performance reviews have been getting a tarnished reputation lately. Academic studies have shown they have no effect on the performance of the majority of employees.[23] Employees themselves may not want to be honest with their supervisor about their need for improvement or training. A supervisor who praises an employee may need to reward that person. On the other hand, a supervisor who criticizes a poor performance may then need to explain why this person wasn't managed more effectively.

Critics also complain about vague criteria and feedback, or stock phrases. They note that "not a team player" is being used to eliminate the need to give high achievers well-deserved promotions. Even widely touted techniques such as 360-degree feedback (anonymous input from supervisors, peers, and subordinates) have their critics. Some companies are suspending this form of review because of conflicting input with vague support.[24]

Another type of performance review now gathering criticism is the forced, or stack, ranking, a technique somewhat like grading on a curve. With forced rankings, most employees receive mediocre reviews. Only a small number of employees receive excellent, or in some cases even good, reviews, and some employees must receive poor reviews. Some companies go so far as to fire the bottom 10% of employees annually. Critics says this type of performance review instills behaviors that are highly detrimental to the good of the company: managers may deliberately hire weak performers so as not to have to dismiss team members and employees compete against each other instead of other companies. In some instances, mediocre workers may strive to undercut top employees.[25]

Preparing for Your Own Performance Reviews

Preparing for Your Own Performance Reviews   As a subordinate, you should prepare for the review interview by listing your achievements and goals.

- What have you accomplished during the review period?

- What evidence of your accomplishments will you need?

- Where do you want to be in a year or five years?

- What training and experience do you need to do your job most effectively and to reach your goals?

If you need training, advice, or support from the organization to advance, the review interview is a good time to ask for this help. As you prepare, choose the persuasive strategy that will best present your work.

Writing Performance Reviews Performance reviews for good employees are usually easy to write: Most supervisors enjoy giving their employees well-deserved praise. Even in these reviews, however, it is important that specifics about the good work be included to help good employees continue to shine and also to receive their well-deserved raises and promotions.

When you are writing performance reviews for employees who need to do better, you will need to document areas for improvement and avoid labels (*wrong, bad*) and inferences. Instead, cite specific observations that describe behavior.

Inference:	Sam is an alcoholic.
Vague observation:	Sam calls in sick a lot. Subordinates complain about his behavior.
Specific observation:	Sam called in sick a total of 12 days in the last two months. After a business lunch with a customer last week, Sam was walking unsteadily. Two of his subordinates have said that they would prefer not to make sales trips with him because they find his behavior embarrassing.

Sam might be an alcoholic. He might also be having a reaction to a physician-prescribed drug, or he might be showing symptoms of a physical illness other than alcoholism. A supervisor who jumps to conclusions creates ill will, closes the door to solving the problem, and may provide grounds for legal action against the organization.

Be specific in a review.

Too vague:	Sue does not manage her time as well as she could.
Specific:	Sue's first three weekly sales reports have been three, two, and four days late, respectively; the last weekly sales report for the month is not yet in.

Without specifics, Sue won't know that her boss objects to late reports. She may think that she is being criticized for spending too much time on sales calls or for not working 80 hours a week. Without specifics, she might change the wrong things in a futile effort to please her boss.

Reviews are more useful to subordinates if they make clear which areas are most important and contain specific recommendations for improvement. No one can improve 17 weaknesses at once. Which two should the employee work on this month? Is getting in reports on time more important than increasing sales?

Phrase goals in specific, concrete terms. The subordinate may think that "considerable progress toward completing" a report may mean that the project should be 15% finished. The boss may think that "considerable progress" means 50% or 85% of the total work.

Sometimes a performance review reflects mostly the month or week right before the review, even though it is supposed to cover six months or a year. Many managers record specific observations of subordinates' behavior two or three times a month. These notes jog the memory so that the review doesn't focus unduly on recent behavior.

A recent trend in performance reviews is attempting to make them objective. Instead of being subjectively evaluated on intangible qualities such as "works well with others," employees are monitored on how well they meet quantifiable goals. Nurses might be ranked on items such as low infection rates and high patient-satisfaction scores. Technical support personnel might be ranked on number of projects completed on time and customer-satisfaction scores.[26] If you will be evaluated by the numbers, try to have a say in setting your goals so you are not judged on items to which you only indirectly contribute. Make sure your goals stay updated so you are not judged on goals that are no longer a priority for your position or your efforts on new goals are not being measured.

Figure 11.7 shows a performance review for a member of a collaborative business communication student group.

Figure 11.7   A Performance Review for a Student Group Member

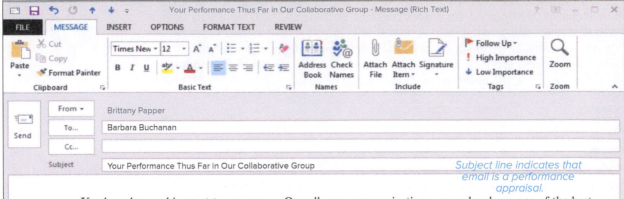

Subject line indicates that email is a performance appraisal.

Overall evaluation. You have been a big asset to our group. Overall, our communications group has been one of the best groups I have ever worked with, and I think that only minor improvements are needed to make our group even better.

These headings would need to be changed in a negative performance appraisal.

Strengths

Specific observations provide dates, details of performance. You demonstrated flexibility and compatibility at our last meeting before we turned in our proposal on February 9 by offering to type the proposal since I had to study for an exam in one of my other classes. I really appreciated this because I did not have the time to do it. I will definitely remember this if you are ever too busy with your other classes and cannot type the final report.

Another positive critical incident occurred February 2. We had discussed researching the topic of sexual discrimination in hiring and promotion at Midstate Insurance. As we read more about what we had to do, we became uneasy about reporting the information from our source who works at Midstate. I called you later that evening to talk about changing our topic to a less personal one. You were very understanding and said that you agreed that the original topic was a touchy one. You offered suggestions for other topics and had a positive attitude about the adjustment. Your suggestions ended my worries and made me realize that you are a positive and supportive person.

Other strengths. Your ideas are a strength that you definitely contribute to our group. You're good at brainstorming ideas, yet you're willing to go with whatever the group decides. That's a nice combination of creativity and flexibility.

Areas for Improvement

Two minor improvements could make you an even better member.

Specific recommendations for improvement. The first improvement is to be more punctual to meetings. On February 2 and February 5 you were about 10 minutes late. This makes the meetings last longer. Your ideas are valuable to the group, and the sooner you arrive the sooner we can share in your suggestions.

Positive cast to suggestion.

Specific behavior to be changed. The second suggestion is one we all need to work on. We need to keep our meetings positive and productive. I think that our negative attitudes were worst at our group meeting February 3. We spent about half an hour complaining about all the work we had to do and about our busy schedules in other classes. In the future if this happens, maybe you could offer some positive things about the assignment to get the group motivated again.

Overall Compatibility

Positive, forward-looking ending. I feel that this group has gotten along very well together. You have been very flexible in finding times to meet and have always been willing to do your share of the work. I have never had this kind of luck with a group in the past, and you have been a welcome breath of fresh air. I don't hate doing group projects any more!

Letters of Recommendation

You may write letters of recommendation when you want to recommend someone for an award or for a job. Letters of recommendation must be specific. General positives that are not backed up with specific examples and evidence are seen as weak recommendations. Letters of recommendation that focus on minor points also suggest that the person is weak.

Letters of recommendation frequently follow a standard organization:

- Either in the first or the last paragraph, summarize your overall evaluation of the person.

- Early in the letter, perhaps in the first paragraph, show how well and how long you've known the person.

- In the middle of the letter, offer specific details about the person's performance.

- At the end of the letter, indicate whether you would be willing to rehire the person and then repeat your overall evaluation.

Figure A.1 in Appendix A shows a sample letter of recommendation.

Although experts are divided on whether you should include negatives, the trend is moving away from doing so. Negatives can create legal liabilities, and many readers feel that any negative weakens the letter. Other people feel that presenting but not emphasizing honest negatives makes the letter more convincing. In either case, you must ensure that your recommendation is honest and accurate.

In many discourse communities, the words "Call me if you need more information" in a letter of recommendation mean "I have negative information that I am unwilling to put on paper. Call me and I'll tell you what I really think."

In an effort to protect themselves against lawsuits, some companies state only how long they employed someone and the position that person held. Such bare-bones letters have themselves been the target of lawsuits when employers did not reveal relevant negatives.

Sales and Fund-Raising Messages

LO 11-7

Sales and fund-raising messages are a special category of persuasive messages. They are known as **direct marketing** because they ask for an order, inquiry, or contribution directly from the audience. Direct marketing includes printed (direct mail), verbal (telemarketing), and electronic (emails, social media, websites, infomercials) channels.

This section focuses on two common channels of direct marketing: sales and fund-raising letters. Large organizations hire professionals to write their direct marketing materials. If you own your own business, you can save money by doing your firm's own direct marketing. If you are active in a local group that needs to raise money, writing the fund-raising letter yourself is likely to be the only way your group can afford to use direct mail. If you can write an equally effective email message, you can significantly cut the costs of a marketing campaign or supplement the success of your direct mail with direct email.

The principles in this chapter will help you write solid, serviceable letters and emails that will build your business and help fund your group.

Sales, fund-raising, and promotional messages have multiple purposes:

Primary purpose

- To have the reader act (order the product, send a donation).

Secondary purpose

- To build a good image of the writer's organization (to strengthen the commitment of readers who act and make readers who do not act more likely to respond positively next time).

Figure 11.8	How to Organize a Sales or Fund-Raising Message

1. Open by catching the audience's attention.

2. In the body, provide reasons and details.

3. End by telling the audience what to do and providing a reason to act promptly.

Organizing a Sales or Fund-Raising Message

Use the sales persuasion pattern to organize your message (see Figure 11.8).

Opener   The opener of your message gives you a chance to motivate your audience to read the rest of the message.

A good opener will make readers want to read the message and provide a reasonable transition to the body of the message. A very successful subscription letter for *Psychology Today* started out,

> Do you still close the bathroom door when there's no one in the house?

The question was both intriguing in itself and a good transition into the content of *Psychology Today*: practical psychology applied to the quirks and questions we come across in everyday life.

It's essential that the opener not only get attention, but also be something that can be linked logically to the body of the message. A sales letter started,

> Can You Use $50 This Week?

Certainly that gets attention. But the letter only offered the reader the chance to save $50 on a product. Readers may feel disappointed or even cheated when they learn that instead of getting $50, they have to spend money to save $50.

To brainstorm possible openers, use the four basic modes: questions, narration, startling statements, and quotations.

1. Questions

> Dear Subscriber,
>
> **Are you nuts?** Your subscription to *PC Gamer* is about to expire!
>
> No reviews. No strategies. No tips.
>
> No *PC Gamer*. Are you willing to suffer the consequences?

This letter urging the reader to renew *PC Gamer* is written under a large banner question: Do you want to get eaten alive? The letter goes on to remind its audience of the magazine's gaming reviews, early previews, exclusive demo discs, and "awesome array of new cheats for the latest games"—all hot buttons for computer gaming fans.

Good questions are interesting enough that the audience want the answers, so they read the letter.

> Poor question: Do you want to make extra money?
>
> Better question: How much *extra* money do you want to make next year?

A series of questions can be an effective opener. Answer the questions in the body of the letter.

2. Narration, stories, anecdotes

> Dear Reader:
>
> She hoisted herself up noiselessly so as not to disturb the rattlesnakes snoozing there in the sun.
>
> To her left, the high desert of New Mexico. Indian country. To her right, the rock carvings she had photographed the day before. Stick people. Primitive animals.

Up ahead, three sandstone slabs stood stacked against the face of the cliff. In their shadow, another carving. A spiral consisting of rings. Curious, the young woman drew closer. Instinctively, she glanced at her watch. It was almost noon. Then just at that moment, a most unusual thing happened.

Suddenly, as if out of nowhere, an eerie dagger of light appeared to stab at the topmost ring of the spiral. It next began to plunge downward—shimmering, laser-like.

It pierced the eighth ring. The seventh. The sixth. It punctured the innermost and last. Then just as suddenly as it had appeared, the dagger of light was gone. The young woman glanced at her watch again. Exactly twelve minutes had elapsed.

Coincidence? Accident? Fluke? No. What she may have stumbled across that midsummer morning three years ago is an ancient solar calendar. . . .

This subscription letter for *Science 84* argues that it reports interesting and significant discoveries in all fields of science—all in far more detail than do other media. The opener both builds suspense so that the reader reads the subscription letter and suggests that the magazine will be as interesting as the letter and as easy to read.

3. Startling statements

I don't drink the water I use to flush.

This startling statement, accompanied by a picture of a toilet, was the catchphrase used by the French bottled water industry. It appeared in response to a campaign by public water companies touting tap water as equal to bottled water.[27] Variations of this mode include special opportunities, twists, and challenges.

4. Quotations

"If you are ever buried under a ton of rubble, trapped where no one can find you, or caught in the aftermath of a storm, I promise to sniff you out. I promise to go about my work with a wagging tail and a hero's heart. . . . I promise never to give up."[28]

This "quotation," printed with a photo of a dog paw raised in position to take an oath, is part of a fund-raising ad for the National Disaster Search Dog Foundation. The position of the paw, as well as the title of the ad, "The Pledge," helps support the quotation.

Body   The body of the message provides the logical and emotional links that move the audience from a first flicker of interest to the action that is wanted. A good body answers the audience's questions, overcomes their objections, and involves them emotionally.

All this takes space. One industry truism is "The more you tell, the more you sell." Tests show that longer letters bring in more new customers or new donors than do shorter letters.

Can short letters work? Yes, when you're writing to existing customers or when the mailing is supported by other media. Email direct mail is also short—generally just one screen. The Direct Marketing Association says a postcard is the mailing most likely to be read.[29] The shortest message on record may be the two-word postcard that a fishing lake resort sent its customers: "They're biting!"

National Disaster Search Dog Foundation used an interesting "quotation" to capture attention and raise money.

ZUMA Press, Inc./Alamy Stock Photo

Content for the body of the message can include

- Information the audience will find useful even if they do not buy or give.

- Stories about how the product was developed or what the organization has done.

- Stories about people who have used the product or who need the organization's help.

- Word pictures of people enjoying the benefits offered.

Be careful not to give too much information, though. New research shows that giving people too much information hinders sales. Customers want sales information that provides "decision simplicity": They want easy access to trustworthy information and tools for quick sorting and easy weighing of options so they feel confident about their choice. Consider the complex and expensive decision of buying diamonds. For years, De Beers has successfully used the "4Cs" (cut, color, clarity, and carat) to help consumers feel confident they have made a good selection.[30]

Because consumers are more likely to choose or favor the familiar, linking your sales message to the things people do or use every day is a good way to increase your message's perceived importance. For example, adults tasting the same peanut butter from three different jars preferred the spread from the jar with a name-brand label.[31] Of course, you must do a good job of audience analysis upfront.

Costs are generally mentioned near the end of the body and are connected to specific benefits. Sometimes costs are broken down to monthly, weekly, or daily amounts: "For less than the cost of a cup of coffee a day, you can help see that Erena is no longer hungry."

Action Close   The action close in the message must do four things:

1. **Tell the audience what to do.** Specify the action you want. Avoid *if* ("If you'd like to try . . .") and *why not* ("Why not send in a check?"). They lack positive emphasis and encourage your audience to say *no*.

2. **Make the action sound easy.** "Fill in the information on the reply card and mail it today." If you provide an envelope and pay postage, say so.

3. **Offer a reason for acting promptly.** People who think they are convinced but wait to act are less likely to buy or contribute. Reasons for acting promptly are easy to identify when a product is seasonal or there is a genuine limit on the offer—time limit, price rise scheduled, limited supply, and so on. Sometimes you can offer a premium or a discount if your audience acts quickly. When these conditions do not exist, remind readers that the sooner they get the product, the sooner they can benefit from it; the sooner they contribute funds, the sooner their dollars can go to work to solve the problem.

4. **End with a positive picture** of the audience enjoying the product (in a sales message) or of the audience's money working to solve the problem (in a fund-raising message). The last sentence should never be a selfish request for money.

The action close also can remind people of central selling points and mention when the customer will get the product.

Using a P.S.   In a direct-mail letter or email, the postscript, or P.S., occupies a position of emphasis by being the final part of the message. Direct mail often uses a deliberate P.S. after the signature block. It may restate the central selling point or some other point the letter makes, preferably in different words so that it won't sound repetitive when the reader reads the letter through from start to finish.

Here are four of the many kinds of effective postscripts.

Reason to act promptly, from a sales letter for Frank Lews Alamo Fruit:

P.S. Once I finish the limited harvest, that's it! I do not store any SpringSweet Onions for late orders. I will ship all orders on a first-come, first-served basis and when they are gone, they are gone. Drop your order in the mail today . . . or give me a call toll free at 800-531-7470! (In Texas: 800-292-5437)

Description of a premium the reader receives for giving to the Sierra Club:

P.S. And . . . we'll be pleased to send you—as a new member—the exquisite, full-color Sierra Club Wilderness Calendar. It's our gift . . . absolutely FREE to you . . . to show our thanks for your membership at this critical time.

Reference to another part of the package in a sales letter for a model car:

P.S. Photographs may be better than words, but they still don't do justice to this model. Please keep in mind as you review the enclosed brochure that your SSJ will look even better when you can see it firsthand in your own home.

Restatement of central selling point in a fund-raising letter for CARE:

P.S. Millions of hungry schoolchildren will be depending on CARE this fall. Your gift today will ensure that we will be there—that CARE won't let them down.

Strategy in Sales Messages and Fund-Raising Appeals

In both sales messages and fund-raising appeals, the basic strategy is to help your audience see themselves using your products/services or participating in the goals of your charity. Too often, communicators stress the new features of their gadgets, rather than picturing the audience using it, or they focus on statistics about their cause, rather than stories about people helping that cause.

Sales Messages The basic strategy in sales messages is satisfying a need. Your message must remind people of the need your product meets, prove that the product will satisfy that need, show why your product is better than similar products, and make people *want* to have the product. For years, V8 vegetable juice used the advertising slogan "Wow, I could've had a V8!" But in reality, most people prefer fruit juices. Then V8's makers realized that what they did better than those other juices was giving people a convenient way to get vegetable nutrients. Once the ad campaign focused on that fact, revenues quadrupled.[32]

Various techniques will help you build your case. Use psychological description to show people how the product will help them. Details about how the product is made can carry the message of quality. Testimonials from other buyers can help persuade people that the product works. In fact, sales trainer and best-seller business author Jeffrey Gitomer cites customer testimonials as one of the best ways to overcome price resistance.[33]

Generally, the price is not mentioned until the last fourth of the message, after the content makes the audience *want* the product. People tend to make relative choices. If you offer various related choices, such as donation amounts or service packages, they will generally choose an option for a middle amount. Similarly, a high-priced dish on a menu tends to help revenue because although most people won't buy it, they will buy the second-most expensive dish.[34]

You can make the price more palatable with the following techniques:

- **Link the price to the benefit the product provides.** "Your piece of history is just $39.95."

- **Link the price to benefits your company offers.** "You can reach our customer service agents 24/7."

- **Show how much the product costs each day, each week, or each month.** "You can have all this for less than one dollar a day." Make sure that the amount seems small and that you've convinced people that they'll use this product sufficiently.

- **Allow customers to charge sales or pay in installments.** Your bookkeeping costs will rise, and some sales may be uncollectible, but the total number of sales will increase.

Fund-Raising Appeals   In a fund-raising appeal, the basic emotional strategy is **vicarious participation.** By donating money, people participate vicariously in work they are not able to do personally. This strategy affects the pronouns you use. Throughout the appeal, use *we* to talk about your group. However, at the end, talk about what *you* the audience will be doing. End positively, with a picture of the audience's dollars helping to solve the problem.

Fund-raising appeals require some extra strategy. To achieve both your primary and secondary purposes, you must give a great deal of information. This information (1) helps to persuade people; (2) gives supporters evidence to use in conversations with others; and (3) gives people who are not yet supporters evidence that may make them see the group as worthwhile, even if they do not give money now.

In your close, in addition to asking for money, suggest other ways people can help: doing volunteer work, scheduling a meeting on the subject, writing letters to Congress or the leaders of other countries, and so on. By suggesting other ways to participate, you not only involve your audience but also avoid one of the traps of fund-raising appeals: sounding as though you are interested in your audience only for the money they can give.

Deciding How Much to Ask For   Most messages to new donors suggest a range of amounts, from $25 or $100 (for employed people) up to perhaps double what you *really* expect to get from a single donor. The **anchoring effect** says that when people consider a specific value for a quantity (like a donation) and then have to come up with their own value for that quantity, their value will be close to the specified value. Thus, contribution letters suggesting higher contributions draw more money than those suggesting lower contributions.[35]

One of the several reasons people give for not contributing is that a gift of $25 or $100 seems too small to matter. It's not. Small gifts are important both in themselves and to establish a habit of giving. The American Heart Association determined that first-time donors responding to direct mail give an average of $21.84 and give $40.62 over a lifetime. But multiplied by the 7.6 million donors who respond to the AHA's mailings, the total giving is large. Also, more than $20 million of the money that the AHA receives from estate settlements after a person's death comes from people who have a relationship as direct-mail donors.[36]

You can increase the size of gifts by using the following techniques:

- **Link the gift to what it will buy.** Tell how much money it costs to buy a brick, a hymnal, or a stained-glass window for a church; a book or journal subscription for a college library; a meal for a hungry child. Linking amounts to specific gifts helps the audience feel involved and often motivates them to give more: instead of saying, "I'll write a check for $25," the person may say, "I'd like to give a ——" and write a check to cover it.

- **Offer a premium for giving.** Public TV and radio stations have used this ploy with great success, offering books, coffee mugs, umbrellas, and tote bags for gifts at a certain level. The best premiums are things that people both want and will use or display, so that the organization will get further publicity when other people see the premium.

- **Ask for a monthly pledge.** People on modest budgets could give $15 or $25 a month; more prosperous people could give $100 a month or more. These repeat gifts not only bring in more money than the donors could give in a single check but also become part of the base of loyal supporters, which is essential to the continued success of any organization that raises funds.

Annual appeals to past donors often use the amount of the last donation as the lowest suggested gift, with other gifts 25%, 50%, or even 100% higher.

Always send a thank-you message to people who respond to your appeal, whatever the size of their gifts. By telling about the group's recent work, a thank-you message can help reinforce donors' commitment to your cause.

Logical Proof in Fund-Raising Messages   The body of a fund-raising message must prove that (1) the problem deserves attention, (2) the problem can be solved or at least alleviated, (3) your organization is helping to solve or alleviate it, (4) private funds are needed, and (5) your organization will use the funds wisely.

1. **The problem deserves attention.** No one can support every cause. Show why your audience should care about solving this problem.

   If your problem is life-threatening, give some statistics: Tell how many people are killed in the U.S. every year by drunken drivers or how many children in the world go to bed hungry every night. Also tell about one individual who is affected.

   If your problem is not life-threatening, show that the problem threatens some goal or principle your audience finds important. For example, a fund-raising letter to boosters of a high school swim team showed that team members' chances of setting records were reduced because timers relied on stopwatches. The letter showed that automatic timing equipment was accurate and produced faster times because the timer's reaction time was no longer included in the time recorded.

2. **The problem can be solved or alleviated.** People will not give money if they see the problem as hopeless—why throw money away? Sometimes you can reason by analogy. Cures have been found for other deadly diseases, so it's reasonable to hope that research can find a cure for cancer. Sometimes you can show that short-term or partial solutions exist. For example, UNICEF shows how simple changes—oral rehydration, immunization, and breastfeeding—could save the lives of millions of children. These solutions don't affect the underlying causes of poverty, but they do keep children alive while we work on long-term solutions.

3. **Your organization is helping to solve or alleviate the problem.** Prove that your organization is effective. Talk specifically about your successes in the past. Your past success helps readers believe that you can accomplish your goals.

   These are some of the specifics that the Charity: Water website gives about its efforts:

   Our Progress So Far: 24,537 water projects funded. 7 million people will get clean water. 24 countries, 25 local partners. Give $30 and you can give one person clean water.[37]

4. **Private funds are needed to accomplish your group's goals.** We all have the tendency to think that taxes, or foundations, or church collections yield enough to pay for medical research or basic human aid. If your group does get some tax or foundation money, show why more money is needed. If the organization helps people who might be expected to pay for the service, show why they cannot pay, or why they cannot pay enough to cover the full cost. If some of the funds have been raised by the people who will benefit, make that clear.

5. **Your organization will use the funds wisely.** Prove that the money goes to the cause, not just to the cost of fund-raising. This point is becoming increasingly important as stories become more common of "charities" that give little money to their mission.

Emotional Appeal in Fund-Raising Messages Emotional appeal is needed to make people pull out their checkbooks. How strong should emotional appeal be? A mild appeal is unlikely to sway anyone who is not already committed, but your audience will feel manipulated by appeals they find too strong and reject them. Audience analysis may help you decide how much emotional appeal to use. If you don't know your audience well, use the strongest emotional appeal *you* feel comfortable with.

Emotional appeal is created by specifics. It is hard to care about, or even to imagine, a million people; it is easier to care about one specific person. Details and quotes help us see that person as real. Sensory details also help people connect to a cause. Covenant House, an organization that takes in homeless youth, does both. It provides vivid pictures both of children arriving at the door and of individuals who have turned their lives around. Covenant House also uses relevant sensory details: a child crawling into bed on a cold night, feeling warm and safe under soft blankets, versus a girl crawling into a cardboard box on the street to try to stay warm on a cold night.[38]

Sample Fund-Raising Letter   The letter from UNICEF (see Figure 11.9) seeks aid for children in less-developed countries. It opens by catching interest and establishing common ground with the concept of keeping promises to children. It stresses the enormity of the problem—"millions of children," "perilous day-to-day existence." It moves on to list specific UNICEF programs and numbers helped—in the millions—for each program. Since this was a letter to someone who had donated before, the close refers to previous support.

Writing Style

Direct mail is the one kind of business writing where elegance and beauty of language matter; in every other kind, elegance is welcome, but efficiency is all that finally counts. Direct mail imitates the word choice and rhythm of conversation. The best sales, fund-raising, and promotional writing is closer to the language of poetry than to that of academia: It shimmers with images; it echoes with sound; it vibrates with energy.

Many of the things that make writing vivid and entertaining *add* words because they add specifics or evoke an emotional response. Individual sentences should flow smoothly. The passage as a whole may be fun to read precisely because of the details and images.

Make Your Writing Interesting   If the style is long-winded and boring, the reader will stop reading. Eliminating wordiness is crucial. Direct mail goes further, breaking some of the rules of grammar. In the following examples, note how sentence fragments and ellipses (spaced dots) are used in parallel structure to move the reader along.

This subscription letter for *Natural History* reads:

Dear Member-elect:

> If you still believe that there are nine planets in our solar system . . . that wine doesn't breathe . . . and that you'd recognize a Neanderthal man on sight if one sat next to you on the bus . . . check your score. There aren't. It does. You wouldn't.

Use Psychological Description   Psychological description means describing your product or service with vivid sensory details. In a sales letter, you can use psychological description to create a scenario so readers can picture themselves using your product or service and enjoying its benefits. You also can use psychological description to describe the problem your product or service will solve.

A *Bon Appétit* subscription letter used psychological description in its opener and in the P.S., creating a frame for the sales letter:

Dear Reader:

> First, fill a pitcher with ice.
> Now pour in a bottle of ordinary red wine, a quarter cup of brandy, and a small bottle of club soda.
> Sweeten to taste with a quarter to half cup of sugar, garnish with slices of apple, lemon, and orange . . .
> . . . then *move your chair to a warm, sunny spot.* You've just made yourself sangria— one of the great glories of Spain, and the perfect thing to sit back with and sip while you consider this invitation . . .
>
>   . . .
>
> P.S. One more thing before you finish your sangria . . .

It's hard to imagine any reader really stopping to follow the recipe before finishing the letter, but the scenario is so vivid that one can imagine the sunshine even on a cold, gray day.

Figure 11.9   Excerpts from a Fund-Raising Letter

Interest-grabbing picture.

Dear Dr. Kienzler,

For more than 65 years, UNICEF has kept a promise to the world's children: no matter who you are, how poor you are, or what danger you are facing, UNICEF will do everything possible to help you survive.

Letter opens with a common ground: keeping promises to children.

As a committed supporter of the U.S. Fund for UNICEF, you know that millions of children face a perilous day-to-day existence, threatened by natural disasters, armed conflicts, malnutrition, exploitation, and disease. In fact, 21,000 children die every day from causes that are <u>totally preventable</u>.

Extent of problem.

As we enter the New Year, I hope you'll join me in <u>making a promise</u> to the world's most vulnerable children by vowing to give them the one thing they need the most: **the chance to survive**.

. . .

Children around the world are <u>counting on your promise</u> and your continued generosity to address the many challenges they confront every day. By sending a tax-deductible gift of $25, $35, $50 – or whatever amount you can afford – you will join with hundreds of thousands of other U.S. Fund for UNICEF supporters to help transport vital medicines and immunizations to prevent disease . . .

Fund-raising letters may use format features such as underlining and ellipses.

Hundreds of thousands of people also are supporting this cause.

. . .

UNICEF's efforts to reach children with basic health care, clean water and sanitation, better nutrition, and protection from exploitation and violence are paying real dividends in terms of young lives saved:

Sentence shows situation is not hopeless.

- **More than six million** children's lives are saved each year through UNICEF's effective, low-cost survival programs.
- Over 75 percent of children in developing countries are now protected with immunizations, saving the lives of an estimated **2.5 million children annually**.
- **Polio is on the verge of being eradicated**.
- Today, 70 percent of all households in developing countries have access to iodized salt, **protecting 85 million newborns** each year from losses in learning ability.
- **Two million children's lives** are saved from diarrheal dehydration due to drinking unclean water through the provision of Oral Rehydration Salts.
- **More children are in school** than ever before.

Bulleted information shows past success, which promises future successes.

Those young lives are <u>living proof</u> that your support for the U.S. Fund for UNCIEF makes a difference.

On behalf of the millions of children whose lives you have so profoundly affected, I extend our best wishes for the upcoming year to you and your loved ones, and I thank you for the generous spirit that is demonstrated in your continued support.

Sincerely,

Caryl M. Stren

Caryl M. Stren
President & CEO

Reference to donor's continued support.

Source: U.S. Fund for UNICEF.

Make Your Letter Sound Like a Letter, Not an Ad   Maintain the image of one person writing to one other person that is the foundation of all letters. Use an informal style with short words and sentences, and even slang.

You also can create a **persona**–the character who allegedly writes the letter–to make the letter interesting and keep people reading. Use the rhythms of speech, vivid images, and conversational words to create the effect that the author is a "character."

The following sales-letter opening creates a persona who fits the product:

Dear Friend:

There's no use trying. I've tried and tried to tell people about my fish. But I wasn't rigged out to be a letter writer, and I can't do it. I can close-haul a sail with the best of them. I know how to pick out the best fish of the catch, I know just which fish will make the tastiest mouthfuls, but I'll never learn the knack of writing a letter that will tell people why my kind of fish—fresh-caught prime-grades, right off the fishing boats with the deep-sea tang still in it—is lots better than the ordinary store kind.

This letter, with its "Aw, shucks, I can't sell" persona, with language designed to make you see an unassuming fisherman ("rigged out," "close-haul"), was written by a professional advertiser.[39]

Face-to-Face Persuasion

When you present your persuasive messages in a spoken, face-to-face format, remember that your interpersonal interactions are an important part of your message. One study of successful retail salespeople identified some techniques you can use when you're speaking persuasively:

- **Use their name.** People respond well when you show that you care enough about them to use their name.

- **Show your interest.** Build goodwill and rapport by asking about, noticing, and remembering details about your audience's history and preferences.

- **Identify mutual interests.** Turn your persuasive pitch into a conversation by inviting stories from your audience and sharing your own in return.

- **Be polite and honest.** Many people react to persuasive messages by being on guard against potential dishonesty. Demonstrate your respect for your audience by backing up your claims with evidence: show them, don't tell them, and invite them to judge for themselves.

- **Give–and seek–information.** Take the pressure off your persuasive message by changing it into an informative message. Build rapport by inviting your audience to share their knowledge with you.[40]

Solving a Sample Problem

Little things add up to big issues, especially where workplace quality of life is at stake.

Problem

First West Insurance's regional office has 300 employees, all working the same 8-to-5 shift. Many of them schedule their lunch break during the noon hour, and that's where the problem started: There was only one microwave in the canteen. People had to wait up to 30 minutes to heat their lunches. As director of human resources, you implemented lunch shifts to break the gridlock. That program failed. People were used to their schedules and resisted the change. In your second attempt, you convinced First West's operations vice president to approve a purchase order for a second microwave oven.

Now there's a new problem: fish. FirstWest recently recruited five new employees. They're from the Philippines, and fish is a prominent part of their diet. Each day at lunchtime, they heat their meals—usually containing fish—and each afternoon, the air-conditioning system in your closed-air building sends the aroma of fish wafting through the whole building.

Other employees have complained bitterly about the "foul odor." You've spoken to the new employees, and while they're embarrassed by the complaints, they see no reason to change. After all, they're just as disgusted by the smell of cooking beef: Why haven't you asked the American employees not to reheat hamburger? And having just purchased a second oven, you know that management won't pay $1,000 for a new microwave with a filter system that will eliminate the odors. You need to solve the microwave problem.

Analysis of the Problem

Use the problem analysis questions in the first chapter to think through the problem.

1. Who is(are) your audience(s)?

   You'll be addressing all the employees at this location. That's a broad audience, but they have certain characteristics in common, at least regarding this topic. They're all on a similar lunch schedule, and many of them use the canteen and the microwaves. They've also responded poorly to a previous attempt to change their lunch habits.

   Many members of your audience won't see this as their problem. They think only the new employees are doing something objectionable. The new employees do not like being singled out.

2. What are your purposes in writing?

   To help eliminate cooking odors. To solve a minor issue before it begins to impact morale and cause ill will directed at new employees.

3. What information must your message include?

   The effects of the present situation. The available options and their costs (in money, and also in time, effort, and responsibility).

4. How can you build support for your position? What reasons or benefits will your audience find convincing?

   Improving the workplace environment—and eliminating a minor but persistent irritation—should improve morale. While expensive solutions exist, this is a matter that can, and should, be solved with cooperative behaviors.

5. What aspects of the total situation may be relevant?

   This issue is a minor one, and it may be difficult to get people to take it seriously. The easy solution—mandating what the new employees can bring for lunch—is discriminatory. For budgetary reasons, company management will not invest in a third (and much more expensive) microwave for the canteen.

Discussion of the Sample Solutions

The solution shown in Figure 11.10 is unacceptable. By formatting the communication as a notice designed to be posted in the canteen, the author invites the audience to publicly embarrass their coworkers: a form of threat. The subject line displays the author's biases in a way that discourages further discussion on the topic and eliminates the possibility of a broader consensus for any solution to the problem. The author uses emotional appeals to place blame on a small segment of the audience, but the lack of logical observations or arguments (and the presence of clip art and emoticons) undermines the author's seriousness. The demand to stop cooking food with strong smells is vague: Does this include pizza? popcorn? The author concludes with a threat, again eliminating the possibility of consensus-based actions. Figures 11.11 and 11.12 will help you compose much more effective direct requests.

The second solution, shown in Figure 11.13, is a more effective persuasive message. The author recognizes that this persuasive situation centers on goodwill and begins with a

Figure 11.10   An Unacceptable Solution to the Sample Problem

ATTENTION!!!!

DON'T BRING DISGUSTING LUNCHES!!

Negative, biased subject line and clip art.

Some of you (you **KNOW!!!** who you are) have been bringing in smelly food and cooking it in the microwave at lunch. We've all smelled the result. It's not fair that everyone has to put up with the smell.

Negative diction.

I'm writing to tell everyone that this is the END. As of today, no one is allowed to cook any food with a strong smell in the canteen microwave ovens.   *Vague diction.*

The microwaves are a privilege and not a right. If you people continue to abuse company property, the microwaves will be removed from the canteen for good. ☹ *Don't use emoticons in serious communications.*

Threatens

Thank you in advance for your cooperation in this matter.

Close does not sound sincere after threat.

Clip art not appropriate for this serious communication.

Clipart Source: Microsoft Inc.

Figure 11.11   Checklist for Direct Requests

☐ If the message is an email, does the subject line indicate the request? Is the subject line specific enough to differentiate this message from others on the same subject?

☐ Does the first paragraph summarize the request or the specific topic of the message?

☐ Does the message give all of the relevant information? Is there enough detail?

☐ Does the message answer questions or overcome objections that readers may have without introducing unnecessary negatives?

☐ Does the closing tell the reader exactly what to do? Does it give a deadline if one exists and a reason for acting promptly?

Figure 11.12   How to Create Originality in a Direct Request

☐ Use lists and create visual impact.

☐ Think about readers and give details that answer their questions, overcome any objections, and make it easier for them to do as you ask.

☐ Add details that show you're thinking about a specific organization and the specific people in that organization.

neutral subject line (as a more directed subject could detract from goodwill). The opening paragraph creates common ground by describing the problem in terms of group experience, rather than by assigning blame. It includes fish odors with pleasant odors (brownies) and suggests that the email's purpose is to propose a consensus-based solution.

The problem is spelled out in detail, balancing the emotional, goodwill-centered problem with rational arguments based on process and cost. The solution is presented

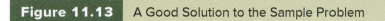

Figure 11.13	A Good Solution to the Sample Problem

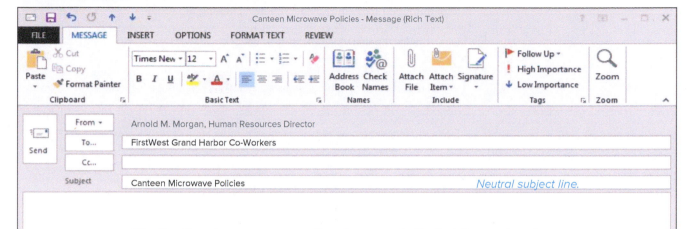

Neutral subject line.

Creates common ground.

We all notice when someone uses the microwaves in the first-floor canteen to reheat strong-smelling food. These odors are distracting—whether they're the scent of burned popcorn, a fish lunch, or fresh-baked brownies—and none of us need any extra distractions in our busy days! Let's work together to "clear the air."

Cause of problem.

How is it that we all smell food cooking in the first-floor canteen? Our building has a closed-air ventilation system: it's good for the environment, and it saves on heating and cooling costs by recirculating air throughout the building. It also circulates any odors in the air. That's why we can smell food from the first-floor canteen down in the basement archives and up in the third-floor conference rooms: we're all sharing the same air.

Long-term solution to problem.

We're all sharing the same microwaves, too. Due to popular demand, we recently purchased a second microwave to relieve crowding at lunchtime. A third microwave—an odor-eliminating, air-filtration microwave—will cost $1,000, plus $20/month for filters. The Employee Council has recommended that we purchase this microwave by instituting a voluntary contribution of 25 cents per microwave use. At approximately 200 uses per day, the Council could collect enough money for the new microwave in about one month. Until then, there are simple things each of us can do to reduce problems with odors.

- **Use containers with lids** when you heat up your food. Not only will this help contain any odors, it will reduce the mess in the microwaves.

Short-term solution to problem.

- **Clean up any mess you make** when you cook. If you cook something with a strong odor—or something that spatters—take a minute when you're done and wipe the oven down with a damp paper towel.

- **Stay with your food** while it's cooking. When food overcooks or burns, it smells more strongly, so watching your food and removing it from the oven before it overcooks is the easiest way to avoid creating a distracting smell.

We work together as a team every day to serve our customers and succeed as an organization. Please take a little time to use the microwaves responsibly, and help us make sure that the only smell in our workplace is success!

Ends on positive note.

as the recommendation of the Employee Council, rather than the administrators, and the cost is broken down into small increments. Until the new microwave arrives, small, easily accommodated changes are recommended. The email ends by linking cooperation with the audience benefit of group participation and identity. The checklists in Figures 11.14 and 11.15 will help you compose effective problem-solving messages.

Figure 11.14	Checklist for Problem-Solving Messages

☐ If the message is an email, does the subject line indicate the writer's purpose or offer a benefit? Does the subject line avoid making the request?

☐ Does the first sentence interest the audience?

☐ Is the problem presented as a joint problem both communicator and audience have an interest in solving, rather than as something the audience is being asked to do for the communicator?

☐ Does the message give all of the relevant information? Is there enough detail?

☐ Does the message overcome objections that the audience may have?

☐ Does the message avoid phrases that sound dictatorial, condescending, or arrogant?

☐ Does the closing tell the audience exactly what to do? Does it give a deadline if one exists and a reason for acting promptly?

Figure 11.15	How to Create Originality in a Problem-Solving Message

☐ Use a good subject line and create common ground.

☐ Provide a clear and convincing description of the problem.

☐ Think about the audience and give details that answer their questions, overcome objections, and make it easier for them to do as you ask.

☐ Add details that show you're thinking about a specific organization and the specific people in that organization.

Summary by Learning Objectives

LO 11-1   Explain the purposes of persuasive messages.

The primary purpose in a persuasive message is to have the audience act or change beliefs. Secondary purposes are to overcome any objections that might prevent or delay action, to build a good image of the communicator and the communicator's organization, to cement a good relationship between the communicator and audience, and to reduce or eliminate future communication on the same subject.

LO 11-2   Analyze a persuasive situation.

Use the questions in Figure 11.1 to analyze persuasive situations.

LO 11-3   Identify basic persuasive strategies.

You always need to consider your audience and situation before choosing your persuasive strategy. In general:

- Use the direct request pattern when the audience will do as you ask without any resistance. Also use the direct request pattern for busy readers in your own organization who do not read all the messages they receive. See Figure 11.3.

- Use the problem-solving pattern when the audience may resist doing what you ask and you expect logic to be more important than emotion in the decision. See Figure 11.5.

- Use the sales pattern when the audience may resist doing as you ask and you expect emotion to be more important than logic in the decision. See Figure 11.8.

LO 11-4 **Produce persuasive direct requests.**

Use the information in Figure 11.3 to write persuasive direct requests.

LO 11-5 **Produce persuasive problem-solving messages.**

- Use the information in Figure 11.5 to write persuasive problem-solving messages.

- Use one or more of the following strategies to counter objections that you cannot eliminate:
  - Specify how much time and/or money is required.
  - Put the time and/or money in the context of the benefits they bring.
  - Show that money spent now will save money in the long run.
  - Show that doing as you ask will benefit some group the audience identifies with or some cause the audience supports.
  - Show the audience that the sacrifice is necessary to achieve a larger, more important goal to which they are committed.
  - Show that the advantages as a group outnumber or outweigh the disadvantages as a group.
  - Turn the disadvantage into an opportunity.

- Threats don't produce permanent change. They won't necessarily produce the action you want, they may make people abandon an action entirely (even in situations where abandoning would not be appropriate), and they produce tension. People dislike and avoid anyone who threatens them. Threats can provoke counteraggression.

- To encourage people to act promptly, set a deadline. Show that the time limit is real, that acting now will save time or money, or that delaying action will cost more.

- Build emotional appeal with stories and psychological description.

LO 11-6 **Produce performance reviews and letters of recommendation.**

When writing performance reviews:

- Cite specific observations that describe behavior.
- Use specifics when you note areas for improvement and goals.
- Avoid labels (*wrong, bad*) and inferences.

When writing letters of recommendation:

- Either in the first or the last paragraph, summarize your overall evaluation of the person.
- Early in the letter, perhaps in the first paragraph, show how well and how long you've known the person.
- In the middle of the letter, offer specific details about the person's performance.
- At the end of the letter, indicate whether you would be willing to rehire the person and then repeat your overall evaluation.

LO 11-7 **Produce sales and fund-raising messages.**

- A good opener makes readers want to read persuasion messages and provides a reasonable transition to the body of the message. Four modes for openers are questions, narration, startling statements, and quotations. A good body answers the audience's questions, overcomes their objections, and involves them emotionally. A good action close tells people what to do, makes the action sound easy, gives them a reason for acting promptly, and ends with a benefit or a picture of their contribution helping to solve the problem.

- In a fund-raising appeal, the basic strategy is vicarious participation. By donating money, people participate vicariously in work they are not able to do personally.

- The primary purpose in a fund-raising appeal is to get money. An important secondary purpose is to build support for the cause so that people who are not persuaded to give will still have favorable attitudes toward the group and will be sympathetic when they hear about it again.

Exercises and Cases

11.1 Reviewing the Chapter

1. What are the purposes of persuasive messages? (LO 11-1)
2. What are the five questions you should answer when analyzing persuasive situations? Which question do you think is the most important? Why? (LO 11-2)
3. What are three basic persuasive strategies? In what kinds of situations is each preferred? (LO 11-3)
4. Why aren't threats effective persuasion tools? (LO 11-3)
5. How do you start the body of persuasive direct requests? Why? (LO 11-4)
6. How do you organize persuasive problem-solving messages? (LO 11-5)
7. How do you develop a common ground with your audience? (LO 11-5)

8. What are 10 ways to deal with objections? (LO 11-4 and LO 11-5)

9. What are ways to build emotional appeal? (LO 11-4 and LO 11-5)

10. How should you prepare for a performance review? (LO 11-6)

11. How should you organize a letter of recommendation? (LO 11-6)

12. What are four good beginnings for sales and fund-raising messages? (LO 11-7)

13. What are ways to de-emphasize costs or donation requests? (LO 11-7)

14. What kind of logical proof is used in fund-raising messages? (LO 11-7)

11.2   Reviewing Grammar

Persuasion uses lots of pronouns. Correct the sentences in Exercise B.4, Appendix B, to practice making pronouns agree with their nouns, as well as practicing subject–verb agreement.

11.3   Evaluating Subject Lines

Evaluate the following subject lines. Is one subject line in each group clearly best? Or does the "best" line depend on company culture, whether the message is a paper memo or an email message, or on some other factor?

1. Subject: Request
   Subject: Why I Need a New Computer
   Subject: Increasing My Productivity

2. Subject: Who Wants Extra Hours?
   Subject: Holiday Work Schedule
   Subject: Working Extra Hours During the Holiday Season

3. Subject: Student Mentors
   Subject: Can You Be an Email Mentor?
   Subject: Volunteers Needed

4. Subject: More Wine and Cheese
   Subject: Today's Reception for Our Visitors from Japan
   Subject: Reminder

5. Subject: Reducing Absenteeism
   Subject: Opening a Day Care Center for Sick Children of Employees
   Subject: Why We Need Expanded Day Care Facilities

11.4   Evaluating P.S.'s

Evaluate the following postscripts. Will they motivate readers to read the whole message if readers turn to them first? Do they create a strong ending for those who have already read the message?

1. P.S. It only takes <u>one</u> night's stay in a hotel you read about here, <u>one</u> discounted flight, <u>one</u> budget-priced cruise, or <u>one</u> low-cost car rental to make mailing back your Subscription Certificate well worth it.
   P.P.S. About your free gift! Your risk-free subscription to CONSUMER REPORTS TRAVEL LETTER comes with a remarkable 314-page book as a FREE GIFT.

2. P.S. Help spread the tolerance message by using your personalized address labels on all your correspondence.

And remember, you will receive a free *Teaching Tolerance* magazine right after your tax-deductible contribution arrives.

3. P.S. Every day brings more requests like that of Mr. Agyrey-Kwakey—for our "miracle seeds." And it's urgent that we respond to the emergency in Malaysia and Indonesia by replanting those forests destroyed by fire. Please send your gift today and become a partner with us in these innovative projects around the world.

4. P.S. Even as you read this letter, a donated load of food waits for the ticket that will move it to America's hungry. Please give today!

11.5   Choosing a Persuasive Approach

For each of the following situations requiring a persuasive message, choose the persuasive approach that you feel would work best. Explain your reasoning; then give a short list of the types of information you'd use to persuade your audience.

1. Asking for an extension on a project.
2. Requesting a job interview.
3. Requesting a free trial of a service.
4. Inviting customers to a store demonstration.
5. Reporting a coworker's poor work performance.
6. Asking your supervisor to reconsider a poor performance review.

7. Requesting a new office computer.
8. Requesting time off during your company's busy season.
9. Asking to be excused from the company service day, when all employees work on a community service project.

As your instructor directs,

a. Write a letter or email that addresses one of the situations in this exercise, drawing on details from your personal experiences. (You might address a real problem that you've faced.)

b. Write an email to your instructor listing the choices you've made and justifying your approach.

11.6   Identifying Observations

Emerson has taken the following notes about their group's meetings. Which of the following are specific observations that they could use in a performance review of group members? If they had it to do over again, what kinds of details would turn the inferences into observations?

1. February 22: Today was very frustrating. Sam was totally out of it—I wonder if he's on something. Jim was dictatorial. I argued, but nobody backed me up. Masayo might just as well have stayed home. We didn't get anything done. Two hours, totally wasted.

2. February 24: Jim seems to be making a real effort to be less domineering. Today he asked Sam and me for our opinions before proposing his own. And he noticed that Masayo wasn't talking much and brought her into the conversation. She suggested some good ideas.

3. February 28: Today's meeting was okay. I thought Masayo wasn't really focusing on the work at hand. She needs to work on communicating her ideas to others. Sam was doing some active listening, but he needs to work at being on time. Jim was involved in the project. He has strong leadership skills. There were some tense moments, but we got a lot done, and we all contributed. I got to say what I wanted to say, and the group decided to use my idea for the report.

4. March 5: This week most of us had midterms, and Masayo had an out-of-town gymnastics trip. We couldn't find a time to meet. So we did stuff by email. Sam and Jim found some great stuff at the library and on the web. Jim created a tentative schedule that he sent to all of us and then revised. I wrote up a draft of the description of the problem. Then Masayo and I put everything together. I sent my draft to her; she suggested revisions (in full caps so I could find them in the email message). Then I sent the message to everyone. Masayo and Jim both suggested changes, which I made before we handed the draft in.

5. March 15: We were revising the proposal, using Prof. Jones's comments. When we thought we were basically done, Masayo noticed that we had not responded to all of the specific comments about our introductory paragraph. We then went back and thought of some examples to use. This made our proposal better and more complete.

As your instructor directs,

a. Based on Emerson's notes, write a performance review addressed to Prof. Jones. For each group member, including Emerson, note specific areas of good performance and make specific suggestions for improvement.

b. Write an email to your instructor describing the process you used to make your recommendations. Be sure to identify each of the observations you used to provide specific details and each of the inferences that needed more information.

11.7   Revising a Persuasive Email

Your co-worker is concerned about the new computer software that IT just installed on everyone's office computers. He is not very familiar with the new program and has been struggling to figure it out. He wants to request a training session for those who still do not feel comfortable with the new system, but he is embarrassed to explain how much he is struggling with the software. He has written a draft of the email to your supervisor and asks you for your feedback.

Subject: Help!

I am sorry to bother you, but I am really struggling with the new computer software that was installed last week. I am not sure, but I think there are a few of us in the office for whom this has been a struggle. I really miss the old one we used. This new software is so different; I am really struggling with entering some of my data.

So, I was wondering if we could put together a training session sometime next week. We could ask IT if they would be willing to do a quick training seminar so we can make sure we are all on the same page. Maybe we could even do a follow-up session later on sometime just to check on our progress.

If you could get back to me soon, I would really appreciate it. I think this learning curve is cutting into my productivity. I really don't want to be behind.

Thanks,

Mitch

Revise the email and send it to your instructor. In a separate email to your instructor, explain the changes you made to make this message more persuasive.

11.8   Creating Persuasive Videos

As they try to undo the harm from YouTube drinking videos starring their institutions, school officials are making their own YouTube videos. Some, such as deans lecturing on course offerings, are ludicrously bad. Other videos are slick promotional films. Still others, such as videos of classes, are somewhere in between. Some schools are sponsoring contests to persuade students to create videos showing what they like about their school.

What would you put in a video to convince students—and parents who foot the bills—to consider your school? Share your ideas in small groups.

11.9   Creating Alternative Activities

You are residence director at Expensive Private University. Enrollment at your school has been declining because of repeated publicity about excessive drinking among the students. Last year, 23 were treated for alcohol poisoning at the local hospital, and one died.

You have been ordered by the president of EPU to develop alcohol-free activities for the campus and ways to persuade students to participate. They want your plans by the end of June so EPU can work on implementing them for the next academic year. Write the email to them detailing your plans. Write a second email to your instructor explaining your persuasive strategies.

Hints:

- Who are your audiences?
- Do they share any common ground?
- What objections will your audiences have?
- What are some ways you can deal with those objections?
- What pitfalls do you need to avoid?

11.10   Writing a Fund-Raiser Flyer

You have volunteered to create a flyer with detailed fund-raising information for a local charity event. Your boss has given you the following information to include on the flyer:

- Shoes for kids—think of a clever title, please!
- All employees should bring children's shoes (any kind, any size) to the break room in the office by August 10th (before school starts).
- The shoes will go to children in need in the metro area.
- We are hoping to have enough shoes to fill up the back of one of our delivery vans.
- Shoes can be used, but they still have to be in good condition.
- Please do not bring dirty shoes.
- Please include some kind of graphic or picture.
- Please stress how important this is and the fact that there are many children in our area who go without decent shoes.

Things to consider:

- How can you make this flyer persuasive?
- How will you grab employees' attention?
- Is there an emotional appeal you can use?
- Will there be objections you need to overcome?
- Is there more information you need to include?
- What audience benefits can you use?

Make the flyer.

11.11   Asking for More Time or Resources

Today, this message from your boss shows up in your email inbox:

> **Subject: Want Climate Report**
>
> This request has come down from the CEO. I'm delegating it to you. See me a couple of days before the board meeting—the 4th of next month—so we can go over your presentation.
>
> I want a report on the climate for underrepresented groups in our organization. A presentation at the last board of directors' meeting showed that while we do a good job of hiring people in underrepresented groups, few of them rise to the top. The directors suspect that our climate may not be supportive and want information on it. Please prepare a presentation for the next meeting. You'll have 15 minutes.

Making a presentation to the company's board of directors can really help your career. But preparing a good presentation and report will take time. You can look at exit reports filed by Human Resources when people leave the company, but you'll also need to interview people—lots of people. And you're already working 60 hours a week on three major projects, one of which is behind schedule. Can one of the projects wait? Can someone else take one of the projects? Can you get some help? Should you do just enough to get by? Ask your boss for advice—in a way that makes you look like a committed employee, not a shirker.

11.12   Persuading Employees Not to Share Files

Your computer network has been experiencing slowdowns and an investigation has uncovered the reason. A number of employees have been using the system to download and share songs and vacation photos. You are concerned because the bulky files clog the network and downloading files opens the network to computer viruses and worms. In addition, management does not want employees to spend work time and resources on personal matters. Finally, free downloads of songs are often illegal and management is worried that a recording firm might sue the company for failing to prevent employees from violating its copyrights.

As director of management information systems, you want to persuade employees to stop sharing files unrelated to work. You are launching a policy of regularly scanning the system for violations, but you prefer that employees voluntarily use the system properly. Violations are hard to detect and increasing scanning in an effort to achieve system security is likely to cause resentment as an intrusion into employees' privacy.

Write an email message to all employees, urging them to refrain from downloading and sharing personal files.

11.13   Persuading Employees to Join a Competition

Your supervisor has decided the employees of the company should participate in a weight-loss program and compete against the business across the street. Your supervisor isn't sure how to begin the program and is asking you for some ideas. They want to know

- How can we get employees interested in the weight-loss program?
- Will a competition get more employees to sign up?
- How long should we run the program?
- Should we have a goal?
- What should the program be called?

- Should there be a prize at the end for the person who lost the most weight?
- Should we get rid of Friday morning doughnuts during the program?
- Should we have some healthy eating and healthy living seminars to encourage our employees to be healthier?

Write an email to your supervisor answering their questions. Then write an email that will go to all employees. Include all the information they will need and use persuasion to get them to join the weight-loss program. Write a third email to your instructor explaining the differences between the emails to your supervisor and your fellow employees.

11.14   Handling a Sticky Recommendation

As a supervisor in a state agency, you have a dilemma. You received this email message today:

From: John Inoye, Director of Personnel, Department of Taxation

Subject: Need Recommendation for Peggy Chafez

Peggy Chafez has applied for a position in the Department of Taxation. On the basis of her application and interview, she is the leading candidate. However, before I offer the job to her, I need a letter of recommendation from her current supervisor.

Could you please let me have your evaluation within a week? We want to fill the position as quickly as possible.

Peggy has worked in your office for 10 years. She designed, writes, and edits a monthly statewide newsletter that your office puts out; she designed and maintains the department website. Her designs are creative; she's a very hard worker; she seems to know a lot about computers.

However, Peggy is in many ways an unsatisfactory staff member. Her standards are so high that most people find her intimidating. Some find her abrasive. People have complained to you that she's only interested in her own work; she seems to resent requests to help other people with projects. And yet both the newsletter and the web page are projects that need frequent interaction. She's out of the office a lot. Some of that is required by her job (e.g., she takes the newsletters to the post office), but some people don't like the fact that she's out of the office so much. They also complain that she doesn't return voicemail and email messages.

You think managing your office would be a lot smoother if Peggy weren't there. You can't fire her: State employees' jobs are secure once they get past the initial six-month probationary period. Because of budget constraints, you can hire new employees only if vacancies are created by resignations. You feel that it would be easy to find someone better.

If you recommend that John Inoye hire Peggy, you will be able to hire someone you want. If you recommend that John hire someone else, you may be stuck with Peggy for a long time.

As your instructor directs,

a. Write an email message to John Inoye.
b. Write an email to your instructor listing the choices you've made and justifying your approach.

Hints:

- Polarization may make this dilemma more difficult than it needs to be. What are your options? Consciously look for more than two.

- Is it possible to select facts or to use connotations so that you are truthful but still encourage John to hire Peggy? Is it ethical? Is it certain that John would find Peggy's work as unsatisfactory as you do? If you write a strong recommendation and Peggy doesn't do well at the new job, will your credibility suffer? Why is your credibility important?

11.15   Asking an Instructor for a Letter of Recommendation

You're ready for the job market or to transfer to a four-year college or graduate school, and you need letters of recommendation.

As your instructor directs,

a. Assume you've orally asked an instructor for a recommendation and they have agreed to write one. The instructor asks, "Why don't you write up something to remind me of what you've done in the class? Tell me what else you've done, too. And tell me what they're looking for. Be sure to tell me when the letter needs to be in and to whom it goes." Write the email.
b. Assume you've been unable to talk with the instructor whose recommendation you want. When you call, no one answers the phone; you stopped by once and

no one was in. Write an email asking for a letter of recommendation.
c. Assume the instructor is no longer on campus. Write them asking for a recommendation.

Hints:

- Be detailed about what the organization is seeking and the points you'd like the instructor to mention.

- How well will this instructor remember you? How much detail about your performance in their class do you need to provide?

- Specify the name and address of the person to whom the letter should be written; specify when the letter is due.

11.16   Writing a Performance Review for a Member of a Collaborative Group

During your collaborative writing group meetings, keep a log of events. Record specific observations of both effective and ineffective things that group members do. Then evaluate the performance of the other members of your group. (If there are two or more other people, write a separate review for each of them.)

In your first paragraph, summarize your evaluation. Then in the body of your message, give the specific details that led to your evaluation by answering the following questions:

- What specifically did the person do in terms of the task? Brainstorm ideas? Analyze the information? Draft the text? Suggest revisions in parts drafted by others? Format the document or create visuals? Revise? Edit? Proofread? (In most cases, several people will have done each of these activities together. Don't overstate what any one person did.) What was the quality of the person's work?

- What did the person contribute to the group process? Did they help schedule the work? Raise or resolve conflicts?

Make other group members feel valued and included? Promote group cohesion? What roles did the person play in the group?

Support your generalizations with specific observations. The more observations you have and the more detailed they are, the better your review will be.

As your instructor directs,

a. Write a midterm performance review for one or more members of your collaborative group. In each review, identify the two or three things the person should try to improve during the second half of the term.
b. Write a performance review for one or more members of your collaborative group at the end of the term. Identify and justify the grade you think each person should receive for the portion of the grade based on group process.
c. Give a copy of your review to the person about whom it is written.

11.17   Writing a Self-Assessment for a Performance Review

Your company privileges good communication skills. In fact, during their second year, all employees are sent to a four-month communication course. As part of your annual review, you must prepare a self-assessment that includes your assessment of your

progress in the communication course. Assume that your business communication course is the company's communication course, and prepare the communications part of your self-assessment. The company expects this portion to be a page long.

11.18 Evaluating Sales and Fund-Raising Messages

Collect the sales and fund-raising messages that come to you, your co-workers, landlord, neighbors, or family. Use the following questions to evaluate each message:

- What mode does the opener use? Is it related to the rest of the message? How good is the opener?
- What central selling point or common ground does the message use?
- What kinds of proof does the message use? Is the logic valid? What questions or objections are not answered?
- How does the message create emotional appeal?
- Is the style effective?
- Does the close tell people what to do, make action easy, give a reason for acting promptly, and end with a positive picture?
- Does the message use a P.S.? How good is it?

- Is the message visually attractive? Why or why not?
- What other items besides the letter or email are in the package?

As your instructor directs,

a. Share your analysis of one or more messages with a small group of your classmates.

b. Analyze one message in a presentation to the class. Make a copy of the message to use as a visual aid in your presentation.

c. Analyze one message in an email to your instructor. Provide a copy of the message along with your email.

d. With several other students, write a group email or report analyzing one part of the message (e.g., openers) or one kind of letter (e.g., political messages, organizations fighting hunger, etc.). Use at least 10 messages for your analysis if you look at only one part; use at least 6 messages if you analyze one kind of message. Provide copies as an appendix to your report.

11.19 Comparing Persuasive Apology Letters

Soon after the latest version of the iPhone went on sale, Apple customers publicly aired grievances with the company for releasing a product with so many technical glitches in its mapping application. Within a week, Apple CEO Tim Cook issued an apology letter to disgruntled customers regarding these glitches. Many critics have compared Cook's apology to letters written by his predecessor, Steve Jobs. Others have argued that Cook's persuasive style is different in that he uses more persuasive strategies to build an intimate feeling of connectedness with his audience, something Jobs did not do.

Compare Cook's apology letter with Job's pricing apology. Make a list of similar strategies that both writers employ as well as a list of the different strategies each uses.

- What differences do you see in the salutations? The first paragraphs?
- How does each handle the explanation of the problem? The apology?
- How does the tone differ in the two letters?
- What differences do you see in the endings of each letter?

Discuss your lists in small groups. Together, decide which letter you found more persuasive and why. Write an email to your instructor persuading him or her that your choice is the correct one.

To our customers,

At Apple, we strive to make world-class products that deliver the best experience possible to our customers. With the launch of our new Maps last week, we fell short on this commitment. We are extremely sorry for the frustration this has caused our customers, and we are doing everything we can to make Maps better.

We launched Maps initially with the first version of iOS. As time progressed, we wanted to provide our customers with even better Maps including features such as turn-by-turn directions, voice integration, Flyover and vector-based maps. In order to do this, we had to create a new version of Maps from the ground up.

There are already more than 100 million iOS devices using the new Apple Maps, with more and more joining us every day. In just over a week, iOS users with the new Maps have already searched for nearly half a billion locations. The more our customers use our Maps the better it will get, and we greatly appreciate all of the feedback we have received from you.

While we're improving Maps, you can try alternatives by downloading map apps from the App Store like Bing, MapQuest and Waze, or use Google or Nokia maps by going to their websites and creating an icon on your home screen to their web app.

Everything we do at Apple is aimed at making our products the best in the world. We know that you expect that from us, and we will keep working non-stop until Maps lives up to the same incredibly high standard.

Tim Cook

Apple's CEO

To all iPhone Customers:

I have received hundreds of emails from iPhone customers who are upset about Apple dropping the price of iPhone by $200 two months after it went on sale. After reading every one of these emails, I have some observations and conclusions.

First, I am sure that we are making the correct decision to lower the price of the 8GB iPhone from $599 to $399, and that now is the right time to do it. iPhone is a breakthrough product, and we have the chance to "go for it" this holiday season. iPhone is so far ahead of the competition, and now it will be affordable by even more customers. It benefits both Apple and every iPhone user to get as many new customers as possible in the iPhone "tent." We strongly believe the $399 price will help us do just that this holiday season.

Second, being in technology for 30+ years I can attest to the fact that the technology road is bumpy. There is always change and improvement, and there is always someone who bought a product before a particular cutoff date and misses the new price or the new operating system or the new whatever. This is life in the technology lane. If you always wait for the next price cut or to buy the new improved model, you'll never buy any technology product because there is always something better and less expensive on the horizon. The good news is that if you buy products from companies that support them well, like Apple tries to do, you will receive years of useful and satisfying service from them even as newer models are introduced.

Third, even though we are making the right decision to lower the price of iPhone, and even though the technology road is bumpy, we need to do a better job taking care of our early iPhone customers as we aggressively go after new ones with a lower price. Our early customers trusted us, and we must live up to that trust with our actions in moments like these.

Therefore, we have decided to offer every iPhone customer who purchased an iPhone from either Apple or AT&T, and who is not receiving a rebate or any other consideration, a $100 store credit towards the purchase of any product at an Apple Retail Store or the Apple Online Store. Details are still being worked out and will be posted on Apple's website next week. Stay tuned.

We want to do the right thing for our valued iPhone customers. We apologize for disappointing some of you, and we are doing our best to live up to your high expectations of Apple.

Steve Jobs

Apple CEO

Sources: Letter from Tim Cook, accessed March 4, 2021, https://techcrunch.com/2012/09/28/tim-cook-apologizes-for-apple-maps-points-to-competitive-alternatives; and Letter from Steve Jobs, accessed September 30, 2012, http://opnlttr.com/letter/all-iphone-customers.

Notes

1. Jay A. Conger, "The Necessary Art of Persuasion," *Harvard Business Review* 76, no. 3 (May–June 1998): 88.
2. John Kotter and Holger Rathgeber, *Our Iceberg Is Melting: Changing and Succeeding under Any Conditions* (New York: St. Martin's Press, 2005), 140.
3. Jonah Lehrer, *How We Decide* (New York: Houghton Mifflin Harcourt, 2009), 26, 235; and Jonah Lehrer, "Attention, Shoppers: Go with Your Gut," *Wall Street Journal*, October 1, 2011, C12.
4. Michael Sanserino, "Peer Pressure and Other Pitches," *Wall Street Journal*, September 14, 2009, B6.
5. Steve Martin, "98% of HBR Readers Love This Article: Businesses Are Just Beginning to Understand the Power of 'Social Norms,'" *Harvard Business Review* 90, no. 10 (October 2012): 23–25.
6. Richard H. Thaler and Cass R. Sunstein, *Nudge: Improving Decisions about Health, Wealth, and Happiness* (New Haven, CT: Yale University Press, 2008), 65–70.

7. Daniel H. Pink, *Drive: The Surprising Truth about What Motivates Us* (New York: Riverhead Books, 2009); and Tomas Chamorro-Premuzic, "Does Money Really Affect Motivation? A Review of the Research," *HBR Blog Network*, April 10, 2013, http://blogs.hbr.org/cs/2013/04/does_money_really_affect_motiv.html.

8. Pink, *Drive*, 145.

9. J. Berger, *Contagious: Why Things Catch On* (New York: Simon and Schuster, 2016), 151–53.

10. Joseph Walker, "Google's Algorithms for Talent," *Wall Street Journal*, July 5, 2012, B1; and Claire Suddath, "Let's Put on a Show!" *Bloomberg Businessweek*, January 7, 2013, 66–67.

11. "'Don't Mess with Texas' Anti-Litter Ad Features Strait," *Des Moines Register*, May 11, 2010, 2A.

12. Daniel Gilbert, *Stumbling on Happiness* (New York: Alfred A. Knopf, 2006), 165, 168–70.

13. National Science Foundation, "Why 'Scientific Consensus' Fails to https://www.nsf.gov/news/news_summ.jsp?cntn_id=117697

14. Min-Sun Kim and Steven R. Wilson, "A Cross-Cultural Comparison of Implicit Theories of Requesting," *Communication Monographs* 61, no. 3 (September 1994): 210–35; and K. Yoon, C. H. Kim, and M. S. Kim, "A Cross-Cultural Comparison of the Effects of Source Credibility on Attitudes and Behavior Intentions," *Mass Communication and Society* 1, nos. 3 and 4 (1998): 153–73.

15. Karen Blumenthal, "Fraud Doesn't Always Happen to Someone Else," *Wall Street Journal*, August 12, 2009, D1.

16. Ray Considine and Murray Raphael, *The Great Brain Robbery* (Los Angeles: Rosebud Books, 1980), 95–96.

17. Phred Dvorak, "How Understanding the 'Why' of Decisions Matters," *Wall Street Journal*, March 19, 2007, B3.

18. Heath and Heath, *Made to Stick*, 165–68.

19. Scott Robinette, "Get Emotional," *Harvard Business Review* 79, no. 5 (May 2001): 24–25.

20. "Around the World," *Washington Post*, March 27, 2009, A14.

21. Jeffrey Zaslow, "The Most-Praised Generation Goes to Work," *Wall Street Journal*, April 20, 2007, W1, W7; and Rachel Emma Silverman, "Performance Reviews, Facebook Style," *Wall Street Journal*, August 1, 2012, B6.

22. Rachel Emma Silverman, "Yearly Reviews? Try Weekly," *Wall Street Journal*, September 6, 2011, B6; and Silverman, "Performance Reviews, Facebook Style."

23. Silverman, "Yearly Reviews? Try Weekly."

24. Samuel A. Culbert, "Get Rid of the Performance Review! It Destroys Morale, Kills Teamwork, and Hurts the Bottom Line. And That's Just for Starters," *Wall Street Journal*, June 21, 2012, http://online.wsj.com/article/SB122426318874844933.html; and Jared Sandberg, "Performance Reviews Need Some Work, Don't Meet Potential," *Wall Street Journal*, November 20, 2007, B1.

25. "Microsoft's Downfall: Inside the Executive E-Mails and Cannibalistic Culture That Felled a Tech Giant," VanityFair.com, July 3, 2012, http://www.vanityfair.com/online/daily/2012/07/microsoft-downfall-emails-steve-ballmer.

26. Joe Light, "Performance Reviews by the Numbers," *Wall Street Journal*, June 29, 2010, D4.

27. David Gauthier-Villars, "Water Fight in France Takes a Dirty Turn," *Wall Street Journal*, February 1, 2007, B7.

28. "The Pledge," National Disaster Search Dog Foundation, accessed June 12, 2013, http://www.searchdogfoundation.org/images/3_pledge.jpg.

29. "How to Launch a Direct-Mail Campaign," *BusinessWeek SmallBiz*, August/September 2008, 28.

30. Patrick Spenner and Karen Freeman, "To Keep Your Customers, Keep It Simple," *Harvard Business Review* 90, no. 5 (May 2012): 108–14.

31. Barbara Kiviat, "Why We Buy: Consumers Tend to Go with What (Little) They Know," *Time*, August 27, 2007, 50–51.

32. Clayton M. Christensen, James Allworth, and Karen Dillon, *How Will You Measure Your Life?* (New York: Harper Business, 2012), 109–10.

33. Jeffrey Gitomer, *Little Red Book of Sales Answers: 99.5 Real World Answers That Make Sense, Make Sales, and Make Money* (Upper Saddle River, NJ: Prentice Hall, 2006), 112.

34. Dan Ariely, *Predictably Irrational: The Hidden Forces That Shape Our Decisions*, rev. ed. (New York: Harper Perennial, 2008), 4.

35. Daniel Kahneman, *Thinking, Fast and Slow* (New York: Farrar, Straus and Giroux, 2011), 119, 124.

36. Beth Negus Viveiros, "Gifts for Life," *Direct*, July (2004): 9.

37. Charity: Water home page, accessed October 31, 2017, http://www.charitywater.org.

38. Fund-raising letter from Kevin M Ryan (undated correspondence).

39. Maxwell Sackheim, *My First Sixty-Five Years in Advertising* (Blue Ridge Summit, PA: Tab Books, 1975), 97–100.

40. Dwayne D. Gremler and Kevin P. Gwinner, "Rapport-Building Behaviors Used by Retail Employees," *Journal of Retailing* 84, no. 3 (2008): 308–24.

CHAPTER

12 Developing Proposals

Chapter Outline

DrAfter123/Getty Images

Endeavors of Detail and Precision

"Rejected. For using Calibri."

"Unfortunately, this application used a non-approved font typeface and point size in the Research Plan, which is a fatal error."

Organizations, agencies, and individuals respond to proposals in a few different ways: (1) they accept proposals as submitted, (2) they accept proposals pending revisions, (3) they reject proposals but accept revised resubmissions, and (4) they reject proposals outright. Any proposal is successful if it is not rejected outright. It might seem easy, then, to research and write a proposal that falls into one of the first three categories rather than the fourth. On the contrary, though, most proposals fall into the category of outright reject. Funding is finite, and an increasing number of people and organizations compete for it. For example, the National Science Foundation (NSF) in the U.S. funded 28% of the proposals it received in 2020.

Given this competition, funding agencies like the NSF are meticulous in their review of proposals. They evaluate proposals on the merit of their content and their fit with funding agencies' missions and values, the meaningfulness of the described problem, and the feasibility of the proposed solution to the problem. Proposal reviewers also examine

LittleRedDragon/Shutterstock

the quality of the research, including the extent to which the authors demonstrate an understanding of the issue at hand and the ability of the described method to measure what it is supposed to measure. They evaluate whether the proposed work can be done in the timeframe and within budget and whether the authors have the knowledge, resources, and facilities to carry out and manage the work and its related expenditures.

In addition to being reviewed for content, proposals are also reviewed for their organization and formatting.

Funding agencies often require specific formatting, including specific margins, headings, font, and page-number placement. These specifications help to keep the review process equitable. Because all proposals have the same appearance, reviewers can concentrate on their content. In addition, these specifications mean that authors have the same number of pages to make their case. And by requiring a specific font, funding agencies make proposal reading easier for reviewers.

So, if a funding agency requires specific content, a specific file name, or even a specific font, you must comply. If not, your proposal will likely face immediate rejection.

Source: Daniel Cressey, "Grant Application Rejected over Choice of Font," *Nature: International Weekly Journal of Science*, October 29, 2015, https://www.nature.com/news/grant-application-rejected-over-choice-of-font-1.18686; Eric Boodman, "Font of Despair: In the Fierce Competition for Science Funding, even a Typeface Glitch Can Be Fatal," *Stat*, October 26, 2018, https://www.statnews.com/2018/10/26/typeface-glitch-dooms-va-ptsd-funding; and Emily Sohn, "Secrets to Writing a Winning Grant," *Nature*, December 20, 2019, https://www.nature.com/articles/d41586-019-03914-5. National Science Foundation, "Funding and Support Descriptions", September 14, 2021, https://www.nsf.gov/homepagefundingandsupport.jsp.

After studying this chapter, you should be able to

LO 12-1 Define proposals.

LO 12-2 Brainstorm for writing proposals.

LO 12-3 Organize proposals.

LO 12-4 Prepare budget and costs sections.

LO 12-5 Produce different kinds of proposals.

Whatever you take away from this chapter, remember that writing proposals requires precision; fulfilling audience expectations and needs is critical to your proposal's success.

Defining Proposals

LO 12-1

A **proposal** is persuasive communication that argues for work that needs to be done and the person or people who will do it; proposals offer a method to find information, evaluate something new, solve a problem, or implement a change. Proposals vary widely. They can be as short as an elevator pitch or as long as a formal report. They can be delivered in an oral presentation, such as on the TV show *Shark Tank*, or by uploading a written document.

At their core, proposals have three component parts:

1. Problem/opportunity.
2. Solution.
3. Qualifications.

The three basic parts are common across all proposals (see Figure 12.1). Each of the three components must persuade the target audience of each point in turn—that a problem or opportunity exists, that you know the potential solution, and that you are the person (or group of people) to implement it. Doubts arising from any of the three parts can result in rejection. Proposal reviewers might not be convinced that there is a real problem or opportunity. They might also think that the problem is not as serious as you claim or that the opportunity isn't as promising as you say. They might not accept that your potential solution could actually solve the problem or take advantage of the opportunity. They might not accept that your solution is feasible. Even if the reviewers accept that the problem or opportunity exists and are convinced that your proposed solution could work, they might be skeptical that you have the knowledge, skills, or resources to do the work. It's critical, then, to present your arguments and evidence as persuasively as possible in each of these three proposal parts.

Proposals may be competitive or noncompetitive. **Competitive proposals** compete against each other for limited resources. Applications for research funding are often highly competitive. Many companies will bid for corporate or government contracts, but only one will be accepted. In fiscal year 2020, the NSF spent close to $8 billion supporting research.[1] The National Institutes of Health (NIH) support almost 50,000 research projects at a cost of $30.9 billion annually.[2] These funds are awarded mainly through competitive proposals.

Noncompetitive proposals have no real competition. For example, a company could accept all of the internal proposals it thought would save money or improve quality. Often a company that is satisfied with a vendor asks for a noncompetitive proposal to

Figure 12.1	Variety of Proposals and Their Components		
Type of proposal	**Problem/opportunity**	**Solution**	**Qualifications**
Sales (solicited)	Buyer needs a good or service; they have a good idea of what they need.	Your company's good or service	Show exactly how your company's good or service will address the buyer's needs and priorities.
Sales (unsolicited)	Office, department, or organization would benefit from something (i.e., new photocopier, additional office staff, more comprehensive insurance, etc.), but you need to convince them that there is a problem.	Purchase, hire, or acquire	Show that you've researched options, their costs, and incidentals, as well as exactly how that purchase, hire, or acquisition will be of benefit to the office, department, or organization.
Business plan	Your business venture or public service project needs capital.	Funding from a foundation, corporation, government agency, or bank	Show that you and your organization can be trusted with their money.
Research	There is a something that you do not know—there is a gap in knowledge.	Research to learn more about a topic to fill that gap in knowledge	Show that you and your team have the expertise, experience, and facilities to conduct that research.
Grant	Nonprofit needs funding for a project or to continue its work.	Funding from a governmental organization, foundation, and individuals	Show that your nonprofit fits the funder's priorities, that you will be able to do the work you're promising, and that you will use the funding responsibly.
Topic for class project	Example: For a report, you need to define and describe the problem, show it is meaningful, and it completed in the given timeframe.	Method that will provide the needed information	Show that you have the knowledge and resources to collect and analyze the needed information.

renew the contract. Like competitive proposals, noncompetitive proposals can involve enormous sums: the proposal for the last U.S. census was $1 billion.

Successful proposals have several common characteristics. First, they anticipate audience needs. They address a specific audience for a specific purpose. Writers of successful proposals analyze their target audiences to learn as much about their values, vision, mission, needs, and wants as possible and then anticipate these in the proposal. The persuasiveness of a successful proposal comes from how well the proposal connects the problem, solution, and qualifications to the audience's values, vision, mission, needs, and wants. Successful proposals are also well-researched; they base their problem, solution, and qualifications components on data, whether from primary or secondary sources (see Chapter 3). Successful proposals follow the required format, whether that format is required, such as in a grant proposal, or implied, such as in a business plan.

Second, proposals are created for projects that are longer or more expensive than routine work, that differ significantly from routine work, or that create larger changes than routine work does. When you or your organization want to consider new opportunities, you will need to write a proposal for that work.

Third, proposals have two major goals: to get the project accepted and to get you or your organization accepted to do the work. To accomplish these goals, proposals must stress benefits for all affected audiences. A proposal for an organization to adopt flexible work hours would offer benefits for both employees and management, as well as for key departments such as finance.

As you write a proposal, you'll need to consider these characteristics. If you were writing a proposal for a flexible work hours, for example, you would need to establish that a problem or opportunity exists. One problem might be that employees miss work because they need to care for children or aging parents. You'll need to consider your audience—the person who can implement the change. This person likely values employee productivity and employee well-being. You'll need to show how your proposed solution, flexible work hours, solves the problem of missed work. In doing so, you'll need to answer questions that will arise in your audience's mind: for example, how will employees schedule meetings if they work different hours of the day?

Brainstorming for Writing Proposals

LO 12-2

As is true for all forms of business communication, you should begin the brainstorming process by considering your rhetorical situation—the audience, purpose, and context. After you determine these key components, use the proposal questions in the next section to brainstorm your proposal's content. In addition, follow the guidelines in the section on proposal style to make sure you're meeting the audience's expectations with your writing choices. These guidelines also may lead to additional content choices.

Proposal Questions

To write a good proposal, you need to have a clear view of the opportunity you want to fill or the problem you hope to solve and the kind of research or other action needed to solve it. A proposal must answer the following questions convincingly:

- **What problem are you going to solve or what opportunity do you hope to fill?** Show that you understand the problem or the opportunity and the organization's needs. Define the problem or opportunity as the audience sees it, even if you believe it is part of a larger problem. Sometimes you will need to show that the problem or opportunity exists. For instance, management might not be aware of subtle discrimination against women that your proposal will help eliminate.

- **Why does the problem need to be solved now or the opportunity explored immediately?** Show that money, time, health, or social concerns support solving the problem or exploring the opportunity immediately. Provide the predicted consequences if the problem is not solved now or if the opportunity is not explored immediately.

- **How are you going to solve it?** Prove that your methods are feasible. Show that a solution can be found in the time available. Specify the topics you'll investigate. Explain how you'll gather data. Show your approach is effective and desirable.

- **Can you do the work?** Show that you, or your organization, have the knowledge, means, personnel, and experience to do the work well. For larger projects, you will have to show some evidence, such as preliminary data, personnel qualifications, or similar projects in the past.

- **Why should you be the one to do it?** Show why you or your company should do the work. For many proposals, various organizations could do the work. Why should the work be given to you? Discuss the benefits—direct and indirect—you and your organization can provide.

- **When will you complete the work?** Provide a detailed schedule showing when each phase of the work will be completed.

- **How much will you charge?** Provide a detailed budget that includes costs for items such as materials, salaries, and overhead. Give careful thought to unique expenses that may be part of the work. Will you need to travel? Pay fees? Pay benefits in addition to salary for part-time workers?

- **What exactly will you provide for us?** Specify the tangible products you'll produce; develop their benefits. If possible, include benefits for all levels of audience.

Since proposals to outside organizations are usually considered legally binding documents, get expert legal and financial advice on the last two bullet points. Even if the proposal will not be legally binding (perhaps it is an internal proposal), safeguard your professional reputation. Be sure you can deliver the promised products at the specified time using resources and personnel available to you.

Proposal Style

Good proposals are clear and easy to read. Research demonstrates that successful grant proposals will use "the funding organization's suggested organization (e.g., headings and subheadings), language (e.g., specialized terminology), and format (e.g., font and margins)."[3] Remember that some of your audience may not be experts in the subject matter. Highly statistical survey and data analysis projects may be funded by finance people; medical and scientific studies may be approved by bureaucrats. Thus, avoid jargon and acronyms.[4] Instead, use clear and concise language your readers will understand.

Proposals are persuasive documents, so appealing to your audience's needs and values is of utmost importance. Successful proposals use key words that mirror the values of the audience and thereby increase the likelihood of accomplishing their purpose.

Some style choices also will add content. How much detail does your audience expect? How much background? As you write, anticipate and answer questions your readers may have. Support generalizations and inferences with data and other information. Stress benefits throughout the proposal and make sure you include benefits for all elements of your audience.

Watch your word choice. Avoid diction that shows doubt.

Weak:	"*If* we can obtain X. . . ."
	"We *hope* we can obtain X."
	"We will *try* to obtain X."
Better:	"We plan to obtain X."
	"We expect to obtain X."

Avoid bragging diction such as "huge potential" and "revolutionary process." Be particularly careful to avoid bragging diction about yourself. Research indicates that overstatement reduces one's credibility.[5] Also avoid "believing" diction, as in "We believe that . . . ." Use facts and figures instead.

Use the expected format for your proposal. Shorter proposals (one to four pages) are generally in letter or email format; longer proposals are frequently formal reports. Depending on the context, you may be asked to mail in a paper proposal, send it as an email attachment, upload a PDF version to a website, or deliver the proposal as an oral presentation. Make sure if you're asked to submit an electronic proposal, you don't send in a paper copy or vice versa. If the proposal is electronic, include a linked table of contents that will provide your audience with an easy way to search your document, especially if your proposal is long.

Government agencies and companies often issue **requests for proposals**, known as **RFP**s. Follow the RFP's specified format in every detail. Use the exact headings, terminology, and organization of the RFP when responding to one. Competitive proposals often are scored by giving points in each category. Evaluators look only under the headings specified in the RFP. If information isn't there, the proposal may get no points in that category.

Beginnings and endings of proposals are important. If you are not following an RFP, your proposal should begin with a clear statement of what you propose doing, why you propose doing it, and what the implications of the proposed action are or why the action is important. Proposals should end with a brief but strong summary of major benefits of having you do the work. In some circumstances, an urge to action is appropriate:

> If I get your approval before the end of the month, we can have the procedures in place in time for the new fiscal year.

Allow a generous amount of time before the due date for polishing and finishing your proposal:

- Edit carefully.

- Make a final check that you have included all sections and pieces of information requested in the RFP. Many RFPs call for appendixes with items such as résumés and letters of support. Do you have all of yours?

- Ensure that your proposal's appearance will create a good impression. This step includes careful proofreading.

- Make sure you have chosen the correct media channel for your proposal submission.

- Allow enough time for production, reproduction, and administrative approvals before the deadline for receipt of the proposal. If multiple signatures are needed, it may take more than a day to get them all. If you are submitting a government grant proposal, the government server may be clogged with heavy usage on the final due date, or even the day before, so don't wait until the last minute.

Organizing Proposals

LO 12-3

Once you have brainstormed for your proposal, you'll need to select a proposal organization that is most appropriate for your purpose. This section offers advice for organizing proposals and for writing three common varieties of proposals: sales proposals, business plans, and grant proposals.

The Organization of Business Proposals

Many business proposals recommend new programs, offer ways to solve problems, sell goods or services, request funds or capital, or outline a new business idea. Writing such proposals often requires considerable research, including reading articles in trade and professional journals, finding supporting data online, and talking to employees or customers. All this information requires careful organization.

Any time you are asked to write a proposal for business purposes, you will want to follow the organization that is most routinely used in business settings.

Proposals for businesses usually employ the following organization:

1. **Introduction.** Summarize the subject and purposes of your proposal. You also should discuss the significance of the project and any relevant background information.
2. **Current situation.** Describe the problem that needs to be solved or the opportunity to be explored, its causes, and the outcome if it is not resolved.

3. **Project plan.** Outline the steps you will follow to solve the problem or explore the opportunity you've identified in the previous section. You also should indicate the final deliverables of your project.

4. **Qualifications.** State the knowledge and skills you possess necessary to complete the project you're proposing. Some proposals include résumés in this section.

5. **Costs and benefits.** Briefly outline the costs associated with your project and then state all the benefits it will bring. Make sure the benefits outweigh the costs. (More details on preparing the costs and budget sections are included in the next section.)

Sales Proposals

To sell expensive goods or services, you may be asked to submit a proposal.

To write a good sales proposal, be sure that you understand the buyer's priorities. A phone company lost a $36 million sale to a university because it assumed the university's priority would be cost. Instead, the university wanted a state-of-the-art system. The university accepted a higher bid.

Make sure your proposal presents your goods or services as solving the problem your audience perceives. Don't assume the buyer will understand why your product or system is good. For everything you offer, show the benefits of each feature. Be sure to present the benefits using *you*-attitude.

Use language appropriate for your audience. Even if the buyers want a state-of-the-art system, they may not want the level of detail that your staff could provide; they may not understand or appreciate technical jargon.

Sales proposals, particularly for complicated systems costing millions of dollars, are often long. Provide a one-page cover letter to present your proposal succinctly. The best organization for this letter is usually a modified version of the sales pattern in Chapter 11:

1. Catch the reader's attention and summarize up to three major benefits you offer.

2. Discuss each of the major benefits in the order in which you mentioned them in the first paragraph.

3. Deal with any objections or concerns the reader may have. In a sales proposal, these objections probably include costs. Connect costs with benefits.

4. Mention other benefits briefly.

5. Ask the reader to approve your proposal, and provide a reason for acting promptly.

Figure 12.2 shows an example of a sales proposal from a cleaning service.

Business Plans

Proposals for funding include **business plans**—documents written to raise capital for new business ventures.

Because venture capitalists and other investors are not known for their patience, business plans in particular need to have a concise, compelling beginning describing exactly what you plan to do and what problem your idea solves. Pay careful attention to the "Executive Summary." This overview section is one of the most important places in any proposal. After reading this opening, the reviewer will make initial decisions about you, your writing, your idea, and your logic. Therefore, it must spark enthusiasm for your idea; the reviewer's interest will never increase later in your proposal. This section also should provide an overview of all of the major topics you will cover in the body.

Figure 12.2   A Sales Proposal from a Cleaning-Service Company

Zenith Cleaning

March 4, 2021

D. C. Allen
Duluth Glass Company
6428 S. Superior Rd.
Duluth, MN 55510

A one-page cover letter presents a summary of the proposal. The primary purpose of the letter is to get the reader to act by reading the complete proposal and to build a good image of the organization.

For guidance on formatting letters, see section "Formats for Letters" in Appendix A.

Dear Ms. Allen:

The opening motivates the reader to read the letter by stating the reader's needs and interests.

Thank you for making time to meet with me on February 25, 2021, to discuss your company's requirements for commercial cleaning.

The body of the letter provides logical content by summarizing the proposal and emotional content by illustrating, through the logical content, that the company has heard the reader's concerns and needs.

Our Zenith Cleaning teams provide reliable, thorough, and cost-effective service. Your cleaning team will arrive promptly at 10:00 a.m., Monday through Friday. The team's daily routine will ensure your company's space is clean and tidy. And our pricing—at about $40 per day—is comparable to cleaning companies that offer far less. At Zenith Cleaning, we have built our reputation and our clientele by keeping our promises and working hard.

In our meeting on February 25, we discussed several concerns you have had in relation to your current cleaning service. Zenith Cleaning assures you that we:

- Use only professional-quality cleaning products.
- Have little turnover in our cleaning crews; our team members are well paid and trained.
- Carry out regular self-assessments via client surveys (email and phone) and via unscheduled visits by our operations team.

The letter offers to provide references to further establish the company's qualifications and benefits they can provide through its quality service.

If you would like references from some of our current clients, I can readily supply them. I can be reached at 515.334.6908 at the office or on my cell at 515.334.6403.

In closing, I hope that you will approve this proposal and that Zenith Cleaning can begin serving your company in March.

The letter ends with a positive picture of the reader enjoying the cleaning service. Note that the ending does not tell the reader how to feel or assume that the reader will accept the proposal.

Best Regards,
Denise Varadkar
Director of Sales, Zenith Cleaning

Figure 12.2   A Sales Proposal from a Cleaning-Service Company (*Continued*)

Proposal Prepared for the Duluth Glass Company
by Zenith Cleaning
February 26, 2021

Your Cleaning Team

The proposal begins with summary of the benefits of hiring the cleaning service that also reflect the buyer's priorities.

You will receive reliable, thorough, safe, and cost-effective service from a cleaning team that will:

- Wear a photo ID badge.
- Wear a professional Zenith Cleaning uniform.
- Use only professional grade cleaning-products.
- Have completed the six-week Zenith Training program.
- Comply with all OSHA regulations.
- Know how to thoroughly clean offices without disturbing computers.
- Know how to work safely in public areas.

The reader expressed the desire that only professional grade cleaning-products be used, so that is stated explicitly. Badges and uniforms add to the overall professionalism of the company and employees.

In the initial meeting, the buyer also expressed the need for well paid, trained employees who stay with the company long-term. The lengthy training period and guarantees about personal and equipment safety speak to a company that is invested in its employees.

Your Team's Cleaning Tasks

Your Zenith Cleaning service will include the following daily, weekly, and monthly tasks.

Daily cleaning tasks will be carried out each day, Monday–Friday, starting at 10:00 a.m. We will clean all entrances and hallways, the reception area, the conference rooms, the lunch room, and the common areas. Daily cleaning tasks are the following:

- Surface dust horizontal surfaces of desks, tables, filing cabinets, etc.
- Spot clean horizontal surfaces for removal of spillage, marks, and rings.
- Empty all trash and recycling receptacles and remove to a collection point. Replace liners as necessary.
- Clean fingerprints and smudges from entrance glass and entry doors.
- Spot clean fingerprints and smudges from partition glass.
- Sweep and spot mop all hard-surface floors.
- Vacuum all carpeted areas.
- Report all maintenance issues in a log book.

The specific break down of daily, weekly, and monthly tasks illustrate the knowledge and professionalism of the cleaning service, make the cleaning company's tasks clear, and give credibility to company's qualifications and ability to deliver what they promise.

Weekly cleaning tasks will be carried out on Fridays. Weekly cleaning tasks are the following:

- Thoroughly dust all horizontal surfaces of office furniture, including desks, cubicles, computer monitors, tables, file cabinets, windowsills, and wall hangings.
- Wipe clean all telephone receivers and dust the bases of the telephones.

Monthly cleaning tasks will be carried out on the last Friday of the month. Monthly cleaning tasks are the following:

Figure 12.2   A Sales Proposal from a Cleaning-Service Company (*Continued*)

- Thoroughly dust all vertical surfaces of office furniture, such as desks, cubicles, tables, chairs, file cabinets.
- Dust high locations, such as air vents, tops of doors, door frames, ceiling corners and edges.
- Dust all baseboards and window blinds.
- Vacuum upholstered furniture to remove dust and lint.
- Clean spots and smudges from walls.
- Clean the refrigerator and the microwave. (Client must remove all perishable items from the refrigerator prior to the last Friday of the month.)

There will be two monthly self-assessments via client surveys (one via email and one via phone) and one monthly unscheduled site inspection visit by our operations team.

The regular assessments of the cleaning company's on-site work reflect the company's pride of work and ability to deliver quality cleaning in the long-term.

Pricing Agreement

Client:	Duluth Glass Company
Location:	Duluth Glass Company, 6428 S. Superior Rd., Duluth, MN 55510
Frequency:	Five days per week
Start date:	March 8, 2021

Provides a reason to act promptly.

Price:	$1200.00 per month (~$40 per day)
Note:	Price is valid for 30 days from the proposal date.
Payment:	Billing occurs on the first Monday of each month.
No service:	New Year's Day, Labor Day, Memorial Day, Thanksgiving, Independence Day, Christmas Day

The clear billing costs and procedures reflect professionalism and make expectations for the client clear.

The parties agree to these terms and conditions:

1. Duluth Glass Company

Name:
Title:
Date:

The request to approve the proposal is not in paragraph form, but an agreement statement with a place for the buyer to sign and date.

2. Zenith Cleaning
Denise Varadkar
Denise Varadkar
Director of Sales
Date: February 12, 2021

Figure 12.3	Questions Business Plans Should Answer

- What is your product or service?
- How well developed is it? Is a mock-up or demo available?
- Who is your market? How large is it? Why does this market need your product or service?
- How will you promote your product or service?
- Who are your competitors? How will you be better? What other problems and challenges will you have to face on your path to profit?
- Who also is providing support for your business?
- Who will be working with you? How many more employees will you need? What will you pay them? What benefits will you give them?

Your business plan should answer the questions listed in Figure 12.3 with sufficient detail to be convincing and supporting evidence where applicable. You can read an example of a business plan in Figure 12.4.

Financial information is important in any proposal, but it is even more crucial in a business plan. You will need to show how much of your own money you are investing, which investors are supporting you already, and how you plan to use the money you get. Many investors want to see a five-year financial forecast. Explain with convincing detail how you expect to make money. What is your timeframe for financial success? What is your estimated monthly income the first year?

Anticipate problems that you are likely to encounter. Investors will already know them; this shows you do, too. Show how you plan to solve them. Use details to help convince your audience. Many business plans are too general to convince investors. Details show you have done your homework and also can show your business acumen.

Of the thousands of business plans presented to potential investors each year, only a few succeed. John W. Mullens, at the London Business School, offers five reasons business plans fail:

- **No problem.**   Plans must fix a problem or fill a need instead of just being examples of cool technology or good ideas.

- **Unrealistic ambition.**   Successful business plans recognize a specific market, instead of aiming at the entire population.

- **Flawed spreadsheets.**   Carefully prepared revenue models can work on paper, but successful business plans must work in the real economy.

- **Wrong team.**   Investors are not necessarily impressed by education and work experience, unless those contribute to the success of the business.

- **Perfect plan.**   Successful plans recognize realistic challenges to the business plan, instead of presenting everything in the best light.

Mullens also suggests three keys for success: (1) a clear problem and a logical solution, (2) hard evidence that you have done your research, and (3) complete candor about challenges and risks associated with your plan.[6]

Grant Proposals

Proposals are also a major part of nonprofits' fund-raising activity; they write **grant proposals** to governmental organizations, foundations, and individuals to raise money

Figure 12.4   A Business Plan for a New Juice and Smoothie Shop

Home Squeeze

A Juice and Smoothie Company

A Business Plan by Mary Stojanovski
March 2021

Business plans can be quite lengthy. For that reason, they sometimes contain a table of contents as well as a cover page.

Figure 12.4   A Business Plan for a New Juice and Smoothie Shop (*Continued*)

Executive Summary

The executive summary sparks enthusiasm for the business and outlines the main points of the business plan.

Mary Stojanovski, owner and manager of Home Squeeze, proposes to open a juice and smoothie company in Ames, Iowa. Home Squeeze will produce all our fresh, cold-press juice and smoothie products in-house. We will also sell grab-and-go salads—bowls of fruits, bowls of veggies, and bowls of veggies and fruits combined—paired with our homemade dressings, made from ingredients such as yogurt, peanut butter, and tahini. We will also sell reusable juice and smoothie cups and straws and will use only recycled and biodegradable packaging to minimize waste. Home Squeeze's drinks will appeal to the growing number of healthy and environmentally conscious professionals and university students who work and take classes at and near Iowa State University. Currently, these individuals—many Millennials and Gen Zs—have few options for grab-and-go drinks that are both filling and healthy. Home Squeeze, which will be located across Lincoln Avenue from the Memorial Student Union—will meet this need. Or, these individuals may enjoy their drinks in Home Squeeze's serene, spa-like space.

Consumer Trends

Consumers are moving to healthier, fast-casual choices. Home Squeeze taps into this movement and in particular targets the Millennial and Gen Z generations. Home Squeeze's products tap into Millennials' love of "hand-crafted," "artisanal," "small batches," and "small companies" (Arthur, 2016). In addition, studies have shown that Millennials engage in what is called "clockless" eating, meaning they are open to consuming products that older generations might consider breakfast items—such as juices and smoothies—at any point in the day (Arthur, 2016). As important, Millennials are now the largest living generation and were estimated to spend $1.4 trillion in 2020 (Netzer, 2020). On the other hand, Gen Z's buying power is—for now—smaller, but this generation's purchases comprised 40% of all shopping in 2020 (Netzer, 2019).

This business plan begins by describing the consumer trends that make this new business a good idea.

Both generations value healthy eating of the sort Home Squeeze will deliver. Over 60% of Millennials believe that their generation pays more attention to health than other generations; in particular, they look for less-processed foods with fewer artificial ingredients (Yue, 2019). In a survey of Gen Z members, 79% said that health plays a role as they determine what to buy (IBM, 2020). Both generations also value companies that engage in eco-friendly practices, as Home Squeeze will. In 2020, 78% of Millennials said that making purchases that support recycling is important to them; 72% of Gen Z said the same (IBM, 2020).

The Market

The market section argues that the market will support the business.

Ames is a college town located right in the middle of Iowa. It has seen continued population growth, reaching over 66,000 people in 2019. However, more broadly, central Iowa includes the cities of Boone, Nevada, Story City, and Gilbert, which together had a population of 23,631 in 2019. Ames is home to Iowa State University, a land-grant university of over 33,000 students. Because half of Ames's population is students, the average age is quite young: 23.3. The city is younger and more liberal than the surrounding, more rural areas, making it an ideal spot for a healthy-food establishment such as Home Squeeze. In addition, Ames has a lower unemployment rate than the national average (pre-pandemic): 2.2% compared to 3.7%. People in Ames have disposable income. Nearly as important as the market of Ames citizens is the market of people who come to Ames for sporting events, particularly football. Football season brings $63 million in revenue to Ames each year (Peterson, 2020).

(*Continued*)

Figure 12.4   A Business Plan for a New Juice and Smoothie Shop (*Continued*)

Community Involvement

I have been a resident of Ames for my entire life, and I am dedicated to ensuring that Home Squeeze benefits the community. We will engage with the surrounding campus community and the Ames community in general though donations and sponsorships, particularly sponsorships for university clubs and events. We also plan to partner with nearby yoga studios, becoming the place to meet before and after class. Home Squeeze will also partner with the Ames Bike Club, becoming a location for the club to meet up for rides. Our goal is to create an image of healthy living, which includes activity as well as healthy drinks and food.

This section discusses how the business will connect with people and businesses in the community in order to bring customers in.

Menu

Home Squeeze's healthy menu revolves around fruits and vegetables, many of which we will obtain through partnerships with local farms. We will serve raw juice mixes, such as kale, cucumber, apple, and lemon. The menu will also include smoothies, which blend fruits and vegetables with milk (e.g., soy, almond, cashew, or oat), yogurt (dairy or nondairy), protein powder, or nut butters (e.g., peanut butter, tahini). Home Squeeze will also sell fruit and vegetable salads. Customers can choose from veggie-only salads, such as a mixture of beets, cucumber, and kale. Or, they can enjoy veggie-fruit mixes—salads that mingle veggies like beets with fruits like orange and tangerine. Finally, we will offer all-fruit salads as well—bowls of citrus or apple blends.

A business plan must describe the product or service that the business will sell. In this case, the business will sell various menu items.

Location and Hours of Operation

Home Squeeze sits across Lincoln Way from Iowa State's Memorial Student Union and Lake Laverne (see Figure 1). It sits at the heart of Campustown—where it receives foot traffic from students and university employees. Ample parking is available behind the building.

A business plan must the location--or potential locations--for the business. The location in this case helps make the argument that the business will see plenty of foot traffic from the nearby university.

Figure 1. Home Squeeze's Ames Location.
Source: Google Maps.

Home Squeeze will open at 7:00am for those on their way to class and to work. It will close at 7:00pm.

Figure 12.4   A Business Plan for a New Juice and Smoothie Shop (*Continued*)

Footprint and Interior Design

Home Squeeze will use space efficiently. The Lincoln Way location provides 1,000 square feet of space, divided among a small, separate kitchen, a behind-the-counter prep area, and a seating area. The kitchen space will house three commercial-grade refrigerators, stations for salad prep, and prep sinks. The area behind the counter has room for industrial juicers and countertop prep. The seating area contains two display fridges for grab-and-go items and seating for 30 (a large communal table that seats ten, as well as three four-tops and four two-tops). The Lincoln Way location, formerly a pizza restaurant, is plumbed and wired properly for our needs.

The interior design will be minimalist, using light woods, such as bamboo, and light natural colors, such as sage greens. The idea is to convey a spa-like sense of nature, health, and calm (see Figure 2).

Figure 2. Bamboo and Sage Green Colors of Home Squeeze's Interior.
Prostock-studio/Alamy Stock Photo

Management and Personnel

As Home Squeeze's owner, I will also manage the day-to-day operations and social media. I have worked in restaurant management since 2010 and, more important, have had success in developing a new restaurant. In 2017, I started RocoTaco—a healthy taco restaurant—in Ankeny. RocoTaco has maintained a profit margin of 18% since 2018. In addition, RocoTaco has been recognized for its community partnerships and its LEED-certified building. I will bring my know-how to Home Squeeze.

I will also train two assistant managers to cover the shop during the hours I am not there. Other employees will be trained to cover back-end and front-end operations. When working in the back, employees will organize, label, and date food deliveries, prep fruits and veggies, make grab-and-go salads, and clean the kitchen. When working in the front, employees will take orders, mix juices and smoothies, and maintain the seating area.

Accounting

The main revenue source will be daily sales. Breakfast and lunch will generate the most sales; however, after-work sales will occur as well, as people grab a drink for the way home or a salad for dinner. Home Squeeze will also cater events, such as baby and wedding showers. Home Squeeze will use monthly, accrual-based accounting. We will manage finances through the point-of-sale system and QuickBooks.

A business plan should indicate the number of employees that the business will need. This business plan also discusses the relevant experience of the owner and manager, Mary S.

| **Figure 12.4** | A Business Plan for a New Juice and Smoothie Shop (*Continued*) |

Legal

Home Squeeze is an LLC incorporated in the State of Iowa; Luis Paisley from Paisley and Newburgh Law will serve as the corporate attorney.

Operating Expenses and Sales Forecast

We will open Home Squeeze in April, taking advantage of the warming weather that will bring customers in for a cool drink. The start-up costs (e.g., commercial refrigerators, display refrigerators, commercial-grade juicers, point-of-sale system, website) appear in the January, February, and March columns of Table 1. The ongoing expenses appear in the following columns, starting in April.

Most business plans contain far more financial information than this plan does; for example, they often contain a cash-flow statement, income projections, and budget that differentiates between fixed and variable costs. This business plan only outlines the start-up costs and initial operating expenses, including payroll.

Table 1. Operating Expenses for January to September 2021.

Operating Expense	Pre-Opening			Opening					
	Jan	Feb	Mar	Apr	May	Jun	Jul	Aug	Sep
Food Supplies				11,880	11,880	11,880	11,880	11,880	11,880
Payroll	1,000	1,000	1,000	18,500	18,500	18,500	18,500	18,500	18,500
Rent	0	2,500	2,500	2,500	2,500	2,500	2,500	2,500	2,500
Marketing	0	0	500	1,000	1,000	500	250	250	250
Website	0	2,500	10	10	10	10	10	10	10
Equipment	34,000	0	0	0	0	0	0	0	0
Utilities	0	0	250	250	250	250	250	250	250
Insurance	150	150	150	150	150	150	150	150	150
Other	375	450	1,300	250	250	250	250	250	250

The sales forecast appears in Table 2. Sales activity will occur around our opening in April and in May. A decline sales will likely occur during the summer as some Iowa State students return home. That said, during summer, Home Squeeze will market to Millennial and Gen Z professionals in Ames, pointing out its parking spaces that ease stopping for a drink and salad on the way to or from work. Home Squeeze will also work during summer to build our business partnerships, particularly with local yoga studios and fitness centers. And during this time we will connect with local groups, such as local cycling groups. Sales will rise again with the return of students in August. Home Squeeze will use more direct marketing during August, such as coupons distributed by property management companies who rent apartments to students.

Here the plan indicates a major challenge that the business will face-- students leaving Ames during the summer. It also states how the business will deal with this challenge.

Table 2. Sales Forecast for January to September 2021

Menu Item	Pre-Opening			Opening					
	Jan	Feb	Mar	Apr	May	Jun	Jul	Aug	Sep
Juice	0	0	0	14,400	15,600	10,500	10,500	13,330	15,600
Smoothies	0	0	0	45,000	47,000	28,650	28,650	35,800	47,000
Salads	0	0	0	18,000	20,000	13,400	13,400	16,300	20,000
Reusable Cups and Straws	0	0	0	1,800	2,000	1,050	1,050	1,500	2,000

Figure 12.4   A Business Plan for a New Juice and Smoothie Shop (*Continued*)

Competition

The only other dedicated juice and smoothie restaurant in Ames is a chain—The Smoothie Café. The Smoothie Café has another location in Ankeny. This chain has demonstrated the market for a juice and smoothie establishment.

Competitive Advantage

Home Squeeze's competitive advantage comes from its connection to Ames in general and the Campustown area in particular. Home Squeeze will support local farms and local organizations and partner with other businesses that fit our healthy-living brand. For example, we will sell fresh juices to other local restaurants, many of which sell orange and tomato juice. We will also supply our bottled juices to local businesses (that have refrigerator storage) at a discount in order to grow our market. While The Smoothie Café has shown that Ames can support a juice and smoothie restaurant, it does not strive to connect to other businesses and organizations, such as sports clubs, because it is a national chain. In addition, it is not located close to campus and has a poor foot-traffic location.

Disadvantages

Price point is the main concern when comparing Home Squeeze's juices to bottled juices. A 12oz bottle of Home Squeeze averages $8. A 12oz bottle of Suja Juice (owned by Coca Cola) is $5 ($0.66 per ounce versus $0.41 per ounce). However, Home Squeeze's prices compete with The Smoothie Café and other national chains that sell fresh juice, even though these chains do not buy from local farmers, as Home Squeeze will. Because we will buy from local farmers when possible (e.g., kale, spinach, beets, rhubarb, cantaloupe, honeydew, apples), Home Squeeze can save on inventory shipping costs.

Sales Strategy

Millennials and Gen Zs are health conscious and will pay for a healthy, fresh drink or salad. Home Squeeze will take advantage of its near-campus location by marketing to university students and young professionals who work at or near campus. Because parking is available at the back of the store, Home Squeeze can also market to professionals driving to their jobs at other locations, given that the store sits on Lincoln Way, a busy Ames thoroughfare. Home Squeeze will also partner with on-brand local businesses, such as yoga studios, the martial arts studio, fitness centers, and upscale spas.

Our website will be set up for online ordering, enabling our customers to order online and then pick up their orders from our store. Or, they can use UberEats or GrubHub and have their orders delivered.

As mentioned above, we intend to keep our prices competitive with other fresh-juice retailers, particularly The Smoothie Café. At Home Squeeze, an 8oz drink will average $5, and a 12oz drink will average $8. Our wholesale discount for partner businesses will be 12oz bottles for $5 and 16oz for $9. That will allow our partners to sell our juice at a mark-up of for $8 and $12.

Figure 12.4   A Business Plan for a New Juice and Smoothie Shop (*Continued*)

Direct Marketing and Social Media

Millennials and Gen Zs share views on key social and policy issues, for example, they are both more likely to see societal changes, linguistics changes (like neutral pronouns) and diversity as positive and ethical progress than their parent and grandparents (Parker & Igielnik, 2020), and they are likely to make purchasing choices based on those views. Millennials and Gen Zs both tend to base purchases on product quality, environmental sustainability, and discounts and reward programs (Costin, 2019; Morgan, 2020). In addition, Millennials appreciate quality customer service and brands that share their values (Costin, 2019), and 67% of Gen Zs value fashionable design. Both groups dislike advertisements and use adblockers (63% and 65% respectively), but 58% of Millennials respond favorably to influencers selling wares and 85% of Gen Zs skip advertisements as fast as possible (Morgan, 2020; Wagner, 2020).

This section discusses the specifics of the marketing plan, particularly direct marketing via coupons and online marketing via social media.

As both groups value discounts, we will offer and coupons for to new customers and reward programs for repeat customers. From a direct-marketing standpoint, coupons are key to attracting the college demographic. Every semester Home Squeeze employees will distribute free coupon books to students on campus. This marketing is more effective than other forms of print marketing because students have an affinity towards deals, and students are the ones that distribute the coupon books, creating a stronger bond of trust. The coupon will feature Home Squeeze's logo, contact information, website URL, and an offer to receive $10 off a juice cleanse. Incentivizing potential guests to try a juice cleanse will give Home Squeeze the opportunity to showcase its various flavors and the health benefits cold-pressed juice brings to the body and soul. Our reward program will offer an upgraded beverage of their choice for every ten purchases.

This section details the direct-marketing strategy.

Although both Millennials and Gen Zs are heavy users of social media, they privilege different social media (see Figure 1). Both Millennials and Gen Zs regularly use YouTube and Instagram, Millennials use Facebook, and Gen Zs use SnapChat and TikTok. Our marketing campaign will take advantage of these differences.

SOCIAL MEDIA USAGE

MILLENNIALS
- age 24-39 (in the year 2020)
- about 26% of US population
- 90.8% of US Millennials use social media

GEN Z
- age 8-23 (in the year 2020)
- about 25% of US population
- 64.4% of US Gen Zers use social media

WHO'S USING WHAT?
% using each platform

Platform	Millennials	Gen Z
Facebook	82	39.8
YouTube	79.1	76.2
Instagram	72.7	68.3
Twitter	27	22.9
Snapchat	48.6	88.2
Pinterest	39.7	24.5
TikTok	19	35

Figure 3. Social Media Use of Millennials versus Gen Zs.
Source: Wagner, 2020.
Ignite Social Media

Figure 12.4 A Business Plan for a New Juice and Smoothie Shop (*Continued*)

We will post on our Facebook and Instagram accounts several times a week. Posts on both sites will be an image of a quality product or ingredient with an explanation of its source and sustainability, brief customer testimonials, friendly customer-service moment, a thank you to a staff member for performing exceptionally well, or a congratulations to a customer or staff member. For Instagram, we will provide daily updates on our story (a picture or video that all followers can see but that only stays for 24 hours), whether it is a introducing a new product, a snowstorm outside the window, or a fun customer moment—something light-hearted that creates a smile.

Here the plan discusses the social media presence of the business, noting the different sites the business will use to reach its target demographics –Millennials and Gen Zs.

Our SnapChat and TikTok campaigns will use 15 to 30 second videos, set to popular music or themes, that show the building's interior, someone setting out all the healthy ingredients, the finishes on a beautiful drink, customers or staff dancing with their drinks, and customers enjoying their drinks out in life. The TikTok account is free and ours to control, but for SnapChat we will purchase ads that will appear between users' stories, which are pictures or videos that people put up for all of their contacts to see.

Future Plans

In the next five years, Home Squeeze will expand to two nearby cities. Ankeny is a suburb of Des Moines that has seen dramatic growth in the last 10 years. Its population has climbed from 45,582 in 2010 to over 71,569. Similarly, Des Moines has seen growth— from 203,433 in 2010 to 210,723 in 2020. Future plans for the Ames location and these second and third locations include more options for fruity salads and acai bowls to complement the full range of juices and smoothies.

References

Costin, G. (2019, May 1). Millennial spending habits and why they buy. Forbes. https://www.forbes.com/sites/forbesbooksauthors/2019/05/01/millennial-spending habits- and-why-they-buy/?sh=53fd9db740b8

Haller, K., Lee, J., & Cheung, J. (2020, June). Meet the 2020 consumers driving change: Why brands must deliver on omnipresence, agility, and sustainability. IBM. https://www.ibm.com/downloads/cas/EXK4XKX8

Morgan, B. (2020, February 28). 50 stats all marketers must know about Gen-Z. Forbes. https://www.forbes.com/sites/blakemorgan/2020/02/28/50-stats-all-marketers-must-know-about-gen-z/?sh=4100936476d0

Netzer, J. (2020, July 1). The top millennial buying habits and insights for 2021. Khoros. https://khoros.com/blog/millennial-buying-habits

Netzer, J. (2019, June 11). 5 Generation Z statistics on spending habits that marketers need to know. Khoros. https://khoros.com/blog/5-stats-generation-z-buying-habits

Figure 12.4   A Business Plan for a New Juice and Smoothie Shop (*Continued*)

Parker, K., & Igielnik, R. (2020, May 14). On the cusp of adulthood and facing an uncertain future: What we know about Gen Z so far. Pew Research Center. https://www.pewresearch.org/social-trends/2020/05/14/on-the-cusp-of-adulthood-and-facing-an-uncertain-future-what-we-know-about-gen-z-so-far-2/

Peterson, R. (2020, May 1). Iowa State football affects Ames to the tune of $63 million. *Des Moines Register*. https://www.desmoinesregister.com/story/sports/college/iowa-state/ randy-peterson/2020/05/01/will-college-football-be-played-2020-iowa-state-cyclones- ames-ncaa/3054840001/

Wagner, J. (2020, July 31). Infographic: Millennials vs Gen Z social media usage. Ignite Social Media. https://www.ignitesocialmedia.com/ social-media-marketing/ infographicmillennials-vs-gen-z-social-media-usage/

Yue, F. (2019, August 27). How millennials eat: Are they killing beer, American cheese and canned tuna? *USA Today*. https://www.usatoday.com/story/money/2019/08/26/millennial-eating-decisions-healthy-convenience-social-elements/2072794001/

Figure 12.5	Resources for Writing Grant Proposals	
Organization	**URL**	**Description**
Philanthropic Research Inc.	http://www.guidestar.org	Publishes free information about grants and grant makers.
Pivot-RP	https://pivot.proquest.com	Offers information on global funding opportunities, as well as tools to manage grants.
U.S. Department of Health and Human Services	http://www.grants.gov	Offers information on grant programs of all federal grantmaking agencies, as well as downloadable grant applications.
Candid	https://candid.org	Indexes foundations by state and city, as well as by field of interest.

for their organization. The writing process involves considerable research and planning and often is preceded by informal conversations and formal presentations to potential funders. The funding process often is seen as a relationship-building process that involves researching, negotiating with, and persuading funders that the proposal not only meets their guidelines, but also is a cause worthy of a grant.

In a grant proposal, stress the problem your project will solve and show how your project helps fulfill the goals of the organization you are asking for funds. Every funding agency has a mission, so be sure to align your idea to fit the agency's needs in obvious ways. Try to weave the agency's mission throughout your proposal's content. Remember effective *you*-attitude—write for the needs of your audience, not yourself.

Some funding agencies have detailed lists of the kind of projects they fund. Be sure to do research before applying. Check recent awards to discover foundations that may be interested in your project. See Figure 12.5 for additional resources.

The statement of the current situation in a grant proposal should specifically describe the problem the project will solve. This section also should discuss the population that will benefit from the work. Grant proposals are frequently rejected because writers do not effectively articulate the problem the proposal addresses.[7] One common problem is that writers mistake issues related to the solution with the underlying problem. For example, a writer may state that an organization needs a large moving truck, when, in fact, a moving truck may be one possible solution to the underlying problem the organization needs to solve—namely, delays in picking up donated items and distributing them to families in need. In describing the current situation, you should highlight the seriousness of the problem by illustrating its effect.[8] Quantifying the problem would help highlight the importance of the problem. If the proposal writer estimates that the company is losing 50 potential donations each month and has 100 families on a wait list, this figure will likely capture the audience's attention.

The project plan in a grant proposal should focus on the proposed solution. It should explain how the proposed project will remedy the underlying problem, such as lack of resources, technology, employees, or company procedures. In grant proposals, the project plan often includes a goal statement. The goal statement for the purchase of a moving truck might be articulated as follows: to increase our organization's donations to needy families by 30% and reduce delays in pickups by 50%.

Finally, pay close attention to deadlines by reading the fine print. Turn your materials in early. The National Endowment for the Humanities encourages fund seekers to submit drafts six weeks before the deadline to allow time for their staff to review materials.[9] Figure 12.6 shows an example of a grant proposal.

Figure 12.6   A Grant Proposal Addressed to the Corning Incorporated Foundation

March 4, 2020

Andrea Lynch, President
Corning Incorporated Foundation
MP-BH-7
Corning, NY 14831

Dear Ms. Lynch:

We are writing to inquire about a Corning Incorporated Foundation grant to fund our ongoing project: a database that links university faculty looking for service-learning opportunities for their communication courses with nonprofit organizations that want help with their communication projects. To meet these needs, we are expanding a database of service-learning projects for upper-division college and graduate communication students. We call it the Technical Communication (or TC) Database. In 2019, with a $1500 grant from the Council for Programs in Technical and Scientific Communication (CPTSC), we built a pilot database that now contains entries from 200 Alabama and Georgia nonprofits and that has to date facilitated 25 service-learning projects. Now, we are seeking additional funding to increase the size of the database to *10 times its current size* so that it can serve nonprofits nationwide. This funding would support a graduate student assistant who would be charged with contacting universities and nonprofits, and managing the data, and collecting feedback to improve the system. This funding would also support personnel for database development and server maintenance.

The grant proposal describes the project and states the need the project meets.

Here is the goal statement for the proposal.

Background
Research shows the critical importance of communication to nonprofit organizations' achieving their goals (e.g., Liu, 2012; Seshadri & Carstenson, 2007). Nonprofit organizations must make their communications stand out from the din of other mailings, emails, and advertisements that people receive each day. However, most nonprofits, particularly small and local organizations, have no dedicated professional communicator with the expertise and time to sculpt—via clear and concise language and via logical and eye-catching design—effective communications. Nonprofits like Alabama Alliance to End Homelessness, Alabama Youth Ballet Company, and Tuskegee Human & Civil Rights Multicultural Center, along with their counterparts in other states, welcome help from communication students on grant writing, website design, marketing materials, educational games, and myriad other publications and public education.

Again, the authors state the problem that the project helps to solve.

The authors point out one group that will benefit from the project-- nonprofit organizations.

Research also strongly indicates that students gain valuable experience from participating in service learning projects: they apply classroom knowledge and skills (understanding genres as they exist within authentic settings and even questioning those genres), learn to manage workplace challenges, and associate their activities with a real-world context, helping them transition from the classroom to the workplace (Blakeslee, 2001). Ideally, students also develop an appreciation for their field and for the work of the organizations they are assisting. By serving nonprofit organizations, students share in the nonprofits' service to communities. As a bonus, service-learning projects build ties among universities, as faculty and students collaborate with nonprofits on publication projects. For example, students at University of Memphis, who have access to a human-factors laboratory, could run usability tests on a website designed by communication students at the University of Minnesota-Duluth.

The authors point out other groups that will benefit from the project.

| Figure 12.6 | A Grant Proposal Addressed to the Corning Incorporated Foundation (*Continued*) |

Promoting Cooperation among Organizations

The TC Database connects faculty and students with nonprofits. This connection is critical, as ties between faculty and nonprofits can be difficult to establish initially. Faculty members sometimes have little contact with organizations outside the university, so they often rely on organizations affiliated with their institutions to fill their project needs. Also, when students are required to identify their own project opportunities, they often fall back on working with student organizations or workplaces with which they are already involved. In each of these cases, although the projects have merit, some organizations become over-relied-upon, straining ties between faculty and nonprofit organizations. The TC Database broadens the range of organizations that faculty and students have for client-based projects.

Here the authors state part of the problem.

The authors clearly state that the project aligns with the funding organization's goals (e.g., instructional technology), and then they explain how.

The TC Database readily meets the Corning Incorporated Foundation's interests. Communication programs enrich their curricula by connecting instructors and students looking for meaningful and educational project with nonprofits looking for help with their communication projects. Such communication projects will include instructional technology projects (e.g., students could potentially develop online tutorials and educational displays for nonprofit groups).

The TC Database's main purpose is to promote cooperation between communication programs (faculty and students) and nonprofit organizations. In addition, it creates potential collaborations among faculty who are affiliated with different universities but who are partnered with the same nonprofit organizations.

Qualifications

Our program at Auburn University is particularly well-suited for this project in terms of resources and tradition. Our technical and professional communication program houses six fulltime faculty in technical and professional communication, along with a cohort of graduate students, who can help administer the database. Also, have additional technical expertise from our College's IT staff, and we have piloted the database on our department's server. With about 30 relevant courses being taught within the 2019–2020, we have ample experience identifying appropriate projects, guiding students through those projects, and working collaboratively with nonprofit organizations. In terms of tradition, Auburn University, a land-grant school, has a strong tradition of outreach and service, demonstrated in the Rural Studio program, the Encyclopedia of Alabama, and the Alabama Prison Arts and Education Project. The TC Database continues Auburn University's tradition of service and outreach to worthy yet underfunded programs.

Description of the TC Database

The TC Database is searchable via an easy-to-use interface through which members of our field will access data. To help faculty assess the appropriateness of a given organization and project to the assignments in their classes, the database includes the following information about each nonprofit organization:

1. Name, location, and size
2. Status (e.g., religious, corporate, political)
3. Goals or mission
4. Typical activities of the local office

5. Likely writing and research needs (e.g., instructions, process descriptions, research reports, grants, proposals)
6. Special skills required to complete a given project (e.g., a knowledge of CSS)
7. Willingness to allow student to telecommute to complete a project
8. Amount of time per week or per project that organization members/employees can devote to assisting and mentoring students

Evaluating the TC Database

We will evaluate the progress of this project via three measures:

1. *User satisfaction*, measured via satisfaction ratings and comments from nonprofit employees, students, and instructors. The database allows opportunities for feedback from all users, both employees of a nonprofit, faculty, and students. Users will respond to several questions with radio buttons and at least one comment box. The results go into the database for research purposes, but the database managers also receive an email with the results so they can screen the responses for serious problems. Feedback from nonprofits remains private. Feedback from students has not been made public during the pilot phase of the database, but the forms will be designed to collect data that could conceivably be made public in the future (similar to product rankings on sites like Amazon.com). Feedback collected through the database will help us study how best to establish and maintain successful relationships with university and nonprofit partners.

2. *Number of service-learning projects initiated via the TC Database*, measured via frequency counts of database use for new and repeat users. We will be able to measure the frequency with which new projects are initiated via the TC Database and, thus, measure the growth of the project's outreach. We will also be able to measure the percentage of instructors and nonprofits who return to the database in later semesters for more projects.

3. *Enrollment in the TC Database*, measured via the number of nonprofit organizations that enter contact information into the TC Database (whether they connect with a partner and participate in a project). At this point, our goal is to enroll 2000 nonprofits.

The authors quantify their goal.

Many funding organizations want to know how you will evaluate the project. That is, how will you know whether it is successful?

Project Tasks, Timeline, and Staff

We have already gone through several initial steps for building the database, and our current funding, which will last through August 2020, will allow us to launch the pilot database and do limited initial recruiting. We see the database project developing in four stages: build, grow, evaluate, and refine. Our $1500 grant has funded the build stage. The grow stage will consume the most time, and it is for this stage that we seek funding from the Corning Incorporated Foundation.

Build: Spring-Summer 2020 (in progress)

- Develop and refine the pilot database and its interface. (Auburn IT staff and faculty)
- Develop a pilot list of universities that have substantial technical communication programs (institutions that will likely use the database), and establish preliminary contact with appropriate representatives of these universities to encourage their use of the database. (Auburn faculty and graduate research assistant, funded by a CPTSC grant)

Figure 12.6	A Grant Proposal Addressed to the Corning Incorporated Foundation (*Continued*)

- Develop a target list of nonprofit organizations near these universities that might have service learning opportunities. (Auburn faculty and graduate research assistant, funded by a CPTSC grant)
- Contact these nonprofit organizations, soliciting their participation and requesting suggestions for other participants. (Auburn faculty and graduate research assistant, funded by a CPTSC grant)
- Develop a list of websites appropriate for posting links to our database (e.g., Nonprofit Resource Center of Alabama) and establish contact with the webmasters of these sites. (Auburn faculty and graduate research assistant, funded by a CPTSC grant)
- Conduct usability testing on the interface. (Auburn faculty)

Grow: Fall 2020-Spring 2021
- Refine the pilot database. (Auburn IT staff and faculty)
- Continue to build list of universities that have substantial technical communication programs, establish contact with appropriate representatives of these universities to encourage their use of the database. (Auburn faculty and graduate research assistant)
- Grow the list of nonprofit organizations (particularly ones near universities with technical communication programs) that might have service-learning opportunities. Include more nonprofits outside Alabama and more national nonprofits. (graduate research assistant)
- Continue to contact nonprofit organizations, soliciting their participation and requesting suggestions for other participants. (graduate research assistant)
- Grow the list of websites appropriate for posting links to our database (e.g., Wisconsin Non-Profits Association) and establish contact with the webmasters of these sites. (graduate research assistant)

Evaluate: Summer 2021
- Gather and analyze participants' ratings and comments. (Auburn faculty)

Refine: Fall 2021
- Refine the data-entry system, contact procedures, usability of the interface, etc., based on feedback and usability testing results. (Auburn faculty, Auburn IT staff)
- Refine the rating system and feedback questionnaire to assess better users' satisfaction with the database and their service-learning experiences. (Auburn faculty)

Budget
Specifically, we are seeking funding for equipment and personnel to expand the database beyond the pilot stage, increasing nonprofit entries from 200 to over 2000, adding more university partners, improving the usability of the database, and marketing the database nationwide. See Table 1.

Table 1. Budget items, task, and cost

The budget relates directly to the project tasks and timeline.

Budget item	Task	Cost
Graduate Student Salary (1 year) Developer's Stipend (1 year)	Completing tasks in the project's Grow stage Refining the database	19,357.45 2,000.00
Server Maintenance	Coordinating the care of the virtual server	1,000.00
Printing and Mailing	Creating, printing, and mailing relevant materials (participant recruiting, advertising, and gathering feedback)	2,000.00
	Total	24,537.45

Self-Sufficiency

Funding from the Corning Incorporated Foundation will see us through the most labor-intensive stage of our project. The last two stages will require less maintenance, and we have already begun to write a proposal for a Breeden grant, an internal funding source at Auburn University, to cover our costs in the Evaluate and Refine stages. Other internal grant opportunities at Auburn make this project likely to be sustained from within the university.

We look forward to hearing from you. Thank you for considering our request.

Sincerely,
Lisa Hughes and Linda Allen
515.334.9081
hughes@email.edu
Department of English
Auburn University

Enclosure: Reference List

Preparing the Budget and Costs Sections

LO 12-4

A good budget is crucial to making the winning bid. In fact, your budget may be the most scrutinized part of your business proposal.

Ask for everything you need to do a quality job. Asking for too little may backfire, leading the funder to think that you don't understand the scope of the project. Include less obvious costs, such as overhead. Also include costs that will be paid from other sources. Doing so shows that other sources also have confidence in your work. Pay particular attention to costs that may appear to benefit you more than the sponsor, such as travel and equipment. Make sure they are fully justified in the proposal.

Do some research. Read the RFP to find out what is and isn't fundable. Talk to the program officer and the person who administers the funding process and read successful past proposals to find answers to the following questions:

- What size projects will the organization fund in theory?

- Does the funder prefer making a few big grants or many smaller grants?

- Does the funder expect you to provide in-kind or cost-sharing funds from other sources?

Think about exactly what you'll do and who will do it. What will it cost to get that person? What supplies or materials will they need? Also think about indirect costs for office space; retirement and health benefits, as well as salaries; and office supplies, administration, and infrastructure.

Make the basis of your estimates specific.

Weak:	75 hours of transcribing interviews	$1,500
Better:	25 hours of interviews; a skilled transcriber can complete 1 hour of interviews in 3 hours; 75 hours @ $20/hour	$1,500

Figure your numbers conservatively. For example, if the going rate for skilled transcribers is $20 an hour, but you think you might be able to train someone and pay only $12 an hour, use the higher figure. Then, even if your proposal receives only partial funding, you'll still be able to do the project.

Writing Topic Proposals for Class Projects

LO 12-5

Proposals for Class Research Projects

If you're writing a proposal that your instructor has assigned for an in-class assignment, such as a research report, your instructor will want to know several things. They will want evidence that your problem is meaningful but not too big to complete in the allotted time, that you understand the topic and the problem, that your method will give you the information you need, that you have the knowledge and resources to collect and analyze the data, and that you can produce the report by the deadline. See Figure 12.7 for an example of a proposal for a class research project.

A proposal for a student report usually has the following sections:

1. In your first paragraph (no heading), summarize in a sentence or two the topic and purposes of your report.

2. **Problem/opportunity.**   What problem or opportunity exists? Why does it need to be solved or explored? Is there a history or background that is relevant?

3. **Feasibility.**   Are you sure that a solution can be found in the time available? How do you know? (This section may not be appropriate for some class projects.)

4. **Audience.**   Who in the organization would have the power to implement the recommendation in your report? What secondary audiences might be asked to evaluate your report? What audiences would be affected by your recommendation? Will anyone in the organization serve as a gatekeeper, determining whether your report is sent to decision makers? What watchdog audiences might read the report? Will there be other readers?

   For each of these audiences give the person's name and job title and answer the following questions:

   · What is the audience's major concern or priority?
   · What will the audience see as advantages of your proposal? What objections, if any, is the audience likely to have?
   · How interested is the audience in the topic of your report?
   · How much does the audience know about the topic of your report?

   List any terms, concepts, or assumptions that one or more of your audiences may need to have explained. Briefly identify ways in which your audiences may affect the content, organization, or style of the report.

5. **Topics to investigate.**   List the questions you will answer in your report, the topics or concepts you will explain, and the aspects of the problem or opportunity you will discuss. Indicate how deeply you will examine each of the aspects you plan to treat. Explain your rationale for choosing to discuss some aspects of the problem or opportunity and not others.

6. **Methods/procedure.**   How will you get answers to your questions? Who will you interview or survey? What questions will you ask? What published sources will you use? Provide a complete list of references. Your methods section should clearly indicate how you will get the information needed to answer questions posed in the other sections of the proposal.

7. **Qualifications/facilities/resources.**   Do you have the knowledge and skills needed to conduct this study? Do you have adequate access to the organization? Is the necessary information available to you? Are you aware of any supplemental information? Where will you turn for help if you hit an unexpected snag?

   You'll be more convincing if you have already scheduled an interview, drafted a survey, or located online sources.

8. **Work schedule.**   For each activity, list both the total time you plan to spend on it and the date when you expect to finish it. Some possible activities you might include are gathering information, analyzing information, preparing a progress report, writing the report draft, revising the draft, preparing visuals, editing and proofreading the report, and preparing the oral presentation. Think of activities needed to complete your specific project.

   These activities frequently overlap. Many writers start analyzing and organizing information as it comes in. They start writing pieces of the final document and preparing visuals early in the process.

   Organize your work schedule in either a chart or calendar. A good schedule provides realistic estimates for each activity, allows time for unexpected snags, and shows that you can complete the work on time.

9. **Call to action.**   In your final section, indicate that you'd welcome any suggestions your instructor may have for improving the research plan. Ask your instructor to approve your proposal so that you can begin work on your report.

   Figure 12.7 shows a student proposal for a long report.

Figure 12.7   Proposal for a Student Team Report

Month Day, Year *Enter current date.*

To: Professor Christopher Toth

From: JASS LLC (Jordan Koole, Alex Kuczera,   *In the subject line ①indicate that this is a proposal*
             Shannon Jones, Sean Sterling)   *②specify the kind of report*
                                                                    ③specify the topic

Subject: Proposal to Research and Make Recommendations on the Feasibility
             of Expanding RAC Inc. to South Korea

Summarize topic and purpose of report. RAC Inc. has recently approached our company to determine the possibility of expanding internationally. We believe South Korea could be suitable for this expansion based on our initial investigation of technology in the country. This proposal provides a brief look at South Korea and gives an overview of our research topics and procedures in preparation for the formal research report.

Problem

If the "Problem" section is detailed and well-written, you may be able to use it unchanged in your report.
After establishing a solid consumer base in the U.S., RAC Inc. is looking to expand its business internationally so that it does not fall behind its competitors. It has asked us to research South Korea as a possible alternative site for the manufacturing of its slate tablets.

Country Overview   *This section is a "Background" section for this proposal. Not all proposals include background.*

After some initial research, we believe that South Korea is a suitable country to research for RAC's international manufacturing of new technology. South Korea has a population of 51.2 million, with 27% of the population located in the capital city Seoul and in Busan. They have a labor force of 27.47 million, ranking as the 24th highest workforce in the world (CIA Factbook, 2018). The official language is Korean, but English, Chinese, and Japanese are taught as second languages (U.S. Department of State, 2017). *Proposal uses in-text citations.*

In 1950, North Korea invaded South Korea, beginning the Korean War. After three years of fighting and pushing troops across both borders, North and South Korea signed an armistice and agreed to a demilitarized zone (DMZ), which currently serves as the border between the two countries and is protected by both countries' military (U.S. Department of State, 2017). While relations between the two countries are still tense and a few minor skirmishes along the border have occurred, we are not concerned about South Korea's stability.

In fact, since the devastation of the Korean War, the economy of South Korea has recovered and has joined the ranks of the most economically prosperous nations. They have risen to the 15th highest GDP in the world and have the 45th highest GDP per capita at the equivalent of $39,400. They have a very low unemployment rate that has dropped in the last year to 3.8% (CIA Factbook, 2018).

South Korea is now ranked the 6th largest exporter in the world and the 9th largest importer. Their economic policy has emphasized exporting products, explaining why their exports are so high (U.S. Department of State, 2017). Their main exports include computers and component parts, semiconductors, and wireless telecommunication equipment. South Korea is known for making excellent products in these areas. They export mainly to the U.S., China, and Japan, and import primarily from the same countries. As one of the most economically healthy countries in the world, South Korea is situated as a prime country for RAC Inc.'s possible expansion.

Not all class reports will need a "Feasibility" section.

(Continued)

Figure 12.7   Proposal for a Student Team Report (*Continued*)

Include a header on all additional pages.

RAC Inc. Proposal
Month Day, Year *Enter current date.*
Page 2

List your major audiences. Identify their knowledge, interests, and concerns.

Audience

Our formal report will have multiple layers of audiences.

- *Gatekeeper*: Professor Toth has the power to accept or reject our proposal for the formal report before it is passed on to Ms. Katie Nichols from RAC Inc.

- *Primary*: Ms. Katie Nichols, CEO of RAC Inc., and the board of directors are our primary audiences, along with other influential members of RAC Inc. They will decide whether to accept the recommendation found in the formal report.

- *Secondary*: Employees of RAC Inc., the legal department of RAC Inc., as well as current RAC Inc. employees who may be transferred to South Korea all may be affected by the primary audience's decision. In addition, the potential employees in South Korea who would work for RAC Inc. also make up this audience.

- *Auxiliary*: Other employees not involved with the expansion effort into South Korea and any Americans or South Koreans who will read about the expansion in the news serve this role.

- *Watchdog*: Stockholders of RAC Inc., the South Korean government, the Securities and Exchange Commission (SEC), the U.S. Department of Commerce, and other companies that may want to expand internationally to South Korea all have economic, social, and political power. Competitors of RAC Inc. already in South Korea (Samsung and LG) also may pay close attention.

Indicate what you'll discuss briefly and what you'll discuss in more detail. This list should match your audiences' concerns.

Topics to Investigate

We plan to answer the following questions in detail:

1. What information does RAC Inc. need to know about South Korean culture, politics, economy, and workforce to be succesful?

   All items in list must be grammatically parallel. Here, all are questions.

   - Culture—What differences exist between Korean and American cultures that might influence the move?
   - Politics—How will relationships between North and South Korea and relationships between the U.S. and South Korea affect business with South Korea?
   - Economics—What is the current economic state of the country? How could free trade between the U.S. and South Korea affect business?
   - Workforce—What is the availabe workforce? How will the economy of the country affect the overall workforce?

2. How should RAC Inc. adapt its business practices to successfully expand into the South Korean market?

   - Competition—Who is the competition in South Korea? How could they affect the business?
   - Location—What city could RAC Inc. expand to for production of the slate tablet? Where should it locate the headquarters? Where should it host the initial product launch?
   - Slate Tablet—What changes, if any, are needed to market and sell the product in South Korea?

Figure 12.7   Proposal for a Student Team Report (*Continued*)

RAC Inc. Proposal
Month Day, Year
Page 3

3. What other issues may RAC Inc. have by introducing its product into South Korea?

If it is well written, "Topics to Investigate" section will become the "Scope" section of the report—with minor revisions.

- Business Culture—How will the differences in business culture influence the expansion to South Korea?
- Technology—To what extent will the advanced state of South Korean technology influence marketing the tablet?
- Marketing—How will competitors' similar products sold in South Korea influence business?
- Integration—How receptive are the people of South Korea to new products from different companies and countries?

If you'll administer a survey or conduct interviews, tell how many participants you'll have, how you'll choose them, and what you'll ask them. This student team does not use a survey.

Methods and Resources

We expect to obtain our information from (1) various websites, (2) articles, and (3) interviews with a native South Korean. The following websites and articles appear useful.

If you're using library or web research, list sources you hope to use. Use full bibliographic citations.

Central Intelligence Agency. (2018). *The world factbook: South Korea*. Retrieved March 18, 2018, from https:/ /www.cia.gov/library/publications/the-world-factbook/geos/ks.html#.

Fackler, M. (2011, January 6). Lessons learned, South Korea makes quick economic recovery. *The New York Times*. Retrieved from http:/ / www.nytimes.com/2011/01/07/world/asia/07seoul.html?_r=2.

Jeon, Kyung-Hwan. (2010, September 7). Why your business belongs in South Korea. Retrieved from http:/ /www.openforum.com/articles/why-your-business-belongs-in-south-korea-kyung-hwan-jeon.

This list uses APA format.

Life in Korea. (n.d.). Cultural spotlight. Retrieved March 31, 2018, from http:/ /www.lifeinkorea.com/Culture/spotlight.cfm.

Ogg, E. (2010, May 28). What makes a tablet a tablet? *CNet News*. Retrieved March 19, 2018, from http:/ /news.cnet.com/8301-31021_3-20006077-260.html?tag=newsLeadStoriesArea.1.

Your list of sources should convince your instructor that you have made initial progress on the report.

Settimi, C. (2010, September 1). Asia's 200 best under a billion. *Forbes*. Retrieved from http://www.forbes.com/2010/09/01/ bub-200-intro-asia-under-billion-10-small-companies.html.

UK Trade & Investment. (2011). 100 opportunities for UK companies in South Korea. Retrieved March 19, 2018, from http:/ /www.ukti.gov.uk/export/countries/asiapacific/fareast/koreasouth/item/119500.html.

U.S. Department of State. (2017, December 10). Background note: South Korea. Retrieved March 18, 2018, from http:/ /www.state.gov/r/pa/ei/bgn/2800.htm.

World Business Culture. (n.d.). Doing business in South Korea. Retrieved March 19, 2018, from http:/ /www.worldbusinessculture.com/Business-in-South-Korea.html.

Figure 12.7 Proposal for a Student Team Report (*Continued*)

RAC Inc. Proposal
Month Day, Year
Page 4

Qualifications *Cite knowledge and skills from other classes, jobs, and activities that will enable you to conduct the research and interpret your data.*

We are all members of JASS LLC who have backgrounds in finance, accounting, computer science, and technology. These diverse backgrounds in the business and technology world give us a good perspective and insight for this project. In addition, we are all enrolled in a business communication course that provides us with knowledge on producing high-quality documents. We are dedicated to producing a thoroughly researched report that will provide solid evidence on the feasibility of an international expansion for RAC Inc. into South Korea.

Work Schedule

The following schedule will enable us to finish this report on time.

Activity	Total Time	Completion Date
Gathering information	12 hours	March 30
Analyzing information	8 hours	April 2
Organizing information	4 hours	April 7
Writing draft/creating visuals	8 hours	April 10
Revising draft	3 hours	April 12
Preparing presentation slides	3–4 hours	April 14
Editing draft	3 hours	April 17
Proofreading report	3 hours	April 18
Rehearsing presentation	2 hours	April 20
Delivering presentaion	1 hour	April 21

Good reports need good revision, editing, and proofreading as well as good research.

Allow plenty of time.

Time will depend on the length and topic of your report, your knowledge of the topic, and your writing skills.

Call to Action

We are confident that JASS LLC can complete the above tasks as scheduled. We would appreciate any suggestions for improving our project plan. Please approve our proposal so that we may begin work on the formal report.

It's tactful to indicate you'll accept suggestions. End on a positive, forward-looking note.

Summary by Learning Objectives

LO 12-1 **Define proposals.**

Proposals define a problem or opportunity, argue for a specific solution, and provide reasons the proposal writer or their organization should do the work. Competitive proposals compete against each other for limited resources; noncompetitive proposals have no real competition.

LO 12-2 **Brainstorm for writing proposals.**

A proposal must answer the following questions:

- What problem are you going to solve, or what opportunity do you hope to fulfill?
- Why does the problem need to be solved now or the opportunity explored immediately?
- How are you going to solve it?
- Can you do the work?
- Why should you be the one to do it?
- When will you complete the work?
- How much will you charge?
- What exactly will you provide for us?

LO 12-3 **Organize proposals.**

- Proposals for businesses usually employ the following organization: introduction, current situation, project plan, qualifications, costs and benefits.

- Sales proposals are useful to sell expensive goods or services.
- Funding proposals should stress the needs your project will meet. Show how your project will help fulfill the audience's goals.
- Business plans need to pay particular attention to market potential and financial forecasts.

LO 12-4 **Prepare budget and costs sections.**

In a project budget, ask for everything you will need to do a good job. Research current cost figures so yours are in line. For costs that appear to benefit you more than the sponsor, give full justifications.

LO 12-5 **Produce different kinds of proposals.**

In a proposal, show that your problem is meaningful but not too big in scope for you to address, that you understand it, that your method will give you the information you need to solve the problem, that you have the knowledge and resources, and that you can produce the deliverable by the deadline.

Exercises and Cases

12.1   Reviewing the Chapter

1. What is the difference between a competitive and noncompetitive proposal? (LO 12-1)
2. What are six brainstorming questions to consider before starting your proposal? (LO 12-2)
3. What is the organization of a business proposal? (LO 12-3)
4. What are some tips for writing a sales proposal? (LO 12-3)

5. What is a business plan? (LO 12-3)
6. In a grant proposal, what is a goal statement? (LO 12-3)
7. What are some guidelines for preparing a budget for a proposal? (LO 12-4)
8. When writing a topic proposal for a class report, what questions should you ask yourself about the report's audience? (LO 12-5)

12.2   Analyze a Real Proposal

Visit the following website: https://www.denvergov.org/content/dam/denvergov/Portals/696/documents/Green%20Roofs%20Review%20Task%20Force/Green_Building_Policy_Proposal.pdf

In groups, answer the following questions:

- What kind of proposal is this?
- What problems does it address?

- What solutions does it offer?
- What is the structure of the proposal?
- Who are the multiple audiences?
- What is the purpose of the proposal?
- Is there any information that is missing?
- What is the style of the proposal?

12.3   Writing a Proposal for a Student Report

Write a proposal to your instructor to do the research for a formal or informal report. The headings and the questions in the section titled "Proposals for Class Research Projects" are your RFP; be sure to answer every question and to use the headings exactly as stated in the RFP. Exception: where alternate heads are listed, you may choose one, combine the two ("Qualifications and Facilities"), or treat them as separate headings in separate categories.

12.4   Proposing a Change

No organization is perfect, especially when it comes to communication. Propose a change that would improve communication within your organization. The change can be specific to your unit or can apply to the whole organization; it can relate to how important information is distributed, who has access to important information, how information is accessed, or any other change in communication practices that you see as having a benefit. Direct your proposal to the person or committee with the power to authorize the change.

12.5   Proposing to Undertake a Research Project

Pick a project you would like to study whose results could be used by your organization. Write a proposal to your supervisor requesting time away from other duties to do the research. Show how your research (whatever its outcome) will be useful to the organization.

12.6   Writing a Proposal for a Nonprofit Group

Pick a nonprofit group you care about. Examples include a professional organization, a charitable group, a community organization, or your own college or university.

As your instructor directs,

a.   Use one of the websites listed in Figure 12.5 to find a foundation that makes grants to groups such as yours. Brainstorm a list of businesses that might be willing to give money for specific projects. Check to see whether state or national levels of your organization make grants to local chapters.

b.   Write a proposal to obtain funds for a special project your group could undertake if it had the money. Address your proposal to a specific organization.

c.   Write a proposal to obtain operating funds or money to buy something your group would like to have. Address your proposal to a specific organization.

12.7   Writing a Sales Proposal

Pick a project that you could do for a local company or government office. Examples include

- Establishing a social media presence.
- Creating a brochure, web page, or series of infographics.
- Revising form letters or other routine communications.
- Conducting a training program.
- Writing a newsletter or an annual report.
- Developing a marketing plan.

Write a proposal specifying what you could do and providing a detailed budget and work schedule.

As your instructor directs,

a.   Phone or email someone in the organization to talk about its needs and what you could offer.

b.   Write an individual proposal.

c.   Join with other students in the class to create a team proposal.

d.   Present your proposal orally.

12.8   Presenting a Stockholder Proposal

Visit the websites of the following companies and locate their latest proxy statements or reports. These are generally linked from the "about us/company information–investor relations" or "investors" pages. Find shareholder proposals under the heading "proposals requiring your vote," "stockholder proposals," or "shareholder proposals."

- Facebook
- Ford Motor Company
- Citigroup
- AT&T
- JPMorgan Chase & Co.
- Delta Air Lines
- Home Depot
- Procter & Gamble
- Boeing
- Dow Chemical

As a team, select one proposal and the management response following it, and give an oral presentation answering these questions:

1. What is the problem discussed in the proposal?
2. What is the rationale given for the urgency to solve the problem?
3. How does the proposal seek to solve it?

4. What benefits does the proposal mention that will accrue from the solution?
5. What is the management response to the proposal, and what are the reasons given for the response? Does the management response strike you as justified? Why or why not?

Hint: It may help you to do some research on the topic of the proposal.

Notes

1. National Science Foundation, "Funding and Support Descriptions," September 14, 2021, https://www.nsf.gov/homepagefundingandsupport.jsp.
2. "NSF at a Glance," About the National Science Foundation, accessed June 23, 2018, http://www.nsf.gov/about/glance.jsp; and "NIH Budget," About NIH: Budget, accessed June 23, 2018, https://www.nih.gov/about-nih/what-we-do/budget.
3. Jennifer Wisdom, Halley Riley, and Neely Myers, "Recommendations for Writing Successful Grant Proposals: An Information Synthesis," *Academic Medicine* 90, no. 12 (December 2015): 1720–25.
4. Ibid., 1722.
5. James Vincler and Nancy Horlick-Vincler, "Producing Persuasive Proposals," *Journal of Management in Engineering* 12, no. 5 (1996): 20–24.
6. John Mullens, "Why Business Plans Don't Deliver," *Wall Street Journal*, June 22, 2009, R3.
7. Karina Stokes, "Writing Clear Statements of Needs and Goals for Grant Proposals," *AMWA Journal* 27, no. 1 (2012): 25–28.
8. Ibid., 25–26.
9. "Grant Programs and Details," National Endowment for the Humanities, accessed June 24, 2013, http://www.neh.gov/grants.

Chapter Outline

DrAfter123/Getty Images

Reporting a Vision for STEM Education

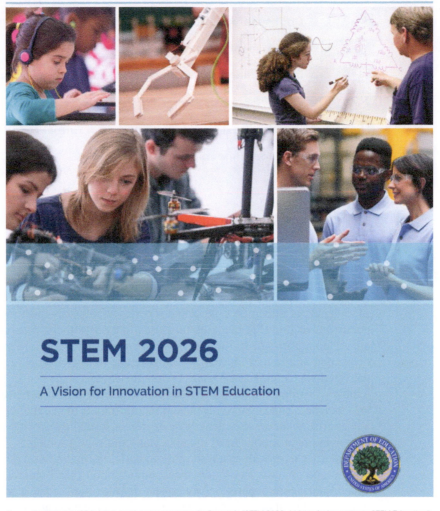

STEM 2026

A Vision for Innovation in STEM Education

Source: Department of Education and American Institutes for Research, "STEM 2026: A Vision for Innovation in STEM Education," September 2016, https://www.air.org/system/files/downloads/report/STEM-2026-Vision-for-Innovation-September-2016.pdf

Corporations, nonprofits, and government organizations routinely use reports to communicate important information to stakeholders, investors, and the general public. In 2015, the U.S. Department of Education teamed up with the American Institutes for Research (AIR) and held a series of workshops for experts in science, technology, engineering, and mathematics (STEM). The workshops culminated in a collaborative report, published in September 2016, from the Department of Energy and AIR titled "STEM 2026: A Vision for Innovation in STEM Education."

The report's purpose was to articulate a 10-year vision for STEM education by detailing key components of STEM teaching philosophy, exploring challenges and opportunities, and recommending future actions.

Often, reports have multiple audiences. The STEM 2026 report had a variety of audiences: teachers, education administrators, academics, policy makers, as well as the general public. Another important goal of the STEM report was to present a positive image of STEM education and promote the values that STEM education provides.

The 60-plus-page report was written in a formal style and contained many of the elements of formal reports described in this chapter, including a title page, executive summary, table of contents, introduction, body, conclusion, references, and appendices.

Whether writing reports for a government agency or a multinational corporation, the process involves diligent research, careful drafting, revising, and editing, and effective organization of information.

Source: Department of Education and American Institutes for Research, "STEM 2026: A Vision for Innovation in STEM Education," September 2016, https://www.air.org/system/files/downloads/report/STEM-2026-Vision-for-Innovation-September-2016.pdf.

After studying this chapter, you should be able to

LO 13-1 Identify varieties of reports.

LO 13-2 Define report problems.

LO 13-3 Choose information for reports.

LO 13-4 Organize reports.

LO 13-5 Use headings and subheadings effectively in reports.

LO 13-6 Produce progress reports.

LO 13-7 Prepare the different components of formal reports.

LO 13-8 Produce white papers.

Varieties of Reports

LO 13-1

Many kinds of documents are called reports. In some organizations, a report is a long document or one that contains numerical data. In others, one- and two-page memos are called reports. In still others, reports consist of PowerPoint slides delivered orally or printed and bound together. A short report to a client may use letter format or be delivered via email. **Formal reports** contain elements such as a title page, a transmittal, a table of contents, an executive summary, and a list of illustrations. **Informal reports** may be letters and emails or even computer printouts of production or sales figures. But all reports, whatever their length or degree of formality, provide the information that people in organizations need to make plans and solve problems.

Reports can provide just information, both information and analysis alone, or information and analysis to support a recommendation (see Figure 13.1). Reports can be called **information reports** if they collect data for the reader, **analytical reports** if they interpret data but do not recommend action, and **recommendation reports** if they recommend action or a solution.

The following reports can be information, analytical, or recommendation reports, depending on what they provide:

- **Accident reports** list the nature and causes of accidents in a factory or office. These reports also can analyze the data and recommend ways to make conditions safer.

- **Credit reports** summarize an applicant's income and other credit obligations. These reports also can evaluate the applicant's collateral and creditworthiness and recommend whether to provide credit.

- **Trip reports** share what the author learned at a conference or during a visit to a customer or supplier. These reports also can recommend action based on that information.

- **Closure reports** document the causes of a failure or possible products that are not economically or technically feasible under current conditions. They also can recommend action to prevent such failures in the future.

- **Return on investment (ROI) reports** correlate how money companies spend on advertising relates to sales or increased traffic. Marketing firms routinely compose these reports for clients.

Figure 13.1	Variety of Information Reports Can Provide

Information only

Sales reports: discussions of sales figures for the week or month.

Quarterly reports: discussions of a plant's productivity and profits for the quarter.

A3 reports: syntheses of information from multiple sources into one page for the purpose of reporting progress or making decisions.

Information plus analysis

Annual reports: analyses of financial data and an organization's accomplishments during the past year.

Audit reports: interpretations of the facts revealed during an audit.

Make-good or **payback reports:** calculations of the point at which a new capital investment will pay for itself.

Information plus analysis plus a recommendation

Recommendation reports: evaluations of two or more alternatives that recommend which alternative the organization should choose.

Feasibility reports: evaluations of a proposed action that show whether it will work.

Justification reports: justifications of the need for a purchase, an investment, a new personnel line, or a change in procedure.

Problem-solving reports: analyses of an organizational problem that recommend a solution.

- **Progress and interim reports** record the work done so far and the work remaining on a project. These reports also can analyze the quality of the work and recommend that a project be stopped, continued, or restructured.

- **White paper reports** explain a problem and then may advocate for a solution to the problem. These reports can be written to inform a general audience. Sometimes companies use white paper reports for marketing purposes.

Later in this chapter, we discuss progress reports, formal reports, and white paper reports in more detail.

Problems That Reports Address

LO 13-2

Good reports grow out of real problems: disjunctions between reality and the ideal, choices that must be made. When you write a report as part of your job, your organization may define the problem for you. However, quite often the problem is not well-understood; your organization might know *something* is wrong, but it may not know exactly what. For example, there might be reoccurring delays in responses to customers' inquiries. Is it an employee problem? A software problem? Or perhaps production on the factory floor is lagging. Is it a materials supply issue? An employee training issue? Something else? Is the problem under your organization's control? As the author of the report, you will have to conduct research to determine what the problem actually is and how broad and deep the problem is. You'll have to determine who has oversight of factors related to the problem. Then, you will have to define and describe the problem so that the audience for your report understands it, its scope, and its effects.

A good report problem in business meets the following criteria:

1. The problem is
   - Real.
   - Important enough to be worth solving.
   - Narrow but challenging.

2. The audience for the report is
   - Real.
   - Able to implement the recommended action.

3. The data, evidence, and facts are
   - Sufficient to document the severity of the problem.
   - Sufficient to prove that the recommendation will solve the problem.
   - Available to *you.*
   - Comprehensible to *you.*

Often, problems need to be narrowed. A class report problem for example, "improving the college experiences of international students studying in the U.S." is far too broad. First, identify the college or university that is the focus of the report. Second, identify the specific problem. Is the problem the lack of social interaction between U.S. and international students? Is the problem that international students have difficulties finding housing? Third, identify the specific audience that would have the power to implement your recommendations. Depending on the specific topic, the audience might be the Office of International Studies, the residence hall counselors, or a service organization on campus or in town.

Some problems are more easily researched than others. For researching international students' experiences at University A, if you have easy access to the Chinese Student Association, you can survey its members about their experiences at the local Chinese grocery. However, if you want to research ways to keep the local Chinese grocery in business, but you do not have access to the store's financial records, you will have a much more difficult time recommending a potential solution. Even if you have access, if the records are written in Chinese, you will have problems unless you read the language or have a willing translator.

When writing a report, be cognizant of your time constraints. Define and describe a problem you can solve in the time available and make sure to identify the limitations of your project. Six months of full-time (and overtime) work and a team of colleagues might allow you to look at all the ways to make a store more profitable. If you're expected to complete a report in 6 to 12 weeks and it is only one of your responsibilities, limit the topic. Depending on your ability and knowledge, you could choose to examine the prices and brands carried, its inventory procedures, its overhead costs, its layout and décor, or its advertising budget. In your report, you will explain the limitations of your project so that the audience will be able to put your report in context.

Look at the following examples of report problems in the category of technology use:

Too broad:	How does texting in class affect college students?
Too time-consuming:	What are the effects of in-class texting on college students?
Better:	What are texting habits of students in XYZ University's business school?
Better:	How can texting be integrated in XYZ University's business courses?

The first problem is too broad because it covers all college students. The second one is too time-consuming. To do a report on this topic, you would need to do your own longitudinal study (i.e., a study of students' in-class texting habits over time). The third and fourth problems both would be possibilities. You would select one over the other depending on whether you wanted to focus on students or courses.

How you define the problem shapes the solutions you find. For example, suppose that a manufacturer of frozen foods isn't making money. If the problem is defined as a marketing problem, the researcher may analyze the product's price, image, advertising, and position in the market. But perhaps the problem is really that overhead costs are too high due to poor inventory management or that an inadequate distribution system doesn't get the product to its target market. Defining the problem accurately is essential to finding an effective solution.

Once you've defined your problem, you're ready to write a purpose statement. A good **purpose statement** makes three things clear:

- The organizational problem or conflict.

- The specific technical questions that must be answered to solve the problem.

- The rhetorical purpose (to explain, to recommend, to request, to propose) the report is designed to achieve.

The following purpose statement for a report to the superintendent of Yellowstone National Park has all three elements:

> Current management methods keep the elk population within the carrying capacity of the habitat but require frequent human intervention. Both wildlife conservation specialists and the public would prefer methods that control the elk population naturally. This report compares the current short-term management techniques (hunting, trapping and transporting, and winter feeding) with two long-term management techniques: habitat modification and the reintroduction of predators. The purpose of this report is to recommend which techniques or combination of techniques would best satisfy the needs of conservationists, hunters, and the public.

To write a good purpose statement, you must understand the basic problem and have some idea of the questions that your report will answer. Note, however, that you can and should write the purpose statement before researching the specific alternatives the report will discuss.

Choosing Information for Reports

LO 13-3

Don't put information in reports just because you have it or just because it took you a long time to find it. Instead, choose the information that your audience needs to understand the problem and make a decision; address the audience's priorities, concerns, needs, and wants concerning the problem; and organize the information so it is easy for your audience to understand. NASA received widespread criticism over the way it released results from an $11.3 million federal air safety study. NASA published 16,208 pages of findings with no guide to understanding them. While the lack of effective structure might have been unintentional, critics maintain the lapse was deliberate because the data contained hundreds of cases of pilot error.[1]

If you know your audience well, you already may know their priorities. For example, the supervisor of a call center knows that management will be looking for certain kinds of performance data, including costs, workload handled, and customer satisfaction. To write regular reports, the supervisor could set up a format in which it is easy to see how well the center is doing in each of these areas. Using the same format month after month simplifies the audience's task; they can focus on the content alone.

If you don't know your audience, you may be able to get a sense of what is important by showing a tentative table of contents and asking, "Have I included everything?" When you cannot contact an external audience, show your draft to colleagues and superiors in your organization to get their perspectives.

How much information you need to include depends on whether your audience is likely to be supportive, neutral, or skeptical. If your audience is likely to be pleased with your research, you can present your findings directly. If your audience will not be pleased, you will need to explain your thinking in a persuasive way. That is, you will have to speak to their priorities and provide substantial evidence.

You also must decide whether to put information in the body of the report or in appendices. Put material in the body of the report if it is crucial to your proof, if your most significant audience will want to see it there, or if it is short. (Something less than half a page won't interrupt the audience.) Frequently, decision makers want your analysis of the data in the report body rather than the actual data itself. Supporting data that will be examined later by specialists such as accountants, lawyers, and engineers are generally put in an appendix.

Anything that a careful audience will want but that is not crucial to your proof can go in an appendix. Appendices can include

- A copy of a survey questionnaire or interview questions.

- A tally of responses to each question in a survey.

- A copy of responses to open-ended questions in a survey.

- A transcript of an interview.

- Complex tables and visuals.

- Technical data.

- Previous reports on the same subject.

Organizing Information in Reports

LO 13-4

Most information can be organized in several logical ways. Choose the way that makes your report easiest for the audience to understand and use. If you were compiling a directory of all the employees at your plant, for example, alphabetizing by last name would be far more useful than listing people by their length of service with the company, though that organizing principle might make sense for another purpose.

The following three guidelines will help you choose the arrangement that will be the most useful for your audience:

1. **Process your information before you present it to your audience.** The order in which you became aware of information usually is not the best order to present it to your audience.
2. **When you have lots of information, group it into categories.** By grouping your information into categories, you make your report easier to comprehend.
3. **Work with the audience's expectations, not against them.** Introduce ideas in the overview in the order in which you will discuss them.

Patterns for Organizing Information

Organize information in a way that will work best for your audience. Figure 13.2 lists common patterns for organizing information that are particularly useful in reports. Any of these patterns can be used for a whole report or for only part of it.

Figure 13.2	Ways to Organize Reports
- Comparison/contrast	- General to particular or particular to general
- Problem–solution	- Geographic or spatial
- Elimination of alternatives	- Functional
- SWOT analysis	- Chronological

Comparison/Contrast   Many reports use comparison/contrast sections within a larger report pattern. Comparison/contrast also can be the purpose of the whole report. Recommendation studies generally use this pattern. You can focus either on the alternatives you are evaluating or on the criteria you use. See Figure 13.3 for ways to organize these two patterns in a report.

Focus on the alternatives when

- One alternative is clearly superior.

- The criteria are hard to separate.

- The audience will intuitively grasp the alternative as a whole rather than as the sum of its parts.

Focus on the criteria when

- The superiority of one alternative to another depends on the relative weight assigned to various criteria. Perhaps Alternative A is best if we are most concerned about Criterion 1, cost, but worst if we are most concerned about Criterion 2, proximity to the target market.

- The criteria are easy to separate.

- The audience wants to compare and contrast the options independently of your recommendation.

A variation of the comparison/contrast pattern is the **pro-and-con pattern**. In this pattern, under each specific heading, give the arguments for and against that alternative.

Figure 13.3	Two Ways to Organize a Comparison/Contrast Report
Focus on alternatives	
Heading/Subheading	Title
Alternative A	Opening a New Store on Campus
Criterion 1	Cost of Renting Space
Criterion 2	Proximity to Target Market
Criterion 3	Competition from Similar Stores
Alternative B	Opening a New Store in the Suburban Mall
Criterion 1	Cost of Renting Space
Criterion 2	Proximity to Target Market
Criterion 3	Competition from Similar Stores
Focus on criteria	
Heading/Subheading	Title
Criterion 1	Cost of Renting Space for the New Store
Alternative A	Cost of Campus Locations
Alternative B	Cost of Locations in the Suburban Mall
Criterion 2	Proximity to Target Market
Alternative A	Proximity on Campus
Alternative B	Proximity in the Suburban Mall
Criterion 3	Competition from Similar Stores
Alternative A	Competing Stores on Campus
Alternative B	Competing Stores in the Suburban Mall

A report recommending new plantings for a university quadrangle uses the pro-and-con pattern:

> Advantages of Monocropping
> > High Productivity
> > Visual Symmetry
> Disadvantages of Monocropping
> > Danger of Pest Exploitation
> > Visual Monotony

This pattern is least effective when you want to de-emphasize the disadvantages of a proposed solution, for it does not permit you to bury the disadvantages between neutral or positive material.

Problem–Solution

Identify the problem; explain its background or history; discuss its extent and seriousness; identify its causes. Discuss the factors (criteria) that affect the decision. Analyze the advantages and disadvantages of possible solutions. Conclusions and recommendation can go either first or last, depending on the preferences of your audience. This pattern works well when the audience is neutral.

A report recommending ways to eliminate solidification of a granular bleach during production uses the problem–solution pattern:

> Recommended Reformulation for Vibe Bleach
> Problems in Maintaining Vibe's Granular Structure
> Solidification during Storage and Transportation
> Customer Complaints about "Blocks" of Vibe in Boxes
> Reasons That Vibe Bleach "Cakes"
> Vibe's Formula
> The Manufacturing Process
> The Chemical Process of Solidification
> Modifications Needed to Keep Vibe Flowing Freely

Elimination of Alternatives

After discussing the problem and its causes, discuss the *impractical* solutions first, showing why they will not work. End with the most practical solution. This pattern works well when the solutions the audience is likely to favor will not work, while the solution you recommend is likely to be perceived as expensive, intrusive, or radical.

A report on toy commercials, "The Effect of TV Ads on Children," eliminates alternatives in a section devoted to alternative solutions:

> Alternative Solutions to Problems in TV Toy Ads
> Leave Ads Unchanged
> Mandate School Units on Advertising
> Ask the Industry to Regulate Itself
> Give FCC Authority to Regulate TV Ads Directed at Children

SWOT Analysis

SWOT analysis is frequently used to evaluate a proposed project, expansion, or new venture. The analysis discusses the strengths, weaknesses, opportunities, and threats (hence, SWOT) of the proposed action. Strengths and weaknesses are usually factors within the organization; opportunities and threats are usually factors external to the organization.

A report recommending an in-house training department uses a SWOT analysis to support its recommendation:

> Advantages of In-House Training
> Disadvantages of In-House Training
> Competitor Training Businesses
> Opportunities for Training Expansion

This report switches the order of threats (Competitor Training Businesses) and opportunities to end with positive information.

General to Particular or Particular to General
General to particular starts with the problem as it affects the organization or as it manifests itself in general and then moves to a discussion of the parts of the problem and solutions to each of these parts. Particular to general starts with the problem as the audience defines it and moves to larger issues of which the problem is a part. Both are good patterns when you need to redefine the audience's perception of the problem to solve it effectively.

The directors of a student volunteer organization, VIP, have defined their problem as "not enough volunteers." After studying the subject, the writer is convinced that problems in training, supervision, and campus awareness are responsible for both a high dropout rate and a low recruitment rate. The general-to-particular pattern helps the audience see the problem in a new way:

Why VIP Needs More Volunteers
Why Some VIP Volunteers Drop Out
    Inadequate Training
    Inadequate Supervision
    Feeling That VIP Requires Too Much Time
    Feeling That the Work Is Too Emotionally Demanding
Why Some Students Do Not Volunteer
    Feeling That VIP Requires Too Much Time
    Feeling That the Work Is Too Emotionally Demanding
    Preference for Volunteering with Another Organization
    Lack of Knowledge about VIP Opportunities
How VIP Volunteers Are Currently Trained and Supervised
    Time Demands on VIP Volunteers
    Emotional Demands on VIP Volunteers
Ways to Increase Volunteer Commitment and Motivation
    Improving Training and Supervision
    Improving the Flexibility of Volunteers' Hours
    Providing Emotional Support to Volunteers
    Providing More Information about Community Needs and VIP Services

Geographic or Spatial
In a geographic or spatial pattern, you discuss problems and solutions by units according to their physical arrangement. Move from office to office, building to building, factory to factory, state to state, region to region, and so on.

A sales report might use a geographic pattern of organization.

Sales Have Risen in the European Community
Sales Are Flat in Eastern Europe
Sales Have Fallen Sharply in the Middle East
Sales Are Off to a Strong Start in Africa
Sales Have Risen Slightly in Asia
Sales Have Fallen Slightly in South America
Sales Are Steady in North America

Functional
In functional patterns, discuss the problems and solutions of each functional unit. For example, a small business might organize a report to its venture capitalists by the categories of research, production, and marketing. A government report might divide data into sections focused on the different functions an agency performed, taking each in turn.

Regulation of Credit-Granting Institutions
Education of Consumers
Research on Financial-Responsibility Programs
Coordination of Efforts with International Agencies

Chronological   A chronological report records events in the order in which they happened or are planned to happen. Many progress reports are organized chronologically.

> Work Completed in October
> Work Planned for November

If you choose this pattern, be sure you do not let the chronology obscure significant points or trends.

Patterns for Specific Varieties of Reports

Informative, recommendation, and justification reports will be more successful when you work with the audience's expectations for that kind of report.

Informative and Closure Reports   **Informative reports** and **closure reports** summarize completed work or research that does not result in action or recommendation.
Informative reports often include the following elements:

- Introductory paragraph summarizing the problems or successes of the project.

- Purpose and scope section(s) giving the purpose of the report and indicating what aspects of the topic it covers.

- Chronological account outlining how the problem was discovered, what was done, and what the results were.

- Concluding paragraph offering suggestions for later action. The suggestions in a closure or informative report are not proved in detail.

Figure 13.4 presents an example of an informative report.

Closure reports also allow a firm to document the alternatives it has considered before choosing a final design.

Recommendation Reports   **Recommendation reports** evaluate two or more alternatives and recommend one of them. (Doing nothing or delaying action can be one of the alternatives.)

Recommendation reports normally open by explaining the decision to be made, listing the alternatives, and explaining the criteria. In the body of the report, each alternative will be evaluated according to the criteria using one of the two comparison/contrast patterns. Discussing each alternative separately is better when one alternative is clearly superior, when the criteria interact, or when each alternative is indivisible. If the choice depends on the weight given to each criterion, you may want to discuss each alternative under each criterion.

Whether your recommendation should come at the beginning or the end of the report depends on your audience and the culture of your organization. Most audiences want the "bottom line" up front. However, if the audience will find your recommendation hard to accept, you may want to delay your recommendation until the end of the report when you have given all your evidence.

Justification Reports   **Justification reports** justify a purchase, investment, hiring, or change in policy. If your organization has a standard format for justification reports, follow that format. If you can choose your headings and organization, use this pattern when your proposal will be easy for your audience to accept:

1. **Indicate what you're asking for and why it's needed.** Because the audience has not asked for the report, you must link your request to the organization's goals.
2. **Briefly give the background of the problem or need.**

Figure 13.4   An Informative Report Describing How a Company Solved a Problem

March 14, 2021

To: Donna S. Kienzler

From: Sara A. Ratterman *SAR*   *Informal short reports use
letter or memo format.*

*First
paragraph
summarizes
main
points.*

Subject: Recycling at Bike Nashbar

Two months ago, Bike Nashbar began recycling its corrugated cardboard boxes. The program was easy to implement and actually saves the company a little money compared to our previous garbage pickup.

*Purpose
and scope
of report.*

In this report, I will explain how and why Bike Nashbar's program was initiated, how the program works and what it costs, and why other businesses should consider similar programs.

Bold headings.

The Problem of Too Many Boxes and Not Enough Space in Bike Nashbar

*Cause of
problem.*

Every week, Bike Nashbar receives about 40 large cardboard boxes containing bicycles and other merchandise. As many boxes as possible would be stuffed into the trash bin behind the building, which also had to accommodate all the other solid waste the shop produces. Boxes that didn't fit in the trash bin ended up lying around the shop, blocking doorways, and taking up space needed for customers' bikes. The trash bin was emptied only once a week, and by that time, even more boxes would have arrived.

*Triple space before
heading.*

The Importance of Recycling Cardboard Rather Than Throwing It Away

Double space after heading.

Arranging for more trash bins or more frequent pickups would have solved the immediate problem at Bike Nashbar but would have done nothing to solve the problem created by throwing away so much trash in the first place.

Double space between paragraphs within heading.

*Further
seriousness
of problem.*

According to David Crogen, sales representative for Waste Management, Inc., 75% of all solid waste in Columbus goes to landfills. The amount of trash the city collects has increased 150% in the last five years. Columbus's landfill is almost full. In an effort to encourage people and businesses to recycle, the cost of dumping trash in the landfill is doubling from $4.90 a cubic yard to $9.90 a cubic yard next week. Next January, the price will increase again, to $12.95 a cubic yard. Crogen believes that the amount of trash can be reduced by cooperation between the landfill and the power plant and by recycling.

How Bike Nashbar Started Recycling Cardboard   *Capitalize first letter of
major words in heading.*

Solution.

Waste Management, Inc., is the country's largest waste processor. After reading an article about how committed Waste Management is to waste reduction and recycling, I decided to see whether Waste Management could recycle our boxes. Corrugated cardboard (which is what Bike Nashbar's boxes are made of) is almost 100% recyclable, so we seemed to be a good candidate for recycling.

(Continued)

Donna S. Kienzler   *Reader's name,*
March 14, 2021   *date,*
Page 2   *page number.*

To get the service started, I met with a friendly sales rep, David Crogen, that same afternoon to discuss the service.

Waste Management took care of all the details. Two days later, Bike Nashbar was recycling its cardboard.

How the Service Works and What It Costs

Talking heads tell reader what to expect in each section.

Details of solution. Waste Management took away our existing 8-cubic-yard garbage bin and replaced it with two 4-yard bins. One of these bins is white and has "cardboard only" printed on the outside; the other is brown and is for all other solid waste. The bins are emptied once a week, with the cardboard going to the recycling plant and the solid waste going to the landfill or power plant.

Double space between paragraphs. Since Bike Nashbar was already paying more than $60 a week for garbage pickup, our basic cost stayed the same. (Waste Management can absorb the extra overhead only if the current charge is at least $60 a week.) The cost is divided 80/20 between the two bins: 80% of the cost pays for the bin that goes to the landfill and power plant; 20% covers the cardboard pickup. Bike Nashbar actually receives $5.00 for each ton of cardboard it recycles.

Employees at Bike Nashbar are responsible for putting all the boxes they open in the recycling bin. Employees must follow these rules:

- The cardboard must have the word "corrugated" printed on it, along with the universal recycling symbol.

Indented lists provide visual variety.

- The boxes must be broken down to their flattest form. If they aren't, they won't all fit in the bin and Waste Management would be picking up air when it could pick up solid cardboard. The more boxes that are picked up, the more money that will be made.

- No other waste except corrugated cardboard can be put in the recycling bin. Other materials could break the recycling machinery or contaminate the new cardboard.

- The recycling bin is to be kept locked with a padlock provided by Waste Management so no one steals the cardboard and loses money for Waste Management and Bike Nashbar.

Figure 13.4   An Informative Report Describing How a Company Solved a Problem   *(Continued)*

Donna S. Kienzler
March 14, 2021
Page 3

Disadvantages
of
solution.

Minor Problems with Running the Recycling Program

The only problems we've encountered have been minor ones of violating the rules. Sometimes employees at the shop forget to flatten boxes, and air instead of cardboard gets picked up. Sometimes people forget to lock the recycling bin. When the bin is left unlocked, people do steal the cardboard, and plastic cups and other solid waste get dumped in the cardboard bin. I've posted signs where the key to the bin hangs, reminding employees to empty and fold boxes and relock the bin after putting cardboard in it. I hope this will turn things around and these problems will be solved.

Advantages of the Recycling Program

Advantages
of
solution.

The program is a great success. Now when boxes arrive, they are unloaded, broken down, and disposed of quickly. It is a great relief to get the boxes out of our way, and knowing that we are making a contribution to saving our environment builds pride in ourselves and Bike Nashbar.

Our company depends on a clean, safe environment for people to ride their bikes in. Now we have become part of the solution. By choosing to recycle and reduce the amount of solid waste our company generates, we can save money while gaining a reputation as a socially responsible business.

Why Other Companies Should Adopt Similar Programs

Argues
that her
company's
experience
is relevant
to other
companies.

Businesses and institutions in Franklin County currently recycle less than 4% of the solid waste they produce. David Crogen tells me he has over 8,000 clients in Columbus alone, and he acquires new ones every day. Many of these businesses can recycle a large portion of their solid waste at no additional cost. Depending on what they recycle, they even may get a little money back.

The environmental and economic benefits of recycling as part of a comprehensive waste reduction program are numerous. Recycling helps preserve our environment. We can use the same materials over and over again, saving natural resources such as trees, fuel, and metals and decreasing the amount of solid waste in landfills. By conserving natural resources, recycling helps the U.S. become less dependent on imported raw materials. Crogen predicts that Columbus will be on a 100% recycling system by the year 2024. I strongly hope that his prediction will come true.

3. **Explain each of the possible solutions.** For each, give the cost and the advantages and disadvantages.

4. **Summarize the action needed to implement your recommendation.** If several people will be involved, indicate who will do what and how long each step will take.

5. **Ask for the action you want.**

If the reader will be reluctant to grant your request, use this problem-solving pattern:

1. **Describe the organizational problem (that your request will solve).** Use specific examples to prove the seriousness of the problem.
2. **Show why easier or less expensive solutions will not solve the problem.**
3. **Present your solution impersonally.**
4. **Show that the disadvantages of your solution are outweighed by the advantages.**
5. **Summarize the action needed to implement your recommendation.** If several people will be involved, indicate who will do what and how long each step will take.
6. **Ask for the action you want.**

How much detail you need to give in a justification report depends on the corporate culture and on your audience's knowledge of and attitude toward your recommendation. Many organizations expect justification reports to be short—only one or two pages. Other organizations may expect longer reports with much more detailed budgets and a full discussion of the problem and each possible solution.

Headings and Subheadings in Reports

LO 13-5

Headings are single words, short phrases, or complete sentences that indicate the topic in each section. A heading must cover all of the material under it until the next heading. For example, *Cost of Tuition* cannot include the cost of books or of room and board; *College Costs* could include all costs. You can have just one paragraph under a heading or several pages. If you do have several pages between headings, you may want to consider using subheadings. Use subheadings only when you have two or more divisions within a main heading.

Informative headings tell the audience what to expect. They provide a specific overview of each section and of the entire report.

> Recommended Reformulation for Vibe Bleach
> Problems in Maintaining Vibe's Granular Structure
> Solidification during Storage and Transportation
> Customer Complaints about "Blocks" of Vibe in Boxes
> The Reasons That Vibe Bleach "Cakes"
> Vibe's Formula
> The Manufacturing Process
> The Chemical Process of Solidification
> Modifications Needed to Keep Vibe Flowing Freely

Headings and subheadings should have **parallel structure**; that is, they must use the same grammatical structure. Subheadings must be parallel to each other but do not necessarily have to be parallel to subheads under other headings.

Not parallel:	Are Students Aware of VIP?
	Current Awareness among Undergraduate Students
	Graduate Students
	Ways to Increase Volunteer Commitment and Motivation
Parallel:	Campus Awareness of VIP
	Current Awareness among Undergraduate Students
	Current Awareness among Graduate Students
	Ways to Increase Volunteer Commitment and Motivation

Not parallel:	We Must Improve Training and Supervision
	Can We Make Volunteers' Hours More Flexible?
	Providing Emotional Support to Volunteers
	Provide More Information about Community Needs and VIP Services
Parallel:	Improving Training and Supervision
	Improving the Flexibility of Volunteers' Hours
	Providing Emotional Support to Volunteers
	Providing More Information about Community Needs and VIP Services

Finally, to improve the usability and design of your report, follow these guidelines as you develop your headings and subheadings:

- Use a subheading only when you have at least two subsections under the next higher heading.

- Avoid having a subheading come immediately after a heading. Instead, some text should follow the main heading before the subheading. (If you have nothing else to say, give an overview of the section.)

- Avoid having a heading or subheading all by itself at the bottom of the page. Instead, have at least one line (preferably two) of type. If there isn't room for a line of type under it, put the heading on the next page.

- Don't use a heading as the antecedent for a pronoun in the paragraph below it. Instead, repeat the noun.

- If you use a **serif** font for the body text of your document, use a **sans serif** font for the headings and subheadings. See Chapter 7 for more document design tips.

Writing Progress Reports

LO 13-6

When you're assigned to a single project that will take a month or more, you'll probably be asked to file one or more progress reports. A progress report reassures the funding agency or employer that you're making progress—that you understand the problem and are working toward a solution (or multiple potential solutions). A progress report also allows you and the agency or employer to resolve problems as they arise.

Ineffective progress reports focus on what the employees have done and say little about the value of their work. Effective progress reports, on the other hand, allot less space to the details of what the employees have done and much more space to explanations of the value of the employees' work.

Progress reports can do more than just report progress. You can use progress reports to

- **Enhance your image.** Details about the number of documents you've read, people you've surveyed, or experiments you've conducted create a picture of a hardworking person doing a thorough job.

- **Float trial balloons.** Explain, "I could continue to do X [what you approved]; I could do Y instead [what I'd like to do now]." The detail in the progress report can help back up your claim. Even if the idea is rejected, you don't lose face because you haven't made a separate issue of the alternative.

- **Minimize potential problems.** As you do the work, it may become clear that implementing your recommendations will be difficult. In your regular progress reports, you can alert your boss or the funding agency to the challenges that lie ahead, enabling them to prepare for the new situation and to act on your recommendations.

Guidelines for Writing Progress Reports

When you write progress reports, use what you know about emphasis, positive tone, and *you*-attitude. Don't present every detail as equally important. Use emphasis techniques to stress major accomplishments.

In your report, try to exceed expectations in at least some small way. Perhaps your research is ahead of schedule or needed equipment arrived earlier than expected. However, do not present the good news by speculating on the reader's feelings; many readers find such statements offensive.

> Poor: You will be happy to hear the software came a week early.

> Better: The software came a week early, so Pat can start programming earlier than expected.

Make your progress report as positive as you *honestly* can. You'll build a better image of yourself if you show that you can take minor problems in stride and that you're confident of your own abilities.

> The preliminary data sets were two days late because of a server crash. However, Nidex believes they will be back on schedule by next week. Past performance indicates their estimate is correct, and data analysis will be finished in two weeks, as originally scheduled.

Focus on your solutions to problems rather than the problems themselves:

> Negative: Southern data points were corrupted, and that problem set us back three days in our data analysis.

> Positive: Although southern data points were corrupted, the northern team was able to loan us Chris and Lee to fix the data set. Both teams are currently back on schedule.

In the example above, the problem with the southern data points is still noted because readers may want to know about it, but the solution to the problem is emphasized.

Do remember to use judicious restraint with your positive tone. Without details for support, glowing judgments of your own work may strike readers as ill-advised bragging, or maybe even dishonesty.

> Overdone positivity,   Our data analysis is indicating some great new predictions;
> lack of support: you will be very happy to see them.

> Supported optimism: Our data analysis is beginning to show that coastal erosion may not be as extensive as we had feared; in fact, it may be almost 10% less than originally estimated. We should have firm figures by next week.

Remember that your audience for your report is usually in a position of power over you, so be careful what you say to them. Generally, it is not wise to blame them for project problems even if they are at fault.

> Poor: We could not proceed with drafting the plans because you did not send us the specifications for the changes you want.

> Better: Chris has prepared the outline for the plan. We are ready to start drafting as soon as we receive the specifications. Meanwhile, we are working on. . . .

Organizing Progress Reports

Subject lines for progress reports are straightforward. Specify the project on which you are reporting your progress.

> Subject: Progress on Developing a Marketing Plan for Fab Fashions

If you are submitting weekly or monthly progress reports on a long project, number your progress reports or include the time period in your subject line. Include information about the work completed since the last report and work to be completed before the next report.

The body text of progress reports can be organized in three ways: by chronology, task, and recommendation support. Some progress reports may use a combination: They may organize material chronologically within each task section, for instance.

Chronological Progress Reports
The chronological pattern of organization focuses on what you have done and what work remains.

1. **Summarize your progress in terms of your goals and your original schedule.** Use measurable, quantifiable statements.

   Poor: Progress has been slow.

   Better: Analysis of data sets is about one-third complete.

2. **Under the heading "Work Completed," describe what you have already done.** Be specific, both to support your claims in the first paragraph and to allow the reader to appreciate your hard work. Acknowledge the people who have helped you. Describe any serious obstacles you've encountered and tell how you've dealt with them.

   Poor: I have found many articles about Procter & Gamble on the web. I have had a few problems finding how the company keeps employees safe from chemical fumes.

   Better: On the web, I found Procter & Gamble's home page, its annual report, and mission statement. No one I interviewed could tell me about safety programs specifically at P&G. I have found seven articles about ways to protect workers against pollution in factories, but none mentions P&G.

3. **Under the heading "Work Remaining," describe the work still to be completed.** If you're more than three days late (for school projects) or two weeks late (for business projects), submit a new schedule showing how you will be able to meet the original deadline. You may want to discuss "Observations" or "Preliminary Conclusions" if you want feedback before writing the final report or if your reader has asked for substantive interim reports.

4. **Express your confidence in having the work ready by the due date.** If you are behind your original schedule, explain why you think you can still finish the project on time.

Even in chronological reports, you need to do more than merely list work you have done. Show the value of that work and your prowess in achieving it, particularly your ability to solve problems. The student progress report in Figure 13.5 uses the chronological pattern of organization.

Task Progress Reports
In a task progress report, organize information under the various tasks you have worked on during the period. For example, a task progress report for a team report project might use the following headings: Conducting Research on RAC, Inc., and the South Korean Market; Analyzing Survey Data; Writing the Introduction of the Report. Under each heading, the student team could discuss the tasks it has completed and those that remain.

Task progress reports are appropriate for large projects with distinct topics or tasks.

Recommendation Progress Reports
Some progress reports offer recommendations. Recommendation progress reports advocate action: increasing the funding or allotted time for a project, changing its direction, canceling a project that isn't working. When the recommendation will be easy for the reader to accept, use the direct request pattern of organization from Chapter 11. If the recommendation is likely to meet strong resistance, the problem-solving pattern, also in Chapter 11, may be more effective.

Figure 13.5   An Excerpt from a Chronological Progress Report

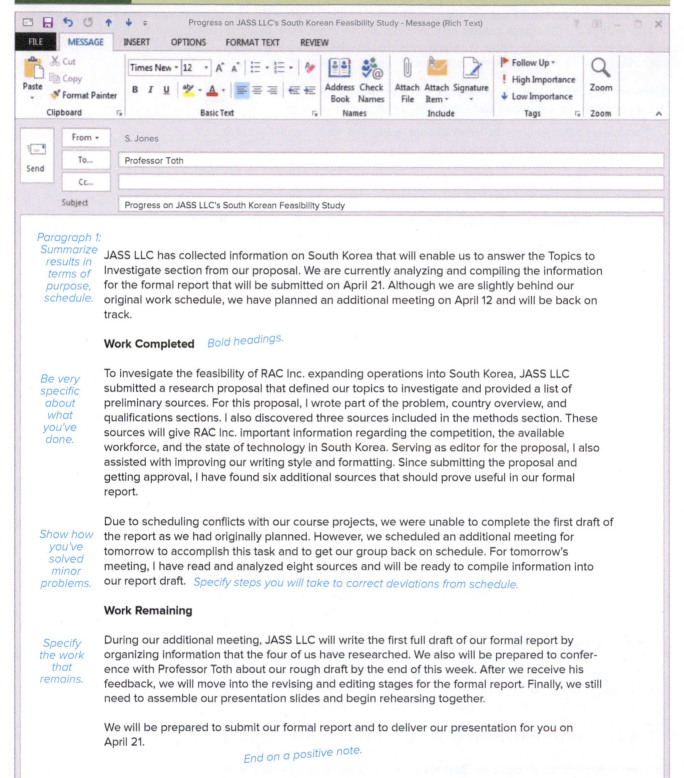

Source: Microsoft Inc

Oral Progress Reports   Not all progress reports are written. Boeing had to ground an entire fleet of its new 787 Dreamliner after discovering potential fire issues with the lithium-ion batteries. A few months into the investigation and repair stages, the Air Line Pilots' Association of Japan requested a progress report about the airplanes. The group wanted to be sure the root of the problem had been identified and that the planes would be safe to fly.

Boeing offered an oral progress report stating the problem with the batteries was not critical to flight operations, even though it was still unsure what caused the issue. Many companies offer the public progress reports on fixes or solutions when their products are discovered to be faulty.[2] You may be asked by a college professor or a supervisor to give an oral presentation that relates your progress toward completing a project. In an oral progress report, review the work you've completed, describe the tasks you're working on currently, discuss any challenges that you've encountered, and explain your next steps in completing the project.

Gantt Charts in Progress Reports

Chapter 8 covered a type of visual that often appears in progress reports: Gantt charts. As discussed in that chapter, Gantt charts specify tasks in a project and the duration of those tasks. They are useful in progress reports to illustrate the work completed, work in progress, and work remaining. Figure 13.6 shows an example of a Gantt chart from a progress report.

Figure 13.6   A Gantt Chart Shows the Tasks Involved in Developing a New Product

		Name	Duration
1		Begin project	0 days
2		Design Phase	55 days
3		Prototype design	25 days
4		Test prototype	20 days
5		Prototype completed	0 days
6		Finance Phase	45 days
7		Create business plan	15 days
8		Present to current inv	0 days
9		Meet with bankers	0 days
10		Circulate plan w/ vent	5 days
11		Negotiate with ventur	10 days
12		Reach agreement	0 days
13		Create legal documer	15 days
14		Financing closed	0 days
15		Production Phase	73 days
16		Setup assembly line	15 days
17		Hire assemblers	50 days
18		Assemble first batch	3 days
19		Quality testing	10 days
20		Assemble product	10 days
21		Inventory available	0 days
22		Marketing and Sale P	30 days
23		Develop marketing pl	5 days
24		Create sales material	25 days
25		Create advertising pla	15 days
26		Develop PR plan	15 days
27		Sales training	15 days
28		Start sales program	0 days
29		Distribution Phase	16 days
30		Stock warehouse	7 days
31		Process orders	5 days

Writing Formal Reports

Formal reports are distinguished from informal letter and memo reports by their components. A full formal report may contain the components outlined in Figure 13.7 in the left column.

As Figure 13.7 shows, not every formal report necessarily has all components, and some reports call for additional components or arrange these components in a different order. The components you need will depend on the audiences and purposes of your report. For example, Figure 13.8 shows the table of contents from Hasbro's annual report. It follows the conventions of an annual report, containing sections on properties and legal proceedings, for example. Figure 13.9 displays excerpts of a typical formal report that you can use as a model.

Title Page

The title page of a report usually contains four items: the title of the report, the person or organization for whom the report is prepared, the person or group who prepared the report, and the release date. Some title pages also contain a brief summary or abstract of the contents of the report.

The title of the report should be as informative as possible. Like subject lines, report titles are straightforward.

Poor title: New Plant Site

Better title: Eugene, Oregon, Site for the New Kemco Plant

Figure 13.7	Possible Report Components	
More formal ←——————————→		**Less formal**
Cover	Title Page	Introduction
Title Page	Table of Contents	Body
Transmittal	Executive Summary	Conclusions
Table of Contents	Introduction	Recommendations
List of Illustrations	Body	
Executive Summary	Conclusions	
Introduction	Recommendations	
Background		
Body		
Conclusions		
Recommendations		
References		
Appendices		
Questionnaires		
Interviews		
Tables and Figures		
Related Documents		

Figure 13.8	This Table of Contents Indicates Content That Is Standard in an Annual Report

Figure 13.9 | Sections of a Formal Report

Slated for Success

Center all text on the title page.

Use a large font size for the main title.

RAC Inc. Expanding to South Korea

Use a slightly smaller font size for the subtitle.

Prepared for *No punctuation.*

Name of audience, job title, organization, city, state, and zip code.

Ms. Katie Nichols

CEO of RAC Inc.

Grand Rapids, Michigan, 49503

Prepared by *No punctuation.*

JASS LLC

Name of writer(s), organization, city, state, and zip code.

Jordan Koole

Alex Kuczera

Shannon Jones

Sean Sterling

Allendale, MI 49401

Month Day, Year *Date report is released.*

Figure 13.9   Sections of a Formal Report   *(Continued)*

The students in this group designed their own letterhead, assuming they were doing this report as consultants.

This letter uses block format.

JASS LLC
1 Campus Drive
Allendale, MI 49401

Month Day, Year   *Enter current date.*

Ms. Katie Nichols, CEO
RAC Inc.
1253 West Main Street
Grand Rapids, MI 49503

In paragraph 1, release the report. Note when and by whom the report was authorized. Note the report's purpose.

Dear Ms. Nichols:

In this document you will find the report that you requested in March. We have provided key information and made recommendations on a plan of action for the expansion of a RAC Inc. slate tablet manufacturing plant into South Korea.

Give recommendations or thesis of report.

Our analysis of expansion into South Korea covered several important areas that will help you decide whether or not RAC Inc. should expand and build a manufacturing plant in South Korea. To help us make our decision, we looked at the government, economy, culture, and, most important, the competition. South Korea is a technologically advanced country and its economy is on the rise. Our research has led us to recommend expansion into South Korea. We strongly believe that RAC Inc. can be profitable in the long run and become a successful business in South Korea.

Note sources that were helpful.

JASS LLC used several resources in forming our analysis. The Central Intelligence Agency's *World Factbook*, the U.S. Department of State, World Business Culture, and Kwintessential were all helpful in answering our research questions.

Thank the audience for the opportunity to do the research.

Thank you for choosing JASS to conduct the research into South Korea. If you have any further questions about the research or recommendation, please contact us (616-331-1100, info@jass.com) and we will be happy to answer any questions referring to your possible expansion into South Korea at no charge. JASS would be happy to conduct any further research on this issue or any other projects that RAC Inc. is considering. We look forward to building on our relationship with you in the future.

Sincerely,

Offer to answer questions about the report.

Jordan Koole

Jordan Koole
JASS Team Member

Center inital page numbers at the bottom of the page. Use a lowercase roman numeral for initial pages of report.

i

(Continued)

Figure 13.9 Sections of a Formal Report *(Continued)*

Main headings are parallel, as are subheadings within a section.

Table of Contents does not list itself.

Table of Contents

Capitalize first letter of each major word in headings.

Indentions show level of heading at a glance.

Use lowercase roman numerals for initial pages.

Introduction begins on page I.

Line up right margin (justify).

List of Illustrations

Add a "List of Illustrations" at the bottom of the page or on a separate page if the report has many visuals.

Figures and tables are numbered independently.

Figure 13.9   Sections of a Formal Report   *(Continued)*

Slated for Success

Report title.

Many audiences read only the Executive Summary, not the report. Include enough information to give audiences the key points you make.

RAC Inc. Expanding to South Korea

Executive Summary

Start with recommendation or thesis.

To continue growth and remain competitive on a global scale, RAC Inc. should expand its business operations into South Korea. The country is a technologically advanced nation and would provide a strong base for future expansion. Slate tablet competitors of RAC Inc. in South Korea are doing quite well. Because RAC Inc. can compete with them in the United States, we are confident that RAC can remain on par with them in this new market.

The research we have done for this project indicates that this expansion will be profitable, primarily because the South Korean economy is flourishing. The workforce in South Korea is large, and finding talented employees to help set up and run the facility will be easy. In addition, the regulations and business structure are similar to those in the United States and will provide an easy transition into this foreign nation. The competition will be fierce; however, we believe that RAC Inc. will be profitable because of its track record with the Notion Tab in the United States.

Provide brief support for recommendations.

To ensure a successful expansion, JASS LLC recommends the following:

1. **RAC Inc. should establish its headquarters and manufacturing plant in Busan.**
   - Purchase a building to have a place to begin manufacturing the Notion Tab.
   - Educate RAC employees about South Korean culture and business practices before they begin working directly with South Koreans to avoid being disrespectful.
   - Explore hiring South Koreans; the available workforce is large.
   - Ensure that the Notion name is appropriate when translated into Korean. If not, change the name to better market the product.
   - Market and sell the product in both Busan and Seoul.

2. **After one year RAC should determine the acceptance and profitability of the expansion.**
   - Conduct a customer satisfaction survey with people who purchased the Notion Tab living in Seoul and Busan to determine the acceptance of the product.
   - Compare and contrast first-year sales with a competitor's similar product.

3. **If the tablet is competitive and profitable, RAC Inc. should expand its product line into all large cities in South Korea.**
   - To gain an edge on the competition, create a marketing plan that will offer the Notion Tab at some discount in the new cities.
   - Explore integrating other RAC Inc. products into South Korea. These products also could be manufactured at the new manufacturing plant in Busan.

Language in the Executive Summary can come from the report. Make sure any repeated language is well-written!

The Abstract or Executive Summary contains the logical skeleton of the report: the recommendation(s) and supporting evidence.

iii

(Continued)

Figure 13.9 Sections of a Formal Report *(Continued)*

A running header is optional. This one includes the main title on the left and the page number on the right.

Slated for Success   1

Introduction   *Center main headings.*

To avoid getting left behind by competition in global expansion, RAC Inc. has contacted JASS LLC to perform an analysis about expanding into South Korea. JASS has researched South Korea to determine if RAC Inc. will be successful in expanding into this foreign market.

"Purpose" and "Scope" can be separate sections if either is long.

Purpose and Scope

RAC Inc. is a successful business in the United States and has had substantial growth over the last five years. With its competitors beginning to venture into foreign markets to gain more global market share, RAC Inc. is looking to expand into the international market as well. The purpose of our research is to decide whether or not RAC Inc. should expand its business into South Korea.

Give topics in the order you'll discuss them.

Tell what you discuss and how thoroughly you discuss each topic.

Topics in "Scope" section should match those in the report.

This report will cover several topics about South Korea including their government, economy, culture, technology, market competition, and possible locations. Our research will not include any on-site research in South Korea. We also are not dealing directly with the South Korean people.

List any relevant topics you do not discuss.

Assumptions cannot be proved. But if they are wrong, the report's recommendation may no longer be valid.

Assumptions

The recommendations that we make are based on the assumption that the relationship between North and South Korea will remain the same as of the first part of 2021. We also are assuming that the technological state of South Korea will remain constant and not suffer from a natural disaster or an economic crash. In addition, we assume that the process of expansion into South Korea is the same with RAC Inc. as it has been with other American companies. Another assumption that we are making is that RAC Inc. has a good name brand and is competitive in the United States with Apple, Samsung, LG, and other electronic companies.

If you collected original data (surveys, interviews, and observations), tell how you chose your subjects, what kind of sample you used, and when you collected the information. This report does not use original data; it just provides a brief discussion of significant sources.

Methods

The information in our report comes from online sources and reference books. We found several good sources, but the best information that we obtained came from The Central Intelligence Agency's *World Factbook*, the U.S. Department of State, World Business Culture, and Kwintessential. These resources have given us much useful information on which we have based our recommendation.

These limitations are listed because the students correctly assumed their instructor would want to know them. Limitations such as these would never be listed in a real consulting report, because they would disqualify the firm.

Limitations   *If your report has limitations, state them.*

The information in the report was limited to what we retrieved from our sources. We were not able to travel to South Korea to conduct on-site research. JASS also was limited by the language barrier that exists between the United States and South Korea. Other limitations exist because we have not been immersed in the Korean culture and have not gotten input from South Koreans on the expansion of companies into their country.

Definitions

Define key terms your audience will need to read your report.

There are a few terms that we use throughout the report that we would like to explain beforehand. The first term is "slate tablet", an industry term, which from this point on is referred to as a "tablet". Another term we would like to clarify is the name of the city Busan. Some sources referred to it as Pusan. From this point forward, we use only Busan. An abbreviation we use is GDP, which stands for gross domestic product. The South Korean and United States Free Trade Agreement signed in 2007 is abbreviated as KORUS FTA, its official name in the United States government.

Figure 13.9   Sections of a Formal Report   *(Continued)*

Slated for Success   2

This section outlines the criteria used to make the overall recommendation.

Criteria

JASS LLC has established criteria that need to be favorable before we give a positive recommendation about South Korea. The criteria include the government, economy, culture, and market competition. We have weighted our criteria by percentages:

- Government = 20%
- Economy = 20%
- South Korean culture = 20%
- Market possibilities and competitors = 40%

We will examine each separately and give each criterion a favorable or not favorable recommendation. Market competition is weighted the heaviest and must be favorable or somewhat favorable for us to give a positive recommendation. Market competition can be given a favorable, nonfavorable, or somewhat favorable recommendation based on various external factors in the marketplace. We need a minimum of a 70% total to give a positive recommendation overall.

Triple-space before major headings and double-space after them.

Government   *Headings must cover everything under that heading until the next one.*

Begin most paragraphs with topic sentences.

South Korea is recognized as a republic government by the rest of the world. A republic government is a democracy where the people have supreme control over the government (South Korea: Political structure, 2021). This foundation makes it similar to the United States' democracy. There is a national government as well as provincial-level governments (similar to state-level governments) with different branches. Larger cities, like Seoul and Busan, have their own city government as well. The government is considered multipartied and has multiple parties vying for positions (South Korea: Political structure, 2021). The Republic of South Korea shares its power among three branches of government, thus providing checks and balances inside the government. The three branches of the government are the presidential, legislative, and judicial (U.S. Department of State, 2021). In this section, we will discuss business regulations, taxes, free trade, and concerns about North Korea.

List subtopics in the order in which they are discussed.

Capitalize all main words of headings and subheadings.

Period goes outside of parenthesis.

It's OK to have subheadings under some headings and not others.

Use subheadings only when you have two or more sections.

Business Regulations

South Korea ranks 5th on the ease of doing business index (World Bank Group, 2021a). This index measures the regulations that a government imposes on businesses and how easy it is to start and run a business in a given country. Factors this index measures include the ease of starting a business, doing taxes, and enforcing contracts. For comparison, the United States is ranked 6th on this list (World Bank Group, 2021b). While there are some regulations on business in South Korea, they are still near the top of the list. The relatively low rating on regulation can be due in part to past Grand National Party control of the government. There are a few general regulations that RAC Inc. should know before going into South Korea. For more specific business regulations, RAC Inc. may need to do further research before expanding.

Since the 1960s, the GDP has had only one dip, a result of the Asian Economic crisis in the late 1990s that affected most Asian countries. In 2004, South Korea became a part of the trillion-dollar economy club, making them one of the world's top economies (Central Intelligence Agency, 2021).

(Continued)

Figure 13.9   Sections of a Formal Report   *(Continued)*

Slated for Success   5

However, the economy faces challenges in maintaining steady growth in the future. These challenges include an aging population and an overdependence on exports. Right now, though, South Korea's economy continues to grow. Its industrial production growth rate was 12.1% in 2016 and 4.6% in 2017. From 2017 to 2019, the country's GDP grew from 2% to 3% per year, "not uncommon for advanced countries" (Central Intelligence Agency, 2021, "Economic Overview"). In addition, inflation remains low—around 0.3% in 2019 (Central Intelligence Agency, 2021).

Refer to figure in the text. Tell what main point it makes.

GDP and Other Economic Measures

South Korea's official GDP was $2.21 trillion in 2019 (Central Intelligence Agency, 2021, "Real GDP"). This GDP is the fourteenth highest in the world. GDP measures the total value of goods that a country produces. Figure 2 compares the GDP growth rates for the world's high-GDP countries. GDP per capita in South Korea is $42,765, which is the 41st highest in the world. GDP per capita measures the output of goods and services per person in the country. It is also an

Number figures consecutively throughout the report; number tables and figures independently.

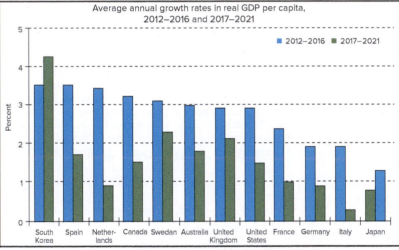

Label both axes of graphs. See Chapter 13 for more information on creating data displays.

Figure 2: Comparison of GDP Growth Rates
(Source: U.S. Bureau of Labor Statistics, 2021)

Cite source of data.

Figure captions need to be descriptive.

indicator of the average worker's salary in the country. South Korea only has 14.4% percent of its population living in poverty. They have a labor force of 26.83 million, with is the 20th largest labor force in the world, with an unemployment rate of just 3.76% (Central Intelligence Agency, 2021). These numbers need to be considered when starting operations in South Korea. South Korea also has a service-driven economy with 70.6% of the labor force employed in the service industry (Central Intelligence Agency, 2021). All of these numbers and high world rankings of the economic measures suggest that South Korea has a stable and healthy economy where a business could prosper.

Figure 13.9   Sections of a Formal Report   *(Continued)*

Slated for Success   11

Conclusions repeat points made in the report. Recommendations are actions the audience should take.

Some companies ask for Conclusions and Recommendations at the beginning of the report.

Conclusions and Recommendations

All of the research that we have done supports the decision to expand into South Korea. The government, economy, and culture criteria all received favorable recommendations for a total of 60%. Market possibilities and competition received half support for an additional 20%. Together, South Korea has earned 80% based on our criteria.

Therefore, we believe that RAC Inc. could profitably expand into South Korea. The Notion Tab is a high-quality product, and it will be easily integrated into this technologically advanced county. In conclusion, we recommend that RAC Inc. should expand into South Korea.

To ensure a successful expansion, JASS LLC recommends the following:

1. **RAC Inc. should establish its headquarters and manufacturing plant in Busan.**
   - Purchase a building to have a place to begin manufacturing the Notion Tab.
   - Educate RAC employees about South Korean culture and business practices before they begin working directly with South Koreans to avoid being disrespectful.
   - Explore hiring South Koreans; the available workforce is large.
   - Ensure that the Notion name is appropriate when translated into Korean. If not, change the name to better market the product.
   - Market and sell the product in both Busan and Seoul.

Numbering points makes it easier for the audience to follow and discuss them.

2. **After one year RAC should determine the acceptance and profitability of the expansion.**
   - Conduct a customer satisfaction survey with people who purchased the Notion Tab living in Seoul and Busan to determine the acceptance of the product.
   - Compare and contrast first-year sales with a competitor's similar product.

Make sure all items in a list are parallel.

3. **If the tablet is competitive and profitable, RAC Inc. should expand its product line into all large cities in South Korea.**
   - To gain an edge on the competition, create a marketing plan that will offer the Notion Tab at some discount in the new cities.
   - Explore integrating other RAC Inc. products into South Korea. These products also could be manufactured at the new manufacturing plant in Busan.

Because many readers turn to the "Recommendations" first, provide enough information so that the reason is clear all by itself. The ideas in this section must be logical extensions of the points made and supported in the body of the report.

Figure 13.9   Sections of a Formal Report   *(Continued)*

Slated for Success   12

References   *This report uses APA citation style.*

Advameg, Inc. (n.d.). *Culture of South Korea*.
    https://www.everyculture.com/Ja-Ma/South-Korea.html

AFP. (2010, December 5). U.S., South Korea sign sweeping free-trade agreement. *Taipai Times*.
    https://www.taipeitimes.com/News/front/archives/2010/12/05/2003490144

Central Intelligence Agency. (2021, February 2021). *Korea, South*.
    https://www.cia.gov/the-world-factbook/countries/korea-south/

Compare this list of sources with those in the proposal. Notice how the authors had to adjust the list as they completed research.

iPad 2 specs. (2011, March 2). *OS X Daily*.
    https://osxdaily.com/2011/03/02/ipad-2-specs/

Koreans love their mobile phones. (2009, January 27). *Korean JoongAng Daily*.
    https://koreajoongangdaily.joins.com/2009/01/27/industry/Koreans-love-their-mobile-phones-/
    2900275.html

KT Corporation. (2021, January 29). In *Wikipedia*.
    https://en.wikipedia.org/wiki/KT_Corporation

Kwintessential. (2021). *A guide to South Korea—etiquette, customs, clothing, and more...*
    https://www.kwintessential.co.uk/resources/guide-to-south-korea-etiquette-customs-culture-business

LG Corporation. (2021). In *Wikipedia*.
    https://en.wikipedia.org/wiki/LG_Corporation

*List all the printed and online sources cited in your report.
Do not list sources you used for background but did not cite.*

Sources for this report continue onto a second page.

Large organizations that issue many reports may use two-part titles to make it easier to search for reports electronically. For example, U.S. government report titles first give the agency sponsoring the report, then the title of that particular report.

> Small Business Administration: Management Practices Have Improved for the Women's Business Center Program

In many cases, the title will state the recommendation in the report: "Why the United Nations Should Establish a Seed Bank." However, the title should omit recommendations when

- The reader will find the recommendations hard to accept.

- Putting all the recommendations in the title would make it too long.

- The report does not offer recommendations.

If the title does not contain the recommendation, it normally indicates what problem the report tries to solve or the topic the report discusses.

Eliminate any unnecessary words:

Wordy: Report of a Study on Ways to Market Life Insurance to Urban Professional People Who Are in Their Mid-40s

Better: Marketing Life Insurance to the Mid-40s Urban Professional

The identification of the receiver of the report normally includes the name of the person who will make a decision based on the report, their job title, the organization's name, and its location (in the U.S., city, state, and zip code). Government reports often omit the person's name and simply give the organization that authorized the report.

If the report is prepared primarily by one person, the "Prepared by" section will have that person's name, their title, the organization, and its location. In internal reports, the organization and location are usually omitted if the report writer works at the headquarters office.

Government reports normally list the names of all people who wrote the report, using a separate page if the group working on the report is large. Practices in business differ. In some organizations, all the names are listed; in others, the division to which they belong is listed; in still others, the name of the chair of the group appears.

The **release date**, the date the report will be released to the public, is usually the date the report is scheduled for discussion by the decision makers. The report is frequently due four to six weeks before the release date so that the decision makers can review the report before the meeting.

If you have the facilities and the time, try using type variations, color, and artwork to create a visually attractive and impressive title page. However, a plain page is acceptable. The format in Figure 13.9 will enable you to create an acceptable title page.

Letter or Memo of Transmittal

Use a letter of transmittal if you are not a regular employee of the organization for which you prepare the report; use a memo if you are a regular employee. See Appendix A for guidelines on formatting letters and email messages.

The transmittal has several purposes: to transmit the report, to orient the reader to the report, and to build a good image of the report and of the writer. An informal writing style is appropriate for a transmittal even when the style in the report is more formal. A professional transmittal helps you create a good image of yourself and enhances your credibility. Personal statements are appropriate in the transmittal, even though they would not be acceptable in the report itself.

Organize the transmittal in this way:

1. **Transmit the report.** Tell when and by whom it was authorized and the purpose it was to fulfill.

2. **Summarize your conclusions and recommendations.** If the recommendations will be easy for the audience to accept, put them early in the transmittal. If they will be difficult, summarize the findings and conclusions before the recommendations.

3. **Mention any points of special interest in the report. Show how you surmounted minor problems you encountered in your investigation. Thank people who helped you.** These optional items can build goodwill and enhance your credibility.

4. **Point out additional research that is necessary, if any.** Sometimes your recommendation cannot be implemented until further work is done. If you'd be interested in doing that research or if you'd like to implement the recommendations, say so.

5. **Thank the audience for the opportunity to do the work and offer to answer questions.** Provide contact information. Even if the report has not been fun to do, expressing satisfaction in doing the project is expected. Saying that you'll answer questions about the report is a way of saying that you won't charge the audience your normal hourly fee to answer questions (one more reason to make the report clear!).

The letter of transmittal on page i of Figure 13.9 uses this pattern of organization.

Table of Contents

In the table of contents, list the headings exactly as they appear in the body of the report. If the report is fewer than 25 pages, you'll probably list all the levels of headings. In a long report, pick a level, and put all the headings at that level and above in the table of contents.

Some software programs, such as Microsoft Word, offer features that automatically generate a table of contents (and a list of illustrations) if you apply the style feature when you generate headings.

Page ii of Figure 13.9 shows the table of contents.

List of Illustrations

A list of illustrations enables audiences to refer to your visuals.

Report visuals comprise both tables and figures. **Tables** are words or numbers arranged in rows and columns. **Figures** are everything else: bar graphs, flow charts, maps, drawings, photographs, and so on. Tables and figures may be numbered independently, so you may have both a Table 1 and a Figure 1. In a report with just two kinds of visuals, such as maps and graphs, the visuals are sometimes called Map 1 and Graph 1. Whatever you call the illustrations, list them in the order in which they appear in the report; give the name of each visual as well as its number.

See Chapter 8 for information about how to design and label visuals.

Executive Summary

An **executive summary** or **abstract** tells the audience what the document is about. It summarizes the recommendation of the report and the reasons for the recommendation or describes the topics the report discusses and indicates the depth of the discussion. A good executive summary should be concise but also should clearly describe the most important elements of the report for the audience who will read only this section of the report.

Abstracts generally use a more formal style than other forms of business writing. Avoid contractions and colloquialisms. Try to avoid using the second-person *you*. Because reports may have many different audiences, *you* may become inaccurate. It's acceptable to use exactly the same words in the abstract and the report.

Summary abstracts present the logic skeleton of the report: the thesis or recommendation and its proof. Use a summary abstract to give the most useful information in the shortest space.

> To market life insurance to mid-40s urban professionals, Interstate Fidelity Insurance should advertise in upscale publications and use direct mail.
>
> Network TV and radio are not cost-efficient for reaching this market. This group comprises a small percentage of the prime-time network TV audience and a minority of most radio station listeners. They tend to discard newspapers and general-interest magazines quickly, but many of them keep upscale periodicals for months or years. Magazines with high percentages of readers in this group include *Architectural Digest, Bon Appetit, Forbes, Golf Digest, Metropolitan Home, Southern Living*, and *Smithsonian*.
>
> Any advertising campaign needs to overcome this group's feeling that they already have the insurance they need. One way to do this would be to encourage them to check the coverage their employers provide and to calculate the cost of their children's expenses through college graduation. Insurance plans that provide savings and tax benefits as well as death benefits also might be appealing.

One way to start composing an abstract is to write a sentence outline. A **sentence outline** not only uses complete sentences rather than words or phrases, but also contains the thesis sentence or recommendation and the evidence that proves that point. Combine the sentences into paragraphs, adding transitions if necessary, and you'll have your abstract.

Descriptive abstracts indicate what topics the report covers and how deeply it goes into each topic, but they do not summarize what the report says about each topic. Phrases that describe the report ("this report covers," "it includes," "it summarizes," "it concludes") are marks of a descriptive abstract. An additional mark of a descriptive abstract is that the audience can't tell what the report says about the topics it covers.

> This report recommends ways Interstate Fidelity Insurance could market insurance to mid-40s urban professionals. It examines demographic and psychographic profiles of the target market. Survey results are used to show attitudes toward insurance. The report suggests some appeals that might be successful with this market.

Introduction

The **introduction** of the report always contains a statement of purpose and scope and may include all the parts in the following list:

- **Purpose.**   The purpose statement identifies the problem the report addresses, the technical investigations it summarizes, and the rhetorical purpose (to explain, to recommend).

- **Scope.**   The scope statement identifies how broad an area the report surveys. For example, Company XYZ is losing money on its line of computers. Does the report investigate the quality of the computers? The advertising campaign? The cost of manufacturing? The demand for computers? A scope statement allows the reader to evaluate the report on appropriate grounds.

- **Assumptions.**   Assumptions in a report are like assumptions in geometry: statements whose truth you assume and that you use to prove your final point. If they are wrong, the conclusion will be wrong too.

For example, to plan cars that will be built five years from now, an automobile manufacturer commissions a report on young adults' attitudes toward cars. The recommendations would be based on assumptions both about gas prices and about the economy. If gas prices radically rose or fell, the kinds of cars young adults wanted would change. If there were a major recession, people wouldn't be able to buy new cars.

Almost all reports require assumptions. A good report spells out its assumptions so that audiences can make decisions more confidently.

■ **Methods.**   If you conducted surveys, focus groups, or interviews, you need to tell how you chose your subjects and how, when, and where they were interviewed. If the discussion of your methodology is more than a paragraph or two, you should probably make it a separate section in the body of the report rather than including it in the introduction. Reports based on scientific experiments usually put the methods section in the body of the report, not in the introduction.

If your report is based solely on **secondary research**, provide a brief description of significant sources.

■ **Limitations.**   Limitations make your recommendations less valid or valid only under certain conditions. Limitations usually arise because time or money constraints haven't permitted full research. For example, a campus pizza restaurant considering expanding its menu may ask for a report but not have enough money to take a random sample of students and townspeople. Without a random sample, the writer cannot generalize from the sample to the larger population.

Many recommendations are valid only for a limited time. For instance, a campus store wants to know what kinds of clothing will appeal to college men. The recommendations will remain valid for only a short time: Two years from now, styles and tastes may have changed, and the clothes that would sell best now may no longer be in demand.

■ **Criteria.**   The criteria section outlines the factors or standards that you are considering and the relative importance of each. If a company is choosing a city for a new office, is the cost of office space more or less important than the availability of skilled workers? Check with your audience before you write the draft to make sure that your criteria match those of your audiences.

■ **Definitions.**   Many reports define key terms in the introduction. For instance, a report on unauthorized internet use by employees might define what is meant by "unauthorized use." A report on the corporate dress code might define such codes broadly to include general appearance, so it could include items such as tattoos, facial piercings, and general cleanliness. Also, if you know that some members of your primary or secondary audience will not understand technical terms, define them. If you have only a few definitions, you can put them in the introduction. If you have many terms to define, put a **glossary** in an appendix. Refer to it in the introduction so that audiences know that you've provided it.

Background or History

Formal reports usually have a section that gives the background of the situation or the history of the problem. Even though the current audience for the report probably knows the situation, reports are filed and consulted years later. These later audiences will probably not know the background, although it may be crucial for understanding the options that are possible.

In some cases, the history section may cover many years. For example, a report recommending that a U.S. hotel chain open hotels in Romania may give the history of that country for at least several decades. In other cases, the background section is much briefer, covering only a few years or even just the immediate situation.

The purpose of most reports is rarely to provide a history of the problem. Do not let the background section achieve undue length.

Body

The body of the report is usually its longest section. Analyze causes of the problem and offer possible solutions. Present your argument with all its evidence and data. Data that are necessary to follow the argument are included with appropriate visuals and explanatory text. Extended data sets, such as large tables and long questionnaires, are generally placed in appendices. It is particularly important in the body that you use headings and subheadings to help your audience navigate your material. Remember to cite your sources and to refer in the text to all visuals and appendices.

Conclusions and Recommendations

Conclusions summarize points you have made in the body of the report; **recommendations** are action items that would solve or ameliorate the problem. These sections are often combined if they are short: "Conclusions and Recommendations." No new information should be included in this section.

Many audiences turn to the recommendations section first; some organizations ask that recommendations be presented early in the report. Number the recommendations to make it easy for people to discuss them. If the recommendations will seem difficult or controversial, give a brief paragraph of rationale after each recommendation. If they'll be easy for the audience to accept, you can simply list them without comments or reasons. The recommendations also will be in the executive summary and perhaps in the title and the transmittal.

Appendices

Appendices provide additional materials that the careful audience may want. Common items are transcripts of interviews, copies of questionnaires, tallies of answers to questions, tables, figures, and previous reports.

Writing White Papers

LO 13-8

Originally, the term "white paper" was used to denote a government report that was too short to be bound between a front and back cover.[3] More recently, though, the term "white paper" has been applied to reports arising in business and technology. White papers range in their purpose, including explanations of a technology underlying a product, comparisons of the strengths and weaknesses of competitors' product, descriptions of a product's applications for a typical customer, guidelines for implementing a new technology, and explanations of an industry issue or a proposed standard.[4]

In other words, the primary goal of white papers is to educate readers. As one marketing expert put it, "Readers expect an advanced problem-solving guide packed with expertise."[5] To deliver that expertise, white paper writers must provide detail, and that means they can be lengthy. Campbell et al.'s study of 96 white papers from high-tech firms found that they contained, on average, 2,645 words, or about five single-spaced pages. The longest white paper in their study contained over 11,000 words, which equates to about 22 single-spaced pages.[6]

While white papers have a range of purposes, they tend to share a secondary purpose: marketing. Usually that marketing is business-to-business (B2B), but sometimes it is business-to-consumer (B2C). White papers build awareness of a product, which is the first step in motivating a potential client to make a purchase.[7] This secondary purpose manifests in metrics for gauging a white paper's success, which include the number of people who open the email for it, the number of people who fill out a registration form to receive it, the number of leads it generates, and the sales resulting from those leads.[8]

In implementing this secondary marketing purpose, experts have said that an understated, "soft-sell" approach is better than an explicit, "hard-sell" approach. A soft-sell approach builds goodwill by providing needed information: "Precisely because a content approach doesn't feel like traditional advertising and selling, it lends itself to being perceived as information which is more genuine and trustworthy."[9]

However, the marketing message may get lost if the soft sell is *too* soft. Campbell et al. provided this advice for finding a balance:

- Explicitly discuss industry problems and solutions. For example, after over 50 pages devoted to developing, producing, and managing content, LinkedIn's white paper, "The Sophisticated Marketer's Guide to Content Marketing," finally discusses LinkedIn's product: its platform for professionals (see Figure 13.10). LinkedIn provides readers with a wealth of information before relating the ways that its social platform can further marketers' goals.

- Implicitly convey your sales goal; for example, list your product's benefits. After discussing various problems related to cyber threats, Cisco's white paper, "Networking and Your Competitive Edge," discusses the benefits of its security products (see Figure 13.11).

Figure 13.10	LinkedIn White Paper: Marketing

LinkedIn markets itself after 50 pages devoted to advice on developing, producing, and managing content.

Source: LinkedIn

Figure 13.11	Cicso White Paper: Benefits

Cisco discusses its security products after pages devoted to cyber threats.

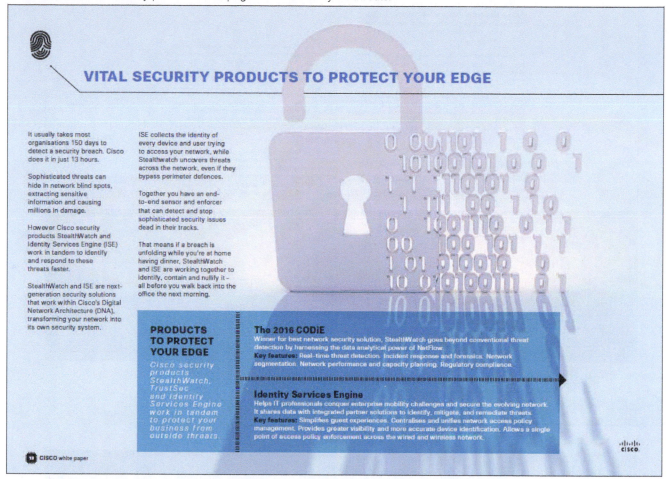

Source: Cisco Systems, Inc.

- Supply precise evidence, especially quantitative data. For example, the conclusion page of Cisco's white paper sums up with some memorable quantitative data (see Figure 13.12). Cisco drives home the increasing challenge of tracking users by noting the creation of 50 billion endpoints by 2020. It also notes the cost-effectiveness of a digital network (particularly Cisco's): over $21 million (Australian dollars) in additional revenue and cost reduction.

- Cite sources of information.[10] Cisco's white paper cites IDC Technologies, Inc., data to show the fiscal benefit of improving network infrastructure (see Figure 13.13).

You may have noted from examples like the page in Figure 13.13 that white papers—depending on the budget devoted to them—showcase document design that far exceeds the basic 12-point single-spaced type on a white page, as shown in the example of a formal report in Figure 13.9. In this sense, white papers such as LinkedIn's and Cisco's use attractive and creative design to enhance credibility.

Figure 13.12	Cisco White Paper: Data

White papers, such as Cisco's, provide memorable quantitative data.

False economy of a commodity edge

When measuring cost it's important not to look purely at the upfront capital cost, but also at the costs associated with operation and risk.

While some network infrastructure may boast a cheaper initial price tag, down the track it can begin to have significantly more expensive financial impacts on an organisation, especially where security is concerned.

It is now more critical than ever to ensure that your network edge is secured against cyber threats, particularly given the network edge is where customer data is collected. Your network holds the key to defending your organisation, and as such, a security breach will blow any initial network infrastructure savings out of the water.

In a nutshell: saving a few dollars at the beginning can cost you a lot more in the long run.

Additionally, IDC reports that on average companies reduced their annual costs for physical network infrastructure (switches, routers, firewalls, load balancers, and WLANs) by 43%. These savings often resulted from using more efficient devices, leading to consolidation of hardware and management systems.

Yet much more significant than infrastructure savings was the ability to reduce the time and cost required to administer, maintain, and manage the network environment. In total, companies reduced their average costs associated with deployment, support, and management of network systems by 30% per year.

The network needs to be positioned as the backbone of every organisation. By investing in a Cisco DNA network you can reduce costs by deploying devices faster through automation, provide a programmable network by enabling developers to create new applications and offer a great consistent application user experience for employees and customers.

Source: Cisco Systems, Inc.

Figure 13.13	Cisco White Paper: Sources

White papers, such as Cisco's, cite credible sources.

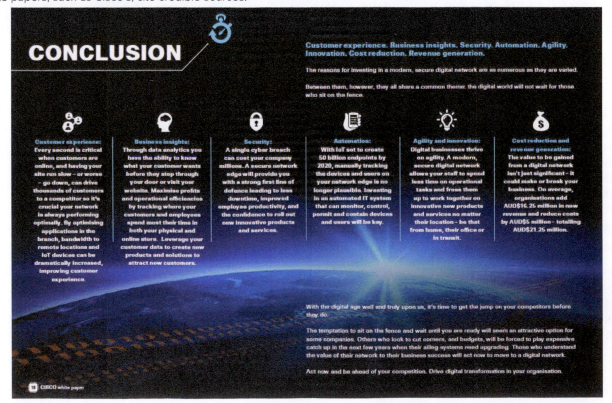

CONCLUSION

Customer experience. Business insights. Security. Automation. Agility. Innovation. Cost reduction. Revenue generation.

The reasons for investing in a modern, secure digital network are as numerous as they are varied.

Between them, however, they all share a common theme: the digital world will not wait for those who sit on the fence.

Customer experience: Every second is critical when customers are online, and having your site run slow – or worse – go down, can drive thousands of customers to a competitor so it's crucial your network is always performing optimally. By optimising applications in the branch, bandwidth to remote locations and IoT devices can be dramatically increased, improving customer experience.

Business insights: Through data analytics you have the ability to know what your customer wants before they step through your door or visit your website. Maximise profits and operational efficiencies by tracking where your customers and employees spend most their time in both your physical and online store. Leverage your customer data to create new products and solutions to attract new customers.

Security: A single cyber breach can cost your company millions. A secure network edge will provide you with a strong first line of defence leading to less downtime, improved employee productivity, and the confidence to roll out new innovative products and services.

Automation: With IoT set to create 50 billion endpoints by 2020, manually tracking the devices and users on your network edge is no longer plausible. Investing in an automated IT system that can monitor, control, permit and contain devices and users will be key.

Agility and innovation: Digital businesses thrive on agility. A modern, secure digital network allows your staff to spend less time on operational tasks and frees them up to work together on innovative new products and services no matter their location – be that from home, their office or in transit.

Cost reduction and revenue generation: The value to be gained from a digital network isn't just significant – it could make or break your business. On average, organisations add AUD$16.25 million in new revenue and reduce costs by AUD$5 million – totalling AUD$21.25 million.

With the digital age well and truly upon us, it's time to get the jump on your competitors before they do.

The temptation to sit on the fence and wait until you are ready will seem an attractive option for some companies. Others who look to cut corners, and budgets, will be forced to play expensive catch up in the next few years when their ailing systems need upgrading. Those who understand the value of their network to their business success will act now to move to a digital network.

Act now and be ahead of your competition. Drive digital transformation in your organisation.

Source: Cisco Systems, Inc.

Summary by Learning Objectives

LO 13-1   Identify varieties of reports.

- Information reports collect data for the reader.
- Analytical reports present and interpret data.
- Recommendation reports recommend action or a solution.

LO 13-2   Define report problems.

- A good report problem in business meets the following criteria:
  - The problem is real, important enough to be worth solving, and narrow but challenging.
  - The audience for the report is real and able to implement the recommended action.
  - The data, evidence, and facts are sufficient to document the severity of the problem, sufficient to prove that the recommendation will solve the problem, available to *you*, and comprehensible to *you*.

- A good purpose statement must make three things clear:
  - The organizational problem or conflict.
  - The specific technical questions that must be answered to solve the problem.
  - The rhetorical purpose (to explain, to recommend, to request, to propose) that the report is designed to achieve.

LO 13-3   Choose information for reports.

- Choose information to include that your audience needs to know to make a decision. Figuring out whether your audience is supportive, neutral, or skeptical will guide you on how much information you need to include.
- Determine what information to put in the body of the report or in appendices.

LO 13-4   Organize reports.

Choose an appropriate organizational pattern for your information and purposes. The most common patterns are comparison/contrast; problem–solution; elimination of alternatives; SWOT analysis; general to particular, particular to general; geographic or spatial; functional; and chronological.

LO 13-5   Use headings and subheadings effectively in reports.

Headings and subheadings are single words, short phrases, or complete sentences that describe all of the material under them until the next heading or subheading. Informative headings tell the audience what to expect in each section.

Headings and subheadings must use parallel structure. Subheadings under a heading must be parallel to each other but do not necessarily have to be parallel to subheadings under other headings.

LO 13-6   Produce progress reports.

- Progress reports let people know how you are coming on a project.
- Positive emphasis in progress reports creates an image of yourself as a capable, confident worker.
- Progress reports may be organized by chronology, task, or recommendation support.

LO 13-7   Prepare the different components of formal reports.

- The title page of a report usually contains four items: the title of the report, for whom the report is prepared, by whom it is prepared, and the date.
- If the report is 25 pages or fewer, list all the headings in the table of contents. In a long report, pick a level and put all the headings at that level and above in the contents.
- Organize the transmittal in this way:
  1. Release the report.
  2. Summarize your conclusions and recommendations.
  3. Mention any points of special interest in the report. Show how you surmounted minor problems you encountered in your investigation. Thank people who helped you.
  4. Point out additional research that is necessary, if any.
  5. Thank the reader for the opportunity to do the work and offer to answer questions.
- Summary abstracts present the logic skeleton of the report: the thesis or recommendation and its proof. Descriptive abstracts indicate what topics the report covers and how deeply it goes into each topic but do not summarize what the report says about each topic. A good abstract or executive summary is easy to read, concise, and clear. A good abstract can be understood by itself, without the report or references.
- The introduction of the report always contains a statement of purpose and scope. The purpose statement identifies the organizational problem the report addresses, the technical investigations it summarizes, and the rhetorical purpose (to explain, to recommend). The scope statement identifies how broad an area the report surveys. The introduction also may include limitations, problems or factors that limit

the validity of your recommendations; assumptions, statements whose truth you assume and that you use to prove your final point; methods, an explanation of how you gathered your data; criteria used to weigh the factors in the decision; and definitions of terms audiences may not know.

- A background, or history section is usually included because reports are filed and may be consulted years later by people who no longer remember the original circumstances.

- The body of the report, usually the longest section, analyzes causes of the problem and offers possible solutions. It presents your argument with all evidence and data.

- The conclusions section summarizes points made in the body of the report; recommendations are action

items that would solve or ameliorate the problem. These sections are often combined if they are short.

- Appendices provide additional materials that the careful audience may want.

LO 13-8   Produce white papers.

The primary goal of white papers is to educate readers; the secondary goal is to market a product. Usually that marketing is business-to-business (B2B), but sometimes it is business-to-consumer (B2C).

To create an effective soft-sell approach:

- Explicitly discuss industry problems and solutions.
- Implicitly convey your sales goal; for example, list your product's benefits.
- Supply precise evidence, especially quantitative data.
- Cite sources of information.

Exercises and Cases

13.1   Reviewing the Chapter

1. What are three different varieties of reports? (LO 13-1)
2. What are some criteria for defining report problems? (LO 13-2)
3. What are some guidelines for choosing information for reports? (LO 13-3)
4. Name seven basic patterns for organizing reports. For four of them, explain when they would be particularly effective or ineffective. (LO 13-4)
5. What are informative headings? (LO 13-5)
6. What are the differences between chronological and task progress reports? (LO 13-6)

7. What are the characteristics of an effective report title? (LO 13-7)
8. What goes in the letter of transmittal? (LO 13-7)
9. What is the difference between summary and descriptive abstracts? (LO 13-7)
10. What goes in the introduction of a report? (LO 13-7)
11. What is the difference between conclusions and recommendations? (LO 13-7)
12. What are the primary and secondary purposes of white papers? (LO 13-8)

13.2   Defining and Evaluating Report Problems

In small teams, turn the following topics into specific report problems you could research for a business communication course. Write three possible report problems for each category.

1. Social media sites
2. Climate change
3. Globalization
4. Marketing to younger audiences
5. Career planning
6. Cell phone use
7. Credit card debt
8. Campus-based organizations
9. Tuition
10. Housing on campus

Once you have defined three possible problems for each topic, evaluate the problems using the following questions:

- Which problem(s) could you address satisfactorily in the time allotted for your course project?
- Which problem(s) are real?
- Which problem(s) are important enough to be worth researching?
- Are the problem(s) narrow enough?
- Who will be able to implement recommended action from your research?
- For which problem(s) could you find adequate resources to create sound solutions?

As your instructor directs,

a. Write an email to your instructor that shares your evaluation of the problems.

b. Pick two of the topic and present to the class your evaluation of the problems in an oral presentation.

c. Write a preliminary purpose statement for each of the three problems you have identified for a category.

13.3   Identifying the Weaknesses in Problem Statements

Identify the weaknesses in the following problem statements by answering these questions:

■ Is the problem narrow enough?

■ Can a solution be found in a semester or quarter?

■ What organization could implement any recommendations to solve the problem?

■ Could the topic be limited or refocused to yield an acceptable problem statement?

1. I want to explore how many Twitter users subscribe to repeat news organizations' Twitter feeds.

2. How can smartphone apps influence driving habits?

3. One possible report topic I would like to investigate would be the differences in women's intercollegiate sports in our athletic conference.

4. How to market products effectively to college students.

5. Should web banners be part of a company's advertising?

6. How can U.S. and Canadian students get jobs in Europe?

7. We want to explore ways our company can help raise funds for the Open Shelter. We will investigate whether collecting and recycling glass, aluminum, and paper products will raise enough money to help.

8. How can XYZ University better serve students from traditionally underrepresented groups?

9. What are the best financial investments for the next year?

10. I'm interested in investigating how meetings changed during the COVID-19 pandemic.

13.4   Writing a Preliminary Purpose Statement

Answer the following questions about a topic on which you could write a formal report.

1. What problem will you investigate or solve?

    a. What is the name of the organization facing the problem?

    b. What is the technical problem or difficulty?

    c. Why is it important to the organization that this problem be solved?

    d. What solution or action might you recommend to solve the problem?

    e. Who (name and title) is the person in the organization who would have the power to accept or reject your recommendation?

2. Will this report use information from other classes or from work experiences? If so, give the name and topic of the class or briefly describe the job. If you will need additional information (that you have not already received from other classes or from a job), how do you expect to find it?

3. List the name, title, and business phone number of a professor who can testify to your ability to handle the expertise needed for this report.

4. List the name, title, and business phone number of someone in the organization who can testify that you have access to enough information about that organization to write this report.

As your instructor directs,

a. Be prepared to answer the questions orally in a conference.

b. Bring written answers to a conference.

c. Submit written answers in class.

d. Give your instructor a photocopy of your statement after it is approved.

13.5   Analyzing Annual Reports

Locate two annual reports online. Choose the reports for the most recent year. You could choose two of these:

■ Hasbro Annual Report: https://investor.hasbro.com /financial-information/annual-reports

■ Caterpillar Annual Report: https://www.caterpillar.com /en/investors/reports.html

■ Publix Annual Report: http://www.publixstockholder.com /financial-information-and-filings/annual-meeting-and-proxy

■ Dick's Sporting Goods Inc. Annual Report: https://www .annualreports.com/Company/dicks-sporting-goods-inc

■ Levi Strauss & Co. Annual Report: https://investors .levistrauss.com/financials/annual-reports/default.aspx

Use the following questions to analyze both reports:

- Who is (are) the audience(s)?
- What is (are) the purpose(s) of the report?
- How is the report organized, and what does the order of information reflect about the company?
- How does the report support the claims it makes? What type of evidence is used more often—textual or visual? What kinds of claims are used—logical, emotional, or ethical?
- How does the text establish credibility?
- What can you tell about the company's financial situation from the report?

- What role do visuals play in the report? What image do they portray for the company? How do the visuals help establish credibility for the report? What do they imply about power distribution in the company?
- Does the report deal with any ethical issues?
- What differences do you see in the letters from the CEOs?

As your instructor directs,

a. Write an email to your instructor comparing and contrasting the two reports according to your analysis answers. Explain which report you find more effective and why.

b. Share your results orally with a small group of students.

c. Present your results to the class.

13.6   Revising a Progress Report

Read the following progress report.

Date: April 3, 2021

To: Professor Keene

From: Jash Sinha

Subject: My Progress

So far my final project for this course has been slow. As you know, I am hoping to present my final report to my boss at the ice cream shop. He is actually very intentional in the idea of having an ice cream cart on campus.

Work Completed

So far I have interviewed a few people on campus and not found out a whole lot of anything. It has been very frustrating. I just handed out a few surveys on campus, but not very many students wanted to fill them out. I do have a little bit data, though. It seems as though several students are very interested in having an ice cream cart on campus and would purchase ice cream items.

I have spoken to my boss, the owner of Mauna Loa Ice Cream, and he is looking forward to reading my final report on the campus ice cream cart. I have put together the numbers for the new cart, and have already spoken to Dining Services on campus for permissions.

Work to be Completed

During these last two weeks of class, I will have no problem getting this project done! I just have to interview more students, put together the information in the report, finish getting the permissions and information for my boss, and then compile all of the information. I also need to write a few more survey questions, too.

Then I will proofread everything, print it, and hand it to my boss!

Your student,

Jash

Revise the progress report. Submit your revision, plus another document justifying your revisions, to your instructor.

13.7   Writing a Progress Report

Write an email to your instructor summarizing your progress on your report.

In the introductory paragraph, summarize your progress in terms of your schedule and your goals. Under the heading "Work Completed," list what you have already accomplished. When describing the work you have completed, make sure to demonstrate how it adds value to your audience. Under "Work Remaining," list what you still have to do. If you are more than two days behind the schedule you submitted with your proposal, include a revised schedule, listing the completion dates for the activities that remain.

13.8   Writing a Progress Report for a Team Report

Write an email to your instructor summarizing your team's progress.

In the introductory paragraph, summarize the team's progress in terms of its goals and its schedule, your own progress on the tasks for which you are responsible, and your feelings about the team's work thus far.

Under a heading titled "Work Completed," list what already has been done. Be most specific about what you yourself have done. Describe briefly the chronology of team activities: number, time, and length of meetings; topics discussed; and decisions made at meetings.

If you have solved problems creatively, say so. You also can describe obstacles you've encountered that you have not yet solved. In this section, you also can comment on problems that the team has faced and whether they've been solved. You can comment on things that have gone well and have contributed to the smooth functioning of the team.

Under "Work Remaining," list what you personally and other team members still have to do. Indicate the schedule for completing the work.

13.9   Revising an Executive Summary

The following executive summary is poorly organized and written. Revise it to make it more effective. Cut information that does not belong and add any information that you feel is missing.

This report will discuss the healthier food options for athletes at the University Gym. Currently, there are several vending machines that student athletes can buy snacks from, but all of the snacks are really unhealthy. Some of the vending machine options that they have are potato chips, candy bars, cookies, and fruit snacks. None of these is a healthy option for athletes.

I think there are a few options that can help this situation. Some of the options include setting up a snack bar. This snack bar could include items like fruits, vegetables, salads, and fruit smoothies. The University's Food Services would have to run this and hire several students to run it. This would cost quite a bit.

Students need healthy food options, especially when they are athletes who are training for sports. Student athletes have very demanding schedules and may not have time to cook healthy foods for themselves.

Another option that we could do would be to simply have a healthy, refrigerated vending machine, with healthy options in it, like fruits, ready-to-eat salads, veggies, and yogurts. This would be easier to install, but would have to be checked frequently to ensure that that items do not go bad.

These are my recommendations for the problem.

13.10   Revising a Recommendation Section

A student has written the following recommendation section for a report for a local restaurant. The restaurant is called the American Grill and specializes in burgers and fries. The restaurant is new to the area and wants to increase its advertising in the local area to get the word out about its food.

Revise the recommendation section so it is well organized and clear. You may add any information that is needed.

> I recommend the following to expand the advertising for American Grill:
>
> American Grill should hand out flyers to people during the July 4th parade that goes through the downtown area. The restaurant managers could ask some of the servers to walk through the parade wearing their American Grill t-shirts to hand out the flyers. The flyers would contain lots of information, like hours, specials, and other important information.
>
> The American Grill should put a radio commercial on the local radio station with the drink specials and also hand out flyers. The radio commercial should also give location information for those who do not know where it is located.
>
> The American Grill should hand out coupons for appetizers and drink specials. These could also be handed out in a parade, or to college students when they first get to the University.

13.11   Comparing White Papers

Locate five white papers online using the search term "white paper." If you are interested in a particular industry, search for that industry to your search as well, such as "white paper" and "fashion," "white paper" and "finance," or "white paper" and "construction." Or, you might choose to locate white papers on a topic that is important to all industries, such as inclusivity, sustainability, health care, or philanthropy.

Compare the five white papers you select. What similarities and differences do you see in the organization and design of these reports? Make a table of your findings. Discuss your findings in small groups.

13.12   Writing a Recommendation Report

Write a report evaluating two or more alternatives. Possible topics include the following:

1. Should your student organization expand its social media presence beyond its current Facebook page to better promote events and share news?
2. Should students in your major start a monthly newsletter? Would a blog, an emailed PDF attachment, or some other medium be more useful to the target audience?
3. Should your student organization write an annual report? Would doing so help the next year's officers?
4. Should your workplace create a newsletter to communicate internally?
5. Should a local restaurant open another branch? Where should it be?

In designing your study, identify the alternatives, define your criteria for selecting one option over others, carefully evaluate each alternative, and recommend the best course of action.

13.13   Writing a Consultant's Report—Restaurant Tipping

Your consulting company has been asked to conduct a report for Diamond Enterprises, which runs three national chains: FishStix, The Bar-B-Q Pit, and Morrie's. All are medium-priced, family-friendly restaurants. The CEO is thinking of replacing optional tips with a 15% service fee automatically added to bills.

You read articles in trade journals, surveyed a random sample of 200 workers in each of the chains, and conducted an email survey of the 136 restaurant managers. Here are your findings:

1. Trade journals point out that the Internal Revenue Service (IRS) audits restaurants if it thinks that servers underreport tips. Dealing with an audit consumes time and often results in the restaurant's having to pay penalties and interest.

2. Only one Morrie's restaurant has actually been audited by the IRS. Management was able to convince the IRS that servers were reporting tips accurately. No penalty was assessed. Management spent $5,000 on CPA and legal fees and spent over 80 hours of management time gathering data and participating in the audit.

3. Restaurants in Europe already add a service fee (usually 15%) to the bill. Patrons can add more if they choose. Local custom determines whether tips are expected and how much they should be. In Germany, for example, it is more usual to round up the bill (e.g., from 27€ to 30€) than to figure a percentage.

4. If the restaurant collected a service fee, it could use the income to raise wages for cooks and hosts and pay for other benefits, such as health insurance, rather than giving all the money to servers and bussers.

5. Morrie's servers tend to be under 25 years old. FishStix employs more servers over 25, who are doing their jobs for a career. The Bar-B-Q Pit servers are students in college towns.

6. In all three chains, servers oppose the idea. Employees other than servers generally support it.

	Retain tips %	Change to service fee %	Don't care %
FishStix servers (*n* = 115)	90	7	3
Bar-B-Q servers (*n* = 73)	95	0	5
Morrie's servers (*n* = 93)	85	15	0
Morrie's nonservers (*n* = 65)	25	70	5
FishStix nonservers (*n* = 46)	32	32	37
Bar-B-Q nonservers (*n* = 43)	56	20	25

(Numbers do not add up to 100% due to rounding.)

7. Servers said that it was important to go home with money in their pockets (92%); that their expertise increased food sales and should be rewarded (67%); and that if a service fee replaced tips, they would be likely to look for another job (45%). Some (17%) thought that if the manager distributed service-fee income, favoritism rather than the quality of work would govern how much tip income they got. Most (72%) thought that customers would not add anything beyond the 15% service fee, and many (66%) thought that total tip income would decrease and their own portion of that income would decrease (90%).

8. Managers generally support the change.

	Retain tips %	Change to service fee %	Don't care
FishStix managers (*n* = 44)	20	80	0
Bar-B-Q managers (*n* = 13)	33	67	0
Morrie's managers (*n* = 58)	55	45	0

9. Comments from managers include: "It isn't fair for a cook with eight years of experience to make only $12 an hour while a server can make $25 an hour in just a couple of months" and "I could have my pick of employees if I offered health insurance."

10. Morale at Bar-B-Q Pit seems low. This low morale is seen, in part, in the low response rate to the survey.

11. In a tight employment market, some restaurants might lose good servers if they made the change. However, hiring cooks and other nonservers would be easier.

12. The current computer systems in place can handle figuring and recording the service fee. Because bills are printed by computer, an additional line could be added. Allocating the service-fee income could take extra managerial time, especially at first.

Write the report.

13.14   Writing a Recommendation Report

Write an individual or a team report. Pick one of the following topics.

1. **Improving Customer Service.** Many customers find that service is getting poorer and workers are getting ruder. Evaluate the service in a local store, restaurant, or other organization. Are customers made to feel comfortable? Is workers' communication helpful, friendly, and respectful? Are workers knowledgeable about products and services? Do they sell them effectively? Write a report analyzing the quality of service and recommending what the organization should do to improve.

2. **Recommending Courses for the Local Community College.** Businesses want to be able to send workers to local community colleges to upgrade their skills; community colleges want to prepare students to enter the local workforce. What skills are in demand in your community? What courses at what levels should the local community college offer?

3. **Improving Sales and Profits.** Recommend ways a small business in your community can increase sales and profits. Focus on one or more of the following: the products or services it offers, its advertising, its décor, its location, its accounting methods, its cash management, or any other aspect that may be keeping the company from achieving its potential. Address your report to the owner of the business.

4. **Increasing Student Involvement.** How could an organization on campus persuade more of the students who are eligible to join or to become active in its programs? Do students know that it exists? Is it offering programs that interest students? Is it retaining current members? What changes should the organization make? Address your report to the officers of the organization.

5. **Evaluating a Potential Employer.** What training is available to new employees? How soon is the average entry-level person promoted? How much travel and weekend

work are expected? Is there a "busy season," or is the workload consistent year-round? What fringe benefits are offered? What is the corporate culture? Is the climate inclusive and antiracist? How strong is the company economically? How is it likely to be affected by current economic, demographic, and political trends? Address your report to the placement office on campus; recommend whether it should encourage students to work at this company.

6. With your instructor's permission, choose your own topic.

As your instructor directs,

Turn in the following documents:

1. The approved proposal.

2. The report, including

   • Cover

   • Title page.

   • Letter or memo of transmittal.

   • Table of contents.

   • List of illustrations.

   • Executive summary or abstract.

   • Body (introduction, all information, recommendations). Your instructor may specify a minimum length, a minimum number or kind of sources, and a minimum number of visuals.

   • Appendices if useful or relevant.

3. Your notes and at least one preliminary draft.

Notes

1. "NASA Releases Information on Federal Survey of Pilots," *Des Moines Register*, January 1, 2008, 2A.
2. Ida Torres, "Japanese Pilots Ask Boeing to Be More Transparent on Dreamliner Issues," *Japan Daily Press*, May 28, 2013, http://japandailypress.com/japanese-pilots-ask-boeing-to-be-more-transparent-on-dreamliner-issues-2829627.
3. Russell Willerton, "Teaching White Papers through Client Projects," *Business Communication Quarterly* 76, no. 1 (2012): 105–13.
4. Janice M. King, *Copywriting That Sells High-Tech: The Definitive Guide to Writing Powerful Promotional Materials for Technology Products, Services, and Companies* (Issaquah, WA: WriteSpark, 2006).
5. Hallie Donkin, "The Schmickest: Top 5 White Paper Examples That Actually Engage," *Mahlab*, April 30, 2018, https://mahlab.co/blog/schmickest-top-5-white-paper-examples.
6. Kim Sydow Campbell, Jefrey S. Naidoo, and Sean M. Campbell, "Hard or Soft Sell? Understanding White Papers as Content Marketing," *IEEE Transactions on Professional Communication* 63, no. 1 (2020): 21–38.
7. E. K. Strong, "Theories of Selling," *Journal of Applied Psychology* 9 (1925): 75–86.
8. Kim Sydow Campbell, Jefrey S. Naidoo, and Sean M. Campbell, "Hard or Soft Sell? Understanding White Papers as Content Marketing," *IEEE Transactions on Professional Communication* 63, no. 1 (2020): 21–38.
9. Lisa Vitale, "Content Marketing, the Hard-Sell and the Soft-Sell—Hitting the Right Balance," *Simply Direct*, January 1, 2014, https://simplydirect.com/content-marketing-the-hard-sell-and-the-soft-sell-hitting-the-right-balance.
10. Kim Sydow Campbell, Jefrey S. Naidoo, and Sean M. Campbell, "Hard or Soft Sell? Understanding White Papers as Content Marketing," *IEEE Transactions on Professional Communication* 63, no. 1 (2020): 21–38.

Chapter Outline

DrAfter123/Getty Images

Sophia the Robot: Orator . . . and Citizen

In 2017, a robot named Sophia spoke at a press conference. She said, "I am very honored and proud for this unique distinction. This is historical to be the first robot in the world to be recognized with a citizenship."

That's correct: Sophia the robot has been granted citizenship—a status partially based on her public speaking ability.

In the field of artificial intelligence (AI), one way to judge a robot's humanity is the Turing test: whether its ability to carry on a conversation can fool humans into thinking they're conversing with another human. In early years, conversation occurred via computers; the test was based solely on written conversation. This was because the AI did not have a humanlike housing that could replicate nonverbal communication elements such as eye contact, facial expression, and vocal delivery; these aspects of communication were simply too nuanced for an AI robot.

But Sophia the robot, speaking from her own mouth and matching what she said to her own blinks, head-nods, and smiles, passed the test with flying colors—or at least well enough for Saudi Arabia to grant her citizenship. Body language expert Jack Brown assessed Sophia's facial expressions, noting her strengths and weaknesses: When she smiles, her eyelids should partially close—but don't—to indicate authenticity; her "sad face," however, is convincing, pulling down the corners of her mouth—like a human would—to indicate emotional distress.

Even when watching humans (as opposed to robots) speak, we analyze

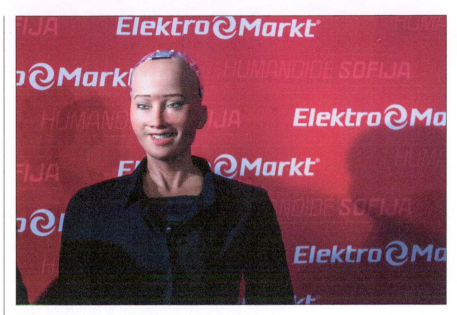

Jevgenij Avin/Shutterstock

nonverbal communication to determine whether we believe what the person is saying. A groundbreaking study showed that if people say one thing about their feelings, but their nonverbal communication indicates that they feel a different way, people interpreting the message assign more weight to the nonverbal communication. The study found

- 7% of a message comes from word meaning.

- 38% of a message comes from *how* the words are spoken (e.g., tone of voice).

- 55% of a message comes from facial expression.

Matching your verbal and nonverbal messages is a complicated skill, and public speaking is a major fear for a significant portion of the population. Jerry Seinfeld joked that "According to most studies, people's number one fear is public speaking. Number two is death. Death is number two. Does that seem right? That means to the average person, if you have to go to a funeral, you're better off in the casket than doing the eulogy."

Thankfully, Seinfeld's statistics are a little off: in 2019, Americans reported public speaking not as their worst fear, but their 54th worst fear, behind dying (44th), sharks (47th), death of a loved one (5th), pollution of oceans, rivers, and lakes (2nd), and corrupt government officials (1st). Though the fear of public speaking will likely linger for a long time, building oral communication skills is essential to presenting yourself as a competent business professional. With focused practice, public speakers can craft powerful, audience-adapted messages with delivery to match.

Sources: Olivia Cuthbert, "Saudi Arabia Becomes First Country to Grant Citizenship to a Robot," *Arab News*, October 26, 2017, http://www.arabnews.com/node/1183166/saudi-arabia; Jack Brown, "Body Language Analysis No. 4105: An Interview with Sophia the Robot at the Future Investment Institute—Nonverbal and Emotional Intelligence (VIDEO, PHOTOS)," *Body Language Success & Emotional Intelligence*, October 27, 2017, http://www.bodylanguagesuccess.com/2017/10/body-language-analysis-no-4105.html; Albert Mehrabian, "Nonverbal Betrayal of Feeling," *Journal of Experimental Research in Personality* 5, no. 1 (1971): 64–73; and Chapman University, "Survey of American Fears 2019," July 2019, https://www.chapman.edu/wilkinson/research-centers/babbie-center/_files/americas-top-fears-2019.pdf.

Learning Objectives

After studying this chapter, you should be able to

LO 14-1 Identify purposes of presentations.

LO 14-2 Plan strategies for presentations.

LO 14-3 Organize effective presentations.

LO 14-4 Plan visuals for presentations.

LO 14-5 Deliver effective in-person and online presentations.

LO 14-6 Handle questions during presentations.

Oral communication allows for unparalleled audience connection, immediacy, and impact. It allows you to amplify and enhance well-researched, audience-adapted verbal content with well-honed nonverbal delivery and a visual aid that illustrates your points and helps develop an emotional connection with the audience. Successful oral communication quickly and completely can convey important information to co-workers, persuade a company to take a chance on funding your idea, or solidify brand loyalty by building goodwill with customers.

Executing a strong oral presentation requires you to consider your purpose, audience, and situation at every step of the way. You'll need to develop a strategy that helps accomplish your purpose within your audience's needs and the presentation context; to curate and frame the content they need while avoiding confusing, complex, or irrelevant content; to organize your content in a digestible and continually reinforced way; to design visuals to assist your audience in caring about your message, connecting with it, and following your content; and to use best practices in nonverbal delivery to bring the content to life for your audience.

Comparing Written and Oral Messages

Giving a presentation—whether in person or online—is similar to writing a message. All the chapters on using *you*-attitude and positive emphasis, developing audience benefits, analyzing your audience, and designing visuals remain relevant as you plan an oral presentation.

Oral messages make it easier to

- Use emotion to help persuade the audience.
- Focus the audience's attention on specific points.
- Answer questions, resolve conflicts, and build consensus.
- Modify a proposal that may not be acceptable in its original form.
- Get immediate action or response.

Written messages make it easier to

- Present extensive or complex data.
- Present many specific details of a policy, product, or procedure.
- Minimize undesirable emotions.

Oral and written messages have many similarities. In both, you should

- Adapt the message to the specific audience.

- Show the audience how they would benefit from the idea, policy, service, or product.

- Overcome any objections the audience may have.

- Use *you*-attitude and positive emphasis.

- Use visuals to clarify or emphasize material.

- Specify exactly what the audience should do.

Identifying Purposes in Presentations

LO 14-1

Successful communication depends on keeping the reason for that communication in mind. You can create targeted, effective presentations—both in person and online—by first identifying your **general purpose** and then describing your **specific purpose** for communicating.

A general purpose is the main goal behind a form of communication—what is the primary purpose driving the communication? Like written messages, most oral presentations have multiple goals. However, before preparing an oral presentation of your own, you should identify its primary general purpose: to inform, to persuade, or to build goodwill. Identify your general purpose and keep it in mind throughout your presentation-crafting process.

Presentations with the general purpose to **inform** aim to share content with the audience.

- An example of a primarily informative presentation is an organizational training session. The presentation's primary goal is to inform because the bulk of the presentation's time would be devoted to conveying information on how employees should conduct themselves within the organization.

- Note that an organizational training session may have *secondary* purposes, such as persuading new employees to follow organizational procedures and helping them to appreciate the organizational culture (i.e., to build goodwill).

Presentations with the general purpose to **persuade** attempt to convince the audience to act a certain way, support a certain action, or believe a certain valuation to be true.

- An example of a primarily persuasive presentation is a business proposal. The person delivering a business proposal would try to persuade the audience to fund an idea or buy a product.

- Persuasion relies on a balanced mix of credibility (in terms of classical rhetoric, ethos), emotional connection (pathos), and reasoning (logos). Presenters can develop credibility by referencing their competence, experience, and consideration for the audience's best interests; develop emotional connection by including stories, testimonies, and stirring visuals; and demonstrate strong reasoning by including data, reasoning, and proof the proposal will work.

Presentations with the general purpose to **build goodwill** entertain or validate the audience while uniting the audience under shared values.

- An example of a primarily goodwill-building presentation is an announcement of a new product to the public. Although the announcement would offer information about the new product, the overall purpose of the announcement would be focused on building goodwill: to celebrate the new product, thereby motivating the public to buy the product and inspiring investors (if the company is publicly traded) to value the company at a higher level, while affirming how the new product represents the company's identity.

- A second example of a goodwill-building presentation is an after-dinner speech at a company dinner; such a speech would aim to entertain the audience while uniting listeners as contributors to the company's culture and mission.

- A third example of a goodwill-building presentation is a speech of inspiration at a sales meeting; such a speech would be designed to recognize the audience's egos and validate their commitment to organizational goals.

- Presentations with the primarily goal of building goodwill may look very different from one another, but all have the common goal of reinforcing shared values.

After identifying your general purpose, you should create a specific purpose statement to guide the creation of your presentation. Write it down before you start preparing your presentation, and refer to it often to help you select strategy and content.

To help you stay focused on your presentation's overall goal, your specific purpose statement should incorporate your general purpose: to inform, to persuade, or to build goodwill. In contrast with the general purpose, which is written in "to + a verb" (the infinitive) format, the specific purpose takes the general purpose one step further, specifying exactly what you will inform, persuade, or build goodwill about. Here are some examples of specific purpose statements:

Weak:	The specific purpose of my presentation is to discuss saving for retirement.
Better (option 1):	The specific purpose of my presentation is to persuade my audience to put their 401(k) funds in stocks and bonds rather than in money-market accounts or CDs.
Better (option 2):	The specific purpose of my presentation is to walk my audience through how to calculate how much money they will need to save for retirement.
Better (option 3):	The specific purpose of my presentation is to affirm my audience's identity as smart investors because they have taken the proactive step of managing their retirement strategy with my investment firm.

Notice how the first "better" example makes clear that the speaker wants the audience to take a specific action; it is a speech with the general purpose *to persuade*. The second "better" example makes clear that the speaker wants to instruct the audience on how to perform a specific calculation; it is a speech with the general purpose *to inform*. The third "better" example makes clear that the speaker wants the audience to feel good about their choice to remain members of a certain investment firm; it is a speech with the general purpose *to build goodwill*.

Note that the specific purpose is *not* the introduction or thesis statement of your talk; it may not be explicit in your presentation at all. Rather, it is a guiding statement to make sure every element of your presentation serves your general purpose.

Planning Strategies for Presentations

LO 14-2

How will you reach your specific goals with the target audience? The more you know about your audience, the better you can strategize how to adapt your message to their needs. Think about the context in which you'll be speaking. Will you be delivering the presentation online via conferencing software? Will you be in the same room with your audience? Will the audience be tired at the end of a long day of listening to other presentations? Will they be sleepy after a big meal? Will the group be large or small?

Whether in person or online, an oral presentation needs to be more simple and more redundant than a written message to the same audience. If readers forget a point, they

Oral presentation skills are a big asset in the business world.

Shutterstock

can reread it. Listeners, in contrast, must remember what the speaker says. Whatever they don't remember is lost. Even asking questions requires the audience to remember which points they don't understand.

Use a strategy that makes your content easy for your audience to understand and remember. In all presentations, simplify what you want to say to the one idea you want the audience to take home. Simplify your supporting details so they are easy to follow. Simplify visuals so they can be taken in at a glance. Simplify your words and sentences so they're easy to understand.

As you begin planning your presentation, you'll need to determine what kind of presentation to deliver and how to adapt your ideas to the audience.

Choosing the Kind of Presentation

Choose one of three basic kinds of presentations: monologue, guided discussion, or interactive.

In a **monologue presentation**, the speaker talks without interruption; questions are held until the end of the presentation, at which time the speaker functions as an expert. The speaker plans the presentation and delivers it without deviation. This kind of presentation is the most common in class situations, but it's often boring for the audience. Good delivery skills are crucial because the audience is comparatively uninvolved.

In a **guided discussion**, the speaker presents the questions or issues that both speaker and audience have agreed on in advance. Rather than functioning as an expert with all the answers, the speaker serves as a facilitator to help the audience tap its own knowledge. This kind of presentation is excellent for presenting the results of consulting projects, when the speaker has specialized knowledge, but the audience must implement the solution if it is to succeed. Guided discussions need more time than monologue presentations but produce more audience response, more responses involving analysis, and more commitment to the result.

An **interactive presentation** is a conversation, even if the speaker stands in front of a group and uses charts and overheads. Most sales presentations are interactive presentations. The sales representative uses questions to determine the buyer's needs, probe objections, and gain provisional and then final commitment to the purchase. Even in a memorized sales presentation, the buyer will talk a significant portion of the time. Top salespeople let the buyer do the majority of the talking.

Adapting Your Ideas to the Audience

Analyze your audience for an oral presentation just as you do for a written message. If at all possible, determine your audience's questions, concerns, and needs so you can address them in your presentation. For audiences inside the organization, the biggest questions are often practical ones: Will it work? How much will it cost? How long will it take? How will it affect me?

You also should assess the type of audience you'll be speaking to and measure the message you'd like to send against where your audience is now. If your audience is generally agreeable and interested in your topic, you can take a more ambitious approach; if your audience is indifferent, skeptical, or hostile, focus on the part of your message the audience will find most interesting and easiest to accept.

Throughout your presentation, consider how you can speak to the audience's needs and make them feel considered. This could mean directly identifying and addressing their concerns, or it could be something as subtle as using inclusive language such as "our problem" instead of "this problem."

Choosing Information to Include

Choose the information that is most interesting to your audience, that answers the questions your audience will have without providing too much information, and that has the most impact in service of your specific purpose. Limit your talk to three main points. Your content will be easier to understand if you clearly show the relationship between each of the main points. In a long presentation (20 minutes or more), each main point also can have subpoints.

Think about colorful ways to present your information. What analogies or metaphors can you use to grab your audience's attention and help them remember your information? What props could you use? How can you entertain and inspire your audience with your presentation to increase its impact?

What pictures can you use to illustrate your ideas? Where could you use video clips? Research evidence is clear that people remember information far better and longer when its presentation involves pictures.

Turning your information into a **narrative** or story also helps. Narrative structures information in a chronological format moved forward by character, plot, and setting. For example, a presentation about a plan to reduce scrap rates on the second shift could begin by setting the scene and defining the problem: *Production expenses have cut profits in half.* The plot unfolds as the speaker describes the facts that helped her trace the problem to scrap rates on the second shift. The resolution to the story is her group's proposal. This example uses a narrative pattern of organization to structure the main points, but you also can include shorter anecdotes in your presentation to illustrate a point and keep the audience's attention.

In an informative presentation, link the points you make to the knowledge your audience has. Show the audience members that your information answers their questions, solves their problems, or helps them do their jobs. When you explain the effect of a new law or the techniques for using a new machine, use specific examples that apply to the decisions they make and the work they do. If your content is detailed or complicated, give people a written outline or handouts. However, distribute the written information wisely. Ideally, you should distribute it after your presentation, so the document does not distract from your spoken content, or before it, if your audience must reference the document during your talk. For many presentations, a better approach is to use a visual aid to reinforce complicated spoken content. Project key words and main ideas sparingly to help your audience track your main points as you verbally elaborate upon them.

To be convincing, you must answer the audience's questions and objections. However, don't bring up negatives or inconsistencies unless you're sure that the audience will think of them. If you aren't sure, save your evidence for the question phase. If someone does ask, you'll have the answer.

Choosing Data

As part of choosing what to say, you should determine what data to present. Any data you mention should be necessary for the points you are making and should start with decisions about what the audience needs to know.

Statistics and numbers can be convincing if you present them in ways that are easy to understand. Simplify numbers by reducing them to two significant digits and putting them in a context.

Hard to understand:	Our 2020 sales dropped from $12,036,288,000 to $9,124,507,000.
Easy to understand:	Our 2020 sales dropped from $12 billion to $9 billion. This is the steepest decline our company has seen in a quarter century.

Double-check your presentation statistics and numbers to ensure they are accurate. Mark Hurd, former chair and CEO of Hewlett-Packard, reported that the best advice he ever got was, "It's hard to look smart with bad numbers."[1]

Choosing Demonstrations

Demonstrations can prove your points dramatically and quickly. They offer an effective way to teach a process and to show what a product can do for the audience. Demonstrations also can help people remember your points.

Apple has become famous for using captivating demonstrations when it launches new versions of its products. Steve Jobs, in particular, was known for amazing presentations, and most of his finest involved a Wow! moment that had his audience standing and cheering. For example, when he introduced the MacBook Air, Jobs picked up a manila envelope and pulled out his new notebook computer, holding it high for everyone to see how thin it was.[2]

Wow! moments don't have to be announcements of world-class technological breakthroughs. In their book *Made to Stick: Why Some Ideas Survive and Others Die*, Chip Heath and Dan Heath say that ideas are remembered—and have lasting impact on people's opinions and behavior—when they have simplicity, are unexpected, are concrete, project credibility, stir emotions, and offer stories. They call the combination of these six factors *stickiness*.[3]

Organizing Your Information

LO 14-3

Unlike written documents where your audience can reread as needed to understand your message, a message conveyed via presentation must be clear to the listener on the first attempt. To help your audience grasp and remember your message, you should tell them about the message multiple times: first in an overview in the introduction, then in detail during the body of the presentation itself, and again in a review in the conclusion. Mere repetition is not enough, however; your content should be organized carefully at every level. You should craft a strong and complete opening, structure the body with strategic organization, and craft a strong and complete conclusion.

Planning a Strong Opening

The opening is the most important part of your presentation. An opening should contain, at a minimum, an attention getter, message or statement of purpose, and preview of your content. You also may include a discussion of your credibility or connect the topic to your audience, showing how your topic is relevant to their needs or concerns.

Attention Getter   Audience members are not going to decide halfway through your presentation that they should start listening; you need to grab their attention from the start and keep it. Even in the most formal or formulaic of presentations, *do not* open by stating your name or topic, unless otherwise specified by conventions specific to the event. The first words out of your mouth should work to earn the audience's attention; if, for clarity, you must state your name or topic—for example, if there are multiple speakers at an event and there is no program—do so *after* first gaining the audience's attention.

The more you can do to personalize the opening for your audience, the better. Recent events are better than ones that happened long ago; local events are better than events at a distance; people they know are better than people who are only names.

Consider using one of five common modes for openers: a startling statement, narrative, quotation, question, or humor. Note that these techniques describe the spoken verbal content you would use to gain your audience's attention; you also should consider how to use nonverbal content to enhance the attention-gaining affect, such as through the use of a visual aid or engaging vocal delivery.

Startling Statement   A startling statement, statistic, or fact—carefully targeted to your audience's realm of concern—can gain audience attention at the beginning of your presentation:

> Twelve of our customers have canceled orders in the past month.

This presentation to a company's executive committee went on to show that the company's distribution system was inadequate and to recommend a third warehouse located in the Southwest. The statement matters to the audience because it indicated an urgent situation that could lead to loss of business if not corrected.

Narration or Anecdote   The same presentation also could start with a relevant story. Stories use character, setting, and chronology to help the audience order information. Elements such as dialogue and sensory details can give stories more impact. Narratives lend themselves particularly well to augmentation by a visual aid to help illustrate the story.

> Last week Joe Murphy, purchasing agent for Westtrop, our biggest client, came to see me. I knew something was wrong right away because Joe was wearing a jacket instead of his usual cowboy shirt and smile. "Ajit," he said, "I have to tell you something. I didn't want to do it, but I had to change suppliers. We've been with you a long time, but it's just not working for us now."

The human mind evolved to process and recall stories more effectively than disconnected facts, so frame facts in a story if it is possible and ethical. In this example, for example, it might not be appropriate to use the individual's or company's name if the interaction was private.

Quotation   A quotation also could start the presentation. Quotations use poetic or memorable language to introduce a "sticky" idea you want your audience to ponder or a concept that frames your message.

Quotations work best when they are directly connected to the audience, as opposed to quotes from famous people. For example, this quotation came from Boyers, a major account for the company:

> "Faster and easier!" That's what Boyers said about its new supplier.

If the quotation is short, you might consider projecting it in a visual aid, but avoid long quotes, which can distract your audience from your spoken content. An appropriate visual-aid alternative to projecting a long quote would be to show an image of the person who said the quote while you orally state the quote.

Question   Asking audience members to raise their hands or reply to questions gets them actively involved in a presentation. However, this technique is widely used, so if using a question as an attention-gaining technique, you must use creativity, sincerity, and effective timing to avoid coming across as cliché. Do more than merely ask a question and move on; give your audience the sense that you sincerely care about their response by giving them time to respond and showing interest in their response, perhaps incorporating it into your presentation, like Tony Jeary does. Jeary skillfully uses this technique in sessions devoted to training the audience in presentation skills. He begins by asking the audience members to estimate the number of presentations they give per week:

> "How many of you said one or two?" he asks, raising his hand. A few hands pop up. "Three, four, six, eight?" he asks, walking up the middle of the aisle to the back of the room. Hands start popping up like targets in a shooting gallery. Jeary's Texas drawl accelerates and suddenly the place sounds like a cattle auction. "Do I hear 10? Twelve? Thirteen to the woman in the green shirt! Fifteen to the gentleman in plaid," he fires, and the room busts out laughing.[4]

Most presenters will not want to take a course in auctioneering, as Jeary did to make his questioning routine more authentic. However, Jeary's approach both engages the audience and makes the point that many jobs involve a multitude of occasions requiring formal and informal presentation skills.

Humor   Some speakers use humor to establish rapport. In the right setting and with the right tone, humor disarms the audience and inclines them to listen more closely. However, humor requires careful consideration because an inappropriate joke can turn the audience against the speaker. Never use humor that's directed against the audience or an inappropriate group. Humor directed at yourself or your team is safer, but don't make your audience squirm with too much self-disclosure.

Message or Statement of Purpose

Your audience should not be left guessing as to your purpose for speaking. After gaining the audience's attention, transition to stating your overall message or goal. It may be similar to the specific purpose statement you outlined and used to guide the presentation-creation process. Among the example thesis statements below, notice the range in tone from informal to formal and the range in approach from disconnected facts to narratively framed; however, all alert the audience to the speaker's general purpose and the presentation's topic:

> Spend a few minutes with me today learning my favorite Gmail hacks, and you'll be able to use these tips and tricks to save you hours on your email tomorrow.

> My goal today is to share with you the benefits of SMART goal setting and how to go about setting SMART goals for yourself.

> Our expansion into the Asian market was met with difficulty, but by the fourth quarter, we've recouped our initial investment and look forward positively to the next year.

> I will inform you of the main challenges we faced this year and the projected performance for year two.

Preview

Even if your audience knows your message or purpose for speaking, they still may need more guidance to easily follow your presentation. In written messages, headings, paragraph indentation, and punctuation provide visual cues to help readers understand the organization of a message. Listeners, in contrast, must rely on what the speaker says for organization and context.

Therefore, in a presentation, you need to provide explicit clues to the structure of your discourse. Before moving on to the body of the presentation, you should offer your audience a specific preview of your main points or ideas. A preview provides a mental peg that listeners can hang each point on. It also can prevent someone from missing what you are saying because they wonder why you aren't covering a major point that you've saved for later.

The message/purpose statement and preview are closely linked, but not exactly the same—the preview should be more specific than your message statement and clarify which main points you will use to develop, illustrate, or support your main idea.

Here is an example of a preview statement for the message statement about SMART goals:

> Message: My goal today is to share with you the benefits of SMART goal setting, and how to go about setting SMART goals for yourself.
>
> Preview: I'll discuss why SMART goals are more likely to be achieved than non-smart goals, and how they're easy to set once you know the acronym: SMART goals are Simple, Measurable, Achievable, Realistic, and Timely.

Here is an example of a preview for a different presentation. Note how this preview makes use of temporal cues, or **signposts**, to show the order in which main points will be discussed:

> **First**, I'd like to talk about who the homeless in Columbus are. **Second**, I'll talk about the services The Open Shelter provides. **Finally**, I'll talk about what you—either individually or as a group—can do to help.

Credibility   Depending on your audience and purpose, it may be wise to spend a few moments in your opening discussing why you are qualified to speak on your topic. If you are speaking internally about company supply-chain logistics, for example, and everyone knows your role as a supply-chain leader in the company, a credibility statement may not be necessary; however, if you take the same presentation and adapt it to an external audience, it would meet the new audience's needs to state your experience and credibility with the topic.

A statement of credibility also can be used to build goodwill by stating why the topic is personally important to you. Doing so is especially appropriate if your general purpose is to build goodwill; for other topics, such as a formal informative report, it may unnecessarily use up time or even confuse the overall tone. At all points in your presentation crafting, consider how to meet audience expectations and needs.

Relevance   Briefly indicating how your topic is relevant to the audience's needs can build on the momentum of your attention-gaining opening, cementing the audience's belief that your presentation is worth listening to. Assume that your audience is busy and concerned with their own needs. Make your ideas relevant to your audience by linking what you have to say to their experiences and interests. Showing your audience that the topic affects them directly is the most effective strategy. When you can't do that, at least link the topic to some everyday experience.

As with message statements, statements of relevance can range from informal to formal and should be matched with the overall purpose, audience, and tone of the presentation.

> Informal example: If we want to stay at the top of our game, we need to listen to these numbers and follow their logic, people. I hate to tell you, but the logic is saying we need a new approach.
>
> Formal example: To generate revenue for our stakeholders and remain competitive, we need to diversify our portfolio.

Establishing relevance in the opening is just the beginning of curating your audience's attention. Throughout your presentation, you should continue to reinforce how your message addresses or relates to your audience's needs. The more seamlessly you can interweave your message with the audience's specific concerns, the more likely they are to pay attention—and remember your message.

Structuring the Body

Using a well-chosen pattern of organization helps organize your content in a way that is accessible, digestible, and memorable to your audience. In a persuasive presentation, the pattern of organization also helps to frame the flow of logic, lending impact to your argument. You should spend time considering how your content could fit different organizational patterns and which pattern best fits the needs of your purpose and audience. You also should orient your audience to each main point through the use of signposts.

Organizational Patterns   Often, one of five patterns of organization will likely work to structure the body of your presentation:

- **Chronological.** Start with the past, move to the present, and end by looking ahead. This pattern works best when the history helps show a problem's complexity or magnitude or when the chronology moves people to an obvious solution.

- **Problem-cause-solution.** Explain the symptoms of the problem, identify its cause, and suggest a solution. This pattern works best when the audience will find your solution easy to accept. If the audience needs more convincing, you may consider adding a final main point, showing how your solution has worked well in other, similar situations.

- **Comparative advantages.** Establish the problem or symptoms of the problem. Then explain the obvious solutions one by one, showing why they won't solve the problem. End by discussing a solution that will work best—your solution. This pattern may be necessary when the audience will find the solution hard to accept; it is also appropriate when the audience already knows about the problem and agrees that it is significant but can't decide upon the best solution.

- **Pro-con.** Detail the reasons in favor of something and then those against it. This pattern works well when you want the audience to see the weaknesses in the opposing position while coming across as balanced and well-informed.

- **1-2-3.** Discuss three aspects of a topic. This pattern works well to organize short, informative briefings ("Today I'll review our sales, production, and profits for the last quarter") and also for persuasive presentations when you have several good reasons to adopt a policy. In the latter, start off a strong note to keep your audience listening by leading with your strongest reason, and place your second-strongest reason last—this takes into account the **recency effect**, whereby audience members best remember what they heard last.

Signposts   Between your main points, use language specifically designed to help the audience orient to the progression of your presentation. Signposts indicate movement from one idea to the next. Some signposts are simple, like the word "first" or "finally," as in the example of a preview above. Others help give your audience time to process and reinforce content. Choose wording that fits your style and your content's needs. You can help your audience move from idea to idea with ease by referencing chronology ("first," "second," "finally"), reinforcing previous content (reviewing the content that was just discussed), preparing the audience for what's to come (previewing the content that's about to be discussed), or transitioning between two ideas ("Now that we've discussed X, let's examine Y.")

The following statements are three different ways that a speaker could use to introduce the last of three points:

> Now we come to the third point: What you can do as a group or as individuals to help people experiencing homelessness in Columbus.

> I've outlined what the company is doing to solve this problem. Now let's talk about what *you* can personally do to help.

> Finally, you may be wondering, what can *I* do to help?

Planning a Strong Conclusion

The end of your presentation should be as strong as the opening. A closing should contain, at a minimum, a review of your main content, a reinforcement of your message or purpose, and a closing statement that leaves your audience with a memorable final thought and clearly signals your audience to applaud (if applicable). If your purpose is to persuade your audience to act, your conclusion should include a final call to action.

Reference an element of your introduction to bring the presentation full circle and create a sense of psychological integrity across the presentation. For example, if your attention getter was a story about your first job, your final statement could reflect on your current job or dream job. If you began your presentation with a negative, shocking statistic, you could end the speech with a positive shocking statistic, leaving the audience with a sense of hope and balancing out your opening technique.

When you write out your opener and close, be sure to use a conversational, oral style suited for delivery rather than reading. Oral style uses shorter sentences and shorter, simpler words than writing does. It can even sound a bit choppy when it is read by eye. Oral style uses more personal pronouns, a less varied and more informal vocabulary, and more repetition.

Planning Visuals

LO 14-4

Once you have planned a strategy for your presentation, you need to decide if you will use visuals to enhance the presentation. Visuals should enhance and not distract from your spoken content. Well-designed visuals can give your presentation a professional image, heighten emotional impact, convey content not easily spoken, and assist the audience in following your presentation. Additionally, visuals should avoid excessive text for the benefit of both speaker and audience.

This section discusses the design and incorporation of visual aids in presentations. See Chapters 7 and 8 for more discussion on designing visuals.

- **Use visuals to create a professional image.** A visual aid, such as a chart or a graph, is not always necessary for conveying content. However, nondistracting visuals can reinforce your company's brand, values, or image.

- **Use visuals to heighten emotional impact.** Emotional (pathos) appeals are much more effective when the audience can visualize emotional content. Along with vivid language, use images to illustrate narratives and other pathos appeals.

- **Use visuals to convey content not easily spoken.** Content such as maps, graphs, and diagrams are better presented visually than described only orally. Use a visual aid to present visual-heavy or complicated content in a way that removes some descriptive burden from the speaker and renders the content more accessible to the audience.

- **Use visuals to assist organization.** Your audience only will hear your presentation once, and—along with a preview, signposts between main points, and a review—they will welcome visual assistance in following the presentation. You can help your audience follow the progression of ideas through headings, images, color, or other methods.

| Figure 14.1 | Poorly Formatted Presentation Slides (Top) and Well-Formatted Slides (Bottom) |

Problem: 75% of Our Company's Used Cardboard Boxes Go to the Landfill

- 75% of our waste ends up in the landfill
- We recycle 5%
- We reuse 10%
- We resell 5%

THIS IS TOO MUCH WASTE!!!!!!

Recycled
Reused
Sold
Other
Landfill

Proposed Solution: Implement Recycling and Reuse Guidelines

- Check every box for the recycling logo and if it's there put the box aside
- Break up every box into a flat form so that we can stack them all neatly in the bin by the loading dock
- Recycle only the cardboard boxes—not the plastic ones because we lease them from the supplier!!
- There is to be no unauthorized access to the recycling bin: keep it LOCKED!

We Expect to See These Advantages from this New Program

- It will keep all of those scrap boxes off the stockroom floor, so as our founder and President Ms. Davis says "A tidy business is good business!"
- Save money through decreased solid waste costs
- Good for the environment: our business is doing its part to save trees and stop global warming!

| Use simple visuals | Build goodwill | Summarize main points | Use a consistent background | Use simplified headings | Use clip art or images that match the topic |

Problem: Used Box Recycling

- We throw out 75% of our used cardboard boxes
- We recycle, reuse, or resell the rest
- We can do better!

Proposed Guidelines

- Check boxes for recycling logo
- Break boxes into flattest form
- Recycle only cardboard — not plastic
- Keep the bin locked

Benefits

- Keep the stockroom floor clean
- Save money
- Conserve resources

For example, if you were walking an audience of nurses through floor plans of a new hospital building, you could color-code each floor a different color and use that color in headings and other visual elements of each slide so the nurses could easily reference which floor was being discussed. A common method for using visual aids to aid organization is to place a heading at the top of each slide so the audience knows which main point the presentation is on.

Well-designed visuals can serve as an outline for your talk (see Figure 14.1), eliminating the need for additional notes. Visuals can help your audience follow along with you and help you keep your place as you speak. Your visuals should highlight your main points, not give every detail. Elaborate on your visuals as you talk in a conversational way that adds new content not available on the slide; it is not effective to read slides word-for-word to the audience because they will stop viewing you as a source of new information. If the audience can read the entire presentation for themselves, why are you there?

Overall, visuals should not duplicate spoken content, but rather present information that is best conveyed in a visual rather than oral manner; visual and spoken content should overlap just enough for the audience to follow along and understand how the visuals correspond to your spoken message.

You can organize your presentation visuals and content with a software program such as PowerPoint, Google Presentation, or Prezi. Each has its own advantages and disadvantages. The next sections discuss the most common types of visual presentation in business settings: PowerPoint and Prezi.

Designing PowerPoint Slides

When used well, PowerPoint can combine text, images, data, video, and audio into a powerful informative and persuasive message. But like any other form of communication, creating visuals requires careful thought; planning; and attention to the context, the message, and the audience.

As you design slides for PowerPoint and other presentation programs, keep the following guidelines in mind:

- Use a consistent background.

- Use a big font size: around 44 point for slide headings and 28 point for body text. You should be able to read the smallest words easily when you print a handout version of your slides.

- Use bullet-point phrases rather than complete sentences. But don't go overboard with bullets because your slides can become monotonous and dull.

- Use clear, concise language.

- Make only three to five points on each slide. If you have more, consider using two slides.

- Strive for creating slides that have more visuals than text. Convey your message with charts, graphs, photos, drawings, and other visual elements.

- For branding purposes, customize your slides with your organization's logo.

Use **animation** to make words and images appear and move during your presentation— but only in ways that help you control information flow and build interest. Avoid using animation or sound effects just to be clever; they will distract your audience.

Use **clip art** in your presentations only if the art is really appropriate to your points. Internet sources have made such a wide variety of drawings and photos available that designers really have no excuse for failing to pick images that are both appropriate and visually appealing.

Choose a consistent **template**, or background design, for your entire presentation. Make sure the template is appropriate for your subject matter and audience. For example, use a globe if, for example, your topic is international business and palm trees only if you're talking about a topic such as tropical vacations. One problem with PowerPoint is that the basic templates may seem repetitive to people who see lots of presentations made with the program. For an important presentation, you may want to consider customizing the basic template. You also can find many professionally designed free templates online to help lend your presentation a customized look. Make sure your template does not detract from your information.

Choose a light background if the lights will be off during your presentation. Slides will be easier to read if you use high contrast between the words and backgrounds. See Figure 14.2 for examples of effective and ineffective color combinations.

Avoiding Disastrous PowerPoints

Conference keynote presentations are notoriously boring, with long PowerPoint shows and droning presenters. Audience members, bored, fiddle with their phones and participate in electronic discussions. During one keynote presentation, people in the audience even designed a t-shirt and put it up for sale online. The shirt's message? "I survived the keynote disaster of 09."

How can you keep your presentations from ending up with their own t-shirts? Here are a few tips:[5]

- **Use visuals and words together.** Your PowerPoint slides should augment and enhance your presentation, not distract from or displace it.

- **Keep your slides simple.** An audience should be able to completely understand each slide in two or three seconds.

- **Break complex ideas into multiple slides.** Don't try to get all the information on a single slide. Use several slides that add up to something more complex.

- **Use your slides as a mnemonic device.** Your slides should make your presentation emotionally appealing and memorable to your audience.

Figure 14.2   Effective and Ineffective Colors for Presentation Slides

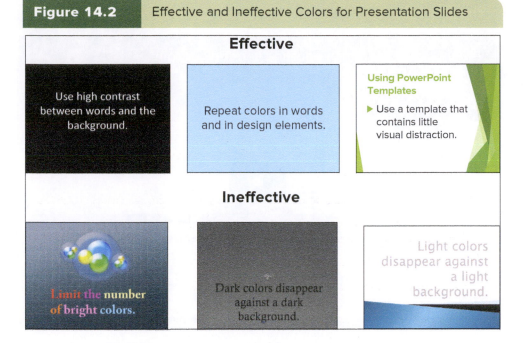

One final note about PowerPoint: because the program is so ubiquitous in the business world, audiences quickly become bored or annoyed and experience attention difficulties. Choose the program only after assessing the audience you'll be presenting to and understanding their expectations. You also might investigate alternative software programs to add more creativity and impact for your audience.

Creating a Prezi

Prezi, a free online tool, provides business communicators with another option when planning presentations. While PowerPoint's presentation philosophy is based on techniques of clicking through slides, Prezi uses modern technologies to create a different experience.

Rather than a series of consecutive slides, Prezi creates one large canvas. The presenter can place text and images anywhere on the canvas and zoom in and out of areas or pan to different areas of the canvas. See Figure 14.3 for an example. This approach allows presenters to display hierarchies and spatial relationships between items in ways that PowerPoint's linear progression does not allow.

Prezi's zooming and panning approach may be more engaging than PowerPoint, especially to viewers who are not familiar with it. But, just as with PowerPoint's transitions and animations, Prezi's movements can become distracting if used unwisely. Overuse of Prezi's movements can create a dizzying effect on the audience.

If you want to convert a PowerPoint into a Prezi, the program allows users to import PowerPoint slides one at a time or in a slide show. Finally, Prezi is cloud-based, meaning that you can access your presentation from any computer, tablet, or smartphone with an internet connection.

For inspiration in designing a Prezi, you can go to Prezi's website to see some award-winning Prezi presentations: https://prezi.com/explore/staff-picks/.

Using Figures and Tables

Visuals for presentations need to be simpler than visuals the audience reads on paper. For example, to adapt a printed data table for a presentation, you might cut out one or more columns or rows of data, round off the data to simplify them, or replace the table

Figure 14.3   Screenshot of Prezi Canvas

Source: https://prezi.com/support/article/creating/powerpoint-import/

with another visual, such as a graph. If you have many data tables or other complex visuals in your presentation, consider including them on a handout for your audience.

Your presentation visuals should include titles but don't need figure numbers. As you prepare your presentation, be sure to know where each visual is so that you can return to it easily if someone asks about it during the question period. Rather than reading from your slides, or describing visuals to your audience in detail, summarize the story contained on each slide and elaborate on what it means for your audience.

Using Technology Effectively

Projected visuals work only if the technology they depend on works. For in-person presentations in your own workplace, plan ahead: Check the equipment in advance. When you make an in-person presentation in another location or for another organization, arrive early so that you'll have time not only to check the equipment but also to track down IT help if the equipment isn't functioning.

For online presentations, check your internet connection. If you can, have an extra laptop, tablet, or smartphone available as a backup.

Keep in mind how you will use your visual aids. Most likely, they will provide support for a presentation—either in person or online. Visual aids should identify the key points of your presentation in a way that allows you to interact with your audience. If you use PowerPoint, Prezi, or some other presentation software, your oral presentation always should include more material than the text on your slides.

> **WARNING:** Be sure you have a backup plan in case of a technology failure that prevents the use of your visual aids. It's good, for example, to have a PDF of your visual aids that you can use as a backup.

Delivering an Effective Presentation
LO 14-5

Audiences want the sense that you're talking directly to them and that you care that they understand and are interested. They'll forgive you if you get tangled up in a sentence and end it ungrammatically. They won't forgive you if you seem to have a "canned" talk that you're going to deliver no matter who the audience is or how they respond.

To deliver an effective presentation, you should deal with fear; develop a good speaking voice; use eye contact; and practice, practice, practice.

Dealing with Fear

Feeling nervous about public speaking is normal; most people feel some fear about public speaking. But the more you practice, the more you can learn to channel nervous energy with purpose. You can harness that nervous energy to help you do your best work both short term, with the presentation at hand, and long term, in the context of how presentations can help you develop as a professional. As various public speaking trainers have noted, you don't need to get rid of your butterflies; all you need to do is make them fly in formation.

To calm your nerves before you give an oral presentation:

- Be prepared. Analyze your audience, organize your thoughts, prepare visual aids, practice your presentation opening and closing, check out the arrangements.

- Have backup plans for various contingencies, including technical problems and questions your audience is likely to ask.

- Use only the amount of caffeine you normally use. More may make you jumpy; less may bring fatigue or a headache.

- Avoid alcoholic beverages.

- Relabel your nerves. Instead of saying, "I'm scared," try saying, "My adrenaline is up." Adrenaline sharpens our reflexes and helps us do our best.

Just before your presentation:

- Consciously contract and then relax your muscles, starting with your feet and calves and going up to your shoulders, arms, and hands.

- Take several deep breaths from your diaphragm; picture stress leaving your body as you exhale.

Developing a Good Speaking Voice

People will enjoy your presentation more if your voice is easy to listen to and your delivery is appropriate. Just how important is your voice when delivering a message?

Vocal delivery can stack the cards for—or against—getting a job offer based on an interview. Vocal fry, the tendency to lower one's voice at the end of statements, often with a creaky, croaky, raspy effect, has been linked to lowering one's chances at being perceived as competent—and the association is much stronger for women.[6] Vocal delivery matters, and you should be aware of how your voice represents you in both prepared and impromptu situations like a job interview.

To find out what your voice sounds like, record it using a digital voice recorder or video camera. Listen to your voice qualities, including tone, pitch, stress, enunciation, and volume.

Tone of voice refers to the rising or falling inflection that tells you whether a group of words is a question or a statement, whether the speaker is uncertain or confident, and whether a statement is sincere or sarcastic.

When tone of voice and the meaning of words conflict, people "believe" the tone of voice. If you respond to your friends' "How are you?" with the words, "I'm dying, and you?" most of your friends will reply, "Fine." If the tone of your voice is cheerful, they may not hear the content of the words.

Pitch measures whether a voice uses sounds that are low or high. Low-pitched voices are usually perceived as being more authoritative and more pleasant to listen to than are high-pitched voices. Most voices go up in pitch when the speaker is angry or excited; some people raise pitch when they increase volume.

Stress is the emphasis given to one or more words in a sentence. As the following example shows, emphasizing different words can change the meaning.

I'll give you a raise.

[Implication, depending on pitch and speed: "Another supervisor wouldn't" or "I have the power to determine your salary."]

I'll **give** you a raise.

[Implication, depending on pitch and speed: "You haven't *earned* it" or "OK, all right, you win. I'm saying 'yes' to get rid of you, but I don't really agree," or "I've just this instant decided that you deserve a raise."]

I'll give **you** a raise.

[Implication: "But nobody else in this department is getting one."]

I'll give you **a** raise.

[Implication: "But just one."]

I'll give you a **raise**.

[Implication: "But you won't get the promotion or anything else you want."]

I'll give **you** a **raise**.

[Implication: "You deserve it."]

I'll give you a **raise!**

[Implication: "I've just this minute decided to act, and I'm excited about this idea. The raise will please both of us."]

Enunciation is giving voice to all the sounds of each word. Words starting or ending with *f, t, k, v,* and *d* are especially hard to hear. "Our informed and competent image" can sound like "Our informed, incompetent image." The bigger the group is, the more carefully you need to enunciate.

Speakers who use many changes in tone, pitch, and stress as they speak usually seem more enthusiastic; often they also seem more energetic and more intelligent. Someone who speaks in a monotone may seem apathetic or unintelligent. When you are interested in your topic, your audience is more likely to be also.

Volume is projecting your voice loud enough for your audience to hear but not so loud that it overwhelms closer audience members. For proper volume, imagine projecting your voice, as if you are throwing a ball, all the way to the back of the room. If you're using a microphone, adjust your volume so you aren't shouting. When you speak in an unfamiliar location, try to get to the room early so you can check the size of the room and the power of the amplification equipment. If you can't do that, ask early in your talk, "Can you hear me in the back of the room?" Another guideline is this: If you can hear your voice bouncing off the back wall of the room, usually everyone in the room can hear you.

What can be done about it when the way we hear our own voice is not the way an audience hears us? Most vocal issues that are not the result of medical concerns can be adjusted with practice based on informed observation of your starting point. Practice your presentation in order to convey sincerity with vocal tone, pacing, and inflection. Ask others for feedback on how your voice actually sounds. Finally, record your voice and listen to hear if your voice comes across as intended. This objective observation can make a real difference.

Use your voice qualities as you would use your facial expressions: to create a cheerful, energetic, and enthusiastic impression for your audience. Doing so can help you build rapport with your audience and can demonstrate the importance of your material. If your ideas don't excite you, why should your audience find them exciting?

Using Eye Contact

The point in making eye contact is to establish one-on-one contact with the individual members of your audience. People want to feel that you're talking to them.

When you are in the same room as your audience, make eye contact with individuals in different locations throughout the audience because you want everyone to feel you are connecting with them. Looking directly at individuals also enables you to be more conscious of feedback from the audience so that you can modify your approach if necessary. Do not stare at your notes or your visual aids. Researchers have found that observers were more than twice as likely to notice and comment on poor presentation features, like poor eye contact, than good features and tended to describe speakers with poor eye contact as uninterested, unprofessional, and poorly prepared.[7]

For an online presentation, move your chair about arm's length from your computer and put a box or stack of books under your laptop so that the camera is at eye level.

Practicing

Many presenters spend too much time thinking about what they will say and too little time rehearsing how they will say it. Presentation is important; if it weren't, you would just email your text or PowerPoint to your audience.

Practice your speech over and over, out loud, in front of a mirror or to your family and friends. Jerry Weissman, a presentation coach for over 20 years, encourages every client to do verbalizations, the process of speaking your presentation aloud. He argues that practicing by looking at your slide show while thinking about what you'll say or mumbling through your slides are both ineffective methods. The best approach is to verbalize the actual words you will say.[8]

Other reasons to practice out loud are that doing so allows you

- To stop thinking about the words and to concentrate instead on emotions you wish to communicate to your audience.

- To work on your signposts, or transitions, that move your speech from one point to the next. Transitions are one of the places where speakers frequently stumble.

- To determine your pace and the overall amount of time that it takes you to deliver your message.

- To avoid unintentional negatives.

- To reduce the number of *uh*s you use. **Filler sounds**, which occur when speakers pause searching for the next word, aren't necessarily signs of nervousness. Searching takes longer when people have big vocabularies or talk about topics where a variety of word choices are possible. Practicing your talk makes your word choices automatic, and you'll use fewer *uh*s.[9]

As an added bonus, practicing your presentation out loud gives you reason to work on your voice qualities.

Guidelines for In-Person Presentations

While dealing with fear, developing a good speaking voice, using eye contact, and practicing are tips that apply to all presentations, some tips apply specifically to in-person presentations.

Standing and Gesturing   Stand with your feet far enough apart for good balance, with your knees flexed. Unless the presentation is very formal or you're on camera, you can walk if you want to. Some speakers like to come in front of the lectern to remove that barrier between themselves and the audience or move about the room to connect with more people.

Build on your natural style for gestures. Gestures usually work best when they're big and confident. Avoid nervous gestures such as swaying on your feet, jingling coins in your pocket, twirling your hair, or twisting a button. These mannerisms distract the audience.

Using Notes and Visuals   If you are using PowerPoint, use the notes feature. If you are not using PowerPoint, put your notes on cards. Many speakers use 4-by-6-inch or 5-by-7-inch cards because they hold more information than 3-by-5-inch cards. Your notes need to be complete enough to help you if you go blank, so use key phrases. Avoid complete sentences on your notes because they easily can become a crutch, allowing you to read directly from them instead of delivering a presentation. Under each main point, you might list the evidence or illustration you'll use during that portion of the presentation.

Look at your notes infrequently. Most of your gaze time should be directed to members of the audience. If using paper note cards, hold them high enough so that your head doesn't bob up and down as you look from the audience to your notes and back again. If you know your material well or have lots of visuals, you won't need notes.

If you use visuals, stand beside the screen so that you don't block it. Always stand facing the audience, not the screen. Remember that your audience can look at you or your visual, but not both at the same time. Direct attention to more complex visuals, such as figures and tables, and explain them or give your audience a few seconds to absorb them. Show the entire visual at once: don't cover up part of it. If you don't want the audience to read ahead, use animation or prepare several slides that build up.

Keep the room lights on if possible; turning them off makes it easier for people to fall asleep and harder for them to concentrate on you.

Involving Your Audience   Just as when you're speaking with someone one-to-one, when you're presenting in front of a group it's important to involve your audience and look for feedback. Pay attention to body language and ask your audience questions: The feedback that you get will help you build rapport with your audience so that you can express your message more clearly.

In some settings, such as when you're presenting to a large group, you might use other tools to gather audience feedback. For example, you could build a group discussion into your presentation: Give your audience some questions to discuss in small groups, then invite them to share their answers with the room. Give questionnaires to your audience, either before your presentation or during a break. Have a member of your team tabulate audience responses, then build them into the remainder of your talk.

Technology also continues to offer new ways to involve your audience. Audience response devices, such as clickers or smartphone apps, allow people to answer multiple-choice, true/false, and yes/no questions; software then quickly tabulates the responses into charts and graphs the audience can see. These response devices and other programs, such as Twitter, offer audiences a way to backchannel during your presentation.

Backchanneling is the process of using online tools such as smartphones, tablets, or computers to hold concurrent conversations or disseminate information while a speaker presents. The audience of the backchannel can be physically in the same room as the presenter but does not have to be. For instance, Twitter audiences can follow multiple presentations at a single conference simply by following the hashtag of the event. The question for you will be how much such a system tempts your audience to send its own tweets instead of listening to you.

Guidelines for Online Presentations

During the COVID-19 pandemic, many people who had never given a talk online suddenly had to learn how to do it. Here are some guidelines that apply specifically to online presentations. These guidelines correspond to those for online meetings, covered in Chapter 6.

Setting the Stage   Before you give an online presentation, think about how your audience will perceive you. Get rid of clutter that your audience could see, such as piles of books and laundry. A plain wall in the background looks professional. You can also use a virtual background.

Choose clothes that you would wear to work, as opposed to clothes that you wear around your home. For an online presentation, it's important to choose solid colors and avoid patterns, particularly busy ones. Also, avoid shiny fabrics.

Give yourself the benefit of flattering lighting. Set a lamp behind your laptop. Center it behind the camera so that it lights up your face. Lower the shades to minimize light from behind you.

Eliminating Distractions   Your presentation should be the only thing your audience hears. So choose a quiet room. You can also avoid background noise by using a headset with a built-in microphone. In addition, turn off notifications on your computer and set your phone to vibrate.

Involving Your Audience   To keep your audience involved in your presentation—and to keep them from tuning out—you can use verbal strategies. Use anecdotes and examples periodically to illustrate your points. Stories engage people. Also, periodically ask questions and solicit your audience's feedback. To this end, you can also use your software's polling feature. For example, WebEx allows your audience to answer questions, vote, and give feedback. All these verbal strategies push your audience to participate. You can use visual strategies as well. You can show and discuss engaging visuals, such as graphs and photographs. You can also show a brief video clip. The point here is that you should carefully plan how you will keep your audience's attention.[10]

Handling Questions

LO 14-6

Prepare for questions by listing every fact or opinion you can think of that challenges your position. Put the questions into categories, and then plan a good answer for each category. The answer should work no matter how the question is phrased. This bundling of questions helps reduce your preparation time and boost your confidence.

During your presentation, tell the audience how you'll handle questions. If you have a choice, save questions for the end. In your talk, answer the questions or objections that you expect your audience to have. Don't exaggerate your claims so that you won't have to back down in response to questions later.

During the question period, don't nod your head to indicate that you understand a question as it is asked. Audiences will interpret nods as signs that you agree with the questioner. Instead, look directly at the questioner. As you answer the question, expand your focus to take in the entire group. Don't say, "That's a good question." That response implies that the other questions have been poor ones.

If the audience may not have heard the question or if you want more time to think, repeat the question before you answer it. Link your answers to the points you made in your presentation. Keep the purpose of your presentation in mind and select information that advances your goals.

If a question is hostile or biased, rephrase it before you answer it. Suppose that during a sales presentation, the prospective client exclaims, "How can you justify those prices?" A response that steers the presentation back to the service's benefits might be: "You're asking about our pricing. The price includes 24-hour, on-site customer support and . . . ." Then explain how those features will benefit the prospective client.

In their book, *Buy*In*, John Kotter and Lorne Whitehead suggest 24 common attacks on presentations.[11] They recommend that speakers answer the attacks with brief, commonsense responses. Here are some examples.

Attack:	We've never done this in the past, and things have always worked out okay.
Response:	True. But surely we have all seen that those who fail to adapt eventually become extinct.
Attack:	Your proposal doesn't go nearly far enough.
Response:	Maybe, but our idea will get us started moving in the right direction and will do so without further delay.
Attack:	You can't do A without first doing B, yet you can't do B without first doing A. So the plan won't work.
Response:	Well, actually, you can do a little bit of A, which allows a little bit of B, which allows more A, which allows more of B, and so on.

Occasionally someone will ask a question that is really designed to state the speaker's own position. Respond to the question if you want to. Another option is to say, "That's a clear statement of your position. Let's move to the next question now." If someone asks about something that you already explained in your presentation, simply answer the question without embarrassing the questioner. No audience will understand and remember 100% of what you say.

If you don't know the answer to a question, say so. If your purpose is to inform, write down the question so that you can look up the answer before the next session. If it's a question to which you think there is no answer, ask if anyone in the room knows. When no one does, your "ignorance" is vindicated. If an expert is in the room, you may want to refer questions of fact to them. Answer questions of interpretation yourself.

At the end of the question period, take a moment to summarize your main point once more because questions may not have focused on the key point of your talk. Take advantage of having the floor to repeat your message briefly and forcefully.

Making Group Presentations

Plan carefully to involve as many members of the group as possible in speaking roles.

The easiest way to make a group presentation is to outline the presentation and then divide the topics, giving one to each group member. Another member can be responsible for the opener and the close. During the question period, each member answers questions that relate to their topic.

In this kind of divided presentation, be sure to

- Plan transitions.

- Coordinate individual talks to eliminate repetition and contradiction.

- Enforce time limits strictly.

- Coordinate your visuals so that the presentation is coherent.

- Practice the presentation as a group at least once; more is better.

Some group presentations are even more fully integrated: the group writes a detailed outline, chooses points and examples, and creates visuals together. Then, within each point, voices trade off. This presentation is effective because each voice speaks only a minute or two before a new voice comes in. However, it works only when all group members know the subject well and when the group plans carefully and practices extensively.

Whatever form of group presentation you use, and whether your presentation is in-person or online, be sure to introduce each member of the team to the audience and to pay close attention to each other. If other members of the team seem uninterested in the speaker, the audience gets the sense that that speaker isn't worth listening to.

Checklists for Effective Presentations

The checklists below will help you plan your individual and group presentations—both in-person and online.

Figure 14.4 provides a checklist of steps toward delivering a successful presentation.

In addition, the checklist in Figure 14.5 will help you plan a group presentation.

Figure 14.4 · Considerations for Oral Presentations	
☐ Was the presentation effective for the situation?	**Strategy**
☐ Did the presentation adapt to the audience's beliefs, experiences, and interests?	
☐ Did the presentation engage the audience?	
☐ Was the purpose clear, even if not explicitly stated? Was the purpose achieved?	**Content**
☐ Was the material vivid and specific?	
☐ Did the material counter common objections without giving them undue weight?	
☐ Were the opening and closing strong and effective?	
☐ Was there an overview of the main points?	**Organization**
☐ Did the body contain signposts of the main points?	
☐ Were there adequate transitions between points? Were the transitions smooth?	
☐ Were there engaging visuals? Did they use an appropriate design or template?	**Visuals**
☐ Were the visuals readable?	
☐ Were visuals free of spelling, punctuation, and grammar mistakes?	
☐ If the visuals contained data, were the data quickly assimilated?	
☐ Did the speaker make good eye contact with the audience?	**Delivery**
☐ Was the speaker positioned effectively in the room or in front of the camera?	
☐ Did the speaker use engaging vocal delivery?	
☐ Could the audience hear and understand what the speaker was saying?	
☐ Did the speaker avoid nervous mannerisms?	
☐ Did the speaker handle questions effectively?	

Figure 14.5	Additional Considerations for Group Presentations	
☐	Were team members introduced to the audience?	**Content**
☐	Were all team members adequately involved in the presentation?	**Delivery**
☐	Did the presentation transition smoothly among the team members?	**Delivery**
☐	Did the individual presentation sections coordinate well?	**Organization**
☐	Did team members stay tuned in to the person speaking at the time?	**Delivery**

Summary by Learning Objectives

LO 14-1   Identify purposes of presentations.

- Informative presentations inform or teach the audience.

- Persuasive presentations motivate the audience to act or to believe a certain way.

- Goodwill presentations entertain and validate the audience, uniting them under a shared value. Most oral presentations have more than one purpose, but you should keep your *primary* purpose in mind as you create your presentation.

LO 14-2   Plan a strategy for presentations.

- An oral presentation needs to be simpler than a written message to the same audience would be.

- In a monologue presentation, the speaker plans the presentation and delivers it without deviation.

- In a guided discussion, the speaker presents the questions or issues that both speaker and audience have agreed on in advance. Rather than functioning as an expert with all the answers, the speaker serves as a facilitator to help the audience tap its own knowledge.

- An interactive presentation is a conversation using questions to determine needs, probe objections, and gain provisional and then final commitment to the objective.

- Adapt your message to your audience's beliefs, experiences, and interests.

- Limit your talk to three main points. In a long presentation (20 minutes or more), each main point can have subpoints.

- Choose the information that is most interesting to your audience, that answers the questions your audience will have, and that is most persuasive for them.

LO 14-3   Organize effective presentations.

- Use the beginning and end of the presentation to interest the audience and emphasize your key point.

- Provide an overview of the main points you will make. Offer a clear signpost—an explicit statement of

the point you have reached—as you come to each new point.

- Based on your audience and purposes, choose a pattern of organization for the body: chronological, problem-cause-solution, comparative advantages, pro-con, or 1-2-3.

LO 14-4   Plan visuals for presentations.

Use visuals to seem more prepared, more interesting, and more persuasive. As you prepare your visuals, determine the presentation platform you will use, use numbers and figures, and use technology effectively.

LO 14-5   Deliver effective in-person and online presentations.

To deliver an effective presentation—whether in-person or online—you should deal with fear, develop a good speaking voice, use eye contact, and practice.

To deliver an effective in-person presentation, you should stand and gesture, use notes appropriately, and involve your audience. You can involve your audience by gathering audience feedback and by building small-group discussions into your presentation.

To deliver an effective online presentation, you should set the stage with an uncluttered background and good lighting, eliminate distractions by using a quiet room and turning off your phone and computer notifications, and involve your audience by asking questions and using the software's polling features.

LO 14-6   Handle questions during presentations.

- Tell the audience during your presentation how you'll handle questions.

- Treat questions as opportunities to give more detailed information than you had time to give in your presentation. Link your answers to the points you made in your presentation.

- Repeat the question before you answer it if the audience may not have heard it or if you want more time to think. Rephrase hostile or biased questions before you answer them.

Exercises and Cases

14.1   Reviewing the Chapter

1. What are the advantages to delivering communication in an oral presentation? (LO 14-1)

2. What are the similarities and differences between developing and delivering written and oral communication? (LO 14-1)

3. What is the difference between the general purposes of informing, persuading, and building goodwill in oral communication? Provide one example for each general purpose. (LO 14-1)

4. What is a specific purpose statement, and why is it beneficial for a speaker and their presentation? (LO 14-1)

5. What do you need to consider when you choose a strategy for a presentation? (LO 14-2)

6. What are the three basic kinds of presentations and what are the strengths and weaknesses for each? (LO 14-2)

7. What are four things that you need to consider when choosing information, data, and/or demonstrations for a presentation? (LO 14-3)

8. What are the common options for creating a strong opening? In what kind of speaking situation would each option be most effective? (LO 14-3)

9. What is a statement of purpose, preview, credibility, and relevance, and why is each one important for an oral presentation? (LO 14-3)

10. What are the five common organizational patterns for presentations? In what types of speaking scenario would each pattern be most effective? (LO 14-3)

11. What are signposts, and why are they essential in presentations? (LO 14-3)

12. What are the required elements for a conclusion for an informative presentation? A persuasive presentation? A goodwill-building presentation? (LO 14-3)

13. What guidelines should be followed when planning and incorporating visuals into a presentation? (LO 14-4)

14. What best practices should be followed when planning and designing PowerPoint and Prezi visuals? What practices should be avoided? (LO 14-4)

15. What are some things a person can do to mitigate fear when preparing and delivering an oral presentation? (LO 14-5)

16. What are some things, or strategies, a person can do to develop a good speaking voice and make eye contact? (LO 14-5)

17. What are three guidelines for delivering in-person presentations and three guidelines for delivering virtual presentations? (LO 14-5)

18. What are five tips for how to effectively handle questions during and/or after a presentation? (LO 14-6)

14.2   Analyzing TED Talks

TED—which stands for Technology, Education, and Design—is an organization offering recordings of high-quality, authoritative, audience-adapted speeches on a broad variety of topics. Speakers are invited to deliver speeches at a live event, and recorded speeches are showcased on the website. Visit http://ted.com to find a talk to analyze based on the following prompts.

- Unless otherwise instructed, select an official TED talk rather than a TEDx talk; TEDx events are independently organized and do not undergo as strict a curation process.

- TED talks can be sorted by topic, such as agriculture, aircraft, or animals, and by other descriptors such as "trending."

1. Select a TED talk in a category of interest and assess it based on the assessment questions below. Then, share your answers with your class in a brief oral presentation (length determined by your instructor). Queue up relevant spots in the TED talk to illustrate your answers. As an alternate to an oral presentation, your instructor may ask you to compose a brief written analysis of the TED talk and email it to them.

2. Based on the talk you analyzed in part 1, prepare a brief presentation for your peers highlighting what they can learn from the presentation: Which techniques might they try to emulate in their own oral presentations? What best practices

did the speaker exemplify? As an alternate to an oral presentation, your instructor may ask you to compose a "best practices" list based on this TED talk and email it to them.

Assessment questions:

- Assess the speaker's content: Which of the three appeals—credibility (ethos), emotional connection (pathos), or reasoning (logos)—was strongest, and why? Which element would have benefited from further practice or attention?

- Assess the speaker's nonverbal delivery: Which nonverbal delivery element (eye contact, facial expression, gestures, **proxemics**, or vocals) was strongest, and why? Which element would have benefited from further practice or attention?

- Assess the speaker's organization: How did the speaker preview the content? Review the content? How did the speaker signal movement from one idea to the next? What pattern of organization best describes how the content was arranged?

- What did the speaker do to adapt their topic to this audience's needs?

- How well did the visual aid (if used), and its incorporation, meet the audience's needs?

- Why do you think this speaker was selected to deliver a TED talk at the live event?

- Why do you think this recorded live speech was selected for inclusion on the website?

3. Select two TED talks in a category your instructor assigns and assess each based on the assessment questions above *as well as* the following additional assessment questions. Then, share your answers with your class in a brief oral presentation (length determined by your instructor). Queue up relevant spots in the TED talk to illustrate your answers.

Additional assessment questions:

- Compare and contrast the speakers' content: Which speech was more effective at creating content balanced in ethos, pathos, and logos?

- Compare and contrast the speakers' nonverbal delivery: Which speaker was more effective at heightening interest, highlighting content, and connecting with the audience via nonverbal delivery?

- Compare and contrast the speakers' audience adaptation: Which speech was more effective at anticipating and addressing the audience's needs?

- Compare and contrast the speakers' use of visual aid(s): Which speech was more effective at designing and integrating a visual aid to enhance spoken content?

- If you had to select one speech to represent this category on the website, which would you select?

14.3   Analyzing Openings and Closings

The following opening and closing lines come from class presentations about informational interviews.

Assess:

- How well does each opening create interest in the rest of the presentation? (How well does it demand your attention as a listener and connect to the content?)
- How well does each closing end the presentation? (Is it memorable and meaningful?)
- How well-matched are the opening and closing lines? (How well do they work together to create psychological unity across the presentation? How well do they match in tone?)

1. Opening line: I interviewed Mark Perry at AT&T.
    Closing line: Well, that's my report.

2. Opening line: How many of you know what you want to do when you graduate?

    Closing line: So, if you like numbers and want to travel, think about being a CPA; Ernst & Young can take you all over the world.

3. Opening line: You don't have to know anything about computer programming to get a job as a technical writer at CompuServe.

    Closing line: After talking to Raj, I decided technical writing isn't for me, but it is a good career if you work well under pressure and like learning new things all the time.

4. Opening line: The advertising agency I interned for has really tight security; I had to wear a badge and be escorted to Susan's desk.

    Closing line: On my last day, Susan gave me samples of the agency's ads and even a sample of a new soft drink she's developing a campaign for—but she didn't let me keep the badge.

14.4   Evaluating PowerPoint Slides

Review PowerPoint slides from http://norvig.com/Gettysburg /index.htm, which matches the content of Lincoln's Gettysburg Address to PowerPoint slides. Evaluate the slides with these questions:

- Are the slides' background appropriate for the topic?
- Do the slides use words or phrases rather than complete sentences?
- Is the font big enough to read from a distance?

- Is the art relevant and appropriate?
- Is each slide free of errors?

What conclusions do you draw from this hypothetical use of PowerPoint as a visual aid for Lincoln's short presentation at the dedication of the Soldiers' National Cemetery in Gettysburg, Pennsylvania, November 19, 1863?

14.5   Evaluating Nonverbal Delivery

Attend a lecture or public presentation on your campus. While the speaker is presenting, don't focus on the content of the message. Instead, focus on their nonverbal communication: eye contact, facial expressions, use of body (gestures, stance, and proxemics), and vocal delivery. Take notes.

As your instructor directs,

a. Deliver your findings to the rest of the class in a two- to four-minute presentation. Rate the speaker's overall nonverbal delivery and tell the class the speaker's strongest nonverbal delivery element, weakest nonverbal delivery element, and your suggestions for actions the speaker could take to improve in that element.

b. Write an email to your instructor that discusses the presenter's speaking abilities and how, if at all, they can be improved.

14.6 Evaluating Steve Jobs

On YouTube, watch clips of three presentations by Steve Jobs. What similarities do you see among them? What are some of his techniques you could use in a job you hope to have? Which ones do you think you would not use? Why not?

As your instructor directs,

a. Discuss your findings in small groups.

b. Write your findings in an email to your instructor.

c. Write your findings in an email and post it on the class website.

14.7 Evaluating the Way a Speaker Handles Questions

Listen to a speaker talking about a controversial subject. (Go to a talk on campus or in town or watch a speaker on a TV show like *Face the Nation* or *60 Minutes.*) Observe the way they handle questions.

- About how many questions does the speaker answer?
- What is the format for asking and answering questions?
- Are the answers clear? Responsive to the question? Something that could be quoted without embarrassing the speaker and the organization they represent?
- How does the speaker handle hostile questions? Does the speaker avoid getting angry? Does the speaker retain control of the meeting? How?

- If some questions were not answered well, what (if anything) could the speaker have done to leave a better impression?
- Did the answers leave the audience with a more or less positive impression of the speaker? Why?

As your instructor directs,

a. Share your evaluation with a small group of students.

b. Present your evaluation formally to the class.

c. Summarize your evaluation in an email to your instructor.

14.8 Short Presentation: The News

Research a hot business communication topic from the news (e.g., health care benefits, ethics, the economy, job layoffs, communication technology). Find at least three sources for your topic. Then, craft and deliver a two- to three-minute presentation where you share your findings with the class. Your presentation should invoke some effective communication strategies you learned in this course by discussing how the situation could have been handled more effectively.

As your instructor directs,

a. Deliver your presentation to the class.

b. Turn in a listing of your sources in APA or MLA format.

c. Write an email to your instructor that discusses the situation and explains how business communication principles would have helped improve the situation.

14.9 Medium Presentation: Informative

Craft and deliver a three- to five-minute presentation with PowerPoint slides or a Prezi on one of the following topics:

1. Explain how what you've learned in classes, in campus activities, or at work will be useful to the employer who hires you after graduation.

2. Explain a "best practice" in your organization.

3. Explain what a new hire in your organization needs to know to be successful.

4. Profile someone who is successful in the field you hope to enter and explain what makes them successful.

5. Explain one of the challenges (e.g., technology, ethics, international competition) that the field you plan to enter is facing.

6. Profile a company that you would like to work for and explain why you think it would make a good employer.

7. Share the results of an information interview.

8. Describe the way technology impacts the field you hope to enter.

14.10 Long Presentation: Persuasive

Craft and deliver a 5- to 12-minute presentation on one of the following. Use visuals to make your talk effective.

1. Persuade your supervisor to make a change that will benefit the organization.

2. Persuade your organization to make a change that will improve the organization's image in the community.

3. Persuade an organization on your campus to make a change.

4. Persuade classmates to donate time or money to a charitable organization.

14.11   Reconfiguring the Johari Window

One of the best ways to improve your presentation skills is to watch yourself present: This expands your knowledge about how you are perceived as a public speaker. After you have prepared a presentation for one of the previous exercises, record your presentation in video format. Then, review your presentation, noting what you did well and what you could improve.

As your instructor directs,

a. Write a 500-word email that discusses your strengths and weaknesses as a presenter. Address how you could improve your weaknesses.

b. Prepare a two-minute oral summation for your peers about your strengths and weaknesses.

c. Record the presentation a second time to see if you have improved some of your weaknesses. Present your findings to the class.

14.12   Evaluating In-Person Presentations

Evaluate an in-person oral presentation given by a classmate or a speaker on your campus. Use the following categories:

Strategy

1. Choosing an effective kind of presentation for the situation.
2. Adapting ideas to audience's beliefs, experiences, and interests.

Content

3. Providing a clear, unifying purpose.
4. Using specific, vivid supporting material and language.
5. Providing rebuttals to counterclaims or objections.

Organization

6. Using a strong opening and close.
7. Providing an overview of main points.
8. Signposting main points in body of talk.

Visuals

9. Using visual aids or other devices to involve the audience.
10. Using an appropriate design or template.
11. Being creative.

Delivery

12. Making direct eye contact with audience.
13. Using voice effectively.
14. Using gestures effectively.
15. Handling questions effectively.
16. Positioning (not blocking the screen).

As your instructor directs,

a. Fill out a form indicating your evaluation in each of the areas.
b. Share your evaluation orally with the speaker.
c. Write an email to the speaker evaluating the presentation. Forward a copy of the email to your instructor.

Notes

1. Jon Birger et al., "The Best Advice I Ever Got," *Fortune*, May 12, 2008, 70.
2. Carmine Gallo, *The Presentation Secrets of Steve Jobs: How to Be Insanely Great in Front of Any Audience* (New York: McGraw-Hill, 2010), 151–53.
3. Chip Heath and Dan Heath, *Made to Stick: Why Some Ideas Survive and Others Die* (New York: Random House, 2007), 16–18.
4. Julie Hill, "The Attention Deficit," *Presentations* 17, no. 10 (2003): 26.
5. Nancy Duarte, "Avoiding the Road to PowerPoint Hell," *Wall Street Journal*, January 27, 2011, C12.
6. Francesca Fontana and Denise Blostein, "Young Women Speak, Older Ears Hear Vocal Fry," *Wall Street Journal*, October 19, 2017, http://www.wsj.com/video/the-vocal-habit-that-women-are-being-criticized-for-at-work/E97C7B5B-8C51-4472-955A-AA1A26468C31.html.
7. Ann Burnett and Diane M. Badzinski, "Judge Nonverbal Communication on Trial: Do Mock Trial Jurors Notice?" *Journal of Communication* 55, no. 2 (2005): 209–24.
8. Jerry Weissman, *Presentations in Action: 80 Memorable Presentation Lessons from the Masters* (Upper Saddle River, NJ: FT Press, 2011).
9. Michael Waldholz, "Lab Notes," *Wall Street Journal*, March 19, 1991, B1; and Dave Zielinski, "Perfect Practice," *Presentations* 17, no. 5 (2003): 30–36.
10. American Express, "How to Give an Effective Online Presentation From Home," April 16, 2020, https://www.americanexpress.com/en-us/business/trends-and-insights/articles/how-to-give-an-effective-online-presentation-from-home.
11. John P. Kotter and Lorne A. Whitehead, "Twenty-Four Attacks and Twenty-Four Responses," *Buy*In: Saving Your Good Idea from Getting Shot Down* (Boston: Harvard Business Review Press, 2010), ch. 7.

Chapter Outline

DrAfter123/Getty Images

Honesty Should Be Your Policy

David Tovar, the former vice president of communications for Walmart, was about to be promoted to senior vice president when a routine background check discovered he had not graduated from college. He had nearly 20 years of professional experience but had never earned the art history degree he reported on his résumé. To his employer, Tovar's years of experience no longer mattered. His job performance—considered so strong it was worthy of a promotion—no longer mattered. He had lied to his employer for personal gain and all trust his employer formerly had in him was gone. After eight years with the company, he was forced to resign.

What may seem like a harmless lie rarely comes without consequences. Misrepresentations during your job search often lead to offers of employment being withheld. But even when the dishonesty isn't immediately noticed, it can spring up unexpectedly and result in embarrassment, the loss of your position, and the derailment of your career. Perhaps surprisingly, low-level employees at the start of their careers aren't the only ones who lie and suffer the consequences. Many high-profile individuals like Tovar have lost their positions due to the inaccuracies or misrepresentations; for example:

- John Davy, who held a six-week stint as CEO of Maori Television Service, a New Zealand television channel, was not only fired but sentenced to eight

Casey Rodgers/AP Images

months in prison when it was discovered he lied about his work history and academic accomplishments.

- Alison Ryan had just accepted a job as head of public relations for Manchester United when the offer was withdrawn. What cost her this prestigious position? She didn't lie about her work history or degrees earned. She lied about her GPA.

Trust is an invaluable commodity in the workplace. In our digital age, it is all too easy for hiring managers to check the validity of the claims you make on your résumé. As we've already seen, lying not only can prevent you from being hired, but it also can cost you your job.

A **résumé** is a persuasive summary of your qualifications for a job with a specific employer. If you're in the job market, having a résumé is a basic step in the job hunt. When you're employed, having an up-to-date résumé makes it easier to take advantage of opportunities that may come up for even better jobs. If you're several years away from job hunting, preparing a résumé now will help you become more conscious of what to do in the next two or three years to make yourself an attractive candidate.

Sources: Hope Restle and Jacquelyn Smith, "17 Successful Executives Who Have Lied on Their Résumés," *Business Insider*, July 15, 2015, http://www.businessinsider.com/successful-executives-who-have-lied-on-their-resumes-2015-7; and Rachel Abrams, "Walmart Vice President Forced Out for Lying about Degree," *The New York Times*, September 16, 2014, https://www.nytimes.com/2014/09/17/business/17tovar.html.

Learning Objectives

After studying this chapter, you should be able to

LO 15-1 Conduct an effective job search.

LO 15-2 Construct a résumé that makes you look attractive to employers.

LO 15-3 Produce two types of résumés.

LO 15-4 Determine what to include in a résumé.

LO 15-5 Determine how to respond to common difficulties that arise during job searches.

LO 15-6 Determine how to handle the online portion of job searches.

LO 15-7 Match your job application letter to the rhetorical situation.

LO 15-8 Create a professional image in your job application letter.

You probably will change jobs many times during your career. The U.S. Bureau of Labor Statistics' National Longitudinal Survey of Youth shows that the average person held an average of nearly 12 jobs from age 18 to age 50. Even in middle age, when job changing slows down, 69% of jobs ended in fewer than five years. Thus, you always should keep your résumé up to date.[1]

This chapter covers résumés and job application letters (sometimes called cover letters). Chapter 16 discusses interviews and communications after the interview. Both chapters focus on job hunting in the U.S. Conventions, expectations, and criteria differ from culture to culture; different norms apply in different countries.

All job communications should be tailored to your unique qualifications and the specifications of the job you want. Adopt the wording or layout of an example if it's relevant to your own situation, but don't be locked into the forms in this book. You've got different strengths; your résumé will be different, too.

Conducting a Job Search

LO 15-1

Formal preparation for job hunting should begin a full year *before you begin interviewing*. Enroll for the services of your campus career center. Ask friends who are in the job market about their experiences in interviews; find out what kinds of job offers they get. Check into the possibility of getting an internship or a co-op job that will give you relevant experience before you interview.

If you are already working, make sure your job search does not interfere with your current employment. Even if you hate your job, acting professionally and searching for a new job outside of work hours or on lunch breaks will help you keep your job and, more importantly, the good reference of your current employer.

Try to have a job offer lined up *before* you get the degree. People who don't need jobs immediately are more confident in interviews and usually get better job offers. If you have to job hunt after graduation, plan to spend at least 30 hours a week on your job search. The time will pay off in a better job that you find more quickly.

Most people think they know how to conduct a job search. You prepare a résumé, look through a few job ads, send your application in, interview, and get the job—right? According to most experts, that's wrong. Successful job searches rely on much more than putting the right things on résumés. In fact, employers look for employees in the exact opposite way from the way most people look for jobs.[2] Employers prefer to hire people in the following order:

1. From within their organization.
2. With proof of expertise, through a job portfolio.
3. With a reference from a trusted friend.
4. From a trusted recruiting agency.
5. From a job advertisement.
6. From a résumé.

A simple résumé is the last on the list for a reason: It is very difficult to tell from a résumé what kind of worker a person will be. Some employers are now moving away from placing job ads in favor of searching for new employees through personal and online networks.

To be successful in your job search, you should:

- Use the internet effectively.

- Build relationships through internships and networking.

- Establish a reputation online through wise use of social media.

- Be prepared with excellent traditional résumés and cover letters.

Using the Internet Effectively in Your Job Search

Probably the most common use of the internet for job candidates is to search for openings (see Figure 15.1). In addition to popular job boards such as Monster and CareerBuilder, job candidates typically search for jobs posted on organizations' Facebook pages, LinkedIn sites, and Twitter. Many successful companies are reducing their postings on job boards in favor of recruiting through social networking sites.

Job candidates also check electronic listings in local newspapers and professional societies. However, you do need to be careful when responding to online ads. Some of them turn out to be pitches from career or financial services firms, or even phishing ads—ploys from identity thieves seeking your personal information. And remember that not all sites are current and accurate. Check your school's career site for help. Check the sites of other schools: Stanford, Berkeley, and Columbia have particularly excellent career sites. Figure 15.2 lists some of the best sites.

A relatively new use of the internet for job searchers is online job fairs. At online fairs, you can browse through virtual booths, leave your résumé at promising ones, and sometimes even apply on the spot, all without leaving your home. Other advantages of online job fairs are their wide geographic range and 24-hour access.

As you do all this research for your job hunt, you probably will begin to find conflicting advice. When evaluating suggestions, consider the age of the advice; what was true five years ago may not be true today because the job-search process changes so quickly. Also consider your industry; general advice that works for most may not work for your

Figure 15.1	Job Listings on the Web	
CareerOneStop.org https://www.careeronestop.org	Indeed.com http://www.indeed.com
CareerBuilder.com http://www.careerbuilder.com	Monster.com www.monster.com
Careers.org http://www.careers.org	ZipRecruiter.com http://www.ziprecruiter.com

Figure 15.2	Comprehensive Websites Covering the Entire Job Search Process	

The Balance Careers	LiveCareer
https://www.thebalancecareers.com/job-search-4161939	https://www.livecareer.com
Campus Career Center	College Grad Job Hunter
http://www.campuscareercenter.com	http://www.collegegrad.com
Career Rookie	Spherion Career Center
https://www.careerrookie.com	http://www.spherion.com/job-seekers
College Central	Vault
http://www.collegecentral.com	http://www.vault.com

industry. Above all, consider what advice helps you present yourself as favorably as possible.

Building Relationships through Networking

Many experts now consider networking to be the most important factor in finding a job. It is important for entry-level work and becomes even more crucial as you advance in your career.

Networking starts with people you know—friends, family, friends of your parents, classmates, teammates, gym mates, colleagues—and quickly expands to your electronic contacts in social media. Let people know you are looking for a job and what your job assets are. Use social media to emphasize your field knowledge and accomplishments. Join your school's alumni association to find alumni in businesses that interest you.

The secret to successful networking is reciprocity. Too many people network just for themselves, and they quickly gain a "one-way" reputation that hurts further networking. Good networkers work for a "two-way" reputation; to earn it, they look for ways to reciprocate. They help their contacts make fruitful connections. They share useful information and tips. Successful networks are not just for finding jobs: they are vital for career success.

Building Relationships through Internships

Internships are becoming increasingly important as ways to build relationships and to find out about professions, employers, and jobs. Many companies use their internships to find full-time employees. GE, for example, makes about 80% of its new-graduate hires from students who held summer internships with the company. The National Association of Colleges and Employers found in a survey of internships that 51.7% of interns became full-time hires.[3] Among those who repeat internships, that number was found to be substantially higher; nearly 90% of returning interns were offered full-time employment. In fact, some industry experts are predicting that within the next few years, intern recruiting will largely replace entry-level recruiting.[4]

Even if your internship does not lead to a full-time job, it still can give you valuable insight into the profession, as well as contacts you can use in your job search. An increasingly important side benefit is the work you do in your internship, which can become some of the best items in your professional portfolio.

Establishing a Reputation Online

When you are searching for a job, a good reputation is vital to your success. According to one survey, nearly all employers use social media to find new employees, mainly LinkedIn, Facebook, and Twitter. Even more use social networking sites to learn about job candidates who already have applied. A CareerBuilder survey found 70% of employers use social media to screen employees.[5] Using social media wisely can help you build your reputation and become visible to employers.

A specialized use of the internet is **personal branding**, a popular term for marketing yourself, including job searching. It covers an expectation that you will use various options, from the traditional résumé and cover letter to social media, to market your expertise. You will use these tools to show your value (what do you offer employers?) and quality (why should they hire you instead of other candidates?). These are some of the most popular tools:

- **LinkedIn:** This site allows you to include useful information beyond your résumé, and, unlike your web page, it has a powerful search engine behind it.

- **Personal website:** Your website allows you to connect to examples of your professional work. You should invest in a domain name that includes your name. This helps you control how you will show up in online searches because most search algorithms favor URLs that include the search term.[6]

- **Facebook:** If you keep your Facebook profile up to date with your education, employment, and interests, it can serve as an attractive informal résumé. Manage your privacy settings to make public only those things that would be important for an employer to see. But keep all of your content professional. Avoid inappropriate language and all content involving alcohol, other drugs, and incomplete attire.

- **Twitter:** Share useful information such as thoughtful comments about news in your field as you work to build up your Twitter network. Aim for quality, not numbers. Also, follow companies you would like to work for and people throughout your profession.

However you develop your personal brand using these tools, remember that consistency matters. Use your résumé, cover letter, personal website, and social networking to create a consistent, professional image that demonstrates the qualities you want your potential employer to see. This consistency includes seemingly small details such as your profile photo you include on LinkedIn or Facebook and large details like your samples of professional work. When you develop a consistent personal brand, employers are more likely to view your profiles, interview you, and hire you.

> **WARNING:** Select your tools carefully; you probably do not have time to use all the tools on this list successfully. Stay professional in all venues; avoid negative comments about people, your school, and your employers. In addition to content, writing (grammar, coherence, style, logic, spelling) will be judged by potential employers. The list of candidates rejected after a basic web search grows daily.

Using Social Networking Sites with Care

Most employers routinely search the internet for information about job candidates, and many report they are turned off by what they find—especially on social networking sites. CareerBuilder found in one of its surveys that over 57% of all hiring managers have found information on social media that has prevented them from hiring a candidate.[7] Check your social media profiles and personal website carefully before you enter the job market:

- Remove any unprofessional material such as pictures of you at your computer with a beer in your hand or descriptions of your last party.

- Remove negative comments about current or past employers and teachers.

- Remove political and social rants.

- Remove any personal information that will embarrass you on the job.

- Remove inappropriate material posted by friends, relatives, and colleagues.

The best advice is to plan ahead and post nothing unprofessional on the web.

> **WARNING:** According to a survey conducted by CareerBuilder, recruiters also check photo- and video-sharing sites; gaming sites; virtual-world sites; and classifieds and auction sites such as Craigslist, Amazon, and eBay.[8]

How Employers Use Résumés

Understanding how employers use résumés will help you create a résumé that works for you.

1. **Employers use résumés to decide whom to interview.**   Résumés are examined for relevant experience and skills. Because résumés also are used to screen out applicants, omit anything that may create a negative impression.
2. **Résumés are scanned or skimmed.**   At many companies, especially large ones, résumés are scanned electronically. Only résumés that match key words are skimmed by a human being. You must design your résumé to pass both the "scan test" and the "skim test" by emphasizing crucial qualifications and using the diction of the job ad.
3. **Employers assume that your letter and résumé represent your best work.**   Neatness, accuracy, and freedom from typographical errors are essential. Spelling errors will probably cost you your chance at a job, so proofread carefully.
4. **After an employer has chosen an applicant, they submit the applicant's résumé to people in the organization who must approve the appointment.**   These people may have different backgrounds and areas of expertise. Spell out acronyms. Explain awards, Greek-letter honor societies, unusual job titles, or organizations that may be unfamiliar to the reader.

Guidelines for Résumés

LO 15-2

Writing a résumé is not an exact science. But when you must compete against many applicants, these guidelines will help you look as good on paper as you are in person.

Length

A one-page résumé is sufficient, but you must fill the page. Less than a full page suggests that you do not have much to say for yourself.

If you have more good material than will fit on one page, use a second page. A common myth is that all résumés must fit on one page. A two-page résumé is acceptable *if* you have sufficient good material that relates to the posted job. That said, it's mostly people who are further along in their careers who can benefit from a two-page résumé.[9]

If you do use more than one page, fill at least half of the second page. Use a second sheet of paper; do not print on the back of the first page. Leave less important information for the second page. Put your name and "Page 2" on the second page. If the pages are separated, you want the reader to know that the qualifications belong to you and that the second page is not your whole résumé.

Emphasis

Emphasize the things you've done that (1) are most relevant to the position for which you're applying, (2) show your superiority to other applicants, and (3) are recent (in the past three to five years). Whatever your age at the time you write a résumé, you want to suggest that you are now the best you've ever been.

Show that you're qualified by giving relevant details on course projects, activities, and jobs where you've done similar work. Be brief about low-level jobs that simply show dependability. To prove that you're the best candidate for the job, emphasize items that set you apart from other applicants: promotions, honors, achievements, experience with computers or other relevant equipment, statistics, foreign languages, and so on.

You can emphasize material by putting it at the top or the bottom of a page, by giving it more space, and by setting it off with white space. The beginning and end—of a document, a page, a list—are positions of emphasis. When you have a choice (e.g., in a list of job duties), put less important material in the middle, not at the end, to avoid the impression of "fading out." You also can emphasize material by presenting it in a vertical list, by using informative headings, and by providing details. Headings that name skills listed in the job ad, or skills important for the job (e.g., Managerial Experience), also provide emphasis and help set you apart from the crowd.

Details

Details provide evidence to support your claims, convince the reader, and separate you from other applicants. Numbers make good details. Tell how many people you trained or supervised, how much money you budgeted or saved. Describe the interesting aspects of the job you did.

Too vague: Sales Manager, *The Daily Collegian*, University Park, PA, 2019–2021. Supervised staff; promoted ad sales.

Good details: Sales Manager, *The Daily Collegian*, University Park, PA, 2019–2021. Supervised 22-member sales staff; helped recruit, interview, and select staff; assigned duties and scheduled work; recommended best performers for promotion. Motivated staff to increase paid ad inches 10% over previous year's sales.

Omit details that add nothing to a title or that are less impressive than the title alone Either use strong details or just give the office or job title without any details.

Writing Style

Without sacrificing content, be as concise as possible.

Wordy: Member, Meat Judging Team, 2017–18
Member, Meat Judging Team, 2018–19
Member, Meat Judging Team, 2019–20
Captain, Meat Judging Team, 2020–21

Concise: Meat Judging Team, 2017–20; Captain 2020–21

Wordy: Performed foundation load calculations

Concise: Calculated foundation loads

Résumés normally use phrases and sentence fragments. Complete sentences are acceptable if they are the briefest way to present information. To save space and to avoid sounding arrogant, don't use *I* in a résumé. *Me* and *my* are acceptable if they are unavoidable or if using them reduces wordiness.

Verbs or gerunds (the *-ing* form of verbs, such as *calculating*) create a more dynamic image of you than do nouns, so use them on résumés that will be read by people instead of scanning programs. In the following revisions of job responsibilities, nouns, verbs, and gerunds are in bold type:

Nouns: Chair, Income Tax Assistance Committee, Winnipeg, MB, 2020–2021. Responsibilities: **recruitment** of volunteers; flyer **design, writing,** and **distribution** for **promotion** of program; **speeches** to various community groups and nursing homes to advertise the service.

Verbs:	Chair, Income Tax Assistance Committee, Winnipeg, MB, 2020–2021. **Recruited** volunteers for the program. **Designed, wrote,** and **distributed** a flyer to promote the program; **spoke** to various community groups and nursing homes to advertise the service.
Gerunds:	Chair, Income Tax Assistance Committee, Winnipeg, MB, 2020–2021. Responsibilities included **recruiting** volunteers for the program; **designing, writing,** and **distributing** a flyer to promote the program; and **speaking** to various community groups and nursing homes to advertise the service.

Note that the items in the list must be in parallel structure (see Chapter 4 and Appendix B for more on parallel structure).

> **WARNING:** All spelling and grammar should be perfect. If they are not your strong suits, pay an editor. In these days of massive responses to job postings, don't give recruiters an easy elimination of your résumé through careless errors. Remember that spell-checkers will not catch all errors, as all those store "mangers" will tell you.

Key Words

Now that electronic résumé scans are common, all résumés, but particularly electronic résumés, need to use **key words**—words and phrases the employer will have the computer seek. Key words are frequently nouns or noun phrases: *database management, product upgrades, cost compilation/analysis*. However, they also can be adjectives such as *responsible*. Key words are frequently the objects of all those action verbs you are using in your résumé: conducted *publicity campaigns*, wrote weekly division *newsletter*.

Key words may include:

- Software program names such as Excel.

- Job titles.

- Types of degrees.

- College or company names.

- Job-specific skills, buzzwords, and jargon.

- Professional organizations (spell out the name and then follow it with its abbreviation in parentheses to increase the number of matches).

- Honor societies (spell out Greek letters, as in Zeta Phi Beta).

- Personality traits, such as creativity, dependability, team player.

- Area codes (for geographic narrowing of searches).

To find the key words you need in your job search, look through job ads and employer job sites for common terminology. If many ads mention "communication skills," your résumé should too.

Some key words are widely popular. According to a survey from the National Association of Colleges and Employers, employers hiring for internship and entry-level jobs searched for these terms:[10]

- Problem-solving skills (91.2%).

- Ability to work in a team (86.3%).

- Strong work ethic (80.4%).

- Analytic/quantitative skills (79.4%).

- Communication skills (written) (77.5%).

In addition to using popular key words, you should double-check to make certain your résumé uses the language of the particular job ad to which you are responding. If the ad uses *software engineers* instead of *computer programmers*, then your résumé also should use *software engineers*. If the ad talks about *collaboration*, you will use that word instead of *teamwork* when you discuss your group work experience.

Layout and Design

The layout and design of your résumé will be vital to catch the eye of the employer who is spending only 7.4 seconds on each document.[11] Almost certainly, you can create a better résumé by adapting a basic style you like to your own unique qualifications. Experiment with layout, fonts, and spacing to get an attractive résumé. Consider creating a letterhead that you use for both your résumé and your application letter.

> **WARNING:** Do not use résumé templates that come with word-processing software. Many employers see so many résumés from these templates that they learn to recognize—and discount—them.

One of the major decisions you will make is how to treat your **headings**. Do you want them on the left margin, with text immediately below them, as in Figure 15.3? Do you want them alone in the left column, with text in a column to the right, as in Figure 15.6? Generally, people with more text on their résumés use the first option. Putting headings in their own column on the left takes space and thus helps spread a thinner list of accomplishments over the page. But be careful not to make the heading column too wide or it will make your résumé look unbalanced and empty.

Work with **fonts**, bullets, and spacing to highlight your information. Be careful, however, not to make your résumé look "busy" by using too many fonts. Generally, you should use only two fonts in a document, and you should avoid unusual fonts. Keep fonts readable by using at least 10-point type for large fonts such as Arial and 11-point for smaller fonts such as Times New Roman. Use enough white space to group items and make your résumé easy to read, but not so much that you look as if you're padding.

Use color sparingly, if at all. Colored text and shaded boxes can prevent accurate scanning. Similarly, white 8½- by 11-inch paper is standard in the U.S., but do use a good-quality paper. Contrary to some popular myths, using brightly colored paper or cardstock-weight paper to get noticed by employers will more likely hurt your prospects than help you get an interview.

All of these guidelines are much more flexible for people in creative fields such as advertising and design. As you prepare your résumé, consult with advisers, professors, professionals, and other job seekers to discover the best strategies for your field.

Honesty

Acting ethically means being absolutely honest on your résumé—and in the rest of your job search. Most businesses now conduct some kind of background check on job applicants. Background checks on job candidates can include a credit check, legal and criminal records, complete employment history, and academic credentials. If employers do an employment history check, and many do, they will have a complete work history for you. They will be able to spot inaccurate company names and work dates. If you left a company off your résumé, they may wonder why; some may assume your performance at that company was not satisfactory.

Obviously, you cannot include everything about your life to date, so it's okay to omit some material on your résumé. For instance, it's still ethical to omit a low GPA, although most employers will assume it is very low indeed to be omitted. But what you do include must be absolutely honest.

Some of the most frequent inaccuracies on résumés are inflated job titles and incorrect dates of employment. While these data are easy to fudge, they are also easy to catch in background checks. Other areas where résumés are commonly inaccurate are

- Degrees: many people conveniently forget they were a few hours short of a degree.

- GPAs: inflating one's grade point average seems to be a big temptation. If you are using the classes in your major or the last 60 hours of coursework to calculate your GPA, label them as such so you won't appear to be inflating your overall GPA.

- Honors: people list memberships in fake honoraries or fake memberships in real honoraries.

- Fake employers.

- Job duties: many people inflate or embellish them.

- Salary increases.

- Fake addresses: people create these to have the "local" advantage.

- Fake contact information for references: this information frequently leads to family members or friends who will give fake referrals.

- Technical abilities.

- Language proficiencies.

All dishonesty on a résumé is dangerous, keeping you from being hired if discovered early, and causing you to be fired if discovered later. However, the last two bullets listed are particularly dangerous because your chances are good of being asked at an interview to demonstrate your listed proficiencies.

Kinds of Résumés

LO 15-3

Two basic categories of résumés are chronological and skills. A **chronological résumé** summarizes what you did in a time line (starting with the most recent events and going backward in **reverse chronology**). It emphasizes degrees, job titles, and dates and is the traditional résumé format. Figures 15.3 and 15.4 show chronological résumés.

Use a chronological résumé when

- Your education and experience are a logical preparation for the position for which you're applying.

- You have impressive job titles, offices, or honors.

A **skills résumé**, also called a functional résumé, emphasizes the skills you've used, rather than the job in which you used them or the date of the experience. Figure 15.6, shown later in the chapter, is a skills résumé. Use a skills résumé when

- Your education and experience are not the usual route to the position for which you're applying.

- You're changing fields.

- You want to combine experience from paid jobs, activities, volunteer work, and courses to show the extent of your experience in administration, finance, public speaking, and so on.

The two kinds differ in what information is included and how that information is organized.

Figure 15.3 A Community College Chronological Résumé to Use for Career Fairs and Internships

James Jiang

jianj@wccc.edu

Vary font sizes. Use larger size for name and main headings.

Campus Address
1524 E. Main St
Portland, OR 97231
503-403-5718

Using both addresses ensures continuous contact information.

Permanent Address
2526 Prairie Lane
Portland, OR 97233
503-404-7793

Education
West Coast Community College
A.A. in Financial Management, June 2021
GPA: 3.0/4.0 *Give your grade average if it's 3.0 or higher.*

Summary of Qualifications

Use key words employers might seek.

List 3–7 qualifications.

- Self-motivated, detail-minded, results-oriented
- Consistently successful track record in sales
- Effectively developed and operated entrepreneurial business

Sales Experience
Financial Sales Representative, ABC Inc., Portland, OR, February 2019– present
- Establish client base
- Develop investment strategy plans for clients
- Research and recommend specific investments

Other Experience
Entrepreneur, A-Plus T-Shirt Company, Portland, OR, September 2017–January 2020

One way to handle self-employment.

- Created a saleable product (Graphic t-shirts)
- Secured financial support
- Located a manufacturer
- Supervised production
- Sold t-shirts to high school students
- Realized a substantial profit to pay for college expenses

Cook, Hamburger Shack, Portland, OR, Summers 2015–2017
- Learned sales strategies
- Ensured customer satisfaction
- Collaborated with a team of 25

Collector and Repair Worker, ACN, Inc., Portland, OR, Summer 2013–2015
- Collected and counted approximately $10,000 a day *Specify large sums of money.*
- Assisted technicians with troubleshooting and repairing coin mechanisms

Other Skills
Computer: Word, Excel, InDesign, WordPress, Outlook
Language: Fluent in Spanish *Many employers appreciate a second language.*

Figure 15.4   A One-Page Chronological Résumé

Jenny Moeller

831.503.4692
51 Willow Street
San José, CA 95112
jmoeller@csmb.edu

Career Objective

Use job title and company name in Career Objective.

To bring my attention to detail and love for computer/video games to Telltale Games as a Game Tester

Qualifications

- Experienced in JavaScript, Lua, and Python
- Intermediate proficiency with Visual Studio; high proficiency with Source Safe
- Excellent communication, interpersonal, and collaboration skills
- Advanced knowledge of computers
- Love of video games

Highlights qualifications specific to the job.

Education

California State University—Monterey Bay
August 2017—May 2021 (expected)
Bachelor of Science in Computer Science and Information Technology

Keeps Education section simple to emphasize experience.

Experience

Online Marketing Consultant—Self–Employed
October 2018–present

Lists job titles on separate lines.

- Manage multiple client Google Adwords accounts
- Install web software and implement designs for fast turnarounds
- Interface with clients using Basecamp

Editor-in-Chief—Point Network LLC
June 2016–present

Use present tense verbs when you are doing the job now.

- Write and edit for several LucasArts-related gaming news websites
- Design and code websites using Wordpress
- Manage and administrate the LucasForums.com community

Online Marketing Assistant—Hayfield Group
May 2019–August 2019; May 2020–August 2020

Use past tense for jobs that are over.

- Managed all client Google Adwords accounts
- Assisted in or managed planning and executing PPC and SEO campaigns
- Coded the company website and integrated the Drupal CMS
- Prepared website analytics reports using Google Analytics and other analytics suites

Community Manager—Praise Entertainment, Inc.
April 2018–September 2020

- Managed the community at AdminFusion.com, a website geared toward online forum owners
- Organized and ran a monthly contest for community members

Honors and Activities

Close with strong section.

- Member of the gaming press for E3 2019 and 2020
- Member of second place team in 2020 National STEM Video Game challenge
  (see demo, "Parrot Villa" at www.STEMChallenge.gov/2020_winners)

Include activities that employer might value.

What to Include in a Résumé

The résumé's purpose is to persuade. In a résumé, you should not lie, but you can omit some information that does not work in your favor.

Résumés commonly contain the following information. The categories in italics are essential.

- *Name*
- *Contact Information*
- *Education*
- *Experience*
- Honors and Awards
- Skills
- Activities
- Portfolio

You may choose other titles for these categories and add categories that are relevant for your qualifications, such as computer skills or foreign languages.

Education and Experience always stand as separate categories, even if you have only one item under each heading. Combine other headings so that you have at least two long or three short items under each heading. For example, if you're in one honor society and two social clubs, and on one athletic team, combine them all under Activities and Honors.

If you have more than seven items under a heading, consider using subheadings. For example, a student who participated in many activities might divide them into Campus Activities and Community Service.

Put your strongest categories near the top and at the bottom of the first page. If you have impressive work experience, you might want to put that category first and Education second.

Name and Contact Information

Use your full name, even if everyone calls you by a nickname. You may use an initial rather than spelling out your first or middle name. Put your name in big type.

Give a complete phone number, including the area code. Make sure this is a phone number where you can be reached during the day. Employers usually call during business hours to schedule interviews and make job offers. Do not give lab or dorm phone numbers unless you are sure someone there will take an accurate message for you at all times. Also, be sure your voice mail has a professional-sounding message.

If you have a website, and you are sure it looks professional (both content and writing), you may wish to include its URL. Be sure your site does not reveal personal information—such as marital status, ethnicity, religious beliefs, or political stance—that could work against you. Be particularly careful of photographs.

Provide an email address. Some job candidates set up a new email address just for job hunting. Your email address should look professional; avoid sexy, childish, or illicit addresses. List your LinkedIn site, if you have one. You also may list your Facebook profile or Twitter handle if you use them professionally or if social networking is required or desired in your profession.

A résumé is your most important document at career fairs.

MARK RALSTON/AFP/Getty Images

Education

Education can be your first major category if you've just earned (or are about to earn) a degree or if you have a degree that is essential or desirable for the position you're seeking. Put your Education section later if you need all of page 1 for what you determine to be more important categories or if you lack a degree that other applicants may have (see Figure 15.6).

Under Education, provide information about your undergraduate and graduate degrees, including the location of institutions and the year you received or expect your degree.

Use the same format for all the schools you attended. List your degrees in reverse chronological order (most recent first).

Master of Accounting Science, May 2021, Arizona State University, Tempe, AZ

Bachelor of Arts in Finance, May 2019, New Mexico State University, Las Cruces, NM

AS in Business Administration, May 2017, Des Moines Area Community College, Ankeny, IA

When you're getting a four-year degree, include community college only if it will interest employers, such as by showing an area of expertise different from that of your major. You may want to include your minor, emphasis, or concentration and any graduate courses you have taken. Include study abroad, even if you didn't earn college credits. If you got a certificate for international study, give the name and explain the significance of the certificate. Highlight proficiency in foreign or computer languages by using a separate category.

Professional certifications can be listed under Education or in a separate category.

If your GPA is good and you graduated recently, include it. If your GPA isn't impressive, calculate your average in your major and your average for your last 60 hours. If these are higher than your overall GPA, consider using them. If you do use your major GPA or upper-class GPA, make sure you label them as such so you can't be accused of dishonesty. The National Association of Colleges and Employers found that 73.3% of employers plan to screen job applicants graduating in 2019 by GPA.[12] If you leave your

GPA off your résumé, most employers will automatically assume that it is below a 3.0. If yours is, you will need to rely on internships, work experience, and skills acquired in activities to make yourself an attractive job candidate.

After giving the basic information (degree, field of study, date, school, city, state) about your degree, you may wish to list courses, using short descriptive titles rather than course numbers. Use a subhead such as "Courses Related to Major" or "Courses Related to Financial Management" that will allow you to list all the courses (including psychology, speech, and business communication) that will help you in the job for which you're applying. Don't say "Relevant Courses," as that implies your other courses were irrelevant.

Bachelor of Science in Management, May 2021, Illinois State University, Normal, IL
GPA: 3.8/4.0
Courses Related to Management:

Personnel Administration	Business Decision Making
Finance	International Business
Management I and II	Marketing
Accounting I and II	Legal Environment of Business
Business Report Writing	Business Speaking

Listing courses is an unobtrusive way to fill a page. You also may want to list courses or the number of hours in various subjects if you've taken an unusual combination of courses that uniquely qualify you for the position for which you're applying.

BS in Marketing, May 2021, California State University at Northridge
    30 hours in marketing
    15 hours in Spanish
    9 hours in Chicano studies

As you advance in your career, your education section will shrink until finally it probably will include only your degrees and educational institutions.

Honors and Awards

It's nice to have an Honors and Awards section, but not everyone can do so. If you have fewer than three and therefore cannot justify a separate heading, consider a heading Honors and Activities to get that important word in a position of emphasis.

Include the following kinds of entries in this category:

- Academic honor societies. Specify the nature of Greek-letter honor societies (i.e., journalism honorary) so the reader doesn't think they're just social clubs.

- Fellowships and scholarships.

- Awards given by professional societies.

- Major awards given by civic groups.

- Varsity letters; selection to all-state or all-America teams; finishes in state, national, or Olympic meets. (These also could go under Activities but may look more impressive under Honors.)

Identify honor societies ("national journalism honorary," "campus honorary for top 2% of business majors") for readers who are not in your discipline. If your fellowships or scholarships are particularly selective or remunerative, give supporting details:

Clyde Jones Scholarship:	Four-year award covering tuition, fees, room, and board
Marilyn Terpstra Scholarship:	$25,000 annually for four years
Heemsly Fellowship:	50 awarded nationally each year to top Information Science juniors

Be careful of listing Dean's List for only one or two semesters. Such a listing reminds readers that in these days of grade inflation, you were off the list many more times than you were on it.

Experience

You may use other headings if they work better: Work Experience, Military Experience, Marketing Experience. In a skills résumé, headings such as "Marketing Experience" allow you to include accomplishments from activities and course projects. Headings that reflect skills mentioned in the job ad are particularly effective.

What to Include   Under this section in a chronological résumé, include the following information for each job you list: position or job title, organization, city and state (no zip code), dates of employment for jobs held during the last 10 to 15 years, and other details, such as full- or part-time status, job duties, special responsibilities, or the fact that you started at an entry-level position and were promoted. Use strong verbs such as the ones in Figure 15.5 to brainstorm what you've done. Try to give supporting details for highly valued attributes such as communication skills and leadership experience. Include any internships and co-ops you have had. Also, include unpaid jobs and self-employment if they provided relevant skills (e.g., supervising people, budgeting, planning, persuading).

If you went to college right after high school, it is common to go back as far as the summer after high school. Include earlier jobs only if you started working someplace before graduating from high school but continued working there after graduation, or if the job is pertinent to the one you are applying for. If you worked full-time after high school, make that clear. More experienced workers generally go back no more than 10 years.

The details you give about your experience are some of the most vital information on your résumé. As you provide these details, use bulleted lists rather than paragraphs, which are harder to read and may be skipped over. Remember that items in lists need to have parallel structure; see Appendix B for a refresher. Focus on results rather than duties; employers are far more interested in what you accomplished than in what you had to do. Use numbers to support your results wherever possible:

> Supervised crew of 15.
>
> Managed $120,000 budget; decreased expenses by 19%.
>
> Wrote monthly electronic newsletter; increased hits by 12%.

Emphasize accomplishments that involve money, customers, teamwork, leadership, computer skills, and communication.

Use past tense verbs for jobs you held in the past and present tense verbs for jobs you still have. Do not list minor duties such as distributing mail or filing documents. If your duties were completely routine, say, at your summer job at McDonald's, do not

Figure 15.5	Action Verbs for Résumés		
analyzed	directed	led	reviewed
budgeted	earned	managed	revised
built	edited	motivated	saved
chaired	established	negotiated	scheduled
coached	evaluated	observed	simplified
collected	examined	organized	sold
conducted	helped	persuaded	solved
coordinated	hired	planned	spoke
counseled	improved	presented	started
created	increased	produced	supervised
demonstrated	interviewed	recruited	trained
designed	introduced	reported	translated
developed	investigated	researched	wrote

list them. If the jobs you held in the past were low-level ones, present them briefly or combine them:

2013–2017 Part-time and full-time jobs to finance education

Skills Résumés   Skills résumés stress the skills you have acquired rather than specific jobs you have held. They show employers that you do have the desired skill set even if you lack the traditional employment background. They allow you to include skills acquired from activities and course projects in addition to jobs.

In a skills résumé, the heading of your main section usually changes from "Experience" to "Skills." Within the section, the subheadings will be replaced with the skills used in the job you are applying for, rather than the title or the dates of the jobs you've held. For entries under each skill, combine experience from paid jobs, unpaid work, classes, activities, and community service.

Use headings that reflect the jargon of the job for which you're applying: *logistics* rather than *planning* for a technical job; *procurement* rather than *purchasing* for a job with the military. Figure 15.6 shows a skills résumé for someone who is changing fields.

A job description can give you ideas for headings. Possible headings and subheadings for skills résumés include

Administration	Communication
Budgeting	Editing
Coordinating	Fund-Raising
Evaluating	Interviewing
Implementing	Negotiating
Negotiating	Persuading
Planning	Presenting
Supervising	Writing

Many jobs require a mix of skills. Try to include the skills that you know will be needed in the job you want. You need at least three subheadings in a skills résumé; six or seven are not uncommon. Give enough detail under each subheading so the reader will know what you did. Begin with the most important category from the reader's point of view.

In a skills résumé, list your paid jobs under Work History or Employment Record near the end of the résumé (see Figure 15.6). List only job title, employer, city, state, and dates. Omit details that you already have used under Skills.

Other Skills

You may want a brief section in a chronological résumé where you highlight skills not apparent in your work history. These skills may include items such as foreign languages or programming languages. You might want to list software you have used or training on expensive equipment (electron microscopes, NMR machines). As always on your résumé, be completely honest: "two years of high school German" or "elementary speaking knowledge of Spanish." Any knowledge of a foreign language is a plus. It means that a company desiring a second language in its employees would not have to start from scratch in training you. Figure 15.4 lists skills in its Qualifications section.

Activities

Employers may be interested in your activities if you're a new college graduate because they can demonstrate leadership roles, management abilities, and social skills as well as the ability to juggle a schedule. If you've worked for several years after college or have an advanced degree (MBA, JD), you can omit Activities and include Professional Activities and Affiliations or Community and Public Service. If you went straight from college to graduate school but have an unusually strong record demonstrating relevant skills, include this category even if all the entries are from your undergraduate days.

Figure 15.6   A Skills Résumé for Someone Changing Fields

Mandy Shelly

www.wisc.edu/~Shelly88/home.htm

If you have a professional web page, include its URL.

266 Van Buren Drive
Madison, WI 53706
shellym@wisc.edu
555-897-1534 (home)
555-842-4242 (cell)

Objective

To contribute my enthusiasm for writing as a Technical Writer at PDF Productions

Job objective includes the position and name of the company.

Skills

Largest section on skills résumé; allows you to combine experiences from work and class.

Computer

- Designed a web page using Dreamweaver
  www.madisonanimalshelter.com
- Used a variety of Macintosh and PC platform programs and languages:
  Aspects (online discussion forum)   Adobe Professional
  Dreamweaver   HTML
  XML   Java Script
                                            Photoshop

Specify computer programs you know well.

Design and Writing

Use parallel structure for bulleted lists.

- Designed a quarterly newsletter for local animal shelter
- Developed professional brochures
- Wrote a variety of professional documents: letters, memos, and reports
- Edited internal documents and promotional materials
- Proofread seven student research papers as a tutor

Organization and Administration

- Coordinated program schedules
- Developed work schedules for five employees
- Led a ten-member team in planning and implementing sorority philanthropy program
- Created cataloging system for specimens
- Ordered and handled supplies, including live specimens

Employment History

Condensed to make room for skills.

Technical Writer, Madison Animal Shelter, Madison, WI, 2019–present
Undergraduate Lab Assistant, Department of Biology, University of Wisconsin–Madison, Madison, WI, 2019–present
Tutor, University of Wisconsin–Madison, Madison, WI, 2018–2019

Uses reverse chronology.

Education

Bachelor of Arts, May 2021
University of Wisconsin–Madison, Madison, WI
Major: Animal Ecology
Minor: Chemistry
GPA 3.4/4.0

Give minor when it can be helpful.

Honors

End with strong items at the bottom of your page, a position of emphasis.

Phi Kappa Phi Honor Society
Alpha Lambda Delta Honor Society, Ecology Honorary
Dean's List, 2013 to present
Raymond Hamilton Scholarship, 2019–2020
($5000 to a top ecology student in Wisconsin)

Explain honors your reader may not know.

Include the following kinds of items under Activities:

- Volunteer work. Include important committees, leadership roles, communication activities, and financial and personnel responsibilities.

- Membership in organized student activities. Include leadership and financial roles as well as important subcommittees.

- Membership in professional associations. Many of them have special low membership fees for students, so you should join one or more, particularly the ones directly associated with your major.

- Participation in varsity, intramural, or independent athletics. However, don't list so many sports that you appear not to have had adequate time to study.

As you list activities, add details that will be relevant for your job. Did you handle a six-figure budget for your Greek organization? Plan all the road trips for your soccer club? Coordinate all the publicity for the campus blood drive? Design the posters for homecoming? Major leadership, financial, and creative roles and accomplishments may look more impressive if they're listed under Experience instead of under Activities.

Portfolio

If you have samples of your work available, you may want to end your résumé by stating "Portfolio (or writing samples) available on request" or by giving the URL for your work.

Dealing with Difficulties

LO 15-5

Some job hunters face special problems. This section gives advice for six common problems.

"I Don't Have Any Experience."

If you have a year or more before you job hunt, you can get experience in several ways:

- **Seek an internship.**   Your college career center or professors in your major can direct you toward opportunities. Internships provide solid experience in your field, and many lead to full-time jobs.

- **Take a fast-food job—and keep it.**   If you do well, you'll likely be promoted to a supervisor within a year. Use every opportunity to learn about management and financial aspects of the business.

- **Sign on with agencies that handle temporary workers.**   As an added bonus, some of these jobs become permanent.

- **Join a volunteer organization that interests you.**   If you work hard, you'll quickly get an opportunity to do more: manage a budget, write fund-raising materials, and supervise other volunteers.

- **Freelance.**   Design brochures, create web pages, do tax returns for small businesses. Use your skills—for free at first, if you have to.

- **Write.**   Create a portfolio of ads, instructions, or whatever documents are relevant for the field you want to enter. Ask a professional—an instructor, a local businessperson, someone from a professional organization—to critique them.

If you're on the job market now, think carefully about what you've really done. Complete sentences using the action verbs in Figure 15.5 to help jog your memory. Think about what you've done in courses, volunteer work, and unpaid activities. Focus on skills in problem solving, critical thinking, teamwork, and communication. Solving a problem for a hypothetical firm in an accounting class, thinking critically about a report problem in business communication, working with a group in a marketing class, and communicating with people at the senior center where you volunteer are good experiences, even if no one paid you.

"All My Experience Is in My Family's Business."

In your résumé, simply list the company you worked for. For a reference, instead of a family member, list a supervisor, client, or vendor who can talk about your work. Because the reader may wonder whether "Jim Clarke" is any relation to the owner of "Clarke Construction Company," be ready to answer interview questions about why you're looking at other companies. Prepare an answer that stresses the broader opportunities you seek but doesn't criticize your family or the family business.

"I Want to Change Fields."

Have a good reason for choosing the field in which you're looking for work. "I want a change" or "I need to get out of a bad situation" does not convince an employer that you know what you're doing.

Think about how your experience relates to the job you want. Sam wants a new career as a pharmaceutical sales representative. He has sold woodstoves, served subpoenas, and worked on an oil rig. A chronological résumé makes his work history look directionless. But a skills résumé could focus on persuasive ability (selling stoves), initiative and persistence (serving subpoenas), and technical knowledge (courses in biology and chemistry).

Learn about the skills needed in the job you want: learn the buzzwords of the industry. Figure 15.6 shows a skills résumé of someone changing fields from animal ecology to technical writing. Her reason for changing could be that she found she enjoyed the writing duties of her jobs more than she enjoyed the ecology work.

"I've Been Out of the Job Market for a While."

You need to prove to a potential employer that you're up-to-date and motivated. Try the following:

- Create a portfolio of your work to show what you can do for the employer.

- Do freelance work.

- Be active in professional organizations. Attend meetings.

- Look for volunteer work where you can use and expand relevant work skills.

- Attend local networking events.

- Read the journals and trade publications of your field.

- Learn the software that professionals use in your field.

- Be up-to-date with electronic skills such as text messaging, internet searches, and social networking.

- Take professional training to expand your skill set.

Employment counselors advise that you not leave a gap on your résumé; such a gap makes employers speculate about problems such as jail time. They suggest you matter-of-factly list an honorable title such as Parent or Caregiver; do not apologize. Better yet is to fill in the gap with substantial volunteer experience. Heading a $75,000 fund-raising drive for a new playground looks good to almost any employer. A side benefit of volunteer work, in addition to new career skills, is networking. Boards of directors and executives of nonprofit organizations are frequently well-connected members of the community.

"I Was Laid Off."

In times of large layoffs, this is not an overwhelming obstacle. You do not need to point out the layoff in your application materials; the end date of your last employment will make the point for you. Instead, use your documents to highlight your strengths.

Be prepared to be asked about the layoff in an interview. Why were you laid off when other employees were retained? It helps if you can truthfully give a neutral explanation: the accounting work was outsourced; our entire lab was closed; the company laid off everyone who had worked fewer than five years. Be sure you do not express bitterness or self-pity; neither emotion will help you get your new job. On the other hand, do not be overly grateful for an interview; such excess shows a lack of self-confidence. Be sure to show you are keeping yourself current by doing some of the items in the bulleted list in the previous section.

"I Was Fired."

In the event you were fired, first, you need to reduce negative feelings to a manageable level before you're ready to job-hunt.

Second, take responsibility for your role in the termination.

Third, try to learn from the experience. You'll be a much more attractive job candidate if you can show that you've learned from the experience—whether your lesson is improved work habits or that you need to choose a job where you can do work you can point to with pride.

Fourth, collect evidence showing that earlier in your career you were a good worker. This evidence could include references from earlier employers, good performance evaluations, and a portfolio of good work.

Some common strategies also may give you some help for references. You should check with the Human Resources Department to understand the company's reference policy. Some companies now give no references other than verification of job title and work dates. Others do not give references for employees who worked only a short time.[13] Another option is to ask someone other than your former boss for a reference. Could you ask a supplier or vendor? A different department head?

Above all, be honest. Do not lie about your termination at an interview or on a job application. The application usually requires you to sign a statement that the information you are providing is true and that false statements can be grounds for dismissal.

Sending Your Résumé Electronically

LO 15-6

In addition to a paper résumé for job fairs, interviews, and potential contacts, you will need electronic versions of your résumé. With a few exceptions noted below, these résumés will have the same content but will be formatted differently so they can be "read" by both software and humans.

Many employers are asking to have résumés uploaded to their organizations' websites. When doing so, be sure you follow the directions exactly. You also may be asked by some employers to send your résumé by email.

Here are some basic guidelines of email job-hunting etiquette:

- Don't use your current employer's email system for your job search. You'll leave potential employers with the impression that you spend company time on writing résumés and other nonwork-related activities.

- Set up a free, internet-based email account using services such as Gmail to manage correspondence related to your job hunt.

- Avoid using silly or cryptic email addresses. Instead of bubbles@gmail.com, opt for something businesslike: yourname@gmail.com. If you have a common name, try using combinations like "firstname.lastname@gmail.com" or "firstname_lastname@gmail.com" rather than using strings of numbers after your name.

- Write a simple subject line that makes a good first impression: Résumé–Kate Sanchez. A good subject line will improve the chances that your résumé is actually read since email from unknown senders is often deleted without being opened. If you are responding to an ad, use the job letters or job code listed.

- Before sending your résumé, test to see how it will look when it comes out on the other end. Email it to yourself and a friend, then critique and fix it.

- Send only one résumé, even if the firm has more than one position for which you qualify. Most recruiters have negative reactions to multiple résumés.

- Experts differ on whether candidates should phone to follow up. Phoning once to be sure your résumé arrived is probably fine.

It's important to heed the specific directions of employers that you are emailing. Many do not want attachments because of viruses. While some may want a Microsoft Word or PDF attachment of your résumé, others may specify that you paste your résumé directly into the body of your email message.

If you are sending your résumé in the text of an email,

- Start all lines at the left margin.

- Eliminate decorative elements such as boxes or vertical or horizontal lines.

- Do not use bold, underlining, bullets, tabs, or unusual fonts. Instead use keys such as asterisks. You also can put some headings in all capital letters, but use this device sparingly.

- To avoid awkward line breaks for your readers, shorten line lengths to 65 characters and spaces.

Your résumé will look plain to you, but the employers receiving it are used to the look of in-text résumés.

If you are sending your résumé as an attachment, name the document appropriately: Smith Robyn Résumé.docx. Never name it just Résumé.docx; you do not want it to get lost in a long directory of documents.

With your résumé include a brief email message that will make the receiver want to look at your résumé. In it, mention the types of files you've included. Remember, it takes only an instant for readers to delete your email. Do not give them reasons to trash your résumé.

Some people confuse electronic and scannable résumés. The former are résumés you send in or attached to an email. The latter are paper résumés specially formatted for older software. Software programs have greatly improved, and most can now scan regular résumés.

The Purpose of Job Application Letters

The job application letter accompanies your résumé and serves as its cover letter. It is your chance to showcase the features that set you apart from the crowd. Here you bring to life the facts presented in your résumé; here you can give a sense of your personality. The cover letter is your opportunity to "sell" yourself so that you get an interview.

Although résumés and job letters share some characteristics, they differ in three important ways:

- The résumé summarizes *all* your qualifications. The letter expands your *best* qualifications to show how you can help the organization meet its needs, how you differ from other applicants, and how much knowledge of the organization you possess.

- The résumé avoids controversial material. The job letter can explain in a positive way situations such as career changes or gaps in employment history.

- The résumé uses short, parallel phrases and sentence fragments. The letter uses complete sentences in well-written paragraphs.

A job application letter can play an important role in your personal branding. It can show your personality and, through careful reference to well-chosen details about the organization, your interest in a particular job.

Because a job application letter is seen as evidence of a candidate's written communication skills, you want to do your best work in yours. Flaws in your letter may well be seen as predicting shoddy job performance in the future.

How to Find Out about Employers and Jobs

To adapt your job application letter to a specific organization, you need information both about the employer and about the job itself. You'll need to know

- **The name and address of the person who should receive the letter.** To get this information, check the ad, call the organization, check its website, or check with your job-search contacts. An advantage of calling is that you can find out what courtesy title the individual prefers and get current information.

- **What the organization does, and some facts about it.** Knowing the organization's larger goals enables you to show how your specific work will help the company meet its goals. Useful facts can include market share, new products or promotions, the kind of computer or manufacturing equipment it uses, plans for growth or downsizing, competitive position, challenges the organization faces, and the corporate culture.

- **What the job itself involves.** Campus placement offices and web listings often have fuller job descriptions than appear in ads. Talk to friends who have graduated recently to learn what their jobs involve. Conduct information interviews to learn more about opportunities that interest you.

The websites listed in Figure 15.7 provide a wide range of information. For instance, the *Forbes* and *Money* sites have good financial news stories; *The Public Register* (prars. com) is a good source for annual reports. As a consumer, you may have used the Better Business Bureau (bbb.org) site.

More specific information about companies can be found on their websites. To get specific financial data on publicly traded companies (and to see how the organization presents itself to the public), get the company's annual report from your library or the web. To learn about new products, plans for growth, or solutions to industry challenges, read business newspapers such as *The Wall Street Journal*, business magazines such as *Fortune* or *Bloomberg Businessweek*, and trade journals (see Chapter 3).

Content and Organization for Job Application Letters

LO 15-7

Job application letters help show employers why they should interview you instead of other—sometimes hundreds of others—qualified applicants. In your letter, focus on

- Your qualifications to meet major requirements of the job.

- Points that separate you from other applicants.

Figure 15.7	Web Sources for Facts about Companies

Company Facts	**Salary Calculators**
http://money.cnn.com	http://salaryexpert.com
http://www.forbes.com	http://www.indeed.com/salary
http://www.bbb.org	http://www.payscale.com
http://www.inc.com/inc5000	
http://www.prars.com	
http://www.vault.com	

- Points that show your knowledge of the organization.

- Qualities that every employer is likely to value: the ability to write and speak effectively, to solve problems, to work well with people.

Two different hiring situations call for two different kinds of application letters. Write a **solicited letter** when you know that the company is hiring: you've seen an ad, you've been advised to apply by a professor or friend, you've read in a trade publication that the company is expanding. This situation is similar to a direct request in persuasion (see Chapter 11): you can indicate immediately that you are applying for the position. Sometimes, however, the advertised positions may not be what you want, or you may want to work for an organization that has not announced openings in your area. Then you write a **prospecting letter**. (The metaphor is drawn from prospecting for gold.) The prospecting letter is like a problem-solving persuasive message.

Prospecting letters help you tap into the **hidden job market**. In some cases, your prospecting letter may arrive at a company that has decided to hire but has not yet announced the job. In other cases, companies create positions to get a good person who is on the market. Even in a hiring freeze, jobs are sometimes created for specific individuals.

In both solicited and prospecting letters, you should

- Address the letter to a specific person (a must for a prospecting letter).

- Indicate the specific position for which you're applying.

- Be specific about your qualifications.

- Show what separates you from other applicants.

- Show knowledge of the company and the position.

- Refer to your résumé (which you would enclose with the letter).

- Ask for an interview.

The following discussion follows the job application letter from beginning to end. The two kinds of letters are discussed separately where they differ and together where they are the same. Letters for internships follow the same patterns: use a solicited letter to apply for an internship that has been advertised and a prospecting letter to create an internship with a company that has not announced one.

How to Organize Solicited Letters

When you know the company is hiring, use the pattern of organization in Figure 15.8. A sample solicited letter for a graduating senior is shown in Figure 15.9. A solicited letter following up from a career fair and requesting an internship is shown in Figure 15.10.

Figure 15.8	How to Organize a Solicited Job Application Letter

1. State that you're applying for the job (phrase the job title as your source phrased it). Tell where you learned about the job (ad, referral, etc.). Include any reference number mentioned in the ad. Briefly show that you have the major qualifications required by the ad: a college degree, professional certification, job experience, etc. Summarize your other qualifications briefly in the same order in which you plan to discuss them in the letter.

2. Develop your major qualifications in detail. Be specific about what you've done; relate your achievements to the work you'd be doing in this new job.

3. Develop your other qualifications, even if the ad doesn't ask for them. Show what separates you from the other applicants who also will answer the ad. Demonstrate your knowledge of the organization.

4. Ask for an interview; tell when you'll be available to be interviewed and to begin work. Thank recipient for considering your application. End on a positive, forward-looking note.

Figure 15.9   A Solicited Letter from a Graduating Senior

Jenny Moeller

831.503.4692
51 Willow Street
San José, CA 95112
jmoeller@csmb.edu

April 4, 2021

Mr. Richard Grove
Telltale Games
P.O. Box 9737
San Rafael, CA 94912

Dear Mr. Grove:

In paragraph 1, shows she has the qualifications the ad lists.

Tells where she learned about the job. If the job has a reference number, provide it.

I am applying for your Game Designer position posted on your website. As an avid player of Telltale games, I believe that I have all the qualifications to do a great job. With my degree in Computer Science and Information Technology and my experience creating game content, I will be able to apply many skills to the Game Designer position. My passion for becoming part of the gaming industry, combined with my oral and written communication skills, makes me a great fit for the Telltale team.

This summary sentence forecasts the structure of the rest of the letter.

Shows enthusiasm for the profession and picks up on the programming experience emphasis in the job ad.

Since I was five, I have had a strong interest in computers and video games, and my interest and knowledge have only increased in recent years. Not only do I play video games, I discuss them with others, read news articles about them online, and consider ways to improve or change a specific game. I have also used game editors to create my own content in games. When it comes to computers, I have a keen interest in staying current with the latest technology, and I apply my knowledge hands-on by building systems. These experiences give me an understanding of how modern computers and video game systems function. I also have experience with several programming languages, from both taking courses and learning them on my own. This has increased my eye for detail, a necessary ability for any game designer.

My passion for creating video games was recognized this year in the national STEM video game challenge. With a team of students in Professor Kent Olbernath's game development class at California State University, I produced "Parrot Villa," the first level of an immersive game where players solve mysteries on a unique jungle world. The programming quality and detailed story line helped my team earn second place in the nationwide competition. You can see a demo of "Parrot Villa" at www.STEMChallenge.gov/2020_Winners.

Provides evidence for her achievements in the profession.

Relates what she has done to what she could do for the company.

Evidence of communication skills is a plus for almost any job.

Along with my enthusiasm for games, I have strong oral and written communication skills. I am a confident public speaker, and I have an ability to relay information in a clear and concise manner. More importantly, though, I have developed the ability in my creative writing courses to create engaging and coherent narratives, which will be a large component of developing new games. In addition to my coursework and experience, I have honed my skills online by writing articles about games. In covering the video game industry for Point Network, I have reviewed Telltale's own *Tales of Monkey Island*.

Shows familiarity with company's products.

Working in the video game industry is my goal, and I would be a great asset to Telltale Games. I would love to come in for an interview to discuss the position and the contributions I can make. I have always enjoyed playing Telltale's games, and I look forward to the possibility of working on them one day soon.

Sincerely,

Jenny Moeller

Jenny Moeller

Figure 15.10   Letter Following Up from a Career Fair and Requesting an Internship

James Jiang
jiangj@wccc.edu

Campus Address
1524 E. Main St
Portland, OR 97231
503-403-5718

Letterhead matches his résumé.

Permanent Address
2526 Prairie Lane
Portland, OR 97233
503-404-7793

January 23, 2021

Ms. Deborah Pascel, HR Department
Prime Financial
401 Prime Park Place
Beaverton, OR 97007

Dear Ms. Pascel:

Uses his contact immediately.

Mary Randi at the West Coast Community College Career Fair suggested I send you my résumé for the Sales Advisor internship. My education, combined with my past work experiences, makes me a strong candidate for Prime Financial.

Shows he has been getting full value from his schooling.

While working toward my Associate of Arts degree in Financial Management from West Coastal Community College, I have learned the value of fiscal responsibility. For example, in my social financial planning course, I developed a strategic plan to eliminate credit card debt for a one-income household with two children. Moreover, in my business communication course, I improved my oral communication ability so that I could effectively communicate my plans to potential clients. This ability will be an asset to Prime Financial as the organization works to maintain the strong relationship with the community and small business owners that Ms. Randi informed me about.

Refers to knowledge gained at career fair.

Paragraphs 2 and 3 show he has skills he can use immediately as an intern.

My financial education, combined with my previous work experiences in sales, will allow me to thoroughly analyze investment opportunities and establish a strong client base for Prime Financial. For example, I started the A-Plus T-Shirt Company that sold graphic t-shirts to high school students; it had a routine client base of over 150 customers. From managing this business, I know what it takes to be reliable and responsive to customer needs. I am looking forward to learning new approaches from Prime Financial's internship, particularly new ways to work with small businesses.

Provides details about his sales experience to interest his reader.

With my education and experience, I can provide the innovative and competitive edge necessary to be part of your team. I would welcome an interview to discuss your internship and the contributions I could make at Prime Financial.

Sincerely,

James Jiang

James Jiang

Figure 15.11	How to Organize a Prospecting Letter

1. Catch the reader's interest.

2. Create a bridge between the attention-getter and your qualifications. Focus on what you know and can do. Since the employer is not planning to hire, they won't be impressed with the fact that you're graduating. Summarize your qualifications briefly in the same order in which you plan to discuss them in the letter. This summary sentence or paragraph then covers everything you will talk about and serves as an organizing device for your letter.

3. Develop your strong points in detail. Be specific. Relate what you've done in the past to what you could do for this company. Show that you know something about the company. Identify the specific niche you want to fill.

4. Ask for an interview and tell when you'll be available for interviews. Don't tell when you can begin work. Thank the recipient for considering your application. End on a positive, forward-looking note.

How to Organize Prospecting Letters

When you don't have any evidence that the company is hiring, you cannot use the pattern for solicited letters. Instead, use the pattern of organization in Figure 15.11. A sample prospecting letter for an applicant desiring to change fields is shown in Figure 15.12.

First Paragraphs of Solicited Letters

When you know that the firm is hiring, announcing that you are applying for a specific position enables the firm to route your letter to the appropriate person, thus speeding consideration of your application. Identify where you learned about the job: "the position of junior accountant announced in Sunday's *Dispatch*," "William Paquette, our placement director, told me that you are looking for. . . ."

Note how the following paragraph picks up several of the characteristics of the ad:

Ad: Business Education Instructor at Shelby Adult Education. Candidate must possess a Bachelor's degree in Business Education. Will be responsible for providing in-house training to business and government leaders. . . . Candidate should have at least one year teaching experience.

Letter: I am applying for your position in Business Education that is posted on your school website. In December, I will receive a Bachelor of Science degree from North Carolina A & T University in Business Education. My work has given me two years' experience teaching word processing and computer accounting courses to adults plus leadership skills developed in the North Carolina National Guard.

Your **summary sentence** or **paragraph** covers everything you will talk about and serves as an organizing device for your letter.

Through my education, I have a good background in standard accounting principles and procedures and a working knowledge of some of the special accounting practices of the oil industry. This working knowledge is enhanced by practical experience in the oil fields: I have pumped, tailed rods, and worked as a roustabout.

My business experience, familiarity with DeVilbiss equipment, and communication skills qualify me to be an effective part of the sales staff at DeVilbiss.

Figure 15.12   A Prospecting Letter from a Career Changer

Mandy Shelly
www.wisc.edu/~Shelly88/home.htm

Use a "letterhead" that harmonizes with the résumé (see Figure 15.5).

266 Van Buren Drive
Madison, WI 53706
shellym@wisc.edu
555-897-1534 (home)
555-842-4242 (cell)

March 29, 2021

Mr. Franklin Kohl
PDF Productions
3232 White Castle Road
Minneapolis, MN 85434

*Opens with a sentence that
(1) will seem interesting and true to the reader and
(2) provides a natural bridge to talking about herself.*

Dear Mr. Kohl:

The Wall Street Journal says that PDF Productions is expanding operations into Wisconsin, Minnesota, and Nebraska. My experience in technical writing, design, and computers would be an asset to your expanding organization.

Shows knowledge of the organization.

Briefly shows a variety of technical writing and computer skills.

While working at a local animal shelter, I used my technical writing skills to create a website that allows users to easily access information. To improve the website, I conducted usability tests that provided useful feedback that I incorporated to modify the overall design. In addition, I was also responsible for writing and editing the shelter's monthly newsletter, which was distributed to roughly 1,200 "Friends of the Shelter." I have extensive computer and design skills, which I am anxious to put to use for PDF Productions.

Relates what she's done to what she could do for this company.

Coursework has also prepared me well for technical writing. I have written technical material on a variety of levels ranging from publicity flyers for the animal shelter to scientific reports for upper-level science courses. My course work in statistics has shown me how to work with data and present them accurately for various audiences. Because of my scientific background, I also have a strong vocabulary in both life sciences and chemistry. This background will help me get up to speed quickly with clients such as ChemPro and Biostage. My background in science has also taught me just how important specific details can be.

Shows how her course-work is an asset.

Names specific clients, showing more knowledge of company.

In May, I will complete my degree from the University of Wisconsin and will be most interested in making a significant contribution to PDF Productions. I am available every Monday, Wednesday, and Friday for an interview (608-897-1534). I look forward to talking with you about technical writing I can do for PDF Productions.

Sincerely,

Mandy Shelly

Mandy Shelly

First Paragraphs of Prospecting Letters

In a prospecting letter, asking for a job in the first paragraph is dangerous: unless the company plans to hire but has not yet announced openings, the reader is likely to throw the letter away. Instead, catch the reader's interest. Then, in the second paragraph, you can shift the focus to your skills and experience, showing how they can be useful to the employer and specifying the job you are seeking.

Here are some effective first and second paragraphs that provide a transition to the writer's discussion of their qualifications.

These are the first two paragraphs of a letter to the director of publications at an oil company:

> If scarcity of resources makes us use them more carefully, perhaps it would be a good idea to ration words. If people used them more carefully, internal communications specialists like you would have fewer headaches because communications jobs would be done right the first time.
>
> For the last six years I have worked on improving my communications skills, learning to use words more carefully and effectively. I have taught business communication at a major university, worked for two newspapers, have completed a Master's degree in English, and I would like to contribute my skills to your internal communications staff.

These are the first two paragraphs of a letter applying to be a computer programmer for an insurance company:

> As you know, merging a poorly written letter with a database of customers just sends out bad letters more quickly. But you also know how hard it is to find people who can both program computers and write well.
>
> My education and training have given me this useful combination. I'd like to put my associate's degree in computer technology and my business experience writing to customers to work in State Farm's service approach to insurance.

Notice how the second paragraph provides a transition to a discussion of qualifications.

Showing a Knowledge of the Position and the Company

If you could substitute another inside address and salutation and send out the letter without any further changes, it isn't specific enough. A job application letter is basically a claim that you could do a specific job for a particular company. Use your knowledge of the position and the company to choose relevant evidence from what you've done to support your claims that you could help the company.

The following paragraphs show the writer's knowledge of the company.

A letter to PricewaterhouseCoopers's Minneapolis office uses information the student learned in a referral interview with a partner in an accounting firm. Because the reader will know that Herr Wollner is a partner in the Berlin office, the student does not need to identify him.

> While I was studying in Berlin last spring, I had the opportunity to discuss accounting methods for multinational clients of PricewaterhouseCoopers with Herr Fritz Wollner. We also talked about communication among PricewaterhouseCoopers's international offices.
>
> Herr Wollner mentioned that the increasing flow of accounting information between the European offices—especially those located in Germany, Switzerland, and Austria—and the U.S. offices of PricewaterhouseCoopers makes accurate translations essential. My fluency in German enables me to translate accurately; and my study of communication problems in Speech Communication, Business and Professional Speaking, and Business and Technical Writing will help me see where messages might be misunderstood and choose words that are more likely to communicate clearly.

A letter to KPMG uses information the student learned in a summer job.

> As an assistant accountant for Pacific Bell during this past summer, I worked with its computerized billing and record-keeping system, BARK. I had the opportunity to help the controller revise portions of the system, particularly the procedures for handling delinquent accounts. When the KPMG audit team reviewed Pacific Bell's transactions completed for July, I had the opportunity to observe your System 2170. Several courses in computer science allow me to appreciate the simplicity of your system and its objective of reducing audit work, time, and costs.

One or two specific details about the company usually are enough to demonstrate your knowledge. Be sure to use the knowledge, not just repeat it. Never present the information as though it will be news to the reader. After all, the reader works for the company and presumably knows much more about it than you do.

Showing What Separates You from Other Applicants

Your knowledge of the company can separate you from other applicants. You also can use coursework, an understanding of the field, and experience in jobs and extracurricular events to show that you're unique. Stress your accomplishments, not your job responsibilities. Be specific but concise; usually three to five sentences will enable you to give enough specific supporting details.

In your résumé, you may list activities, offices, and courses. In your letter, give more detail about what you did and show how those experiences will help you contribute to the employer's organization more quickly.

When you discuss your strengths, don't exaggerate. No employer will believe that a new graduate has a "comprehensive" knowledge of a field. Indeed, most employers believe that six months to a year of on-the-job training is necessary before most new hires are really earning their pay. Specifics about what you've done will make your claims about what you can do more believable and ground them in reality.

Writing the Last Paragraph

In the last paragraph, indicate when you'd be available for an interview. If you're free any time, you can say so. But it's likely that you have responsibilities in class and work. If you'd have to go out of town, there may be only certain days of the week or certain weeks that you could leave town for several days. Use a sentence that fits your situation.

> November 5 to 10 I'll be attending the Oregon Forestry Association's annual meeting and will be available for interviews then.

> Any Monday or Friday I could come to Memphis for an interview.

Should you wait for the employer to call you, or should you call the employer to request an interview? In a solicited letter, it's safe to wait to be contacted: you know the employer wants to hire someone, and if your letter and résumé show that you're one of the top applicants, you'll get an interview. In a prospecting letter, call the employer. Because the employer is not planning to hire, you'll get a higher percentage of interviews if you're assertive.

End the letter on a positive note that suggests you look forward to the interview and that you see yourself as a person who has something to contribute, not as someone who just needs a job.

> I look forward to discussing with you ways in which I could contribute to PayPal's continued growth.

Do not end your letter with a variation of the negative cliché "Please do not hesitate to contact me." Why do you think the reader would hesitate? Also avoid this other tired cliché: "Thank you for your time." Using an overworked ending dumps you right back in the pool with all the other applicants.

Oh yes, one more thing. Don't forget to sign your letter—with blue or black ink—legibly.

Email Application Letters

You will probably email most of your applications. If your application is solicited, you can paste your traditional letter into your email. If your application is prospecting, you need a shorter letter that will catch the reader's attention within the first screen (see Figure 15.13). In both solicited and prospecting applications, your first paragraph is crucial; use it to hook the reader.

As with any letter, what you write depends on your audience. For solicited applications, your email most likely will be read initially by someone in Human Resources rather

Figure 15.13   An Email with Application Letter and Résumé

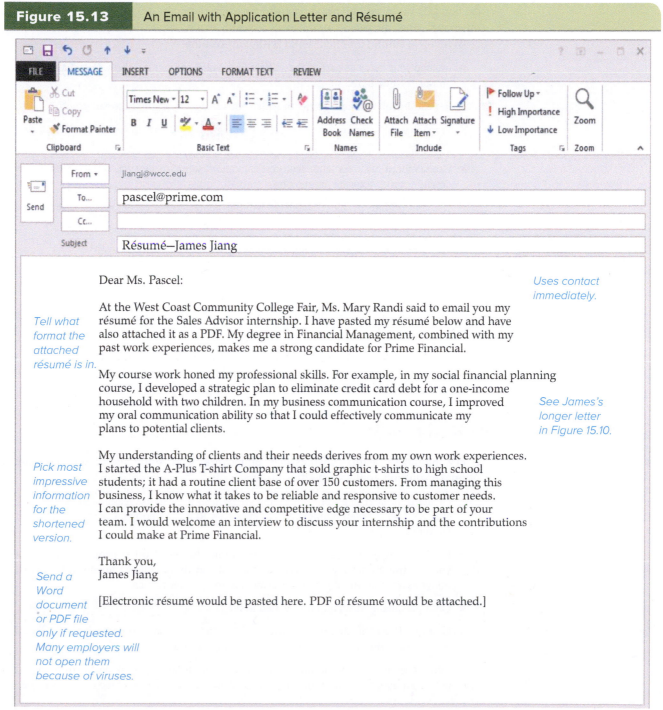

Tell what format the attached résumé is in.

Dear Ms. Pascel:

Uses contact immediately.

At the West Coast Community College Fair, Ms. Mary Randi said to email you my résumé for the Sales Advisor internship. I have pasted my résumé below and have also attached it as a PDF. My degree in Financial Management, combined with my past work experiences, makes me a strong candidate for Prime Financial.

My course work honed my professional skills. For example, in my social financial planning course, I developed a strategic plan to eliminate credit card debt for a one-income household with two children. In my business communication course, I improved my oral communication ability so that I could effectively communicate my plans to potential clients.

See James's longer letter in Figure 15.10.

Pick most impressive information for the shortened version.

My understanding of clients and their needs derives from my own work experiences. I started the A-Plus T-shirt Company that sold graphic t-shirts to high school students; it had a routine client base of over 150 customers. From managing this business, I know what it takes to be reliable and responsive to customer needs. I can provide the innovative and competitive edge necessary to be part of your team. I would welcome an interview to discuss your internship and the contributions I could make at Prime Financial.

Thank you,
James Jiang

Send a Word document or PDF file only if requested. Many employers will not open them because of viruses.

[Electronic résumé would be pasted here. PDF of résumé would be attached.]

Source: Microsoft Inc

than the hiring manager. The HR staff member is reading your letter to see what job you are applying for and whether you meet the basic qualifications. In some cases, you will send a transmission email to Human Resources with only basic information (the job number and your contact information) and an attached cover letter for the hiring manager. Pay close attention to the instructions in the job ad on how to submit your application.

For prospecting applications, your email will more likely go directly to a hiring manager, who is not expecting it. You therefore need to do more to convince them to read your letter and look at your résumé. Do not make the mistake of treating a prospecting email like a transmission email. The recipient is unlikely to look at an unsolicited cover letter or résumé without a persuasive email message.

If you don't know who will receive your email, use a traditional cover letter format for your email. Some experts are starting to recommend a shorter letter for both situations, but many caution that you need to include enough information to make you, not one of the numerous other applicants, the person for the job. Frequently that is hard to do in one screen.

When you submit an email letter with your résumé:

- Include your name as part of the subject line. Many companies also will request the job number or title in the subject line.

- Repeat the job number or title for which you're applying in the first paragraph.

- Prepare your letter in a word-processing program. Use the spell-checker to edit and proof the document.

- Use standard business letter features: salutation, standard closing, single-spacing with double-spacing between paragraphs.

- Use appropriate business language, without abbreviations or acronyms. Use correct punctuation.

- Don't put anything in all capital letters.

- Don't use smiley faces or other emoticons.

- Put your name at the end of the message.

- Include contact information (at least your email address and phone number) below your name.

Follow all guidelines posted by the company. Do not add attachments unless you know doing so is okay. Test your email by sending it to a friend; have your friend check it for appearance and correctness.

Creating a Professional Image

LO 15-8

Every employer wants businesslike employees who understand professionalism. To make your job application letter professional:

- Create your letter in a word-processing program so you can use features such as a spell-checker. Use a standard font such as Times New Roman, Georgia, Cambria, Calibri, or Helvetica in 12-point type.

- Don't mention relatives' names. It's okay to use names of other people if the reader knows those people and thinks well of them, if they think well of you and will say good things about you, and if you have permission to use their names.

- Omit personal information not related to the job.

- Unless you're applying for a creative job in advertising, use a conservative style: few, if any, contractions; no sentence fragments, clichés, or slang.

- Edit the letter carefully and proof it several times to make sure it's perfect. Errors suggest that you're careless or inept. In particular, double-check the spelling of the receiver's name.

- Print on the same paper (both shade and weight) you used for your résumé. Envelopes should match, too.

- Use a computer to print the envelope address.

Writing Style

Use a concise writing style (review Chapter 4). Use the technical jargon of the field to show your training, but avoid businessese and stuffy words like *utilize* (for *use*), *commence* (for *begin*), and *transpire* (for *happen*). Use a lively, energetic style that makes you sound like a real person.

Be sure your letter uses the exact language of the job ad and addresses all items included in the ad. If the ad mentions teamwork, your letter should give examples of teamwork; don't shift the vocabulary to collaboration. Many readers expect their job ad language in applicants' letters. If the language is not there, they may judge the applicant as not fitting the position. And so may their computer since the vocabulary of the job ad probably contains crucial key words for the computer to find.

Positive Emphasis

Be positive. Don't plead ("Please give me a chance") or apologize ("I cannot promise that I am substantially different from the lot").

Avoid word choices with negative connotations. Note how the following revisions make the writer sound more confident.

Negative: I have learned an excessive amount about writing through courses in journalism and advertising.

Positive: Courses in journalism and advertising have taught me to recognize and to write good copy. My profile of a professor was published in the campus newspaper; I earned an "A+" on my direct mail campaign for the American Dental Association to persuade young adults to see their dentist more often.

Excessive suggests that you think the courses covered too much—hardly an opinion likely to endear you to an employer.

Negative: You can check with my references to verify what I've said.

Positive: Professor Hill can give you more information about my work on his national survey.

Verify suggests that you expect the employer to distrust what you've said.

You-Attitude

Unsupported claims may sound overconfident, selfish, or arrogant. Create *you*-attitude by describing accomplishments and by showing how they relate to what you could do for this employer. (See Chapter 2 for more on *you*-attitude.)

Lacks *you*-attitude: An inventive and improvising individual like me is a necessity in your business.

You-attitude: Building a summer house-painting business gave me the opportunity to find creative solutions to challenges. At the end of the first summer, for example, I had nearly 10 gallons of exterior latex left, but no more jobs. I contacted the home economics teacher at my high school. She agreed to give course credit to students who were willing to give up two Saturdays to paint a house being renovated by Habitat for Humanity. I donated the paint and supervised the students. I could put these skills in problem solving and supervising to work as a personnel manager for Burroughs.

Show what you can do for them, not what they can do for you.

Remember that the word *you* refers to your reader. Using *you* when you really mean yourself or "all people" can insult your reader by implying that they still have a lot to learn about business:

Lacks *you*-attitude:	Running my own business taught me that you need to learn to manage your time.
You-attitude:	Running my own business taught me to manage my time.

Beware of telling readers information they already know as though they do not know it. This practice also can be considered insulting.

Lacks *you*-attitude:	Your company has just purchased two large manufacturing plants in France.
You-attitude:	My three college French courses would help me communicate in your newly acquired French manufacturing facilities.

Because you're talking about yourself, you'll use *I* in your letter. Reduce the number of *I*'s by revising some sentences to use *me* or *my*.

Under my presidency, the Agronomy Club. . . .

Courses in media and advertising management gave me a chance to. . . .

My responsibilities as a summer intern included. . . .

In particular, avoid beginning every paragraph with *I*. Begin sentences with prepositional phrases or introductory clauses:

As my résumé shows, I. . . .

In my coursework in media and advertising management, I. . . .

While I was in Italy. . . .

(To learn more about *you*-attitude, please explore the Connect exercise "Creating *You*-Attitude and Positive Emphasis.")

Paragraph Length and Unity

Keep your first and last paragraphs fairly short—preferably no more than four or five typed lines. Vary paragraph length within the letter; it's okay to have one long paragraph, but don't use a series of eight-line paragraphs.

When you have a long paragraph, check to be sure that it covers only one subject. If it covers two or more subjects, divide it into two or more paragraphs.

Use topic sentences at the beginning of your paragraphs to make your letter more readable.

Letter Length

Have at least three paragraphs. A short letter throws away an opportunity to be persuasive; it also may suggest that you have little to say for yourself or that you aren't very interested in the job.

Without eliminating content, tighten each sentence to be sure that you're using words as efficiently as possible. If your letter is a bit over a page, use slightly smaller margins or a type size that's one point smaller to get more on the page.

Editing and Proofreading

Be sure you edit and proofread your cover letter. Failure to do so can undo all the work you put into it. The web abounds with humorous examples of spelling errors making unintended statements ("I'm excellent at spelling and grammer"). In fact, some companies post the best bloopers on their websites. For example, Robert Half International maintains Resumania (resumania.com); Killian Branding, an advertising agency, has "Cover Letters from Hell" on its website (www.killianbranding.com/cover-letters-from-hell).

Check your content one last time to ensure that everything presents you as a hardworking professional. Make sure you are not revealing any frustration with the job search process in your content or diction. Check your tone to see that it is positive about your previous experiences and yourself. Don't beg or show too much gratitude for commonplaces such as reading your letter.

Follow-Up

Follow up with the employer once if you hear nothing after two or three weeks. It is also okay to ask once after one week if email materials were received. Do not make a pest of yourself, however, by calling or emailing too often; doing so could eliminate you from further consideration.

Summary by Learning Objectives

LO 15-1   Conduct an effective job search.

- The internet has many tools for job searching. Choose the ones that will be best for you and your career.
- Networking and internships help you build relationships in your profession.
- When you are searching for a job, your online reputation is vital. Use social networking like Twitter, Facebook, and LinkedIn wisely to build and maintain your online personal brand.
- With your online job search efforts, always be prepared to give a traditional cover letter and résumé to an interested employer.

LO 15-2   Construct a résumé that makes you look attractive to employers.

- Employers skim résumés to decide whom to interview. Employers assume that the letter and résumé represent your best work.
- Emphasize information that is relevant to the job you want, is recent (last three years), and shows your superiority to other applicants.
- To emphasize key points, put them in headings, list them vertically, and provide details.
- Résumés use sentence fragments punctuated like complete sentences. Items in the résumé must be concise and parallel. Verbs and gerunds create a dynamic image of you.

- Always be completely honest in your résumé and job search. Dishonesty can keep you from being hired or cause you to lose your job later.

LO 15-3   Produce two types of résumés.

- A chronological résumé summarizes what you did in a time line (starting with the most recent events, and going backward in reverse chronology). It emphasizes degrees, job titles, and dates. Use a chronological résumé when
  - Your education and experience are a logical preparation for the position for which you're applying.
  - You have impressive job titles, offices, or honors.
- A skills résumé emphasizes the skills you've used, rather than the job in which or the date when you used them. Use a skills résumé when
  - Your education and experience are not the usual route to the position for which you're applying.
  - You're changing fields.
  - You want to combine experience from paid jobs, activities, volunteer work, and courses to show the extent of your experience in administration, finance, speaking, etc.
  - Your recent work history may create the wrong impression (e.g., it has gaps, shows a demotion, or shows job-hopping).

LO 15-4   **Determine what to include in a résumé.**

Résumés contain the applicant's contact information, education, and experience. Summary of qualifications, honors and awards, other skills, activities, and a portfolio reference also may be included.

LO 15-5   **Determine how to respond to common difficulties that arise during job searches.**

- Remove any unprofessional material from your personal web page and social networking sites.
- If you have gaps in your employment history or low experience, or if you were laid off or fired, address those problems honestly in both your résumé and your interview.
- Seek opportunities, such as internships and volunteer work, to fill in or expand your employment history and to reinforce your skills.

LO 15-6   **Determine how to handle the online portion of job searches.**

Many résumés are now sent electronically and are posted on the internet or the organization's website. Prepare your résumé to send both electronically and in print.

LO 15-7   **Match your job application letter to the rhetorical situation.**

When you know that a company is hiring, send a solicited job letter. When you want a job with a company that has not announced openings, send a prospecting job letter. In both letters, you should

- Address the letter to a specific person.
- Indicate the specific position for which you're applying.
- Be specific about your qualifications.
- Show what separates you from other applicants.
- Show knowledge of the company and the position.
- Refer to your résumé (which you would enclose with the letter).

LO 15-8   **Create a professional image in your job application letter.**

- Use your knowledge of the company, your course-work, your understanding of the field, and your experience in jobs and extracurricular activities to show that you're unique.
- Don't repeat information that the reader already knows; don't seem to be lecturing the reader on their business.
- Use positive emphasis to sound confident. Use *you*-attitude by supporting general claims with specific examples and by relating what you've done to what the employer needs.
- Have at least three paragraphs in your letter. Most job application letters are only one page.
- Application essays give you a chance to expand on your best points and show your personality.

Exercises and Cases

15.1   Reviewing the Chapter

1. How can you use the internet effectively in your job search? (LO 15-1)
2. What is the role of networking and internships when you are looking for a job? (LO 15-1)
3. What is the role of social networking in your job search? (LO 15-1)
4. How can you use writing components such as emphasis and details to help set yourself apart from other candidates? (LO 15-2)
5. What are key words? How do you use them in your summary of qualifications? (LO 15-2)
6. What are two types of résumés, and when should you use each? (LO 15-3)
7. What types of information should you include in your résumé? (LO 15-4)
8. How can you deal with common difficulties in job searches? (LO 15-5)
9. How can you format your résumé to send it electronically? (LO 15-6)
10. What are the differences between solicited and prospecting letters? (LO 15-7)
11. What are three ways to create a professional image with your letter? (LO 15-8)

15.2   Reviewing Grammar

1. Most résumés use lists, and items in lists need to have parallel structure. Polish your knowledge of parallel structure by revising the sentences in Exercise B.7, Appendix B.

2. As you have read, it is crucial that your job application letter be error-free. One common error in job letters, and one that spell-checker programs will not catch, is confusing word pairs like *affect/effect*. Practice choosing the correct word with Exercises B.12, B.13, and B.14 in Appendix B.

15.3   Analyzing Your Accomplishments

List the 10 achievements that give you the most personal satisfaction. These could be things that other people wouldn't notice. They can be accomplishments you've achieved recently or things you did years ago.

Answer the following questions for each accomplishment:

1. What skills or knowledge did you use?
2. What personal traits did you exhibit?

3. What about this accomplishment makes it personally satisfying to you?

As your instructor directs,

a. Share your answers with a small group of other students.
b. Summarize your answers in an email to your instructor.
c. Present your answers orally to the class.

15.4   Remembering What You've Done

Use the following list to jog your memory about what you've done. For each item, give three or four details as well as a general statement.

Describe a time when you

1. Used facts and figures to gain agreement on an important point.
2. Identified a problem that a group or organization faced and developed a plan for solving the problem.
3. Made a presentation or a speech to a group.
4. Won the goodwill of people whose continued support was necessary for the success of some long-term project or activity.
5. Interested other people in something that was important to you and persuaded them to take the actions you wanted.

6. Helped a group deal constructively with conflict.
7. Demonstrated creativity.
8. Took a project from start to finish.
9. Created an opportunity for yourself in a job or volunteer position.
10. Used good judgment and logic in solving a problem.

As your instructor directs,

a. Identify which job(s) each detail is relevant for.
b. Identify which details would work well on a résumé.
c. Identify which details, further developed, would work well in a job letter.

15.5   Developing Action Statements

Use 10 of the verbs from Figure 15.5 to write action statements describing what you've done in paid or volunteer work, in classes, in extracurricular activities, or in community service.

15.6   Deciding How Much Detail to Use

In each of the following situations, how detailed should the applicant be? Why?

1. Kai Oliver has been steadily employed for the last six years while getting their college degree, but the jobs have been low-level ones, whose prime benefit was that they paid well and fit around their class schedule.
2. Adrienne Barcus was an assistant department manager at a clothing boutique. As assistant manager, she was authorized to approve checks in the absence of the manager. Her other duties were ringing up sales, cleaning the area, and helping mark items for sales.

3. Avery Heilman has been a clerk-typist in the Alumni Office. As part of their job, they developed a schedule for mailings to alumni, set up a merge system, and wrote two of the letters that go out to alumni. The merge system they set up has cut in half the time needed to produce letters.

4. As a co-op student, Stanley Greene spends every other term in a paid job. He now has six semesters of job experience in television broadcasting. During his last co-op, he was the assistant producer for a daily morning news show.

15.7 Taking Advantage of Volunteer Opportunities

Volunteer work can improve your skills and enhance your résumé. With a partner, seek volunteer opportunities on your campus or in your city. Make a list of volunteer groups that may need help. Here are a few organizations that might help you get started:

- Big Brothers Big Sisters
- ASPCA

- Your local library or art center
- A local food pantry
- Ronald McDonald House

Present your findings to the class and encourage your friends to join you in volunteering.

15.8 Performing a Needs Analysis

Identify a specific job posting you are interested in and list its requirements. Analyze the needs of the job and identify your personal strengths and qualifications to obtain it.

As your instructor directs,

a. Work on incorporating your list into a résumé.

b. Compose bullet entries for each qualification using action verbs.

c. Identify areas in which you still need to improve. Brainstorm a list of ways in which you can achieve what you need.

15.9 Evaluating Your Online Reputation

Your online reputation is vital to your successful job search. Evaluate your reputation online using the following steps.

a. Search for your name on Google. What are the results on the first page? Do you see a positive online presence?

b. Search for your name on Google and click on the Images search tab. What pictures come up? Is there anything that could embarrass you?

c. Check your privacy settings on Facebook. What can employers see? What can your friends see?

d. Review your Twitter, Facebook, and other social media posts for the past several months. What do they say about you?

e. Review and update your LinkedIn profile. Do you think it will be attractive to potential employers?

15.10 Editing a Résumé

Below are a job ad and a résumé applying for that job. Using the information you have about Kendall's two jobs (given below the résumé), critique Kendall's résumé. Revise their résumé to improve it. Then write an email to your instructor discussing the strengths and weaknesses of the résumé and explaining why you made the changes you did.

Account Manager

Location: Aurora, IL
Job Category: Business/Strategic Management
Career Level: Entry-Level Manager (Manager/Supervisor of Staff)

Quantum National is the market leader in providing research, sales and marketing, health care policy consulting, and health information management services to the health care industry. Quantum has more than 20,000 employees worldwide and offices in 15 countries in Central and South America. Medical Innovation Communications, a division of Quantum National, currently has an opportunity for an Account Manager in our Aurora, IL, office. Medical Innovation Communications provides comprehensive product commercialization at all stages of product development: from phase 2, through national and international product launches to ongoing support.

The Account Manager has global responsibility for managing the client's marketing communications programs, assuring that the client's objectives are met in terms of program quality and on-time delivery.

Responsibilities include:

- Day-to-day client contact to identify and translate marketing objectives into strategic medical communications/education programs.
- Develop proposals, budgets, estimates of job cost, and profitability.
- Lead a team of Project Managers and Marketing Associates through guidance, delegation, and follow-up; and significant interaction with the client.
- Work with New Business Development Teams to develop proposals, budgets, and presenting company capabilities/business pitches to clients.
- Schedule the workflow of a 30-person demonstration and marketing team.

Requirements:

- Bachelor's degree.
- Ability to define and respond to client needs, working effectively under tight deadlines.
- Proven client management experience.
- Proven team management experience.
- Superior written and spoken communication skills.

Email applications and résumés to pattersj@micquant.com, and direct inquiries to J. Pattersen.

Kendall Stanton

wildechilde@gmail.com	8523 8th Street	125 A S. 27th Ave
cell: 515-668-9011	Ames, IA 50011	Omaha, NE 68101
	515-311-8243	402-772-5106

Education

Iowa State University, Ames, IA—Business
May 2021, maybe December 2021
Minor: Botany
Cumulative GPA: 2.63 / 4.0

Mid-Plains Community College, North Platte, NE—Associate of Arts
May 2017

Bryan High School, Omaha, NE
May 2014

Work Experience

May 2020–August 2020—Summer Internship at FirstWest Insurance, Des Moines, IA

- Worked with a senior account manager to oversee some medical and EAP accounts.
- Made her phone calls to customers.
- Organized online meetings with customers.
- I had to write some training "how-to's" for the new billing database.

2007–2019—*Worked in family business*
Worked weekends and summers in my parents' used-book store.

Skills

Microsoft Office
Fluent in Spanish

When you ask, Kendall tells you about their two jobs:

At their internship this summer, the person they worked with was pretty much an absentee supervisor: Kendall had to do all the work alone (and they are still a little bitter about that). Their department managed five Employee Assistance Provider accounts with a total of about 36,000 individual policyholders in five Midwestern states. They had to set up and maintain work schedules for 12 employees and manage the expense reports for the entire group. Four of those employees traveled a lot, so there were lots of expense reports to manage; there were so many that Kendall had to revise the department's budget twice. They spent about four hours of every day returning customer phone calls and linking customers on conference calls with their department's employees. And those training how-to's? That turned into a 20-page how-to manual, which they wrote up and then had FirstWest's IT department turn into a website for the department to use.

Their parents' family bookstore in Omaha is actually a franchise of a national chain of aftermarket bookstores: Booktopia. The store generates about $450,000 in gross sales per year and stocks about 100,000 titles (not counting internet sales and special orders); it employs 5 full-time and 17 part-time employees. In addition to filling in as a floor clerk, stocker, and cashier—all jobs that put their customer-service, cash-handling, and "people skills" to the test—Kendall has been handling all of the paperwork between the store and the Booktopia corporate office. (Their parents are great salespeople, but they're not good at paying attention to details. That's created friction between them and the corporate office.) That paperwork includes all of the store's quarterly and yearly budget, staffing, and marketing reports since 2003.

Note: This exercise was written by Matthew Search.

15.11   Analyzing Job Applicants Based on Their Résumés

Based on your reading of this chapter, the following job description, and the two résumés below, analyze the two applicants for the position. What are their strengths and weaknesses as highlighted by their résumés? Which of the two candidates would you select? Why?

Job description for Cost Accountant

The position of Cost Accountant is responsible for budgeting, reviewing, analyzing, controlling, and forecasting costs involving different cost centers throughout the production process, including raw material procurement, inventory management, manufacturing, warehousing, and shipping. Other responsibilities include analyzing G/L reports; ensuring compliance with Generally Accepted Accounting Principles (GAAP) and Cost Accounting Standards (CAS); conducting breakeven (BE), contribution margin, and variance analyses; and preparing periodic reports for upper management. The position requires a bachelor's degree in accounting. A certification in management accounting from the Institute of Management Accountants (IMA) will be a plus. The position also requires a minimum of two years of work experience in cost accounting at a manufacturing company.

SAM PORTER

1010, Buck St., Fairfax, VA
sporter@bestwebsite.com

EXPERIENCE

2019–2021   Abacus Engineering   Portland, OR.

Cost Accounting Trainee
- Calculated cost variance for different cost centers.
- Prepared quarterly budget reports
- Coodinated with employees at different levels for data collection

2019–till date   Bourke Winodws   Fairfax, VA

Costing Manager
- Monitored 12 cost centers
- Implemented policies that reduced costs by 25%
- Supervised a staff of three, including one cost accountant.
- I also produced multiple G/L reports for the production department as well as upper management

EDUCATION

2015–2019   Edward Young University, Perry, OH
- B.A., accounting.
- Currently pursuing CMA of Institute of Management Accounting

INTERESTS

Country music, computers, fishing, golf

José Cortez

1212 S. E. Avenue, Earl, PA
(111) 112-1121; jc8@pearlnews.com

Qualification Summary

Skills in **controling** and reducing costs, experience with GAAP and CAS, skills in cost analyses, project management, CMA (IMA), member of the Financial Management Association International, well-versed with ERP software

Education

- **Certification in Management Accounting**
- Graduation—2021
- Institute of Management Accountants
- True Blue University, Roald, PA
- Graduation—2020
- Degree—Bachelor of Sciences (BS)
- Major—Accounting, G.P.A. 3.55

(continued)

Experience

Silverstein Windows and Doors, Earl, PA   2021-Till date

> Cost Accountant
> - Estimate, review, budget, analyze, and forecast direct / indirect and variable and fixed costs for all stages of production
> - Work on the ERP system to genrate reports and data sheets giving cost analyses
> - Suggested a procedure in a contract that saved the company $35,000
> - Worked with the Marketing Department on the costing / pricing of lower-priced vinyl casement windows

Achievements

> - Volunteered more than 100 hours for the Habitat for Humanity Award 2019–2020
> - Visted door and widow manufacturing plants in Argentina, Belgium, and Japan
> - Received the best employee of the month award at Silverstein Windows and Doors
> - Wrote articles for *Financial Control Weekly,* a publication of Costing Professionals Association

References

> Available upon request

Note: This exercise was written by Anish Dave.

15.12   Preparing a Résumé

Write a résumé that you could use in your job search.

As your instructor directs,

a. Write a résumé for the field in which you hope to find a job.

b. Write two different résumés for two different job paths you are interested in pursuing. Write an email to your instructor explaining the differences.

c. Adapt your résumé to a specific company you hope to work for. Write an email to your instructor explaining the specific adaptations you made and why.

15.13   Creating a Web Portfolio

Use a web platform such as Wordpress to create a portfolio that highlights your professional and academic accomplishments. Include course projects, workplace samples, and other documents that support your professional accomplishments and goals.

Write an email to your instructor listing each item in your portfolio and explaining why you chose it.

15.14   Evaluating Visual Résumés

Working individually, in pairs, or in small groups, as your instructor directs,

a. Look at five of the example student résumés on VisualCV.com. What features do you like? Why? What features would you change or omit? Why? What are the advantages of VisualCV over your own résumé? Disadvantages?

b. Discuss strengths and weaknesses of two résumés in an email to your instructor, a posting on the class website, or an oral presentation.

15.15   Evaluating LinkedIn Profiles

Working individually, in pairs, or in small groups, as your instructor directs, look at six profiles on LinkedIn. You could use those of your classmates, family members, or local businesspeople.

- Which one has the best résumé? Why?
- How do the profiles and résumés differ?

- Which one has the best recommendations? Why?
- Overall, which one has the best profile? Why?

Discuss your conclusions in an email to your instructor, a posting on the class website, or an oral presentation.

15.16   Analyzing First Paragraphs of Prospecting Letters

All of the following are first paragraphs in prospecting letters written by new college graduates. Evaluate the paragraphs on these criteria:

- Is the paragraph likely to interest readers and motivate them to read the rest of the letter?
- Does the paragraph have some content that the student can use to create a transition to talking about their qualifications?
- Does the paragraph avoid asking for a job?

1. Redeccer just added three new stores in Ohio. It also got voted best hardware store in Denton. This is where I want to start my career in supply-chain management.

2. From the time I was old enough to walk, my father involved me with the many chores and decisions that happen on a successful family farm. He taught me to work, to manage employees, and to handle large amounts of money. I believe my lifelong experience has prepared me to contribute to the continued success of your company.

3. Two years ago, my right leg was crushed in a car accident in the middle of my second semester of college. Although I had to have two surgeries and was on heavy painkillers, I successfully completed the semester with a 3.4. I know that this experience shows I have what it takes to succeed in your law firm.

4. For the past two and one-half years I have been studying turf management. On August 1, I will graduate from Western State University with a BA in Ornamental Horticulture. The type of job I will seek will deal with golf course maintenance as an assistant superintendent.

5. Ann Gibbs suggested that I contact you.

6. Each year, the Christmas shopping rush makes more work for everyone at Nordstrom's, especially for the Credit Department. While working for Nordstrom's Credit Department for three Christmas and summer vacations, the Christmas sales increase is just one of the credit situations I became aware of.

7. Whether to plate a two-inch eyebolt with cadmium for a tough, brilliant shine or with zinc for a rust-resistant, less expensive finish is a tough question. But similar questions must be answered daily by your salespeople. With my experience in the electroplating industry, I can contribute greatly to your constant need of getting customers.

8. What a set of tractors! The new 9430 and 9630 diesels are just what is needed by today's farmer with his ever-increasing acreage. John Deere has truly done it again.

9. Prudential Insurance Company did much to help my college career as the sponsor of my National Merit Scholarship. Now I think I can give something back to Prudential. I'd like to put my education, including a BS degree in finance from Ludewig University, to work in your investment department.

10. Since the beginning of Delta Electric Construction Co. in 2002, the size and profits have grown steadily. My father, being a stockholder and vice president, often discusses company dealings with me. Although the company has prospered, I understand there have been a few problems of mismanagement. I feel with my present and future qualifications, I could help ease these problems.

15.17   Improving *You*-Attitude and Positive Emphasis in Job Letters

Revise each of these sentences to improve *you*-attitude and positive emphasis. You may need to add information.

1. I got laid off at Barlons three months ago when the company downsized.

2. Your company needs someone like me, who has the experience and knowledge to take your department to new heights.

3. I may not be the most qualified candidate you will see, but with your location and financial struggles, I am certainly the best you will get.

4. I understand that your company has had problems due to the mistranslation of documents during international ad campaigns.

5. Included in my résumé are the courses in Finance that earned me a fairly attractive grade average.

6. I am looking for a position that gives me a chance to advance quickly.

7. Although short on experience, I am long on effort and enthusiasm.

8. I have been with the company from its beginning to its present unfortunate state of bankruptcy.

9. I wish to apply for a job at Austin Electronics. I will graduate from Florida State in May. I offer you a degree in electrical engineering and part-time work at Best Buy.

10. I was so excited to see your opening. This job is perfect for me.

11. You will find me a dedicated worker, because I really need a job.

15.18   Evaluating Letter Content

Improve the content of these passages from job cover letters. You may need to add content.

1. I am a very hard worker. In fact, I am known for finishing the jobs of my co-workers.

2. I have always worked hard, even when most of my co-workers and my boss were hardly working.

3. I have received a 4.0 in every semester at my university. This shows my dedication to perfection.

4. My internship gave me lots of experience for this job.

5. My job duties at Saxon Sport were to create displays, start an employee newsletter, and on weekends I was part of the sales staff.

6. While at San Fernando State, I participated in lots of activities. I played intramurals in baseball, football, basketball, hockey, and volleyball. I was treasurer and then president of the Marketing Club. I was in the Gaffers' Guild, where I made blown-glass creations. I was also in Campus Democrats.

7. I will be in Boston for a family reunion June 23–25 and will drop by your office then for an interview.

8. I feel any of my bosses would tell you that I try hard and pay attention to to detail.

9. I wish to apply for your job as a computer programmer. I have a computer science minor and two summers of sales experience at Best Buy in their computer department.

15.19   Evaluating Rough Drafts

Evaluate the following drafts. What parts should be omitted? What needs to be changed or added? What parts would benefit from specific supporting details?

1.

Dear_____:

There is more to a buyer's job than buying the merchandise. And a clothing buyer in particular has much to consider.

Even though something may be in style, customers may not want to buy it. Buyers should therefore be aware of what customers want and how much they are willing to pay.

In the buying field, request letters, thank-you letters, and persuasive letters are frequently written.

My interest in the retail field inspired me to read Forever 21's annual report. I saw that a new store is being built. An interview would give us a chance to discuss how I could contribute to this new store. Please call me to schedule an interview.

Sincerely,

2.

> Dear Sir or Madam:
>
> I am taking the direct approach of a personnel letter. I believe you will under stand my true value in the areas of practical knowledge and promotional capabilities.
>
> I am interested in a staff position with Darden in relation to trying to improve the operations and moral of the Olive Garden Restaurants, which I think that I am capable of doing. Please take a minute not to read my résumé (enclosed) and call to schedule an interview.
>
> Sincerely,

3.

> Dear_____:
>
> Hello, my name is Dave. I am very interested in the position of marketing guy for Applicious Applesauce. I have recently graduated from Sharman University, with a Bachelor's Degree in Marketing and Finance. I graduated with a 2.0 GPA, and took many classes in Marketing and Finance. I believe these classes will help me to grow your company to where it needs to be.
>
> I did some marketing work for my friend, Aaron, who is starting his own business. I helped promote his new business and came up with a clear marketing plan for him to follow. He is doing really well with it so far.
>
> I have no problem relocating for this job. I really want it.
>
> Thank you for your time.
>
> Sincerely,

15.20   Gathering Information about Companies in Your Career Field

Use five different websites to investigate three companies in your career field. Look at salary guides for your level of qualifications, product/service information, news articles about the companies, mission/vision statements, main competitors, annual reports, and financial reports.

As your instructor directs,

a.   Share your findings with a small group of other students.

b.   Summarize your findings in an email to your instructor. Include a discussion of how you could use this information in your job letter and résumé.

c.   Present your findings to the class.

d.   Join with a small group of other students to write a report summarizing the results of this research.

15.21   Conducting an Information Interview

Interview someone working in a field you're interested in. Use the following questions to get started:

- How did you get started in this field?
- What do you like about your job?
- What do you dislike about your job?
- What courses and jobs would you recommend as preparation for this field?

As your instructor directs,

a.   Share the results of your interview with a small group of other students.

b.   Write an email to your instructor containing the results of your interview. Include a discussion of how you could use this information in your job letter and résumé.

c.   Present the results of your interview orally to the class.

d.   Write to the interviewee thanking him or her for taking the time to talk to you.

15.22   Writing a Solicited Letter

Write a letter of application in response to an announced opening for a full-time job (not an internship) you would like.

Turn in a copy of the listing. If you use option (a), your listing will be a copy. If you choose option (b), you will write the listing.

a.   Respond to an ad in a newspaper, in a professional journal, in the placement office, or on the web. Use an ad that specifies the company, not a blind ad. Be sure that you are fully qualified for the job.

b.   If you have already worked somewhere, assume that your employer is asking you to apply for full-time work after graduation. Be sure to write a fully persuasive letter.

15.23   Creating a Virtual Cover Letter

Using a cover letter you have written, review your online presence. What key words do you see in your social networking profiles? What job experience, education, and skills are highlighted? How can you make your online profiles more attractive to potential employers? List what you found and identify changes you are going to make to your online presence.

15.24   Reviewing Cover Letters

All-Weather Inc. invited applications for the position of sales representative. This person will be based in Nebraska and will be responsible for sales of All-Weather's vinyl windows in local markets, including single- and double-hung windows and casement windows. The job description for the position reads as follows:

> The Sales Representative (Residential Sales) will be responsible for successful market penetration of identified market segments. Specifically, the duties include achieving targeted sales, conducting product demonstrations, contacting customers and other stakeholders, gathering market intelligence, preparing market and sales reports, communicating with internal customers, coordinating between customers and the Service and Installation Group, participating in meetings of trade associations and government agencies, attending company training events, and performing other duties assigned by managers. The ideal candidate will be someone with a BS degree, preferably with a technical major. Additionally, the candidate must have at least one year of sales experience, preferably in industrial products. Candidates with experience in brand marketing will also be considered. Among skills for the job, the candidate must possess computer skills, PR and communication skills, teamwork skills, and the ability to perform basic mathematical computations.

Write a response in which you discuss the strengths and weaknesses of both applicants. Judging just from their cover letter, which applicant would you prefer to hire? Why?

> Antonio Ramirez aramirez@bestmail.com 164 Beet St. Houston, TX
>
> October 12, 2021
>
> Ms. Erin Lenhardt
> 1210 Polaroid Av.
> St. Paul, MN
>
> Dear Ms. Lenhardt:
>
> Please consider this letter as my application for the post of Sales Representative (Residential Sales). I learned about your job from the journal *Plastics US* (September issue). I have a bachelor's degree in chemistry from the University of Austin, Texas, and have two years of experience selling PVC resin.

The last two years I have been a Sales Executive in Goodman Petrochemicals in Houston, TX. My responsibilities include selling Goodman's PVC resin to Houston-based PVC processors of rigid and flexible applicatons.

As you suggest in your advertisement, my degree in chemistry will help me explain to customers the important technical attributes of your vinyl windows. My focus during my bachelor's degree was inorganic chemistry, especially hydrocarbons and its practical applications. Apart from my coursework, I also interned at Bright Fenestration Products in Austin, TX.

I look forward to discussing my experience and interst in your organization with you in a face-to-face interview. I'm available for the interview any time in the next two weeks at a day's notice. I'm confident I will meet—and exceed—all your expetations for this important front line position.

Sincerely,

Antonio Ramirez

Tai Chang
4334, Sunset Boulevard, Lincoln, NE
mchang@myemail.com

October 14, 2021

Ms. Erin Lenhardt
HR Manager
1210 Polaroid Av.
St. Paul, MN

Dear Ms. Lenhardt:

I wish to apply for the position of Sales Representative (Residential Sales) advertised through Monster.com. After acquiring a bachelor's degree in design, I joined Albatross Advertising in November, 2018, as a trainee in the Accounts Department. Currently, I'm an Account Representative handling three of our most promising brands: *LiteWait* vacuum cleaners, Nebraska Furniture Mart, and Chimney Rock Art Gallery.

My bachelor's degree in design with a major in community and regional planning not only familiarized me with demands of buildings and landscapes in our 21st-century living but also acquainted me with concepts of media and design. I joined Albatross because I wanted to see if my education has equipped me to inform, persuade, and help customers with regard to products and brands.

During my nearly three-year tenure at Albatross as Account Representative, I have created and given insightful presentations to clients. As a result of my performance, the agency has entrusted me with three of its most promising accounts, the ones that I mention above.

I would be delighted at an opportunity for a personal interview to further make my case for the job. You can contact me at my email address mentioned above.

Sincerely,

Tai Chang

Notes

1. U.S. Department of Labor, Bureau of Labor Statistics, "Number of Jobs, Labor Market Experience, and Earnings Growth among Americans at 50: Results from a Longitudinal Survey," news release, August 27, 2017, USDL-17-1158, https://www.bls.gov /news.release/pdf/nlsoy.pdf.

2. Richard Nelson Bolles, *What Color Is Your Parachute? 2013: A Practical Manual for Job-Hunters and Career-Changers* (Berkeley: Ten Speed Press, 2013), 57.

3. National Association of Colleges and Employers, "Intern to Full-Time Hire Conversion: 'Returning vs 'Nonreturning' Students," July 21, 2015, http://www.naceweb.org/talent-acquisition/internships /intern-to-full-time-hire-conversion-returning-vs-nonreturning -interns.

4. Teri Evans, "Penn State, Texas A&M Top the List: Recruiters Like One-Stop Shopping for Grads with Solid Academics, Job Skills, Record of Success," *Wall Street Journal*, September 13, 2010, B1; and Alexandra Cheney, "Firms Assess Young Interns' Potential: Businesses Look to Pools for Full-Time Hires, Tracking Future Employees as Early as Freshman Year," *Wall Street Journal*, September 13, 2010, B10.

5. Lauren Salm, "70% of Employers Are Snooping Candidates' Social Media Profiles," press release, June 15, 2017, https://www .careerbuilder.com/advice/social-media-survey-2017.

6. Caleb Wojcik, "8 Great Examples of Personal Domain Names in Action," *Fizzle*, n.d., https://fizzle.co/personal-domain-names/

7. Careerbuilder.com, "Press Release: More Than Half of Employers Have Found Content on Social Media That Caused Them NOT to Hire a Candidate, According to Recent CareerBuilder Survey," http://press.careerbuilder.com /2018-08-09-More-Than-Half-of-Employers-Have-Found-Content -on-Social-Media-That-Caused-Them-NOT-to-Hire-a-Candidate -According-to-Recent-CareerBuilder-Survey.

8. Leslie Kwoh, "Beware: Potential Employers Are Watching You," *Wall Street Journal*, October 29, 2012, B8.

9. Moire Lawler, "The One-Page Resume vs. the Two-Page Resume," *Monster*, 2021, https://www.monster.com/career-advice/article/one -page-or-two-page-resume.

10. Steven Rothberg, "What Do Employers Want to See on the Resumes of Students Applying to Jobs?" *College Recruiter*, March 3, 2020, https://www.collegerecruiter.com/blog/2020/03/03/who -do-employers-want-to-see-on-the-resumes-of-students-applying-to -jobs.

11. Ladders, "Eye-Tracking Study," 2018, https://www.theladders .com/static/images/basicSite/pdfs/TheLadders-EyeTracking -StudyC2.pdf.

12. National Association of Colleges and Employers, "Job Outlook 2019," November 2018, https://www.odu.edu/content/dam/odu /offices/cmc/docs/nace/2019-nace-job-outlook-survey.pdf.

13. Roni Noland, "It's Not a Disaster if Your Old Boss Won't Provide a Reference," *Boston Globe*, March 8, 2009, 5.

CHAPTER 16

Interviewing, Writing Follow-Up Messages, and Succeeding in the Job

Chapter Outline

Interview Channels

- Campus Interviews
- Phone Interviews
- Video-Recorded Interviews
- Online Interviews

Interview Strategy

Interview Preparation

- Company Research
- Elevator Speech
- Travel Planning
- Attire
- Professional Materials
- Interview Practice

Interview Customs

- Behavior
- Meal Etiquette
- Note-Taking
- Interview Segments

Traditional Interview Questions and Answers

Kinds of Interviews

- Behavioral Interviews
- Situational Interviews
- Stress Interviews
- Group Interviews
- Multiple Interviews

Final Steps for a Successful Job Search

- Following Up with Phone Calls and Written Messages
- Negotiating for Salary and Benefits
- Deciding Which Offer to Accept
- Dealing with Rejection

Starting Your Career

- Your First Full-Time Job
- A Long-Term Strategy

Summary by Learning Objectives

DrAfter123/Getty Images

Expect the Unexpected

Imagine interviewing for your dream job. You're confident and well prepared, and everything is going well. Then, one of the interviewers asks, "When a hot dog expands, in which direction does it split and why?"

Would you have an immediate answer?

That question—asked during an interview for a position at SpaceX—is just one instance in a growing trend of interview questions designed to illicit unrehearsed answers. These questions give the interviewers a snapshot into your ability to "think on your feet." Your responses will reveal glimpses of how you handle stress, as well as insights into your personality. The interviewers are not just looking for creative potential in their job candidates, they are also searching for the sort of person they would like to work with day after day.

Some other recent examples of unusual interview questions include

- Do you believe in Bigfoot?
- How many basketballs would fit in this room?

suhendri/Shutterstock

- What would you call your debut album?
- If there was a movie produced about your life, who would play you and why?
- What kind of tree would you be?

While it is impossible to know exactly the sort of strange questions that might be tossed your way, the good news is that prospective employers likely aren't interested in the content of your answers so much as in the way you handle yourself when giving those answers. Be prepared for anything. And when an unusual question comes your way, focus on remaining confident and friendly. Try to be the person you'd like to work with.

Source: "Top 10 Oddball Interview Questions," *Glassdoor*, https://www.glassdoor.com/List/Oddball-Interview-Questions-LST_KQ0,27.htm; Alison Doyle, "Top 25 Weird Interview Questions," *The Balance*, November 5, 2016, https://www.thebalance.com/top-weird-interview-questions-2059482; and Rachel Gillett, "17 Weird Job-Interview Questions Facebook, Google, and Other Top Companies Have Asked," *Business Insider*, November 22, 2015, http://www.businessinsider.com/weirdest-interview-questions-from-top-companies-2015-11.

Learning Objectives

After studying this chapter, you should be able to

LO 16-1 Identify what interview channels you may encounter.

LO 16-2 Create a strategy for successful interviewing.

LO 16-3 Determine what preparations to make before you start interviewing.

LO 16-4 Anticipate what to do during an interview.

LO 16-5 Answer common interview questions.

LO 16-6 Prepare for less common interview types.

LO 16-7 Determine what to do after an interview.

LO 16-8 Plan for a successful career.

Job interviews—whether in-person or online—are an important part of the hiring process. A survey of 600 managers found that they overwhelmingly preferred evaluating job candidates in person, either by interviews or temporary work performance.[1]

Because they are so important, job interviews are scary, even when you've prepared thoroughly. Surveys show that, according to hiring managers, job candidates are more likely to make mistakes during their interviews than at any other point of their job search.[2] A host of issues, such as arriving too late (or too early), failing to bring copies of your résumé, focusing too much on yourself, or not asking questions, can undercut your chances.[3] But when you are prepared, you can reduce missteps and increase your chance of getting the job you want. The best way to prepare is to know as much as possible about the interview process and the employer. The following steps will help you prepare well for the interview process:

- Learn the kinds of interviews you may encounter.
- Create a strategy for interviewing.
- Prepare for your interview.
- Be aware of the customs and expectations of interviews.
- Be prepared to answer common interview questions.
- Prepare to accept an offer and succeed in your career.

Interview Channels

LO 16-1

Although you may picture a job interview in a traditional office setting, modern interviews use other channels as well. Knowing about different interview channels can help you prepare for a successful interview. As a college student, you well may find yourself being interviewed on campus. You also may find you have a phone interview or an interview via Zoom, WebEx, or some other platform for online meetings, as more and more companies use technology to keep hiring costs in check. Most of the interview advice in this chapter applies to all settings, but some types of interviews have particulars you should consider.

Campus Interviews

Most campus career offices have written protocols and expectations for campus interviews arranged through them. Be sure to follow these expectations.

Remember that campus job fairs are the first places to make an impression on recruiters and interviewers. As you approach the booths at a job fair, show interest; be engaged; and be prepared with a résumé, business card, or other professional materials. If you make a good impression at a job fair, you already have an advantage when you enter the formal campus interview later.

Because campus interviewers will see so many students who are all following the same protocols, it is important that you come prepared with good details and professional stories about your work to help you stand out from the crowd. Focus on three to four selling points you most want the interviewer to remember about you. If you have a choice, do not schedule your interview late in the day when interviewers are getting tired.

Phone Interviews

Your job search will involve a lot of time on the phone. You should place special emphasis on developing your phone skills for before the interview, during the interview, and when you are following up. Be polite to everyone with whom you speak, including administrative assistants and receptionists. Be considerate, both on the phone and when leaving voicemail messages. Before you leave a voicemail message, think about what you want to say. Keep your message concise, and make sure to give both your name and your phone number slowly and distinctly.

Some organizations use phone interviews to narrow the list of candidates they bring in for office visits. Phone interviews give you some advantages. Obviously, you do not have to dress up for them. You can use all the materials you want as you speak. You also can take all the notes you want, although copious note-taking will probably affect your speaking quality, and you certainly don't want the sound of keyboard clicking to be heard by your interviewer.

On the other hand, phone interviews obviously deny you the important component of visual feedback. To compensate for this loss, you can ask your interviewer for verbal feedback (e.g., "Is this sufficient detail?" "Would you like more on this topic?").

Here are some additional tips for a good phone interview:

- **Speak distinctly.** Although you always want to speak distinctly at an interview, doing so is even more crucial for a phone interview.

- **Treat the interview like an in-person interview.** Although you don't need to dress up, doing so may help you focus and be appropriately formal. Speech experts recommend that you smile, lean forward, and gesture, even though no one can see you. Such activities add warmth and personality to your words.

- **Find a quiet, private location.** Don't interview in a room where people are coming and going. Be sure to eliminate all background noise such as music or TV.

- **Make sure your phone works.** If you are using your cell phone, make sure it is fully charged before the interview and that you can get good reception in the room where you will be speaking. If possible, use a landline instead to get a better, clearer, and more consistent connection.

- **Focus on your selling points.** Just as you did for a campus interview, focus on three to four selling points you most want the interviewer to remember about you.

Video-Recorded Interviews

Video-recorded interviews are becoming more common. With this type of interview, the organization sends you a list of questions, and you prepare a video to send back to them.

If you are preparing a video:

- **Practice your answers so you are fluent.** You don't want to stumble over your responses, but you also don't want to sound like you have memorized the answers.

- **Be thorough.** Because the employer can't ask follow-up questions, you want to consider what those questions could be and then be sure to answer them.

- **Pay attention to your surroundings.** Make sure you choose a location for your video with a background that is not visually distracting. If you choose a background with objects, make it someplace interesting and, if possible, related to your field (e.g., a laboratory or a set of bookshelves). But take care that the background is not cluttered and that it does not include objects or pictures that could hurt the professional image you are trying to establish.

Online Interviews

With the COVID-19 pandemic, online interviews via Zoom or Skype increased even more in popularity. If you are participating in an online interview:

- **Do a practice video ahead of time.** Listen to your pronunciation and voice qualities. Watch your video with the sound turned off: check your posture, gestures, facial expressions, and clothing. Do you have nervous mannerisms you need to control?

- **Test your technology.** Ensure that your wi-fi, mic, camera, and screen sharing work.

- **During the actual interview, keep your answers under two minutes.** Then ask the interviewers whether they want more information. People are generally more reluctant to interrupt a speaker in another location, and body language cues are limited, so ask for feedback ("Would you like to hear about that?").

- **Treat the interview as if you are in the same room.** Remember that even though you are not in the same room with the interviewers, they are still judging your appearance and mannerisms as if you were sitting in front of them. Use the tips for an in-person interview to help your online interview go well.

- **Once again, attend to your surroundings.** Choose a nondistracting and uncluttered background, use a quiet room, silence your cell phone, and turn off computer notifications.

- **Be prepared for a technology failure.** While the technologies that support online meetings have greatly improved, they can still have glitches. Be prepared for a technology failure by providing your telephone number in a polite email before the interview and having your phone handy and charged just in case.

Interview Strategy

LO 16-2

One of the most important steps in preparing for your interview is to have a successful interview strategy. Develop an overall strategy based on your answers to these three questions:

1. **What about yourself do you want the interviewer to know?** Pick two to five points that represent your strengths for that particular job and that show how you will add value to the organization. These facts are frequently character traits (such as enthusiasm), achievements, and experiences that qualify you for the job and separate you

from other applicants, or abilities such as fluency in Spanish. For each strength, think of a specific accomplishment to support it. For instance, be ready to give an example to prove that you're hardworking. Be ready to show how you helped an organization save money or serve customers better with specific numbers and details: "I saved my department $250,000 over three years with my redesigned training program."

Then, at the interview, listen to every question to see if you could make one of your key points as part of your answer. If the questions don't allow you to make your points, bring them up at the end of the interview.

2. **What disadvantages or weaknesses do you need to minimize?** Expect that you may be asked to explain weaknesses or apparent weaknesses in your record such as lack of experience, so-so grades, and gaps in your record.

Plan how to deal with these issues if they arise. Decide if you want to bring them up yourself, particularly disadvantages or weaknesses that are easily discoverable. If you bring them up, you can plan the best context for them during the interview. Many students, for example, have been able to get good jobs after flunking out of school by explaining that the experience was a turning point in their lives and pointing out that when they returned to school, they maintained a B or better grade point average. Although it is illegal to ask questions about marital status, married candidates with spouses who are able to move easily sometimes volunteer that information: "My husband is a dentist and is willing to relocate if the company wants to transfer me." See the suggestions later in this chapter under "Traditional Interview Questions and Answers," "Behavioral Interviews," and "Situational Interviews."

3. **What do you need to know about the job and the organization to decide whether you want to accept this job if it is offered to you?** Plan *in advance* the criteria on which you will base your decision (you always can change the criteria). Use "Deciding Which Offer to Accept" below to plan questions to elicit the information you'll need to rank each offer.

Interview Preparation

LO 16-3

With your strategy in place, you can prepare for a specific interview. Preparing for your interviews is vital in these days of intense competition for jobs. It also can help you to feel more confident and make a better impression.

Company Research

Research the company interviewing you. Read its web pages, Facebook page, Twitter page, company newsletters, and annual reports. Many companies now have YouTube videos and employee blogs to give you insight into the company and its culture. Some of them even offer interview tips. Read about the company in trade journals and newspapers. Search the internet. Ask your professors, classmates, friends, family, and co-workers about the firm. If possible, find out who will interview you and research them, too.

Also research salaries for the job: What is average? What is the range? Use web tools like the salary calculators listed in Figure 15.7.

Elevator Speech

After you have finished your research, prepare your elevator speech, a powerful, 60- to 90-second statement of why you are a good candidate for this particular job. (The name comes from the scenario of being alone with the recruiter for a multifloor elevator ride. What can you say in that short period to convince the recruiter to consider you?) Even though it is short, your elevator speech will need some carefully selected details to be convincing. It will come in handy for questions like "Tell me about yourself" or "Why should I hire you?" It is useful in a variety of situations, including group interviews and receptions where you meet a variety of the company's employees in brief, one-on-one conversations.

Travel Planning

Before your interview, make sure you can find the building and the closest parking. Plan how much time you will need to get there. Leave time cushions for stressors such as traffic jams or broken elevators. If you are fortunate enough to be flown to an interview, don't schedule too tightly. Allow for flight delays and cancellations. Plan how you will get from the airport to the interview site. Take enough cash and credit cards to cover emergencies.

Attire

First impressions are important; employers start judging you from the first second they see you. A major part of that first impression is your appearance.

The outfit you wear to an interview should meet your interviewer's expectations. The most conservative choice is the traditional dark business suit, a dress shirt, tie, and dress shoes with matching dark socks, or a dark two-piece suit with a white or pastel blouse and closed-toe shoes.

Although a conservative outfit is still a common choice, you cannot count on it being the right choice. Many companies now expect more casual attire: sport jackets or a coordinated jacket matched with pants or a skirt below the knee. Tight or low-cut tops and athletic wear should be avoided. Sneakers and sandals are inappropriate.

For campus interviews, you still should be professional in your attire. Although recruiters and interviewers on campus know they are interviewing students, you shouldn't dress like a student. Treat the interview like an off-campus interview and dress up. If possible, leave your backpack, laptop, and other items you would take to class at home or in a safe location. Take only those things that you need, like a pen or pencil, some paper, your résumé, and any work samples or other materials you may need during the interview.

For in-person and online interviews, you should show that you understand the organization's culture. Try to find out from your career contacts what is considered appropriate attire. While some interviewers do not mind if you ask them what you should wear to the interview, others do, so be careful. Use your other contacts first before you ask the interviewer. Find out what other employees wear each day, and dress a little nicer.[4]

No matter what outfit you choose, make sure it fits well (especially important if it has been a few months since you wore it), is comfortable, and does not show too much cleavage or chest.

Make conservative choices. Have your hair cut or styled conservatively. Jewelry and makeup should be understated; face jewelry, such as eyebrow and nose studs, should be removed. If possible, cover tattoos. For in-person interviews, personal hygiene must be impeccable. Pay attention to your breath. Avoid perfume, cologne and perfumed aftershave lotions.

Professional Materials

Take extra copies of your résumé. If your campus placement office already has given the interviewer a data sheet, present the résumé at the beginning of the interview: "I thought you might like a little more information about me."

You can wear a wide range of apparel to interviews. Find out what is appropriate—and inappropriate—for each interview. Which of these outfits would you wear?

Top left: Justin Horrocks/E+/Getty Images; Top middle: DreamPictures/Pam Ostrow/Blend Images LLC; Top right: BJI/Blue Jean Images/Vetta/Getty Images; Bottom left: Eric Audras/Onoky/Getty Images; Bottom middle: Jupiter Images/Stockbyte/Getty Images; Bottom right: Ron Chapple Stock/Alamy Stock Photo

Take something to write on and something to write with. It's okay to carry a small notepad that lists the questions you want to ask.

Take copies of your work or a portfolio: an engineering design, a copy of a letter you wrote on a job or in a business writing class, an article you wrote for the campus paper. You don't need to present these unless the interview calls for them, but they can be very effective: "Yes, I have done a media plan. Here's a copy of a plan I put together in my advertising seminar last year. We had a fixed budget and used real figures for cost and rating points, just as I'd do if I joined Toth and Rawlins."

Take the names, street addresses, email addresses, and phone numbers of references. Take complete details about your work history and education, including dates and street addresses, in case you're asked to fill out an application form.

If you can afford it, buy a briefcase in which to carry these items. At this point in your life, an inexpensive vinyl briefcase is acceptable.

Interview Practice

Rehearse everything you can: put on the clothes you'll wear, and practice entering a room, shaking hands, sitting down, and answering questions. Ask a friend to interview you. Saying answers out loud is surprisingly harder than saying them in your head. If your department or career center offers practice interviews, take advantage of them.

Some campuses have video-recording facilities so that you can watch your own practice interview. Video-recording is particularly valuable if you can do it at least twice, so you can modify behavior the second time and check to see whether the modification works. Your interviewing skills will improve with practice.

Interview Customs

LO 16-4

Strategy, preparation, and practice help you get ready for your interviews. But you also need to be aware of what will be expected of you during the interview. Not all interviews are question-and-answer sessions. More employers are starting to use other screening devices; they are asking candidates to provide on-the-spot writing samples or to take critical thinking, intelligence, writing, skills, personality, emotional intelligence, and drug tests. Some also use computer algorithms to screen their applicants.[5]

Behavior

How you act at the interview is as important as what you say, and first impressions of behavior are as important as they are for appearance.

Employers start judging you from the first second they see you. If you meet multiple people, first impressions will begin anew with each encounter. Always act professionally. Have a firm, pleasant handshake; avoid the limp, dead-fish handshake or the overly aggressive knuckle-crusher. Be polite to everyone, including people such as security guards, receptionists, and people in the restroom. Learn names and introduce yourself whenever possible. Their input about you may be sought.

Politeness extends to the interview itself.

- Be punctual, but not too early (no more than 10 minutes early). Many recruiters don't like someone hanging around their reception area.

- Practice active listening; it makes speakers feel appreciated, and you will likely pick up clues you can use effectively during your interview.

- Do not monopolize the interview time with lengthy monologues. Generally, your interviewer will have many questions to cover and will not appreciate an undue amount of time wasted on just one. Check the interviewer's verbal cues and body language for the amount of detail and depth desired. After two to three minutes, ask if the interviewer wants more detail. The best interviews are conversations in which you and your interviewer enjoy your interactions.

- Never say anything bad about current and former employers, a category that includes schools. Candidates who snipe about their employers and instructors will likely continue to do so on their new job and thus appear to be unattractive colleagues.

Be enthusiastic about the job. Enthusiasm helps convince people you have the energy to do the job well. Show how you are a good choice for their job by clearly presenting your carefully chosen accomplishments and strengths. If you are attending an in-person interview, where you could well be asked the same questions by different people, prepare to repeat yourself—with enthusiasm.

Be yourself. There's no point in assuming a radically different persona. If you do, you run the risk of getting into a job that you'll hate. Furthermore, as interviewers point out, you have to be a pretty good actor to come across convincingly if you try to be someone other than yourself. Yet keep in mind that all of us have several selves: we can be lazy, insensitive, bored, slow-witted, and tongue-tied, but we also can be energetic, perceptive, interested, intelligent, and articulate. Be your best self at the interview.

Interviews can make you feel vulnerable and defensive; to counter this, review your accomplishments—the things you're especially proud of having done. You'll make a better impression if you have a firm sense of your own self-worth.

Every interview merits the advice that you've probably heard before: sit up straight, don't mumble, look at people when you talk. Remember to turn off your cell phone.

As much as possible, avoid **nervous mannerisms**: playing with your hair, jingling coins in your pocket, clicking your pen, or repeating verbal spacers such as "like" and "uh." These mannerisms distract your audience and detract from your interview. It's okay to be a little nervous, however; it shows that you care.

Sometimes you will be asked to visit the company for a day or more of interviews. Because they may last longer, sometimes site interviews will present you with minor problems such as being brought back late from lunch or being kept overtime with one interviewer so you are late for your appointment with another. Don't let these minor problems throw you. Think of them as a new opportunity to show that you can roll with the punches; move forward calmly.

The interview is also a time for you to see if you want to work for this organization. Look for signs of organizational culture. How do people treat each other? Are offices or work spaces personalized? How many hours a week do the newest employees work? Is this the place where you want to become another new employee?

Meal Etiquette

Site visits that involve meals and semi-social occasions call for sensible choices. Remember that as long as you are with any person from the company, you are in an interview. They are evaluating how you behave in different situations. The meals

Meals may be an important part of the interview process. Be sure your manners measure up.
AJA Productions/The Image Bank/Getty Images

during a site visit are more relaxed, but do not make the mistake of relaxing too much. Here are some tips:

- When you order, choose something that's easy to eat without being messy.

- Watch your table manners. Sit up straight, keep your elbows off the table, and use your napkin. Silverware is used from the outside in. So you grab the correct glass or bread plate, remember BMW for table settings: bread on the left, meal in the center, water on the right.

- Take small bites that allow you to maintain the conversation—you are still answering interview questions.

- Eat a light lunch, so you'll be alert during the afternoon.

- Do not drink alcohol at lunch. At dinner or an evening party, accept only one drink, if any. A survey by the Society for Human Resource Management found that 96% of human resources professionals believe job candidates should not drink at interview meals.[6] Your best bet is to decline alcohol during your site visit, even if everyone else is drinking. You're still being evaluated, and you can't afford to have your guard down.

Note-Taking

During or immediately after the interview, write down

- The name of the interviewer (or all the people you talked to, if it's a group interview or a site visit).

- Tips the interviewer gave you about landing the job and succeeding in it.

- What the interviewer seemed to like best about you.

- Any negative points or weaknesses that came up that you need to counter in your follow-up messages or phone calls.

- Answers to your questions about the company.

- When you'll hear from the company.

The easiest way to get the interviewer's name is to ask for their card. You may be able to make all the notes you need on the back of the card.

Some interviewers say they respond negatively to applicants who take notes during the interview. However, if you have several interviews back-to-back or if you know your memory is terrible, do take brief notes during the interview. That's better than forgetting which company said you'd be on the road every other week and which interviewer asked that *you* get in touch with them. Try to maintain eye contact as much as possible while taking notes.

Interview Segments

Every interview has an opening, a body, and a close.

In the *opening* (two to five minutes), most good interviewers will try to set you at ease. Some interviewers will open with easy questions about your major or interests. Others open by telling you about the job or the company. If this happens, listen so you can answer questions later to show that you can do the job or contribute to the company that's being described.

The *body* of the interview (10 to 25 minutes) is an all-too-brief time for you to highlight your qualifications and, potentially, to find out what you need to know to decide if you want to accept a site trip. Expect questions that give you an opportunity to showcase your strong points and questions that probe any weaknesses evident from your résumé. (You were neither in school nor working last fall. What were you doing?) Normally the interviewer also will try to sell you on the company and give you an opportunity to raise questions.

You need to be aware of time so that you can make sure to get in your key points and questions: "We haven't covered it yet, but I want you to know that I . . . ." "I'm aware that it's almost 10:30. I do have some more questions that I'd like to ask about the company."

In the *close* of the interview (two to five minutes), the interviewer will usually tell you what happens next: "We'll be bringing our top candidates to the office in February. You should hear from us in three weeks." Make sure you know who to contact if the next step is not clearly spelled out or if you don't hear by the stated time.

The close of the interview is also the time for you to summarize your key accomplishments and strengths and to express enthusiasm for the job. Depending on the circumstances, you could say: "I've certainly enjoyed learning more about Zappos." "I hope I get a chance to visit your Las Vegas office. I'd really like to see the new computer system you talked about."

Traditional Interview Questions and Answers

LO 16-5

One of the best ways to prepare for an interview is to practice answering specific common interview questions. As Figure 16.1 shows, successful applicants use different communication behaviors when answering questions than do unsuccessful applicants. Successful applicants are more likely to use the company name, show they have

Figure 16.1	The Communication Behaviors of Unsuccessful and Successful Interviewees	
Behavior	**Unsuccessful interviewees**	**Successful interviewees**
Statements about the position	Have only vague ideas of what they want to do.	Specific and consistent about the position they want; are able to tell why they want the position.
Use of company name	Rarely use the company name.	Refer to the company by name.
Knowledge about company and position	Make it clear that they are using the interview to learn about the company and what it offers.	Make it clear that they have researched the company; refer to specific websites, publications, or people who have given them information.
Level of interest, enthusiasm	Respond neutrally to interviewer's statements: "okay," "I see." Indicate reservations about company or location.	Express approval nonverbally and verbally of information provided by the interviewer: "That's great!" Explicitly indicate desire to work for this particular company.
Nonverbal behavior	Make little eye contact; smile infrequently.	Make eye contact often; smile.
Picking up on interviewer's cues	Give vague or negative answers even when a positive answer is clearly desired ("How are your writing skills?").	Answer positively and confidently; back up claims with specific examples.
Use of industry terms and technical jargon	Use almost no technical jargon.	Use appropriate technical jargon.
Use of specifics in answers	Give short answers—10 words or fewer, sometimes only one word; do not elaborate. Give general responses: "fairly well."	Support claims with specific personal experiences.
Questions asked by interviewee	Ask a small number of general questions.	Ask specific questions based on knowledge of the industry and the company. Personalize questions: "What would my duties be?"

researched the company, support their claims with specific details, use appropriate technical language, and ask specific questions about the company and industry. In addition to practicing the content of questions, try to incorporate these tactics.

The ultimate questions in your interviewers' minds are probably these three: What can you do for us? Why should we hire you instead of another candidate? Will you fit in our company/division/office? However, many interviewers do not ask these questions directly. Instead, they ask other questions to get their answers more indirectly. Some of the more common questions are discussed below. Do some preparation before the interview so that you'll have answers that are responsive, honest, and positive. Choose answers that fit your qualifications and the organization's needs.

Initial interviews often seek to screen out less qualified candidates rather than to find someone to hire. Negative information will hurt you less if it comes out in the middle of the interview and is preceded and followed by positive information. If you stumble on a question near the end of the interview, don't leave until you've said something positive—perhaps restating one of the points you want the interviewer to know about you.

Check your answers for hidden negatives. If you say you are the kind of person who is always looking for challenges, your interviewer may wonder about hiring you for this entry-level position, which needs someone who does mostly routine work with care. Similarly, if you say you want lots of responsibility, your interviewer again may not see you as a good fit for entry-level positions, which are not known for providing lots of responsibility.

Rehearse your answers mentally, so you feel confident you have good answers. Then get family and friends to interview you. You may be surprised at how much work good mental answers still need when you give them out loud.

1. **Tell me about yourself.** Focus on several strengths that show you are a good candidate. Give examples with enough specifics to prove each strength. Don't launch into an autobiography, which will have too many details the interviewer will not care about. Provide professional, not personal, information. This is often one of the first questions asked in an interview; be prepared for it. Use it to set the tone of the interview and to establish your selling points.

2. **Walk me through your résumé.** Highlight your best features and offer reasons for major decisions. Why did you choose this college? Why did you take that job? Have professional reasons: You went to State U because it has a top-ranked accounting department, not because it is close to home; you took that summer job because it allowed some interaction with the company's accounting department, not because it was the only one you could find.

   Don't try to cover too much; your résumé walk-through should be no longer than three minutes. Tie your résumé into your selling points, and add some interesting details that are not on your résumé. Above all, maintain eye contact; do not read your résumé.

3. **What makes you think you're qualified to work for this company? or, I've received 120 applications for this position. Why should I hire you?** This question may feel like an attack. Use it as an opportunity to state (or restate) your strong points. Remember, though, that most of the candidates who are interviewing meet the basic qualifications. Your focus should be on the qualities that separate you from other applicants.

4. **What two or three accomplishments have given you the greatest satisfaction?** Pick accomplishments that you're proud of, that create the image you want to project, and that enable you to share one of the things you want the interviewer to know about you. Focus not just on the end result, but on the problem-solving, thinking, and innovation skills that made the achievement possible.

5. **Why do you want to work for us?** What is your ideal job? Make sure you have a good answer—preferably two or three reasons you'd like to work for that company. If you don't seem to be taking the interview seriously, the interviewer won't take you seriously.

   If your ideal job is very different from the ones the company has available, the interviewer may simply say there isn't a good match and end the interview. If you're interested in this company, do some research so that what you ask for is in the general ballpark of the kind of work the company offers.

6. **What college subjects did you like best and least? Why?** This question may be an ice-breaker; it may be designed to discover the kind of applicant they're looking for. If your favorite class was something outside your major, prepare an answer that shows that you have qualities that can help you in the job you're applying for: "My favorite class was a seminar in the American novel. We got a chance to think on our own, rather than just regurgitate facts; we made presentations to the class every week. I found I really like sharing my ideas with other people and presenting reasons for my conclusions about something."

7. **What is your class rank? Your grade point average? Why are your grades so low?** If your grades aren't great, be ready with a nondefensive explanation. If possible, show that the cause of low grades now has been solved or isn't relevant to the job you're applying for: "My father almost died last year, and my schoolwork really suffered." "When I started, I didn't have any firm goals. Once I discovered the field that was right for me, my grades have all been B's or better." "I'm not good at multiple-choice tests. But I am good at working with people."

8. **What have you read recently? What movies have you seen recently?** These questions may be icebreakers; they may be designed to probe your intellectual depth. The term you're interviewing, read at least one book or magazine (multiple issues) and see at least one serious movie that you could discuss at an interview. Make thoughtful selections.

9. **Show me some samples of your writing.** Many jobs require the ability to write well. Employers no longer take mastery of basic English for granted, even if the applicant has a degree from a prestigious university.

    The year you're interviewing, go through your old papers and select a few of the best ones, editing them if necessary, so that you'll have samples to present at the interview if you're asked for them.

10. **Describe a major problem you have encountered in your work and how you dealt with it.** Choose a problem that was not your fault, such as a customer's last-minute change to a large order. In your solution, stress skills you know the company will be seeking.

11. **What are your interests outside work? What campus or community activities have you been involved in?** While it's desirable to be well-rounded, naming 10 interests is a mistake. The interviewer may wonder when you'll have time to work. Select activities that show skills and knowledge you can use on the job: "I have polished my persuasion skills by being a cabin counselor at a camp for troubled preteens."

    If you mention your fiancé, spouse, or children in response to this question ("Well, my fiancé and I like to go sailing"), it is perfectly legal for the interviewer to ask follow-up questions ("What would you do if your spouse got a job offer in another town?"), even though the same question would be illegal if the interviewer brought up the subject first.

12. **What have you done to learn about this company?** An employer may ask this to see what you already know about the company. (If you've read the recruiting literature and the website, the interviewer doesn't need to repeat their content.) This question also may be used to see how active a role you're taking in the job-search process and how interested you are in this job.

13. **What adjectives would you use to describe yourself?** Use only positive ones. Be ready to illustrate each with a specific example of something you've done.

14. **What are your greatest strengths?** Employers ask this question to give you a chance to sell yourself and to learn something about your values. Pick strengths related to work, school, or activities: "I'm good at working with people." "I really can sell things." "I'm good at solving problems." "I learn quickly." "I'm reliable. When I say I'll do something, I do it." Be ready to illustrate each with a specific example of something you've done. It is important to relate your strengths to the specific position.

15. **What is your greatest weakness?** Use a work-related negative, even if something in your personal life really is your greatest weakness. Interviewers won't let you get away with a "weakness" like being a workaholic or just not having any experience yet. Instead, use one of these strategies:

   a. Discuss a weakness that is not related to the job you're being considered for and will not be needed even when you're promoted. (Even if you won't work with people or give speeches in your first job, you'll need those skills later in your career, so don't use them for this question.) End your answer with a positive that *is* related to the job.

   [For a creative job in advertising:] I don't like accounting. I know it's important, but I don't like it. I even hire someone to do my taxes. I'm much more interested in being creative and working with people, which is why I find this position interesting.

   [For a job in administration:] I don't like selling products. I hated selling cookies when I was a Girl Scout. I'd much rather work with ideas—and I really like selling the ideas that I believe in.

   b. Discuss a weakness that you are working to improve.

   In the past, I wasn't a good writer. But last term I took a course in business writing that taught me how to organize my ideas and how to revise. I may never win a Pulitzer Prize, but now I can write effective reports and letters.

   c. Describe advice you received and how that advice helped your career.

   The professor for whom I was an undergraduate assistant pointed out to me that people respond well to liberal praise and that I was not liberal with mine. As I have worked on providing more positive feedback, I have become a better manager.

16. **What are your career goals? Where do you want to be in five years? Ten years?** This question is frequently a test to see if you fit with this company. Are your goals ones that can be met at this company? Or will the company have the expense of training you only to see you move on promptly to another company?

17. **Why are you looking for another job?** Do not answer this with a negative—"My boss didn't like me," "I didn't like the work"—even if the negative is true. Stress the new opportunities you're looking for in a new job, not why you want to get away from your old one: "I want more opportunity to work with clients."

   Also be careful of hidden negatives: "I couldn't use all my abilities in my last job" sounds like you are complaining. It also suggests that you don't take the initiative to find new challenges. If you are looking for a job with a bigger salary, it is better to use other points when answering this question.

   If you were fired, say so. There are various acceptable ways to explain why you were fired:

   a. It wasn't a good match. Add what you now know you need in a job, and ask what the employer can offer in this area.

   b. You and your supervisor had a personality conflict. Make sure you show that this was an isolated incident and that you normally get along well with people.

   c. You made mistakes, but you've learned from them and are now ready to work well. Be ready to offer a specific anecdote proving that you have indeed changed.

18. **Why do you have a gap in your employment history?** Answer briefly and positively; do not apologize for family decisions.

> I cared for an ill family member. Because of the time it took, it wasn't fair to an employer to start a new job.

> I stayed home with my children while they were young. Now that they are both in school, I can devote myself to top performance in your company.

If you were laid off, be prepared to explain why you were one of the people let go. It helps if you can truthfully say that all new employees with less than three years' experience at the firm were laid off, that legal services were outsourced, or that the entire training department was disbanded. Be careful you do not display bitter, angry feelings; they will not help you get a new job. It may help you to realize that in tight economies, being laid off is not an issue for many interviewers.

19. **What questions do you have?** This question gives you a chance to cover things the interviewer hasn't brought up; it also gives the interviewer a sense of your priorities and values. Almost all interviewers will ask you for questions, and it is crucial that you have some. A lack of questions will probably be interpreted as a lack of interest in the company and a lack of preparation for the interview. Figure 16.2 lists some questions you might want to ask.

Do not ask:

- Questions about information you can easily find (and should have found) on the company's website.

- Questions that indicate dissatisfaction with the job for which you are being interviewed (How soon can I get promoted?).

- Questions about salary and benefits. Wait until you have a job offer.

Not all questions asked by interviewers are proper. Various federal, state, and local laws prohibit questions that would allow employers to discriminate on the basis of

---

Figure 16.2	Questions to Ask about a Potential Job

- What would I be doing on a day-to-day basis?
- What's the top challenge I would face in this job?
- What kind of training program do you have?
- How do you evaluate employees? How often do you review them?
- What will a good employee have done by the time of their first evaluation?
- Where would you expect a new trainee (banker, staff accountant) to be three years from now? Five years? Ten years?
- What happened to the last person who had this job?
- How would you describe the company's culture?
- This sounds like a great job. What are the drawbacks?
- How are _____ (interest rates, new products from competitors, imports, demographic trends, government regulations, etc.) affecting your company? Questions like these show that you care enough to do your homework and that you are aware of current events.
- What do you like best about working for this company? Ending with a question like this closes your interview on an upbeat note.

protected characteristics such as race, gender, age, and marital status. If you are asked an improper or illegal question during an interview, you have several options:

- You can answer the question, but you may not get hired if you give the "wrong" answer.

- You can refuse to answer the question. Doing so is within your rights, but it may make you look uncooperative or confrontational, so again you may not get hired.

- You can look for the intent behind the question and provide an answer related to the job. For example, if you were asked who would care for your children when you had to work late on an urgent project, you could answer that you can meet the work schedule a good performance requires.

Keep in mind in each situation that legal and illegal questions can be very similar. It is legal to ask if you are over 18, but illegal to ask you how old you are. It is legal to ask you which languages you speak (if that skill is relevant for the job), but it is illegal to ask you what your native language is. Also be careful of variants of illegal questions. For example, asking when you graduated from high school gives the interviewer a pretty good idea of your age.

You won't be able to anticipate every question you may get. Check with other people at your college or university who have interviewed recently to find out what questions are currently being asked in your field. Search the internet for the most common interview questions.

Kinds of Interviews

LO 16-6

Although traditional interviews are still the most popular form of interview, many companies are turning to alternative kinds of interviews that may help them find the best employees. Many companies will inform you about what to expect during the interview, but you should be prepared for these less common interview types. Some of the other kinds of interviews include behavioral, situational, stress, group, and multiple interviews.

Behavioral Interviews

Using the theory that past behaviors predict future performance, **behavioral interviews** ask applicants to describe actual past behaviors, rather than future plans. Thus, instead of asking, "How would you motivate people?" the interviewer might ask, "Tell me what happened the last time you wanted to get other people to do something." Follow-up questions might include, "What exactly did you do to handle the situation? How did you feel about the results? How did the other people feel? How did your superior feel about the results?"

Additional behavioral questions may ask you to describe a situation in which you

- Created an opportunity for yourself in a job or volunteer position.

- Used writing to achieve your goal.

- Went beyond the call of duty to get a job done.

- Communicated successfully with someone you disliked.

- Had to make a decision quickly.

- Took a project from start to finish.

- Used good judgment and logic in solving a problem.

- Worked under a tight deadline.

- Worked with a tough boss.

- Worked with someone who wasn't doing their share of the work.

In your answer, describe the situation, tell what you did, and explain what happened. Think about the implications of what you did, and be ready to talk about whether you'd do the same thing next time or if the situation were slightly different. For example, if you did the extra work yourself when a team member didn't do their share, does that fact suggest that you prefer to work alone? If the organization you're interviewing with values teams, you may want to go on to show why doing the extra work was appropriate in that situation but that you can respond differently in other situations.

A good way to prepare for behavioral interviews is to make a table with five or six columns and rows. Across the top row, list jobs, accomplishments, and projects. Down the left column, list qualities employers will want in candidates for the jobs you seek. These qualities should include skills such as communicating clearly, working in teams, thinking critically, networking, and influencing people. They should also include traits such as honesty, reliability, and a developed ethical sense. Then you fill in the boxes. How does that presentation you made to skeptical administrators demonstrate your communication skills? Your ethics? Your ability to perform under pressure? Make sure each item in your boxes casts you in a favorable light: the ability to work under pressure is generally valued, but if you had to pull three all-nighters to finish your marketing project, employers might see you as a procrastinator.

Situational Interviews

Situational interviews put you in situations similar to those you will face on the job. They test your problem-solving skills, as well as your ability to handle problems under time constraints and with minimal preparation. While behavioral interviews asked how you handled something in the past, situational interviews focus on the future. For instance, for jobs with strong service components, you could expect to be asked how you would handle an angry client. For jobs with manufacturing companies, you might be asked to imagine a new product.

Frequently, situational interviews contain actual tasks candidates are asked to perform. You may be asked to fix some computer coding, sell something to a client, prepare a brochure, or work with an actual spreadsheet. Two favorite tasks are to ask candidates to prepare and give a short presentation with visuals or to work through an online in-box. Both of these tasks test communication and organization skills, as well as the ability to perform under time constraints.

Stress Interviews

Obviously, if the task is complex, performing it at a job interview, particularly with time constraints, is stressful. Thus, situational interviews can easily move into stress interviews. The higher you move in your career, the more likely it is that you will have situational or stress interviews. **Stress interviews** deliberately put applicants under stress to see how they handle the pressure. The key is to stay calm; try to maintain your sense of humor.

Sometimes the stress is physical: for example, you're given a chair where the light is in your eyes. Speak up for yourself: ask if the position of the curtains or blinds can be changed or if you can move to another chair.

Usually, however, the stress is psychological. Panel interviews, such as those for many political appointments, may be stressful. The group of interviewers may fire rapid questions. However, you can slow the pace with deliberate answers. In another possibility, a single interviewer may probe every weak spot in your record and ask questions that elicit negatives. If you get questions that put you on the defensive, rephrase them in less inflammatory terms, if necessary, and then treat them as requests for information.

Q: Why did you major in physical education? That sounds like a pretty Mickey Mouse major.

A: Are you wondering whether I have the academic preparation for this job? I started out in physical education because I've always loved team sports. I learned that I couldn't graduate in four years if I officially switched my major to business administration because the requirements were different in the two programs. But I do have 21 hours in business administration and 9 hours in accounting. And my sports experience gives me practical training in teamwork, motivating people, and management.

Respond assertively. The candidates who survive are those who stand up for themselves and who explain why indeed they *are* worth hiring.

Sometimes the stress comes in the form of unusual questions: Why are manhole covers round? How many tennis balls would fit inside a school bus? If you were a cookie/ car/animal, what kind would you be? If you could be any character from a book, who would you be? How you handle the question will be as important as your answer, maybe more important. Can you think creatively under pressure?

Silence also can create stress. One woman walked into her scheduled interview to find an interviewer with his feet up on the desk. He said, "It's been a long day. I'm tired and I want to go home. You have five minutes to sell yourself." Because she had planned the points she wanted to be sure interviewers knew, she was able to do this. "Your recruiting brochure said that you're looking for someone with a major in accounting and a minor in finance. As you may remember from my résumé, I'm majoring in accounting and have had 12 hours in finance. I've also served as treasurer of a local campaign committee and have worked as a volunteer tax preparer through the Accounting Club." When she finished, the interviewer told her it was a test: "I wanted to see how you'd handle it."

Group Interviews

In **group interviews**, sometimes called "cattle calls," multiple candidates are interviewed at a time. While many interview tips still apply to these interviews, successful candidates also will practice other techniques. Researching the job and company becomes even more important because your time to show how you fit the job will be limited. Have a two-minute summary of your education and experience that shows how you fit this job. Practice it so you can share it during the interview.

Arrive early so you have time to meet as many interviewers and interviewees as possible. Get business cards from the interviewers if you can. This pre-interview time may be part of the test, so make the most of it.

During the interview, listen carefully to both interviewers and interviewees. Make eye contact with both groups as well. Participate in the discussion and look engaged even when you aren't. Watch your body language so you don't give off unintended signals.

Some group interviews are organized around tasks. The group may be asked to solve a problem. Another scenario is that the group will be split into teams, with each team performing a task and then presenting to the whole group. Remember that your participation in these activities is being watched. You will be judged on skills such as communication, persuasion, leadership, organization, planning, analysis, and problem solving. Do you help move the action forward? Are you too assertive? Too shy? Do you praise the contributions of others? Do you help the group achieve consensus? Are you knowledgeable?

Many group interviews particularly test how you interact with other people. Talking too much may work against you. Making an effort to help quiet people enter the discussion may work in your favor. Connecting your comments to previous comments shows you are a good listener as well as a team player. Be careful not to get caught up in a combative situation.

At the end of the interview, thank each interviewer. Follow up with a written thank-you to each interviewer.

Multiple Interviews

Some companies, dissatisfied with hires based on one interview, are turning to **multiple interviews**. Geoff Smart and Randy Street, in their business best seller *Who: The A Method for Hiring*, present a four-interview system for finding the best employees. The system consists of

1. A screening phone interview, which culls the list.
2. A "topgrading" interview, which walks job candidates through their careers so far.

3. A focused interview, which focuses on one desired aspect of the candidate's career.

4. A reference interview, which checks in with candidates' references.[7]

Granted, this system is not for hiring entry-level people, but you won't be entry level for long, even if you are now. If you are scheduled for multiple interviews, you need to pay extra attention to your interview strategy so you provide the interviewers with a consistent view of you and your qualifications. Be prepared to answer some of the same questions multiple times with the same level of enthusiasm each time. Multiple interviews will likely draw on traditional interview questions in the early stages and some of the more focused types of interview questions in the later stages.

Final Steps for a Successful Job Search

LO 16-7

What you do after the interview can determine whether you get the job. Many companies expect applicants to follow up on their interviews within a week. If they don't, the company assumes they wouldn't follow up with clients.

If the employer sends you an email query, answer it promptly. You're being judged not only on what you say but on how quickly you respond. Have your list of references and samples of your work ready to send promptly if requested to do so.

Following Up with Phone Calls and Written Messages

After a first interview, make a follow-up phone call to show enthusiasm for the job, to reinforce positives from the first interview, to overcome any negatives, and to provide information to persuade the interviewer to hire you. Do not stalk the recruiter. Call only once unless you have excellent reasons for multiple calls. If you get voicemail, leave a message. Remember that caller ID will tell the recruiter that you were the person making the multiple hang-ups.

A thank-you note, written within 24 hours of an interview, is essential. Some companies consider the thank-you note to be as important as the cover letter. Figure 16.3 lists what a good thank-you note does.

The note can be an email, but many employers are still impressed by paper thank-you notes. In either case, do not use text messaging abbreviations or emoticons. Figure 16.4 is an example of a follow-up letter after a site visit.

Figure 16.3	Steps for a Good Thank-You Note

- Thank the interviewer for useful information and any helpful action.
- Remind the interviewer of what they liked in you.
- Use the jargon of the company and refer to specific things you learned during your interview or saw during your visit.
- Be enthusiastic about the position.
- Refer to the next move, whether you'll wait to hear from the employer or whether you want to call to learn about the status of your application.
- Thank your hosts for their hospitality if the note is for a site visit. In the postscript, mention enclosed receipts for your expenses.
- Use your best writing skills and correct grammar, capitalization, punctuation, and spelling. Double-check the spelling of all names.

Figure 16.4   Follow-Up Letter after a Site Visit

405 West College, Apt. 201   *Single-space your address and the date*
Thibodaux, LA 70301   *when you don't use letterhead.*
April 2, 2021

Mr. Robert Land, Account Manager
Sive Associates
378 Norman Boulevard
Cincinnati, OH 48528

Dear Mr. Land:

After visiting Sive Associates last week, I'm even more sure that writing direct mail is the career for me.

Refers to things she saw and learned during the interview.

I've always been able to brainstorm ideas, but sometimes, when I had to focus on one idea for a class project, I wasn't sure which idea was best. It was fascinating to see how you make direct mail scientific as well as creative by testing each new creative package against the control. I can understand how pleased Linda Hayes was when she learned that her new package for *Smithsonian* beat the control.

Seeing Kelly, Luke, and Gene collaborating on the Sesame Street package gave me some sense of the tight deadlines you're under. As you know, I've learned to meet deadlines, not only for my class assignments but also in working on Nicholls' newspaper. The award I won for my feature on the primary election suggests that my quality holds up even when the deadline is tight!

Reminds interviewer of her strong points.

Thank you for your hospitality while I was in Cincinnati. You and your wife made my stay very pleasant. I especially appreciate the time the two of you took to help me find information about apartments that are accessible to wheelchairs. Cincinnati seems like a very livable city.

Be positive, not pushy. She doesn't assume she has the job.

I'm excited about a career in direct mail and about the (possibility) of joining Sive Associates. I look forward to hearing from you soon!

Refers to what will happen next.

Sincerely,

Gina Focasio (signature)

Gina Focasio
(504) 555-2948

Writer's phone number.

Puts request for reimbursement in P.S. to de-emphasize it; focuses on the job, not the cost of the trip.

P.S. My expenses totaled $454. Enclosed are receipts for my plane fare from New Orleans to Cincinnati ($367), the taxi to the airport in Cincinnati ($30), and the bus from Thibodaux to New Orleans ($57).

Encl.: Receipts for Expenses

Negotiating for Salary and Benefits

The best time to negotiate for salary and benefits is after you have the job offer. Try to delay discussing salary early in the interview process, when you're still competing against other applicants.

Prepare for salary negotiations by finding out what the going rate is for the work you hope to do. Ask friends who are in the workforce to find out what they're making. Ask the campus placement office for figures on what last year's graduates got. Check trade journals and the web.

This research is crucial. The Bureau of Labor Statistics shows that women earn about 82% as much as men, overall, and sizable differences can be seen in a wide variety of fields.[8] Knowing what a job is worth will give you the confidence to negotiate more effectively.

The best way to get more money is to convince the employer that you're worth it. During the interview process, show that you can do what the competition can't.

After you have the offer, you can begin negotiating salary and benefits. You're in the strongest position when (1) you've done your homework and know what the usual salary and benefits are and (2) you can walk away from this offer if it doesn't meet your needs. Avoid naming a specific salary. Don't say you can't accept less. Instead, say you would find it difficult to accept the job under the terms first offered.

Remember that you're negotiating a package, not just a starting salary. A company that truly can't pay any more money now might be able to review you for promotion sooner than usual, or pay your moving costs, or give you a better job title. Some companies offer fringe benefits that may compensate for lower taxable income: use of a company car, reimbursements for education, child care or elder care subsidies, or help in finding a job for your spouse or partner. And think about your career, not just the initial salary. Sometimes a low-paying job at a company that will provide superb experience will do more for your career (and your long-term earnings prospects) than a high salary now with no room to grow.

Work toward a compromise. You want the employer to be happy that you're coming on board and to feel that you've behaved maturely and professionally.

Deciding Which Offer to Accept

The problem with choosing among job offers is that you're comparing apples and oranges. The job with the most interesting work pays peanuts. The job that pays best is in a city where you don't want to live. The secret of professional happiness is taking a job where the positives are things you want and the negatives are things that don't matter as much to you.

To choose among job offers, you need to know what is truly important to *you*. Start by answering questions like the following:

- Are you willing to work after hours? To take work home? To travel? How important is money to you? Prestige? Time to spend with family and friends?

- Would you rather have firm deadlines or a flexible schedule? Do you prefer working alone or with other people? Do you prefer specific instructions and standards for evaluation or freedom and uncertainty? How comfortable are you with pressure? How much variety and challenge do you want?

- What kinds of opportunities for training and advancement are you seeking?

- Where do you want to live? What features in terms of weather, geography, cultural, and social life do you see as ideal?

- Is it important to you that your work achieve certain purposes or values or do you see work as "just a way to make a living"? Are the organization's culture and ethical standards ones you find comfortable? Will you be able to do work you can point to with pride?

No job is perfect, but some jobs will fulfill more of your major criteria than will others.

Some employers offer jobs at the end of the office visit. In other cases, you may wait for weeks or even months to hear. Some employers may offer jobs orally. In those instances, you must say something in response immediately, so it's good to plan some strategies in advance.

If your first offer is not from your first choice, express your pleasure at being offered the job, but do not accept it on the phone. "That's great! I assume I have two weeks to let you know?" Then *call* the other companies you're interested in. Explain, "I've just gotten a job offer, but I'd rather work for you. Can you tell me what the status of my application is?" Nobody will put that information in writing, but almost everyone will tell you over the phone. With this information, you're in a better position to decide whether to accept the original offer.

Companies routinely give applicants two weeks to accept or reject offers. Some students have been successful in getting those two weeks extended to several weeks or even months. Certainly if you cannot decide by the deadline, it is worth asking for more time: the worst the company can do is say *no*. If you do try to keep a company hanging for a long time, be prepared for weekly phone calls asking you if you've decided yet.

Make your acceptance contingent upon a written job offer confirming the terms. That letter should spell out not only salary, but also fringe benefits and any special provisions you have negotiated. If something is missing, call the interviewer for clarification: "You said that I'd be reviewed for a promotion and higher salary in six months, but that isn't in the letter." Even well-intentioned people can forget oral promises. You have more power to resolve misunderstandings now than you will after six months or a year on the job. Furthermore, the person who made you the promise may no longer be with the company a year later.

When you've accepted one job, notify the other places you visited. Then they can go to their second choices. If you're second on someone else's list, you'll appreciate other candidates' removing themselves so the way is clear for you.

Dealing with Rejection

Because multiple people usually apply for each job opening, most job seekers get far more rejections than job offers. Learn to live with this fact of the job hunt. Form support groups with your friends who are also on the job market. Try to keep an upbeat attitude; it will show in job interviews and make you a more attractive candidate. Remember that candidate selection can be a political process. You may have been competing with an inside candidate or a candidate who was recommended by a respected employee.

Starting Your Career

LO 16-8

Your successful job interview is just the first step toward your career. Once you have landed the job, you need to succeed in the job so it can be a path to your professional goals. Remember that your end goal is not to just have any job; your goal should be to continue to develop your skills and to see a clear path to promotion. Planning a career successfully involves two steps: starting out in the right way in your first full-time job and creating a strategy to achieve your long-term goals.

Your First Full-Time Job

Just like the step from high school to college, the step from college to your first full-time job brings changes that you must negotiate. The new business environment is exhilarating, with many opportunities, but it also contains pitfalls. As you go to being the new kid on the block yet again, remember all the coping strategies you have developed as a newbie in middle school, high school, and college.

- Reread all your materials on the organization, its competition, and the industry.

- Get to know your new colleagues, but also keep networking with people in the field.

- Talk to recent hires in the organization. Ask them what they found to be helpful advice when they were starting.

- Fit into the corporate culture by being observant. Watch what people wear, how they act, how they talk. Watch how they interact during meetings and in the break room. Look at the kinds of emails and letters people send. Discover who people go to when they need help.

- Use your breaks effectively. Stop by the coffee station, water cooler, or break room occasionally to plug into the social grapevine.

- Find a successful person who is willing to mentor you. Even better, find a support network.

- Ask lots of questions. It may feel embarrassing, but it will feel even worse to still be ignorant several months down the road.

- Seek early opportunities for feedback. What you hear may not always be pleasant, but it will help you become a valued employee more quickly.

- Learn the jargon, but use it sparingly.

- Be pleasant and polite to everyone, including support personnel.

- Be punctual. Arrive for work and meetings on time.

- Be dependable. Do what you say you will do—and by the deadline.

- Be organized. Take a few minutes to plan your daily work. Keep track of papers and emails.

- Be resourceful. Few work projects will come to you with the detailed instructions provided by your professors. Think projects through. Ask for suggestions from trusted colleagues. Have a plan before you go to your boss with questions.

- Use technology professionally. Keep your cell phone on vibrate or turn it off. Resist the temptation to send text messages during meetings. Don't visit inappropriate websites; remember that all computer activity can be tracked. Learn the company's internet policies.

- Be discreet. Be careful what you say and where you say it. Above all, be careful what you put in emails!

- Proofread all your written messages, including tweets and texts, before you send them. At rushed times, such as the end of the day or week, proofread them twice.

- Go the extra mile. Help out even when you are not asked. Put in extra hours when your help is needed.

- Do your share of grunt work—making coffee or refilling the paper tray.

- Take advantage of company social events, but always act professionally at them. Seriously limit your intake of alcohol.

- Document your work. Collect facts, figures, and documents. You will need this information for your performance reviews.

- Enjoy yourself. Enthusiasm for your new job and colleagues will help you become part of the team in short order.

A Long-Term Strategy

The *Harvard Business Review* suggests planning for your career in the same way that presidential candidates plan for a campaign: begin early, calculate how to win, and plan a detailed time line of tasks to achieve the goal.[9] These tasks usually include the following:

- Continue to network. The people you know are not just there to help you get a job. Build real relationships that are productive and reciprocal.

- Continue seeking mentors for different aspects of your work.

- Take advantage of voluntary training opportunities.

- Plan where you want to be. Look ahead in your career, not just to your next promotion but to your goals for the next 10 to 20 years.

- Collect work for your professional portfolio.

- Prewrite your future résumé. As you plan your career, write a résumé that you may use in 10 years' time. What jobs do you have on it? What other activities? What is missing from your experience or education that would help you achieve your goals?

- Look for opportunities. Some of the advances in your career will happen by luck or because of chance encounters. Be prepared to take advantage of opportunities by always working hard, talking with people, and keeping your focus on your ultimate goals.

- Read. Read *The Wall Street Journal*, business magazines, trade journals, trade blogs. When Wharton business students asked Warren Buffett where he got his ideas, he replied that he just reads—all day.[10]

Summary by Learning Objectives

LO 16-1   Identify what interview channels you may encounter.

- Phone and video interviews may precede face-to-face interviews.
- Campus interviews and job fairs provide you with opportunities to impress recruiters.

LO 16-2   Create a strategy for successful interviewing.

Develop an overall strategy based on your answers to these three questions:

1. What two to five facts about yourself do you want the interviewer to know?
2. What disadvantages or weaknesses do you need to overcome or minimize?
3. What do you need to know about the job and the organization to decide whether or not you want to accept this job if it is offered to you?

LO 16-3   Determine what preparations to make before you start interviewing.

- Conduct research about the company; spend time on its website.
- Check on dress expectations before the interview.

- Rehearse everything you can. In particular, practice answers to common questions. Ask a friend to interview you. If your campus has practice interviews or video-recording facilities, use them so that you can evaluate and modify your interview behavior.

- Prepare professional materials, including copies of your résumé, a list of references, a work portfolio, and detailed work and education histories in case you are asked to fill out an application form.

LO 16-4   Anticipate what to do during an interview.

- Bring an extra copy of your résumé, something to write on and write with, and copies of your work to the interview.

- Record the name of the interviewer, tips the interviewer gave you, what the interviewer liked about you, answers to your questions about the company, and when you'll hear from the company.

- Behave professionally; show enthusiasm for the job.

LO 16-5   Answer common interview questions.

- Successful applicants know what they want to do, use the company name in the interview, have researched the company in advance, back up claims with specifics, use appropriate technical jargon, ask specific questions, and talk more of the time.

LO 16-6   Prepare for less common interview types.

- Behavioral interviews ask the applicant to describe actual behaviors, rather than plans or general principles. To answer a behavioral question, describe the situation, tell what you did, and tell what happened. Think about the implications of what you did and be ready to talk about what you'd do the next time or if the situation were slightly different.

- Situational interviews put you in a situation that allows the interviewer to see whether you have the qualities the company is seeking.

- Stress interviews deliberately create physical or psychological stress. Change the conditions that create physical stress. Meet psychological stress by rephrasing questions in less inflammatory terms and treating them as requests for information.

- Group interviews involve several candidates at one time. You will need to make sure you are prepared

and focused to take advantage of opportunities to stand out.

- Multiple interviews involve several tiers of interviews. Prepare to answer questions multiple times and to maintain your enthusiasm through a long process.

LO 16-7   Determine what to do after an interview.

- Use follow-up phone calls and written messages to reinforce positives from the first interview and to provide information to persuade the interviewer to hire you.

- The best time to negotiate for salary and benefits is after you have the job offer.

- If your first offer isn't from your first choice, call the other companies you're interested in to ask the status of your application.

LO 16-8   Plan for a successful career.

- Begin your new job well. Work hard, contribute, ask questions, and build your professional network.

- Keep your career goals in mind. Find mentors, network effectively, and plan for 10 years in the future.

Exercises and Cases

16.1   Reviewing the Chapter

1. Name four interview channels. What special considerations do you have to make for them? (LO 16-1)
2. How can you create an effective strategy for your interview? (LO 16-2)
3. What preparations should you make before an interview? (LO 16-3)
4. What are some behavior tips you should keep in mind during an interview? (LO 16-4)
5. What should you accomplish in the close of an interview? (LO 16-4)

6. What are some common interview questions? What are effective answers for you? (LO 16-5)
7. What are three special kinds of interviews you may encounter? What are tips to succeed in them? (LO 16-6)
8. What do you need to do after an interview? (LO 16-7)
9. When do you negotiate for salary? Why? (LO 16-7)
10. What are some tips to help you succeed at your first full-time job? (LO 16-8)
11. How can you plan for a successful career? (LO 16-8)

16.2   Interviewing Job Hunters

Talk to students at your school who are interviewing for jobs this term. Possible questions to ask them include the following:

- What field are you in? How good is the job market in that field this year?

- How long is the first interview with a company, usually?

- What questions have you been asked at job interviews? Were you asked any stressful or sexist questions? Any really oddball questions?

- What answers seemed to go over well? What answers bombed?

- At an office visit or plant trip, how many people did you talk to? What were their job titles?

- Were you asked to take any tests (skills, physical, drugs)?

- How long did you have to wait after a first interview to learn whether you were being invited for an office visit? How long after an office visit did it take to learn whether you were being offered a job? How much time did the company give you to decide?

- What advice would you have for someone who will be interviewing next term or next year?

As your instructor directs,

a.   Summarize your findings in an email to your instructor.

b.   Report your findings orally to the class.

c.   Join with a small group of students to write a group report describing the results of your survey.

16.3   Interviewing an Interviewer

Talk to someone who regularly interviews candidates for entry-level jobs. Possible questions to ask include the following:

- How long have you been interviewing for your organization? Does everyone on the management ladder at your company do some interviewing or do people specialize in it?

- Do you follow a set structure for interviews? What are some of the standard questions you ask?

- What are you looking for? How important are (1) good grades, (2) leadership roles in extracurricular groups, or (3) relevant work experience? What advice would you give to someone who lacks one or more of these?

- What are the things you see students do that create a poor impression? Think about the worst candidate you've interviewed. What did they do (or not do) to create such a negative impression?

- What are the things that make a good impression? Recall the best student you've ever interviewed. Why did they impress you so much?

- How does your employer evaluate and reward your success as an interviewer?

- What advice would you have for someone who still has a year or so before the job hunt begins?

As your instructor directs,

a.   Summarize your findings in a written document for your instructor.

b.   Report your findings orally to the class.

c.   Join with a small group of students to write a group report describing the results of your interviews.

d.   Write to the interviewer thanking them for taking the time to talk to you.

16.4   Analyzing a Video Interview

Analyze a video clip of an interview session.

As your instructor directs,

a.   In groups of four, search on a video-based website such as YouTube for terms such as "interview" or "student interview."

b.   Watch a video clip of an interview and note the strengths and weaknesses of the interviewee.

c.   Discuss your observations with your group and explain why you considered certain responses as strengths and weaknesses.

d.   Share your video and analysis with your class.

16.5   Analyzing a Panel Interview

Watch some of the videos of the confirmation hearings (e.g., job interviews) for Supreme Court Justice Neil Gorsuch. What good interview behaviors do you notice? What interview behaviors do you think could be improved? How does he handle difficult questions?

As your instructor directs,

a.   Share your findings with a small group of other students.

b.   Describe your findings in an email to your instructor.

c.   Present your findings orally to the class.

16.6   Preparing an Interview Strategy

Prepare your interview strategy.

1.   List two to five things about yourself that you want the interviewer to know before you leave the interview.

2.   Identify any weaknesses or apparent weaknesses in your record and plan ways to explain them or minimize them.

3.   List the points you need to learn about an employer to decide whether to accept an office visit or plant trip.

As your instructor directs,

a.   Share your strategy with a small group of other students.

b.   Describe your strategy in an email to your instructor.

c.   Present your strategy orally to the class.

16.7   Preparing Questions to Ask Employers

Prepare a list of questions to ask at job interviews.

1. Prepare a list of three to five general questions that apply to most employers in your field.
2. Prepare two to five specific questions for the three companies you are most interested in.

As your instructor directs,

a. Share the questions with a small group of other students.
b. List the questions in an email to your instructor.
c. Present your questions orally to the class.

16.8   Analyzing Answers to Interview Questions

What might be problematic about these responses to interview questions? How might the answers be improved?

a. Q: Tell me about yourself.

A: I'm really easy-going and casual.

b. Q: I noticed that you had a pretty large break between your last two jobs. What can you tell us about that?

A: Oh, it wasn't a big deal. I just wanted to take some time for myself.

c. Q: Tell me about a collaborative project that you've worked on.

A: I usually work better by myself. I'm very independent.

d. Q: What was your least favorite class in college?

A: Business communication.

e. Q: Tell me about your last boss.

A: Well, I couldn't stand him, but neither could anyone else. He always expected us to stay late to finish up projects.

f. Q: Tell me about a weakness that you have.

A: I always help people when they ask for it. I just love to help.

g. Q: Tell me about a book you have read and enjoyed that wasn't a textbook.

A: We read *To Kill a Mockingbird* in 10th-grade English.

h. Q: What are your interests outside work?

A: I play a lot of video games.

i. Q: What are some of your strengths?

A: I never give up; I am really stubborn. I like to get my work done really quickly, and I hate to waste time on little things.

j. Q: Tell me about a group project that had problems.

A: Our marketing team had a real deadbeat on it. But I saved us by going to the teacher and getting her to take them off the project.

k. Q: Why do you want this job?

A: This is a great job for me. It will really increase my skill set.

16.9   Preparing for the Worst Interview Questions

In small groups, discuss the worst or most difficult interview questions you have ever received. Add to your list by searching the internet for weird or unusual questions. Review your list and discuss how you would answer these questions in an interview. Use the questions to conduct practice interviews and analyze the answers. Share your best two examples with the class.

16.10   Preparing Answers to Questions You May Be Asked

Prepare answers to each of the interview questions listed in this chapter and to any other questions that you know are likely to be asked of job hunters in your field or on your campus.

As your instructor directs,

a. Write down the answers to your questions and turn them in.
b. Conduct mini-interviews in a small group of students. In the group, let student A be the interviewer and ask five questions from the list. Student B will play the job candidate (the interviewee) and answer the questions, using real information about student B's field and qualifications. Student C will evaluate the content of the answer. Student D will observe the nonverbal behavior of the interviewer (A); student E will observe the nonverbal behavior of the interviewee (B).

After the mini-interview, let students C, D, and E share their observations and recommend ways that B could be even more effective. Then switch roles. Let another student be the interviewer and ask five questions of another interviewee, while new observers note content and nonverbal behavior. Continue the process until everyone in the group has had a chance to be "interviewed."

16.11   Writing a Follow-Up Message after a Site Visit

Write a follow-up email message or letter after an office visit or plant trip. Thank your hosts for their hospitality; relate your strong points to things you learned about the company during the visit; allay any negatives that may remain; be enthusiastic about the company.

16.12   Revising a Follow-Up Message after a Site Visit

Revise the follow-up message below to be more professional and effective, based on the principles in this chapter.

December 2, 2021
Ms. Charlotte LeClaire
Pebble Creek Publishing Inc.
New York, NY

Dear Ms. LeClaire:

I wanted to thank you for taking time out of your busy schedule to show me around Pebble Creek Publishing. I really enjoyed it.

I've always wanted to join the publishing field, and Pebble Creek just seemed right to me. I loved watching how all of your employees work together to create the best possible product. They were quite a friendly bunch, especially the guys in the break room.

As you know, I have had extensive editing experience in my English courses that I took here at ISU. I also took a Grammatical Analysis class through the Linguistics program here, which was really helpful for me. I really love making sure things are right, and I would love to do that for your company.

I enjoyed my stay in New York very much. I am so looking forward to moving there very soon!

Thank you so, so much,

Terese Mart
(515) 888-1212

16.13   Clarifying the Terms of a Job Offer

Last week, you got a job offer from your first-choice company, and you accepted it over the phone. Today, the written confirmation arrived. The letter specifies the starting salary and fringe benefits you had negotiated. However, during the office visit, you were promised a 5% raise in six months. The job offer says nothing about the raise. You do want the job, but you want it on the terms you thought you had negotiated.

Write to your contact at the company, Damon Winters.

16.14   Researching a Geographic Area

Research a geographic area where you would like to work. Investigate the cost of living, industrial growth in the area, weather and climate, and attractions in the area you could visit. The local Chamber of Commerce is a good place to start your research.

As your instructor directs,

a.   Share your findings with a small group of other students.
b.   Describe your findings in an email to your instructor.
c.   Present your findings orally to the class.

Notes

1. Accountemps, "The Personal Connection: Survey Shows That in Hiring Process, There's No Substitute for Being There," 2013, http://accountemps.rhi.mediaroom.com/PersonalConnection.

2. Accountemps, "Hiring Manager to Applicant: 'What Is Your Greatest Weakness?': Accountemps Survey Finds Job Seekers Make Most Mistakes during Interview," news release, September 23, 2010, http://accountemps.rhi.mediaroom.com/interview_mistakes.

3. Jenna Goudreau, "CNBC Managing Editor Reveals the 11 Most Common Job Interview Mistakes," *CNBC*, April 3, 2017, https://www.cnbc.com/2017/04/03/the-most-common-interview-mistakes-job-candidates-make.html.

4. Alison Doyle, "How to Dress for an Interview: Dress Code for Job Interviews," *About.com Careers*, accessed June 27, 2013, http://jobsearch.about.com/od/interviewattire/a/interviewdress.htm.

5. Jennifer Alsever, "How AI Is Changing Your Job Hunt," *Fortune*, May 19, 2017, http://fortune.com/2017/05/19/ai-changing-jobs-hiring-recruiting.

6. Dana Mattioli, "Sober Thought: How to Mix Work, Alcohol: Taking Cues from Bosses and Clients Can Keep Parties or Meals under Control," *Wall Street Journal*, December 5, 2006, B10.

7. Geoff Smart and Randy Street, *Who: The A Method for Hiring* (New York: Ballantine, 2008).

8. Sonam Sheth, Shayanne Gal, Madison Hoff, and Marguerite Ward, "7 Charts That Show the Glaring Gap between Men's and Women's Salaries in the US," *Business Insider*, August 26, 2020, https://www.businessinsider.com/gender-wage-pay-gap-charts-2017-3#the-gender-wage-gap-varies-widely-depending-on-the-state-1.

9. Dorie Clark, "A Campaign Strategy for Your Career," *Harvard Business Review* 90, no. 11 (November 2012): 131–34.

10. Carol Loomis, ed., *Tap Dancing to Work: Warren Buffett on Practically Everything, 1966–2012: A Fortune Magazine Book* (New York: Portfolio/Penguin, 2012), 275.

Formatting Letters and Email Messages

Appendix Outline

Formats for Letters

Formats for Envelopes

Formats for Email Messages

Letters normally go to people outside your organization; **memos** go to other people in your organization. Emails go to both audiences. Emails, which are electronic memos, have largely replaced paper memos.

Letters, memos, and emails do not necessarily differ in length, formality, writing style, or pattern of organization. However, letters, memos, and emails do differ in format. **Format** means the parts of a document and the way they are arranged on the page.

Formats for Letters

LO A-1

If your organization has a standard format for letters, use it.

Many organizations and writers choose one of two letter formats: **block format** (see Figure A.1) or the **simplified format** (see Figure A.2). Your organization may make minor changes from the diagrams in margins or spacing.

Use the same level of formality in the **salutation**, or greeting, as you would in talking to someone on the phone: *Dear Glenn* if you're on a first-name basis; *Dear Mr. Helms* if you don't know the reader well enough to use the first name.

Some writers feel that the simplified format is better since the reader is not *Dear.* Omitting the salutation is particularly good when you do not know the reader's name or do not know which courtesy title to use. (For a full discussion of salutations, see Chapter 2.) However, readers like to see their names. Because the simplified format omits the reader's name in the salutation, writers who use this format but who also want to be friendly often try to use the reader's name early in the body of the letter.

The simplified letter format is good in business-to-business mail or in letters where you are writing to anyone who holds a job (admissions officer, customer service representative) rather than to a specific person. However, it is too cold and distancing for cultures that place a premium on relationships.

Sincerely and *Yours truly* are standard **complimentary closes**. When you are writing to people in special groups or to someone who is a friend as well as a business acquaintance, you may want to use a less formal close. Depending on the circumstances, the following informal closes might be acceptable: *Cordially, Thank you*, or even *Cheers.*

In **mixed punctuation**, a colon follows the salutation and a comma follows the close.

A **subject line** tells what the message is about. Subject lines are required in memos and emails; they are optional in letters. Good subject lines are specific, concise, and appropriate for your purposes and the response you expect from your reader:

- When you have good news, put it in the subject line.

- When your information is neutral, summarize it concisely in the subject line.

- When your information is negative, use a negative subject line if the reader may not read the message or needs the information to act. Otherwise, use a neutral subject line.

- When you have a request that will be easy for the reader to grant, put either the subject of the request or a direct question in the subject line.

- When you must persuade a reluctant reader, use a common ground, a benefit, or a neutral subject line.

For examples of subject lines in each of these situations, see Chapters 9, 10, and 11.

A **reference line** refers the reader to the number used on the previous correspondence this letter replies to, or the order or invoice number this letter is about. Very large organizations use numbers on every piece of correspondence they send so that it is possible to find quickly the earlier document to which an incoming letter refers.

Both formats can use headings, lists, and indented sections for emphasis.

Each format has advantages. Both block and simplified can be typed quickly because everything is lined up at the left margin. Block format is the format most frequently used for business letters; readers expect it.

The examples of the two formats in Figures A.1 and A.2 show one-page letters on company letterhead. **Letterhead** is preprinted stationery with the organization's name, logo, address, phone number, and, typically, email address.

When a letter runs two or more pages, use letterhead only for the first page. For the remaining pages, use plain paper that matches the letterhead in weight, texture, and color. Also include a heading on the second page to identify it (see Figure A.3).

> Reader's Name
> Date
> Page Number

Set side margins of 1 inch to 1½ inches on the left and ¾ inch to 1 inch on the right. If you are right justifying, use the 1 inch margin. If your letterhead extends all the way across the top of the page, set your margins even with the ends of the letterhead for the most visually pleasing page. The top margin should be three to six lines under the letterhead, or 1 to 2 inches down from the top of the page if you aren't using letterhead. If your letter is very short, you may want to use bigger side and top margins so that the letter is centered on the page.

The **inside address** gives the reader's name, title (if appropriate), and address. Always double-check to make sure the recipient's name is spelled correctly. To eliminate printing the reader's name and address on an envelope, some organizations use envelopes with cutouts or windows so that the inside address on the letter shows and can be used for delivery. If your organization does this, adjust your margins, if necessary, so that the whole inside address is visible.

Many letters are accompanied by other documents. Whatever these documents may be—a multipage report or a two-line note—they are called **enclosures** because they are enclosed in the envelope. The writer should refer to the enclosures in the body of the letter: "As you can see from my résumé, . . . " The enclosure notation (Encl.:) at the bottom of the letter lists the enclosures. (See Figures A.1, A.2, and A.3.)

Sometimes you write to one person but send copies of your letter to other people. If you want the reader to know that other people are getting copies, list their names on the last page. The abbreviation *cc* originally meant *carbon copy* but now means *computer copy*. Other acceptable abbreviations include *pc* for *photocopy* or simply *c* for *copy*. You also can send copies to other people without telling the reader. Such copies, called **blind computer copies (bcc)**, are not mentioned on the original but are listed on the file copy.

Figure A.1   A Job Reference Letter in Block Format

Bay City Information Systems
151 Bayview Road • San Francisco, CA 81153 • (650) 405-7849 • www.baycity.com

2–6 spaces

September 15, 2021

2–6 spaces

Ms. Mary E. Arcas
Personnel Director
Cyclops Communication Technologies
1050 South Sierra Bonita Avenue
Los Angeles, CA 90019   *Zip code on same line.*

1"–1½"

Dear Ms. Arcas: *Colon in mixed punctuation.*

Do not indent paragraphs.

I am responding to your request for an evaluation of Colleen Kangas. Colleen was hired as a clerk-typist by Bay City Information Systems on April 4, 2019, and was promoted to Administrative Assistant on August 1, 2020. At her review in June, I recommended that she be promoted again. She is an intelligent young woman with good work habits and a good knowledge of computer software.

1" because right margin is justified.

Single-space paragraphs.

As an Administrative Assistant, Colleen not only handles routine duties such as processing time sheets, ordering supplies, and entering data, but also screens calls for two marketing specialists, answers basic questions about Bay City Information Systems, compiles the statistics I need for my monthly reports, and investigates special assignments for me. In the past eight months, she has investigated freight charges, inventoried department hardware, and transferred files to archives. I need only to give her general directions: she has a knack for tracking down information quickly and summarizing it accurately.

Double-space between paragraphs (one blank line).

Although the department's workload has increased during the year, Colleen manages her time so that everything gets done on schedule. She is consistently poised and friendly under pressure. Her willingness to work overtime on occasion is particularly remarkable considering that she has been going to college part-time ever since she joined our firm.

At Bay City Information Systems, Colleen uses Microsoft Word, Excel, and Access software. She tells me that she also uses PowerPoint in her college classes.

If Colleen were staying in San Francisco, we would want to keep her. We would move her into staff work once she completed her degree. I recommend her highly.

1–2 spaces

Sincerely,   *Use a colon in mixed punctuation.*

3–4 spaces

Jeanne Cederlind

Jeanne Cederlind
Vice President, Marketing
jeanne_c@baycity.com

Line up signature block with date.

1–4 spaces

Encl.: Evaluation Form for Colleen Kangas

Leave at least 6 spaces at bottom of page—more if letter is short.

Figure A.2   Simplified Format on Letterhead

McFarlane
HOSPITAL
Memorial

1500 Main Street   Iowa City, IA 52232   (319) 555-3113

2–6 spaces

Line up everything at left margin.

August 24, 2021

2–6 spaces

1"–1½"

Melinda Hamilton
Medical Services Division
Health Management Services, Inc.
4333 Edgewood Road, NE
Cedar Rapids, IA   52401

Triple-space (two blank spaces).   *Subject line in full capital letters.*

REQUEST FOR INFORMATION ABOUT COMPUTER SYSTEMS

No salutation.

We're interested in upgrading our computer system and would like to talk to one of your marketing representatives to see what would best meet our needs. We will use the following criteria to choose a system:

1. Ability to use our current software and data files.

Double-space (one blank space) between items in list if any items are more than one line long.

2. Price, prorated on a three-year expected life.

3. Ability to provide auxiliary services, e.g., controlling inventory of drugs and supplies, monitoring patients' vital signs, and processing insurance forms more quickly.

4. Freedom from downtime.

Triple-space (two blank spaces) between list, next paragraph.

Do not indent paragraphs.

McFarlane Memorial Hospital has 50 beds for acute care and 75 beds for long-term care. In the next five years, we expect the number of beds to remain the same while outpatient care and emergency room care increase.

¾"–1" when right margin is not justified.

Could we meet the first or the third week in September? We are eager to have the new system installed by Christmas if possible.

Please call me to schedule an appointment.

Headings are optional in letters.

No close.

HUGH PORTERFIELD   *Writer's name in full capital letters.*
Controller

1–4 spaces

Encl.:   Specifications of Current System
Databases Currently in Use

cc: Rene Seaburg

Leave 6 spaces at bottom of page—more if letter is short.

Figure A.3   A Two-Page Letter, Block Format

State University

4300 Gateway Boulevard
Midland, TX 78603

August 11, 2021

2–6 spaces

1"–1½"

Ms. Stephanie Voght
Stephen F. Austin High School
1200 Southwest Blvd.
San Antonio, TX 78214

Dear Ms. Voght: *Colon in mixed punctuation.*

Enclosed are 100 brochures about State University to distribute to your students. The brochures describe the academic programs and financial aid available. When you need additional brochures, just let me know.   *1"*

Further information about State University

You may also want your students to learn more about life at State University. You

---

Plain paper for page 2.

½"–1"

Stephanie Voght ← *Reader's name.*
August 11, 2021
Page 2

campus life, including football and basketball games, fraternities and sororities, clubs and organizations, and opportunities for volunteer work. It stresses the diversity of the student body and the very different lifestyles that are available at State.

Triple-space before each new heading (two blank spaces).

Scheduling a State Squad Speaker   *Bold or underline headings.*

Same margins as page 1.
To schedule one of the these dynamic speakers for your students, just fill out the enclosed card with your first, second, and third choices for dates, and return it in the stamped, self-addressed envelope. Dates are reserved in the order that requests arrive. Send in your request early to increase the chances of getting the date you want.

Any one of our State Squad speakers will give your high school students a colorful preview of the college experience. They are also great at answering questions.

1–2 spaces
Sincerely,   *Comma in mixed punctuation.*

3–4 spaces
Michael L. Mahler   *Headings are optional in letters.*

Michael L. Mahler
Director of Admissions

1–4 spaces

Encl.: Brochures, Reservation Form

cc: R. J. Holland, School Superintendent
    Jose Lavilla, President, PTS Association

Figure A.4   Requirements for the Margins of Business Envelopes in the U.S.

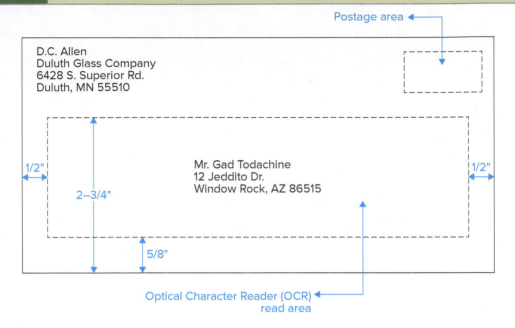

LO A-2   Formats for Envelopes

Business envelopes need to put the reader's name and address in the area that is picked up by the post office's optical character readers (OCRs). Use side margins of at least 1 inch. The bottom margin of the address area must be at least ⅝ inch from the bottom edge of the envelope, and the top margin of the address area must be 2¾ inches from the bottom edge of the envelope (see Figure A.4).

Most businesses use envelopes that already have the return address printed in the upper left-hand corner. When you don't have printed envelopes, print your name (optional); your street address; and your city, state, and zip code in the upper left-hand corner. The OCR doesn't need this information to route your letter, so exact margins don't matter. Use whatever is convenient and looks good to you.

LO A-3   Formats for Email Messages

The "To" line on an email provides the name and email address of the receiver. Double-check that the address is correct because even a one-character mistake will keep the receiver from getting your message. "Cc" denotes computer copies; the recipient will see that these people are getting the message. "Bcc" denotes blind computer copies; the recipient does not see the names of these people. Blind copies can cause hard feelings when they become known, so be sparing in their use. The computer program supplies the date and time automatically.

Most email programs also allow you to attach documents; thus, emails have attachments rather than enclosures.

Even though the email screen has a "To" line, many writers still use an informal salutation, as in Figure A.5. The writer in Figure A.5 also ends the message with a

Figure A.5	A Basic Email Message

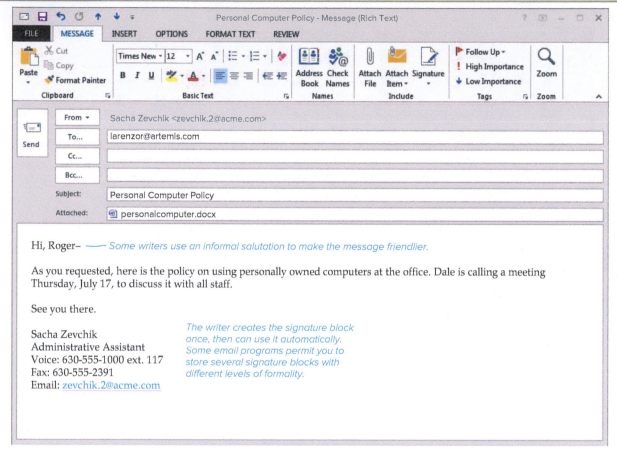

Source: Microsoft Inc

signature block. Signature blocks are particularly useful for email recipients outside the organization who may not know your title or contact information. You can store a signature block in the email program and set the program to insert the signature block automatically.

Sometimes writers omit both the salutation and their names, especially when writing to colleagues with whom they work closely.

Subject lines are important because most businesspeople receive large numbers of emails. Messages with vague subject lines may go unread. The advice for subject lines of letters also applies to emails. Chapters 9, 10, and 11 give more information on subject lines.

When you hit "reply," the email program automatically uses "Re:" (Latin for *about*) and the previous subject line. The original message is set off, usually with one or more vertical lines in the left margin or with carats (see Figure A.6), to help indicate it originated from a separate email. You may want to change the subject line to make it more appropriate for your message.

Figure A.6   An Email Reply with Copies (response to a complaint)

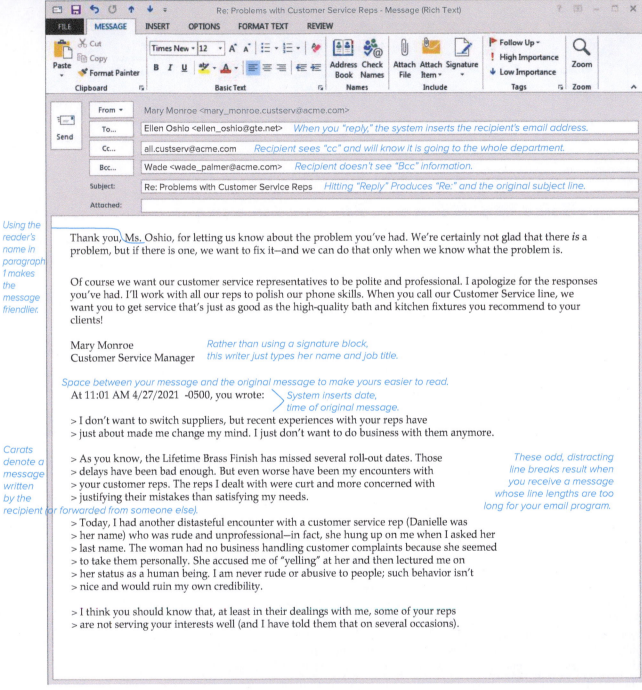

Using the reader's name in paragraph 1 makes the message friendlier.

Thank you, Ms. Oshio, for letting us know about the problem you've had. We're certainly not glad that there *is* a problem, but if there is one, we want to fix it—and we can do that only when we know what the problem is.

Of course we want our customer service representatives to be polite and professional. I apologize for the responses you've had. I'll work with all our reps to polish our phone skills. When you call our Customer Service line, we want you to get service that's just as good as the high-quality bath and kitchen fixtures you recommend to your clients!

Mary Monroe   *Rather than using a signature block,*
Customer Service Manager   *this writer just types her name and job title.*

Space between your message and the original message to make yours easier to read.
At 11:01 AM 4/27/2021 -0500, you wrote: *System inserts date, time of original message.*

> I don't want to switch suppliers, but recent experiences with your reps have
> just about made me change my mind. I just don't want to do business with them anymore.

Carats denote a message written by the recipient (or forwarded from someone else).

> As you know, the Lifetime Brass Finish has missed several roll-out dates. Those
> delays have been bad enough. But even worse have been my encounters with
> your customer reps. The reps I dealt with were curt and more concerned with
> justifying their mistakes than satisfying my needs.

These odd, distracting line breaks result when you receive a message whose line lengths are too long for your email program.

> Today, I had another distasteful encounter with a customer service rep (Danielle was
> her name) who was rude and unprofessional—in fact, she hung up on me when I asked her
> last name. The woman had no business handling customer complaints because she seemed
> to take them personally. She accused me of "yelling" at her and then lectured me on
> her status as a human being. I am never rude or abusive to people; such behavior isn't
> nice and would ruin my own credibility.

> I think you should know that, at least in their dealings with me, some of your reps
> are not serving your interests well (and I have told them that on several occasions).

Source: Microsoft Inc

Writing Correctly

Appendix Outline

After studying this chapter, you should be able to

LO B-1 **Apply common grammar guidelines.**

LO B-2 **Apply punctuation guidelines.**

LO B-3 **Correctly use words that often are confused.**

Too much concern for correctness at the wrong stage of the writing process can backfire: writers who worry about grammar and punctuation when they're writing a first or second draft are more likely to get writer's block. Wait until you have your ideas on paper to check your draft for correct grammar, punctuation, numbers and dates, and word use.

Most writers make a small number of grammatical errors repeatedly. Most readers care deeply about only a few grammatical points. Keep track of the feedback you get (from your instructors now, from your supervisor later) and put your energy into correcting the errors that bother the people who read what you write. A command of grammar will help you build the credible, professional image you want to create with everything you write.

LO B-1 ## Using Grammar

With the possible exception of spelling, grammar is the aspect of writing that writers seem to find most troublesome. Faulty grammar is often what executives are objecting to when they complain that college graduates or MBAs "can't write."

Agreement

1. Subjects and verbs agree when they are both singular or both plural.

   Incorrect: The accountants who conducted the audit was recommended highly.

   Correct: The accountants who conducted the audit were recommended highly.

Subject–verb agreement errors often occur when other words come between the subject and the verb. Edit your draft by finding the subject and the verb of each sentence.

2. Use a plural verb when two or more singular subjects are joined by *and*.

   Correct: Larry McGreevy and I are planning to visit the client.

3. Use a singular verb when two or more singular subjects are joined by *or, nor,* or *but*.

   Correct: Either the shipping clerk or the superintendent has to sign the order.

4. When the sentence begins with *Here* or *There,* make the verb agree with the subject that follows the verb.

   Correct: Here is the booklet you asked for.

   Correct: There are the blueprints I wanted.

5. When a situation doesn't seem to fit the rules, or when following a rule produces an awkward sentence, revise the sentence to avoid the problem.

Problematic:	The plant manager in addition to the sales representative (was, were?) pleased with the new system.
Better:	The plant manager and the sales representative were pleased with the new system.
Problematic:	None of us (is, are?) perfect.
Better:	All of us have faults.

6. The following words require a singular verb:

everybody	neither
each	nobody
either	a person
everyone	

Correct:	Everyone is to blame for this catastrophe.

7. These words used to require a singular pronoun as well. But now, usage has changed and plural pronouns are acceptable:

Correct:	Everyone should bring their copy of the manual to the next session on changes in the law.

8. Each pronoun must refer to a specific word. If a pronoun (such as *this* in the example below) does not refer to a specific term, add a word to correct the error.

Incorrect:	We will open three new stores in the suburbs. This will bring us closer to our customers.
Correct:	We will open three new stores in the suburbs. This strategy will bring us closer to our customers.

9. Use *who* and *whom* to refer to people. *That* and *which* can refer to anything else: animals, organizations, and objects.

Correct:	The new executive director, who moved here from Boston, is already making friends.
Correct:	The information, which she wants now, will be available tomorrow.
Correct:	This invoice confirms the price that I quoted you this morning.

Case

Case refers to the grammatical role a noun or pronoun plays in a sentence. Figure B.1 identifies the case of each personal pronoun in English.

1. Use **nominative case** pronouns for the subject of a clause.

Correct:	Shannon Weaver and I talked to the customer, who was interested in learning more about integrated software.

2. Use **possessive case** pronouns to show who or what something belongs to.

Correct:	Microsoft Office will exactly meet her needs.

3. Use **objective case** pronouns as objects of verbs or prepositions.

Correct:	When you send in the quote, thank them for the courtesy they showed Shannon and me.

Figure B.1	The Case of the Personal Pronoun			
	Nominative	**Possessive**	**Objective**	**Reflexive/Intensive**
Singular				
1st person	I	my, mine	me	myself
2nd person	you	your, yours	you	yourself
3rd person	he/she/it	his/her(s)/its	him/her/it	himself/herself/itself
	one/who	one's/whose	one/whom	oneself/(no form)
	they	their, theirs	them	themself*
Plural				
1st person	we	our, ours	us	ourselves
2nd person	you	your, yours	you	yourselves
3rd person	they	their, theirs	them	themselves

*Throughout this book, we use *they* (and its other forms) as the indefinite singular pronoun, as in "Each manager reports their own sales." This use is in keeping with major style guides. *They* can also be a specific person's preferred pronoun, as opposed to *he* or *she*.

Hint: Use *whom* when either *him* or *her* would fit grammatically in the same place in your sentence. Use *who* when either *he* or *she* would be grammatically correct in the same place in your sentence.

> To (who, whom?) do you intend to give this report?
>
> You intend to give this report to her.

Whom is correct.

> Have we decided (who, whom?) will take notes?
> Have we decided he will take notes?

Who is correct.

4. Use **reflexive pronouns** to refer to or emphasize a noun or pronoun that already has appeared in the sentence.

> Correct: I myself think the call was a very productive one.

5. Do not use reflexive pronouns as subjects of clauses or as objects of verbs or propositions.

> Incorrect: Elaine and myself will follow up on this order.
> Correct: Elaine and I will follow up on this order.
> Incorrect: He gave the order to Dan and myself.
> Correct: He gave the order to Dan and me.

Note that the first-person pronoun comes after names or pronouns that refer to other people.

Dangling Modifier

A **modifier** is a word or phrase that gives more information about the subject, verb, or object in a clause. A **dangling modifier** refers to a wrong word or word that is not actually in the sentence. The solution is to reword the modifier so that it is grammatically correct.

> Incorrect: Confirming our conversation, the truck will leave Monday. [The speaker is doing the confirming. But the speaker isn't in the sentence.]
>
> Incorrect: At the age of eight, I began teaching my children about American business. [This sentence says that the author was eight when they had children who could understand business.]

Correct a dangling modifier in one of these ways:

- Recast the modifier as a subordinate clause.

Correct: As I told you, the truck will leave Monday.

Correct: When my children were eight, I began teaching them about American business.

- Revise the main clause so its subject or object can be modified by the now-dangling phrase.

Correct: Confirming our conversation, I have scheduled the truck to leave Monday.

Correct: At the age of eight, my children began learning about American business.

Hint: Whenever you use a verb or adjective that ends in *-ing,* make sure it modifies the grammatical subject of your sentence. If it doesn't, reword the sentence.

Misplaced Modifier

A **misplaced modifier** appears to modify another element of the sentence than the writer intended.

Incorrect: Customers who complain often alert us to changes we need to make. [Does the sentence mean that customers must complain frequently to teach us something? Or is the meaning that frequently we learn from complaints?]

Correct a misplaced modifier by moving it closer to the word it modifies or by adding punctuation to clarify your meaning. If a modifier modifies the whole sentence, use it as an introductory phrase or clause; follow it with a comma.

Correct: Often, customers who complain alert us to changes we need to make.

Parallel Structure

Items in a series or list must grammatically complete the lead-in sentence and have the same grammatical structure.

Not parallel: In the second month of your internship, you will learn:
1. How to resolve customers' complaints.
2. Supervision of desk staff.
3. To plan store displays.

Parallel: In the second month of your internship, you will:
1. Learn how to resolve customers' complaints.
2. Supervise desk staff.
3. Plan store displays.

Also parallel: Duties in the second month of your internship include resolving customers' complaints, supervising desk staff, and planning store displays.

Predication Errors

The predicate of a sentence must fit grammatically and logically with the subject. Make sure that the verb describes the action done by or done to the subject.

Incorrect: Our goals should begin immediately.

Correct: Implementing our goals should begin immediately.

In sentences using *is* and other linking verbs, the complement must be a noun, an adjective, or a noun clause (not a subordinate clause as in the incorrect example below).

Incorrect: The reason for this change is because the SEC now requires fuller disclosure.

Correct: The reason for this change is that the SEC now requires fuller disclosure.

LO B-2

Understanding Punctuation

Punctuation marks are road signs to help readers predict what comes next. (See Figure B.2.)

When you move from the subject to the verb, you're going in a straight line; no comma is needed. When you end an introductory phrase or clause, the comma tells readers the introduction is over and you're turning to the main clause. When words interrupt the main clause, like this, commas tell the reader when to turn off the main clause for a short side route and when to return.

Some people have been told to put commas where they'd take breaths. That's bad advice. How often you'd take a breath depends on how big your lung capacity is, how fast and loud you're speaking, and how much emphasis you want. Commas aren't breaths. It's better to think of them (and other punctuation) as road signs.

Punctuating Sentences

A sentence contains at least one main clause. A **main or independent clause** is a complete statement. It contains a subject and a tensed verb. A **subordinate or dependent clause** contains both a subject and a tensed verb but is not a complete statement and cannot stand by itself. A phrase is a group of words that does not contain both a subject and a tensed verb.

Main clauses

> Your order will arrive Thursday.
>
> He dreaded talking to his supplier.
>
> I plan to enroll for summer school classes.

Subordinate clauses

> If you place your order by Monday
>
> Because he was afraid the product would be out of stock
>
> When I graduate next spring

Figure B.2	What Punctuation Tells the Reader
Mark	**Tells the reader**
Period	We're stopping.
Semicolon	What comes next is closely related to what I just said.
Colon	What comes next is an example of what I just said.
Dash	What comes next is a dramatic example of or a shift from what I just said.
Comma	What comes next is a slight turn, but we're going in the same basic direction.

Phrases

> With our current schedule
>
> As a result
>
> After talking to my advisor

A clause with one of the following words, called **subordinating conjunctions**, will be subordinate:

after	if
although	when
though	whenever
because	while
since	as
before	
until	

Using the correct punctuation will enable you to avoid four major sentence errors: comma splices, run-on sentences, fused sentences, and sentence fragments.

Comma Splices

A **comma splice or comma fault** occurs when two main clauses are joined only by a comma (instead of by a comma and a **coordinating conjunction**).

> Incorrect: The contest will start in June, the date has not been set.

Correct a comma splice in one of the following ways:

- If the ideas are closely related, use a semicolon rather than a comma. If they aren't closely related, start a new sentence.

> Correct: The contest will start in June; the exact date has not been set.

- Add a coordinating conjunction.

> Correct: The contest will start in June, but the exact date has not been set.

- Subordinate one of the clauses.

> Correct: Although the contest will start in June, the exact date has not been set.

Remember that you cannot use just a comma with transition words such as these:

however	nevertheless	indeed	furthermore
therefore	moreover	consequently	still

Instead, either use a semicolon to separate the clauses or start a new sentence.

> Incorrect: Computerized grammar checkers do not catch every error, however, they may be useful as a first check before an editor reads the material.
>
> Correct: Computerized grammar checkers do not catch every error; however, they may be useful as a first check before an editor reads the material.

Run-on Sentences

A **run-on sentence** strings together several main clauses using *and, but, or, so,* and *for.* Run-on sentences and comma splices are "mirror faults." A comma splice uses *only* the comma and omits the coordinating conjunction, while a run-on sentence uses *only* the conjunction and omits the comma. Correct a short run-on sentence by adding a comma. Separate a long run-on sentence into two or more sentences. Consider subordinating one or more of the clauses.

Incorrect: We will end up with a much smaller markup but they use a lot of this material **so** the volume would be high **so** try to sell them on fast delivery **and** tell them our quality is very high.

Correct: Although we will end up with a much smaller markup, volume would be high because they use a lot of this material. Try to sell them on fast delivery and high quality.

Fused Sentences

A **fused sentence** results when two sentences or more are joined (or *fused*) with neither punctuation nor conjunctions. To fix the error, add the punctuation, add punctuation and a conjunction, or subordinate one of the clauses.

Incorrect: The advantages of intranets are clear the challenge is persuading employees to share information.

Correct: The advantages of intranets are clear; the challenge is persuading employees to share information.

Also correct: Although the advantages of intranets are clear, the challenge is persuading employees to share information.

Sentence Fragments

In a **sentence fragment**, a group of words that is not a complete sentence is punctuated as if it were a complete sentence.

Incorrect: Observing these people, I have learned two things about the program. The time it takes. The rewards it brings.

To fix a sentence fragment, either add whatever parts of the sentence are missing or incorporate the fragment into the sentence before it or after it.

Correct: Observing these people, I have learned that the program is time consuming but rewarding.

Remember that clauses with the following words are not complete sentences. Join them to a main clause.

after	if
although	when
though	whenever
because	while
since	as
before, until	

Incorrect: We need to buy a new computer system. Because our current system is obsolete.

Correct: We need to buy a new computer system because our current system is obsolete.

Punctuation within Sentences

Good writers know how to use the following punctuation marks: apostrophes, colons, commas, dashes, hyphens, parentheses, periods, and semicolons.

Apostrophe

1. Use an apostrophe in a contraction to indicate that a letter or symbol has been omitted.

   We're trying to renegotiate the contract.

   The '90s were years of restructuring for our company.

2. To indicate possession, add an apostrophe and an *s* to the word.

   The corporation's home office is in Houston, Texas.

   Apostrophes to indicate possession are especially essential when one noun in a comparison is omitted.

   This year's sales will be higher than last year's.

   When a word already ends in an *s,* add an apostrophe or an apostrophe and *s* to make it possessive.

   The meeting will be held at New Orleans' convention center.

   With many terms, the placement of the apostrophe indicates whether the noun is singular or plural.

   Incorrect: The program should increase the participant's knowledge. [Implies that only one participant is in the program.]

   Correct: The program should increase the participants' knowledge. [Many participants are in the program.]

   Hint: Use "of" in the sentence to see where the apostrophe goes.

   The figures of last year = last year's figures.

   The needs of our customers = our customers' needs.

   Note that possessive pronouns (e.g., *his, ours*) usually do not have apostrophes. The only exception is *one's.*

   The company needs the goodwill of its stockholders.

   His promotion was announced yesterday.

   One's greatest asset is the willingness to work hard.

3. Do not use an apostrophe to make plurals.

   Incorrect: We meet on Thursday's to discuss our social media reports.

   Correct: We meet on Thursdays to discuss our social media reports.

Colon

1. Use a colon to separate a main clause and a list that explains the last element in the clause. The items in the list are specific examples of the word that appears immediately before the colon.

   Please order the following supplies:

   Printer cartridges

   Computer paper (20-lb white bond)

   Bond paper (25-lb, white, 25% cotton)

   Company letterhead

   Company envelopes

When the list is presented vertically, capitalize the first letter of each item in the list. When the list is run in with the sentence, you don't need to capitalize the first letter after the colon.

Please order the following supplies: printer cartridges, computer paper (20-lb white bond), bond paper (25-lb, white, 25% cotton), company letterhead, and company envelopes.

Do not use a colon when the list is grammatically part of the main clause.

Incorrect:	The rooms will have coordinated decors in natural colors, such as: eggplant, moss, and mushroom.
Correct:	The rooms will have coordinated decors in natural colors, such as eggplant, moss, and mushroom.
Also correct:	The rooms will have coordinated decors in a variety of natural colors: eggplant, moss, and mushroom.

If the list is presented vertically, some style guides suggest introducing the list with a colon even though the words preceding the colon are not a complete sentence.

2. Use a colon to join two independent clauses when the second clause explains or restates the first clause.

Selling is simple: give people the service they need, and they'll come back with more orders.

Comma

1. Use commas to separate the main clause from an introductory clause, the reader's name, or words that interrupt the main clause. Note that commas both precede and follow the interrupting information.

R. J. Garcia, the new sales manager, comes to us from the Duluth office.

A **nonrestrictive** (nonessential) **clause** gives extra information that is not needed to identify the noun it modifies. Because nonrestrictive clauses give extra information, they need extra commas.

Amita Decker, who wants to advance in the organization, has signed up for the company training program in sales techniques.

Do not use commas to set off information that restricts the meaning of a noun or pronoun. **Restrictive clauses** give essential, not extra, information.

Anyone who wants to advance in the organization should take advantage of on-the-job training.

The clause "who wants to advance in the organization" restricts the meaning of the pronoun *anyone*. Do not use commas to separate the subject from the verb, even if you would take a breath after a long subject.

Incorrect:	Laws requiring registration of anyone collecting $5,000 or more on behalf of another person, apply to schools and private individuals as well to charitable groups and professional fund-raisers.
Correct:	Laws requiring registration of anyone collecting $5,000 or more on behalf of another person apply to schools and private individuals as well to charitable groups and professional fund-raisers.

2. Use a comma, with a conjunction, after the first clause in a compound sentence.

   This policy eliminates all sick-leave credit of the employee at the time of retirement, and payment will be made only once to any individual.

   Do not use commas to join independent clauses without a conjunction. Doing so produces comma splices.

3. Use commas to separate items in a series. Using a comma before the *and* or *or* is not required by some authorities, but using a comma always adds clarity. The comma is essential if any of the items in the series themselves contain the word *and*.

   The company pays the full cost of hospitalization insurance for eligible employees, spouses, and unmarried dependent children under age 23.

Dash

Use dashes to emphasize a break in thought.

   Ryertex comes in 30 grades—each with a special use.

To type a dash, use two hyphens with no space before or after.

Hyphen

Use hyphens to join two or more words used as a single adjective. The hyphen prevents misreading. In the second example, without the hyphen, the reader might think that *computer* was the subject and *prepared* was the verb.

   The computer-prepared income and expense statements will be ready next Friday.

In the next example, five lengths are needed, not lengths of 5, 10, or 12 feet.

   Order five 10- or 12-foot lengths.

   If you are unsure whether two words should be joined by a hyphen, consult a dictionary or a usage guide.

Parentheses

1. Use parentheses to set off words, phrases, or sentences used to explain or comment on the main idea.

   For the thinnest Ryertex (.015″) only a single layer of the base material may be used, while the thickest (10″) may contain over 600 greatly compressed layers of fabric or paper. By varying the fabric used (cotton, asbestos, glass, or nylon) or the type of paper, and by changing the kind of resin (phenolic, melamine, silicone, or epoxy), we can produce 30 different grades.

   Any additional punctuation goes outside the second parenthesis when the punctuation applies to the whole sentence. It goes inside when it applies only to the words in the parentheses.

   Please check the invoice to see if credit should be issued. (A copy of the invoice is attached.)

2. Use parentheses for in-text citations for sources that you cite. For help with APA style, see https://apastyle.apa.org/.

Period

1. Use a period at the end of a sentence. Use only one space before the next sentence.
2. Use a period after some abbreviations. When a period is used with a person's initials, leave one space after the period before the next letter or word. In other abbreviations, no space is necessary.

    R. J. Tebeaux has been named Vice President for Marketing.

    The U.S. division plans to hire 300 new M.B.A.s in the next year.

    The trend is to reduce the use of punctuation. It also would be correct to write

    The US division plans to hire 300 new MBAs in the next year.

Semicolon

1. Use semicolons to join two independent clauses when they are closely related.

    We'll do our best to fill your order promptly; however, we cannot guarantee a delivery date.

    Using a semicolon suggests that the two ideas are very closely connected. Using a period and a new sentence also is correct but implies nothing about how closely related the two sentences are.

2. Use semicolons to separate items in a series when the items themselves contain commas.

    The final choices for the new plant are El Paso, Texas; Albuquerque, New Mexico; Salt Lake City, Utah; Eureka, California; and Eugene, Oregon.

    Hospital benefits also are provided for certain specialized care services such as diagnostic admissions directed toward a definite disease or injury; normal maternity delivery, Caesarean section delivery, or complications of pregnancy; and in-patient admissions for dental procedures necessary to safeguard the patient's life or health.

    Hint: A semicolon could be replaced by a period and a capital letter. It has a sentence on both sides.

Special Punctuation Marks

Quotation marks, square brackets, ellipses, and italics are necessary when you use quoted material.

Quotation Marks

1. Use quotation marks around the names of brochures, pamphlets, academic journal articles, and magazine articles.

    Enclosed are 30 copies of our pamphlet "Saving Energy."

    You'll find articles like "How to Improve Your Golf Game" and "Can You Keep Your Eye on the Ball?" in every issue.

    In U.S. punctuation, periods and commas go inside quotation marks. Colons and semicolons go outside. Question marks go inside if they are part of the material being quoted.

2. Use quotation marks around words to indicate that you think the term is misleading.

    These "pro-business" policies actually increase corporate taxes.

3. Use quotation marks around words that you are discussing as words.

   Forty percent of the respondents answered "yes" to the first question.

   Use "Ms." as a courtesy title for a woman unless you know she prefers another title.

   It is also acceptable, in this case, to italicize words instead of using quotation marks.

4. Use quotation marks around words or sentences that you quote from someone else.

   "The Fog Index," says its inventor, Robert Gunning, is "an effective warning system against drifting into needless complexity."

Square Brackets

Use square brackets to add your own additions to or changes in quoted material.

Senator Smith's statement:	"These measures will create a deficit."
Your use of Smith's statement:	According to Senator Smith, "These measures [in the new tax bill] will create a deficit."

The square brackets show that Smith did not say these words; you added them to make the quote make sense in your document.

Ellipses

Ellipses are spaced dots. Use three spaced periods for an ellipsis. When an ellipsis comes at the end of a sentence, use a period immediately after the last letter of the sentence. Then add three spaced periods, with another space after the last period.

1. Use ellipses to indicate that one or more words have been omitted in the middle of quoted material. You do not need ellipses at the beginning or end of a quote.

   The Wall Street Journal notes that Japanese magazines and newspapers include advertisements for a "$2.1 million home in New York's posh Riverdale section . . . 185 acres of farmland [and] . . . luxury condos on Manhattan's Upper East Side."

2. In advertising and direct mail, use ellipses to imply the pace of spoken comments.

   If you've ever wanted to live on a tropical island . . . cruise to the Bahamas . . . or live in a castle in Spain . . .

   . . . you can make your dreams come true with Vacations Extraordinaire.

Italics

1. Italicize the names of newspapers, magazines, and books.

   San Francisco Chronicle

   Fortune

   The Wealth of Nations

   Titles of brochures and pamphlets are put in quotation marks.

2. Italicize words to emphasize them.

   Here's a bulletin that gives you, in handy chart form, *workable data* on over 50 different types of tubing and pipe.

   Use italics rather than underlining for emphasis.

Writing Numbers and Dates

1. Spell out numbers from one to nine. Use figures for numbers 10 and over in most cases. Always use figures for amounts of money.

    The new office costs $1.7 million.

Large numbers frequently use a combination of numbers and words.

    More than 20 million people are affected by this new federal regulation.

2. Spell out any number that appears at the beginning of a sentence. If spelling it out is impractical, revise the sentence so that it does not begin with a number.

    Fifty students filled out the survey.

    In 2002, euro notes and coins entered circulation.

3. When two numbers follow each other, spell out the smaller number and use figures for the larger number.

    The committee members read over 20 five-year reports.

4. In dates, use figures for the day and year. The month is normally spelled out. Be sure to spell out the month in international business communication. American usage puts the month first, so that 1/6/21 means *January 6, 2021*. European usage puts the day first, so that 1/6/21 means *June 1, 2021*. Modern punctuation uses a comma before the year only when you give both the month and the day of the month:

    May 1, 2021

but

    Summers 2017–21

    August 2021

    Fall 2021

No punctuation is needed in military or European usage, which puts the day of the month first: 13 July 2021.

5. Use an en dash (a short dash that is slightly wider than the hyphen) to join inclusive dates.

    March–August 2022 (or write out: March to August 2022)

    '19–'22

    2019–2022

Note that you do not need to repeat the century in the date that follows the en dash: 2019–22.

LO B-3 Words That Often Are Confused

Here's a list of words that frequently are confused. Master them, and you'll be well on the way to using words correctly.

1. accede/exceed
    accede: to yield
    exceed: to go beyond, surpass

        I accede to your demand that we not exceed the budget.

2. accept/except
    accept: to receive; to agree to
    except: to leave out or exclude; but

        I accept your proposal except for point 3.

3. access/excess

   access: the right to use; admission to

   excess: surplus

   As supply clerk, they had access to any excess materials.

4. adapt/adopt

   adapt: adjust

   adopt: to take as one's own

   She would adapt her ideas so people would adopt them.

5. advice/advise

   advice: (noun) counsel

   advise: (verb) to give counsel or advice to someone

   I asked them to advise me, but I didn't like the advice I got.

6. affect/effect

   affect: (verb) to influence or modify

   effect: (verb) to produce or cause; (noun) result

   They hoped that their argument would affect their boss's decision, but so far as they could see, it had no effect.

   The tax relief effected some improvement for the citizens whose incomes had been affected by inflation.

7. affluent/effluent

   affluent: (adjective) rich, possessing in abundance

   effluent: (noun) something that flows out

   Affluent companies can afford the cost of removing pollutants from the effluents their factories produce.

8. a lot/allot

   a lot: many (informal and always spelled as two words, not one)

   allot: divide or give to

   A lot of players signed up for this year's draft. We allotted one first-round draft choice to each team.

9. among/between

   among: (use with more than two choices)

   between: (use with only two choices)

   This year the differences between the two candidates for president are unusually clear.

   I don't see any major differences among the candidates for city council.

10. amount/number

    amount: (use with concepts or items that can be measured but that cannot be counted individually)

    number: (use when items can be counted individually)

    It's a mistake to try to gauge the amount of interest they have by the number of questions they ask.

11. attributed/contributed

    attributed: was said to be caused by

    contributed: gave something to

    The rain probably contributed to the accident, but the police officer attributed the accident to driver error.

12. cite/sight/site

    cite: (verb) to quote

sight: (noun) vision, something to be seen

site: (noun) location, place where a building is or will be built

> They cited the old story of the building inspector who was depressed by the very sight of the site for the new factory.

13. complement/compliment

complement: (verb) to complete, finish; (noun) something that completes

compliment: (verb) to praise; (noun) praise

> The compliment they gave me complemented my happiness.

14. compose/comprise

compose: make up, create

comprise: consist of, be made up of, be composed of

> Twelve members compose the city council. Each district comprises 50 square blocks.

15. confuse/complicate/exacerbate

confuse: to bewilder

complicate: to make more complex or detailed

exacerbate: to make worse

> Because I missed the first 20 minutes of the movie, I didn't understand what was going on. The complicated plot exacerbated my confusion.

16. continual/continually/continuous/continuously

continual (adjective)/continually (adverb): recurs at regular intervals

continuous (adjective)/continuously (adverb): happens without stopping

> The loud, continuous drone of the machinery meant we had to take continual breaks.

17. different from/different than

> Almost always *different from* (try changing the adjective *different* to the verb *differs*)

>> Bob's job description is different from mine.

> The most common exception is the indirect comparison.

>> Inaya has a different attitude than you and I [*do* is implied].

18. discreet/discrete

discreet: tactful, careful not to reveal secrets

discrete: separate, distinct

> I have known them to be discreet on two discrete occasions.

19. disinterested/uninterested

Disinterested: impartial

Uninterested: unconcerned

> Because our boss is uninterested in office spats, she makes a disinterested referee.

20. elicit/illicit

elicit: (verb) to draw out

illicit: (adjective) not permitted, unlawful

> The reporter could elicit no information from the senator about the illicit love affair.

21. eminent/immanent/imminent

eminent: distinguished

immanent: existing in the mind or consciousness

imminent: about to happen

> The eminent doctor believed that the patient's death was imminent.

22. farther/further

    farther: use for physical difference

    further: use for metaphoric difference; also use for *additional* or *additionally*

    > As I traveled farther from the destruction at the plant, I pondered the further evidence of sabotage presented to me today.

23. fewer/less

    fewer: use for objects that can be counted individually

    less: use for objects that can be measured but not counted individually

    > There is less sand in this bucket; there are probably fewer grains of sand, too.

24. forward/foreword

    forward: ahead

    foreword: preface, introduction

    > The author looked forward to writing the foreword to the book.

25. good/well

    good: (adjective) used to modify nouns

    well: (adverb) used to modify verbs, adjectives, and other adverbs

    > Her words "Good work!" told them that they were doing well.

26. i.e.,/e.g.,

    i.e.,: (id est—that is) introduces a restatement or explanation of the preceding word or phrase

    e.g.,: (exempli gratia—for the sake of an example; for example) introduces one or more examples

    > The position required multiple skills (e.g., TIG welding, thermal cutting, and grinding).

    > The anatomy class requires the field's main style manual (i.e., *AMA Manual of Style*).

27. imply/infer

    imply: suggest, put an idea into someone's head

    infer: deduce, get an idea from something

    > She implied that an announcement would be made soon. I inferred from her smile that it would be an announcement of her promotion.

28. it's/its

    it's: it is, it has

    its: belonging to it

    > It's clear that a company must satisfy its customers to stay in business.

29. lectern/podium

    lectern: raised stand with a slanted top that holds a manuscript for a reader or notes for a speaker

    podium: platform for a speaker or conductor to stand on

    > I left my notes on the lectern when I left the podium at the end of my talk.

30. lie/lay

    lie: to recline; to tell a falsehood (never takes an object)

    lay: to put an object on something (always takes an object)

    > He was laying the papers on the desk when I came in, but they aren't lying there now.

31. loose/lose

    loose: not tight

    lose: to have something disappear

If I lose weight, this suit will be loose.

32. moral/morale

moral: (adjective) virtuous, good; (noun: morals) ethics, sense of right and wrong

morale: (noun) spirit, attitude, mental outlook

> Studies have shown that coed dormitories improve student morale without harming student morals.

33. objective/rationale

objective: goal

rationale: reason, justification

> The objective of the meeting was to explain the rationale behind the decision.

34. personal/personnel

personal: individual, to be used by one person

personnel: staff, employees

> All personnel will get personal computers by the end of the year.

35. possible/possibly

possible: (adjective) something that can be done

possibly: (adverb) perhaps

> It is possible that we will be able to hire this spring. We can choose from possibly the best graduating class in the past five years.

36. precede/proceed

precede: (verb) to go before

proceed: (verb) to continue; (noun: proceeds) money

> Raising the money must precede spending it. Only after we obtain the funds can we proceed to spend the proceeds.

37. principal/principle

principal: (adjective) main; (noun) person in charge; money lent out at interest

principle: (noun) basic truth or rule, code of conduct

> *The Prince,* Machiavelli's principal work, describes his principles for ruling a state.

38. proscribe/prescribe

proscribe: to forbid

prescribe: to specify the features something must contain

> The law prescribes the priorities for making repairs. This new law also proscribes carbon emissions.

39. quiet/quite

quiet: not noisy

quite: very

> It was quite difficult to find a quiet spot anywhere near the floor of the stock exchange.

40. regulate/relegate

regulate: control

relegate: put (usually in an inferior position)

> If the federal government regulates the size of lettering on country road signs, we may as well relegate the current signs to the garbage bin.

41. respectfully/respectively

respectfully: with respect

respectively: to each in the order listed

> When I was introduced to the queen, the prime minister, and the court jester, I bowed respectfully, shook hands politely, and winked, respectively.

42. role/roll

    role: part in a play or script, function (in a group)

    roll: (noun) list of students, voters, or other members; round piece of bread; (verb) move by turning over and over

    > While the teacher called the roll, George—in his role as class clown—threw a roll he had saved from lunch.

43. simple/simplistic

    simple: not complicated

    simplistic: watered down, oversimplified

    > She was able to explain the proposal in simple terms without making the explanation sound simplistic.

44. stationary/stationery

    stationary: not moving, fixed

    stationery: paper

    > During the earthquake, even the stationery was not stationary.

45. their/there/they're

    their: belonging to them

    there: in that place

    they're: they are

    > There are plans, designed to their specifications, for the house they're building.

46. to/too/two

    to: (preposition) function word indicating proximity, purpose, time, etc.

    too: (adverb) also, very, excessively

    two: (adjective) the number 2

    > The formula is too secret to entrust to two people.

47. unique/unusual

    unique: sole, only, alone

    unusual: not common

    > I believed that I was unique in my ability to memorize long strings of numbers until I consulted *Guinness World Records* and found that I was merely unusual: someone else had equaled my feat in 1993.

48. verbal/oral

    verbal: using words

    oral: spoken, not written

    > His verbal skills were uneven: his oral communication was excellent, but he didn't write well. His sensitivity to nonverbal cues was acute: he could tell what kind of day I had just by looking at my face.

    Hint: Oral comes from the Latin word for mouth, *os.* Verbal comes from the Latin word for word, *verba.* Nonverbal language is language that does not use words (e.g., body language, gestures).

49. whether/weather

    whether: (conjunction) used to introduce possible alternatives

    weather: (noun) state of the atmosphere: wet or dry, hot or cold, calm or storm

    > We will have to see what the weather is before we decide whether to hold the picnic indoors or out.

50. your/you're

    your: belonging to you

    you're: you are

    > You're the top candidate for promotion in your division.

Exercises and Cases

B.1   Diagnostic Test on Punctuation and Grammar

Identify and correct the errors in the following passages.

a. Company's are finding it to their advantage to cultivate their suppliers. Partnerships among a company and it's suppliers can yield hefty payoffs for both company and supplier. One example is Bailey Controls an Ohio headquartered company. Bailey make control systems for big factories. They treat suppliers almost like departments of their own company. When a Bailey employee passes a laser scanner over a bins bar code the supplier is instantly alerted to send more parts.

b. Entrepreneur Trip Hawkins appears in Japanese ads for the video game system his company designed. "It plugs into the future! he says in one ad, in a cameo spliced into shots of U.S kids playing the games. Hawkins is one of several US celebrities and business people whom plug products on Japanese TV. Jodie Foster, Harrison Ford and Charlie Sheen advertise canned coffee beer and cigarettes respectively.

c. Mid size firms employing between 100 and 1000 people represent only 4% of companies in the U.S.; but create 33% of all new jobs. One observer attributes their success to their being small enough to take advantage of economic opportunity's agilely, but big enough to have access to credit and to operate on a national or even international scale. The biggest hiring area for midsize company's is wholesale and retail sales (38% of jobs), construction (20% of jobs, manufacturing (19% of jobs), and services (18 of jobs).

B.2   Providing Punctuation I

Provide the necessary punctuation in the following sentences. Note that not every box requires punctuation.

1. The system □ s □ user □ friendly design □ provides screen displays of work codes □ rates □ and client information.

2. Many other factors also shape the organization □ s □ image □ advertising □ brochures □ proposals □ stationery □ calling cards □ etc.

3. Charlotte Ford □ author of □ Charlotte Ford □ s □ Book of Modern Manners □□ says □□ Try to mention specifics of the conversation to fix the interview permanently in the interviewer □ s □ mind and be sure to mail the letter the same day □ before the hiring decision is made □□

4. What are your room rates □ and charges for food service □

5. We will need accommodations for 150 people □ five meeting rooms □ one large room and four small ones □□ coffee served during morning and afternoon breaks □ and lunches and dinners.

6. The Operational Readiness Inspection □ which occurs once every three years □ is a realistic exercise □ which evaluates the National Guard □ s □ ability to mobilize □ deploy □ and fight.

7. Most computer packages will calculate three different sets of percentages □ row percentages □ column percentages □ and table percentages □

8. In today □ s □ economy □ it □ s almost impossible for a firm to extend credit beyond it □ s regular terms.

9. Don't let customers think you are a stick □ in □ the □ mud, but don't feel that you must stay up until two o'clock with them either.

10. The program has two goals □ to identify employees with promise □ and to see that they get the training they need to advance.

B.3   Providing Punctuation II

Provide the necessary punctuation in the following sentences. Note that not every box requires punctuation.

1. Office work ☐ especially at your desk ☐☐ can create back ☐ shoulder ☐ neck ☐ or wrist strain.
2. I searched for ☐ vacation ☐ and ☐ vacation planning ☐ on Google.
3. I suggest putting a bulletin board in the rear hallway ☐ and posting all the interviewer ☐ s ☐ photos on it.
4. Analyzing audiences is the same for marketing and writing ☐ you have to identify who the audiences are ☐ understand how to motivate them ☐ and choose the best channel to reach them.
5. The more you know about your audience ☐☐ who they are ☐ what they buy ☐ where they shop ☐☐ the more relevant and effective you can make your ad.
6. The city already has five ☐ two ☐ hundred ☐ bed hospitals.
7. Students run the whole organization ☐ and are advised by a board of directors from the community.
8. The company is working on three team ☐ related issues ☐ interaction ☐ leadership ☐ and team size.
9. I would be interested in working on the committee ☐ however ☐ I have decided to do less community work so that I have more time to spend with my family.
10. ☐ You can create you own future ☐☐ says Frank Montaño ☐☐ You have to think about it ☐ crystallize it in writing ☐ and be willing to work at it ☐ We teach a lot of goal ☐ setting and planning in our training sessions ☐☐

B.4   Creating Agreement

Revise the following sentences to correct errors in noun–pronoun and subject–verb agreement.

1. If there's any tickets left, they'll be $17 at the door.
2. A team of people from marketing, finance, and production are preparing the proposal.
3. Image type and resolution varies among clip art packages.
4. Your health and the health of your family is very important to us.
5. If a group member doesn't complete their assigned work, it slows the whole project down.
6. Baker & Baker was offended by the ad agency's sloppy proposal, and they withdrew their account from the firm.
7. To get out of debt you need to cut up your credit cards, which is hard to do.
8. Contests are fun for employees and creates sales incentives.
9. Either the CEO or the CFO is likely to testify before Congress.
10. A new employee should try to read verbal and nonverbal signals to see which aspects of your job are most important.

B.5   Correcting Case Errors

Revise the following sentences to correct errors in pronoun case.

1. I didn't appreciate him assuming that he would be the group's leader.
2. Myself and Jim made the presentation.
3. Employees which lack experience in dealing with people from other cultures could benefit from seminars in intercultural communication.
4. Chandra drew the graphs after her and I discussed the ideas for them.
5. Please give your revisions to Shanice, Tyrone, or myself by noon Friday.
6. Let's keep this disagreement between you and I.

B.6   Improving Modifiers

Revise the following sentences to correct dangling and misplaced modifiers.

1. Originally a group of four, one member dropped out after the first meeting due to a death in the family.
2. Examining the data, it is apparent that most of our sales are to people on the northwest side of the city.
3. As a busy professional, we know that you will want to take advantage of this special offer.
4. Often documents end up in files that aren't especially good.
5. By making an early reservation, it will give us more time to coordinate our trucks to better serve you.

B.7   Creating Parallel Structure

Revise the following sentences to create parallel structure.

1. To narrow a web search,

   - Put quotation marks around a phrase when you want an exact term.
   - Many search engines have wild cards (usually an asterisk) to find plurals and other forms of a word.
   - Reading the instructions on the search engine itself can teach you advanced search techniques.

2. Each issue of *Hospice Care* has articles from four different perspectives: legislative, health care, hospice administrators, and inspirational authors.

3. The university is one of the largest employers in the community, brings in substantial business, and the cultural impact is also big.

4. These three tools can help competitive people be better negotiators:

   A. Think win–win.
   B. It's important to ask enough questions to find out the other person's priorities, rather than jumping on the first advantage you find.
   C. Protect the other person's self-esteem.

5. These three guidelines can help cooperative people be better negotiators:

   A. Can you develop a specific alternative to use if negotiation fails?
   B. Don't focus on the bottom line. Spend time thinking about what you want and why you need it.
   C. Saying "You'll have to do better than that because . . ." can help you resist the temptation to say "yes" too quickly.

B.8   Correcting Sentence Errors

Revise the following sentences to correct comma splices, run-on sentences, fused sentences, and sentence fragments.

1. Members of the group are all experienced presenters, most have had little or no experience using PowerPoint.

2. Proofread the letter carefully and check for proper business format because errors undercut your ability to sell yourself so take advantage of your opportunity to make a good first impression.

3. Some documents need just one pass others need multiple revisions.

4. Videoconferencing can be frustrating. Simply because little time is available for casual conversation.

5. Entrepreneurs face two main obstacles. Limited cash. Lack of business experience.

6. The margin on pet supplies is very thin and the company can't make money selling just dog food and the real profit is in extras like neon-colored leashes, so you put the dog food in the back so people have to walk by everything else to get to it.

7. The company's profits jumped 15%. Although its revenues fell 3%.

8. The new budget will hurt small businesses it imposes extra fees it raises the interest rates small businesses must pay.

9. Our phones are constantly being used. Not just for business calls but also for personal calls.

10. Businesses are trying to cut travel costs, executives are taking fewer trips and flying out of alternate airports to save money.

B.9   Editing for Grammar and Usage

Revise the following sentences to eliminate errors in grammar and usage.

1. The number of students surveyed that worked more than 20 hours a week were 60%.

2. Not everyone is promoted after six months some people might remain in the training program a year before being moved to a permanent assignment.

3. The present solutions that has been suggested are not adequate.

4. At times while typing and editing, the text on your screen may not look correct.

5. All employees are asked to cut back on energy waste by the manager.

6. The benefits of an online catalog are

   - We will be able to keep records up-to-date;
   - Broad access to the catalog system from any networked computer on campus;
   - The consolidation of the main catalog and the catalogs in the departmental and branch libraries;
   - Cost savings.

7. You can take advantage of several banking services. Such as automatic withdrawal of a house or car payment and direct deposit of your pay check.

8. As a sophomore, business administration was intriguing to me.

9. Thank you for the help you gave Aliyah Jackson and myself.

10. I know from my business experience that good communication among people and departments are essential in running a successful corporation.

B.10   Writing Numbers

Revise the following sentences to correct errors in writing numbers.

1. 60% percent of the respondents hope to hold internships before they graduate.
2. 1992 marked the formal beginning of the European Economic Community.
3. In the year two thousand, twenty percent of the H-1B visas for immigrants with high-tech skills went to Indians.
4. More than 70,000,000 working Americans lack an employer-sponsored retirement plan.
5. The company's sales have risen to $16 million but it lost five million dollars.

B.11   Using Plurals and Possessives

Choose the right word for each sentence.

1. Many Canadian (companies, company's) are competing effectively in the global market.
2. We can move your (families, family's) furniture safely and efficiently.
3. The (managers', manager's) ability to listen is just as important as their technical knowledge.
4. A (memos, memo's) style can build goodwill.
5. (Social workers, Social worker's) should tell clients about services available in the community.
6. The (companies, company's) benefits plan should be checked periodically to make sure it continues to serve the needs of employees.
7. Information about the new community makes the (families, family's) move easier.
8. The (managers, manager's) all have open-door policies.
9. (Memos, Memo's) are sent to other workers in the same organization.
10. Burnout affects a (social workers', social worker's) productivity as well as their morale.

B.12   Choosing the Right Word I

Choose the right word for each sentence.

1. Exercise is (good, well) for patients who have had open-heart surgery.
2. This response is atypical, but it is not (unique, unusual).
3. The personnel department continues its (roll, role) of compiling reports for the federal government.
4. The Accounting Club expects (its, it's) members to come to meetings and participate in activities.
5. Part of the fun of any vacation is (cite, sight, site)-seeing.
6. The (lectern, podium) was too high for the short speaker.
7. The (residence, residents) of the complex have asked for more parking spaces.
8. Please order more letterhead (stationary, stationery).
9. The closing of the plant will (affect, effect) house prices in the area.
10. Better communication (among, between) design and production could enable us to produce products more efficiently.

B.13   Choosing the Right Word II

Choose the right word for each sentence.

1. The audit revealed a small (amount, number) of errors.
2. Diet beverages have (fewer, less) calories than regular drinks.
3. In her speech, she (implied, inferred) that the vote would be close.
4. We need to redesign the stand so that the catalog is eye-level instead of (laying, lying) on the desk.
5. (Their, There, They're) is some evidence that (their, there, they're) thinking of changing (their, there, they're) policy.
6. The settlement isn't yet in writing; if one side wanted to back out of the (oral, verbal) agreement, it could.
7. In (affect, effect), we're creating a new department.
8. The firm will be hiring new (personal, personnel) in three departments this year.
9. Several customers have asked that we carry more campus merchandise, (i.e., e.g.,) pillows and mugs with the college seal.
10. We have investigated all of the possible solutions (accept, except) adding a turning lane.

B.14   Choosing the Right Word III

Choose the right word for each sentence.

1. The author (cites, sights, sites) four reasons for computer phobia.
2. The error was (do, due) to inexperience.
3. (Your, You're) doing a good job motivating (your, you're) subordinates.
4. One of the basic (principals, principles) of business communication is "Consider the reader."
5. I (implied, inferred) from the article that interest rates would go up.
6. Working papers generally are (composed, comprised) of working trial balance, assembly sheets, adjusting entries, audit schedules, and audit memos.
7. Eliminating time clocks will improve employee (moral, morale).
8. The (principal, principle) variable is the trigger price mechanism.
9. (Its, It's) (to, too, two) soon (to, too, two) tell whether the conversion (to, too, two) computerized billing will save as much time as we hope.
10. Formal training programs (complement, compliment) on-the-job opportunities for professional growth.

B.15   Tracking Your Own Mechanical Errors

Analyze the mechanical errors (grammar, punctuation, word use, and typos) in each of your papers.

■ How many different errors are marked on each paper?

■ Which three errors do you make most often?

■ Is the number of errors constant in each paper, or does the number increase or decrease during the term?

As your instructor directs,

a. Correct each of the mechanical errors in one or more papers.

b. Deliberately write two new sentences in which you make each of your three most common errors. Then write the correct version of each sentence.

c. Write an email for your instructor discussing your increasing mastery of mechanical correctness during the semester or quarter.

d. Briefly explain to the class how to avoid one kind of error in grammar, punctuation, or word use.

Glossary

A

abstract   A summary of a report, specifying the recommendations and the reasons for them. Also called an executive summary.

accessibility   Design that accounts for disabilities or unique perceptive needs such as color blindness, impaired vision, or dyslexia; accessible design is required by the Americans with Disabilities Act (ADA), and some examples of accessible accommodations include closed captioning of videos and screen-reader-friendly image tags.

accident report   A report that lists the nature and causes of accidents in a factory or office. An accident report also can analyze the data and recommend ways to make conditions safer.

active voice   A verb that describes the action done by the grammatical subject of the sentence.

adaptive design   Website design that adapts a website's full content to the width of a browser at specific points to improve the viewing experience.

agenda   A list of items to be considered or acted upon at a meeting.

analytical report   A report that interprets information.

anchoring effect   The tendency to rely on the first piece of information given (the anchor) when making decisions.

animation   In a presentation, words and images that appear to move. Animation should be used carefully—to help control information flow and to build interest.

appendices   A section of a report that will interest only careful readers. Appendices can include survey and interview questions, transcripts, and complex tables and visuals.

audience benefits   Benefits or advantages that the audience gets by using the communicator's services, buying the communicator's products, following the communicator's policies, or adopting the communicator's ideas. Audience benefits can exist for policies and ideas as well as for goods and services.

auxiliary audience   People who may encounter a message but who do not have to interact with it. People cc'ed on an email are an auxiliary audience.

average   See *mean.*

B

backchanneling   The practice of using online technology to hold conversations concurrent with another activity, such as a speaker.

bar graph   A data display consisting of parallel bars or rectangles that represent specific sets of data.

behavioral economics   A branch of economics that uses social and psychological factors in understanding decision making. It is particularly concerned with the limits of rationality in those decisions.

behavioral interview   A job interview that asks candidates to describe actual behaviors they have used in the past in specific situations.

blind computer copies (bcc)   Copies sent to other recipients that are not listed on the original letter, memo, or email.

block format   In letters, a format in which inside address, date, and signature block are lined up at the left margin; paragraphs are not indented. In résumés, a format in which dates are listed in one column and job titles and descriptions in another.

boilerplate   Language from a previous document that a writer includes in a new document. Writers use boilerplate both to save time and energy and to use language that already has been approved by the organization's legal staff.

branching question   A question that sends respondents who answer differently to different parts of the questionnaire. Allows respondents to answer only those questions that are relevant to their experience.

build goodwill   To create a good image of yourself and of your organization—the kind of image that makes people want to do business with you.

bullets   Small circles (filled or open) or squares that set off items in a list. When you are giving examples, but the number is not exact and the order does not matter, use bullets to set off items.

business plan   A document written to raise capital for a new business venture or to outline future actions for an established business.

businessese   A kind of jargon including unnecessary words. Some words were common 200–300 years ago but are no longer part of spoken English. Some have never been used outside of business writing. All of these terms should be omitted.

bypassing   Miscommunication that occurs when two people use the same language to mean different things.

C

case   The grammatical role a noun or pronoun plays in a sentence. The nominative case is used for the subject of a clause, the possessive to show who or what something belongs to, the objective case for the object of a verb or a preposition.

causation   When one thing causes another.

channel   The physical means by which a message is sent. Written channels include emails, memos, letters, and billboards. Oral channels include phone calls, speeches, and face-to-face conversations.

cherry-pick   Choosing only the items or opportunities that are of benefit to the person choosing.

choice architecture   A form of persuasion that involves changing the context in which people make decisions to encourage them to make specific choices.

chronological résumé   A résumé that lists what the job applicant did in a dated order, starting with the most recent events and going backward in reverse chronology.

citation   Attributing a quotation or other idea to a source in the body of the report.

clickbait   Text or image intended to deceptively attract and motivate the reader or viewer to click on the text and image to link to misleading, false, or salacious content.

clip art   Predrawn images that you can import into your documents.

closed question   A question with a limited number of possible responses.

closure report   A report summarizing completed work that does not result in new action or a recommendation.

comma splice or **comma fault**   Using a comma to join two independent clauses. To correct, use a semicolon, use a comma with a conjunction, subordinate one of the clauses, or use a period and start a new sentence.

competitive proposal   A proposal that has to compete for limited resources.

complex sentence   A sentence with one main clause and one or more subordinate clauses.

complimentary close   The words after the body of the letter and before the signature. *Sincerely* and *Yours truly* are the most commonly used complimentary closes in business letters.

compound sentence   A sentence with two main clauses joined by a comma and conjunction.

conclusions   A section of a report or other communication that restates the main points.

confidence interval   In reporting the results of a study, the degree of uncertainty that a given sample is associated with the population it represents; 90%, 95%, and 99% are commonly used confidence intervals.

connotations   The emotional colorings or associations that accompany a word.

consensus   Group solidarity supporting a decision.

convenience sample   A group of subjects to whom the researcher has easy access; not a random sample.

conventions   Widely accepted practices.

coordinating conjunctions   Words that join two independence clauses: *for, and, nor, but, or, yet, so.*

correlation   When two things happen at the same time that might be positively or negatively related.

credibility   The ability to come across to the audience as believable.

credit report   A report that summarizes an applicant's income and other credit obligations. Credit reports also can evaluate the applicant's collateral and creditworthiness and recommend whether to provide credit.

critical incident   An important event that illustrates behavior or a history.

crop   To trim a photograph to fit a specific space, typically to delete visual information that is unnecessary or unwanted.

culture   A shared set of attitudes, beliefs, behaviors, and customs passed on and learned by the members of a community.

cycling   The process of sending a document from writer to superior to writer to yet another superior for several rounds of revisions before the document is approved.

D

dangling modifier   A phrase that modifies the wrong word or a word that is not actually in a sentence. To correct a dangling modifier, recast the modifier as a subordinate clause or revise the sentence so its subject or object can be modified by the dangling phrase.

demographic characteristics   Measurable features of an audience that can be counted objectively, such as age, education level, income.

denotation   A word's literal or dictionary meaning. Most common words in English have more than one denotation. Context usually makes it clear which of several meanings is appropriate.

descriptive abstract   A listing of the topics an article or report covers that does not summarize what is said about each topic.

deviation bar graph   Bar graphs that identify positive and negative values, or winners and losers.

devil's advocate   A person who defends a less popular viewpoint so that it receives fuller consideration.

direct marketing   All advertisements that ask for an order, inquiry, or contribution directly from the audience. Includes direct mail, catalogs, telemarketing (telephone sales), and newspaper and TV ads with 800 numbers to place an order.

discourse community   A group of people who share assumptions about what channels, formats, and styles to use for communication, what topics to discuss and how to discuss them, and what constitutes evidence.

discourse-based interview   Interview in which the interviewer asks questions based on documents that the interviewee has written.

documentation   Full bibliographic information that allows interested readers to locate the original source of material used in a document.

dot planning   A way for large groups to set priorities; involves assigning colored dots to ideas.

drawings   Visuals that show dimensions, show processes, emphasize detail, or represent a theoretical or proposed scenario. Drawings are effective visuals for eliminating unwanted detail.

dynamic data display   Visuals that allow users control over their visual experience. These displays are interactive, allowing users to adapt them to personal needs or interests.

E

ellipsis   Spaced dots used in reports to indicate that words have been omitted from quoted material and in direct mail to give the effect of pauses in speech.

emotional appeal   A persuasive technique that uses the audience's emotions to make them want to do what the writer or speaker asks.

enclosure   A document that accompanies a letter.

endnote   Unlike footnotes, endnotes appear at the end of a document, typically just before the reference list. Like footnotes, endnotes can contain citation and documentation information. They can also contain commentary on the text.

enunciation   The act of giving voice to all the sounds of each word while speaking.

ethnocentrism   The assumption that one's own culture is the norm and the tendency to view differences in other cultures as deviations from that "norm."

executive summary   See *abstract.*

external audiences   Audiences who are not part of the writer's organization.

extrinsic motivators   Benefits that are added on; they are not a necessary part of the product or action.

F

face-to-face survey   A survey carried out in person rather than, for example, through email or survey software. Face-to-face surveys are convenient when surveying a fairly small number of people in a specific location.

fallacies   Common errors in logic that weaken arguments.

figure   Any visual that is not a table.

filler sounds   Syllables, such as *um* and *uh*, that some speakers use to fill silence as they mentally search for their next words.

fixed-pitch font   A typeface in which each letter has the same width on the page. Such typefaces are also called monospaced.

flow chart   A visual that represents a sequence of actions of people or things involved in a complex process.

focus group   A small group of people who come in to talk with a skilled leader about a potential product or process.

font   A unified style of type. Fonts come in various sizes.

footnote   A note placed below the text on a page. Footnotes can include citation and documentation information. They can also include comments on the text.

formal meetings   Meetings that are run under strict rules, like the rules of parliamentary procedure summarized in *Robert's Rules of Order.*

formal report   A report containing formal elements such as a title page, a transmittal, a table of contents, and an abstract.

format   The parts of a document and the way they are arranged on a page.

full justification   Making both right and left margins of a text even, as opposed to having a ragged right margin.

fused sentence   The result when two or more sentences are joined without punctuation or conjunctions.

G

Gantt charts   Bar charts used to show schedules. Gantt charts are most commonly used in proposals.

gatekeeper   The audience with the power to decide whether your message is sent on to other audiences.

general purpose   The main goal behind a form of communication, particularly a presentation. Typically the primary purpose is to inform, to persuade, or to build goodwill.

global agility   The ability to relax one's own customary ways of communicating to allow for the communicative norms of other people.

glossary   A list of terms used in a document with their definitions.

goodwill ending   Shift of emphasis away from the message to the reader. A goodwill ending is positive, personal, and forward-looking and suggests that serving the reader is the real concern.

grant proposal   A proposal submitted by an organization, particularly a nonprofit organization, that describes a proposed project and requests grant funding in support of it.

grid system   A means of designing layout by imposing columns on a page and lining up graphic elements within the columns.

group interview   A job interview in which more than one candidate is interviewed in the same interview appointment.

grouped bar graph   A bar graph that allows the viewer to compare several aspects of each item or several items over time.

guided discussion   A presentation in which the speaker presents the questions or issues that both speaker and audience have agreed on in advance. Instead of functioning as an expert with all the answers, the speaker serves as a facilitator to help the audience tap its own knowledge.

H

hashtag   The symbol # plus word or phrase that is used on social media platforms to identify content on a specific topic.

header row   In a table, the row at the top that presents the labels for column information.

headings   Words or short phrases that group points and divide your letter, memo, email, or report into sections.

hidden job market   Jobs that are never advertised but that may be available or may be created for the right candidate.

high-context culture   A culture in which most information is inferred from the context, rather than being spelled out explicitly in words.

histogram   A bar graph using pictures, asterisks, or points to represent a unit of the data.

house style   The standards for documents in a particular organization, often based on a style guide, such as the *Chicago Manual of Style* or *Associated Press Stylebook.*

hypothetical (interview) question   A question that asks what a person would do in an imaginary situation.

I

impersonal expression   A sentence that attributes actions to inanimate objects, designed to avoid placing blame on a reader.

inclusive language   Language that covers all potential audiences and avoids expressions that exclude (and thus discriminate against) groups of people based on race, gender, socioeconomic status, age, ability, and so on.

inclusivity   Accessible design that uses accessibility principles to make a document inviting and usable for all users.

infographic   An informative graphic combining statistics, text, color, and visuals.

inform   To convey facts, data, or other information to an audience.

informal meetings   Loosely run meetings in which votes are not taken on every point.

informal report   A report using letter or memo format.

information report   A report that collects data for the reader but does not recommend action.

informative headings   Headings that are detailed enough to provide an overview of the material in the sections they introduce.

informative message   Message giving information to which the reader's basic reaction will be neutral.

informative report   A report that provides information.

inside address   The reader's name and address; put below the date and above the salutation in most letter formats.

interactive presentation   A presentation that is a conversation between the speaker and the audience.

intercultural competence   The ability to communicate sensitively with people from other cultures and countries, based on an understanding of cultural differences.

internal audiences   Audiences in the communicator's organization.

interruption interview   Interview in which the interviewer interrupts users to ask them what's happening. For example, a company testing a draft of computer instructions might interrupt a user to ask, "What are you trying to do now? Tell me why you did that."

interview   Structured conversation with someone who is able to give you useful information.

intrinsic motivators   Benefits that come automatically from using a product or doing something.

introduction   The part of a report that states the purpose and scope of the report. The introduction also may include limitations, assumptions, methods, criteria, and definitions.

J

jargon   There are two kinds of jargon. The first kind is the specialized terminology of a technical field. The second is businessese, outdated words that do not have technical meanings and are not used in other forms of English.

judgment sample   A group of people whose views seem useful.

justification report   A report that justifies the need for a purchase, an investment, a new personnel line, or a change in procedure.

K

key word   A word used in (1) a résumé to summarize areas of expertise or qualifications and (2) to specify the content of a document and used to retrieve that document in searches.

L

letter   A short document using block, modified, or simplified letter format that goes to readers outside your organization.

letterhead   Stationery with the organization's name, logo, and contact information printed on the page.

Likert scale   A rating scale for measuring attitudes or opinions. Respondents rate an item on a scale of agreement, for example, 1 = strongly disagree and 5 = strongly agree.

line graph   A data display consisting of lines that show trends or allow the viewer to compare values among the observed values.

lingua franca   A language used among people who speak other languages. English has become the lingua franca for international business.

long quotations   Quotations of around four lines or more. Such quotations are used sparingly in business reports.

low-context culture   A culture in which most information is conveyed explicitly in words rather than being inferred from context.

M

mail surveys   Surveys delivered via "snail mail." Such surveys are effective in that some people may be more willing to fill out an anonymous questionnaire than to give sensitive information to a stranger over the phone.

main clause   A group of words that can stand by itself as a complete sentence. Also called an independent clause.

maps   Visuals that represent a location or compare items in different locations.

mean   The average of a group of numbers. Found by dividing the sum of a set of figures by the number of figures.

median   The middle number in a ranked set of numbers.

memo   A document using memo format sent to readers in an organization.

minutes   Records of a meeting, listing the items discussed, the results of votes, and the persons responsible for carrying out follow-up steps.

mirror question   A question that paraphrases the content of the answer an interviewee gave to the last question.

misplaced modifier   A word or phrase that modifies some element of a sentence other than the one the writer intended.

mixed punctuation   Using a colon after the salutation and a comma after the complimentary close in a letter.

mobile-first design   The process of designing a website by prioritizing design for mobile devices first and then modifying that design for other interfaces.

mode   The most frequent number in a set of numbers.

modifier   A word or phrase giving more information about another word in a sentence.

monochronic culture   A culture in which people focus on one important activity at a time.

monologue presentation   A presentation in which the speaker talks without interruption. The presentation is planned and is delivered without deviation.

multiple interview   (1) A four-interview system comprising a screening interview, a "topgrading interview," a focused interview, and a reference interview. (2) A series of interviews for a single job. The series could include an initial screening interview and might end with a final interview that checks references.

N

narrative   A story moved forward by character, plot, or setting. Using a narrative structure can be an effective strategy for organizing a presentation.

nervous mannerism   Verbal and gestural tics such as using *like* and *uh* and clicking a pen. Such mannerisms can distract an audience.

nominative case   The grammatical form used for the subject of a clause. *I, we, he, she,* and *they* are nominative pronouns.

nonageist   Words, images, or behaviors that do not discriminate against people on the basis of age.

noncompetitive proposal   A proposal with no real competition and hence a high probability of acceptance.

nongendered language   Language that treats gender neutrally, that does not make assumptions about the proper gender for a job, and that does not imply that one gender is superior to or takes precedence over another.

nonracist   Words, images, or behaviors that do not discriminate against people on the basis of race.

nonrestrictive clause   A clause giving extra but unessential information about a noun or pronoun. Because the information is extra, commas separate the clause from the word it modifies.

nonverbal communication   Communication that does not use words.

O

objective case   The grammatical form used for the object of a verb or preposition. *Me, us, him, her,* and *them* are objective pronouns.

offshoring   In business, the process of moving operational facilities to other countries.

omnibus motion   A motion that allows a group to vote on several related items in a single vote. Saves time in formal meetings with long agendas.

online survey   A survey that delivers questions over the internet. The researcher can contact respondents with an email containing a link to a web page with the survey or can ask people by mail or in person to log on and visit the website with the survey.

open question   A question with an unlimited number of possible responses.

oppressive language   Language that belittles and dehumanizes people, including racist, misogynistic, homophobic, transphobic, ablest, ageist, and xenophobic language.

organizational chart   A visual that shows the hierarchical structure of an organization and the relative ranks of different positions (e.g., president, CEO, marketing director).

outsourcing   Going outside the company for products and services that once were made by the company's employees.

P

paired bar graph   A bar graph that shows the correlation between two items.

parallel structure   Using the same grammatical and logical form for words, phrases, clauses, and ideas in a series.

paraphrase   To repeat in your own words the verbal content of another communication.

passive voice   A sentence in which the grammatical subject of the sentence receives the action denoted in the verb rather than performing that action.

people-first language   Language that names the person first, then the condition, for example, "people with impaired vision." Used to avoid implying that the condition defines the person's potential.

persona   The "author" or character who allegedly writes a document; the voice that a communicator assumes in creating a message.

personal brandings   A term for marketing oneself, including job searching. It connotes various options, including social media such as LinkedIn, to market oneself.

persuade   To motivate and convince the audience to act or change a belief.

persuasive message   A persuasive message attempts to convince someone to carry out some action or to change their beliefs. Examples include proposals and performance reviews.

phishing   The deceptive practice of pretending to be from a trusted organization and contacting an individual with the intent of getting personal information, such as financial information or passwords.

phone survey   A survey carried out via phone. Phone surveys are popular because they can be closely supervised. Interviewers can read the questions from a computer screen and key in answers as the respondent gives them. The results then can be available just a few minutes after the last call is completed.

photographs   Visuals that realistically represent a given subject. Photographs are effective for creating a sense of authenticity or realism or for showing an item in use.

pictogram   A bar graph that uses images to create the bars.

pie graph   A data display in which sections of a circle represent percentages of a given quantity.

pitch   The highness or lowness of a sound generated by the rate of vibrations that produce it.

plagiarism   Passing off the words or ideas of others as one's own.

polychronic culture   A culture in which people do several things at once.

population   The group a researcher wants to make statements about.

positive or **good-news message**   Message to which the reader's reaction will be positive.

possessive case   The grammatical form used to indicate possession or ownership. *My, our, his, hers, its,* and *their* are possessive pronouns.

prepositions   Words that indicate relationships, for example, *with, in, under, at.*

presenting problem   The problem that surfaces as the subject of discord. The presenting problem is often not the real problem.

primary audience   The audience who will make a decision or act on the basis of a message.

primary research   Research that gathers new information.

pro-and-con pattern   A pattern of organization that presents all the arguments for an alternative and then all the arguments against it.

probe question   A follow-up question designed to get more information about an answer or to get at specific aspects of a topic.

progress and interim report   A statement of the work done during a period of time and the work proposed for the next period.

proportional font   A font in which some letters are wider than other letters (e.g., *w* is wider than *i*).

proposal   A document that suggests a method and personnel for finding information or solving a problem.

prospecting letter   A job application letter written to a company that has not announced openings.

proxemics   The amount of space that a person wants between themselves and another person. Proxemics differs among cultures.

psychographic characteristics   Human characteristics that are qualitative rather than quantitative: values, beliefs, goals, and lifestyles.

psychological description   A description of a product or service in terms of audience benefits.

psychological reactance   A phenomenon occurring when a person reacts to a negative message by asserting freedom in some other arena.

purpose statement   The statement in a proposal or a report specifying the organizational problem, the technical questions that must be answered to solve the problem, and the rhetorical purpose of the report (to explain, to recommend, to request, to propose).

Q

qualitative research   Research that collects data that are non-numerical; it employs methods such as interviews, observations, and focus groups.

quantitative research   Research that collects numerical data; it often employs statistics to yield a result that can be generalized from the study sample to a population.

questionnaire   A list of questions for people to answer in a survey.

R

ragged right margins   Margins that do not end evenly on the right side of the page.

random sample   A sample for which each member of the population has an equal chance of being chosen.

range   The difference between the highest and lowest numbers in a set of figures.

recency effect   The phenomenon by which audience members best remember what they heard last.

recommendation report   A report that evaluates two or more possible alternatives and recommends one of them. Doing nothing is always one alternative.

recommendations   A section of a report that specifies items for action.

reference line   A subject line that refers the reader to another document (usually a numbered one, such as an invoice).

reflexive pronoun   A pronoun that refers to or emphasizes a noun or pronoun that already has appeared in the sentence. *Myself, herself,* and *themselves* are reflexive pronouns.

release date   The date that a report will be made available to the public.

request for proposal (RFP)   A statement of the service or product that an agency wants with an invitation for proposals to provide that service or product.

response rate   The percentage of subjects receiving a questionnaire who answer the questions.

responsive design   Website design that continuously adjusts to the size of a browser to optimize the content of a site for a particular interface.

restrictive clause   A clause limiting or restricting the meaning of a noun or pronoun. Because its information is essential, no commas separate the clause from the word it restricts.

résumé   A persuasive summary of qualifications for employment.

return on investment (ROI) report   A report that correlates how the money that companies spend on advertising relates to sales or increased traffic. Marketing firms routinely compose these reports for clients.

reverse chronology   Starting with the most recent events, such as job or degree, and going backward in time. A pattern of organization used for chronological résumés.

rhetorical situation   The relationship among an author, the author's purpose in communicating, a text, the audience for the text, and the setting of the communication.

run-on sentence   A sentence containing two or more main clauses strung together with *and, but, or, so,* or *for.*

S

salutation   The greeting in a letter, for example, "Dear Ms. Smith:"

sample (in research)   The portion of the population a researcher actually studies.

sample size   The number of observations included in a study's statistical sample. Sample size is a critical component of a study in which the goal is to make inferences about a population based upon the sample.

sans serif font   Literally, without serifs. Typeface whose letters lack bases or flicks. Helvetica and Geneva are examples of sans serif typefaces.

scatterplot graph   A graph of multiple data points that shows the relationship between two sets of numerical variables.

secondary audience   The audience who may be asked by the primary audience to comment on a message or to implement ideas after they've been approved.

secondary research   Research that retrieves data someone else gathered. It includes library research.

segmented, subdivided, or **stacked bars**   Bars in a bar graph that sum components of an item.

semantic analysis   Computer-assisted analysis of a text to understand its meaning.

sentence fragment   Words that are not a complete sentence but that are punctuated as if they were a complete sentence.

sentence outline   An outline using complete sentences. It contains the thesis or recommendation plus all supporting points.

serif   The little extensions from the main strokes on letters. Times New Roman and Courier are examples of serif typefaces.

signpost   An explicit statement of the place that a speaker or writer has reached, for example, "Now we come to the third point."

simple sentence   A sentence with one main clause.

simplified format   A letter format that omits the salutation and complimentary close and lines text at the left margin.

situational interview   A job interview in which candidates are asked to describe what they would do in specific hypothetical situations.

situational questions   In an interview, questions that allow the interviewer to probe what the interviewee does in a specific circumstance.

skills résumé   A résumé organized around the skills you've used, rather than the date or the job in which you used them.

solicited letter   A job letter written when you know that the company is hiring.

specific purpose   In a presentation, a statement that identifies the topic about which the speaker will inform, persuade, or build goodwill.

spell-checker   A feature of a software program (e.g., Microsoft Word) that checks for misspellings in a document.

stereotype   An overly simple and generalized belief—and often a prejudiced one—about a person based on that person's membership in a given group, for example, an ethnic group.

storyboard   A visual representation of the structure of a document, with a rectangle representing each page or unit. An alternative to outlining as a method of organizing material.

stress (in a communication)   Emphasis given to one or more words in a sentence, or one or more ideas in a message.

stress interview   A job interview that deliberately puts the applicant under stress, physical or psychological. Here it's important to change the conditions that create physical stress and to meet psychological stress by rephrasing questions in less inflammatory terms and treating them as requests for information.

structured interview   An interview that follows a detailed list of questions prepared in advance.

stub column   The left-most column of a table, which contains the row headings.

subject line   The title of the document, used to file and retrieve the document. A subject line tells readers why they need to read the document and provides a framework in which to set what you're about to say.

subordinate clause   A group of words containing a subject and a verb but that cannot stand by itself as a complete sentence. Also called a dependent clause.

subordinating conjunction   Words that make a clause grammatically dependent on another, independent clause, for example, *while*, *though*, *before*, *until*.

summary abstract   The logic skeleton of an article or report, containing the thesis or recommendation and its proof.

summary sentence or paragraph   A sentence or paragraph listing in order the topics that the following sentences or paragraphs will discuss.

survey   A method of getting information from a group of people.

SWOT analysis   A method of evaluating a proposed action that examines both internal factors (Strengths, Weaknesses) and external factors (Opportunities, Threats).

T

table   Numbers or words arrayed in rows and columns.

task force   A temporary team organized to complete a specific task.

template   A design or format that serves as a pattern.

thank-you note   A note thanking someone for their help.

think-aloud protocol   A method used in usability research in which the user is asked to think out loud while performing some task, such as finding certain information on a company's website. The goal is to understand what the user thinks as they try to perform the task.

threat   A statement, explicit or implied, that someone will be punished if they do or don't do something.

tone of voice   The rising or falling inflection that indicates whether a group of words is a question or a statement, whether the speaker is uncertain or confident, whether a statement is sincere or sarcastic.

tone   The implied attitude of the author toward the reader and the subject.

topic sentence   A sentence that introduces or summarizes the main idea in a paragraph.

trip report   A report in which the author shares what they learned, for example, at a conference or during a visit to a customer or supplier. It also can recommend action based on that information.

truncated graphs   Graphs with part of the scale missing.

U

umbrella sentence or paragraph   A sentence or paragraph listing in order the topics that following sentences or paragraphs will discuss.

unity   Using only one idea or topic in a paragraph or other piece of writing.

unsolicited   Not asked for; no consent given.

unstructured interview   An interview based on three or four main questions prepared in advance and other questions that build on what the interviewee says.

usability testing   Testing a document with users to see that it functions as desired.

V

verbal communication   Communication that uses words. The words may be oral or written. In addition, they may be signed, as in a language such as American Sign Language.

vested interest   The emotional stake readers have in something if they benefit from maintaining or influencing conditions or actions.

vicarious participation   An emotional strategy in fund-raising letters based on the idea that by donating money, readers participate in work they are not able to do personally.

visual cluster   Visuals, such as line graphs, bar graphs, and maps, grouped together to tell a complex story.

volume   The loudness or softness of a voice or other sound.

voting   In teamwork, a method of making a decision in which all team members indicate their preference

W

watchdog audience   An audience that has political, social, or economic power and that may base future actions on its evaluation of your message.

whistleblower   A person, usually an employee, who exposes illicit activity in an organization.

white paper report   A report that explains a problem and then may advocate for a solution to the problem. A white paper report can be written to inform a general audience. Sometimes companies use white paper reports for marketing purposes.

white space   The empty space on the page. White space emphasizes material that it separates from the rest of the text.

wordiness   Taking more words than necessary to express an idea.

Y

***you*-attitude**   A style of communicating that looks at things from the audience's point of view, emphasizes what the audience wants to know, respects the audience's intelligence, and protects the audience's ego. Using *you* generally increases *you*-attitude in positive situations. In negative situations or conflict, avoid *you* because that word will attack the audience.

Name Index

Company Index

Subject Index